T0391983

Poetry After Barbarism

....
LITERATURE NOW

LITERATURE NOW

Matthew Hart, David James, and Rebecca L. Walkowitz, Series Editors

Literature Now offers a distinct vision of late twentieth- and early twenty-first-century literary culture. Addressing contemporary literature and the ways we understand its meaning, the series includes books that are comparative and transnational in scope as well as those that focus on national and regional literary cultures.

Alexander Manshel, *Writing Backwards: Historical Fiction and the Reshaping of the American Canon*

Glenda Carpio, *Migrant Aesthetics: Contemporary Fiction, Global Migration, and the Limits of Empathy*

John Brooks, *The Racial Unfamiliar: Illegibility in Black Literature and Culture*

Vidyan Ravinthiran, *Worlds Woven Together: Essays on Poetry and Poetics*

Ellen Jones, *Literature in Motion: Translating Multilingualism Across the Americas*

Thomas Heise, *The Gentrification Plot: New York and the Postindustrial Crime Novel*

Sunny Xiang, *Tonal Intelligence: The Aesthetics of Asian Inscrutability During the Long Cold War*

Jessica Pressman, *Bookishness: Loving Books in a Digital Age*

Heather Houser, *Infowhelm: Environmental Art and Literature in an Age of Data*

Christy Wampole, *Degenerative Realism: Novel and Nation in Twenty-First-Century France*

Sarah Chihaya, Merve Emre, Katherine Hill, and Jill Richards, *The Ferrante Letters: An Experiment in Collective Criticism*

Peter Morey, *Islamophobia and the Novel*

Gloria Fisk, *Orhan Pamuk and the Good of World Literature*

Zara Dinnen, *The Digital Banal: New Media and American Literature and Culture*

For a complete list of books in the series, please see the Columbia University Press website.

Poetry After Barbarism

The Invention of
Motherless Tongues and
Resistance to Fascism

Jennifer Scappettone

Columbia University Press

New York

Columbia University Press
Publishers Since 1893
New York   Chichester, West Sussex
cup.columbia.edu

Copyright © 2025 Jennifer Scappettone
All rights reserved

Library of Congress Cataloging-in-Publication Data
Names: Scappettone, Jennifer author
Title: Poetry after barbarism : The invention of motherless tongues and resistance to fascism / Jennifer Scappettone.
Description: New York : Columbia University Press, 2025. | Includes bibliographical references and index.
Identifiers: LCCN 2025000458 | ISBN 9780231212083 hardback | ISBN 9780231212090 trade paperback | ISBN 9780231559201 ebook
Subjects: LCSH: Poetry, Modern—20th century—History and criticism | Multilingualism and literature | Politics and literature | Experimental poetry—History and criticism | LCGFT: Literary criticism
Classification: LCC PN1059.M8 S33 2025 | DDC 809.1/3581—dc23/eng/20250526
LC record available at https://lccn.loc.gov/2025000458

Printed in the United States of America

Cover design: Chang Jae Lee
Cover image: Etel Adnan, detail of *Rihla ila Jabal Tamalpais (Journey to Mount Tamalpais)*, 2008. Watercolor and India ink on Japanese book, 30 x 10.5 cm x 54 pages: 30 x 567 cm. Copyright Estate of Etel Adnan. Courtesy of Donation Claude & France Lemand, Institut du monde arabe, Paris.

GPSR Authorized Representative: Easy Access System Europe, Mustamäe tee 50, 10621 Tallinn, Estonia, gpsr.requests@easproject.com

FOR THE WORDWEAVING THERESA SCAPPETTONE,
who harbors aloft in new places the syllables of foremothers
I never knew, and for the cherished ever-roving spirits of
Amelia Rosselli, of Milli Graffi, of Lyn Hejinian
and Etel Adnan, all mothers of mine in making
and remaking a language worthy of continuing to live in

The shadows lengthen, the sun-drenched line of arriving strangers are all admitted, seen in the day and not the same at night, host and guest alike.

Two things then, both occurring as the beginner arrives: acceptance and the reconstruction of the world which that acceptance implies.

—Lyn Hejinian, *The Beginner*

. . . this very lyric speech becomes the voice of human beings between whom the barriers have fallen.

—Theodor Adorno, "On Lyric Poetry and Society," trans. Shierry Weber Nicholsen

Contents

Acknowledgments xiii

Abbreviations xix

Introduction: From Babel to a Possible Pentecost: The Abracadabrant Word and the Invention of "Xenoglossia" 1

Prelude: What Is Xenoglossia? 1

Belonging to No Known Language:
Henry James Against the Melting Pot 8

La Xénoglossie at the Turn of the Twentieth Century 13

The Emergence of Pentecostalism: Transgressions of Citizenship 17

From Mother Tongue to Nurse's Tongue:
Xenoglossia's Theoretical Matrices 21

A "Barbarian" Poetics 29

Two "Pentecosts" Within the New Babel:
Fortunato Depero and Amelia Rosselli in New York 42

1. Wireless Imagination: Futurist Delusions of Autarky and the Dream (or Nightmare) of a Transnational Language 51

The Telegraph and the Dawn of a Global Consciousness According to
F. T. Marinetti 51

CONTENTS

Inspiration and Dictation from the War Machine as Holy Spirit: Words-in-Freedom (or Words-in-Thrall) 57

Autarky, Nurse's Milk, and the Troubling of the Mother Tongue Under Italian Colonialism: Marinetti and Munari Compose *The Poem of the Milk Dress* 67

Fatherland as Cataclysm: Unbinding Pentecosts in the Verse of the Baroness Elsa von Freytag-Loringhoven 85

2. Antifascist Philology and the Rejection of Linguistic Purity in Emilio Villa 98

The Turbine of Genesis: A Xenoglossic Hurricane 98

Beyond the Myth of the Aryans 105

Study Under Fascism 110

The Question(s) of a Unitary Language 115

Italian Pentecosts (and the Shadow of Gabriele D'Annunzio) 117

"Os Puristas São Enfadonhos e Inúteis" (Purists Are Tedious and Useless): The "Brazilian Parenthesis" 124

Etymology as Rogue Archaeology: Cuneiformism as a Medium for Poetry 133

An Ideal Nationality: On Twombly 140

A Sphere Without Strangers 144

3. Amelia Rosselli's Disintegrating Canto(n)s and the Holy Ghost of Parental Tongues 155

Songs of the State Versus the Idiolect of Panmusic 155

"Not for I, Not for Me, the Quesit and the Full Bosom": Mother as Void 171

"Cantonidisintegratidella/miavita": Closure and Implosion of the Canto(n) 180

Harmonics of the Translingual Voice: From Una Lingua Vacillante to Overtone as Holy Ghost 203

CONTENTS · XI

4. "Fog Is My Land": Etel Adnan's Painting in Arabic and the Reinvention of Belonging 215

Leporello as Geopoetics 215

To Write and to Paint in a Foreign Language 221

Queer Xenoglossia and the Reimagination of Kinship 228

Tongues of Fire: Veiling and Unveiling in *The Arab Apocalypse* 243

Critical Practices of Unmastery: An Aspirational Collective 255

5. Glottal Stop: Xenoglossic Breathing and Transmutations of the Mother Tongue in LaTasha N. Nevada Diggs 257

Performance Beyond Citizenship, Bodies Beyond the Body Politic 261

The Voice as a Wind Instrument 268

Choreography of Cuts 271

An Orphaned Tongue: Identity and/as Longing 277

Extensions of the Mother/Tongue:
Nurses, Foster Parents, Birth and Adoptive Mamas in *Village* 281

Mother Breath and Pentecostal Insurgence 286

Coda. A Xenoglossic Community to Come: Belonging by Rogue Translation in Sawako Nakayasu and Sagawa Chika's *Mouth: Eats Color* 291

....

Notes *307*

Selected Bibliography *359*

Index *369*

Acknowledgments

One of the arguments of this book is that it takes a village to think—though the form of the academic monograph tends, in line with this society's fetishization of novelty and individual achievement, to obscure the collective genesis of any argument, just as the academy writ large tends to render monolithic the language and culture under investigation in any given discipline. A book like this could never have happened without musing in community, swapping knowledges that are never quite complete. It began in the most intimate of collectives: my one-on-one grappling with the oeuvre of Amelia Rosselli, whose poetry hovers in many ways beyond translation. It developed, year by year, in spaces where readings and debates about poetics and multilingualism flourished within my immediate literary community: in sustaining dialogues and exchanges of material with Nathanaël, Marco Giovenale, Charles Bernstein, Milli and Barbara Graffi, Jen/Eleana Hofer, Lisa Robertson, Juliana Spahr, JD Pluecker, Sarah Riggs, Caroline Bergvall, Susan Schultz, Ghazal Mosadeq, and Mónica de la Torre. It was exhaustively researched as an academic argument about language in conversation with a host of generous colleagues. I have learned the hard way that today's literary culture, with its fast pace, cut-and-pastable internet-borne facts, and ferocious self-marketing, hardly rewards an ethics of citation that would acknowledge the range of one's interlocutors, including those who first researched and translated a "trending" author through long hours spent in the apparent solitude of primary and secondary resources. Although aware that it's impossible to cite every interlocutor, I try to model a different way of moving forward, in full recognition of the limits of disciplines and immensity of influence.

XIV   ❧   ACKNOWLEDGMENTS

The book was enriched immeasurably by the chance to conduct initial research as a Rome Prize Fellow at the American Academy in Rome, and it could never have been finished without the shelter of precious postdoctoral fellowships at the Stanford Center for the Humanities, the Civitella Ranieri Foundation (with the collaboration of the Center for Italian Modern Art), I Tatti, the Harvard University Center for Italian Renaissance Studies, the Getty Research Institute, and the Huntington Library, as well as a National Endowment for the Humanities Summer Grant and the support of the departments of English and romance languages and literatures and research leave granted by the Humanities Division at the University of Chicago.

Thinking through one's second scholarly monograph, without a committee or a deadline, can be terribly isolating, and indeed, I am not sure how anyone who works full time manages to pull it off. As such, I'm grateful to the colleagues near and far who invited me to present substantial, beyond conference-shrunk chunks of the work in progress and of its kernel, *Locomotrix: Selected Poetry and Prose of Amelia Rosselli*, over the past dozen years: Stephen Motika at Poets House; Ammiel Alcalay at City University of New York; Nelson Moe at Barnard; Kevin Craft at the University of Washington in Rome; Jorie Graham and Christina Davis at Harvard; Jen/Eleana Hofer at the University of Houston; Ara Merjian at New York University (NYU); Cathy Wagner and cris cheek at Miami University of Ohio; Ignacio Infante at Washington University; Robert Majzels at the University of Calgary; Franco Baldasso at Bard; Alessandro Cassin at the Primo Levi Center; Brandon Brown at the Bay Area Public School; Giorgio Van Straten and Andrea Raos at the Istituto Italiano di Cultura of New York and of Chicago; Andrea Cortellessa at Poetitaly; Orlando Reade and Joshua Kotin at Princeton; Ellen Alderman at the Graham Foundation; Peggy Pacini at the Transnational Beat Network; Harriet Boyd-Bennett at Christchurch, Oxford; Rebecca Walkowitz at Rutgers and the New York/New Jersey Modernism Seminar; Judah Rubin at the St. Mark's Poetry Project; Alexander Streim and the editors of *ELH: English Literary History* at Johns Hopkins; Luigi Ballerini for Yale's "Those Who from Afar Look Like Flies" launch; Cristina Iuli at "Transatlantic Transfers"; Tae Yamamoto of the Virginia Woolf Society of Japan; Chiara Trebaiocchi, Eloisa Morra, Dalila Colucci, and Valeria Federici at Harvard and Brown; Melih Levi, Shoshana Olidort, Nick Jenkins and Roland Greene at Stanford; Eli Mandel and Jennifer Soong at Princeton; Maria Francesca Stamuli at the Soprintendenza Archivistica e Bibliotecaria della Toscana; the curators of the Chicago Humanities Festival, who staged my generative conversation with Jhumpa Lahiri; Montana Ray and Elisa Biagini at NYU Florence; and Omar Berrada and Simone Fattal in preparing a centenary homage to Etel Adnan. Rachel Levitsky and erica kaufman commissioned my volume for the Belladonna* Elders

ACKNOWLEDGMENTS   XV

Series, jump-starting my friendship with Etel Adnan, an act of imagination and hospitality for which I remain to eternity grateful.

Other readers and interlocutors with whom I had the gift of dialogue over the years include Leonard Schwartz, for *Cross-Cultural Poetics*; Montana Ray, for the *Circumference* podcast; Alexis Almeida and Allegra Rosenbaum, for *Asymptote*; Al Filreis and Anna Stafford Strong, for ModPo; and in live and written forums, Gian Maria Annovi, Chiara Carpita, Don Mee Choi, Andrea Cortellessa, Teresa Fiore, Stefania Heim, Ara Merjian, Chiara Portesine, and Antonio Riccardi. My friends Donato Colli and Marinella Caputo were always up for a chat about the fine weirdnesses of translingual writing. The musicians/musicologists Huck Hodge, Jane Hatter, and Loren Carle all patiently explained the harmonic series to me—armed with props and piano demonstrations.

Chapter 4 would not have been possible without the generous time and conversation of Etel Adnan and Simone Fattal. I am also greatly indebted to those who read or heard versions of that work and provided translations and commentary, in particular Ghenwa Hayek at the University of Chicago; M'barek Bouchichi at Civitella Ranieri; and at Stanford Alexander Key, Omnia El Shakry, Adrien Zakar, and Aamer Ibraheem, who recorded a beautiful recitation of al-Sayyab's "The Mother and the Lost Daughter."

Haun Saussy was my coconspirator in the teaching of several seminars in exploratory translation at the University of Chicago during this period, and in the creation of an international symposium that took place in the middle of the global pandemic. His advocacy and creative camaraderie in the matter of being between languages has provided crucial sustenance. I am indebted to our stupendous hyperpolyglot teaching assistant, Claudio Sansone, for an extended conversation about Emilio Villa's etymological labyrinths. Thanks, too, to the other colleagues who read and commented upon pieces of this work at critical moments: Edgar Garcia, John Wilkinson, Bill Brown, Mark Payne, and Ken Warren.

Being built from the ground up of marginalized sources, this study necessitated travel to archives and libraries on several continents. I'm grateful for the funding that enabled those rare opportunities but also for the archivists and librarians who welcomed me in to see rare and frangible materials, sometimes before they were fully catalogued, especially Chiara Panizzi at the Biblioteca Panizzi, Adriano Accattino at the Museo della Carale, Nicoletta Trotta at the Centro della Tradizione Manoscritta at the University of Pavia, Marvin Sackner at the Ruth and Marvin Sackner Archive of Concrete and Visual Poetry, Matteo Fochessati at the Collezione Wolfsoniana, Anna Carboncini at the Fondazione Bardi, and the staff at the Centro de Pesquisa of the Museu de Arte de São Paulo, the Instituto Lina Bo e P. M. Bardi / Casa de Vidro, the Archivio di Stato of Florence, and the Getty Research Institute.

For valuable help sifting through thousands of archival photos and secondary sources, as well as the years-long labor of securing permissions, I am indebted to a series of brilliant research assistants who worked on this manuscript with me: undergraduates Marina Resende Santos, Didi Chang-Park, Serin Lee, Vivian Lei, and Aidan Goldberg, and doctoral candidate Alessandro Minnucci. David Gutherz's excellent dissertation on postwar "upside-down intellectuals" provided inspiration along the way. Students in my classes orchestrated around these topics, especially Emily Wang, May Huang, Maya Nguyen, and my dissertation advisee Silvia Guslandi, kept me interested. I am also exceedingly grateful to Allie Scholten at the University of Chicago's Visual Resource Center for help with the thicket of images, captions, and permissions.

Slow-cooked on back, front, and para-burners amid the production of translations, books of poetry, performance and video and book-arts projects, two other only apparently unrelated critical monographs, and a rash of other commitments, this book almost didn't come to pass, or rather, it came to pass notwithstanding various interpolations in the form of capital-L Life: travel and displacement, pandemic, lockdown, the passing of my father, illness—so that those whom I need to acknowledge most are the ones who insisted on the human act of bringing me food in the midst of these assaults: my colleagues Amber Ginsburg, Haun Saussy, and Suzanne Buffam with Chicu Reddy.

For keeping me alive and raging notwithstanding all my battles with the genre and machine, I am indebted to my colover of languages and now spouse, whom I met at the very start of this book's official germination in Rome, so that its publication marks another marvelous anniversary: Joshua.

Thanks to heir Francesco Villa for his kind permission to publish the writing and documents of Emilio Villa. Thanks too to the Instituto Lina Bo e P. M. Bardi / Casa de Vidro for their permission to quote from Villa's unpublished correspondence with Pietro Maria Bardi.

Thanks to Alessandro Quasimodo for his permission to publish "Alle fronde dei salici" by Salvatore Quasimodo.

Extracts from *Documento*, *Primi scritti*, *Serie ospedaliera*, *Variazioni belliche*, and *Le poesie* by Amelia Rosselli

© Garzanti Editore s.p.a., 1997
© 2004, Garzanti Libri s.p.a., Milano
Gruppo editoriale mauri Spagnol

ACKNOWLEDGMENTS · XVII

Extracts from Amelia Rosselli's *Sleep* © 1992, 2020, Garzanti s.r.l., Milano Gruppo editoriale mauri Spagnol

Additional permission to publish excerpts from Amelia Rosselli's *Documento* was provided by World Poetry Books.

Extracts from Amelia Rosselli's unpublished writings are reproduced thanks to the kind permission of the Centro per gli Studi sulla Tradizione Manoscritta di Autori Moderni e Contemporanei, Università di Pavia.

Thanks to the Estate of Etel Adnan, and to Simone Fattal and Post-Apollo Press for their kind permission to publish the writings and artwork of Etel Adnan; thanks as well to E. Tracy Grinnell at Litmus Press and Eric Delpont at the Institut du Monde Arabe for rendering texts accessible.

Thanks to LaTasha N. Nevada Diggs for her permission to reproduce extracts from her writings. Much gratitude to Belladonna* Books for their permission to publish extracts from *TwERK* (2012). "Performance," "some sort of alchemy," "items of confectionery," and "hour of the star" are used by permission from *Village* (Coffee House Press, 2023), Copyright © 2023 by LaTasha N. Nevada Diggs.

Thanks to M. NourbeSe Philip for her permission to reproduce fragments of her poetry and prose.

Thanks to Sawako Nakayasu for her permission to reproduce extracts from her poetry and translations.

Earlier versions of certain chapter sections appeared in the following: "The Infinite Cartography of Etel Adnan," Poetry Foundation, *Open Door*, November 2022; "On 'X-RAY,' by 'the Baroness' Elsa von Freytag-Loringhoven," in *The Difference Is Spreading: Fifty Essays on Modern and Contemporary Poems*, ed. Al Filreis and Anna Strong Safford (University of Pennsylvania Press, 2022); "Amelia Rosselli's Disintegrating Cantons: Songs for a Community to Come," in *Exile and Creativity*, ed. Alessandro Cassin (Centro Primo Levi Editions, 2020); "Fog Is My Land: A Citizenship of Mutual Estrangement in the Painted Books of Etel Adnan," in *Reading Experimental Writing*, ed. Georgina Colby (Edinburgh University Press, 2019); "Phrasebook Pentecosts and Daggering Lingua Francas in the Poetry of LaTasha N. Nevada-Diggs," in *The Fate of Difficulty in the Poetry of Our Time*, ed. Charles Altieri and Nicholas D. Nace (Northwestern University Press, 2017); "Chloris in Plural Voices: Performing Translation of 'A Moonstriking Death,'" *Translation Review* 95 (July 2016); " 'Cantonidisintegratidella / miavita': Closure and Implosion of the Canto(n) in Amelia Rosselli, and the Dream (or Nightmare) of a Transnational Language," *Moderna: Semestrale di teoria e critica della letteratura* 15, no. 2 (2015); and "Xenoglossia," a new entry for *The Princeton Encyclopedia of Poetry and Poetics*, ed. Ronald Greene et al. (Princeton University Press, 2012).

Abbreviations

F. T. MARINETTI

TIF: Teoria e invenzione futurista, Meridiano edition, ed. Luciano de Maria [1968] (Mondadori, 2010)

PVL: Poema del vestito di latte, with design by Bruno Munari, ed. Propaganda Office of SNIA Viscosa (Officina Grafica Esperia, 1937)

ELSA VON FREYTAG-LORINGHOVEN

BS: Body Sweats: The Uncensored Writings of Elsa von Freytag-Loringhoven, ed. Irene Gammel and Suzanne Zelazo (MIT Press, 2011)

EMILIO VILLA

OP: L'opera poetica, ed. Cecilia Bello Minciacchi (L'Orma, 2014)

AMELIA ROSSELLI

LP: Le poesie, ed. Emmanuela Tandello [1997] (Garzanti, 2016)

OP: L'opera poetica, Meridiano edition, ed. Stefano Giovannuzzi (Mondadori, 2012)

CI: È vostra la vita che ho perso. Conversazioni e interviste 1963–1995, ed. Monica Venturini and Silvia De March (Le Lettere, 2010)

FVC: La furia dei venti contrari. Variazioni Amelia Rosselli, con testi inediti e dispersi dell'autrice, ed. Andrea Cortellessa (Le Lettere, 2007)

USP: Una scrittura plurale. Saggi e interventi critici, ed. Francesca Caputo (Interlinea, 2004)

ETEL ADNAN

AA: The Arab Apocalypse (Post-Apollo, 1989)

LATASHA N. NEVADA DIGGS

T: TwERK (Belladonna*, 2013)

V: Village (Coffee House, 2023)

FRED MOTEN

ITB: In the Break: The Aesthetics of the Black Radical Tradition (University of Minnesota Press, 2003)

SAWAKO NAKAYASU

MEC: Sawako Nakayasu with Sagawa Chika, *Mouth: Eats Color: Sagawa Chika Translations, Anti-Translations, & Originals* (Rogue Factorial, 2011)

Poetry After Barbarism

Introduction

*From Babel to a Possible Pentecost: The Abracadabrant
Word and the Invention of "Xenoglossia"*

PRELUDE: WHAT IS XENOGLOSSIA?

This book charts the fugitive and dynamic mode of citizenship that can be embedded in poetic language—specifically translingual language, language crossing national lines, aimed directly or indirectly against the jingoistic monolingual agendas that mushroomed and are mushrooming under fascism. The works explored within these pages host a formative if fleeting poesis that undermines the prescriptively homogenous definitions of community innate to modern geopolitics. Such poetic worldmaking takes place in vectors of linguistic stretch and cross-contamination, modeling paths toward alternative republics—republics in which poetry (and its undervalued kith, translation) might assume a central agency.

I name this literary and linguistic work *xenoglossic*, intending to distinguish it from the reputedly seamless code switching of the bilingual native or the polished multilingualism of the cosmopolitan traveler. Both poles of polyglot practice, implying unmarked fluency, have dominated discussions of multilingual literature to this point, though in reality the lion's share of polyglot practice is uneven, incomplete, shored up less by self-possession than by a striving and an attendant anxiety of *belonging less* than one's compatriots, or of not having compatriots at all. Xenoglossic theory as I develop it within these pages distinguishes practices of speaking or writing languages in a condition of unbelonging, unauthorized by some tacit alchemy of the anointed involving blood relation, fluency, and unaccentedness—or else class-dependent mobility and a proper education. The writers that have compelled me to devote years to construing such practices deploy xenoglossia as a literary resource—a site of invention at once aesthetic and, as I will insist, political.

Xenoglossic practice is characterized, as we shall see, by obstructions to legibility that have routinely been relegated, by some ideologically determined instinct, to the category of the opaque (often in the form of the *glossolalic*, or an unintelligible speaking in tongues) or else of the simply wrong: it is shot through by seams and ragged edges where linguistic systems have been sutured together, perceived dysfluencies and awkwardnesses of grammar and of speech, linguistic jerks, hiccups and chokes, cross-encroachments of vocabulary and syntax that betray the way the cohabitation of sign systems within a single person or community inevitably generates friction—and fresh creation. Abject as xenoglossic authors may tend to be in terms of established power structures, their work is characterized by the dazzlingly or difficultly intelligible rather than by opacity. This book proposes that we cross-examine and push past the hermeneutic reflex that leads us to stop reading when confronted by obstructions to legibility. Continuing with yet altering the visual metaphor, we might characterize xenoglossic writing as iridescent—registering that brilliance of motion and encounter that Deborah Bird Rose and, earlier, Howard Morphy thought through in glossing the Aboriginal concept of bir'yun, or shimmer, as a zone of coinventive "reciprocal capture" with Western thought.[1] In these writings, the demi-legibility of a poet's ecstatic deployment of languages "foreign" to their conscripted domain draws in attentive readers to exceed their own domains of fluency, disclosing fresh traffics of thought and of beauty—and triggering mutual transformation of the linguistic cultures in the crosshairs.

Poetry After Barbarism studies xenoglossia as it emerges in twentieth-century literature. It hones in on a series of vivid episodes leading up to and following those notoriously vicious ethnonationalist movements that the West erroneously hoped to have extinguished by defeating the Axis powers at the end of the Second World War. It does not address twenty-first-century neo- or para-fascism directly, instead positing that a combination of lacunae in the modern canon (caused by the passing over of texts in marginalized languages, including those spoken by hundreds of millions of people, like Brazilian Portuguese), deficient archives (caused by the passing over of difficult or noncompliant bodies of work), and the rash resolve of affected nation-states to "move on" from first-wave Fascism (distinguished in this book with a capital F) has resulted in a picture of fascism's manifestations and instances of opposition that lacks key passages. Understanding Fascist ideologies of language and culture is essential if we are to resist the tragedy or farce of permitting history to repeat itself once again, and poetry constitutes an unembedded matrix of resistance that clarifies these ideologies through antagonism to the language in which they are grown. I contend that we must exceed the terms of a collective education that permitted us to end up in the current state of affairs scarcely eight decades later in order to analyze rather than being stupefied by contemporary fascist manifestations, and to invent a shared language in which to rebuke them in the current day.

INTRODUCTION   ❧   3

Fascism relies on impoverishment of the citizenry's linguistic and cultural resources—tactics visible in the "defense" of the Italian language beginning shortly after Mussolini's 1922 March on Rome, encompassing neopurist wars popularly disseminated through a newspaper column and commercially successful book of strategies for "purging" neologisms, "exoticisms," and barbarisms under the title *Barbaro dominio* (*Barbaric Dominion*, 1933), and which resound in the Third Reich's "protection" of the German language beginning in 1933. The reduction of subjects to what German philologist Victor Klemperer, a victim of Nazi anti-Semitism, called "unthinking and docile cattle in a herd driven and hounded in a particular direction" relies on the dulling of their capacity to express themselves as individuals or independently thinking collectives. In *Mein Kampf* Hitler underscored the need for effective propaganda to confine itself to a handful of slogans in line with the masses' limited capacity of understanding and enormous "power of forgetting"; Klemperer sarcastically dubbed the resulting language Lingua Tertii Imperii (LTI), a form of fanatical oratory aimed at stirring emotions, conjuring bankrupt superlatives and a banal sense of historicity. Hitler saw the lack of common blood and a common State language as core elements of the Habsburg monarchy's weakening, and the "de-Germanizing" of villages "slowly but surely thrust into the danger zone of mixed languages" as part of the tragedy that led his glorified "rebels" to rise up against a government that failed to represent "national love for the Fatherland and People."[2] Needless to say, the language of a People conceived as monolith needs to disavow the ineluctably shared histories and futures of speech and writing, which deposit themselves in linguistic resources representing a treasury of exchange impossible to shut down: a perpetual transmutation taking place in the ungovernable work of ears, mouths, and hands absorbing and passing on difference.

Such purist attitudes bespeak dubious programs aimed at walling off language and, by extension, race that pervade nationalisms on the democratic and "liberal" side of the spectrum as well. As president of the newly formed Turkish Republic, in 1928–29, Mustafa Kemal Atatürk initiated a campaign of "Turkification" that has been compared with its contemporary Fascist parallels, as it mandated eliminating Ottoman Arabic script, instruction of Arabic and Persian language in schools, and terms within the Turkish language emerging from these cultures in the name of secular liberal (modern Western) ideals, while ordering Turkish minorities not to speak their native languages in public.[3] In a 1946 article positing that "the present political chaos is connected with the decay of language," George Orwell petitioned the public to "defend" the English language through a number of well-worn rules of simplification, including: always cut words if possible; never use the passive where you can use the active voice; "Never use a foreign phrase, a scientific word or a jargon word if you can think of an everyday English equivalent"; and "Break any of these rules sooner than say anything outright barbarous."[4] In the United States, widespread prejudice and abuse targeting the use and even heritage of languages other than English dates back to the era of boarding schools for Indigenous children (forbidden to speak what were historically approximately five hundred distinct Native tongues); this attitude suffused the hysteria surrounding mass immigration at the turn of the twentieth century as well, and is far from extinct. On the campaign trail, the current president, renowned for the limited vocabulary of his populist fulminations and rally chants and of his 23,000 tweets, tested out a talking point surrounding the menace represented by foreign languages unknown to himself: "We have languages coming into our country. . . . These are languages—it's the craziest thing—they have languages that nobody in this country has ever heard of. It's a very horrible thing."[5] This attitude was consummated in an executive order issued when this book was in press designating English as the "one—and only one" official language of the United States for the first time, part of an effort to "reinforce shared national values"—a startling and legally questionable departure from the heritage of a nation still acclaimed as a melting pot.

The present study homes in on cases that expose such rules not only as hopelessly out of step with the realities of twentieth-century subjects, but as politically and culturally stultifying. Individuals' relations to language are far less stable, this book will show, than myths of the mother tongue and national language—and even the presumptions of "plain language"—allege. Jacques Derrida's *Monolingualism of the Other, or the Prosthesis of Origin* argues that no tongue is exclusively one's "own"; since no master can maintain "relations of property or identity that are natural, national, congenital, or ontological" with language, the master must thus "pretend historically, through the rape of a cultural usurpation" that is "always essentially colonial, to appropriate it in order to impose it as 'his own.'" Poet/translator/theorists in his wake like Pierre Joris operate according to the premise that "Language is the stranger, the other . . . which always, and irremediably so, remains the outside."[6] I focus on authors who, while lacking a common geopolitical identity, share the condition of having been molded (negatively) by nationalism in its most virulent and essentially modern form—as a tribal myth predicated on the homogenization of an ineluctably mixed race, language, and culture or as a settler-colonial construct predicated on the eradication of Indigenous sovereignty and on the statelessness and inhumanity of people whose ancestors were abducted from afar. I study cases in which the prescripts and privileges of full-blooded citizenship and a chance at "mastering" the dominant State language are rejected, fled from, or withdrawn; yet in the sense developed by Édouard Glissant in *Le Discours antillais*, here "non-mastery . . . of an appropriated language" triggers "critical revision" of the authoritarian, prestigious language's hegemony—or to deploy Glissant's original French term, "domesticage."[7] My genealogy therefore exhumes from these authors (and from

INTRODUCTION ❧ 5

the many I might have included had I had several tomes of exposition at my disposal) a solidarity and kinship of orphans whose works constitute testing grounds for future-oriented poetics. I do not treat here an equally crucial subject: the vying for nationhood by minoritized groups who have historically been deprived of that status and whose political recognition would at least trigger hope for a radically different outcome—for some counter to that endpoint of romantic nationalism after which Theodor Adorno declared the composition of lyric poetry to be barbaric.[8]

The core questions of this monograph derive from a dozen years of research toward my 2012 book *Locomotrix*, which having manifested in a lengthy critical introduction and translations of Amelia Rosselli, a refugee from European Fascism, ranging from her first to her final works, had still not exhausted the questions opened up by her invention of a "cubic" poetic stanza aimed at hosting all possible rhythms of all possible languages: Can poetry ever come to constitute a universal language, like its reputed corollaries, music, gesture, and painting? Is it possible to forge a universal poetry in a world of divisive national idioms—a world haunted by the specter of fascism? Are poets who transgress national grammars indeed capable of quashing the political boundaries between cultures that so often doom interchange, or are they fated to the status of the barbarian?

Lacking a "mother" tongue in the ideologically familiar sense, Rosselli invented a "cube-form" as a means of harmonizing the roiling linguistic energies within each of her stanzas—tidal jerks of which are unmistakable in the free verse of sequences not subject to this rule. Rosselli's work has commonly been discussed as multilingual, and indeed, her early experiments manifest the sort of cross-lingual play that we normally associate with that term. The trilingual games of her "Diario in Tre Lingue" comply with this sort of treatment, as the poet positions herself at a high noon of accumulating political and literary geographies:

> midi italien
> Anglais-Américain
> France littéraire
> Italie Classique-Moderne
> Le Chinois
> smattering of German
> > Latin
> > Greek

contraption littéraire

contrazioni (cramps)

hystoire phonetik[9]

6 INTRODUCTION

Smatterings of the "foreign" within a largely French text may well be what triggers the phrase "literary contraption," shot through with suspicion, before morphing into contractions, or birthing cramps, lodged in Italian and English; these are followed by the coinage "phonetik hystery"—mingling "history" with "hysteria" and spelled, as if to creolize, the French phrase with a phonetic -k instead of a -que.

The mature translingual poetic of Rosselli is more disconcerting than any accumulation of foreign smatterings of the sort that she discovered early on in the multilingual modernists and rejected. To distinguish her xenoglossic poetics, it is necessary to attempt analysis of the more subtle discomposure of poems that appear to be composed in a single language. The lyrics of "Poesie," dated to 1959, and published in the collection *Variazioni belliche*, pursue an anachronistic mode with obvious tethers in metaphysical verse and the dolce stil novo. One of various references to Donne's Holy Sonnets appears in a secular prayer about death and reason:

> Fui, volai, caddi tremante nelle
> braccia di Dio, e che quest'ultimo sospiro
> sia tutt'il mio essere, e che l'onda premi,
> stretti in difficile unione, il mio sangue,
> e da quell'inganno supremo mi si renda
> la morte divenuta vermiglia, ed io
> che dalle commosse risse dei miei compagni staccavo
> quell'ansia di morire
> godrò, infine,—l'era della ragione;
> e che tutti i fiori bianchi della riviera, e
> che tutto il peso di Dio
> battano sulle mie prigioni.

> I was, I flew, I fell atremble into the
> arms of God, and may this final sigh
> be my entire being, and may the wave abounty,
> straits in difficult union, my blood,
> and from that supreme ruse may death
> become vermillion be rendered me, and I
> who from the ardent riots of my comrades detached
> that anxiousness to die
> will relish, at last,—the age of reason;
> and may all the white riviera flowers, and
> all the weight of God
> beat at my prisons.[10]

INTRODUCTION &~ 7

At first blush, this lyric is comfortably "Italian," though hailing back to a moment and mode when Italian was hardly a national language. Yet the subjunctive mode here, that of a secular prayer, produces a range of ambiguities that slow reading and hermeneutic operations reveal; we might rashly read them as mistakes before thinking through how these deviations from grammatical expectation become poetically generative. The construction of "e che l'onda premi, / stretti" (following "sia" earlier in the line) leads us to believe both "premi" and "stretti" are meant to be subjunctive verbs qualifying the wave that pushes and pulls tight. "Premi" might read initially as the "premere" or "push" of the wave but ends up resolving as the subjunctive form of the verb "to award/repay/honor," so that we may hear both constructions at once, teetering between the simple present of one verb and the subjunctive mood of another. In propulsion from the preceding subjunctives, one presumes "stretti" to be a verb; however, the subjunctive form of "to grasp/clasp/pull tight" would be "stringa," so it becomes clear that "stretti" is instead a noun ("straits" or musical "strettos"), likely chosen for its assonance with all the "t" sounds of "tutt'il," "tutti" and "tutto," and finally "battano" (batter, à la Donne). In translating I've attempted to twist expectation in another way, hoping "abounty" might get at the awarding and the binding in a single word, as well as the way that "premi, / stretti" trips up reading. That the speaker's blood is marked as hybrid in precisely these phrases, as plural straits (or quickening musical passages) difficultly united, subtends the greater environment of linguistic, cultural, and indeed racial uncertainty that pervades Rosselli's oeuvre—an uncertainty that beplagues all xenoglossic writing and that distinguishes it from more familiar versions of multi- and translingual practice.

The apparently simple, prayerlike "Fui, volai" casts a blood-tinged death as the endpoint of the age of reason. It recalls the fact that Rosselli kept a photograph of her savagely assassinated father and uncle, lying in their own blood in Bagnoles-de-l'Orne, at her desk. (Having learned of this fact, I proposed to publish this image in the biography I developed for *Locomotrix*, but the photograph mysteriously disappeared.) While examples of xenoglossia in Rosselli are innumerable, I foreground this moment sounding her evolved poetics of "phonetik hystery" because the prayer's beating exemplifies her irony surrounding reason writ large. Rosselli's irony—in which death represents the consummation of the age of reason—harmonizes caustically with Horkheimer and Adorno's thesis in *Dialectic of Enlightenment*: that the ultimate consequence of Enlightenment is a new form of death, a new form of barbarism.

The poet must become a barbarian to this barbarity in order to speak back to it. This means that she is bound not to be understood except under duress, for in an age that rewards only ready clarities, translucent luminosity is automatically treated as blockage, as affront. Umberto Eco reinforces in a retrospective analysis of "Ur-Fascism" or "Eternal Fascism" that "all the Nazi or Fascist schoolbooks made use of an impoverished vocabulary, and an elementary syntax, in order to limit the instruments for complex and critical reasoning."[11] The Frankfurt School theorists glossed the ideology of "clarity" from Los Angeles in May of 1944: "By tabooing any thought which sets out negatively from the facts and from the prevailing modes of thought as obscure, convoluted, and preferably foreign, [the concept of clarity] holds mind captive in ever deeper blindness. It is in the nature of the calamitous situation existing today that even the most honorable reformer who recommends renewal in threadbare language reinforces the existing order he seeks to break by taking over its worn-out categorial apparatus and the pernicious power-philosophy lying behind it."[12]

Poetry may seem the most abject of genres when it comes to resisting fascism; poetry that inspires knee-jerk responses of being off-key, awkward, and wrong—the xenoglossic poetry with which we will tarry in the following pages by exemplars Rosselli, Elsa von Freytag-Loringhoven, Emilio Villa, Etel Adnan, LaTasha N. Nevada Diggs, Chika Sagawa, and Sawako Nakayasu—will certainly appear ever so much more powerless to the skeptical reader. In resisting false clarity, however, this poetry casts out into public discourse precious shards of liberty, with critical "remnants of freedom, of tendencies toward real humanity," as Horkheimer and Adorno put it—"even though they seem powerless in face of the great historical trend."[13] Amelia Rosselli's heroic father, too, had publicly acknowledged the apparently abject status of resistance movements against the rise of Fascism. In honoring martyrs such as the recently deceased Antonio Gramsci on May Day of 1937—roughly a month before his own murder—Carlo Rosselli wrote of the new society, "It seems the passage to a higher phase of coexistence is impossible before we have reached the depths of abjection."[14]

In order to comprehend the political and cultural stakes of this poetry and the xenoglossic mode of song and critique that it will develop, we need to understand the linguistic, cultural, and political contexts out of which it emerged. That task must take us back to the dawning international consciousness to be overshadowed by xenophobic political motions ascendant at the turn of the twentieth century.

BELONGING TO NO KNOWN LANGUAGE: HENRY JAMES AGAINST THE MELTING POT

Upon revisiting the city of his birth after two decades of expatriation in Europe, in 1904, Henry James took to recounting his "impressions" surrounding the overwhelming infusion of immigrants into Manhattan with a notorious stupor

INTRODUCTION 9

that nevertheless led him to lucid reflections surrounding the future of language in the New World—and beyond. James's musings, composed amid an upwelling of xenophobic sentiment that accompanied the entry, that decade, of roughly one million foreign nationals to the United States per year, were prompted by his encounter with the "cheerful hum of that babel of tongues" in Central Park, where what James densely refers to as "the alien" seemed quite at home and (quite discomfitingly for the white expatriate) "in possession" of the metropolis of his birth.[15] Ever the self-conscious writer, James articulates the impossibility of comprehending the horde of "facts" transported into New York from remote lands in opaque linguistic terms, facing the countless new "racial ingredients" introduced to the changing metropolis in dumbfoundedness:

> He doesn't *know*, he can't *say*, before the facts, and he doesn't even want to know or to say; the facts themselves loom, before the understanding, in too large a mass for a mere mouthful: it is as if the syllables were too numerous to make a legible word. The *il*legible word, accordingly, the great inscrutable answer to questions, hangs in the vast American sky, to his imagination, as something fantastic and *abracadabrant*, belonging to no known language, and it is under this convenient ensign that he travels and considers and contemplates.[16]

Synthesis of these ambiguously exotic ingredients and facts hovers in the form of an "ensign" under which the newly alienated New York native travels and that is as obscure as a conjuror's charm, "belonging to no known language" and challenging both cognition and expression for the author of prose; knowing and saying are italicized here, emphatic yet simultaneously registering as foreign to the passage. James's coinage to describe this "*il*legible word" is apt: the word *abracadabra* hangs between languages, nonsense, and purely performative spell. A Kabbalistic term, it is riddled with numerous and conflicting folk etymologies and has been claimed to derive from ancient Greek, Aramaic, and Hebrew.[17] The "*abracadabrant*" word hovering over the land in James's hallucination is poignant as an emblem but riddles the classification of any proper "ensign," or national flag.

Through the sangfroid of immigrants strolling uptown, James comes to fathom that "the general queer sauce of New York," which unifies races through taste in the "hot pot" of the metropolis, is actually the concoction of "the alien himself" and that gentlemen such as our guide are already feeding from it: "Is not the universal sauce essentially *his* sauce, and do we not feel ourselves feeding, half the time, from the ladle, as greasy as he chooses to leave it for us, that he holds out?"[18] James's particular form of xenophobia differs from that of popular US representations of selected immigrants as those who would not assimilate; a

FIGURE 0.1 C. J. Taylor, "The Mortar of Assimilation—And the One Element that Won't Mix," *Puck*, June 26, 1889. Collection of the National Museum of American History. A feminized allegory of the United States tries to mix, by pestle, a mortar filled with caricatures of ethnic types, including one unruly figure who rises above the rest, wearing a sash reading "Blaine Irishman."

cartoon published in the humor magazine *Puck* on June 26, 1889, captioned "The Mortar of Assimilation—And the One Element that Won't Mix" features a feminized allegory of the United States attempting to blend caricatured racial types (Black, Indigenous, Ottoman, and European) in a mortar labeled "CITIZENSHIP" with the spoon of equal rights, grimacing at an inassimilable Irishman wielding a bloody knife (figure 0.1). On the other hand, orchestrated scenes such as the graduation ceremonies of the Ford Motor Company English School—wherein students from some thirty-three cultures donning traditional costumes from their homelands were directed to reemerge from a massive "Melting Pot" stage set wearing American dress, fused beneath a banner reading "E PLURIBUS UNUM"—presume that the linguistic histories of these laborer-students will have no impact on the English they have been taught to absorb as a precursor to citizenship and fair pay (figure 0.2).[19] The metaphor of the greasy sauce that fuses cultural elements that James would rather leave distinct lends carnal

INTRODUCTION

FIGURE O.2 Ford Motor Company English School graduation ceremony, Highland Park Plant, 1916, in which students donning traditional costumes emerge from a "Melting Pot" wearing "American" clothing, reflecting their linguistic and cultural assimilation. Image from the Collections of The Henry Ford, Dearborn, Michigan.

expression to the threat represented by ingesting the influence of these subaltern ladlers from the melting pot. That the mouth becomes the locus of taste as opposed to speech in James's ruminations on the "vast hot pot" suggests that when placed among people so culturally remote, the Anglo-American author is not merely rendered speechless: rather, a primal displacement of bodily functions necessary for linguistic function threatens to be undone (since discourse, as Deleuze and Guattari remind us in their work on minor languages, always requires a supersession of eating, or "a deterritorialization of the mouth, the tongue, and the teeth").[20] Whereas Whitman was able to produce ever more and more English to synthesize and absorb such facts (both those surrounding the genocide of Indigenous nations and those hailing from foreign territories) and to insist that all, however curious, are part of the "simple, compact, well-join'd scheme, myself disintegrated, every one disintegrated yet part of the scheme," James understands these to be scenes of unbrotherhood.[21] James's comments were prescient, published a decade before the outbreak of the First World War and two decades before the Asian Exclusion and National Origins Acts that prevented Asians from entry into the United States and set quotas on Eastern and

Southern Europeans. What's more, the novelist understands that the language of the future is opaque to him.

James's parallel encounter with "superlatively southern" Italian landscapers digging at an estate on the Jersey shore leads him to claim that the picturesque "colour" of exotic types encountered by the gentleman excursionist in Europe, on a "rural walk in his England or his Italy, his Germany or his France," falls away in this "land of universal brotherhood" under the work of "a huge whitewashing brush" applied to the foreigner, making the "vague warmth" of sociability impossible for the uncharmed and no longer sovereign gentleman's heart and producing a "puzzle,... for the head."[22] At the same time, James gripes at bottom that despite the efforts of "the on-coming citizen" to assimilate, "there is no claim to brotherhood with aliens in the first grossness of their alienism."[23] James's insistence as "restored absentee" on the brotherhood being manufactured for "millions of little transformed strangers" that arrive in the United States as too mechanistic and banalizing, on the one hand, and beyond consummation, on the other, encapsulates the anxiety surrounding not only the visual identity of the American population he has deserted but also its language.[24] What sort of tongue will emerge from "such a prodigious amalgam, such a hotch-potch of racial ingredients" as is harbored in New York's "huge looseness"?[25] James can only pose a question that will, of necessity, find innumerable answers, most of which would never be committed to writing, let alone standardized as a national language or literary school.

James's vision of the abracadabrant word manifests both the utopian promise of the "'ethnic' synthesis" that was to be achieved in the century to come, emerging through forms as different as skyscrapers of Babel and the wireless "global village," and an anxiety surrounding the integrity of national languages legible in encroaching political motions—from the 1907 Dillingham Commission to the 2017 Reforming American Immigration for Strong Employment (RAISE) Act (both aimed at curtailing US immigration by privileging applicants literate in English).[26] This anxiety would turn into a monolingual agenda more emphatic with the jingoism of the world wars: Theodore Roosevelt would write in 1919, "We have room for but one language in this country, and that is the English language, for we intend to see that the crucible turns our people out as Americans, of American nationality, not as dwellers in a polyglot boarding house."[27] Yet to his credit, James recognizes that if the earth is ever to be of one language and one speech again, as it was before Babel, that speech will not be recognizable to the cosmopolitan author and his assumed audience of literate settler Anglophones. As he muses, "The accent of the very ultimate future, in the States, may be destined to become the most beautiful on the globe and the very music of humanity (here the 'ethnic' synthesis shrouds itself thicker than ever); but whatever we shall

INTRODUCTION &- 13

know it for, certainly, we shall not know it for English—in any sense for which there is an existing literary measure."[28]

As reticulated as James's prose is, it will not burst the existing lexicon or literary measure to that extent in representing this cultural welter; instead, it takes recourse in an audacious proliferation of liquid metaphors—of melting in a hot pot, of being served a greasy foreign sauce, of swimming in a "sallow aquarium," of washing in a "terrible tank."[29] The task of transforming an existing literary measure in the United States and the world over, as migration and conflict abroad lead New York to become but the most renowned example of " 'ethnic' synthesis" in the global metropolis, will in key instances be left to the genre we commonly identify as poetry—a genre in which transformations of reigning narratives more readily unfold through the reformulation of language. Modernist artists across the globe who embraced the linguistic welter being generated by mass migration and global telecommunications would soon consummate James's portents through poetic experimentation as they forged idioms resisting comprehension as national. Despite James's patent xenophobia and his shock at soundscapes such as that of "a Jewry that had burst all bounds" in the murmurs of "the dense Yiddish quarter," the polyglot Jewish modernist poet and translator Louis Zukofsky, for one, would later claim such consummation and adopt as literary ancestor "H. J. intensely in / New York the year I was born."[30]

LA XÉNOGLOSSIE AT THE TURN OF THE TWENTIETH CENTURY

In 1905, the year that James's essay was published in *North American Review*, both references to the myth of Babel and the compensatory dream of a common language were profuse. This was the year that the first World Congress of Esperanto was convened in Boulogne-sur-Mer, France, on the edge of the English Channel. It was also the year that the term *xenoglossia* first appeared in print to describe a phenomenon contrasting starkly with the rationalized mode of debabelization represented by auxiliary languages. "Xénoglossie" was coined by a French physiologist and future Nobel Prize winner to describe the inexplicable experiences of a medium, Madame X, who wrote long sentences in Greek while in a trance, without having studied the language.[31] Xenoglossia (also known as xenolalia) has come to denote the intelligible use of a natural language one has not learned formally or does not know—a concept distinguishable from (though often confused with) glossolalia, or lexically incommunicative utterances. The canonical narrative of this phenomenon in Western literature reaches back to the story of Pentecost in Acts of the Apostles, chapter 2, wherein a burst of divine breath is said to have descended upon the followers of Christ, bestowing upon them suddenly the ability to speak in languages previously alien to them. As the King James edition renders it: "And suddenly there came a sound from heaven as of a rushing mighty wind [πνοῆς/ pnoēs ('blowing, wind, breath')],[32] and it filled all the house where they were sitting. And there appeared unto them cloven tongues like as of fire, and it sat upon each of them. And they were all filled with the Holy Ghost, and began to speak with other tongues, as the Spirit gave them utterance."

The Holy πνοῆ, spirit, breath, or Ghost whose fire descends upon the disciples enables Galileans—who would have been understood by the audience of Acts to be uneducated—suddenly to speak the native languages of pilgrims from the many nations of the Jewish diaspora present for the feast of Pentecost. These groups would have traveled to Jerusalem from every corner of the known world spanning modern Iran to Egypt, and they are named in a list crafted, as biblical scholars have argued, to undermine Rome's claim to universal rule: "Parthians, and Medes, and Elamites, and the dwellers in Mesopotamia, and in Judaea, and Cappadocia, in Pontus, and Asia, / Phrygia, and Pamphylia, in Egypt, and in the parts of Libya about Cyrene, and strangers of Rome, Jews and proselytes, / Cretes and Arabians."[33] Artifacts such as the twelfth-century Cupola of the Pentecost in Saint Mark's Basilica emphasize the harmonizing of nations implicit in this story, picturing in mosaic tesserae the convergence of pairs of young and aged men representing each of the distinct peoples listed in Acts via the rays of the Holy Spirit and divine fire enlightening the preaching followers of Christ (figure 0.3). This event is widely interpreted as a remedy for the confusion of tongues meted out as divine punishment for construction of the Tower of Babel in Genesis 11:5–8: "Go to, let us go down, and there confound their language, that they may not understand one another's speech." Yet unlike Babel, which has become a ubiquitous cliché in the literary criticism and theory of our times, the dream of Babel's resolution in Pentecost through the reconciliation of languages has received very little attention outside of religious contexts.

The story of Pentecost tends to emerge in instances of linguistic confusion when the need for translation is on the rise, and it generates a fascinating tension with the ideology of the mother tongue. My intention in studying its invocation throughout the twentieth century is not to adjudicate the factuality or lack thereof of religious or secular testimonials but to understand the aspirations to channel an unmastered tongue into literature—and to ponder the effects of poems of secular "pentecostal" strain upon their linguistic and political ecologies

FIGURE 0.3 Anonymous Greek masters, Cupola of the Pentecost, Saint Mark's Basilica, Venice, twelfth century. Photo by Dennis G. Jarvis. CC BY-SA 2.0. Depicts the Holy Spirit, Apostles, and representatives of sixteen peoples to whom the apostles preached: labeled, as according to the Acts of the Apostles, *Parthi, Medi, Elamitae, Mesopotamia, Judea, Cappadocia, Pontum, Asiatici, Phrygiam, Pamphiliam, Aegiptum, Libiam, Romani, Judei, Cretes,* and *Arabes.*

of adoption. While presumptions of nationality and nativity continue to govern the reception of literary works, mass migration, colonization, war, and trade place greater and greater stress on the putative intimacy between any given subject and a single mother tongue in the twentieth century, such that in a range of contexts, as Jing Tsu demonstrates in her study of global language exchange and governance in the Sinophone world, "just how one manages to arrive at the inside of language, to command its use and to maneuver its effect, and to become an anointed member of its community of speakers hardly looks easy."[34] Becoming an anointed member of the community against a backdrop of variously unfolding strains of xenophobic racism, in the mildest instances, and, in the most extreme, of waves of "palingenetic ultranationalism" (to cite Roger Griffin's canonical definition of revolutionary fascism) is particularly onerous.[35] The recurrent upwelling of fascist populism across the globe has made clear the importance of the relatively flexible, which is to say ideologically cynical, Italian archetype of this political drive (identified by Eco via "the philosophical weakness of its ideology"), which continues to serve as synecdoche for manifold manifestations of totalitarianism.[36] The Italian case provides a vivid point of critical departure in revealing the peril of origin myths, as a perceived border crisis in an economy of decline revitalizes the appeal to a spectral "Italianity," resulting in a dominant political order (Fratelli d'Italia or Brothers of Italy) that is a direct descendant of the neofascist Movimento Sociale Italiano. I present a range of cases in this study—from that of the Alexandria-born avowed Fascist modernist F. T. Marinetti through contemporary poet-theorists of the rigorously internationalist anticolonial Black diaspora—to propose that the translingual poetry of the unanointed, however marginalized in reception for ideological reasons, should be read as political trial and errantry against this backdrop of shifty, performatively besieged, irrationalist traditionalism.[37] Situating poetic experiments that counter the multifaceted evolution of white supremacy within the longue durée of Pentecostal longing historicizes their reach for communion across entrenched cultural divisions but also their interrogation of concepts of nationhood and of belonging via blood, milk, and soil.

The unstudied or inspired, even divine or otherwise paranormal channeling of natural languages by subjects deemed improper to those languages places on display language's bursting at its imagined seams in accounts of experience that transgress policed national and ethnic divisions—such that the resultant idiolects come across as dissonant, dissident, made for no given group or no yet-extant one, destabilizing the authoritarian dicta and myths of rootedness notoriously enforced over the course of the twentieth century. The disfluency in these poets' use of multiple language systems, however conscious, has a disconcerting effect contrary to the satisfying hermeneutic game of multilingual modernist monuments, which boast masterful pastiches that formed the building blocks of a new canon—and it is wobblier than any fluid act of code switching. Indeed, the eccentric qualities of these texts cause them to seem impossibly bizarre, opaque, and shrouded to hermeneutics, such that despite their uses of natural languages, a critical tic for their analysis becomes not translation but their classification as nonsemantic, leading to the frequent invocation of glossolalia.[38]

Naming these works "xenoglossic" signals their character as translingual and unlearned rather than cleanly macaronic or prone to code switching—less fluid or fluent than the poetry of bilingual authors, yet not authorized as cosmopolitan. I deploy the term to underscore that such poetics, however disorienting, are *not* nonsemantic, distinguishing them from the act of speaking in tongues with which

INTRODUCTION &- 17

they are often confused because of their disobedience toward borders between national languages. As a result of the transmogrified form of literacy they demand, we are compelled to read these poems and the poets that compose them as latent citizens, rather than casting them outside the borders of the overweening national language as barbarians. In the process, these texts perform their own critiques of the sociobiology of blood and reformulate notions of kinship as wrought of intersectional vigilance, solidarity, and mutual recognition in the process.[39] Such poetics achieve a defamiliarizing mode of artistry that we need to reckon with in its translucency (as opposed to invoking by knee-jerk reflex the ubiquitously adopted term from Édouard Glissant, "opacity")—generating glints of refracted meaning that draw in readers of varying remoteness to the language(s) of composition to unlearn natural or national grammars, and to learn again.[40]

This book argues, then, that poets act as forceful agents of linguistic and consequently of cultural change, and that poems poised at the experiential or researched boundaries of language systems make the "translational" elements of all language particularly emphatic, thereby challenging readers to transgress the ideological barriers between one linguistic system and the next imposed by national grammars.[41] Poems composed in "orphan" tongues manifest, often dolorously, their disbelonging to reigning nation-states or fixed communities, while aspiring to craft room for utopian congregations of linguistic and cultural alterity. Such a congregation was formed in literal terms under the name Pentecostalism in the same moment of Henry James's return "home."

THE EMERGENCE OF PENTECOSTALISM: TRANSGRESSIONS OF CITIZENSHIP

In the moment when Ludwik Lazar Zamenhof ("Doktoro Esperanto") was presenting the case for an artificial universal language to an audience of linguists, diplomats, and logicians, a multiracial, multiethnic, and mixed-class group of believers led by the African American preacher William J. Seymour in Los Angeles was claiming, among other gifts of the Holy Ghost, the sudden ability to speak in foreign languages without instruction. In the period of James's reflections on the abracadabrant word, a new form of Pentecostalism was emerging in the United States, driven by African American preachers from the South and based on ecstatic forms of worship that included dancing and speaking and singing in tongues. Catalyzed by what is now known as the Azusa Street Revival in Los Angeles, taking off in April of 1906 in a congregation mixing Black, European, Jewish, Korean, Native

American, and Latino worshippers, Pentecostalism rapidly transgressed national borders, spreading to Asia, Africa, Europe, and Latin America and eventually gaining five hundred million adherents, as studies of the internationalism inherent and implicit in tongues' "Pentecostal process of transnationalisation" attest.[42] Whereas contemporary Pentecostalism is dominated by ecstatic glossolalia, or "tongues," the phenomenon at Azusa Street was represented as a xenoglossic event, whose sociopolitical implications I wish to recuperate for the purposes of this study. Immigrants told of uneducated white and Black members of the congregation suddenly able to speak in and translate from languages such as Hebrew, Yiddish, German, Italian, Arabic, and Spanish, and local newspapers decried the "New Sect of Fanatics" and "Weird Babel of Tongues"—because worshippers were, to their ears, "Breathing strange utterances and mouthing a creed which it would seem no sane mortal could understand" (figure 0.4).[43] According to one key participant, "It seemed as if a vessel broke within me and water surged up through my being, which when it reached my mouth came out in a torrent of speech in the languages which God had given me.... I sang under the power of the Spirit in many languages, the interpretation both words and music which I had never before heard, and in the home where the meeting was being held, the Spirit led me to the piano, where I played and sang under inspiration, although I had not learned to play."[44]

In testifying to channeling a multitude of languages, these seminal gatherings of the mission at Azusa Street came under suspicion for promoting "disgraceful intermingling of the races." The Pentecostal evangelist, missionary, and journalist Frank Bartleman, whose chronicles are credited as being key to Pentecostalism's

FIGURE 0.4 Headline from a front-page article of the *Los Angeles Daily Times* devoted to the Azusa Street revival, April 18, 1906.

global success, affirmed in his 1925 book *How Pentecost Came to Los Angeles* that through these events "the 'color line' was washed away in the blood of Christ."[45] These events represented precisely the sort of racial melting and potential for a transgressive commons at which James finds himself balking when faced with laborers from the Global South strolling in "his" American North: a situation in which the author's cosmopolitan acquaintance with hegemonic European tongues provides little ground on which to broach "the play of mutual recognition," leaving him speechless in the immediate scenario, illiterate in the face of the abracadabrant word, and performatively lacking language at the moment of composition.[46]

Esperantists strove to overcome linguistic difference, but revivalists were perceived as a threat because in acts of tongues and xenoglossia, they occupied zones of linguistic and cultural difference. In 1907, as Jim Crow continued to rage, Seymour, born to recently emancipated laborers and preaching from behind stacked shoeboxes, reinforced that linguistic, racial, and national commingling was central to the purpose of the movement: "One token of the Lord's coming is that He is melting all races and nations together, and they are filled with the power and glory of God."[47] One can imagine how threatening this vision would have been to a white majority and how easily it could have been dismissed as irrational illusion or fakery. One can also easily deduce why academic scholarship and Western theory would shy away from such a concept—while the rational undertaking of building and its deconstruction via Babel would lend itself more easily to theoretical extrapolation.

In a 2016 study titled *Blackpentecostal Breath: The Aesthetics of Possibility*, Ashon T. Crawley elicits from this radical Black tradition of Pentecostalism (within which Crawley was raised, though not without critique) the conditions necessary for unsettling the categorical distinctions of disciplinary knowledge that buttress racist epistemology. He sees in these performances "the perpetual reconfiguration—and, with hope, the dismantling of and building something otherwise—of normative, violative modes of repressive and regulatory apparatuses" that produce the coherence of the state.[48] At the core of this reconfiguration is the phenomenon of tongues, a "linguistic rupture" that for Crawley "announces and enunciates expanded sociality."[49] Crawley foregrounds the question of whether tongues in this tradition is xenolalic or glossolalic and determines that it is the latter, reading xenolalia through its missionizing tendencies as a "settler colonial claim on language."[50] Yet the jubilant adoption of a hegemonic language by a subaltern subject has quite a different effect. While Crawley and scholars such as Frank Macchia have rightly seen in xenoglossia a gesture with colonial implications—implicitly justifying imposition of the Christian Word and doctrine upon a range of Indigenous peoples—I deploy the term here to describe aspirations that invert

20   INTRODUCTION

the evangelizing gestures of empire, undertaken by artists on the frayed margins of belonging.[51] Christine Cooper-Rompato's research on women's xenoglossia in late medieval narratives shows that this miracle's "promise of complete equivalence between languages" addresses anxieties and "questions . . . concerning women's 'appropriate' language acquisition, usage, and access to translation."[52] Turning to a much later moment in which the term "xenoglossia" was coined, I sound the ways that the ecstatic, playfully poetic wielding of language by illegitimate outsiders exposes fears and designs that counter them surrounding authority and definitions of community. Gloria Anzaldúa, too, cast the "inaudible" speech of women of color whose schooling "did not give us the skills for writing nor the confidence that we were correct in using our class and ethnic languages" as an act of speaking in tongues "like the outcast and the insane," and bid her fellow mujeres de color, "Write with your tongues of fire."[53]

I adopt the term xenoglossia as a literary-critical tool to recognize the creative work that individual poets undertake to express themselves in tongues officially foreign to them, within which they have no identifiable authority—transmuting the languages they touch and thereby creating more capacious linguistic mediums and literary forms, albeit ones that will routinely be committed to the margins in their time for being too much, unlearned, agrammatical, dissonant, or outright illegible. By adopting mother tongues that reach beyond the bounds of tradition to which they have been consigned, composing verse from the position of the cultural, lexical, and aesthetic barbarian, these artists imagine and breathe themselves into what the poet-translator-philologist Emilio Villa calls an "ideal nationality."[54] Congregations of linguistic alterity route themselves through individual idiolects that are reversing Babel all the time, albeit in coruscating glimpses, in ways unacknowledged by the academies of national languages and literatures. "World literature" doesn't necessarily take root in academies under the aegis of a discipline founded according to occidental terms of comparison; as abracadabrant operation, it flourishes in the continuum established between one language and the next encountered within independent ears and mouths, individual idiolects striving in deviance toward some common ground, orally and on paper. This work is most prominently displayed and best investigated—because it is focalized— in poetry. Routinely confused in contemporary discourse with glossolalia, or lexically incommunicative utterances, xenoglossia has received scarce critical elaboration as a secular concept despite its unmistakable sociopolitical implications: it represents the incorporation of natural languages by those perceived to be lacking the proper education or birthright—lacking what Jhumpa Lahiri, writing in Italian rather than the Bengali of her parents or the English of her geographical upbringing, calls "una vera padronanza" ("authentic mastery").[55]

INTRODUCTION　　　🙾 21

FROM MOTHER TONGUE TO NURSE'S TONGUE:
XENOGLOSSIA'S THEORETICAL MATRICES

Narratives of miraculous translation evince a yearning for the promise of correspondence between languages and thereby for erased cultural difference, in instances and loci of vexing cultural amalgamation—though the contradiction between the Christian Pentecost as a resolution of the punishment of Babel and a meting out of authority cannot be denied, and poetic attempts at trouncing the confines of national vernaculars often end up producing work more barbarous than universal. Echoes of the pentecostal urge articulated in a moment when a national vernacular was an exile's dream—from Dante's reckoning with the calamity of Babel to the papal resurrection of Pentecost as a missionizing unification tactic to dismantle Protestant revolt—furnish touchstones of another protohistory of the xenoglossic, from utopian poetics to its compromise as entrenched dogma. Dante Alighieri's *De vulgari eloquentia* (ca. 1304) argues through the Latin medium for an illustrious vernacular in a context of vast linguistic confusion, being an early early-modern example of a search for the origins of distinct common idioms in an Adamic tongue, although in practice, such a tongue can only emerge through mutual interference. Dante's comments on the vernacular as "that which we learn without any formal instruction, by imitating our nurses"—not necessarily mothers but nourishers at large—produce tension with modern notions of national language even while arguably being their precursor.[56] My project returns to Dante to decouple mother and tongue, nation and language, for as Gary Cestaro points out, the role of the wet nurse in *De vulgari eloquentia* and its predecessors signals that any originary unity between mother and child is already lost to linguistic experience.[57] This untethering can be productive in dismantling nationalist myths of origins.

The Barbadian poet Kamau Brathwaite, for instance, identifies Dante as the forerunner of antiestablishment "nation language"—a type of vernacular (whose name, hailing from the streets, is also useful in slyly overturning the imposed "national" languages of colonialism) expressing the submerged African aspects of a linguistically prismatic Caribbean experience that emerges in the context of the dispossession of those ancestral native tongues. Brathwaite avows that such a creole, revolutionizing English from within, can make the colonizing language follow calypso rather than iambic rhythms and cause it to "roar" like a hurricane.[58] While taking the poetics of Brathwaite, Édouard Glissant, Daniel Maximin, and other theorists of diasporic avant-gardes as crucial touchstones, this book does not focus on colonized populations who generated shared creoles as broader historical collectives, nor does it track coherent countercultural movements. It turns instead to aspirational or aborted projects taken on by individual poets who lack the intimacy of a household language as a result of historical circumstances triggered or conditioned by fascism and (in the case of my chapter 5) extended outcomes of white supremacy over the longue durée. These poets are thereby compelled to attempt to create, or at least to model, an alternative political community through the allegedly quixotic, generatively abject mechanisms of poetry.[59]

The supple and transitory modality of citizenship that can be embedded in poetic language is theorized by the contemporary poet-essayist Lisa Robertson in a brilliantly compacted "Untitled Essay" on the vernacular that closes her 2012 collection *Nilling*. As a Canadian expatriate in France whose vast intellectual gamut has included translation of such figures as the trobaïritz Na Castelloza and the poet-linguist Henri Meschonnic, Robertson elicits from Dante's poetics of the grammarless vernacular "the collectively accessible speech of the household and the street," a paradigm of mutual, open, and antiauthoritarian political community. Following the theorization of the Aleppo-born French linguist Émile Benveniste, street and household, polis and oikos do not conform in Robertson's handling to the ossified binary oppositions that tend to circulate in canonical discourse: The Latin "domus" indicates everyday operations shared by a port of entry rather than blood, and "civis" indicates not "citizen" but "fellow-citizen" as mutually constituted; rather than a dyadic spatial opposition, the two concepts represent differences in the scale of collective reciprocity for Benveniste and his interpreter.[60] Dante's vernacular, sourced in part from the illustrious mobility of Provençal lyric poetry, models for Robertson the inherently volatile, improvisatory, innovative, and ancient coconstitution of meaning in discourse, which is in turn the basis of an entwined coconstitution of citizens "that vehemently overflows the bordered and policed containment of identity."[61] Casting the poem, in its "urgent social abjection" and thus its institutional and economic evasiveness, as the very "speech of citizenship," Robertson draws both this literary genre and the vernacular away from myths of tradition and of the tribe as closed constructs and draws prosody away from the governance of meter and "measure" (recall here James's "existing literary measure"). Together, poetry and the vernacular form a shapely and shaping, if fleeting, "geopoetics" (a concept leading back to Meschonnic and Maximin) taking place in "wit, excess, plasticity, admixture, surge, caesura, . . . polylinguality and inappropriateness," challenging the Romantic principles of "lexical economy and simplicity" and instead hearkening (with a nod to poet-theorist Lyn Hejinian) to the density experienced when new to a language—to the "native complexity of each beginner as she quickens."[62] Within an ultimately conservative tractate that expresses nostalgia for spontaneous self-expression in an infant tongue, a childhood before exile, the vision of a unified Italian language, and the dream of a space and time before Babel, after all, Dante calls upon poets to desert the "'natural' language learned from mothers and nurses, . . . for that which is 'the property of none' (1.18.2)."[63]

This is a different origin story from that of the modern German philosophy of language, conditioned by a legacy of theorizations ranging from Johann Gottfried Herder (writing in 1772) to Jakob Grimm (lecturing in 1851), with Friedrich Schleiermacher and Wilhelm von Humboldt in between, which buttressed Romantic notions of the nation-state as an expression of the genius of a particular *Volk* and invoked the primordial bonding between mother and child as a social yet quasi-natural "drinking in."[64] As such, the genealogy of the nurse's tongue, with its destabilizing implications for notions of kinship and community, deserves its own analysis that might enrich the understanding of the "post-monolingual" condition established by Yasemin Yildiz in her essential analysis and critique of the German tradition, *Beyond the Mother Tongue*.[65] My hope is that this circuitry of thought offers a fresh inroad into the reading of poetry that arises in immediate response to Fascist tales of the tribe and the policing of identity through language (which were, ironically, quick to take up Dante as precursor and that resound in the current Italian minister of culture's claim of Dante as the "founder of right-wing thought in Italy")—and that it can suggest, in closing, more capacious ways of reading the surge in xenoglossic poetry of the early twenty-first century, which is being composed against a swell of dangerously purist origin stories.[66]

Theorizing the unique stress on distinct tongues endemic to the early modern period as played out between species of Latin and developing "national" vernaculars against the backdrop of the Second World War, Mikhail Bakhtin concluded that the literary consciousness of the Renaissance "was born not in a perfected and fixed linguistic system but at the intersection of many languages and at the point of their most intense interorientation and struggle," thus forging idioms that "had to be shaped in the very process of translation and had to master concomitantly a new world of high ideology and strange . . . concepts, disclosed for the first time in an alien medium."[67] The poetry at the center of my book registers a struggle to forge emergent, nonnational languages of interorientation and what Emilio Villa will call "dis-sense" in the wake of the conflict that led Bakhtin to his literary-historical speculations. These authors trigger instances of poetic convocation that disclose such processes of stress that fascinated Bakhtin even if, like Dante, they may ultimately, because of their very marginalization, be speaking "into the void of an idealized community of the learned and just," to borrow Marianne Shapiro's description of the audience of *De vulgari eloquentia*. These authors are products of exile, cursed by a fresh task of universalism. "Of each and every poet," Shapiro writes, "Dante requires that he follow ... the path of linguistic alienation by deserting the mother tongue."[68]

In *Against World Literature: On the Politics of Untranslatability*, Emily Apter calls on readers and scholars to recognize "the importance of non-translation, mistranslation, incomparability and untranslatability" and endorses world literature only insofar as it deprovincializes the canon and "at its best, ... draws on translation to deliver surprising cognitive landscapes hailing from inaccessible linguistic folds."[69] Though a desire for a universal vehicle of communication pervaded many poetic impulses in a century of global conflict, poets have a distinct commitment to preserving the untranslatable—to stressing that language is not merely abstraction but trenchantly material fact. The poetry surveyed here does not partake of the dream of a universal language, like Esperanto, but instead works toward communion with the flawed and incomplete material of natural languages as bridge,[70] and it conforms less to the category of global literature than to planetarity as conceived by Gayatri Chakravorty Spivak, a concept the theorist develops as unsusceptible to nation-state geopolitics and then suggestively includes in Barbara Cassin's 2004 *Dictionnaire des intraduisibles*.[71] Spivak's *Death of a Discipline* calls for a humbler world literature in which we "imagine ourselves as planetary subjects rather than global agents, planetary creatures rather than global entities." This recasting aims to destabilize the cartography of the globe as defined by a geopolitics relentlessly marshaled by imperial powers, as well as the unevenly distributed information circuitry buttressing this process (a circuitry praised by Marinetti in its primitive forms, as we shall see, and to some extent reproduced in the distant reading practices of world-systems methodology, which comprises significant lapses, particularly regarding languages and literatures of the Global South).[72] Against the knowability and control of the globe that the silicon chip appears to offer, Spivak's planetarity represents an unassuming realm of cultural activism wherein such activities as language learning "distinguished from the learned tradition of language acquisition for academic work" become a crucial part of knowing as a form of solidarity with the subaltern.[73] All of the poets focused upon in my study, after their counterexample Marinetti, engaged in some form of language learning and translation on an autodidactic basis and proceeded to compose in languages without the authority or goal of mastery, while critiquing the ideology of official academies and grammars.[74] We can read their projects as a move toward elective kinship or "kith" (to cite Divya Victor's anti-nationalist, diasporic formation of imagined community) with those siphoned off as "other" in the Manichean understandings that dominate modern culture.[75] Moving further, these poets model the recognition of self and other as a continuum—one manifest carnally within the counterintuitive example of the nurse's tongue.

INTRODUCTION 25

In Spivak, in fact, a relation that I will call non-appropriative kithship with subaltern subjects forms part of a critique of subjectivity: Spivak understands identity as "pluralized as a drop of water under a microscope." This conception of identity as a hybrid eddy destabilizes the tethering of identity and origin and highlights the importance of translation, "as one works with a language that belongs to many others," as an act through which we heed our "responsibility to the trace of the other in the self." These ideas are articulated in Spivak's 1992 essay "The Politics of Translation," which considers the problems with translating into "plain English"—as a story titled "The Wet-nurse"—a 1980 work of fiction by Mahasweta Devi whose Bengali title is "Stanadāyini," or in Spivak's literal translation, "Breast-giver."[76] The "plain English" rendering fully assimilates the work of the world-suckler at the story's heart by invoking a conventional, thus comprehensible title and role; by contrast, the ironic, uncanny original Bengali title and Spivak's literal translation of it defamiliarize and contest the sacrifice implicit in suckling as well as the patriarchal and class/caste ideology of the language in which it is couched. The figure of the wet nurse in Spivak's example is freighted in ways that she does not comment upon explicitly but that are worth glossing for the purposes of my argument against the presumptions of the "mother" tongue. For Spivak, language constitutes "a vital clue to where the self loses its boundaries." By wielding it in "generating" thoughts, one enters into relation with manifold subjects, and such relations are rendered most palpable in the process of translation, where "we feel the selvedges of the language-textile give way." (The term "selvedge" refers to a finished border that prevents the fraying of fabric, and represents a "corruption" of the late Middle English for "self" plus "edge.") The bond with innumerable unakin others implicit in language use becomes manifest carnally as fluid kithship with non-"relations" in the figure of the child suckling at the breast of the nurse rather than the "biological" mother. I recruit the relations of nurse and suckler implicit in Spivak's defamiliarizing translation here in order to revise understandings of the "mother tongue." Spivak points to the "spacy emptiness between two named historical languages" highlighted in translation as a site of the fraying and dissemination of grammar and logic inherent within the act of communication. She does not fail to acknowledge the sense of the unheimlich or "un-homely" introduced when language is spoken in a place outside of its "native" context, or in the "homely" effort of speaking "across two earthly languages": "The experience of contained alterity in an unknown language spoken in a different cultural milieu is uncanny."[77] In conversation with Alfred Arteaga, she speaks of Samuel Beckett's French and J. M. Coetzee's English—species of expression backed by "'no recognizable ethnos whose language of exchange'" is the tongue in which they compose—as products of deliberate distancing from a tongue prescribed as "natural" to the self: in such cases, to get out from under the oppression of identity within a prescribed native language (the overtly colonial English in Beckett's case, Afrikaans in Coetzee's), "One must clear one's throat, . . . clear a space, step away, spit out the mother tongue."[78]

The poet-performer Caroline Bergvall, of French and Norwegian background yet adopting English as a language of composition, builds upon Spivak's conversation with Arteaga to develop a poetics that expectorates the mother tongue as imposition as well as the largely unquestioned presumptions embedded in this concept: "Spitting out the most intimate and most irretrievable, the most naturalised source language, or so-called mother tongue (this gendering always strikes me as deeply problematic), is a dare, it is dangerous, but it also starts a whole process of re-embodying and re-appraisal of language's spaces."[79] Bergvall identifies with the revolutionary internationalist poetics being practiced by a growing number of writers and artists who are new "arrivants" to the cultures in which they traffic and who need to create "an allegiance or a correspondence, sometimes seemingly from scratch, or from access-points hidden from view, . . . to a complex living jigsaw of multiple markers and untranslated biographical circumstances."[80] Such arrivants to language are drawn to "question what linguistic belonging means, what fluency entails" because "to be in language is not only to be caressed, held, nurtured by 'intuitive' or tonal waves of recognition and belonging." (The Beckett example makes that clear; the Irish writer's spitting out of English in favor of French is a political act, a wrested instance of liberation.) In defamiliarizing the breathed mechanics of speech through performed and written work with sound, language stutter and loss, and ultimately linguistic dislocation, these poets are "released from this kind of unquestioned psychosomatic attachment." The voice as trope becomes, in Bergvall's model, a sited physiological act manifesting traffic between ejected and adoptive languages in the throat's conduit, "like a constant transport that takes place in the exchange between one's body, the air, and the world."[81] Such traffic renders strange the "mother" tongues from which these writers supposedly hail and that hail them, performing the clearing out of ideologically naturalized speech "with a cat in the throat" (an expression translated literally from the French "avoir un chat dans la gorge," or as Bergvall incisively points out, to have a frog in one's throat, in English).[82] For Bergvall, the friction indicated by a cat in the throat, purposefully invoked (with the feminized chatte being particularly libidinally charged for the queer author), stands for the "autography" of speech, its accent, its marking as other (and implicitly, for the animal, other than human, or barbarian). We will witness authors playing upon these dynamics of linguistic obstruction, traffic, disgorgement, and estrangement on both figurative and literal levels in xenoglossic poetry. These techniques become channels of unlearning what Bergvall later calls "a voice that speaks for us before we get to speak" in a "confusing, seemingly self-defeating process of dissociation, of 'disloyalty'" that enables new, queer, and subversive forms of kinship and allegiance to emerge.[83]

Such poetics, which occupy the interstices between distinct tongues and media, impart an embodied apprehension of the ways in which language exceeds the transmission of both information and so-called national expression. Our understanding of strategic performances of fragmented grammar can be further enriched by exploring the bases of Antonio Gramsci's conception of the subaltern, which indeed subtends the whole of Spivak's distinguished oeuvre. As political and cultural theory, Gramsci's concept of hegemony is inextricable from his background in linguistics and from his own linguistic upbringing. Gramsci was born to a father of Arbëreshë descent—that of Albanian refugees who fled the Ottoman conquest of Albania—on the island of Sardinia, where, in the year that he moved to the industrial center of Turin on a university scholarship, illiteracy was at 58 percent and standard Italian was experienced as a distant second language.[84] These roots led Gramsci to a dynamic conception of the relation between "spontaneous," fragmented subaltern grammars and "normative" (standard) grammars—one that was potentially revolutionary. In 1918, Gramsci criticized the fabrication of Esperanto as a bourgeois cosmopolitan effort as opposed to a truly international endeavor, opposing its espousal by the Socialist Party: "The advocates of a single language are worried by the fact that while the world contains a number of people who would like to communicate directly with one another, there is an endless number of different languages which restrict the ability to communicate. This is a *cosmopolitan*, not an international anxiety."[85] From early on, Gramsci argued that the creation of a new idiom can only happen from the ground up, not as the result of a top-down formulation like Esperanto. He did, however, advocate for the creation of transnational verbal complexes that could forge solidarity. I propose that the xenoglossic poetry crafted by early readers of Gramsci, such as the polyglot communist refugee Amelia Rosselli, represents a fruit of the philosopher-activist's thinking that he certainly did not anticipate— though both Gramsci and Rosselli, direct enemies and victims of global Fascism, should be more carefully studied if we wish to learn from the most hard-won, suffered varieties of antifascist thought. Another Marxist thinker and poet, Louis Zukofsky, opens his 1943 essay on C. K. Ogden's BASIC English by simply stating the source of the acronym—"British, American, Scientific, International, Commercial"—and goes on implicitly to critique that stance: "Ogden is against 'Babel,' the confusion of many languages. But the refreshing differences to be got from different ways of handling facts in the sound and peculiar expressions of different tongues is not to be overlooked, precisely because they have *international* worth."[86] The "international" in these instances preserves the animate material differences that would appeal to a poet and a materialist. When Eugene Jolas, another protagonist of the avant-garde born in the New Jersey Palisades on the west banks of the Hudson River, and best known as the publisher of *Finnegans Wake*, reconceived of "Atlantica" or "Crucible Language" in the early 1940s as a species of polyglossia that "might bridge the continents and neutralize the curse of Babel," it was not "by being an invention like Esperanto or Interglossia" but by absorbing the grammatical and lexical remnants of innumerable idiolects.[87] This "embryonic language of the future," claimed by Jolas as "the result of the interracial synthesis that is going on in the United States,"[88] was already in use and being constantly invented on the fringes of academic language—both by immigrants and by poets such as Joyce, "individuals with sensitive antennae, sensing linguistic decomposition and conscious of the growing trend to abolish the frontier-posts of words."[89] Michael North rightly pointed out in *Reading 1922* that modernism was conditioned by grappling with the impossibility of an international language—by a move from debabelization (aligned with the grandiose effort of centralization in Babylon's Tower) to rebabelization (aligned with the Tower's inevitable fall into disunity, and resultant babble).[90] My study lingers on the wistful aspiration toward communicability. It recognizes concurrently that poets working across or beyond languages continue to crave understanding beyond the nation in a pentecostal key, *and* that the common tongue they forge often emerges as cryptic and easy to banish as illegible—being poised at the threshold of the unintelligible.[91]

Although I have studied, written about, and taught the modernist multilingual monuments, I have reasons for straying from such artifacts in this volume. Modernist multilingual poetry has tended, at least since the New Criticism, to be so mystified in the academic culture of the United States as to render it the involuted suburb of an elitist canon for which Eliot and Pound provide the template, as cosmopolitan epics groping from an English-language core toward arcane literary sources. In the bleakest of all outcomes, US poetry written in multiple languages from 1922 forward has provided the academic basis for generations of gatekeeping rituals. One might have imagined a different future: pupils like those who attended the "Ezuversity" of Pound's Rapallo were—in the utopian mirage in which Ez's Fascism paradoxically played a part—supposed to constitute an enlightened population of intellectual renegades capable of radicalizing the reigning academic curriculum as *"Kulchur."* Indeed, pathbreaking poets abroad, from the Noigandres group in Brazil to Pier Paolo Pasolini in Italy, regarded these polyglot montages as touchstones for a radically international vernacular language,

INTRODUCTION ❧ 29

transmitting a "volgar'eloquio 又楼" capable of "taking the sense down to the people."[92] ("Volgar'eloquio" is an Italian rendering of "vulgar elocution" and a nod to Dante's *De vulgari eloquentia*; Pasolini chose Pound's phrase as the title of his last public speaking engagement in 1976 at a high school in Lecce on the topic of dialect and the schools.[93]) Despite these tethers in the vernacular, cross-cultural and -historical references in cosmopolitan modernist poems appear to offer but two possibilities of reception: they either repel monolingual Anglophone readers or send those compelled beyond the verse to annotations and, inevitably, institutions to accrue knowledge that might begin to make them adequate to the poetry. This book sets out to propose *unlearning* as a critical stance toward relearning and dis-sense, taking "unlearned" texts as its points of departure.

A "BARBARIAN" POETICS

While the historical examples I have furnished above present narratives of xenoglossia, the spontaneous or strategic deployment of unknown tongues becomes a material component of modernist poetries that register the sudden, unruly copresence of previously remote languages in an environment of increased mobility, urbanization, transoceanic telecommunications, and conflict at the turn of the twentieth century. Against a backdrop of unprecedented scales of global interchange and warfare, the desire for a vehicle of expression that would traverse cultural borders necessarily inflected poetry, the art most self-consciously focused on the word—as did the fervor surrounding technologies that seemed to make it possible, from the telegraph to the World Wide Web. It is worth pondering the politics of poetics tractates such as the Russian Symbolist and translator Konstantin Bal'mont's 1915 *Poetry as Sorcery*, which conducts a transcultural study of magical language that emphasizes "the *physical power of words*" as sheer sound and shape, "every word an impulse on the air," arguing that "there are . . . crystalline moments where the souls of all peoples converge" in expression; it was a corresponding postwar desire of Amelia Rosselli, born a refugee from Italian Fascism, "to enclose myself in the alchemies of a language good at every latitude" that triggered this book project.[94] However, the "ethnic syntheses" provisionally generated through xenoglossic verse fail by design to fall into line with prevailing dictates of citizenship through democratic assimilation or fascist colonization (within and beyond the nation-state); they also resist compliance with the economizing drives of communication under globalization through "international" languages such as English. An even more discomfiting rebuke to received ideologies of language, people, and state resides in their failure to comply with received notions of possessors of minority vernaculars as comfortably native—with understandings, that is, of "coming from" or "belonging to" any localizable home. Unlike nonlexical sound poetry, xenoglossic poetry occupies an uncomfortable space within the perceivable precincts of, yet skidding across or confusing, national and other localizable languages. In fact, the cross-linguistic research and contamination pervading poetries of the historical avant-garde—from Futurist telegraphic verse through Dada and sound poetry, which appropriated African, South Pacific, and other "tribal" lyrics, to Russian Zaum, with its "transrational" investigation of a lost aboriginal tongue in common, and Surrealist automatism—may be read as xenoglossic to some extent. Though normally characterized as glossolalic, these poetries integrate more or less submerged fragments of human languages; they ultimately locate meaning in an elsewhere beyond the conventions of any single dominant idiom as opposed to negating it.[95] These movements presage the poetics on which I focus in balking any straightforward transfer of meaning from one distinct tongue into another. Instead of accommodating a switch between codes, they reveal the partitions between codes to be arbitrary conventions, and ultimately generate material friction countervailing the proposition that "the underlying structure of language is universal and common to all men," an assumption whose underpinnings in Western metaphysics George Steiner set out to quash in his 1975 tour de force *After Babel* and that enabled a future generation of critics to theorize what is now known as translingualism.[96]

Experiments at the fringes of the seemingly aloof, arcane domain of poetics enable us to witness the vital metamorphosis of language and culture in unanticipated ways despite state denials of cultural traffic and flux. A surprising number of critics continue to fall back on a sense inherited from classical stylistics that poetic discourse acts centripetally "to unify and centralize the verbal-ideological world," as Bakhtin charged in *The Dialogic Imagination*, rather than expressing the cultural welter immanent within any national language.[97] Critics and industry tastemakers upholding rigid standards of eloquence propel the genre's "authoritarian, dogmatic and conservative" tendency diagnosed in Bakhtin's canonical yet disputable contrast between poetry and the heteroglossic novel (eliding the radical experiments in "prosification" that Bakhtin recognized in modernist poetry).[98] The critical presumption that poetry is more locally and nationally rooted than prose, which scholars like Jahan Ramazani have continued to battle, artificially extinguishes from the record those poets who reckon with the "Tower-of-Babel mixing of languages" engulfing any object of representation, despite the fact that, as Emilio Villa pointed out in the São Paulo–based journal *Habitat* in 1952, "the . . . most elevated exemplars of human poetry developed, or better,

INTRODUCTION 31

deflagrated precisely at the apex of the most confused linguistic mixtures, in the critical punctums of cosmopolitanism" (with Homer writing in "four strata of dialect, and, in great part, overflows of barbarous, that is to say, not Greek, vocabularies," and Dante mixing Tuscan vernacular "with entire tercets . . . in Provençal, . . . French, . . . Latin, . . . Hebrew").[99]

The once scant scholarship attending to multilingual poetry in the modern and contemporary era of nation-forging myths has until recently tended to reinforce a sense that languages exist in isolation, privileging either the citational, appropriative practices of cosmopolitan modernist collage typified by T. S. Eliot's "The Waste Land" and Ezra Pound's *Cantos* or the fluidly dual self-representation of bilingual speakers cast as ethnic or racial minorities[100]—with less attention to the creolized vernaculars we see theorized in the poetics of Caribbean thinkers such as Édouard Glissant or Kamau Brathwaite.[101] Even less attention is paid to the ways in which poetry as form may host the invention of singular argots through the commingling of idioms that are elsewhere alien to one another. Beyond the prevailing discursive dyad of elite culture sampling and code switching between authentic and imposed tongues hovers a corpus of polyglot texts hazarded by speakers for whom the concept of a mother tongue has been occluded.

Despite the welcome breadth modeled by the evolving scholarly discourse on modern transnational poetics (as refined by Ramazani and others), it tends to address the canonized sectors of global literatures, which often exclude figures who reject or blur the lexical and grammatical norms of national literatures, and to focus on traditional verse, rather than the forms and media unique to the twentieth century. I have laid out an alternative lineage of theorization here that moves from the ground up: from the process of translation and immanent critique of politically committed translingual poetry that does not conform to canonical understandings of literary movements—believing that these case studies pose valuable correctives to disciplinary rifts. It is for this reason that I have routed thinking in this introduction largely through poet-theorists and translator-theorists: Dante, Brathwaite, and Robertson; Gramsci, Spivak, and Bergvall. (In shifting to the contemporary moment, I will turn to Fred Moten, Nathaniel Mackey, and M. NourbeSe Philip, among other touchstones of Black studies, for a different look at the nurse's tongue under conditions of enforced statelessness.)

Poetry After Barbarism hones in on the fraught inheritance of the "founding fathers" of the historical avant-gardes, with their self-consciously international, cross-media tactics, within the work of postwar polyglots whose writing rebukes the rabid nationalism that coursed through the century's first puerile aesthetic revolution through strategic acts of barbarism—moving from the Italian Futurists and the Baroness Elsa von Freytag-Loringhoven through a sequence of uncategorizable prisms, primarily among them Emilio Villa, Amelia Rosselli, Etel Adnan, and LaTasha N. Nevada Diggs, situating each within a broader context of local and planetary experimentation. My title echoes (and makes a Möbius strip of) Theodor Adorno's notorious remark about the barbarism of writing poetry after Auschwitz. Instead, I name the civilization that produced Fascism as barbaric and make room for xenoglossic and "abracadabrant" occupations of the condition of geopolitical outsider, simultaneously resisting any formulation that might suggest that the end of World War II signaled an end to fascism. The polis created by these poets exceeds prevailing territorialisms, thereby rendering the figure of the barbarian obsolete. While F. T. Marinetti's polyglossy and call to regenerate culture through contact with the "barbaric" attached itself to Mussolini's imperialist agenda, poets working through the immediate aftermath of Fascism forged insurgent verse by blasting national languages open to proliferating channels of influence unmastered.[102] Poets on the margins of citizenship's pronouncements whose expression would be cast as the incomprehensible stammering of the "barbarian" (a concept crystallized during Greek conflicts with Persia in the fifth century BCE and reducing the sound of foreign tongues to babble) rework national idioms via linguistic barbarism and solecisms to trigger spellbinding, however transient and confined, revolutions in poetic language. In the process, they render the ideological concept of a "barbarism" as (according to the *American Heritage Dictionary*) "a word or expression that is badly formed according to traditional philological rules, for example a word formed from elements of different languages" as obsolete and moot. These poets accord with the strategic confusion of outside and inside, of xenos as guest and xenos as host, implicit in Lyn Hejinian's literalization of Adorno's dictum, articulated in the 1995 essay "Barbarism": "Poetry after Auschwitz must indeed be barbarian; it must be foreign to the cultures that produce atrocities. As a result, the poet must assume a barbarian position, taking a creative, analytic, and often oppositional stance, occupying (and being occupied by) foreignness—by the barbarism of strangeness."[103] Intensive attention to this poetry in its estranging linguistic and material demi-opacity refracts reigning debates surrounding global and ethnic literature, as its constantly molting language exposes the permeability of linguistic systems and transfigures the volatile yet still largely inviolate concept of a national tongue.

My thesis is meant to challenge prevailing concepts of nation and nativity that still condition discussions of language and literature and that subtend the infrastructure of institutional spaces within and outside of the academy, even in the wake of the transnational and global turns. Rather than dwelling in the strictly contemporary—in a moment when examples of translingual poetry seem to be multiplying exponentially—this thesis insists on the value of grappling

INTRODUCTION &- 33

with the past and future lessons of fascist ultranationalism. At the same time, I swerve from a definition of fascism that is historically restricted to the first half of the twentieth century because yoking fascism too tautly to the definitions that emerged from that period and circumstance leads to specious assumptions about where fascism may later flourish and how it may direct its constitutive passions of brotherhood and racial hatred—as recent manifestations have rendered clear.

This book practices an exploded historicism that argues explicitly and implicitly for a new perspective on geopolitical edge conditions, involving the rejection or, at the very least, the recession of geographical categories governing cultural criticism that isolate languages and cultures from one another, leading recurrently to the exclusion of vital figures, peoples, and histories. In this endeavor, I heed Angela Last's 2015 call for the undoing of geopolitics via geopoetics (reinvoking Maximin's work and Meschonnic's as transported into English by Robertson).[104] Certain illuminating historical connections between apparently remote loci become evident only when we strategically extricate ourselves from national frameworks; as such, it becomes more fruitful to present my authors as born in and removed from the geopolitical vortices of Alexandria (Marinetti), Swinemünde (von Freytag-Loringhoven), Fondo/Pfund/Fón (Depero), Milan (Villa), Paris (Rosselli), Beirut (Adnan), and Harlem (Diggs) than to present them as exemplary of traditional forms of collective identity. Although multiplying examples is tempting (I think of the writing of my contemporaries and in many cases my cherished interlocutors, Nathanaël, Mónica de la Torre, Julian Talamantez Brolaski, Lynn Xu, Don Mee Choi, Edwin Torres, Eugene Ostashevsky, Will Alexander, Tanya Lukin Linklater, Youmna Chala, Uljana Wolf, Renee Gladman, and Cathy Park Hong; elder luminaries Erín Mouré, Cecilia Vicuña, Rosmarie Waldrop, Myung Mi Kim, and Anne Tardos; and the entire output of presses like Wave Books, Action Books and its editors, the Post-Apollo Press initially founded to house Adnan's work and now harbored by Litmus, and the London-, Toronto-, and Tehran-based Pamenar, to name only a handful), I draw away from the attempt to construct a completist account of xenoglossic poetics. That would be a misstep because the concept of a geopolitically consistent genealogy does not apply to the chosen figures and binding them through the formalist genealogy of the cosmopolitan avant-garde would both overstate their identification with canonical aesthetic movements and undercut their political aspirations (aspirations that this book continually exposes, nevertheless, to be tragically unredeemed, fragmentary, transitory, or even illusory). To tarry with these works is to glimpse a different way of fashioning the planetary.

The intensive study of poetic environments in which national languages improperly merge or are unmoored from their ideological "roots" can bring material and affective texture to Anglophone debates surrounding the limitations of mainstream multiculturalism as a management strategy,[105] of cosmopolitanism as a figure for plurality,[106] and of "world literature" as theorized by scholars such as David Damrosch, Rey Chow, Franco Moretti, Pascale Casanova, and Rebecca Walkowitz[107]—debates that have underscored the importance of acknowledging the violence of self-referentiality and reproduced cultural affiliations and differences[108] and of respecting cultural incommensurability,[109] the density of literary artifacts,[110] the intellectual and ethical challenges of undomesticated translation,[111] and untranslatability itself.[112] At times, these debates, purist in their own right, have lost sight of the texture of invention that emerges in what Waïl S. Hassan calls translational literature, the most visible examples of which have been composed by immigrant, exiled, or diasporic authors writing in nonnative tongues. Writing on multilingual literature has often focused on those authors, like Conrad or Nabokov, who mastered an adopted language.[113] Within post- and anticolonial studies, this writing has tended dialectically to contest the debilitating frames of colonizing tongues against tongues regarded as native (extending the charges of Fanon's *Black Skin, White Masks*), whereas diasporic and migration studies have traditionally been committed to models of code switching. A growing minority of literary critics devoted to the term "translingualism" arising out of sociolinguistics have stressed contact and collision rather than dialectics or bilingual fluency, which is to say, they stress the dynamism of linguistic and cultural boundaries, invoking movement not only between and across languages on a spectrum but beyond them, with the *trans-* as a prefix meaning additionally to invoke an epistemic upheaval of the categories traversed. This movement "recognizes difference and promotes plurality while rejecting ideologies of homogeneity and hygiene that govern assumptions about language and how language should be used."[114] As Lydia Liu lays out in *Translingual Practice*, this methodology, which presses beyond the presumptions of equivalence underpinning standard translation practices as well as cultural dichotomies such as East/West, enables us to better observe "the process by which new words, meanings, discourses, and modes of representation arise, circulate, and acquire legitimacy within the host language due to, or in spite of, the latter's contact/collision with the guest language."[115] Such a methodology proves fruitful in observing the "barbarous" linguistic alchemy taking place in experimental poetry, an alchemy that never manages to produce the dreamt-of universal language but that might generate artifacts "buono a ogni latitudine" for those committed to the dance of listening and interpretation—artifacts forged from a language good enough to produce harmonics along the axis of North and South and to reach across each latitudinal spectrum.[116]

INTRODUCTION   35

The scholarship on multilingual literature has long been dominated by the concerns and suppositions of prose; few have challenged Bakhtin's characterization of the novel as the heteroglossic genre par excellence. Ramazani's 2009 and 2020 volumes on transnational and global poetics constituted pathbreaking departures from this generic lacuna, stressing the importance of verse as an essential locus of cross-cultural exchange, fully integrated in rather than aloof to globalization, and acting as more provocative material for thought by sustaining losses in translation.[117] Ironically, although Amitav Ghosh upholds the fluid traffic between imperfectly mastered tongues that takes place in linguistically rich regions such as the Indian subcontinent against the "serial monolingualism" of European cosmopolitans, he proposes that the novel is an inherently monolingual form, whose most innovative author may be "the one who is most economical in suggesting a diversity of tongues." Those writing in dialects, he contends, must submit to the linguistic stasis of the literary marketplace, even if "they are writing about a world that powerfully resists the linguistic stasis that novelistic conventions impose upon it."[118] Ghosh notes that in attempting to convey the dialect of the Bengal Delta in *The Hungry Tide* (2004), he deployed a metrical form, dwipodi poyar, widely used in Bengali devotional poetry, in passages of "verse disguised as prose."[119]

Building upon yet departing from the critical and curatorial work of Werner Sollors on multilingual America and hailing from a community of poet-critics such as Charles Bernstein, Erín Moure, Yunte Huang, Mark Nowak, and Juliana Spahr that has devoted decades of criticism and curation to illuminating multilingual or intralingual writings as sites of "social utterance and social inscription," Sarah Dowling's 2018 volume *Translingual Poetics: Writing Personhood Under Settler Colonialism* devotes itself to North American poets from the 1980s forward rooted in women of color feminism. Dowling stresses the genocidal quality of what she calls "settler monolingualism," framed as a core component of neoliberal multiculturalism that prevails in discussions of multilingual, macaronic, and exophonic texts that package foreignized signifiers for safe incorporation.[120] Dowling focuses on poetic artifacts that embrace untranslatability and noncomprehension in order to trace their complication of theories of personhood. It remains to be seen how the critical writings on translingual poetics by poets, translators, and critics like Eugene Ostashevsky, Johannes Göranssen, and Uljana Wolf, who hail from and are more explicitly linked to non-Anglophone poetics than the above scholars, will affect the critical discourse.[121]

The geopolitical montage of my study differentiates itself from both Ramazani's broad and Dowling's focalized analyses in tracing the collective political visions (and nightmares) embedded in xenoglossic poetry. Hovering between Pentecost and Babel, between the legibility of "universal" exchange and the total illegibility

36   INTRODUCTION

implied by opacity—in the apparent absence of a Holy Ghost that would render all communication transparent—twentieth-century xenoglossic poetry relies on a certain communicability in order to operate on a more-than-individual realm, in order to envision a collective more expansive than the citizenry as currently conceived. Its optics are closer to that of a veil or a fog, to utilize the metaphorics of Etel Adnan, and its sonics "off-key," to quote an early editor of Amelia Rosselli. Xenoglossia's discomfiting quality, I argue, lies precisely in its arduous legibility—a legibility that demands the unlearning of realms of mastery dictated by hegemonic education systems. Departing from the apparent contradiction between aesthetic revolution and compliance with authoritarianism enmeshed in the work of the historical avant-garde, I sound that tainted legacy in the postwar period as an influence rarely named but rather channeled toward utopian ends. These writings flesh out syllable by syllable Steiner's contention that "Language is the main instrument of man's refusal to accept the world as it is".[122]

I draw exempla from a corpus integrating literary, visual, and performed arts and provide historical frames for the ways that successive generations of authors contend with the dual opportunity/threat of global networking and translation; each chapter focuses on artists tapping into a different medium, spanning visual poetry and artists' books, sculpture, music, calligraphic painting, and vocal performance. The artifacts I examine have been difficult to access, both because of their rarity and because poems with emphatic visual or aural traits tend to be treated as eccentric within literary discourse and marginal within art history (though this is finally beginning to change).[123] Situating these inventive modes of expression in an international context of experimental poetry hosting the interchange of European, Asian, Middle Eastern, African, and colonial and Indigenous American languages, the manuscript strives to further unsettle designations of center and periphery through fresh juxtapositions that permit us to think more capaciously about the aftermath and enduring resonance of fascist myths of tribes, and to read language politics now manifest in global neopopulist upheavals through the lens of earlier refusals. Although inspired by the poetics of polyglot practitioners such as Paul Celan, this manuscript highlights the poetic wake of a strain of Fascism that garners less attention within Anglophone contexts—that of the belated nation-state of Italy, where the population's relationship to a newly imposed national language and its accompanying claims as a mother tongue were exceptionally tenuous and fraught.

While scanning varied modes of poetic expression and situating them in an international context of experimental poetry hosting the interchange of global languages, this study focuses on a constellation of paralanguages that interact with English and Italian. English, the vehicle of British colonialism and US-led

INTRODUCTION &- 37

globalization—whose power and ubiquity are so threatening as to trigger Japanese novelist Minae Mizumura to ask, "What will become of all the national languages that are not English?"—is an obvious choice for elaboration, whereas Italian—a seemingly minor European tongue still contending with countless regional dialects, an uncontrolled discharge by emigrants, and the ghost of the Roman Empire—presents an instructive counterexample.[124] By the mid-twentieth century, literary Italian had still not consolidated the cultures of linguistically diverse speakers on the Italian peninsula and islands, despite being theorized and invented by Dante to heal the wound of Babel seven hundred years prior and multipronged Fascist campaigns to standardize and enforce the autarky of language. Moreover, despite a mounting and dynamic if relatively belated critical record, the Italian strain of Fascism—which became a synecdoche for the phenomenon, as Eco reminds us—is still underrepresented as a touchpoint in comparative literary studies and has as much to teach outsiders about violent yearnings toward brotherhood in language and beyond as Nazism. In fact, given that Italian Fascism grows directly out of revolutionary modernism, it constitutes an essential chapter in the relentless pursuit by populist demagogues of what Walter Benjamin called the "aestheticization of politics" (an aestheticization widely interpreted as the "manipulation of cultural symbology to bring about the pervasive nationalization of intellectual, academic, and artistic life," or the engineering of the semblance of a social revolution for the masses ultimately aimed at cynical reactionary ends).[125] As increasing numbers of refugees, asylum seekers, and other migrants arrive on Italian shores, the question of italianità has once again reared its head, calling for reflection on the figures who expressed this literary tradition's inherently polyglot nature and capacity—for the homogenization of idioms effected by mass media in the postwar period (following upon the Fascist project of Italianization) has not quelled the deep-seated clashes of history, disposition, and socioeconomic circumstance reflected in poetry.

My opening chapter, "Wireless Imagination: Futurist Delusions of Autarky and the Dream (or Nightmare) of a Transnational Language," explores the inspiration drawn by first-wave European modernism from a technology that laid the framework for "the globe" as a construct produced by data networks enabling immediate communication and command across national borders: the wireless telegraph, which made possible a new form of military intelligence as well as increased economic and cultural interchange. I explore F. T. Marinetti's Futurist works of "words-in-freedom" inspired by two waves of Italian colonial aggression in Libya and Ethiopia—ventures enabled by the wireless telegraph as well as the weakening of the Ottoman Empire. This chapter explores the apparent contradiction between the cosmopolitan embrace of global telecommunications and Marinetti's early roots in Alexandria, Egypt, and the rapacious forms of nationalism that rendered Futurism so valuable to the Italian Fascist regime. It goes on to detail how Futurism and Fascism colluded to generate a species of supranationalism consonant with colonial expansion in Africa and a program of autarky involving the paranoid expulsion of foreign "contaminants" from a national language that was newly introduced and, in fact, foreign to many of those on the Italian peninsula and islands who were suddenly supposed to speak it as natives. The acme of the Marinetti section focuses on *The Poem of the Milk Dress*, a collaborative artist's book produced with the designer Bruno Munari that glorifies the notorious 1935 Fascist invasion of Ethiopia, taking note of the global outcry by pan-Africanists, Socialists, and the League of Nations that this invasion provoked. I close by contrasting Marinetti's colonial multilingualism with polyglot poetry by an artist-emigré in New York City: as a counterpoint to the Futurists' rabid ultranationalism, I present the "Baroness" Elsa von Freytag-Loringhoven, Dadaist and "future Futurist," as a poet of geopolitically uncertain extraction who presages the xenoglossic writing to be practiced by the writers in the remainder of the volume. This first chapter serves as an admonition that multilingualism and aperture to "global" expression do not necessarily lead to subversion of a fortressed national language and culture; on the contrary, in the majority of Italian Futurist works, "foreign" signifiers and the global reach of the wireless merely prop up a more efficient, accelerated form of supranationalism, which is to say, in this case, white supremacist imperialism.

The heart of the book, in chapters 2 through 4, is devoted to postwar writers operating in the wake of the Fascist decades of ultranationalism encompassing the barbarism of colonial rule and its uneven disintegration. Each author here represents a xenoglossic or unlearned approach to "mother tongues" deemed external to them; each experiments within a different constellation of national, subnational, or anational languages as a result of experience in a different geopolitical situation of exile; and in each chapter, I highlight an artist's turn toward a different medium of composition to create more accommodating stanzas for translingual contact (without reducing each author's body of work to a single schematic form). These media include visual poetry, "oggetti di poesia" or sculptural poems, and the artist's book in Emilio Villa, music and sound in Amelia Rosselli, and painting and calligraphy in Etel Adnan.

Chapters 2 and 3 trace the work of postwar poets whose visual and musicological research unfolded in tandem (and sporadic exchange) with the global evolution of concrete poetry and the Darmstadt School of New Music, in conversations between artists across the globe that strove to elicit the common roots of tongues in a "pure phonetic ideology."[126] These are the book's longest sections because these complex figures and their milieux require substantial introduction for an Anglophone audience, lacking robust bodies of criticism in English despite the rising trends in publication and translation of their work over the past several years. Moreover, the chapters work to flesh out the political and cultural obtrusions of global Fascism and their long shadow beginning with the immediate aftermath. Chapter 2, "Antifascist Philology and the Rejection of Linguistic Purity in Emilio Villa," introduces to the Anglophone comparative context a pathbreaking poet, translator, art critic, and radical philologist whose disgust for Italian authoritarian nationalism led him to a cross-disciplinary venture in the comparative history of planetary art and poetry at the São Paulo Museum of Art. Villa's relentless work through and against what he lampooned as the "Ytalyan" language would include an etymological dictionary aimed at dismantling the phantasm of European coherence and the "myth" of "Romance" languages through research into their Eastern roots; he trained in Semitic languages during the Fascist ventennio, abandoned the academy at the outbreak of war to continue his work in a climate of escalating anti-Semitism, and pursued large-scale comparative or better, transcultural projects for the rest of his life, often in isolation and in flight from academic or mainstream validation. His translation of the first lines of Genesis from the Hebrew represents the "Spirit of God" as Bird-Hurricane-Turbine-God with Mesopotamian and Egyptian antecedents—tropes confusing or suturing Eastern and Western cosmogonies and upending doctrinal notions of the Trinity, whose possible Pentecost and attendant geopolitical implications emerge as undeniably heretical. Villa goes on to forge extraterritorial poetic forms such as the "hydrology"—a sculptural ball filled with water whose screen-printed verses rendering English, Italian, and French hazy are designed to be read in rolling motion, upending "ideology" through a dizzying and estranging linguistic hybridity.

Chapter 3, "Amelia Rosselli's Disintegrating Canto(n)s and the Holy Ghost of Parental Tongues," explores the utopian metrical strategies adopted by the daughter of an assassinated hero of the global antifascist resistance, who developed a "cube-form" into which the rhythms of all languages might be convoked. Although Rosselli, born in Paris as a refugee from Fascist Italy and a "child of the Second World War," lacked a clear mother tongue, she committed to composing her public work largely in Italian for love of the country her father had been murdered in attempting to liberate—or rather, to composing in a singular Italian idiolect bruised by the traces of the French and English in which her mother and grandmother were obliged to raise her in exile. The chapter contrasts Rosselli's tentative adoption of Italy as a literal fatherland with her aspirations to build a stanza, or canto(n), capable of hosting congregations of polyrhythmic "panmusic," and contrasts such dreams of harmony with the discomposure triggered by her notoriously "foreign" performing accent and cadence. If "to write poetry after Auschwitz is barbaric," as Adorno claimed, these poets compose rejoinders to Fascism by seizing upon the barbarism within the Italian language and revealing the residue of the alien, the unintelligible, within it, while dreaming of an ideal nationality.

Chapter 4 shifts the geopolitical constellation to address the aftermath of European colonialism from a different edge of the Mediterranean, via Etel Adnan, a contemporary of Villa and Rosselli whose formative experiences as a writer and painter took root following the efforts of cultural and linguistic homogenization undertaken by both the modern Republic of Turkey and the French Mandate for Syria and the Lebanon. In a 1989 essay, Adnan describes the trajectory of her relationship to Arabic—a tongue associated with shame and sin in the context of her French convent education in Beirut and a script newly purged from the nationalist Turkey of Atatürk in which her parents met, which her Syrian father had her copy from an Arabic-Turkish grammar book in ardent attempts at reparation. Her family's common languages were Turkish and French; Adnan acquired knowledge of Arabic writing through a channel more somatic than semantic. During the Algerian war of independence, when a dream of pan-Arab unity emerged, Adnan's attitude to the languages of her inheritance changed: "I didn't need to write in French anymore, I was going to paint in Arabic." This chapter, "'Fog Is My Land': Etel Adnan's Painting in Arabic and the Reinvention of Belonging," tracks how this dream constitutes itself in Adnan's painting and poetry, and elicits the geopolitical implications of readers' attempts to parse the hybrid sign systems that result. Adnan's queer xenoglossia, merging writing and painting, calligraphy and drawing, and transcription and supralinguistic gesture, compels those who confront it to grapple past their comfort zones of literacy and to revise reigning discursive categories of cultural nativity and affinity, citizenship and statelessness.

Chapter 5, "Glottal Stop: Xenoglossic Breathing and Transmutations of the Mother Tongue in LaTasha N. Nevada Diggs," leaps into the contemporary moment, to the turn of the millennium, which is to say the full-blown moment of globalization, to ask how translingual writing might move beyond the sunny surface multiculturalism propounded by both neoliberal and authoritarian states in this period, producing a field of difference that challenges the uptake of minor tongues by hegemonic colonial languages. This chapter turns to the performance and theorization of breathlessness by women poets of the Black African diaspora to extend the thinking of Fred Moten, Nathaniel Mackey, Saidiya Hartman, and Christina Sharpe on statelessness and transhistorical maternal trauma. It shows how studied incorporation of breathing techniques from non-"mother" tongues

INTRODUCTION 41

opens language to new forms of performative kinship. Diggs's work across languages through gravely ruptured open fields of phonemes invokes Pentecost, yet her poetry proposes an alternative, xenoglossic rather than glossolalic strain of the "radical sociality" Ashon T. Crawley traces to practices of *Blackpentecostal Breath*—a strain in which "speaking in tongues" hosts the arduous splitting and fusing of natural languages produced and lost through settler colonialism, the Atlantic slave trade, and their reverberation through state-sponsored police violence. In Diggs's Blackpentecostal open-field verse, the languages of empire are subjected to performative enunciation acquired through the independent study of Indigenous languages. Without disavowing the Indigenous right to sovereignty or the catastrophic endangerment or disappearance of Native languages, the xenoglossic poetry of Diggs makes an oblique argument not only for language revitalization but also for the forging of solidarities across linguistic difference and specifically across populations of color throughout the world, who are convoked into a new, more capacious "village." Diggs's interpolation of the glottal stop present in Indigenous languages into phrasings from dominant tongues permits the apprehension of what M. NourbeSe Philip calls "prepositional breathing"—breathing for another, as in the experience of motherhood before birth—to rush to the surface while reckoning with the gravity of ancestral breath lost. Such work implicitly revises Charles Olson's individualist and patriarchal theorization of projective composition by field as manifesting "certain laws and possibilities of breath, of the breathing of the man who writes," and proposes that we shift conceptions of language as possession to conceptions of language as modulation of inescapably shared breath, shared bequest.[127]

My coda, "A Xenoglossic Community to Come: Belonging by Rogue Translation in Sawako Nakayasu and Sagawa Chika's *Mouth: Eats Color*," extends the argument beyond my close case studies to ponder how criticism can respond to a growing number of book environments being produced during the twenty-first century in which "we are all orphans," in the words of Don Mee Choi—a condition very different from the rather more straightforward and common claim, "we are all immigrants," as it lacks a clear origin or conciliatory destiny. The emerging body of xenoglossic poetry, I argue, provides the blueprint for a community both past—the heady moment of modernist collectivity and exchange, dampened by ultranationalism—and to come, in which poetic expression may take the form of what Naoki Sakai calls "heterolingual address."[128] Poetic artifacts such as Sawako Nakayasu's *Mouth: Eats Color*, a mischievously ludic translation that is really a collaboration with eclipsed Japanese modernist Sagawa Chika, entreat us as readers and critics to implode our own domains of literacy in order to reconstellate the universe of divided languages and clans—however provisionally and ephemerally. My argument is fundamentally dedicated to reimagining the form and expectation of the academic monograph in order to make such implosion of authorial domain possible through studious unlearning; that is, I try to introduce a more collaborative, speculative, and above all humble dimension to a genre typified by assumptions, demands, and proofs of mastery (which lead in turn to chronic blind spots and provincial self-referentiality in academic discourse). Through the catalyst of *Mouth: Eats Color*, I propose that, over the course of groping at understanding such linguistic collages, the first-person plural may become a vector not of the universality of expression but of the mutual vulnerability in efforts to understand one another across our incongruities.

TWO "PENTECOSTS" WITHIN THE NEW BABEL: FORTUNATO DEPERO AND AMELIA ROSSELLI IN NEW YORK

Before plunging into a thorough study of colonial Futurism, it will prove instructive to come full circle and return to New York for a glimpse of two species of multilingualism analyzed in this book: the supranational and the xenoglossic. As one of the few Italian Futurists who had a lived experience of the cosmopolis of New York, Fortunato Depero (Fondo 1892–Rovereto 1960) represents a fascinating punctum in the landscape of Futurist output, operating more waveringly across nationalist and internationalist ambitions than his elder, the movement's leading instigator, F. T. Marinetti did.[129] Depero hailed from a town in the None Valley of Trentino-Alto Adige/Südtirol that had toponyms in three languages: Italian (as Fondo), German (as Pfund), and the Nones dialect, which has been linked to Ladin and was being suppressed in favor of Italian during the Fascist period of Italianization (as Fón). Early on, he took up his Futurist forebears' idiom-destabilizing call for onomatopoeic compositions, producing what he called "onomalingua," a species of sound poetry that still gestures in some way toward identifiable linguistic cultures (as in one 1916 "Noiseist Song" ("Canzone Rumorista") in a "Chinese rhythm").[130] The sojourn of this second-wave Futurist in what he called "New York New Babel" coincided with a wave of anti-immigrant sentiment culminating in the openly racist restrictive covenants surrounding entry to the United States, introducing interference to the exultant quashing of borders within this plurilingual sound poetry. Depero's frictional Fascist modernism thereby registers as alternatively euphoric and cowed.

Depero traveled from Genoa to New York City with his now-famous bolted book, or portable museum for auto-réclame, on the heels of the US Emergency

INTRODUCTION   43

Quota Act of 1921 and its revision in the Immigration Act of 1924. This legislation, an outgrowth of the Dillingham Commission, aimed to restrict the immigration of Southern and Eastern Europeans, particularly Italians and Jews, to the United States, and to radically reduce African immigration and shut down Asian and Arab immigration altogether. In an understanding atypical within his circle that the metropolis that so impressed, or pressed upon, James with its swarm of cultures was destined to be a new center of art in the West, Depero persevered in his attempt to become a New York success from 1928 to 1930, setting up a short-lived Casa Futurista for display of his own work and dreaming of founding a Futurist school and village on the city outskirts. These plans were ill-timed, equally beleaguered by the stock market crash and the Great Depression. Depero's applications for state funding were largely unsuccessful because Mussolini's regime still enjoyed favor in the United States and, until the Ethiopian Campaign of 1935 featured in chapter 1, the nation of Italy had no exceptional need to instrumentalize contemporary artists in the service of propaganda. To make matters worse, Depero's radical aesthetic did not fit in with the conservative Italian community in the city—and he relied heavily on that community because he had no access to English. Though the trip proved to be a commercial disaster, Depero managed to elevate his experience to the status of myth—even choosing to publish his memoirs in English and to revisit the city after the Second World War.

Depero understood early on that the city of skyscrapers that had inspired the Futurist visions of Antonio Sant'Elia and Umberto Boccioni, and the conglomerate nation whose roiling energies these buildings represented, was an avenue through which Italian artists might "define and re-define their own modernity," as Raffaele Bedarida points out.[131] My interest here is to discuss the hold New York had on Depero's imagination as a New Babel and his politically aestheticized, reactionary response. As transport and technology enabled people and languages to travel ever greater distances and as skyscrapers assuming the proportions of the biblical tower rose to contain them, we can easily understand how the myth of Babel would impassion modernist authors in the West: with the growth of polyglot metropolises condensing the sense of linguistic confusion, the myth continues to be revisited in secular contexts. Babel occupies a crucial role in Fritz Lang's 1927 *Metropolis*, whose set was famously inspired by the director's 1924 trip to New York (figure 0.5), although the film's fanciful rewriting of the fable suggests that the tower was destroyed not because of human hubris and divine retribution but because laborers and ruler, or mind, spoke the same language yet lacked a mediator who would help them comprehend one another's intentions. Depero created his own series of designs and accompanying publicity campaigns for a ballet of moving sets conceived for Broadway's Roxy Theater titled *New York New Babel*,

FIGURE 0.5 The Tower of Babel as depicted in a still from *Metropolis*, directed by Fritz Lang, written by Thea von Harbeau, produced by Erich Pommer, with cinematography by Carl Freund and Günther Rittau, 153 minutes, 1927.

although it was turned down, and Depero's misfortune in the city meant that, like the tower, it was never realized. "In no other place on earth can one find oneself so alone and lost as in New York," he wrote; "one's language is different, one's life different; faces, hearts, mouths and wallets armored" amid "the apocalyptic spectacles of unreachable Babel."[132] In this writing, the multiple Towers of Babel signify metaphorical foils to success in the cruel city of isolated strangers. Depero's visual free-word tableaus try to materialize this allegory, to reconstruct the form and baffling soundscape of the New Babel orthographically. Despite the references to Babel, however, languages foreign to Depero's own appear only rarely, in the proper names of the city and of the buildings he seeks to erect alphabetically.

Depero's visual poem "State of Mind in New York" (figure 0.6) expresses, in the artist's signature visual vocabulary of advertising and propaganda, the paradox of being seduced by Babel as an ambitious young Italian artist following Mussolini's 1922 March on Rome. The iconic visage depicted through line and orthography represents the (Italian) words for CHINEEESE/RUSSIAN/FREENCH and ENGLISH/GREEK/GERMAN permeating its ears and brain and syncretic emblems of Depero's transnational art-business plans raining upon it from above (the token foreign phrase that appears in this poem is the English "A-B-C-OF-ITALIAN-FUTURISM" within this spectrum). The figure's steely face recalls the ubiquitous representations of the dictator himself propagated in

INTRODUCTION 45

FIGURE 0.6 Fortunato Depero, *Stato d'animo a New York* (*State of Mind in New York*), 1930. Private collection. Copyright Archivio Depero.

public space during the Fascist ventennio (figure 0.7); amid the ray- or rodlike lines that issue from the other side of this sort of mediator's head, Depero has crafted a verbal "FLAG OF OPTIMISM" seemingly waving in the wind and saluting the exalted totems of Marinetti and Mussolini (W equals "evviva," or "LONG LIVE MUSSOLINI," "LONG LIVE MARINETTI," in an only faintly heretical key). The words MOLTIPLICARSI (to multiply oneself) and CORAZZARSI (to armor or protect oneself) form the dome of the icon's head; the eyes, mouth, and ears are in fact doubled and quadrupled, creating a typically Futurist sense of motion that here, however, registers as destabilizing vibration or vacillation, aided by the zigzagging onomatopoeic "SSSSSSSS..." and "TRR-RRRRR..." above. The incursion of the foreign into the orifices of hearing has a vaguely threatening, because deracinating, effect. As if to steady the dizziness, the word FERMO (still; steadfast) brands the figure's forehead in a phallic vertical column, and the image's base is formed by the words "AUTO FASCIO DI VOLONTÀ" (auto-fasces of will). The entire ensemble is bundled together in the form of the fasces invoked in this bottom line: the symbolic bundle of rods

FIGURE 0.7 A propaganda poster featuring Mussolini's face overlaid upon the word "yes" repeated dozens of times, erected briefly on Palazzo Braschi in Rome (headquarters of the dictator in Piazza di San Pantaleo) to garner support during the uncontested 1934 Italian general election (which involved a yes–no vote). Anonymous photographer. Courtesy of Archivio Luce, Cinecittà Spa.

surrounding an axe that symbolizes Fascist unity and power, hearkening back to the ancient power literally to inflict corporal or capital punishment through the Roman imperium.[133] (Roman consuls were referred to as "the twelve fasces," in a fascinating symmetry with the later Christian apostles.) This visual fable falls short of true xenoglossia, although it functions visually as a Pentecost with Futurist Fascism or Fascist Futurism standing in for the Christian Holy Ghost.

Born into exile in Paris in 1930, the same year Depero constructed this "State of Mind" and retreated from his New Babel, the young Amelia Rosselli would arrive in New York State (Westchester County to be exact) a decade later with her mother, grandmother, aunt, and cousins: these were the families of Carlo and Nello Rosselli, assassinated heroes of the global Resistance, fleeing from Fascism's stranglehold on their former residences of Italy and France and from the Axis bombardment of England. Amelia would go on to produce one of the most singular bodies of poetry in the postwar period, one oscillating dynamically between

INTRODUCTION ❧ 47

species of Italian and English (and early on, French). Her corpus renders material Gramsci's observation—in his final, 1935 prison notebook surrounding "Grammar and national language" before death under conditional release from detention in Formia's Cusumano clinic—that whereas "'normative grammars' tend ... to create a unitary national linguistic conformism," "il fatto linguistico" ("the linguistic fact," placing uncommon emphasis on fact's active *facture*) "non può avere confini strettamente definiti" ("cannot have national borders strictly defined")—that "non [si] può immaginare la lingua nazionale fuori del quadro delle altre lingue, che influiscono per vie innumerevoli e spesso difficili da controllare su di essa" ("the national language cannot be imagined outside the frame of other languages that exert an influence on it through innumerable channels that are often difficult to control")— adding in a parenthetical, "Who can control the contribution of linguistic innovations indebted to repatriated emigrants, to travelers, to readers of foreign journals and languages, to translators, etc.?"[134] Hazarding the translation of Rosselli's oeuvre, an effort that lasted a dozen years and counting and that could not fully contain its theoretical-political aspirations, was the prod that led me to these pages.

English would be Rosselli's "mother tongue" had she not spat out the concept (though her father was Italian, her mother was English): although she was educated partly in Anglophone institutions, her more copious poetic production grafts itself to Italian, constituting an urge toward a father tongue and faulty patria, or fatherland. It is easy to see in the figure of the "hatchet" within the following 1953 poem composed in English the axe of the Italian fasces[135]:

> What woke those tender heavy fat hands
> said the executioner as the hatchet fell
> down upon their bodily stripped souls
> fermenting in the dust. You are a stranger here
> and have no place among us. We would have you off our list
> of potent able men
> were it not that you've never belonged to it.[136]

This piece appeared in the *Times Literary Supplement* on Bastille Day of 1966. Unlike the multilingual modernist work that incorporates stray foreign signifiers within an overall national linguistic fabric, as in the *Cantos*, and unlike the rowdily translingual linguistic pyrotechnics of *Finnegans Wake*, this poem in a hazily Elizabethan idiolect is couched entirely within English signifiers and yet discomfits. "The multilingual work that has been fashionable from Pound forward does not in fact interest me," Rosselli affirmed in an interview.[137] But something about this lyric seems off-key, constituted from the outside, from the position of the stranger

48 INTRODUCTION

herein banished (or so they would be had they ever belonged to the lyric's locus): the negative subjunctive ("were it not") and the hortative voices from historically afar, for instance. "Pray be away / sang the hatchet as it cut slittingly / purpled with blood."[138] Here and through the term "bodily" above, the placement of an adverb and its subtly estranging diction puts the "native" vaguely at sea; so does the "purpled," a substitution for the more expected "reddened" or "stained," which nevertheless puts us more vividly in mind of royalty and of the hierarchy in general to which the second person is subjected. These choices strike one as erroneous, yet no error can be pinned down, and one cannot resort to a stable, shared vernacular grammar in looking these usages up. They instead amalgamate an idiolect that—in the manner of Deleuze and Guattari's idiot, originally the private, nonexpert outsider, one uninitiated into Greek society—slows the mobilization of civilization and in the process, via micropolitical movements, resists consensus.[139] Hence the utility of the term xenoglossic in this case. The hatchet of the poem's authority—this ascia (hatchet, axe)—recalls the fascio whose Italian signifier haunts the whole composition from just outside the gates. Despite the violently punitive tone of this scene, that axe falls upon "bodily stripped souls": souls that are either incongruously "bodily" (which do indeed go off, perhaps sexually, "to enjoy an hour's agony / with our saintly Maker") or else are stripped of their bodies, already fermenting. That is to say, the hatchet falls upon dust; authority may fall as well as the souls, already immaterial and already "outside," slip out from under its dead weight.

In the opening of a 1965 lyric written in English and published in 1966 in the Paris-based *Art and Literature* under John Ashbery's editorship, the first person echoes Whitman but with a difference: "radioactive confusion bit into my / brain radiant with multitudes."[140] Rather than containing multitudes or steeling the self against confusion as in her male forbears, Rosselli deploys a nuclear metaphor that bites into the integrity of the subject and her mind, rendering the multitudes within the brain radiant. This gnawing, dazzling action could be a figure for Rosselli's operations upon each queasily national language in which she writes. Such biting and corrosion of the subject and mind in favor of multitudes resist the notion of any god or authority who "chancels," to cite my literal translation from the Italian lyric "o dio che ciangelli," which the poet glossed for Pier Paolo Pasolini as an echo of the English term "to chancel" as well as "cangiare," a poetic term for change, or cambiare, and "cianciare" (to chatter), with reference to "cancello" (gate), "augelli" (a poetic term for uccelli, or birds), or "angeli" (angels), as well as "cancellare" (to erase).[141] This constellation of meanings, in forcing flight beyond the partitions of any chancellor's dominion, undoes the authority it names. In the central and in many ways the core chapter of this book, I will ask us to listen for these heretical, (un-)holy ghostings of languages beyond

INTRODUCTION &- 49

national dominion as harmonic in the musicological sense. For now, the reader may wish to listen to the recitation of "What woke those tender heavy fat hands" in English and Italian translation included in broadcast #3 of "With the hatchet at one's back: 10 years without Amelia Rosselli," which I have archived at Penn-Sound|Italiana for safekeeping.[142] The musicality of Rosselli's recitations, with their illocatable "accent" and defamiliarizing accentuation of both languages, nearly sung in ways that cut across sense, causes these pieces to hover above their language(s) of composition on the aural front.

Rosselli's territorially uncontainable voice finds an "abracadabrant" analog in the extended vocal technique that pervades the work of Meredith Monk—both constituting musical parallels to the concord and dissonance of the myriad languages filing into New York that so discomposed James and that inspired Depero's firm "state" of mind. One must imagine—or can simply choose to witness in ongoing history—the secular day to day of encounter between irreconcilable languages in the metropolis encompassing myriad instances of discomposure and self-steeling as Depero portrays, and James before him, leading to countless less cross-examined silences in the written historical and literary record. Meredith Monk gives a different kind of body to such lapses in her 1981 musical film *Ellis Island*, which in reanimating the ruins of the storied processing station prior to its restoration strategically deprives viewers of the diegetic soundscape of Babel generated by turn-of-the-century migrations.[143] Immigrants being asked their names upon arrival are shot from the back, faceless, without an accompanying vocal. Intertitles as of silent film stand in for their mistranscribed voices, while their quantified, measured, and taxonomized identities are set against the disembodied writing hand of an intake functionary (figure 0.8). Immigrants taking dictation in English, being taught nouns for household appliances and Empire State monuments in their language lessons, are shown mouthing a pedantic schoolmarm's audible voicings in absolutely muted mimicry, their live mixing of accents pruned to harsh, even jarring filmic silence. With nearly twelve thousand immigrants passing through Ellis Island on a single day in 1907, as the film's contemporary tour guide narrates amid the dust in a cascade of overlapping languages, one can imagine how many instances of foundering communication would have prevailed in the inspection stations and streets of the day. Monk carves these silences through editing and then punctuates the moments between with overdubbed vibratory, melismatic syllables sung, her deployment of extended vocal technique as piercing as a whistle, yet forging through its multiphonic vowels the effect of multiple languages, accents, and affects. Such effects exist in tension with the more idealistic notion of the "world vocal family" of which Monk speaks in interviews, with the human voice cast as the original instrument that can transcend cultural difference.[144]

FIGURE 0.8 Still from *Ellis Island*, conceived and directed by Meredith Monk, produced and codirected by Bob Rosen, with cinematography by Jerry Pantzer, 28 minutes, 1981.

The implicit chorality produced in Monk's incongruous sporadic voicings provides a correlative for the xenoglossic poetry I am confronting in its vibratory dissonance. The eerie muteness that accompanies Monk's disarmingly moving images—filmed to record the minute vacillations of immigrants standing still to be captured as photographs, files, and specimens for absorption or ejection—underscores the ghosting not only of these individuals but also of the policy of open borders that made Ellis Island a historical crossroads teeming with abracadabrant accents of the future. With the passing of the Emergency Quota Act of 1921 and the Immigration Act of 1924, the era of mass immigration in the United States would come to an abrupt close and the role of the island would shift to that of a detention and deportation processing station. The doubling down on languages of the "tribe" that was soon to follow would pave the way for the fraught reception of the xenoglossic poetries I seek to recover in these chapters—through readings that will cast them not as alien, but as more broadly representative of the homely and unheimlich production of language at the crossroads of entry and expulsion.

I

Wireless Imagination

*Futurist Delusions of Autarky and the Dream
(or Nightmare) of a Transnational Language*

THE TELEGRAPH AND THE DAWN OF A GLOBAL
CONSCIOUSNESS ACCORDING TO F. T. MARINETTI

In the decades preceding Henry James's musings on the dissonance between the Babelic soundscape of immigrants and that of his native New York, the promise of a universal communication system enabled by technology had been spreading, spurred by the lines of message conduction laid by subterranean transatlantic telegraph cables and by the eventual advent of the wireless. It had been obvious in the early published ideology that the development of global telecommunications held the promise to serve as a sort of inverse Pentecost for ascendant nations—disseminating timescapes and geographies of empire in the languages of power from modernized center to periphery (while facilitating the plunder of that periphery's resources and labor). A woodcut catalogued by the Library of Congress as a "crude but engaging picture" commemorating the successful completion of the Atlantic telegraph cable between Newfoundland and Valentia Bay in 1858, and the goodwill between Great Britain and the United States that it buttressed and exemplified, pictures an American youth in an electric handshake with his British uncle under a lightning-filled sky, exclaiming in sovereign English, "May the feeling of Friendship, which comes from my heart, and tingles to the very end of my fingers, be like the electric current which now unites our lands . . .! May our hearts always beat together; and with one pulse—one Purpose, of Peace and Good-Will, we yet shall see ALL NATIONS speaking our Language, blessed with our Liberty!"[1] The first official transatlantic messages celebrated the electric cable as "an additional link between the nations" (in Queen Victoria's words to President James Buchanan) and (in Buchanan's words) aspired that the cable would prove "for ever neutral"; they simultaneously articulated its service as an instrument of domination, "destined by Divine Providence to diffuse religion, civilization, liberty and law throughout the world."[2] In 1904, Sir Sandford Fleming, railway engineer, pioneer of worldwide standard time, and advocate of the expanded trans-Pacific telegraph communication system, would articulate the utility of the projected system of pan-Brittanic cables and telegraphs in stringing subject nations together "like jewels on an epoch-making electric girdle": "All British subjects throughout the world will be kinsmen in the truest sense; trade and commerce will be aided; the Empire will be strengthened in all its parts and made mutually helpful; . . . and this world-wide union of commonwealths will become more and more a civilizing agency making always for the peace of the world and the welfare of mankind."[3] The metaphor of the "girdle" invited by the form of cabling infrastructure accurately expresses this technology's relation to warfare, surveillance, and the power to marshal data, but it overstates the degree to which the language of such communications could be contained by imperial powers. None of these visions anticipate the potential for global communication to forge a form of kinship not predicated on subjection; none anticipates the occupation or interception of these technologies by nondominant nations and peoples or the cross-contamination of cultures and tongues.[4] When Guglielmo Marconi first introduced his wireless telegraph in 1895, crossing across, over, and around all obstacles with long waves simply by using the curvature of the earth, he made possible a different world picture, one potentially more anarchic (though in practice, the technology was most readily appropriated by those in power). Over the next thirty years, signal enhancements and couplings with the storage media of the gramophone and sound strip that made wireless voice transmission possible enabled a new picture of globalization via information to emerge.[5]

Despite the dominance of Anglo-American discourse in media history, it was perhaps most avidly, consistently, and notoriously an Italian poet raised in Alexandria who articulated the revolutionary potential of wireless telecommunicative union in the early twentieth century, outlining the ramifications of this technology in social, aesthetic, and psychic terms: Filippo Tommaso Marinetti.[6] This key practitioner in the historical avant-garde, poet, theorist, performance artist, and propagandist, whose scrapbooks preserve charts of transatlantic telegraph lines that enabled the transmission of messages from the Mediterranean to the Americas (figure 1.1), pioneered in perceiving and clearing channels through which to modernize not only language and literature but, by extension, civilization and the psyche itself.[7] In "Destruction of Syntax—Wireless Imagination—Words-in-Freedom" ("Distruzione della sintassi—Immaginazione senza fili—Parole-in-libertà"), a manifesto composed as an independent leaflet in Italian dated

WIRELESS IMAGINATION

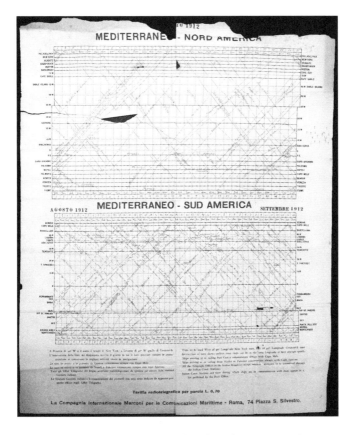

FIGURE 1.1 A chart of transatlantic telegraph lines from the International Marconi Company for Maritime Communications tucked into F. T. Marinetti's scrapbook, 1912. Collections of Getty Research Institute.

May 11, 1913, and shortly thereafter translated for publication in England and France,[8] F. T. Marinetti explicitly bound the fundamental precepts of Futurist poetry and art to the modes of global transit (of persons, goods, and messages) that were revolutionizing consciousness—yet whose consequences for the modern sensibility were being neglected, he argued, by contemporaries who relied on these innovations mindlessly: "Those people who today make use of the telegraph, the telephone, the gramophone, the train, the bicycle, the motorcycle, the automobile, the ocean liner, the dirigible, the airplane, the cinema, the great newspaper (the synthesis of a day in the world's life) are not aware of the decisive influence that these various forms of communication, transportation, and information have on their psyches."[9] Marinetti was hell-bent against the neutralization of phenomena that compose each hurtling "synthesis of a day in the world's life"—offering up Futurist art as a corrective to the bourgeois cosmopolitan's smooth integration of the excitement, anxiety, danger, and sensual pleasure now accessible to ordinary people from all corners of the globe.

> An ordinary man, spending a day's time in the train, can be transported from a small town, dead, . . ., to a great capital bristling with lights, movement, and street cries. By means of the newspaper, the inhabitant of a mountain village can tremble with anxiety every day, following the Chinese in revolt, the suffragettes of London or New York, Doctor Carrel, or the heroic dogsleds of the polar explorers. The pusillanimous and sedentary inhabitant of any provincial town can allow himself the inebriation of danger by going to the movies and watching a great hunt in the Congo. He can admire Japanese athletes, Negro boxers, endless American eccentrics, and very elegant Parisian women by spending a franc to go to the variety theater. Then, tucked up in his bourgeois bed, he can enjoy the distant and costly voice of a Caruso or a Burzio.[10]

These conditions, the initial developments in what David Harvey would later characterize as time-space compression, bring about a "negation of distances and of nostalgic solitudes," giving rise to a "new tourist sensibility of ocean liners and grand hotels (annual synthesis of diverse races)."[11] The imperious "tourist sensibility" in this phrase exists in tension with the leveling parenthetical "synthesis of diverse races," sounding a friction in the consequences of global exchange opened up by the wireless that we will explore in this chapter. Marinetti derived from this early form of time-space compression revamped aesthetic precepts that would enable those fully awake to inhabit the new "sense of the world" possessed by modern "man," who hardly need look backward in time for inspiration; for one now "has only a modest need to know what his forebears have done, but a burning need to know what his contemporaries are doing in every part of the globe," replacing historical awareness with awareness that crosses the planet.[12] Such transcultural and transracial interchange can have radical implications for the lyric. A moody Symbolist musing on solitudes and distance is trounced in favor of the "tragic lyricism of ubiquity and omnipresent speed."[13] The freshly perceived necessity of "communicating with all the peoples of the earth" spurs production of an "orchestral style," choralizing lyricism in visual, aural, and spatial terms, so that it is "at once polychromatic, polyphonic, and polymorphous," as the "Technical Manifesto of Futurist Literature" had claimed.[14] By comparison, even Nicolas Tesla's 1926 declaration, in an interview with *Colliers*, that "when wireless is perfectly applied the whole earth will be converted into a huge brain, which in fact it is, all things being particles of a real and rhythmic whole," appears belated and tame in its syncretism.[15]

Yet the case of Marinetti reveals that the global polyphony to be tapped by the wireless and the "coscienze molteplici" (multiplicate consciousnesses) now harbored within the renovated individual hardly lead straightforwardly to an internationalist sensibility. This author's militant symphonics instead herald how readily expression "link[ed] to the entire universe" could converge with colonizing impulses—encompassing the capitalist's "tourist sensibility" at best and forms of expansionist nationalism at worst, simply updated as a "[m]odification of patriotism, which nowadays has become the heroic idealization of the commercial, industrial and artistic solidarity of a people."[16] The Futurists' aspirations toward revamping society led them to compromises with contemporary politics that typify the failure of the avant-garde utopia of merging art and life as canonically analyzed by Peter Bürger, a failure perhaps nowhere more dazzlingly seen as in Fascist Futurism coinciding with its institutional success; these compromises remain instructive for the poetics and politics of our time.[17] The Futurists' urge to achieve the "solidarity of a people" would drift over the next decade from their early anarcho-syndicalist and libertarian affiliations to provocatory forms of nationalism, culminating, notoriously, in the movement's jagged pact with Fascism.

Futurism and Fascism evolved toward nuptials of mutual exploitation. Claudio Fogu has argued persuasively for Futurism's oscillation between competing poles of a Mediterranean imaginary: that of *emporion*, which occasions the breaking down of cultural barriers through mass communications, and that of *imperium*, which connects the rhetoric of virility, worship of the modern, and eugenicist love of war to the building of a Fascist Italian-Mediterranean empire. Nondialectical oscillation between these impulses, Fogu contends, led to the Italian Futurists' prominence as "a primary point of reference for the fascist completion of the making of Italians."[18] Roger Griffin's classic analysis of modernism, Fascism, and the rhetoric of beginnings synthesized concisely "how extensively Fascism's character was shaped by the diffuse, polycentric, and largely leaderless counter-cultural or 'cultic' cultural milieu of cultural modernists who well before the First World War were calling for Italy's renewal."[19] The Fascist movement's cooptation of Futurist energies and tactics may be emblematized by the fact that the king of Italy's invitation to Mussolini to form a new government was precipitated by Fascist squads' seizure of the post and telegraph offices and by the ensuing media onslaught surrounding a mythically insurrectionary March on Rome on October 29, 1922, which set the national calendar to Year I of Fascist time. (In 1933–1934, Marinetti's wife Benedetta would create *Synthesis of Communications:* five murals devoted to communication by air, radio, sea, land, telegraph, and telephone for the Palermo Central Post Office.) Conversely, the Futurists' compromises with the regime become emblematized by artifacts such as the Janus-faced Futurist *Velocità astratta* (1913) by Giacomo Balla, typifying the most radical years, and his hyperrealistic depiction of Mussolini at the core of the March on Rome painted upside down on the canvas's verso (probably painted for the Mostra della Rivoluzione Fascista of 1932, commemorating the ten-year anniversary of the Fascists' seizure of power)—an eventual cultural embarrassment that, following the Duce's fall, was withheld from public display until the year 2000.[20]

Before turning to the orphan tongues forged by postwar poets in flight from the political and linguistic legacies of Fascism, this book needed to face off against this modernist whose pioneering embrace of the newly international address opened up by radio and whose multinational aesthetic campaigns, from London to St. Petersburg and São Paulo, seemed to point toward the dissolution of geopolitical borders—yet who ended up being a primary voice in the engine buttressing their reinforcement, precisely through expansionism. Marinetti's manifestos can be read, with the help of Harsha Ram's analysis of Futurist geographies, as part of a struggle by aesthetic modernism hailing from a semi-peripheral European state to test the global literary system then coming into being—a system, with Paris at its core, "marked by centers of dominance and restless peripheries, and characterized by increasingly rapid cosmopolitan cultural flows as well as the reaffirmation of cultural and geopolitical boundaries."[21] With this in mind, Marinetti's publishing history in French, the strategic translation of his works into foreign languages, and scattered moments of polylingual or nonlinguistic noise should be read chiefly as an effort to claim a place for Italy at the table in the Darwinian geopolitical struggle of the "world republic of letters," in a far cry from approaching xenoglossic expressions of hybrid cultural allegiance.[22]

Confrontation with Marinetti's aesthetic and political legacy obliges engagement with offensive relics of imperial drive, nearly unreadable at points because of their attitudes toward non-Europeans or toward women, that have for obvious reasons largely dropped out of the recuperation of Futurism by sundry theorists of the avant-garde and the narration of heroic moments that coincided with its centennial, or that have been elided altogether in favor of engagement with more progressive, less problematic modernists. I confront them here on the premise that we cannot understand the xenoglossic before fleshing out which transcultural formations, however pathbreaking in terms of their grasp on the consequences of modern technology or their aesthetics, tend simply toward the appropriationist, colonialist, or veritably Fascist.

INSPIRATION AND DICTATION FROM THE WAR MACHINE AS HOLY SPIRIT: WORDS-IN-FREEDOM (OR WORDS-IN-THRALL)

In reading Futurist texts for xenoglossic impulses, we find that the movement's mission to communicate with all the peoples of the day invites an analogy with the Christian narrative of Pentecost in Acts of the Apostles 2:2 that Marinetti's own imagery induces heretically and that underscores the need to remain wary, with Ashon Crawley, of Pentecostal narratives channeling the ideology of any monolithic overweening Spirit.[23] "Wireless Imagination" represents the evolution and justification of the manifesto in which that phrase first appeared: the "Technical Manifesto of Futurist Literature" (1912), whose mythical dictation to its author by the propeller of an airplane over Milan manifests a typically Marinettian twist of spiritual irony.[24] Here, the wind/breath (πνoή, pnoē) of the biblical Holy Spirit is replaced by the divine wind/breath generated by the transrational machine. Marinetti channels the biplane's internal combustion motor to draw poetic "respirazione" (breathing) and instinct away from that of the lyrical I, transforming these basic human impulses into the capriciously lunging, sputtering, explosive impulses of the mechanism, of the brute matter of metals and wood.[25] Such perversion of the trope of dictation updates a sensibility reaching much farther back than Romanticism; it hails back to the very roots of inspiration (from the Latin for "breathing in") and suggests a global dissemination of utterance and noise by means of the machine that will act as no less than the new gospel.

Such reworkings of pnoē via propeller and wireless telecommunications dictate a newly implosive form of expression, freer than already-defunct free verse, careening in an expanded field. The "Wireless Imagination" manifesto narrates that friends to Futurism gifted with a "lyrical faculty" that enables them to be intoxicated with the world and their own experience of the now will be drawn spontaneously to transmit the shock experiences of modern life with parole-in-libertà, or words-in-freedom. The manifesto elaborates Marinetti's program in the "Technical Manifesto of Futurist Literature" for the renovation of verse: shattering the syntax inherited from Homer and the prison of the Latin period and rejecting the lyricism of a literary I, the qualifying adjective and adverb, and ponderous verb conjugations. In their place, there shall hurtle an assault of unpunctuated paratactic sensations—visual, auditory, and olfactory—held in tension by mathematical signs, "stoplight-adjectives," and "atmosphere-adjectives" in free tableaus making up a "multilineal lyricism."[26] The poem and book must change to accommodate the flux and reflux of sensation and of noise by means of what Marinetti calls a "typographic revolution" of variety in font style and color and of verse form flung open, opposed to any "so-called typographical harmony of the page."[27] Conventional spelling will be thrown to the wayside as the poet taking dictation embraces "a *new orthography* that I call *free expressive*," wherein "it matters little if the deformed word becomes ambiguous," but instead becomes sonic, abstracted from pure emotion or thought.[28] Marinetti presents this elastic form of transcribing words and onomatopoeia as the latest achievement of the evolution of lyric intoxication away from traditional prosody (which had been measured by "fiati uguali" or equal breaths, with sonic effects at preestablished distances), gradually taking liberties with breaths measured by the lungs of earlier poets ("misurati dai polmoni dei poeti precedenti"), toward the elasticity of breath in free verse. Now, declaring free verse dead, unimpeded by syntactical shackles, the Futurist will relaunch and dismantle words beyond recognition with modernized, machinic "breaths that we have invented."[29] Through all these tactics, the narrator gifted with lyricism "will involuntarily link his [sic] sensations to the entire universe as he has known and intuited it" as he "hurl[s] immense networks of analogies across the world"—connecting remote phenomena through the air "*without connecting wires*" (emphasis in original) and assuming "the same economical rapidity that the telegraph imposes on war correspondents and journalists."[30]

The global embrace of the wireless imagination barely obscures geopolitical tensions whose stakes would be heightened in the decades to come. Marinetti, although raised in Alexandria, educated at an international collège run by French Jesuits in Egypt before receiving his baccalaureate at the Sorbonne, and publishing his first texts in French, was spectacularly attuned to charged developments in communications technologies in which his Italian compatriots played a crucial part and that abetted the fledgling nation's expansionism. Radio and aviation were chief among them. As Luca Cottini narrates, within a few months of one another between 1902 and 1903, the tenor Enrico Caruso recorded for RCA Victor despite his misgivings (the Neapolitan is said to have protested in thick dialect, "nun me piace cantá dint' 'o tubo'" ["I don't like singing inside the tube"]),[31] thereby becoming a worldwide operatic sensation and enabling the birth of the flat-disc industry, and Marconi completed the first two-way wireless communication between America and Europe, Cape Cod and Cornwall, President Theodore Roosevelt and King Edward VII, inaugurating a new era of mass communications.[32] Caruso's performance of "Vesti la Giubba" at the Metropolitan Opera would be transmitted in 1910 as the world's first public radio broadcast. Marinetti flaunted an openly nationalist sense of the stakes of diffusing civilization, liberty, and power across the planet, like his precursors in the British Empire advocating for the telegraph cable network, yet was armed with this new medium: the ether. "Wireless Imagination" follows on its description of the ordinary man oblivious to the revolutionary capacity of each technology-driven "synthesis of a day in the world's life" with a violent analogy to the Arabs of Libya in late 1911, depicting them as vacuously unaware that they were about to become the victims of a notorious act of Italian aggression—the first bombs in history to be hurled from planes: "Having become commonplace, such possibilities fail to arouse the curiosity of superficial minds which remain as incapable of grasping their deeper significance as *the Arabs who watched with indifference the first airplanes in the skies above Tripoli*" (emphasis in original).[33] Marinetti's metaphorics of air, ravenous to wrest analogies among the new lyricism, transrational diction, the wireless telegraph, radio, and aviation, transgresses the realm of poetics and the merely theoretical or aesthetic praise for "war, the world's only hygiene" to enter the military realm.[34] Having had his youthful aggression stoked by two months as an embedded war correspondent for the French daily *L'Intransigeant* in the Battle of Tripoli (in October–November 1911), he would have been on the front lines of the world's first aerial bombardment inflicted by the Kingdom of Italy upon Ottoman Libya. These exploits formed the core of Italy's colonial escapades in the Italo-Turkish War, aimed at securing Balkan and North African colonies by exploiting Turkey's weakness and adding Libya in October 1912 to the colonial grab that had spurred Italy's nineteenth-century occupation of Somalia and Eritrea. Widely regarded as a key factor in the prompting of the Great War, this invasion was bolstered by wireless telegraphy stations transported by camels across the desert, visited by Guglielmo Marconi himself, and it was elaborated in aesthetic and perspectival terms by Luca Comerio's innovations in aerial film footage.[35] Seemingly far-flung touchstones of the Italo-Turkish War such as the Battle of Beirut in February 1912 would have stoked the young poet-impresario's colonial imagination equally, aimed as they were at annihilating Ottoman naval forces in the Mediterranean, granting Italy temporary dominance over the southern Mediterranean and the approach to the Suez Canal and therefore ready access to Italy's already extant colonies in Somalia and Eritrea, from which Italy drew troops for further colonial efforts. These were the events that excited the young artist into his most beguiling aesthetic innovations.

In Marinetti's first independent presentation of his reportage, *La Bataille de Tripoli, 26 Octobre 1911, vécue e chantée par F. T. Marinetti*, published as a sort of prose poetry in French by the Milan-based Futurist Editions and in Italian as *La battaglia di Tripoli* ["The Battle of Tripoli (26 October 1911), lived and sung by F. T. Marinetti"] by the same press in 1912, the wind itself becomes a battleground: the Italian imperial assault vows, in closing, to pastoralize "the sands lifted by the torrid *Ghibli*" (enervating winds originating in the Sahara that carry dust and sea humidity accumulated in crossing to the northern Mediterranean coast). Marinetti's narrator declares that the invading Italian collective will immobilize the itinerant desert sand with the footprint of agriculture (in a characteristic "civilizing" narrative), planting barley and clover in trenches excavated by grenade. I cite from both French and Italian editions to give a quick sense of the reckless tone, bent more on dissemination than polish or precision:

> C'est pour de belles salades et de glorieux rosiers qu'une grenade a creusé ce grand trou. Nous en creuserons d'autres. . . . Nous planterons d'autres palmiers, sentinelles avancées qui défendront les nouveaux orges, les nouvelles luzernes étagées stratégiquement contre les sables ameutés par le *ghibli* torride.

> Fu per farvi nascere belle insalate e gloriosi rosai, che una granata scavò quell'ampia buca. . . . E altre, e altre ne scaveremo noi. Pianteremo altri palmizi, sentinelle avanzate che difenderanno i nuovi orzi, i nuovi trifogli dispersi strategicamente contro le sabbie sollevate dal torrido *ghibli*.[36]

> It was to give birth to gorgeous salads and glorious rosebushes that a grenade excavated that ample hole. . . . And we will excavate others. We will plant more palm trees, advanced sentinels that will defend the new barley, the new clover dispersed strategically against the sands lifted by the torrid *Ghibli*.

As with many other Marinetti texts containing foreign terms, the Italianized Libyan Arabic term قِبْلِيّ (qibliyy, coming from the qibla) that replaces the more familiar French or Italian words for this wind, jugo or scirocco, in being subsumed by the adamant imperialist agenda, does not disorient but decorates. It serves to index the poet-reporter's status as insider from an ideological distance, steadied territorially against the flux of sand and cultural multiplicity—as insider, that is, embedded on behalf of Europe, whether assuming the stance of the Italian invaders or the French colonial perspective of the newspaper and the neighboring Maghreb.

Marinetti soon transmuted *La Bataille de Tripoli* into a telegraphic antilyric composed in Italian: *Battaglia / Peso + Odore* (*Battle / Weight + Smell*), the first work of words-in-freedom and expression of the poetics of a wireless imagination, appended to his 1912 "Technical Manifesto of Futurist Literature" as a manifestation of its principles. A brief example of the textual barrage suffices to show how the poet "weave[s] together distant things *without connecting wires*, by means of essential words *in freedom*," quashing syntax.[37] Here the aerial delirium of the avant-garde movement that celebrated the verbal charging of the ether and that would go on to theorize "aeropoetry" and "aeropainting" in ensuing decades becomes leaden with the scents of chemical warfare—the sweetness of perfumes associated with Orientalist fantasies meeting the putridity of food and flesh in a wall of text shot through with rare voids and presented as a mathematical formula:

zaffate lustreggìo cispa puzzo cannella muffa flusso riflusso pepe rissa sudiciume turbine aranci-in-fiore filigrana miseria dadi scacchi carte gelsomino + nocemoscata + rosa arabesco mosaico cagna pungiglioni acciabattìo mitragliatrici = ghiaia + risacca + rane Tintinnìo zaini fucili cannoni ferraglia atmosfera = piombo + lava + 300 fetori + 50 profumi selciato-materasso detriti sterco-di-cavallo carogne flic-flac ammassarsi cammelli asini frastuono cloaca Souk-degli-argentieri dedalo.

stenches lustrousness gunk stench cinnamon mold flux reflux pepper brawl filthiness turbine orange-trees-in-flower filigree misery dice chess cards jasmine + nutmeg + rose arabesque mosaic bitch stings endless shuffling machineguns = gravel + backwash + frogs Jinglejangle backpacks rifles cannons scrap-iron atmosphere = lead + lava + 300 stenches + 50 perfumes pavement-mattress detritus horse-dung carrions flick-flack ammassing camels asses din sewer Souk-of-the-silversmiths maze.[38]

Seeking to reproduce "the countless noises of matter in motion," Marinetti's onslaught of sense images reads like an Orientalist cut-up trained on the exotic and grotesque, stippled with signifiers of calculation and warfare.[39] Despite its peppering of toponyms suggesting privileged intimacy with the Libyan terrain, the text demonstrates that the transnational reach of the wireless does not necessarily lead to an internationalist imagination; on the contrary, it exemplifies how the revolutionary supranationalism of avant-garde ideals proved subject to the marriage of nationalist expansionism and provincialism on many fronts.

The text ends on the satiation of the parched reporter-fighter through a substitute for milk, via the metaphor of the Milky Way yoked by hyphenation to the image of the coconut tree ("via-lattea-albero-di-cocco"), in an action that anticipates further fetishization of this bodily fluid fraught with collective questioning.

monoplano = balcone-rosa-ruota-tamburo trapano-tafano > disfatta-araba bue sanguinolenza macello ferite rifugio oasi umidità ventaglio freschezza siesta **striciamento** germinazione sforzo dilatazione-vegetale sarò-piú-verde-domani restiamo-bagnati serba-questa-goccia-d'acqua bisogna-arrampicarsi-3-centimetri-per-resistere-a-20-grammi-di-

sabbia-e-3000-grammi-di-tenebre via-lattea-albero-di-cocco
stelle-noci-di-cocco
latte grondare succo delizia.

                                       monoplane = balcony-rose-
wheel-drum drill-horsefly > Arab-defeat ox bloodiness slaughter wounds
refuge oasis humidity fan coolness siesta striping germination
urge vegetal-dilation I'll-be-greener-tomorrow
let's-remain-soaked preserve-this-drop-of-water must-climb-3-centimeters-
    to-resist-20-grams-of-
sand-and-3000-grams-of-darkness milky-way-coconut-tree stars-coconuts
milk to ooze juice delight.[40]

Blood, water, and an exotic form of milk acting as surrogate for the sustenance
of the mother's breast form a violent cocktail that enables the soldier-poet to end
the Sisyphean episode of draining expansionism, crammed with the weight of
sand and darkness, on primal delight.

It is easy to be dazzled, to enter a passive aesthetic attitude, in the face of
the textual and sonic shock and awe of *Zang Tumb Tumb: Adrianopoli Ottobre
1912* (1914, but excerpted in *Lacerba* the year before), the apotheosis of words-
in-freedom, and Marinetti's most canonical work of the kind, published with
the framing theoretical texts "Destruction of Syntax—Wireless Imagination—
Words-in-Freedom" and the "Technical Manifesto of Futurist Literature." An
anarchic score for the poet's virtuosic declamations straddling language and
noise at *serate* across Europe in the 1910s, via radio in 1929, and as a phonographic
recording in 1935, the text embodies the ideal of Futurist noise as a discordant
force of fragmentation and conflict in which nonhuman forces and machines
address themselves to a mass audience so as, in Christine Poggi's words, "to rupture the stability of existing bourgeois social codes and to produce a new national
collectivity founded on imperialist politics and the thrills afforded by speed and
war."[41] While sonically and typographically vertiginous in its pursuit of explosive
wireless verse, from the diagonals and curves of the graphic design, to its radical
invention of forms such as the "Simultaneous Map" of sensations perceived by
an aviator in motion or the formation of a captured Turkish balloon with letters (figure 1.2), to its loosening of syntax, to its onomatopoeic transliteration
of the noise of modern battle and its use of other languages ("treno express-ex-
press-expresssssss   press-press   press   press-press-press-press-press-press-press
press-press-presssssss"[42]), all of which undermine a reader's grasp of the Italian

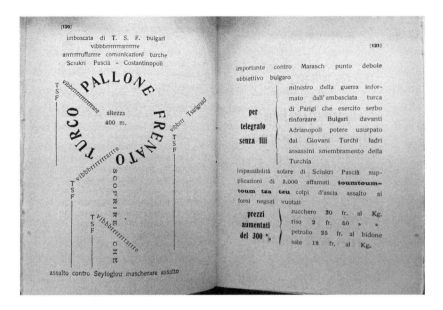

FIGURE 1.2 F. T. Marinetti, from *Zang Tumb Tumb: Adrianopoli ottobre 1912. Parole in libertà* (Edizioni futuriste di "Poesia," 1914), 120–21. A ten-part poem about the Balkan War of 1912–1913, witnessed by Marinetti as reporter, here laying out the use of the wireless in the Bulgarian "assault against Siiloglu masking assault," as the bottom line of page 120 reads, and the capture of a Turkish balloon illustrated typographically.

Photograph by Jennifer Scappettone. Special Collections, Regenstein Library, University of Chicago.

text, the artist's book is straightforwardly nationalist in terms of content. It is aimed at celebrating the continued weakening of the Turkish Ottoman Empire at the strategic gateway city of Adrianople (modern-day Edirne) in the Balkans by the peripheral state of Bulgaria and other members of the Balkan League in an allegiance that eased the way for Italian colonies in the Dodecanese Islands. The page spread in figure 1.2 sports messages sent by the vibrations of the wireless telegraph ("per / telegrafo / senza fili") about a Turkish balloon captured at four hundred meters above ground (on the left)

imboscata di TSF bulgari
vibbbrrrrrrarrrrrre
arrrrrruffarrre comunicazioni turche
Sciukri Pascia—Costantinopoli

ambush of Bulgarian TSF *[Telegraphie Sans Fils]*
vibbbrrrrrrrattttting
rrrrrruffllling Turkish communications
Sciukri Pascia—Constantinople

64   WIRELESS IMAGINATION

and about shops being attacked (on the right: "**toumtoumtoum tza tzu** colpi d'ascia assalto ai forni negozi vuotati"—"**toumtoumtoum tza tzu** blows of axe assault of the emptied ovens shops"), leading to soaring prices of sugar, rice, petroleum, and salt. Both sides feature languageless noise as well as the infinitive, mathematically oriented, clipped communications typical of the telegram.

The emphasis on *libertà* in Futurist poetics may ultimately be misleading, as the loosening of syntax and nihilistic emptying of individual expression merely allow the poet to become a more efficient medium for dictation or the unchecked streaming of signifiers, whether received from state command or the clichés of the Symbolist literary past Marinetti so reviles.[43] Though the Russian Futurists appear to have borrowed from the Italians' typographical experiments, Roman Jakobson (who seems to have received a copy of *Zang Tumb Tumb* by mail in the spring of 1914) wryly cast the Italian Futurists as reforming reportage rather than poetry, undercutting a sense of their imaginative freedom: "it appears that new material and new concepts in the poetry of the Italian Futurists have led to a renewal of the devices of poetry and of artistic forms, and in this way, supposedly, the idea of parole in libertà, . . . for instance, came into being. But this is a reform in the field of reportage, not in poetic language."[44] (Jakobson goes on to draw a contrast with Russian Futurism's focus on the creative shaping of speech and the autonomous, "selfsome" words of a writer like Khlebnikov.)[45] As Campbell notes of developments in telegraphic technology, "What the wireless makes possible on the battlefield, the rapid transmission of orders, it successfully extends in the command to patriotism and attunement between the collective and *il duce*."[46]

Notwithstanding Marinetti's cosmopolitan upbringing and multilingual output and the transcultural origins of others in his ambit, such as Fortunato Depero, Italian Futurists had declared from their first 1910 serata staged in the then-Austro-Hungarian city of Trieste that "[a]ll freedom and all progress occurs within the circle of the Nation!"—acting in the grip of irredentism, or the notion that territories unintegrated by Italy during the formal creation of the modern nation-state in 1860 should be "redeemed" as Italian, whether by diplomacy or force.[47] The bulk of these artists—with notable exceptions in Neapolitan Francesco Cangiullo and Florentine Aldo Palazzeschi—espoused Fascism in the decade following. The historical avant-garde makes it a primary mission to transform the language. Yet within the just-unified and largely undeveloped state of Italy— which Marinetti's early biographer Tullio Pànteo characterized as a "patria classica dell'analfabetismo" (classical fatherland of illiteracy)—the national language still begged to be transformed into an integral phenomenon, as the ubiquitously invoked post-Risorgimento dictum "Fatta l'Italia, bisogna fare gli italiani" (Italy has been made, now it is time to make Italians) elicits.[48] Marinetti, the erstwhile enemy of academies and libraries, ultimately directed his efforts of innovation toward reactionary linguistic ends. Summoned by Mussolini to the newly established Italian Academy in 1929, he was eventually chosen to advance the dictator's call to "defend" the Italian language by inventing new Italian words so as to expel foreign contaminants. The cosmopolitan whose career was launched in French thus became a cog in the machinery of the doomed project of the "autarky of language"—as if any national language could be fortressed against infiltration by other tongues, foreign or local.[49]

In his preface to *L'autarchia della lingua* (*Autarky of Language*; figure 1.3), Marinetti characterizes the expulsion of foreign words and the existence of foreign importations as part of the "holy... campaign directed at the absolute integrity of

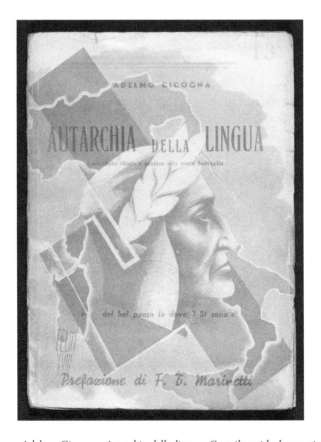

FIGURE 1.3 Adelmo Cicogna, *Autarchia della lingua: Contributo ideale e pratico alla santa battaglia*, with a preface by F. T. Marinetti (Edizioni dell' autore brossura, 1940). Cameo of Dante on the cover.

the Italian language," part of a "combat" against "every form of xenophilia."[50] The Fascist regime built in an ideologically pointed, doctrinaire, and systematic way on efforts of the early twentieth century to nationalize the language of a state that was only a few decades old (unified as a kingdom out of a fragmented set of city-states, kingdoms, duchies, and colonies of other states, including the Papacy) and was inherently multilingual (with Alto Adige and Venezia Giulia being alloglot). It sought to intervene in the linguistic experience of a citizenry for whom the use of local dialect predominated (with linguists coming to the conclusion that at the turn of the twentieth century, no more than 20 percent of the population spoke Italian),[51] imposing a national linguistic norm, both written and spoken/phonetic, through proliferating channels: education; grammars, dictionaries, and encyclopedias; mass media campaigns spanning radio to film; photography and the press; Minculpop (the propaganda of the Ministry of Popular Culture); Italianization of toponyms; and the syncretic, simplistic oratory of Mussolini, crafted for the ears of thronging militarized or paramilitarized assemblies.[52] Pedagogical reforms initially introduced by the Hegelian idealist philosopher of Fascism Giovanni Gentile in 1923—identified by Mussolini as the most Fascist of all the reforms and leading to a high profile within the regime that ended in Gentile's 1944 assassination by partisans—aimed to increase participation in schooling, combat illiteracy (which characterized nearly half the population at the turn of the twentieth century), and move the people "dal dialetto alla lingua" (from dialect to language) through instruction in Italian employing translations of dialect literature, while retaining Latin as an echo of ancient imperial grandeur.[53] That said, Gentile was soon demoted, and postwar linguists have come to see the effects of the regime's linguistic designs as largely rhetorical and ideological: eliminating dialect as the language of instruction in school likely slowed the literacy process, and despite all mystifications surrounding the national language as the "speech of the people," dialect continued to dominate daily life in Italy for two decades after Fascism's fall.[54] (Taking note of the willed omission from the census of statistics about education between 1936 and 1951, scholars conjecture that illiteracy decreased by only 5 percent during the first decade of the regime's hold on power.[55])

The creation of the Accademia Reale d'Italia in 1926 was a lynchpin in the regime's efforts to "fascistize" and marshal culture toward homogenization. Marinetti claimed that his entry signaled "a triumph of Futurism and a multiplication of our innovating and revolutionary forces," but history attests otherwise. Although he managed to convince Mussolini to let him represent Futurism as if it were a full-blown branch of knowledge and to convince the minister of education to open Italian universities to foreigners (with the proposal that they would then be equipped to spread Italian civilization across the globe), in the Academy's inaugural address, its first president, Tommaso Tittoni, underscored that Fascism was "prosecutore e avvalatore della tradizione" (prosecutor and validator of tradition). Marinetti's title did not ultimately impart significant power, which would be entrusted to less volatile personalities.[56] From 1929 forward, Marinetti would be present on the committees tasked with finding Italian terms for foreign terms deemed unacceptable and was involved with production of a new dictionary to fight off the centrifugal influence of dialects, minor languages, and borrowings from foreign tongues: "bar" would become "quisibeve" (youdrinkhere), "cocktail" "polibibita" (polybeverage), and "sandwich" "traidue" (betweenthetwo). This is a key context in which Marinetti continued the efforts of his most pronounced aesthetic and political elder and rival, Gabriele D'Annunzio, as cultural demagogue—in promoting the Italianization of the language. To better grasp the way in which the "deterritorialized cosmopolitanism" that characterized the Alexandria of Marinetti's youth could have led him ultimately to a promotion of autarky, I will now turn to a specific case: his collaboration on a work of words-in-freedom directly serving that political campaign in the period of European sanctions against Italian Fascist aggression.[57]

AUTARKY, NURSE'S MILK, AND THE TROUBLING OF THE MOTHER TONGUE UNDER ITALIAN COLONIALISM: MARINETTI AND MUNARI COMPOSE *THE POEM OF THE MILK DRESS*

Although Marinetti's national identification and its supranational extensions remain unmistakable, it is misleading to characterize him as straightforwardly Italian or even cosmopolitan—a term that might imply that all international capitals enjoyed the same footing in the period of his vociferous aesthetic and political campaigns. His writings position him rather straightforwardly between the cultural capital of Paris and two peripheral metropolises: Milan and Alexandria. Writing as director of what was soon to become a nationalist interventionist journal, *Il Marzocco* (its title taken from D'Annunzio, theorist and illustrious xenophobic poetaster of the Italian "razza" or "stirpe" [race or stock] against the "Barbari" [Barbarians]), the soon-to-be-founder of the Italian Nationalist Association, Enrico Corradini, characterized Marinetti as "twice deracinated": "déraciné [using the French term within an Italian text] insofar as he is Italian and writes in French, déraciné insofar as he writes in

French and lives in Milan. And so this young man . . . has two half-fatherlands and no whole one. . . . [He] is in flesh and bones and in books of prose and poetry a revolution against all our conceptions and preconceptions regarding the bonds between one's birth country and country of residence."[58] This characterization, however discerning of the contradictions sustaining Marinetti as European cosmopolitan, glaringly leaves out the poet's settler Africanity, a crucial aspect of his cultivated persona from his earliest writings, in particular *Mafarka le Futuriste: Roman Africain* (*Mafarka the Futurist: An African Novel*, 1909). Marinetti's father, a lawyer from Piedmont specializing in commercial contracts, settled in Alexandria in 1865, setting up additional offices in Cairo and Khartoum, Sudan, to represent foreign companies and individuals involved in the aggressive modernization plan launched by Isma'il Pasha, ruler of Egypt and Sudan from 1863 to 1879. Isma'il the Magnificent was an ambitious figure granted the semi-sovereign Ottoman title of Khedive (Viceroy), educated in Paris, who was intent on maximizing Egypt's position between Europe and Africa and on Egypt's expansion along the Nile. His costly projects were aimed at reducing the country's dependence on Britain and France yet ended up incurring so much debt that, paradoxically, he lost control over Egyptian finances to European bankers; this situation provoked nationalist uprising against the Khedival government collaborators and British military occupation—as well as Marinetti senior's retreat to Milan in the early 1880s. Isma'il Pasha's development projects had ranged from the construction of the Suez Canal, financed by French investors, to telegraph and transport infrastructure, modernization of agriculture, and education and governmental reforms. Milena Contini summarizes the auspicious conditions triggered by the inauguration of the Suez Canal, motor of globalization, in an industrious and cosmopolitan Alexandria: it represented "an acceleration toward progress wedded perfectly to the futurist movement."[59] Though critically neglected, the parallels between Marinetti's Alexandria and his Milan, economic centers of rapidly modernizing Mediterranean territories, are numerous.

Marinetti capitalizes on images of his childhood in Egypt, concoctions of exoticism and nostalgia, to justify imperial violence throughout his career. His notorious birth as a Futurist narrated in the prologue to "The Founding and Manifesto of Futurism" (1909) landed, famously, on the front page of *Le Figaro* thanks to an Egyptian business associate of his late father and shareholder of the newspaper, the Pasha Mohammed El Rachi.[60] The birth scene takes place following a minor car accident on the industrial periphery of Milan in Filippo Tommaso's new Fiat convertible, where he ends up in a "maternal" trench teeming with factory sludge:

WIRELESS IMAGINATION &~ 69

Tagliai corto, e, pel disgusto, mi scaraventai colle ruote all'aria in un fossato. . . .
Oh! materno fossato, quasi pieno di un'acqua fangosa! Bel fossato d'officina! Io
gustai avidamente la tua melma fortificante, che mi ricordò la santa mammella nera
della mia nutrice sudanese. . . . Quando mi sollevai—cencio sozzo e puzzolente—
di sotto la macchina capovolta, io mi sentii attraversare il cuore, deliziosamente,
dal ferro arroventato della gioia![61]

I stopped short, and to my disgust was hurled into a ditch with my wheels in
the air. . . . Oh! Maternal ditch, nearly full of a muddied water! Beautiful factory ditch! I savored your fortifying sludge, which recalled for me the holy black
breast of my Sudanese nurse. . . . When I raised myself out—a filthy, smelly rag—
from underneath the capsized car, I felt my heart traversed, deliciously, by the
red-hot iron of joy!

What's stunning about this passage is how baldly the Futurist depicts the European, and specifically Italian, need to nurse itself on the colonial exploitation
of Africa in order to propel its culture into the future—while the stress on the
nurse's black skin racializes the scene, underscoring that this maternal caregiver
was Black, from Sudan, and not an Egyptian Arab. In this notorious avant-
garde origin story, Africa supplies the human and natural resources that make
the future possible; elsewhere Marinetti describes the arms and breasts of his
"nutrice sudanese" (Sudanese nurse) in relation to coal, as "color carbone coke,"
coke or petcoke colored.[62] But these resources are simultaneously confused with
the detritus of industrial processes. The slime of industrial waste and the milk
(or petroleum) of origins are imbibed simultaneously in the factory channel to
fuel the phallic surge of the newborn Futurist, who does not emerge immaculate
but cast as a filthy wreck, soaked in a confusion of primordial dirt and contaminated factory fallout. Irradiated with the "imprisoned radiance of electric hearts"
compared to that of the perforated mosque lamps in his father's bourgeois apartment prior to this red-hot release from the maternal ditch, Marinetti condenses
a history of exploitation forming the basis of his fatherland's technological rise.
In a single self-mythologizing image of nursing, the Futurist foretells the Italian colony in Libya to be established several years later and a repercussive century of oil, gas, and refugee flows, from Fascist imperial war in East Africa to the
'Ndrangheta's shipping of toxic and radioactive waste to Somalia.[63] In observing
that the so-called unification of Italy was actually a colonization of the rural Italian south by the developing north, Sardinian Marxist Antonio Gramsci made
use of the figure of the "leech": "The North was concretely a 'leech' ['piovra'] that
enriched itself at the expense of the South [and its] economic-industrial growth

was directly correlated with the impoverishment of the Southern economy and agriculture."[64] He could as well have deployed the figure of the Futurist infant suckling itself at the expense of brutally seized colonies of the Global South—for Marinetti's text allows us to perceive the suckling of milk as another form of resource extraction.

That said, the very choice to stage this return to the scene of suckling in order to birth a new poesis suggests a willed regression—a retraction from grammar as the first of the seven liberal arts that, traditionally, disciplined boys away from primal desire and spontaneous expression in the mother tongue, supervising what Gary Cestaro, in *Dante and the Grammar of the Nursing Body*, identifies as "the transition from immediate in-fant (i.e., speechless) desire to the symbolic obligations of adulthood and speech."[65] Marinetti's will to "destroy syntax" and poeticisms in favor of noise suggests a desire to destroy grammar and, with it, the injunctions of maturity associated with rigor mortis of culture and language by his puerile comrades. To do so, however, he returns phantasmatically to grammar's alleged birthplace (and his own) in Egypt. Cestaro traces how, in the fourteenth-century Italy in which Dante conceived of *De vulgari eloquentia*, grammar had come to be represented as a wet nurse with one breast exposed and a whip in one hand: a veritable embodiment of the conflict between nurturing and discipline embedded in the entry into language. But it signified much more: "Grammatica was the pre-eminent site of social law, the first science of border inscription, a drawer of lines at once linguistic, social, and corporeal." Not only does Marinetti recall in this scene, and confuse through remembrance of suckling, "the basic cultural opposition between the fluid body (female) and the acorporeal rational ego (male)" contoured by Cestaro, but he also meshes together the overdetermined oppositions between European and Black African.[66] Along the way, the Futurist writes himself into an ancient lineage linking the wet nurse's milk to spontaneous gushes of unschooled language, stretching from Quintilian through Jerome and Augustine and reaching its crux in Dante's comments on the vernacular as "that which we learn without any formal instruction, by imitating our nurses" in a tractate nostalgic for a space and time before Babel and a life before exile, desirous of a unified Italian tongue. This is a different "lineage" from that of the modern German philosophy of language, which yoked Romantic conceptions of the nation to the expression of a *Volk*, invoking the infant's nourishment upon the mother's milk as part of a biological phenomenon analogous to the acquisition of national speech, and played an important role in establishing the monolingual paradigm critiqued by Yasemin Yildiz in *Beyond the Mother Tongue*. The genealogy of the nurse's tongue can enrich understandings of what Yildiz names the "post-monolingual" condition, helping us exhume the tensions beneath the surface coherence of any nation-state predicated on colonialism or enslavement as a violent suckling of offshore resources.

Marinetti further denaturalizes the mother tongue by insisting on the color of his nurse's skin, highlighting her difference from his biological mother to his international readership and claiming this difference, this carnal and cultural link with the so-called barbarian, as part of a personal myth ("Go ahead and scream that I am a barbarian, incapable of tasting the divine poetry that bobs upon your enchanting isles!" he taunted the effete Venetians in 1909, in just one early example).[67] Such a link renders his poetic origin story an early complication of any essentializing function of the maternal within the realm of language as will later be operative in Fascist overdeterminations or as found in modes of opposition to Fascism through feminist poetics like that of Julia Kristeva, wherein the maternal *chora* becomes the site of the semiotic before entry into the realm of the Lacanian symbolic order.[68] Along the way, the Futurist highlights how Italian Fascism's opportunistic flexibility in its absorption of the avant-garde and this species of Fascist modernism differed from more familiar forms of control under National Socialism; the latter's language policies would come to a head in the 1943 establishment of a secret "Political Language Bureau" that would rail against various "forms of 'linguistic treason' as high treason against the *Volk*." Such protection of the mother tongue by the fatherland is the natural outgrowth of what Christopher Hutton describes as a "a set of anxieties about cultural transmission, family bonds and kinship, the sexual fidelity of females to their kin-group, and the relation of the individual to wider communities with which that individual might seem to be 'linguistically' related," in which "identity becomes dependent on the state-building capacities of the group" because "in order to secure its boundary, the mother-tongue had to be protected by political power and force if necessary."[69]

Returning to the "petcoke" reference mentioned earlier, which appears in Marinetti's "Self-Portrait," we see metaphors of milk and color invoked to mark the poet's disobedience to political ideals of purity and diplomacy.

> Ebbi una vita tumultuosa, stramba, colorata. Cominciai in rosa e nero; pupo fiorente e sano fra le braccia e le mammelle color carbone coke della mia nutrice sudanese. Ciò spiega forse la mia concezione un po' *negra* dell'amore e la mia franca antipatia per le politiche e le diplomazie al lattemiele.[70]

> I had a tumultuous, outlandish, colored life. I began in pink and black; a flowering and healthy moppet between the arms and teats the color of petcoke of my Sudanese nurse. That perhaps explains my *Blackish* conception of love and my frank antipathy for the politics and diplomacy of milk and honey.

However offensive, the passage claims an outlandish racialized attachment to both Sudan and Egypt that transgresses the boundary between European and African territories derived from modern European biblical interpretation. "The land of milk and honey" can be traced to a passage in Exodus 3:8 in which God says to Moses, "I have come down to rescue them from the hand of the Egyptians and to bring them up out of that land into a good and spacious land, a land flowing with milk and honey—the home of the Canaanites, Hittites, Amorites, Perizzites, Hivites and Jebusites." Invoking Exodus, Marinetti sides with the Egyptians and, in the process, plays on the metaphor of "milk and honey" that, in Italian, indicates a mode of facile ingratiation. The poet's aggressive identification with freighted contrasts of Blackness, whiteness, and pinkness begins with the body of his Sudanese nurse.

As Cestaro points out, the discourse of language acquisition in ancient and medieval European texts is consistently focused on the wet nurse over the mother, making the scene of entry into the symbolic order a postlapsarian one. The role of the wet nurse as opposed to the birth mother in these texts reflects a historical and social reality of care economies, but "this focus also tends to belie the expression 'mother tongue,' or reduce *mamma* to a literal, biological function. . . . The image of an infant at the breast of the wet nurse, in particular, conveys the always partial, supplemental nature of the comforts language has to offer. Mother/not mother, the wet nurse steps in to take the mother's place and thus to represent the object of a desire whose only true perfection remains shrouded in a radically inaccessible, original unity."[71] Marinetti's recollections of his Sudanese nurse appear fixated on demonstrating how his upbringing in Alexandria prepared him for transgression of institutional conventions and propriety in language. In the first century CE, Quintilian, stressing the matriarchal origins of language over language's association with patriarchal discipline, admonished that a child's nurse must speak correctly, lest the infant's speech be contaminated indelibly. Quintilian set milk in direct relation to the child's speech and compared the speech of the nurse with dye that stains an explicitly white virgin wool: "It is the nurse that the child first hears, and her words that he will first attempt to imitate. And we are by nature most tenacious of childish impressions, just as the flavour first absorbed by vessels when new persists, and the colour imparted by dyes to the primitive whiteness of wool is indelible."[72] Marinetti flaunts his disobedience to such attitudes of purism. His dubious primitivist appropriation of the exotic Sudanese nurse will be echoed by his comrade Giacomo Balla in a sound poem, "Discussione di due critici sudanesi sul Futurismo" ("Discussion About Futurism by Two Sudanese Critics"), made up of a "nonexistent, grotesque and paradoxical language" that was reportedly improvised at the opening of an exhibition in Rome by Balla, Marinetti, and Cangiullo around an out-of-tune piano.[73]

We will return imminently to this link between milk, wool, language, and textile.

Between the so-called heroic phase of Futurist manifestos preceding the Great War discussed earlier and the moment of the fascistization of language, the political system of Italy was aggressively overhauled, although a fervor for supranationalist expansionism remained intact—through the revanchist rhetoric of the "vittoria mutilata" of World War I (or mutilated victory, a term coined by Gabriele D'Annunzio in 1918), D'Annunzio's populist seizure of the Croatian port of Fiume with two thousand Italian legionaries in 1919, the histrionics of the 1922 March on Rome (which secured the Fascist regime in myth and in practice), and the 1935 Italian invasion of Ethiopia.[74] It is this last episode on which I will now focus—one often interpreted as paving the way for the Second World War, consolidating support for Fascism within Italy, and signaling the danger of Fascism's spread on a global scale, from Geneva to Harlem. The strategic importance of Ethiopia within Mussolini's imperial program would have echoed the motivations beyond the aerial bombing of Ottoman Libya and allied maneuvers against the Ottoman Empire that jumpstarted Marinetti's experimentation with "wireless" telegraphic verse. Marinetti actually volunteered to serve on the Ethiopian front in late 1935 at sixty years of age.

The Fascist invasion of Ethiopia can be seen as an apotheosis of the nationalist consolidation of Italy achieved by the Libyan (Italo-Turkish) war that had effectively launched Marinetti's most radical aesthetic innovations, and the ability of Italians to use radio for communications was a key element of the technological advantages that enabled them to prevail. Launched in 1911, the Libyan offensive was a cruel campaign that remained unremitting as a result of formidable Berber and Arab resistance, despite declarations of "peace," until 1932, when the assassination of resistance leader Omar al-Mukhtar permitted Italy to occupy the entire country. Lucia Re interprets this war as "a turning point and an important, racially-oriented shift in the process of 'making Italians'"; Re also presents this racialized campaign and its constitutive atrocities as "the clearest evidence of the embarrassing long-term continuity between Liberal and Fascist Italy."[75] I would add that this continuity has been repressed not only by Italians but also by international theorists of the avant-garde eager to recuperate the so-called heroic or avant-guerre production of Futurism during its anarchist phase in a semipalatable light, as the product of a desire "to break down existing economic and political structures and to transcend nationalist barriers" (to quote Marjorie Perloff).[76]

Opposition to the Libyan war by Italian leftists and revolutionary socialists (among whom still stood Mussolini) on the grounds that class rather than race should form the appropriate matrix for conflict led to the left's ultimate loss of popularity and power. Italy as nation was only fifty years old, and it was deeply divided between a civilized north and a peasant south that was cast as feminized, atavistic, and barbarian and racialized as African or Arab. Re outlines the elaborate process by which the war in North Africa unified Italians along the lines of "race":

> The Libyan war press campaign, and the war itself in its largely literary construction, had . . . a paradoxically healing function for the fractured and contested identity of Liberal Italy. It created like never before, and in the face of glaring physical, behavioral, linguistic, religious, and cultural differences among Italians of different sexes, geographical areas, and social classes, the belief (however precarious and illusory) in an ethnic-racial sameness, a shared "essence." A similar process of racialized identification and differentiation through opposition to an inferior "other," promoted through new instruments of mass persuasion, later allowed Italians (including Italian Jews) to feel once again truly "one," and Fascism to reach its peak moment of national consensus during the conquest of Ethiopia in 1935–1936. . . . [A] self-righteous rhetoric exalted Italy's attack as a "war of civilization and liberation" undertaken by a poor but generous proletarian people to find "a place in the sun" while breaking the shackles of primitive slaves in a barbaric land.[77]

Ethiopia's conquest would have signified for Italians a crucial, belated act of redemption against the Kingdom of Italy's ignominious 1896 defeat in the Battle of Adwa in its initial attempt to forcefully impose a protectorate over the African country, which definitively checked the nation's colonial ambitions in the Horn of Africa. Opposition to that act of expansion by socialists and members of the working class, through street demonstrations and rioting in major cities, had also embarrassed leadership by baring the fledgling country's internal rifts, and it led to the collapse of the government of Prime Minister Francesco Crispi.

Worldwide, Ethiopia became a unique rallying point for Black internationalism and for anticolonial, anti-Fascist, and other leftist movements spanning races, ethnicities, and continents.[78] A League of Nations member regarded as Africa's last Black empire and one of few countries on the continent never subject to colonization, Ethiopia became a preeminent symbol of Pan-Africanism or simply

"Ethiopianism"—an earlier, theologically inflected millenarianism of divine retribution for the suffering of African peoples, figuring the country, Christian since antiquity, as an African Zion. These movements were bolstered upon the 1896 defeat of the Italian invaders. Ethiopia's invasion by Mussolini's forces from Eritrea and Somalia on October 3, 1935, thus signified a threat to Black dignity and freedom the world over. Grassroots efforts at military assistance for Ethiopia that rallied from Kingston to Chicago resisted the Italian aggression, while support groups, protests, and labor stoppages effloresced from West African villages to Johannesburg, Rio de Janeiro, Trinidad, Oklahoma, Miami, Chicago, Marseille, and London (to name only a handful of resistance centers).[79] As Ruth Ben-Ghiat has narrated, in August 1935, in a period when Hearst newspapers hosted a column by Mussolini, *Time* magazine featured the dictator with a cover profile, and New York City mayor Fiorello La Guardia contributed to the Fascist invasion with a check for a hundred thousand dollars, twenty-five thousand New Yorkers composed of Pan-Africanists and leftists of various ethnicities and races marched down Harlem's Lenox Avenue in protest of the plan to invade. A rally of ten thousand at Madison Square Garden followed in the weeks to come, featuring speeches by W. E. B. Du Bois and Paul Robeson and the burning of an effigy of Il Duce.[80]

Exiled in England, emperor and spiritual leader Haile Selassie I (also known as Ras Tafari and viewed as messiah by followers of the eponymous movement that emerged in Jamaica after his 1930 coronation) addressed the League of Nations to testify to Italian atrocities in June 1936. Selassie condemned the unprecedented deployment of chemical weapons, averring that "there has never before been an example of any Government proceeding to the systematic extermination of a nation by barbarous means, in violation of the most solemn promises made by the nations of the earth that there should not be used against innocent human beings the terrible poison of harmful gases."[81] Europe was more focused on German anti-Semitic actions than on Italy's violation of the Geneva Conventions in Africa, however, and colonized people of color were again cast aside by a Eurocentric field of concern that resounds today in the reduction of the Ethiopian invasion and its pioneering crimes of chemical warfare to a footnote in history. Between the invasion and the 1941 Italian retreat in the face of Allied forces, four hundred thousand troops were deployed in an immense drain on Italian resources, funded in part by the gold wedding rings donated by scores of ordinary Italian and Italian emigrant women. Two hundred fifty thousand Ethiopians, including as many as thirty thousand civilians, were killed via massacre, aerial bombardments of mustard gas upon both combatants and civilians, deliberate attacks on Red Cross hospitals, and concentration camps.[82] The disturbing pertinence of this episode to the geopolitical landscape of our times is expressed in an April 6, 2022, editorial from the UK newspaper *The Guardian*, stressing that "the UN desperately needs a fresh start. And so, too, does the disintegrating international order. If the UN fails over Putin and Ukraine as the League of Nations did over Mussolini and Ethiopia, then the global consequences, as in the 1930s, may be catastrophic for all."[83]

Italy's invasion of Ethiopia did lead the League of Nations to impose economic sanctions upon the Fascist regime on November 18, 1935. Although these were largely unenforced and feckless, the rhetorical resistance from the first worldwide intergovernmental organization aimed at peace enabled an intense campaign of propaganda that aided in the consolidation of a national identity within Italy. Meanwhile, the seizure of Addis Ababa in May of 1936 led Mussolini to declare through the spectacle of his balcony in Piazza Venezia that "Italy finally has its Empire"—the new Roman Empire that he had promised, encompassing Libya, Eritrea, Somalia, and Ethiopia (as celebrated in figure 1.4).

FIGURE 1.4   Italian Youth of the Littoral (GIL), *Bulletin of the Federal Command of Bologna*, no. 162–63 (May 31, Year XIV of the Fascist era, 1942). © Alma Mater Studiorum Università di Bologna, Biblioteca Universitaria di Bologna, T2118/PER 10220. Cover image of Mussolini inside the African continent, backed by the repeated mantra "Ethiopia Is Italian"—celebrating the dictator's announcement of the Italian Empire on May 9, 1936.

Regardless of their ineffectuality, the economic sanctions prompted the ramping up of a large-scale movement toward Italian autarky, or economic self-sufficiency, announced by Mussolini on August 31, 1935, that was to encompass all elements of daily life, from agriculture to design, coffee to synthetic textiles—including language (figure 1.5). This is the campaign that led Marinetti to declare, in his preface to *Autarchia della lingua*, that "Il Primo problema autarchico è l'italianità

FIGURE 1.5 "18 November: Sanctions. Italians, Remember!" Propagandistic poster commemorating European economic sanctions against Italy and celebrating the resultant autarky campaign. Museo Nazionale Collezione Salce, Direzione regionale Musei Veneto. Courtesy of the Italian Ministry of Culture.

della lingua" (The First autarchic problem is the Italianity of the language).[84] It also led him to pen a manifesto in 1937, "Against Love of the Foreign," aimed at the bourgeoisie, whom he claims to be in love with "the baubles and chatter from over the Alps and overseas" ("Contro l'esterofilia," "alle signore e gli intellettuali"). He also judges mothers who surround their children with foreign words and things harshly because "this way they will learn Italian poorly" while developing a "xenophilic attitude."[85]

I will close this discussion of Marinetti's supranational imagination by troubling both the concept of autarky and that of the mother tongue as embedded in the 1937 artist's book, *Il poema del vestito di latte* (*The Poem of the Milk Dress*).[86] This visually and materially sensational work of words-in-freedom was a collaboration between "Marinetti, accademico d'Italia" (member of the Italian Academy), as proclaimed on the cover, and the pathbreaking young Milanese graphic designer Bruno Munari (Milan 1907–1998), a figure associated with second-wave Futurism since 1927 and generally regarded as apolitical (yet whose early works manifest complicity with the regime). Dissociating himself from the verboten Futurists after World War II, Munari is best known for his far more palatable postwar inventions in design, encompassing visual arts, industrial design, and kinesthetic pedagogy.[87] Commissioned by the propaganda office of Italy's largest producer of synthetic textiles, the Società Nazionale Industria Applicazioni (SNIA) Viscosa, whose facilities Marinetti was invited to visit in 1937, Marinetti's free-word *Poema* constitutes a delirious species of documentary; it juxtaposes fantasias of autarchic manufacturing with battle scenes witnessed during the Ethiopian invasion and spectacles of patriotism in the Italian capital that we might call surreal were they not so coherent with the concurrent pageantry of the state. The industry in question is that of textiles—an arena that had obsessed the Futurists continually since Giacomo Balla's 1914 "Futurist Manifesto of Men's Clothing" and the 1920 "Manifesto of Futurist Women's Fashion" by Volt (pseudonym of Italian Futurist poet Vincenzo Fani Ciotti), wherein, because of war shortages, "one hundred new revolutionary materials" were prophesied to "riot in the piazza."[88] Recalling the primal scene of Futurism's founding at the remembered breast of Marinetti's Sudanese nurse, *The Poem of the Milk Dress* exposes a fascinating yet no less barbaric complication of any purist ideology of the mother tongue that "we learn . . . by imitating our nurses": the work celebrates empire through the Fascist state's autarchic production of milk fiber, while concurrently exposing that industry to be dependent upon the suckling and choking of the Horn of Africa.[89]

The textile industry, in which women constituted the workforce majority, remained a cornerstone of the Italian economy, even as the steel industry was developed; yet wool and cotton both depended on imports, and silk was a luxury market.[90] Even viscose rayon production, in which Italy excelled globally, required high-quality cellulose from Scandinavian wood and fossil fuels that Italy did not possess. Marinetti and Munari's elaborately produced work of propaganda celebrates the invention of Lanital, the first commercially manufactured regenerated protein fiber, patented in 1935 by an Italian chemist. Casein, a protein contained in mammalian milks and thus capable of being proclaimed "native" to Italy, could be processed and pressed through spinnerets to form silk-like viscose fibers. Through a brief reading of this poem and related Futurist works such as the eventual 1940 collection *The Non-Human Poem of Technicisms*, Jeffrey Schnapp brings out that as a key component of industrialization, fabrics had assumed "a central, symbolically charged place in the universe of commodities," acting as "a key indicator of a modern nation-state's ability to project its power at home and abroad"; under the regime, fabric becomes "the technologically enhanced double of a primary skin seen as once enfeebled and enervated but reinvigorated thanks to the fascistization of the Italian body politic."[91] The acutely gendered, racialized, and colonial dynamics of this work fall largely to the byways of Schnapp's compelling analysis of fascist embodiment, however, such that *The Poem of the Milk Dress*, a tour de force of late modernist aesthetics, deserves a closer unblinking look. In this section, we will examine the symbolic and theoretical enmeshments of armed territory and liquidity, the reinforced colonizing body and the maternal fluid of milk, through their entwinement in the story of this fabric's production.

Despite the book's remit to advertise the autarchy of the state, provocative mixed-media montages of organic and military imagery by Munari, overlaid with streams of Marinetti's unpunctuated verse that herald the manufacture of autochthonous fabric, serve to exhume the lawless imperial conquest that is as constitutive of Italy's apparent economic and cultural self-sufficiency as the Sudanese nurse was to the myth of Futurism's birth. Brute juxtaposition bares the ensnarlment of overdetermined oppositions: of militant masculinity and femininity grounded, from the first line, in the matter of milk and iron; of the colonizing body and the maternal fluid vital to its reinforcement; of territory enforced by armaments of steel and shot through with tactical liquidity of natural resources and navigation canals; and finally, of Africa and Europe, Black and white races (figure 1.6). The text can be read productively as a Fascist parallel to Dziga Vertov's Communist kino-eye reverse-time sequence tracing the origins of beef and undoing commodity fetishism in the process—revealing the repressed African substrate of an autarchic body of state. The book strips bare, in other words, the nuptials between an idealized Europe and its colonized others—subtended by

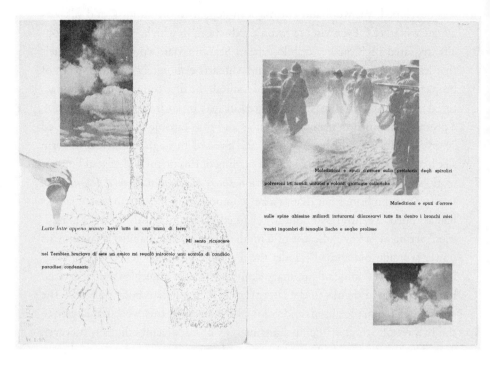

FIGURE 1.6 F. T. Marinetti and Bruno Munari, *Il poema del vestito di latte: parole in libertà futuriste*, ed. Ufficio Propaganda SNIA Viscosa (Officina Grafica Esperia, 1937), first page spread depicting combat in Ethiopia alongside a graphic of lungs and a can of milk. Copyright 1937 Bruno Munari. All rights reserved to Maurizio Corraini s.r.l. Published with the permission of The Wolfsonian—Florida International University (Miami, Florida). © 2024 Artists Rights Society (ARS), New York.

ethnoracial fantasies and fear of cross-contaminated blood, milk, soil, and air laden with toxic dust and mustard gas.

Marinetti's biblically resonant poem, brimming with profane violence, narrates the first-person epic of an embedded reporter/fighter/Futurist (presumably the poet himself) from combat in Tembien, to Khartoum, down the Suez Canal, and onto a train represented as projectile from the southern tip of the Italian peninsula at Reggio Calabria to Rome. The parole-in-libertà composition then fantasticates an extravagant celebration of the "Impero Mussoliniano" (Mussolinian Empire) in the Italian capital based on actual events of 1937–1938. The theme of thirst pervades the text throughout, and mechanical war is corporealized, with orifices of assault weapons rendered teatlike. The text finally transitions into idealized narration of the manufacturing of Lanital, as casein is siphoned off from milk, and machines represented as maternal draw on it to spin their polyphony of colorful thread. The process of creating a textile that will reinforce the Italian state by returning milk to its "pure" wet nurse/machine is represented in semi-onomatopoeic, repetitive, infantile phrasing, the possessively puerile babble of a sacred milk that speaks: "*sono un latte che ritorna beatamente alla sua pura mammella bobina bobina mia mia mia*" (*I am a milk that beatifically returns to its pure breast bobbin bobbin mine mine mine*).[92] The text will conclude on the declaration of

LATTE DI FERRO ARMATO
LATTE IN GUERRA
LATTE MILITARIZZATO

MILK OF ARMED IRON
MILK AT WAR
MILITARIZED MILK[93]

The notion of militarized milk is reinforced by Munari's montage: the verse on the final page of the poem is preceded by the green image of a ship and superimposed over a photograph of raw wool, and the sexualized orifice of a massive duct appears on the adjacent page, canon-like, at once phallic and recalling the udder-like carriage of the tank compared to a cow whose teats drip fire in an earlier scene: "o mucca dai cappezzoli purtroppo gocciano fuoco."[94]

Consisting of fourteen pages of free-word "aeropoetry" designed to mimic the panoramic imagination of the aviator, the book is remarkable for its design innovations.[95] Munari's bold page spreads juxtapose reportage photos with etched graphics, both elements being printed in grayscale and in monochrome Italian national colors of green and red against the white of the page. The book becomes almost sculptural because of the self-referential inclusion of cellophane that creates overlays of aerial and liquid imagery—a rain of bullets in one case, the moths that presumably won't corrode this rayon in another. These groundbreaking facets of the book's design have led its scarce commentators to halt analysis at the pictorial surface, calling attention to the work's stunning use of plastic transparencies and photo collage or to Munari's expression through imagery of "the passage from natural to artificial matter, but also . . . his epistemological perspective of an intrinsic continuity between nature and technology."[96] I resist the temptation not to interpret the content of either the imagery or the poetry, though my revulsion is potent.

Through montage, floating signifiers of the natural world, the cycle of milk's consumption and generation, are wedded to the heavy machinery of war,

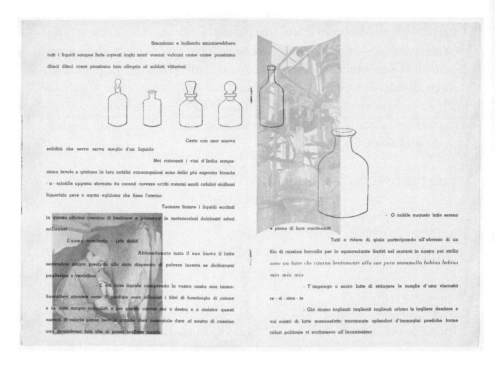

FIGURE 1.7 F. T. Marinetti and Bruno Munari, *Il poema del vestito di latte: parole in libertà futuriste*, ed. Ufficio Propaganda SNIA Viscosa (Officina Grafica Esperia, 1937), fourth page spread montaging a scene of milking alongside a factory scene. Copyright 1937 Bruno Munari. All rights reserved to Maurizio Corraini s.r.l. Published with the permission of The Wolfsonian—Florida International University (Miami, Florida). © 2024 Artists Rights Society (ARS), New York.

farming, and textile production as the work moves from combat in Ethiopia (figure 1.6) to the "autarchic" Italian factory (figure 1.7). Bodily organs suspended in space—the lungs on the first page spread, the stomach on the second—are juxtaposed with clouds, and clouds of dust, in armed combat—presumably of gunfire, possibly of mustard gas; the overall narrative drive targets quenching the thirst of desert combatants and Indigenous African inhabitants with a milk of empire that is literally fortified (figure 1.6). The third page spread features armed tanks and a decorative formation of celebratory attack planes before the work moves on to juxtapose images of cows being milked and pastoral sheep with kitchen or laboratory jars (figure 1.7), and the fifth spread presents the spinnerets that will make national fabric of their maternity. The seventh and final spread juxtaposes the massive duct, a ship, and an oceanic mass of wool or Lanital fiber, with the poet hailing the "immensa e dilagante carezzevole dut-/tilità materna di questa animalità quasi tessile" (immense and rampant caressing maternal duct-/tility of this almost textile animality) as the milk slowly metamorphoses into autarchic commodity.

The poem begins in medias res in battle in the Ethiopian province of Tembien, during an offensive known for its large-scale deployment of mustard gas, with a speaker thirsty and choking on "putrid and stinking dustclouds" who is given "milk just milked . . . in an iron cup": "In Tembien I was burning with thirst a friend miraculously gifted me a can of snow-white condensed paradise" (*Latte latte appena munto* bevo latte in una tazza di ferro / Mi sento ricuocere nel Tembien bruciavo di sete un amico mi regalò miracolo una scatola di candido paradiso condensato") (figure 1.6).[97] Throughout the text, milk's whiteness and its signification as a maternal nurturing fluid will be exploited to palliate and racialize the scene of conquest, as the narrative embarks upon histrionic return to Rome on a "fiery ship" through a corporeal African landscape. The speaker situates himself at the meeting point of three continents, at the confluence of the White and the Blue Nile, in Karthoum, where Marinetti's father had had an office and political unrest led to an Anglo-Egyptian government in Sudan. The "holy dawn milk" that soothes the smoking lungs and satiates the living and dying Italian volunteers will be contrasted with the "thick broth" of the Red Sea cooked by Sudanese women cast offensively as "lustful black [sic] witches"; the throats of the relieved Italians will be contrasted with the "throat" or "chokepoint" of the Suez Canal "lacking candor."[98]

The return to Rome in this text appears to model the 1937–1938 propagandistic celebrations of the two thousandth anniversary of Augustus Caesar's birth being held in Rome's Palazzo delle Esposizioni, in the archaeological Mostra Augustea della Romanità (Augustean Exhibition of Romanity).[99] These spectacles are described in a delirium of overblown white, milkish imagery, although this overdetermined color field is punctuated by the abusively decorative "Truppe di Colore" (Troops of Color)—African reinforcements of empire that are presented as an exotic "Carnival of war" decorated with precious stones and fruits, then "dressed in quicklime," as if to reinforce the white palette through a substance used in ancient chemical warfare.[100] In a hallucinatory scene, Mussolini's reborn empire is feted with a squadron of planes compared to a pack of "aerial scissors" and scrap metal hunks, whose "blabbermouth shadows acrobatically lick the milky Altar of the Fatherland" (the ostentatious white Victor Emmanuel II National Monument in Piazza Venezia, where Mussolini held his mass assemblies)—the dark lapping up light in an outrageously overstated way that will continue in unfortunately racialized terms in subsequent passages. For at the same time, the African sun, represented as "Italianized," "rounds a rosy oven mouth," recalling the outlandish black and pink imagery of Marinetti's infancy, as if to accept the milk of Italy while emitting thirsty sparrows; the "black forest of the gods smokes" under fire, thereby "carbonizing itself" and creating of its blackened leaves "banners of the

84   ◆   WIRELESS IMAGINATION

dark invoking the blessing of the Tiber"; and "bronze dubats," colonial troops of Italian Somaliland, "*spring* out of cream skins and give up *flights /of swallows* wriggling out of the Indigenous night towards the ideal European milk."[101] While peppered with African place-names and terms, strewn with the signature Futurist infinitives, and deprived of obvious punctuation so as to appear "free," this late example of words-in-freedom doggedly manifests a state-sanctioned drive to invert the scene in the founding of Futurism—to domesticate the dubat and to make Africans drink European milk, rather than the other way around.

At the same time, the viscous fluidity and femininity associated with women, communism, and the other that Klaus Theleweit theorized fifty years back as central to the Fascist imagination, an association we see in early modernism across the continents, must be drawn off in order for milk to be "militarized" and adapted for national textile use.[102] One of the speaker's final declarations/admissions will be "I AM THE HARD MAN NOT ADEQUATELY / MILKY WHILE NURSED WITH THE BEST SNOW-WHITE MILK OF THE BEYOND"—making men harder than flesh and milk transubstantial. The text imagines the Colosseum as an "immeasurable sieve" that "skims *cirruses* of cream," the famed Roman monument's holes simultaneously filling with the moths that colonize natural wool, in a decorative spectacle "[t]o celebrate the Mussolinian Empire." Il Duce is represented as a "gourmand" who drinks ecstatically from the horizon: "On the highest terrace an imperial gourmand dominates plazas / and lunatic with his mute mouth turning to sip horizons," before he appears again through the edict, "The man commands—Milk divide yourself."[103] Schnapp points out that this modernist reworking of the separation of land from water in Genesis to narrate "the separation of cheese from whey and casein from water" echoes Aristotle, whose writings lead cheese making to become a Western trope for how semen succeeds in "fixing" the menstrual fluid secreted in the universe.[104]

I would add that, given the geopolitical context, we must see in the division of solid from liquid in this text a sadistic and somewhat masochistic, given Marinetti's roots, parting of the Red Sea, which leads to the crossing of the Israelites and the drowning of Egyptians. In the final page spread, the poem will laud a woolish sea of former milk that breathes and opens to submit to the European navigating ship, while the farms continue to submit their animal resources to the process in a vexingly funereal key:

> *Respirazione lentissima di un laneggiante mare quasi carne vellu-*
> *tata da aprirsi agevolmente colla più garbata prua*
> > *Le fattorie sottopongono*
> *le loro lane vive al lavaggio funebre dei tramonti autunnali spugne scarlatte*

> *Most slow breathing of a wooling sea almost flesh velvet-*
> *ed to open itself easily with the more courteous prow*
> *The farms submit*
> *their live wools to the funereal washing of autumn sunsets scarlet sponges*

Effectively genocidal in its aspirations, this text haunts, resisting the well-founded desire to relegate it once more and definitively to the muteness of a violent history once thought to be overcome, because Marinetti never successfully expels a desire to be both Arab and European, Black and white. That infantile nostalgia for oneness with his nurse exists alongside the desire for conquest of this Global South of "color" by a species of milky-white Europeanness primarily associated with more northerly European nations (those more successful at stockpiling territory toward global empires than Italy had been). The dependence upon Africa so histrionically dramatized in this work ultimately topples the autarchic precepts that commissioned it, leading us through a harm-inducing cultural centrifuge that denaturalizes not only mother's milk and wool textile but also consolidated tongue and text.

FATHERLAND AS CATACLYSM: UNBINDING PENTECOSTS IN THE VERSE OF THE BARONESS ELSA VON FREYTAG-LORINGHOVEN

Having established that cosmopolitanism and a multilingual background can be channeled toward ultranationalist and monstrously colonial ends, it's time to reroute our account of the historical avant-gardes that paved the way for post-war experimentation with poetic language to contour how—by contrast with the Futurists' fanatical and strategic embrace of industrial development and its wars—skepticism surrounding modernization and the military escapades to prop up fatherlands that it enabled did thrive in contemporary artistic circles. The poetry explored in the chapters that follow, far from colluding with nationalist designs to ward off foreign influence in language, will deploy Western languages from an exilic stance. These figures will make a home in the labyrinthine linguistic circumstance of immersion in a language that is culturally remote, blending subaltern and obsolete or endangered tongues with those of ascendant empires in experimental stanzas. Constructing poetic forms that will allow plural linguistic and cultural logics to cohabit the same space, these authors devise unique ways to take liberties with the boundaries of nationalized vernaculars.

The work of the resultant poems on the apparent language of composition exceeds the language of political sovereignty and naturalized conceptions of the mother tongue, though the verse that issues from these processes is, practically by definition, politically orphaned either by design or by error—not efficacious in rounding up coherent or actionable sociopolitical caucuses. The work of itinerant poet, model, and body performance artist, "mother of Dada" and "Future Futurist," the "Baroness" Elsa von Freytag-Loringhoven (Swinemünde 1874–Paris 1927) presages these developments; the Baroness (as I will hereafter identify her) proposes a form of languages-in-freedom that virulently counters Marinetti's nationalism, his embrace of technology, and the expansionist wars enabled by it.[105]

Two 1915 photographs of the itinerant Elsa aged forty-one in her Greenwich Village studio by International News Photography constitute the first portraits of the artist as an exile in New York City. She had arrived in New York via Cincinnati; Sparta, Kentucky; and Pittsburgh in 1913 and, although legally married to the writer, translator, and sometime prisoner-for-fraud Felix Paul Greve (who later, in Canada, renamed himself Frederick Philip Grove), wedded Leopold Karl Friedrich the Baron von Freytag-Loringhoven (who would die in 1919). This act effectively christened her the Baroness—a term that insists ludically on the difference of an aristocratic title within the reputed democracy of the United States and, in its linguistic origins, bears the meaning of "warrior." Donning acrobat's pants, ballerina slippers, a bustier fashioned of ribbon and Ghanaian kente cloth, baubles dangling from the nipples, and an aviator helmet topped by a giant feather mimicking a propeller, this androgynous figure—who had been arrested in Pittsburgh three years earlier for cross-dressing and smoking—forms a warrior of a peculiar kind (figure 1.8). Once a Berlin music-hall performer of tableaux vivants, then simultaneously an artist's model for hire and pioneering body performance artist, sculptor, and poet, Elsa was the creator of innumerable assemblages frequently remarked upon in art scene chatter yet rarely, until our time, dignified as worthy of the archive. These rare, now-famed stills of the artist's athletic enactments memorialize what International News Photography captured as "Elsa von Freytag-Loringhoven's Body Performance Poem"—one that lends itself to interpretation in a geopolitical key. The feather as propeller naturalizes and renders feral the woman's aerodynamic pose, while referring to the plume of writing, cocked at an angle forty-five degrees at odds to the body's direction; such a wing plume parodies the mechanistic society that had invented the military technology essential to the air raids just beginning, at the time of the portraits' capture, tragically to characterize the Great War.

FIGURE 1.8 International News Photography, "Elsa von Freytag-Loringhoven's Body Performance Poem in her Greenwich Village Studio," December 1915.

Visually, the feather refers us not only to aviation but to a bird cage at upper right that, in turn, draws attention to the disheveled domestic environment that surrounds the statuesque pose, strewn with potential and cast-off outfits. This chamber indexes a chaotic existence thrown together in temporary compositions—compositions verbal, sculptural, and corporeal that form a species of counterarchive of the global metropolis wrought of hand-me-downs and foraged garbage. The photo was presumably shot in the Lincoln Arcade studio where the artist was neighbor to Marcel Duchamp, her platonic friend and would-be lover who would go down in history as having invented the readymade through a urinal-cum-"Fountain" that, it now seems plausible, echoed not only in conception but also in subject matter a sculpture belatedly attributed to the Baroness: a plumbing trap-cum-"God."[106]

In understanding her work, which still strikes us as radically dissonant and heretical, it is essential to keep the terms "readymade" and "assemblage" in mind, not only as aesthetic but as geopolitical principles characterized by performative displacement and palpable seams. The Baroness's upbringing in an archipelagic port city subject to constant geopolitical contestation, on the border of states now known as Germany and Poland, and her variously driven cross-continental migrations are particularly riddling to literary-historical classification—shedding light on Marinetti's adamant Italianness as a focalized construct by the son of African colonists. Else Hildegard Plötz was born to a Polish mother and Teutonic father in the border city of Swinemünde—a Pomeranian port on a thin strip of canalized land between the Baltic Sea and the Szczecin Lagoon that had been part of Sweden, Prussia, and, from 1871 on, the German Empire—now known as Swinoujscie, Poland. She spent long periods in Italy with her first "marriage experiment," the architect August Endell; resided in New York between 1910 and 1923; suffered her early fifties in poverty in Berlin from 1923–1926; and lived the last year of her life in Paris until her accidental death or suicide by asphyxiation in 1927.[107] Clearly (dis)rooted in her origins and in resentment for her abusive and tyrannical father, the adult Baroness's political sympathies were strictly contrarian. With Germany and France bitterly at war, the French American painter Louis Bouché attested to her appearing at a Broadway subway station wearing a French poilu's blue trench helmet. Vaunting her adoption of American English in verse, she deployed it mercilessly to parody American ignorance, crassness, and commercialism, its being "nothing but impudently inflated rampantly guideless burgers, ... founded on greed."[108]

Because she was associated with the community of European expatriate artists fleeing the horrors of war for New York City (retroactively named the New York Dada circle), however, critical simplification has warped the Baroness's geopolitical figuration. Even scholars who cleave closely to the careers of cosmopolitan artists tend to distinguish literary movements through the perspectives of national traditions for the sake of coherence and accessibility and, in cases where this is not possible, to associate these artists with single cities, as though figures of this period and type had had the capacity to "settle down." The Baroness is, by extension of her association with New York Dada, described continually as giving rise to a "a strikingly American form of dada"—cultivated through criticism as "the first American dada," "America's first performance artist," and "America's first assemblage artist."[109] Such critical simplification, cleaving to a notion of national literary tradition that the Baroness's work overrides and overturns, occults both her itinerancy and a key function of the geopolitical harbor of cities for modern artists, arguably for women, queer, and Black and Brown artists above all; her confidante and amanuensis Djuna Barnes put it more accurately when she described the Baroness in 1924 as "a citizen of terror."[110]

Although feminist scholars have begun to unearth this artist's importance within the history of the avant-garde, identifying her assemblages as among the first modernist readymades and performance art objects, few have ventured to interpret her poetry, which traversed languages and media, was only published as a proper collected volume in 2011, and presents various methodological difficulties that I will present in this section. Much of the poetry was composed in English because, as she wrote, she found "*American English* . . . a treasure trove" that "newfound must be *cherished and evermore explored*."[111] Yet the verse is laced with defamiliarizing translinguistic assemblages and disfluencies. As a prelude to discussion of the postwar artists in this study, here I present a compact reading of the xenoglossic effects of this poetry, with xenoglossia referring to a use of language unsanctioned by geopolitical belonging or education. Needless to say, it has been more challenging historically for women to receive a proper education, so authorization of their cosmopolitanism has consistently been stymied. Christine Cooper-Rompato has shown how xenoglossia as "miracle" thus figures in the writings of late medieval women writers like Margery Kempe.

Arriving in New York a few years after James's return to the city as disoriented "native," the Baroness helps us understand how an abracadabrant poetry was being forged on these western Atlantic shores: the fruit of a Babel that was not simply exterior, the result of languages pooling in the streets, but interior as well for many immigrants—and tempting the staging of Pentecosts for those able to twist divided language into consonance, however fleetingly. Through its shuttling "betwixt" linguistic systems, the Baroness's poetry alters the terms of sociopolitical belonging, bucking what she calls her eventual aborted "Cataclysmic Undertaking to Join 'Fatherland.'"[112] Xenoglossia provides a useful tool for characterizing the work of an artist who titled her self-portrait in verse "Pfingst Fanfare"—"Pfingst" being the German term for "Pentecost." Though it begins with the line "Proud deep—teutonic—" and plays with pagan figures of Norse mythology, that 1923–1924 poem's relationship to "own" or "owned" tongues was rendered ambiguous from the start, as its subtitle's description reads, "[Translated from my own—into my other own.]"[113] There's a word missing here, and that omission registers as defamiliarizingly awkward, although one understands from this disfluent phrase that what's being "owned" is language. That said, one normally understands one's "own" language to be singular, whereas here, plurality is being insisted upon. English seems to have opened up a medium akin to rebirthing for the Baroness, for, as she expressed in an annotation to another lyric, "Germany has become stupid—inflexible. Brooding on old eggs—unable to brood new ones. Like all genuine stupidity—senile stupidity—it is important."[114] This monstrous maternal imagery in which the mother bird attempts to "brood" aged eggs rather than newly hatched ones expresses impatience both with history and with her "breed"—or even the whole notion of a so-called mother tongue, in a context where mothers do not release their vital offspring. Even the literary offspring of Marinetti register in the face of the Baroness's radical aesthetics as old, retrograde: kitschy pastiches of Roman imperial imagery exaggerated, rather than being replaced with signifiers of a different and truly revolutionary world to come. The morbid aesthetics of lactation's fixing in Marinetti's *The Poem of the Milk Dress* ultimately genuflects, that is, to a museological Romanità at odds with avant-guerre Futurism's radical negativity.[115]

In the June 1929 issue of the pathbreaking, Paris-based, little magazine, *transition*, editor and translingual poet Eugene Jolas formulated a programmatic goal for modern poetry whose manifesto bears clear debts to Futurist calls for the violent destruction of syntax and words-in-freedom. "Poetry is at the crossroads today," he wrote. The poet "will have to abandon completely the attempt to express his universe with the decadent instrument of unpliable and exhausted language matter, or else he will have to try to resuscitate the comatose word." For the poet, such a "renunciation of despair" lies precisely in the degree to which he succeeds in "producing adequately and violently a chemistry in words."[116] As lyric preface to these pronouncements, Jolas chose four poems by the late Baroness, suggesting that she exemplified the new verbal chemistry being summoned. Jolas, who published in French, German, and English and in macaronic and glossolalic modes between and beyond the three, is best known as the first publisher of that translingual monument, "Work in Progress," later to be titled *Finnegans Wake*. He was fond of claiming that "all the acoustics and sonorousness in all the languages of the world can be traced in *Finnegans Wake*."[117]

As part of a quest for the "Pentecostal word" that might reverse the curse of Babel, Jolas would go on to theorize the Atlantic, or Crucible language, as an alternative to Esperanto, which he viewed as the logical result of the mixing of languages that he witnessed as a teen in New York and as an enlisted soldier in the US South: "Not [the language] of the 'educated philistine' who demands signs to simplify his world of communication, not an auxiliary language that will never remind him of his solitude, not a quotidian language of gestures that flees from consecration. But a language that will dance and sing, that will be the vision of the 'troisième oeil,' that will bind the races in a fabulous unity."[118]

As part of this vision, Jolas compiled both an anthology of multilingual poetry and a "Migration Dictionary" consisting of definitions and etymologies of hundreds of invented words, although neither project was ever brought to fruition. His later "Vertigralism," high on modern aeronautics, envisioned a futuristic extraterrestrial language of glyphs beyond translation. *transition*, however, became a key locus where competing possibilities toward the aesthetic realization of a language both common and revolutionary were being worked out in public between 1927 and 1939—plural strains heeding Jolas's somewhat confused call for "the word of movement," "the new vocabulary and the new syntax" that must "help destroy the ideology of a rotting civilization"—characterizing "not a collective being, but a universal being, an harmonious being."[119] Jolas was deeply dissatisfied with contemporary political movements, from anarchism, to tyrannical capitalism, to a communism that apes capitalist economic visions, to Fascism, and turned to art rather than politics for revolutionary solutions. The solutions featured within the pages of *transition* ranged from the stupefyingly virtuosic linguistic omnivorism characterizing the *Wake* to C. K. Ogden's distillation of Basic English as tactic of *Debabelization* (to cite Ogden's 1931 book on the matter, subtitled *With a Survey of Contemporary Opinion on the Problem of a Universal Language*). Deriding synthetic languages as merely contributing to the existing Babel and proposing in their place the "universalization of English," Ogden translated the last four pages of James Joyce's *Anna Livia Plurabelle* into Basic English, publishing the endeavor in *transition*, to make his point that the 850 words in his Basic vocabulary were capable of expressing the full range of thought, from the simplest to the most complex.[120]

The support offered to the Baroness by this public forum goads us to push past the most iconic and canonical figures of *transition*'s stable—and the spectacular but already obsessively trodden and perhaps less exemplary linguistic pyrotechnics of Joyce—to contend with the geopolitically fraught and gendered complexities of her oeuvre: the rattling disfluencies and disharmony as well as the lacunae, which lead more readily to suspicion than to consecrations of genius. For in residing uncomfortably between languages, geographies, and sexual identities, and salvaged notwithstanding its author's life of abuse, poverty, homelessness, and an early death, the Baroness's work has given rise to a spotty reception history—a fact shared by many of the authors in this study for politically inflected reasons. Along the way, through its relentless negativity and insistence on grounded social commentary (not always of a coherent or politically digestible type), the Baroness's oeuvre, ragged around the linguistic edges, also offers oblique ripostes to the monomaniacal aspects of Jolas's fantasy languages that have led Emily Apter to label him a "premier dogma theorist of self-enclosed language worlds."[121]

A materialist approach to the wireless imagination appears in the Baroness's transmedia work, providing an instructive counterpoint to the violent ideological idealism that subtends Marinetti's vociferous stress on the "lyrical obsession with matter."[122] The Baroness's riposte to the wireless imagination is titled variously "X RAY" and "RADIO" and was published by Eugene and Maria Jolas in *transition*'s October 1927 issue; it confounds as it underscores the materiality of this seemingly ethereal medium. "Nature causes brass to oxidize": the Baroness's deceptively baffling poem begins with a perfectly legible statement, delivered in the authoritative rhythm of iambic pentameter, about the patina that develops when copper and its alloys make contact with oxygen in the air.[123] Nature is the poem's protagonist; what another version of the lyric calls nature's "finishing process" develops a coating upon the metal that—contrary to received ideas about corrosion—protects it. Nature also causes "people to amass," and even to "congest," as the poem's revision has it—either through the primal instincts driving sex and reproduction or through death: a congestion not only of cities but also of soil, such as that of the unprecedented mass graves yielded by the recent catastrophic Great War. The text exists in nine versions housed in archives at the University of Maryland and in its published form (with several inexplicable editorial deletions and additions); the only thing that remains the same is this opening statement, with a few minor variants.[124]

The Baroness doesn't assume a heady Futurist reverie in the face of the advancing developments of X-rays and radio; instead, the artist known for dressing herself in garbage grounds a seemingly ethereal medium in earth and the body. In one version, a cluster of compound riffs suggests a marriage of sun and soil through electromagnetic radiation, which is in turn wedded to radio: "SUNS RADIOINFUSED / RADIO'S SOIL / SOILSECRET SUN-MESSAGE SUNIMPREGNATED / DORMANT WITHIN SOIL FOR PROGRESS' / DUMB [BUMB?] RADIOPENETRATED SOIL." The poet, doubtless inspired by the advent of voice broadcasting and the rise of the commercial radio "craze" in the 1920s, conceptually extends the aural rather than visual implications of these scientific discoveries, imagining the sun's electromagnetic radiation penetrating the seemingly silent, secret earth as radio "sunmessage": "Polish— / Kill— / For fastidious / Brilliant boss' 'idée fix' / Sum total : / Radiance" (figure 1.9). "Brilliant boss' 'idée fix' "—note the lack of a final e in "fix," which renders this a translingual phrase in manuscript—is closer to the slang fix of the addict than to the obsession elegantly cast in perfect French. We can assume that a poet as subversive as the Baroness (a "mother" both antipatriarchal and hardly maternal) would distance herself from this brilliant and, in some versions, "fastidious" boss's monomaniacal polish. Though parataxis makes it difficult to determine exactly how the manuscript line "Luxury ornament" fits—the line was in fact deleted (by the editors?) in the published poem—it compels us to remember the Baroness's first *objet trouvé* or found object, *Enduring Ornament* (1913): a rusted iron ring that she found on the street en route to marry the Baron Leo von Freytag-Loringhoven at New York's City Hall

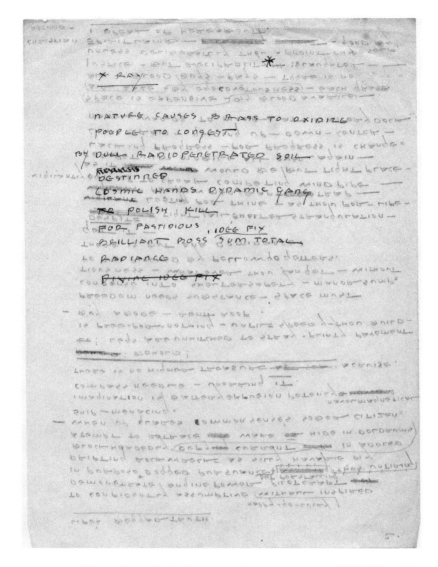

FIGURE 1.9 Elsa von Freytag-Loringhoven, second manuscript version of "X RAY," out of ten. Courtesy of Elsa von Freytag-Loringhoven papers, Special Collections and University Archives, University of Maryland Libraries. Poem was published in *transition* (October 1927): 134–35.

and that she claimed as a symbol of Venus.[125] Despite or because of its rust—another process of oxidation—the Baroness's readymade nuptial ornament is "enduring," treasured in duration, a part of nature. As the makeshift crystal radios of the 1920s and World War II demonstrate, the oxide coatings of many metal surfaces (rusty nails, corroded pennies, and other discarded objects) can act as semiconductors capable of detecting (and rectifying) radio waves. The compulsion to "polish" in the service of creating a "luxury ornament" deprives metal not only of its place in nature but also of its conductive properties.

Indeed, in the compressed yet audacious space of this poem, polishing metal is rendered equivalent to killing off an amassment of people—both aspects of the boss's idea-fixes that are "contra nature" and associated in five versions of the text with "progress." Given what was about to happen in Europe, the United States, and the Pacific theater of war, this seemingly facile analogy makes a reader shudder—and wonder about the contents of the radio's "sunmessage." Arthur Holly Compton, who won the Nobel Prize in Physics for his discovery of the change in the wavelength of X-rays when they collide with electrons in metals, was instrumental in initiating the Manhattan Project, which generated the first atomic bomb. And as Futurist touts make plain, radio itself was deployed initially in the service of killing, not communicating: "Radio . . . was born into a world of jittery jingoism and started life as a weapon in the commercial and military rivalries of the great powers," writes historian Daniel Headrick. "Thus do humans unfairly project their own virtues and vices upon the machines they create."[126]

> Progress is ravishing—
> It doesn't me—
> Nudge it—
> Kick it—
> Prod it—
> Push it—
> Broadcast————
> That's the lightning idea![127]

On December 7, 1924, Djuna Barnes took to writing the preface for a collection of the Baroness's writings, describing her older confidante and spiritual lover as "a citizen of terror, a contemporary without a country" and expressing the hope that in offering some of her works, "a country will inherit her life, offering in return peace, and decency and time."[128] The Baroness did not obtain the privilege of country or peace. She had been the victim of domestic violence at home, was sporadically criminalized and penniless, and was mentally unstable, as her mother had been. At the moment Barnes was writing, Elsa was describing herself as "insane from Germany—as my mother was from 'home.'"[129] She'd left New York and the United States after thirteen years, where she was by turns celebrated as the essence of Dada and left destitute and homeless, frequently jailed at the notorious Manhattan prison "The Tombs" for shoplifting, vagrancy, bathing in public fountains, and other petty offenses. "'Say it with——— / Bolts! / Oh thunder! / Serpentine aircurrents——— / Hhhhhphsssssss! The very word penetrates!"[130] These words from a poetic commentary on radio and sex subversive enough that it wasn't published until 1983 come down to us in vengefully penetrating lines. They transmute radio into what endures and exceeds any aesthetically or ideologically constrictive message: "radiance," passing through any number of cultural obtusenesses and obstructions.

"'Ach—Lieber Kapitän' / But—Dear Captain" is the swan song to New York that the Baroness composed in an amalgam of German and English or, to be more accurate, "betwixt" the two upon her departure to return to Germany via the steamer *SS York* in 1923—or as she puts it in the subtitle, "On My Cataclysmic Undertaking to Join 'Fatherland.'" She defines the occasional poem as a "Reflex" upon being subjected to a lecture by the ship's captain, a German veteran of the Great War.[131] The very word "reflex" substituting the more expected term "reflection," although awkward to a native speaker of English, renders corporeal the poet's disgust at hearing the captain's speech, displacing cerebral response with the autonomic.

She caricatures the ship captain as "V. Mücke," or Mosquito, and describes his unthinking nationalism in the key of doggerel: "Upright / Will he fight / For what he is thought to think / To be right / Battle orb ablaze with blue sheen!" The poem parodies his dialect, suggesting it relays his steadfast commitment to country against a phantom enemy, devoid of questioning, humor, or qualm. She translates the lecturing by his "square bean" (an unmelodious phrase wrangling with American dialect and suggesting "doltish brain") into an uncouth rural English melded to more arcane poetic diction, such as "nary": "Stout as oak / Nor doubt— / Nor joke! / Nary qualm assailing square bean of his'n / As to the foeman's 'utter wrong' / Amongst 'der Weltgeschichte' [world history]."[132] The captain describes his escapades through a desert landscape, which we can imagine as the same one that Marinetti romanticized in his battle poems—the desert of former Ottoman terrain:

>An seiner höchst ureigensten Küste—
>Betwixt seiner persönlichst ererbten
>"Dreckwüste"—
>Trübt das "Hunnengewissen" des
>Kaptäns Mücke!

> Along the coast he calls his own alone—
> *Betwixt* his personally inherited
> "Dirtdesert"—
> Clouds the "Hunconscience" *des*
> Captain Mosquito![133]

The Baroness skewers the claim to inherited land—"his 'right o' way'"—by this merely subordinate soldier, "Lacking originality." The mosquito's pricking embodies by suggestion the puniness of Mücke's masculinity, which she also parodies in propositions that he cannot ride a camel with skill and cannot match the desire of veiled women.

This fantasiless erect captain is nevertheless dismissed as being "Ganz wie ein Mann!"—"Just like a man!": "Transparent to me / As clay.../.../Y'see— / That guy / Will die / With jeer and battlecry / For what he is trained to comprehend." While "His circumscribed horizon is firm / No squirm," the unbound Baroness will prevail through "'Dada' torpedoes high blue soulsea— / Waterlogged hulks to split / ... / That's where *I* hap'n / To be Cap'n"—the "waterlogged hulk" certainly referring to the oafish shipman himself.[134] The image embraces the journey of radical artistry instead of conformist war, suggesting it allows one's soul to be at home at sea. The poem closes on the speaker's calling out to the captain, "Sie rudern— / Sie rudern— / Sie rudern sich hinein," translated by the editors as "You row— / You row— / You row your boat inside." The infantilizing nursery rhyme, an English classic, seems to further diminish the captain's self-importance, whereas the image's sexual connotations imply some childish return to the womb. Supposedly, the Baroness gave the captain a copy of the poem, to which he could not "shoot back," rendering him "more 'at sea' than ever he was before," in her words.[135]

Marcel Duchamp is known to have quipped that the Baroness was not a Futurist but that she *was* the future.[136] By contrast with the fanatical Futurist embrace of modernization and the pervasive nationalism that followed, she cast military escapades to prop up "fatherlands" as the pathetic harvests of unoriginal parasites at best, cataclysmic for art and life, flight and navigation. Blending endangered and subaltern tongues with those of various empires and opening overdetermined notions of the "mother tongue" to question, her verse takes liberties with the boundaries of nationalized vernaculars, treating languages of citizenship with caustic blends of utopianism, skepticism, and disdain and redrafting the terms of community in the process. The work of the Baroness on the apparent language of composition far exceeds naturalized conceptions of the mother tongue and the language of political sovereignty. Rather unakin to Marinetti's late and opportunistic embrace of would-be autarky, the Baroness attempted unsuccessfully to graft herself onto roots in the New World. She embraces this distant soil and imagines blood and milk as having their own wild autonomy. In a late (ca. 1924–1927) poem titled "Purgatory Lilt," which well describes the state of the reader attempting to parse it, von Freytag-Loringhoven describes her inspiration in Germany as a "wheezing," and her Teutonic blood "leaping" out of nation and body in a "swerve" from its ice, toward an "America" where "Belonging" is consummate with "root's" cleavage: "Swerve leaping blood / Off ice casts stunning scale / In sweet soil America / Clove it root / Belonging."[137] As pentecostal fanfare, the Baroness's idiom arguably "made in New York" expresses the pulverizing of circumscribed peoples, classes, genders, and races, unbinding individuals at every turn of phrase from the patriarchal collectives of "jeer and battlecry" that were to dominate the decades after her premature passing—a different kind of barbarism.

2

Antifascist Philology and the Rejection of Linguistic Purity in Emilio Villa

THE TURBINE OF GENESIS: A XENOGLOSSIC HURRICANE

"And the earth was without form, and void; and darkness was upon the face of the deep. And the Spirit of God moved upon the face of the waters." So reads the familiar version of the second verse of Genesis, conveyed to English-language readers in the canonical King James edition of 1611—having been inflected by transit and interpretation from Hebrew through the instruments of Greek and Latin. Yet in a passage dedicated to this creation narrative composed to accompany a radical translation of the Bible channeled directly from Hebrew into Italian, the poet, critic, translator, and philologist Emilio Villa (Affori 1914–Rieti 2003) stresses that "Spirit" hails from a Hebrew term for a natural force. Digging further into possible origins, Villa glosses the word for the air, breath, or wind that passed over the primordial waters—rwh 'lhjm, or ruach Elohim, as voiced aloud with vowels infused—through its links to Sumerian, Akkadian, Ugaritic, and Babylonian cosmogony. The discussion of רוּחַ (ruach) appears in Villa's commentary on Bereshit/Genesis ("Origin") 1:2, where the Hebrew text reads, "וְהָאָרֶץ הָיְתָה תֹהוּ וָבֹהוּ וְחֹשֶׁךְ עַל פְּנֵי תְהוֹם וְרוּחַ אֱלֹהִים מְרַחֶפֶת עַל פְּנֵי הַמָּיִם." Prepared between 1953 and 1986 and rejected by the trade publisher Feltrinelli in 1975, this poet/philologist's translation of Genesis for a general public—had he found editors brave enough to publish it—would have revolutionized understanding of this consecrated text via its insistence, at the level of each transmitted word, that "the historical delirium of Hebrew literature is born of a tangle of mythological notions and inventions regarding the origins of the world."[1] His gloss of ruach defamiliarizes readers from the Spirit of a domesticated Christian Trinity, which derives, he explains, from a patristic doctrine that needed to justify the plural form used for

God, "Elohim," as well as the plural verb forms that often appear in the workings of the creating deity.[2] Villa, who was also responsible for introducing key protagonists of postwar abstraction to the Italian public (Pollock, Burri, Twombly, Rothko, and Matta, to name only a few), steps back from the rewriting of Genesis's averbal wind or breath as rational, human Logos or Word that was articulated in the prologue to the Gospel of John. In the place of the Holy Spirit, he populates Genesis with a hyper- as well as supranatural force, both wind and bird: "A pure mythic *fictio* (a gigantic 'speaking' Bird, a Hurricane, attributed belatedly to rwh-divine, Wind-of-God)" that "represents and founds the inventive value of the creative and performative word."[3] The *fictio* in question is a fashioning, shaping air, then, at the foundations of language, hailing from the primordial forces of wind; its motion is analogous to a fluttering of wings that Villa excavates "figuratively beneath the shadows of the text and etymologizing analogy"—pointing out that the Bird is a cosmogonic being in various archaic creation myths.[4] While Villa as poet is clearly drawn to this origin story because of its links to the creative power of the performative word, ruach precedes human language and its codifications, and he does not hold back from naming this suprahistorical phenomenon anachronistically via the New World idiom of the "Uragano" (Hurricane), from the sixteenth-century colonial Spanish coinage, yet originally hailing from the Caribbean Taíno term for the storms spawned by the angry goddess Guabancex.

The philosopher Adriana Cavarero would argue decades later—in *A più voci: Per una filosofia dell'espressione vocale* (*In Plural Voices: Toward a Philosophy of Vocal Expression*, 2003)—for the disembodying, rationalist repercussions of ruach's translation into Latin. Her vital recuperation of this text's corporeal resonance in the form of breath turns on the fact that the Vulgate version of Genesis "suffers from the Christian rereading of the Old Testament," wherein "ruach," although translated as πνεῦμα (pneuma) in the Septuagint version traced by tradition to the Jewish community of Alexandria, becomes "spirit," whereas qol, or prelinguistic voice, becomes signifying speech.[5] The more ambiguous "spiritus" (meaning breath but also spirit, mind, and energy) of "Et spiritus Dei ferebatur super aquas" was carried forth in the early modern Italian and English translations: Giovanni Diodati's Protestant version of 1603, although the first to be translated from Greek, Hebrew, and Syriac sources in the reformists' new refusal of the Church's mediating interpretation, rendered the passage as "E lo Spirito di Dio si moveva sopra la faccia delle acque," presaging the transmutation enacted by the collective King James translation published several years later. Cavarero focuses on ruach's manifestation as "the divine breath that exhales into the chaos before naming the elements," which also arises in the forms of "wind, breeze, storm, and, above all, as a creative force."[6] Yet the implications of Emilio Villa's interpretation reach farther than this in both space and time. A typescript of his translation of Genesis 1:1–2 bearing the marks of several work phases reads:

First cosmogony {360–300 BCE}
When Elohim began to form
the skies and the land,
the land was Desolation and Void,
and Darkness [Tenebra] over the face of the Primordial-Water,
while the Wind-of-Elohim fluttered
upon the surface of the Waters.[7]

Here Villa reaches "beneath the shadows of the text and of etymologizing analogy," into the resonance of the Hebrew that bestows nonhuman elemental and avian realities upon the divine force, for embedded within the verb "מְרַחֶפֶת" "mə-ra-ḥe-p̄eṯ: (from "tpjrm" and the root "pjr")—translated by Villa as "volteggiava" and as "fluttered" in my translation of his translation—is the idea that "Elohim 'beat their wings' or 'brooded,'" and "is to be understood as residue, or reprovocation [*risentimento*], of the mythical figuration of the god as great primordial Bird."[8] (Another way of translating this passage, retaining the implications of the action of an eagle hovering over a nest in Deuteronomy 32:11, which uses the same verb, would be, "And the divine wind was brooding over the cover of the deep."[9]) Villa points out a possible connection between Jewish and Egyptian myth "in the morphological sense" through the Ptolemaic-era cosmogony of Edfu, in which Horus makes solid earth appear from a bed of reeds.[10] And although Villa's methodology rebukes institutional historicism in the positivist sense, the fact that he appends dates to Genesis (one understands from the wavering penmanship that this was later in life) also overturns doctrinal expectations, anchoring in history what is supposed to transcend it.[11]

Although the translation above appeared in the body of the typescript Villa prepared for Feltrinelli, in his accompanying notes on the translation of Genesis, Villa proposes a more startling, culturally explosive possibility of rendering this biblical cosmogony: "Consider what has been exposed in the note to the first verse; summarizing that information, and beneath the text that is currently available, altered by restructuring and unsettled by spontaneous mutations in oral and written transmission, this is how we propose the probable original intention should be recuperated":

Elohim stette a guardare,
guardò l'Universo Cosmo:
Terra (era) allora la Dimora
delle divinità Tohutohu e Bohu;
il dio Tehom era cappato dalle Tenebre,
mentre il dio Uragano {Vento-Divino}
sbatteva le ali sulla distesa delle Acque.[12]

Elohim was watching,
watched over the Cosmic Universe:
Earth (was) at that time the Dwelling
of the divinities Tohutohu and Bohu;
the god Tehom was cloaked in Shadows,
while the god Hurricane {Divine-Wind}
beat its wings upon the expanse of the Waters.

Villa, then, strips what he calls the "theodynamic conception" behind this divine wind from any monolithic, monotheistic narrative of a single "tribe" of Israel and relates it to the "foundation of every religion," including what he identifies as "a particular and decisive imprint from the more stable and ancient Egyptian theology,"[13] by which he may be referring to Osiris's canonical resurrection through the beating of Isis's wings as raptor (a story dating at least as far back as the twenty-fourth century BCE).[14] These verses make clear that, for Villa, the act of "creation" was one of transcultural poesis, with "poetics" constituting a vocation that encompassed translation, philology, archaeology, anthropology, and speculative historiography.

Perhaps most surprising in Villa's philological approach to Genesis is his relation of Elohim, so often fused with an anthropocentric conception of the Father, to a bird brooding over the world and beating its wings to produce the turbine of wind that will trouble the surface of the waters. We can see these connections brewing as far back as his 1939 translation, in a footnote, of lines from Patesi Gudea, the Sumerian king of Ur: "his force was of the god Wind, bird of the hurricane."[15] That the Holy Spirit of Pentecost is normally represented as avian, traditionally a dove, takes on newly concrete and transcultural foundations in this literary-historiographical context. Pentecost, a feast observed with veneration from at least the fourth century CE, doubtlessly figured in scripture as the miraculous inauguration of the church and of a priestly class, its agents transformed from mere followers of Jesus into spiritual leaders. This narrative also bolstered the conception of Christianity's missionary expansion through the word of God, enjoying an uptick in attention during the Counter-Reformation of papal Rome.[16] The concept of xenoglossia (also known as xenolalia) has therefore rightly been treated with suspicion as a narrative justifying colonization by the theorist of "tongues" Ashon Crawley, who takes pains to distinguish it from the focus of his study with which it is often confused: the nonsemantic phenomenon of glossolalia, as identified in Blackpentecostal practice. "Xenolalic utterances resemble settler colonialist theological-philosophical imperatives," Crawley writes, in which one arrogantly assumes the language of another group; "Xenolalia is theoria, the enunciation of desired pure being, enunciated through the mastery of the language of the Other," implying no transformation of cognition or subjectivity—as if "one could speak in, without having to think in the language of the Other, without having to ever think about the value of the persons that think and speak in that language."[17]

In this book, I explore pentecostal aspirations that undercut such ecclesiastical and political attitudes. In the chapters that follow, we will pass through thickets of poetry whose use of languages foreign to the artist is "inspired" yet unmastered and unordained. The stanzas that issue from this process undermine the national tongues they mobilize, adding strains of alterity to enunciation, cognition, and subjectivity and, in the process, transforming prevailing narratives of belonging and community. This chapter will track the xenoglossic poetics emerging under the sign of Villa's Bird-Hurricane-Turbine-God: a figuration simultaneously suturing and centrifugal, uprooting the domesticated doctrinal form of Holy Spirit. This Vento-Divino registers as geopolitically radical within the immediate context and aftermath of Fascism, achieving a pentecostal alliance with Semitic cultures through poetic language that is transcultural, antinationalist, antipatriarchal, and antiauthoritarian. The implications of this Pentecost transmitted by the divine Bird-Hurricane-Turbine oppose the settler-colonial logics of the mission. Instead of the common sense of the nation, or the non-sense of asemantic sound poetry, Villa generates endless variations on sense, rooted in the incessant transmutation of meaning from remote antiquity. As a young writer in 1937, he will distinguish himself from the "total exclusion of semantic and syntactical values" that he sees in the "arbitrary uplifting of phonetic values" in modernist writing—surely a critique of Futurists' attack on syntax and lionization of onomatopoeia and sheer noise.[18] An unpublished manuscript from the 1960s surrounding the concept of sense defines sense as inherently open, "pure variation": "not 'becoming' but being variable in act, in gesture, in insurrection." This manuscript theorizes the workings of sense inside of a "conch-abyss," or a "field that is a network of all the possible stations of sense."[19] We see this concept mobilized in another poetic manuscript composed largely in English (figure 2.1) that assumes the "conch-abyss" as spiral form without telos; a grid of "simult-sense"s couched within an

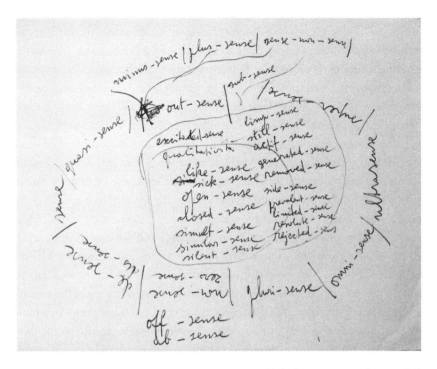

FIGURE 2.1 Emilio Villa, "de-sense/dis-sense." Unpublished manuscript. Photograph by Jennifer Scappettone. Copyright Estate of Emilio Villa. Courtesy of Archivio Emilio Villa, Biblioteca Panizzi di Reggio Emilia. Compound coinages in English spiraling around transmutations of the term "sense," pointing to both signification and sensory experience, and overseen by the contradictory compound "sense-non-sense."

outlined enclosure explodes into a whirl of compound coinages that works its way through plurality of sense and hypersense: from "quasi-sense | minus-sense | plus-sense" through "out-sense | sub-sense | super-sense | ultra-sense | omni-sense | pluri-sense," from "off-sense" and "ab-sense" to "de-sense," and ultimately dissensus, or "dis-sense."[20] Sense's ceaseless transmogrifications, spurred by contact with ever-altering lexicons toward poesis, encompass dissensus and insurrection against both "common sense" and academic strivings to clamp sense down.

Addressing Villa's formation in a religious ambit, through a search for ultimate truths manifest in "a concrete desperation of form," the great poet Andrea Zanzotto, seven years younger than Villa, speaks of the way "the arts of the sign and gesture . . . have affinities with the mantic element and element of wisdom," inspiring a mythic grip that continues to disquiet (Zanzotto's "mantico" means oracular, a mode obsessively researched by Villa, and it is related to "bellows," or the action of bringing air into the divinatory scene).[21] This poetics, Zanzotto proposes, "probes the irrelevance of languages through language, and goes beyond poetry, into a zone visible only 'at the editing machine [alla moviola],' within a sort of capsized pentecostalism."[22] Zanzotto identifies in Villa a *pentecostalismo rovesciato*, issuing from a Pentecost toppled, spilled, knocked over, turned inside out. The younger poet's choice of metaphor is acute: Villa's disquieting, formally outrageous strain of pentecostalism topples once more the arrogant Tower of Babel that the miracle of xenoglossia had supposedly mended or healed in giving the disciples of Christ unmitigated access to the tongues of each nation. Villa's pentecostalism rescatters, redistributing consensus and sense as through a centrifuge. At the same time, Villa's drive to connect the foundations of Hebrew literature with their Mesopotamian echoes undermines the rejection of Babylonia and the Babylonian creation myth implicit in Genesis's story of the toppled Tower of Babel (for Marduk's dominion at the center of the universe in Enūma Eliš is a high tower). Villa's work exposes a continuum that repudiates the myth of cultural division. Zanzotto's remarks about Villa's yearning for a zone beyond language, *through* language(s), aptly conjure the paradox within the postlapsarian xenoglossic impulse; the pentecostal strivings amalgamated and overturned by Villa's scattered projects surrounding common origins become legible only in the borderlines visible at the cinematic editing machine of poesis, via the sutures and tripwires between languages.

Villa's version of Genesis, begun upon his return from Brazil in 1953 and persisting as a passion for over three decades, was never to see the light during his lifetime because the church of that moment would not abide publication of biblical interpretations out of its doctrinal control; his translation of and rich commentary on the entire Hebrew Bible remain published only in fragments to this day (although he did serve as advisor to John Huston's 1966 film *The Bible: In the Beginning*).[23] By understanding Villa's work on Semitic languages historically—first within the period from 1930 to 1945, which saw the flourishing of Indo-European studies under Fascism; then in light of the implementation of racial laws between 1938 and 1945 that led to the deportation and murder of some six thousand Jewish people from Italy; and finally on the heels of these appalling abuses of "science"—we can begin to appreciate the radical implications and unusual reach of both the poet-philologist's deconstruction of the polar opposition between "West" and "East" and of the myth of a monolithic Jewish "tribe" in itself.

BEYOND THE MYTH OF THE ARYANS

In the introduction to his translation of Genesis, Villa points out that what we conventionally call Hebrew was called the "language of Canaan" by its people and was the language spoken in the southern zones of the Syro-Palestinian area, whose most antique phase is Ugaritic, then Phoenician, then various "dialectal motions," and then Moabitic, a literary language, whereas the people themselves spoke a language vaguely defined as Aramaic. Hebrew is therefore, Villa argues, a sacred official idiom consolidated by the "books" that eventually were called the Bible but whose Pentateuch comprises "vast material of spontaneous, collective formation" mediated by articulated hinges or a convoluted series of edits: "compilations, juxtapositions, sutures, inserts, lexical commentaries, supplements, innovations, deletions, ablations, corrections, explicative glosses, annotations, infiltrations, fusions and re-fusions."[24] Villa thereby introduces potential readers of his Genesis into a disorienting philological excavation that upends doctrinal approaches to this most sacred of Judeo-Christian texts. Rooting the creator-divinity in the concreteness of wind, which syntactically suggests what he calls a "wind of enormous proportions; vast turbine," he reaches to trace the remote origins of the text that quash the notion of a coherent monotheism and that, at the same time, given the choice to compare God with "turbine," resound with utter contemporaneity for the atomic age in which he eventually writes.[25] On the heels of a revised Diodati translation commissioned in 1904 and published twenty years later, Villa pivots from Catholic orthodoxy to translate Genesis as a "literary monument"—not only to recuperate its aesthetic qualities, as achieved by later renderings such as Robert Alter's, but to undo what he sees as its belated "dissolution" by means of a patristic Christian doctrine.[26] Rather than the literary whole that translators like Alter will emphasize in the redacted Hebrew book, Villa aims at excavating the chorality of both text and religion; he will claim that in "patriarchal, or ancestral, legends, no theophany issues from a strict condition of cultic etiology."[27]

For Villa, as a fulsome footnote within his introduction to Genesis details, "in the Hebrew imagination, God is Nature; is Fire, is Stone, Rock; is Wood; is Beast and Man; is Atmosphere, Wind, Lightning; is Sulfur and is Bread." The "magic and daemonic" action of this god continues within what he calls "the Miscellany of the 'ceremonial,'" as the god is "accompanied, surrounded, served" by a primordial throng of "daimons" that includes the "largely 'adversarial,' company of the international pantheon, plus the monstrous larvae of primordial divinities of which only the nomenclature generally survives, more or less obliterated as personages related to clamorous cosmogonic gestures."[28] This is how Villa can attempt to revive "the divinities Tohutohu e Bohu" and "the god Tehom" in his notes' outtake to his more official translation of Genesis's opening verses, suggesting provocatively by way of translation that what we understand to be "the deep," from "tehom" [תְּהוֹם], and "desolation and void," from "tohu wa-bohu" (a phrase thought to constitute paronomasia and now imported into various languages to signify "confusion" or, metonymically, "Babylon" [תֹהוּ וָבֹהוּ]), hail back to the proper names of more ancient creator gods. In a moment of cosmological but also ethnoecological comparison, Villa compares the initiating action of Genesis to the work of En-líl, the god of the air and storms responsible for parting the earth from the sky in Sumerian myth, as narrated in the prologue to *Gilgamesh*. He draws further parallels between Genesis and the Babylonian creation myth Enūma Eliš recorded in Akkadian language, which he translated in 1939; here, Marduk, the sky god of creation, deploys a northern wind, Imhullu, as an instrument for overtaking the primordial hermaphroditic monster of the feminine principle, Tiâmat (presumably a precursor of "Tehom"), who inhabits a chaotic abyss of waters that finds its direct counterpart in the Hebrew text.[29] As Villa wrote in the July 1939 preface to his translation of Enūma Eliš Tablet I, "Primordial chaos is, in fact, the alliance/marriage [connubio] of *tiamat*, the salt water where hurricanes sleep, with *apsÛ*, fresh water, of subterranean origin."[30] The presiding keywords of this sentence (primordial, chaos, connubio, hurricane, waters) will occupy Villa for the rest of his life in poetry, as we shall see.

Invoking the doctrine of the Trinity leveraged as justification for the plural verb forms of Elohim that appear in the operations of the creator god of Genesis, yet that might also refer to polytheistic origins, Villa notes that it was Christian exegesis that transmuted "wind" into a figure of the Holy Spirit that moves "super aquas" as part of the same action as the Father-God and the historically rooted son. Even so, he points out that "the mythologistic ideography" of the trinity could itself have entered into Christian theology from other strains of myth, drawing attention to the fact that "the apparition of the divinity as a triad at the primordial margins of the cosmos is part of many mythologies, in both the Mesopotamian and in Mediterranean worlds, and that often the triad is reconstructed as a theomatic and theogonic succession of fathers, sons, grandchildren." Moreover, Villa presents Elohim, compared to Anu and Zeus, as a compound with El, the creator of earth in the Ugaritic texts, with both gods being preceded by "other monstrous, chimerical, formless traces of divinity, identified generically with a whirling, agitated chaos." Therefore, the Hebrew mythology may well preserve, in Villa's argument, "one of the continuous Mesopotamian or Ugaritic-Canaanite mythological-literary influences," in addition to influences from Egypt.[31] This basic foundation of territorialization—an act through which earth, as posited dominion of God and humankind, is separated from the primordial chaos of waters associated with the East through Genesis—will prove animating throughout Villa's publishing (and unpublishing) career and an inspiration behind his eventual sculptural *Hydrologies*; his was a vocation aimed at deterritorializing the roots of Western culture, in the sense developed by Deleuze and Guattari in *Kafka: Toward a Minor Literature*.[32] However the staid philologist may judge the scientific accuracy of his renderings and however one might interrogate Villa's drive to find a more distant origin for this book of origins, we understand that the "theodynamic conception" behind his "Vento-Divino" is rooted in a profound rejection of dogma and tribal heritage, according instead with a concept of cultural bequest akin to, and poetically echoing, *thermo*dynamics in its emphasis on the exchange of energy and entropy.

The consequence of Villa's Genesis consists not only in its aim of disseminating to a wider public a pointedly down-to-earth and culturally capacious Italian-language Bible ("Books," as he puts it, reading the Hebrew literally and thus a touch heretically) but also through the mobilization of this translation's principles via a body of transgenre, translingual, outlandishly experimental poetry. Through this translation and a sprawling range of other scholarly and creative projects to which he dedicated himself for decades, having given up on academia while rejecting as vehemently the ideologically petrified thickets of conventional publishing, Villa invents an approach to philology that he distinguishes from the orthodox species dominated by historical linguistics or theological exegesis.[33] Stripping the Word away from theologians seeking a literal interpretation, Villa opens that Word to infinite "linguistic and anthropological research," inducing us into what his foremost interpreter, Aldo Tagliaferri, identifies as "labyrinths of exhaustive and never concluded exegetical diatribes, into the secrets of the most archaic lexemes, into the plays of false and faux etymologies [paraetimologie] and of pseudo-homophony."[34] Villa's interest in one famed instance of popular or "folk" etymology inheres in the root of Babel itself. As he glosses in his note to Genesis 11:9, the Assyrian Bâb-ilu, properly denoting "portal of divinity," was assimilated to the Semitic b̲l̲l̲, meaning instead "to confound, mix, babble."[35]

Villa's interpretation of the Old Testament counters any monolithic patriarchal orthodoxy in stressing the work's expression, above all, of the pain and misery of a people in abeyance, holding out in "confused hope of liberation"—a theme that would resonate strongly with readers in the postwar period. As a poet, Villa places particular stress on liberation from any Word issued from on high. For him, the war between a precosmic group of divinities separated by an abyss becomes translated into "the primordial refusal of the Word of the divinity by man (a semigod, 'form' of the divinity's blowing breath); and the consequent saga of the passage [*iter*] of humanity toward liberation, or salvation." Villa sees within Genesis an exposure of the abyss that divides the two poles of rebellion and work, or "human initiative," at the foundations of humankind; he thus excavates from Genesis the history and awareness of " 'rebellion' as nature; which is to say as permanent riot against the divinity; and as justification . . . of the human being made up of mud, dust and ashes (elements that are the residue of a divine nature that has been degraded)."[36] Placing this thesis surrounding the rebellion of humankind and the primordial nature of which it is made, suppressing doctrinal overtones of punishment and obedience, in the historical context of Villa's introduction to biblical study under Fascism will help us grasp its political (and micropolitical) overtones.

Villa's oeuvre of interwoven poetry, translation, criticism, research, and visual art is extraordinary in its restless xenoglossic and transmedial reach for cross-cultural and transhistorical connections that trounce the entrenched binary of supposed opposing Völker, Aryan and Semite, that was steering the authoritarian regimes of his time toward violent crusades. It constitutes a rebuke to developments that renewed Herder's theorizing of the Völk, marrying that theorization with research into "Aryan" origins—outgrowths and vulgarizations of the Indo-European thesis popularized by the Orientalist Sir William Jones in a lecture of 1786, whose genealogy and pernicious consequences have been traced by a fulsome literature of greater depth than can be reproduced here.[37] In his research, Villa was influenced by thinkers like Alfredo Trombetti (Bologna 1866–Venice 1929), the controversial comparative linguist who, having grown up in poverty and learned many languages as an autodidact, from German to Arabic, devoted himself to tracing similarities between tongues as remote as Basque and the Caucasian and Sino-Tibetan languages and who became best known for his theory of monogenesis. First published in 1905, Trombetti's thesis posited that all the world's languages could be traced to a single common tongue.[38] On the front of comparative religion, the Eastern roots of the Bible were being researched by figures such as the biblical archaeologist James B. Pritchard, editor of *Ancient Near Eastern Texts Relating to the Old Testament* (first published in 1950).[39] Villa's work responds to broad developments in comparative linguistics, history, archaeology, folklore, comparative religion, and anthropology—all fields of inquiry with which he is relatively obsessed yet that he reinvents, against positivistic classifications and notions of "development," in the grids and vortices of a new poetry.

Villa's nondoctrinal alliance with academic outliers such as Trombetti foretells his own eventual status as exemplary renegade—from translation to criticism to poetry (the three always being linked in his work).[40] Villa himself emerges as a kind of indecipherable myth whose story is etched across the occasional typeset edition, but also (and largely) across catalog scraps, plastic spheres, paper plates, styrofoam stelae, and scrawled-upon stones cast into the Tiber, in writings encompassing Sumerian, Latin, Greek, Brazilian Portuguese, French, Spanish, English, Provençal, Lombard dialect, and (begrudgingly) Italian. Any narrative account of Villa is destined to fall short of or implode the expectations of a work like the scholarly monograph you are reading, expectations of documented linear literary historiography and generic/disciplinary/linguistic uniformity. Any understanding of Villa obliges this protagonist's steadfast rescue from oblivion in the form of strategically rare or irrecuperable, out-of-print, frangible collaborative artists' books, catalogs, broadsides, chapbooks, posters, ephemeral magazines, and anthologies; "oggetti di poesia" (a genre of objects that constitute poems); innumerable poetic and philological fragments often scribbled atop residua of pamphlets and gallery invitations in handwriting that has frequently been literally crossed out by the author in his increasingly reticent old age; barely legible annotations in etymological dictionaries; and piles of entries for a dazzling array of translations and parascholarly works never to be published. This miscellany of writings is dispersed across private collections and archives in six cities on three continents that I have frequented when possible over the course of fourteen years, often only to find myself missing critical pieces of the puzzle, finding just a handful of works in museums, and benefiting from devoted exegesis by the "clandestine" author's foremost lifelong editor, commentator, and biographer Aldo Tagliaferri (himself a product of studying Pound, Joyce, and Beckett at Yale and Berkeley in the late 1950s) and a circle of younger scholars that has finally been widening over the past few years.

Intrepid champion in both prose and verse, in Italian and French, of the abstract visual artists of his day, Villa was embraced by the younger poets of the neoavanguardia yet rejected the term "avant-garde," remaining aloof from groupthink and eminently arcane. As the scholar and editor of the belated 2014 edition of his collected poetry Cecilia Bello Minciacchi puts it, "as much as the Lombard author rejected tradition and codes, he held back equally from avant-gardes that were declared as such, organized, ready to be historicized."[41] Zanzotto, perhaps Villa's most illustrious and oblique inheritor across the fronts of linguistic and/as historical research, put it most succinctly when he spoke of Villa's "persecuted and cultivated crypticity," a blockage to cooptation enacted definitively through "the poisonous and necessary lava flow of languages, which screech amongst themselves [la colata velenosa e necessaria delle lingue, che stridono tra loro], but which in the end cannot do without Italian, or 'blasts' of Italian, . . . so as to make us feel as well the breath of history, and that putrid breath of the history of recent times." Zanzotto proposes that in the end, even if one succeeded in publishing Villa's entire corpus, the poet would manage to "subtract himself from this deviation-destiny, . . . terrain vague in which life and writing launched at who knows what else are confounded, re-boiled [si confondono, ribollono]" (with a strong echo of "rebelled").[42]

STUDY UNDER FASCISM

Born into a working-class family in the hinterlands of Milan in 1914 as the son of a left-leaning mason turned factory steelworker, Emilio Villa was supported early on in his education by his parents, who saw in his studies the hope for a better life. He thus had the chance to study ancient languages at seminary school in the provinces of Lombardy from 1925 to 1932. He developed an interest in prebiblical languages in a moment when the rise of Fascism and the eventual 1938 adoption of anti-Semitic race laws cast a shadow over Semitic study in Italy—studying as *hospes laicus* at the premier site in Italy for Semitic and Mesopotamian studies, the Pontifical Biblical Institute in Rome (beginning in 1934). Villa was further trained in Assyriology and Sumerian and Akkadian philology with teachers such as the German Jesuit Assyriologist Anton Diemel, creator of a Sumerian lexicon published by the institute in the 1930s, whose 1962 edition is richly annotated by Villa as part of his longstanding etymological research.[43] Villa was recognized with a scholarship from the Reale Accademia d'Italia for the study of Phoenician grammar in 1936, the same year he published his first collection of poems, *Adolescenza*, at age twenty. Villa's antipositivist research into the origins and contaminations of language and of religious thought was destined in its heterodoxy and heresy to take root principally in works of experimental poetry rather than the staid fortresses of scholarship or the seminary, where too-avid interest in the Old Testament or in the East was looked upon with suspicion. While following in the footsteps of the controversial Trombetti, to whom he devoted research for another text never to be published, Villa's work on the Hebrew Bible also recalls the unorthodox excavation of a prebureaucratic, primordial Christianity by one of his elders in biblical study, Ernesto Buonaiuti (1881–1946), the excommunicated self-described "*Modernist Priest*" and avowedly anti-Fascist historian of Christianity who was forbidden to teach beginning in 1929 and two years later had his university chair in Rome revoked for refusing to swear the oath of loyalty to the regime required of professors by law (one of only a dozen professors of over 1200 to do so).[44]

Villa abandoned the Pontifical Institute suddenly at the outbreak of World War II without receiving a degree; he ceased his public life at both the institute and in the artistic circles of Milan to flee to the Chianti region.[45] After departure, he studied with Raffaele Pettazoni, a well-known scholar of world religions who would risk vocal critique of the race laws adopted against Italian Jews and African colonists from 1938 through 1943. Between the late 1930s and the 1940s, under the shadow of war, Villa was working on an astounding range of scholarly or parascholarly projects. In tandem with published articles on modern poets such as Rimbaud, Essenin, Ungaretti, Dino Campana, T. S. Eliot, Jorge Carrera Andrade, and Esther de Cáceres (which he translates in fragments), he reviewed anthologies of Argentinian, Chilean, Uruguayan, and Cuban poetry. Amid analyses of books on contemporary figures such as Stalin that offered space for trenchant commentaries on history as "uno sbaglio continuo" (a continual mistake),[46] he reviewed translations of Sumerian hymns and published an argument positing linguistic relations between the cuneiform sign TÌL (life) and the Bible's Eve, as well as his translation, from the Akkadian, of the tablet of Enuma Eliš. Meanwhile in this period, on the front of the visual arts, Villa's praise for young painters such as Corrado Cagli and for the Futurist painter Carlo Carrà alternates with texts that compare Leonardo da Vinci's mechanical genius to that of the young Argentine artist Lucio Fontana.[47]

To avoid being sent for a second time into military service, this time into conflict, Villa had reportedly attempted to burst an eardrum and did his best to become obese. Despite these efforts to stay out of the war, Villa was rounded up into combat but eventually deserted. He was captured and sent to a prison camp in Holland for four months and then in 1944 sent to another military camp in Germany for months before escaping. He eventually took part in the Resistance with a cell of anti-Fascist artists and the communist critic Mario De Micheli in Milan, withstanding injury and searches by the police and hiding under false documents. In late April 1945, he witnessed firsthand the hanging of Mussolini, his mistress, and high-ranking officials in Milan's Piazzale Loreto.[48]

That said, Villa's most lasting rebellion against Fascist dogma took place in language itself—in the spaces of his poetry and scholarship, where readers both perceive and are immersed in linguistic estrangement or exile as an insisted-upon freedom.[49] This rebellion began early, with his resentment against the imposition of a national language at school, which can be understood as colonial, and his accompanying castigation and condemnation to an ineloquent future by a grade school teacher for using dialect expressions in class. Having been raised in a humble environment in which Milanese dialect prevailed and having attended seminary where the language of instruction and community was Latin, Villa developed an intimacy with these languages for reasons both affective and intellectual—in the face of a mounting mandate to speak standard Italian that reinforced the measures taken against regional dialects on the part of the Fascist government, as well as class prejudice. These experiences informed Villa's relationship to Italian, characterized by furious impulses of disgust and refusal. At a 1984 lecture for students in Perugia that provides a rare autobiographical record, he spoke of the way that Milanese dialect was barred from school, from the seminary, and even from home by his parents. He thereby justified his revulsion against a form of servitude to

> a language supporting much disgrace, like the Italian language, for which I often harbor a hatred [la lingua di sostegno di molte vergogne, come l'italiano, che molte volte ho proprio in odio]. Not hatred, but refusal, a blockage against Italian, which is not my language. . . . I spoke Milanese dialect throughout my entire childhood. As a seminarian . . . for many years, my language was Latin, I spoke Latin from morning to night . . . I could not speak Milanese, neither at home nor at the seminary. The Italian language had become an enemy to me, a sign of slavery.[50]

The national idiom that Villa associates with enslavement and shame was the product of an elaborate post-Risorgimento campaign for linguistic purity that had been taken up again as early as 1923 and was popularly disseminated through a war against barbarisms in favor of "speaking and writing Italianly" as a "national action"; Mussolini himself had delivered a public address on March 16, 1931 surrounding the "purity of the idiom of the fatherland." Following the invasion of Ethiopia and autarky campaigns of 1935, this "national action" comprised banning the handshake in favor of the Roman salute, replacing the formal second-person pronoun "lei" (seen as a feminine, foreign imposition) with the putatively Roman "voi," purging non-Italian toponyms, and laws and decrees (disregarded now yet never abolished) prohibiting the use of foreign terms in newspapers, public performances, company names, and advertisements.[51] Following the Fascist ventennio's initial decade of strategic tolerance for dialects, the myriad local vernaculars were eventually removed from school curricula and prohibited in newspapers and periodicals outside of fortressed and policed scholarly contexts. The editors of the *Corriere della Sera* defended the shuttering of all regional associations with the argument that "Dialect, folklore, vernacular theater, and regionalistic novellas can perhaps still have a provisional function as curiosities and as historical culture, but only inasmuch as they demonstrate the slow disappearance of a world"—in line with the reduction of regional culture to what Ruth Ben-Ghiat calls "the realm of the carnival, the occasional festival, and the museum" in the service of a putative underlying ethnic national unity.[52]

ANTIFASCIST PHILOLOGY

Against this backdrop of induced anachronism, Villa pays homage to his native region of Lombardy in a range of modes, jocose and funereal, in his poetry— even, in Fabio Zinelli's formulation, treating it as a "readymade," comparable to the poor discarded popular materials of his eventual collaborator Alberto Burri.[53] A 1936 poem of mourning and remorse, "Any Lombardy" ("Qualsiasi Lombardia") narrates a reversal of Pentecost that Zanzotto, whose own poetics cleaved closely to dialect and regional culture, may have been echoing in his coinage of Villa's "pentecostalismo rovesciato":

> A nuvole di nebbia dei re longobardi,
> si partiva, per le cene, con le torce,
> coi letti, arrugginiti, sulle spalle,
> a fare una pasqua, per i morti,
> senza tregua. E tramontava il giubilo
> di pentecoste, a picco
> sopra il torrente del mio paese,
> una labile, unica Strona.[54]

> To clouds of fog of the Lombard kings,
> we left for our dinners, with torches,
> with our beds, rusted, on our shoulders,
> to make an easter, for the dead,
> without respite. And the jubilation
> of pentecost was setting, plummeting
> over the torrent of my town,
> a labile, singular [River] Strona

This image marries the death of a local culture with rites of easter, while the joy of pentecost itself collapses "a picco": a descent of Spirit in the colors of the sunset here conflated paradoxically, via the violent action of plummeting, with the Tower of Babel. The backdrop of this image is bound up in the speaker's "guai italiani" ("Italian troubles"), imposing a fatuous, tyrannical nationalist memory upon the labile local landscape: "un convoglio di fatui santuari, / negli acquitrini delle risiere in fuga, / perseguiterà fischiando il rimorso dei miei guai italiani" ("a convoy of fatuous sanctuaries, / in the marshlands of the rice mills in flight, / will persecute, whistling the remorse of my Italian troubles").[55]

Yet Villa will become anything but a backward-looking dialect poet. Against this context of agrarian culture in flight, the speaker of "Any Lombardy" imagines an exodus to California through citation of a popular emigrants' song: "Prendi la rocca e il fuso e andiamo in California," with the original lyrics being "Prendi la rocca e 'l fus / che andiamo in California / in California a tappare i buchi" ("get the distaff and spindle [figuratively, 'get everything necessary'] / because we're going to California / to California to stop up holes"). It would be more accurate to observe that Villa's poetics seeks out and *creates* holes—like those of Fontana's canvas slashes or Burri's scorched textile trous—to part the way for a poetics of transnational and cross-historical coextension, characterized by what Villa eventually called a "Hyperpast and Hypopresent."[56]

Villa's search for origins would in fact be accompanied by a search for endgames, for the language of the future—as manifest in California. The long visual poem *Brunt H : Options : 17 eschatological madrigals captured by a sweetromatic cybernetogamig vampire, by Villadrome* (its original title in English) began when Villa visited his son working in Silicon Valley in the late 1960s and beheld for the first time the printed language of computer code of which he couldn't understand *"un H"* (idiomatic for saying he couldn't understand a word), in the critic Aldo Tagliaferri's words.[57] Villa proceeded to assail this H to bear a poetic brunt, to hack into the printed code with handwritten script, typewriter, and typesetting, figuring himself as a "sweetromantic cybernetogamic vampire" in the subtitle of the eventual artist's book: as a figure who had "captured" polyphonic madrigals from an alien language, semi-English, semimachinic—possibly from a universal code language of the future.[58] The frequently reproduced cover constitutes a palimpsest of various page spreads forced into coexistence. Villa here coins the term "CYCLOFLESH," standing in all caps as the punctum of one spread. This postwar dispersion of phonemes brings to mind immediately the cyclotron: the mechanical force of dispersion of atoms and of flesh and quite the syntax-beater. Writing through the discarded printouts of Silicon Valley computers, Villa excavates what he calls in this text "the hyponecrotic Essence of Muscles of Word-Dumps," wallowing in "the Sewer of Member / and Raid's Fluency." Raid—piracy of what is found in a strange land—can make for its own linguistic fluency or flux, exposing the idea of "membership" itself as a stagnant sewer.[59]

Whereas Villa's first collection, *L'Adolescenza*, is written in a "pure" Italian idiom, he subjects his Italian writings increasingly to irruptions by geographical and temporal alterity: Milanese and other dialects; variations on ancient, Romance, and Saxon languages; English; and Edenic tongues of his own forging. These phantom instances of polyglotism and the eventual eclipsing of Italian in favor of compositions in an unhinged French prove more disquieting than those of the storied montages of "foreign" fragments in the Anglophone monuments of Eliot and Pound or the collage tactics of their postwar followers in the neo-avanguardia and throughout Western experimental literature. Villa will come to decompose language syllable by syllable, to exhume sonic and etymological relations across time and geography; this generates texts more akin to those of Joyce and Artaud, in which idioms improperly acquired and deployed become estranged from themselves. Staging microdisplacements of fossilized dead and national languages, Villa's works make palpable the fact that "Italianness," like any nationality, is fundamentally an amalgam of borrowings, piracies, and migrations. In the wake of Fascism, he articulates a more capacious "Italia"—or "Ytalya," as he ludically chose to write it, using two "y"s.[60]

THE QUESTION(S) OF A UNITARY LANGUAGE

The so-called questione della lingua, or language question, was a heavily freighted topic, with centuries of history behind it on the divided Italian peninsula and outlying islands. It is estimated that in the newly founded nation-state of 1861, only between 2.5 and 12 percent of the population spoke anything resembling standard Italian. The Romantic view of language as the basis of national identity was shared by many founding personalities of the Italian nation-state, such as novelist Alessandro Manzoni, and thus had emphatic political implications in both postunification and Fascist Italy.[61] We will recall that the Fascist idealist Giovanni Gentile's pedagogical reforms as minister of public education in the fledgling regime, aimed at the consolidation of a national language, were considered by both the regime and Gentile's eventual Resistance assassins as essential to its workings. Benedetto Croce (Pescasseroli 1866–Naples 1952), another Hegelian, but in the vein of liberalism, broke with Gentile in 1924 as he outwardly rejected Fascism, refusing entry into the Italian Academy, while continuing to regard the work of philosophy on language as a top-down phenomenon. In explicit contrast to these compatriot idealists, Antonio Gramsci (Abas 1891–Rome 1937), the Sardinian philosopher and labor activist trained in historical linguistics at the University of Turin, would reflect on "the Southern question" and the dynamics of hegemony and subalternity through language, seeking a common idiom of uplift that would activate and empower subaltern groups, nationally and internationally.[62]

Critical of both liberal and Fascist idealism, as well as of socialist impositions of Esperanto, Gramsci theorized linguistic contact and sociocultural struggle through the concept of hegemony. As Peter Ives has detailed, he was influenced by his professor Matteo Bartoli's theory of linguistic competition, in which hegemony (egemonia), fascination (fascino), and prestige (prestigio) determined a word's "irradiation" ("irradiazione"). Along the way, Gramsci absorbed the

lessons of Bartoli's teacher Graziadio Isaia Ascoli, the Jewish Friulian "glottolo-
gist" (Ascoli's own coinage, meaning to bring linguistics into conversation with
ethnology, anthropology, and biology). Ascoli critiqued Alessandro Manzoni's
attempts to standardize Italian through the tongue of the Florentine elite, instead
treating dialects as integral languages in and of themselves and theorizing a "substratum" of older linguistic traces within languages in use.[63] In 1918 and beyond,
Gramsci criticized Esperanto as a fanatical bourgeois cosmopolitan imposition
as opposed to a truly international endeavor; he argued that the creation of a unitary language can only happen from the ground up, in "hotbeds of irradiation"
("focolai di irradiazione") propelling either innovation or conformism, such as
schooling, media, public gatherings, conversation across classes, folk verse, and
like phenomena involving the masses.[64] Remarkably, Gramsci's last, twenty-ninth
prison notebook, written under the duress of Fascist detainment and illness and
dated to 1935 (but smuggled out of the country with the other notebooks and
published posthumously by Einaudi between 1948 and 1951), is devoted to grammar; this is less surprising when we realize that Gramsci considered arguments
surrounding language policy to be manifestations of political quarrels. In these
notes, the Marxist philosopher critiques the proposition of any "'exemplary
phase' of language as the 'only' one worthy of becoming, 'organically' and 'in
totalitarian key' [totalitariamente], the common language of a nation," identifying Dante's *De vulgari eloquentia* as a product of elite anxiety, an attempt to
reinforce the language of an intellectual class against the political disintegration
evident in the popular uprisings of the contemporary communes.[65] Gramsci did
advocate for the creation of unitary verbal complexes that could uplift and modernize the peasantry—instruments of solidarity.[66]

What Gramsci cast as the "national battle of a hegemonic culture against
other nationalities or residua of nationalities," and vice versa, inheres in Villa's
poetry with a critical particularity.[67] We see in Villa's verse this "lotta nazionale"
("national battle") at work (and play) in language that spars against itself, and
in Villa's collateral commentaries on language, we see strains of the same influences on his thinking through conflicts and aspirations in historical linguistics
and glottology. Perhaps most illuminating in establishing a context of friction for
Villa's work on language is Gramsci's insistence, in Prison Notebook XI, that "the
starting-point of critical elaboration is . . . 'knowing yourself' as a product of the
historical process to date which has deposited in you an infinity of traces, without
leaving an inventory" ("L'inizio dell'elaborazione critica è . . . un 'conosci te stesso'
come prodotto del processo storico finora svoltosi che ha lasciato in te stesso
un'infinità di tracce accolte senza beneficio d'inventario").[68] Villa's unpublished
dictionaries of etymology and of myth can be regarded as a form of inventory that

ANTIFASCIST PHILOLOGY

yet balks at any form of "chronology." Although Villa launches countless polemics against historicism and would shirk any avowed Marxist affiliation, his interest in what he repeatedly calls the "organic" and "spontaneous" motions of language from below in linguistic unfolding can be fruitfully read in the context of Gramsci's analysis, which pays homage to the work of literature, translation, and popular culture on linguistic innovation. Paralleling Gramsci but in the vein of art and sacrality instead of materialist philosophy and political life, Villa researches the origins and futures of expression as if to manifest that all of poetry, from Babylon through the computing code of the early Silicon Valley, from the high priest to the poet's illiterate grandmother, could potentially conspire as part of an antideterministic "lingua unitaria" (united language),[69] but one aimed squarely against the nation as construct and possibly finding its consummation in silence.

ITALIAN PENTECOSTS (AND THE SHADOW OF GABRIELE D'ANNUNZIO)

It is crucial for our purposes to distinguish Villa's xenoglossic translingualism from the multilingualism of the historical avant-garde of which he was most directly heir. Although F. T. Marinetti, thirty-eight years Villa's senior, dissented publicly against the alliance with Hitler, anti-Semitism, and the racial laws, he continued vociferously, as we have seen, to serve as prop and booster for the regime's other racialized campaigns, participating directly in acts of imperial aggression in Africa and promoting autarky in arenas ranging from textiles to language, even as his narratives continued to produce fantasies of métissage. Marinetti ultimately became an Accademico d'Italia and a cog in the regime's ultranationalist language machinery, even while rejecting the extreme purist stances on blood, soil, and milk that characterized Nazism. By contrast, Villa spent his career blasting what he called "Ytalyan" apart through poetic and philological research, largely deserting the national language as a tool of poetic composition in favor of Latin, a demotic French, English, and other vernaculars of fascination and lived experience as diverse as Milanese and Brazilian Portuguese.

A March 1939 issue of the journal *Letteratura*, to which both writers contributed an homage to the canonical nationalist poet, aesthete, Great War aviator, and sometime colonizer/impresario Gabriele D'Annunzio (who had died a year earlier), renders the difference between these authors, one aged sixty-two years and one twenty-four, ardently apparent. Marinetti takes the opportunity to describe an intimate encounter with D'Annunzio at his sumptuous villa on Lake

Garda days before the older poet's death, gently chiding D'Annunzio's passéist tendencies at the expense of the Futurist ideals that would succeed them, but also naming him as the animating force of aeropoetry and aeropainting, and commemorating "the revolutionary war in Fiume" led by D'Annunzio in 1919 in which the young Marinetti had participated. Here we should remember that D'Annunzio cast that imperial act of aggression in Dalmatia—which harbored anarcho-syndicalist leanings but is seen by many as symbolically anticipating the March on Rome—as the descent of Flame and Spirit in an "Italian Pentecost" that accords with the colonial mode of resurrecting this biblical narrative.[70] In his homage, Marinetti ultimately genuflects to this "tireless poet of the noblest Italianity" within "a Fatherland made enormous by the Great War of the Fascist Revolution and by Mussolini's Fast War" and closes with a note about gifts they exchanged "fascistly Futuristly between imperial poets [fascistamente Futuristamente tra poeti imperiali]."[71]

Villa, on the other hand, occupies the space in seeking out the reasons for which "such an imperious and despotic figuration could have coexisted with a history entirely dissenting from its dominion [una figurazione così imperiosa e perentoria abbia potuto coesistere con una storia tutta dissidente dal suo dominio]," adding between parentheses, "(the one that was not dissident doesn't count) [(quella che non fu dissidente non conta)]."[72] (This dissident history is not clarified but almost certainly refers to the anarcho-syndicalist elements of D'Annunzio's exploits in Fiume, whereas Villa's use of a term like "figuration" in the place of "figure" to describe the imperious typifies a form of circumlocution possibly indebted to the threat of being silenced.) Villa renders clear the tension in Fascism that scholarship can now more distantly classify as, in Arvidsson's words, "conservative ethics combined with revolutionary activism."[73] He ends his piece with a reprimand that is surprising in a young writer whose audience will surely be rife with D'Annunzio's Fascist comrades, stating that D'Annunzio cannot be abandoned or rejected even if he "has continued to disappoint us, with an insisted-upon betrayal which had come to negate all commotion normal to our insurgent movements [ha continuato a venirci meno con un instito tradimento che negava oramai ogni commozione normale ai nostri moti insorgenti]"; instead, "one puts up with him fatally, with all the weight of glory and of disappointment" (the final word being "tristezza," which we might also translate as pity, tragedy, or embarrassment).[74] Villa's tortuous homage to D'Annunzio, rife with ambivalence and barely veiled critique, commences with the phrase "Engaged in a violent combat with that history which is erected in irreparable methods [Impegnati in un violento scombattimento con quella storia che si inalbera in irrimediabili procedimenti]"; this phrase would be taken up by the young poets Luciano Caruso (1944–2002) and Stelio Maria Martini (1934–2016) in

1974 as their opening to a chapbook containing both essays of tribute titled *Dannunziana:* "'Engaged in a violent combat with that history that is erected in irreparable methods,' we would only have to lay out, perhaps haphazardly, the exposé of the revealing moments of the continuum, in parallel to which, as is known, we live in the absence."[75] In other words, by resurrecting this eclipsed collision of Marinetti and Villa in the same discursive space, Caruso and Martini seek to delineate a continuum of the poetic avant-garde rife with contrast—rife with violent combat in the face of an even more irreparable Fascist history.

Readers can ease into Villa's dismantling of any nationalist ideology of language through his more readily legible Italian-language poems published in the immediate aftermath of the war and apprehend the development of his verse from deformation and parody of tradition through the more "barbarous" experimentation with form and language that follows in the 1950s and beyond. In the 1947 collection *Oramai* (*By Now*, a term implying a state of belatedness), Villa expresses disgust with the remnant inertia and harm of patriotism and simultaneously invokes the poet's own rebellious posture of slothfulness in a fatherland that demanded erect compliance (in an uncollected poem composed around 1989, "Poesia è," he will define poetry as, among other things, a "Sloth" hanging with one arm from the Tree of Knowledge, using the Brazilian term "Perguiça").[76] His "Declarations of the Dead Soldier" speaks from beyond the grave impotently: "La guerra è là sull'orlo di finire, / E fui soldato, pigro di patria [The war's over there on the brink of ending, / and I was a soldier, lazy with the fatherland]." The soldier dreams of giving himself up to some mythical folkscape, ambiguously Lombard or German: "I would like to succumb to the arms of a great Teutonic / Spring, at the feet of the holm oak [Io vorrei darmi in braccia, a una grande primavera / teutonica, a pie' de lecci]." He can only hope to consummate his "naia" (slang for the depredations of military service) by dying "con la morte in cuore / e con il cuore in gola [with death in my heart / and with my heart in my mouth]"—in the figure for agitation made concrete by ingestion, with death caught inside the organs most frequently yoked to poetry and passion.[77] In "Il dopoguerra" ("The Postwar [Era]"), Villa continues to lash out at the state of morbidity coursing through the citizenry and at their complicity, churning up dissonance through his vaunted bravura in poetic craft: a base of roughly ten- to twelve-syllable verse (roaming among the syllabic counts of the French alexandrine, the hendecasyllable inherited through Greece and Rome, and the iambic pentameter of English) and a pointedly jagged but prominent rhyme scheme in quatrains (moving at random from abab to abba and then becoming more unpredictable, although constantly circling around this tactic of assonance). Tagliaferri has referred to this mode as "neoalexandrine," emphasizing Villa's act of resuscitation; Gian Paolo Renello, building on the latter, refers to it as "alexandrinism exasperated and pushed to excess."[78]

120 ANTIFASCIST PHILOLOGY

Against this sporadic hammering at mastery in Italian versification, "Il dopoguerra" describes the forced, morbid calm after a storm, pervaded by the smell of "il tramonto di tante nazioni [the sunset of so many nations]," sensed once again through the body of a soldier, although first-person verbs appear belatedly and often in the remote tense. The piece depicts the trauma and avarice of a populace melded together by a false equilibrium of consensus, neither uplifted for their wartime deeds nor brought to justice. My translation here attempts to get at the jangling irregular rhyme scheme, laden with irony:

> son tornato con tutta la pelle,
> con la sciabola al costato,
> fresco e bello, e rivoltelle,
> come se niente fosse stato;
>
> son tornato dalla guerra stolta
> con la piaga stretta in pugno:
> scolta in aria che mugugno,
> che ronfar sulla terra stravolta.
>
> È passata la bufera,
> è accaduto il temporale,
> chi fe' il bene e chi fe' il male
> cerca soldi e bella ciera

(OP, 61)

> I came back with all my flesh,
> with my saber at my chest,
> fresh and gorgeous, and revolvish,
> as if nothing had come to pass;
>
> I came back from the doltish war
> with the wound tight in my fist:
> sculpted in air that I grumble;
> upon the contorted land, what snores.
>
> The tempest has passed,
> as has the storm,
> he who did good & he who did harm
> seeks cash and nice-looking wax;

The cupidity extends to the Machiavellian selling of assassinated finches, birds canonical in European visual culture for their storied role in easing the Passion of Christ, and the bodies of the populace appear parceled out for sale or petty pleasure as well:

> vendevano perfino i cardelli,
> assassinati dentro in gabbia
> con una fina machiavell-
> ica, con un guizzo di rabbia.
>
> Un po' di sangue, un po' di sabbia,
> un po' di tetta e un po' di pene,
> un po' di morte, come conviene
> a chi vuol vita e non ce l'abbia

(*OP*, 64)

> they were even selling the finches,
> assassinated inside the cage
> with a Machiavellian precious-
> ness, with a jolt of rage.
>
> A bit of blood, a bit of sand,
> a bit of tit and a bit of cock,
> a bit of death, as is stock
> for those who want life and are damned;

The speaker prays heretically that "carnal penury" come "to the white man, / ever on his feet [all'uomo bianco, sempre in piedi]"—that such destitution might "carbonize all contours / from our civil parts [che carbonizza tutti i profili / dalle nostre parti civili]," incinerating civility, the bodies and geographies of its citizenry, and that the war martyrs might return to introduce fury to a scene of fell equilibrium: "tornino i Caduti, dementi / e fraterni, dove loro consente / la furia del bene e del male! [may the Fallen return, demented / and fraternal, where the fury / of good / and evil is consented to them!]" (*OP*, 63). Later in the poem, the Fallen reappear to obliquely usher in the symbol of the Fasces—the Etruscan and Roman bundle of rods signifying the power of corporal punishment and, by extension, imperium: "nel volubile / fascheggio dei Caduti, / son quei pioppi d'aria muti [in the voluble / fascistness of the Fallen, / are those mute poplars of air]" (*OP*, 64). This invented "fascheggio" comprises poplar trees made up of air and is thus amalgamated by Villa with the Populus trees that the Romans planted around public meeting places (hence the species name, which indicates "the people, nation") and that, for the Greeks, symbolized the border between earth and the infernal realms. Ironically, the fascistness of the war dead remains "voluble," whereas the verse induces the "Caduti" to rhyme with the Populus trees that are "muti" (mute). Villa will return to the fasces as a complex of sound and air in his writings of the early 1960s on Cy Twombly.

Ultimately, the irony couched in these relatively tight, accomplished verses bursts form, language, and national identification at the seams. "Il dopoguerra" is a kind of swan song to Italy or, more pointedly, a breakup note, which ends,

> Ti ricordi, Italia, quella sera,
> là seduti sui bordi del mare,
> e io ti dissi che in primavera
> ci dovevam lasciare?

(OP, 65)

> Do you remember, Italy, that evening,
> sitting there on the sea's edges,
> and I told you that in spring
> we'd have to leave each other?

A riposte in the form of a macaronic "Ytalyan" appears in the poem "La Tenzone" ("The Tenson"), written in 1948, the year in which Villa moved to Rome (although it was not published until 1964). The piece is written in the tradition of the dispute in Provençal poetry, which was also adopted by Dante and the school of the dolce stil novo—thus paying homage to the vernacular tradition while skewering the national language dreamt by the author of *De vulgari eloquentia*. It thereby invokes the modernist recuperation of Provençal verse by Pound and the more distant echo of Browning's 1904 *Sordello*, but implicitly rejects Pound's accord with Italian Fascism. In Villa's satirical mongrel style, stratifications of corrupted Lombard and southern dialects face off against one another and against the specter of Italian; critic Andrea Cortellessa has usefully identified this poem as "polyvernacular" rather than "polylingual,"[79] honing in on one of the aspects of Villa's xenoglossia that we can spotlight to distinguish it from a more familiar modernist cosmopolitan multilingualism. In a headnote to the piece's initial publication, Villa calls it "a grotesque on the war, defeat, and the postwar period (with its Marshall Plan, Era [European Recovery Plan], Arar [Azienda Rilievo Alienazione Residuati], Unrra [United Nations Relief and Rehabilitation

Administration] etcetera)."[80] This parenthetical invokes the official acronyms of policy, the US occupation (1948–1952), and the Cold War, with their colonizing functionaries, as well as the engines of resettlement for the displaced and the repatriation of machines confiscated in war. Yet Villa's headnote follows by indicating the poem's adherence to the modes and language of the vernacular Sicilian Opera dei Pupi, a popular form that translates Italian chivalric poems of the Renaissance, themselves adaptations of Frankish romantic poems and the Carolingian cycle, into puppet theater—as if to counter the various occupying forces (including those of the Italian state as internal colonizers of the provinces) with carnivalesque chivalric conquest. The poem begins with a slapstickish appearance of the two of spades—the tarot card of duality and division—in which the speaker's legs and those of Italy seem to cross (as if in a battle of marionettes); the backdrop is the death of Christ, merged unmistakably with the hanged duce and king:

> DUE DI SPADE DUE DI SPADE
> LE MIE GAMBE CO LE TUE
> dico di te, Ytalya, dico de te
> in mortem de cristo duce re.

(OP, 309)

> TWO OF SPADES TWO OF SPADES
> MY LEGS W YOURS
> I say of you, Ytaly, I say of you
> in mortem de cristo duce re.

I have attempted a vernacular translation of one representative mongrel stanza, in which deformations of words seem to reproduce the accents of the Sicilian pupari (puppeteers):

> "Ahi, padritaglia, ahi che disdetta!
> ahi scarogna modona sfortuna deslippa
> restar qui così privo de trippa,
> padritaglia!" sclamò rugendo le mascelle en fretta.

(OP, 311)

> "Ow, da-Idily, ow what tough luck!
> ow what a jinx Madunn misfortune de-slippe
> to be stuck here so empty o' tripe,
> da-Idily!" he 'owled roaring his jaws right quick.

The neologism "padritaglia" in "Tenzone" sonically echoes "patria d'Italia" or "fatherland of Italy" yet literally renders as "fathers-cutter" (which I chose to translate as "daIdaly"). This is a fine metaphor for Villa's operations on a language he regarded as enslaved to the pompous academicism of a nationalist elite.

"OS PURISTAS SÃO ENFADONHOS E INÚTEIS" (PURISTS ARE TEDIOUS AND USELESS): THE "BRAZILIAN PARENTHESIS"

"Il dopoguerra" sits in a Brazilian archive alongside a copy of Villa's unpublished "Canzone bislacca / per andare in America" ("Contorted canzone / for going to America"), another poem hailing to a traditional verse genre—one deemed supreme by Dante and yet that is deeply critical of the Italians, who are identified in both the third and the first person plural as enemies and victims: "those crooked Italians [loro storti, loro italiani]," "Ignoratissimi e volgari, noi con le piaghe a bozzo [Massively ignorant and vulgar, us with the bulbous wounds]."[81] Like the poems of *Oramai*, "Canzone bislacca" represents nations as going up in snuff and declares a new Exodus: "Each nation was a leaf of snuff, they were made / without true mythical flesh: now to the passage / of the Red Sea [Ogni nazione era una foglia fiuta, erano fatte / senza vera carne mita: ora al passaggio /del Mar Rosso]."[82] Emilio Villa included a copy of this piece and of "Il dopoguerra" with the inscription "poesia fatta per PM Bardi" (with numerous variants, presumably an earlier version) in an undated letter to Pietro Maria Bardi, an Italian expatriate in Brazil from 1946 forward and an autodidact collector, gallerist, curator, author, and partner to the celebrated architect Lina Bo. It is contained alongside their correspondence from 1947 forward regarding projects for art journals such as *Ulisse* and their collaboration on the Museu de Arte de São Paulo (MASP), an institution founded by Bardi with the patronage of the Brazilian senator and press magnate Francisco de Assis Chateaubriand Bandeira de Melo in 1947.[83]

The making of this self-consciously New World museum, with its sights on the future and its interests in the distant and recent modernist past, involved vigorous dialogue across the Atlantic and the disciplines of art, history, poetry, and architecture in the 1940s through the 1960s. Villa's background in ancient languages and aesthetics and his intellectual adventurousness made him the ideal collaborator on such a project, notwithstanding the fact that neither Bardi nor Villa had previous museological experience. The MASP's pathbreaking inaugural exhibits, aimed at South American citizens, were didactic in nature, aiming to forge a newly global art history encompassing visual and poetic arts: they constituted a somewhat utopian attempt to reconstitute the violent syntheses of nations and "world" effected by the wars.[84] Bardi's vision as director was that no work of art should be presented in isolation, but instead "located in the total historical process by which it is expressed, moulded and ripened, if we want it to reveal the whole world which it comprises." He aimed at representing the "collaboration of all human forces" in his museum, generating no less than "the democratic formation of modern man."[85] Through their publications, building, and programming, the MASP collaborators took up what Bardi called "the task of consolidating the function of the entire past, of making it a common property, of filling and repairing breaches." This was a task resting on the shoulders of the "man of modern culture," but "especially on man manipulating documents of the past."[86] The MASP has been praised, as both edifice and program, for having "flouted European museological and museographical conventions by dissolving structural, temporal and hierarchical boundaries"; Lina Bo Bardi's exhibition architecture has been said to allow the works in the MASP collection, of mixed periods, "to literally stand on their own as objects liberated completely from chronological, connoisseurial and scholarly classification systems."[87] The didactic exhibition panels were experimental, juxtaposing photographs of representative artifacts in Lina Bo's floating glass panels, in transhistorical montages that recall those of Aby Warburg's Mnemosyne Atlas—as well as the collage tactics of Fascist modernism that Bardi, as journalist and gallerist, had practiced between Milan and Rome. In a South American twist attempting performatively to dissolve the boundaries between institution and public as "habitat," these panels were surrounded by tropical plants.

Villa's labor with the Bardis on the inaugural exhibitions in the late 1940s and early 1950s from Rome and his consequent residence in São Paulo dated to approximately 1952–1954 can be traced to a watershed in his poetics but also in postwar Italian art and poetry more generally—because Villa's postwar work across the visual and literary arts, however marginalized by the academy and official verse culture, was met with recognition by a range of artists/interlocutors as different as Alberto Burri, with whom he collaborated, and Carmelo Bene, to whom he dedicated a text, as well as by younger poets, from Nanni Balestrini and Luciano Caruso to Andrea Zanzotto, from Lello Voce to Marco Giovenale. What Aldo Tagliaferri initially named "the Brazilian parenthesis" in Villa's career becomes a key moment in the development of one of the most consequential, however neglected, bodies of anti-Fascist poetry that we have in the Italian context.[88] These were the nascent years of Brazilian concrete poetry and art, exposing Villa to a range of revisions of modernist abstraction, both European and South and North American, that would later be invoked in Adriano Spatola's sweeping study *Verso la poesia totale*. In the aftermath of both world wars and the absorption, cooptation, or expurgation of modernist tactics by authoritarian states, many poets and artists were eager to revisit the supranational proposals of the European historical avant-gardes: many attempted to reconceptualize linguistic and cultural pathways in a new utopian key outside of any "fatherland" through negotiations with the graphic space of poetry. Fueled by debates surrounding universal form in the wake of structuralism, through renegade transdisciplinary methods and a renewed interest in the spatialization or "scoring" of language, the postwar avant-gardes staged attempts to reroute ideological inscription. *Toward Total Poetry*, published in Italian by Spatola in 1969, provides a stunning synthesis of this widespread desire, manifest in various international movements from Concretism to Lettrism to Fluxus, to expand the modernist "necessity of overcoming national linguistic barriers" and to produce poetry as "a total medium," generating a culture "disconnected from strictly national spheres and endowed with laws valid almost everywhere."[89]

Yet the work being done by Villa and his conspirators in São Paulo was anything but presentist: among the exhibitions Villa worked on was one devoted to the history of abstractionism in art from prehistory through Mondrian (figure 2.2), whose title panel juxtaposes the hair of an archaic Greek kouros (dated to 610 BCE and discovered in 1910) with a bronze 1914 Raymond Duchamp-Villon sculpture, *The Horse*, a hybrid animal-dynamo possessing Cubist and Futurist qualities. Meanwhile, the poet imagined other, more imaginative expositions still, as with many of his intellectual inventions never to be executed, proposing to Bardi in unpublished correspondence an atlas of art history, "a history of anatomical conceptions and general aesthetics of the anatomy of animal and human bodies . . . across epochs," "a history of conceptions of space in art," and most tantalizingly for our purposes, a "great panorama of poetry from the prehistoric grottos to Parisian surrealism."[90] Villa takes a more historically grounded, more ludic, and more sacral (although religiously unaffiliated) approach to the remote beginnings and futures of cultures than idealists such as Bardi, from whom he must eventually split in order to pursue less institutionally straightjacketed projects.

Villa started out working on the ground in Rome, gathering objects and images, in correspondence with characters as different as Benedetta Marinetti, the Jewish anti-Fascist historian and theorist of organic architecture Bruno Zevi, and Marcello Piacentini, former official architect of the Fascist regime and modernist planner of Esposizione Universale Roma (EUR). In a letter dated to April 1948, I found his faint complaints that the syncretic work for the didactic expositions undertaken alone should have required ten people at work for half

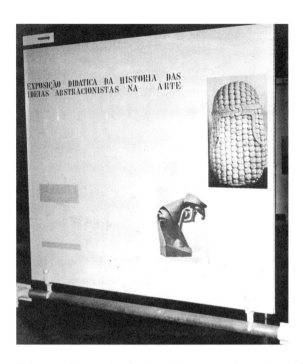

FIGURE 2.2 Unknown photographer from Diários dos Associados, Detail of the Didactic Exhibition on the History of Abstractionist Ideas in Art, 1949, juxtaposing archaic with modernist sculpture. Photo courtesy of Centro de Pesquisa do Museu de Arte de São Paulo Assis Chateaubriand.

a year. That said, Bardi emerges as a kind of patron and possible amanuensis, subsidizing a mode of research toward which Villa, ever in need of funds and finding himself in poor health, is drawn with the (ultimately dashed) hopes of forging a more stable living in South America. While never recognized publicly for their authorship by the ever more powerful, institution-building Bardi, the exhibition texts, written by Villa and to a lesser extent by Flavio Motta, contour a poetics not only of spatial but also of intersubjective and cross-historical relationships—one characterized by what Villa eventually called a "Hyperpast and Hypopresent" in a scrawled note reproduced on the cover of the artist's book *GREEN* (1971).[91]

In Villa's words outlining the exhibition methodology for one of the many panels he composed, devoted to the first Mediterranean cultures after 1000 CE, this "whole world" embraced by curation must be understood at the largest possible categorial scale, and it is always in flux: "Nothing still, stable, definitive exists in this systematization. . . . The incessant contagion of styles, . . . the oscillation and intersection of modes, of intuitions, of improvisations, of returns, of repetitions, are characteristic of the human spirit. A thick cloud of wonders, splendors, errors, elevated achievements and mediocre products, collective popular tendencies and extreme intellectual refinements, hides the motivations and causes of this developing and involving imagination of men from the view of academia."[92] Although it seems clear that the verbo-voco-visual experiments in Brazilian concretism would have opened Villa's horizons to new possibilities for the stanza, his embrace of stylistic "contagion," of spontaneity, of error, of the mediocre, the nebulous, and the popular all distinguish his mature aesthetics from the refined, pristine minimalism of Brazilian concretism.

Beyond the ephemeral opening exhibitions, the founding ideas of MASP were worked out in the pages of *Habitat*, the journal that the Bardis launched upon emigrating from Rome to São Paulo, published between 1950 and 1953. Here too we can see Villa working out the past and future of poesis, both his own and that of "great human currents." He titled an article upholding linguistic mixture and transmogrification pointedly "Os puristas são enfadonhos e inúteis" ("Purists Are Tedious and Useless"), recalling the nineteenth-century debate between classicists and romantics surrounding language in Italy, but also the neopurism that had flourished under Fascism and continued to course through postwar Italian culture, albeit in a less overtly xenophobic vein. The most authoritative mouthpiece of neopurism was the linguist-philologist Bruno Migliorini (Rovigo 1896–Florence 1975), Esperantist in the first decades of the twentieth century, co-founder of the journal *Lingua nostra* (*Our Language*) in 1939, professor and author of the first academic history of the Italian language published in 1960, and president of the Accademia della Crusca, the oldest linguistic academy in the world, founded in Florence in 1583 to "winnow" corruptions from the Italian language (with the metaphorical "crusca" meaning "bran"), from 1949 until 1963.[93] Migliorini identified the essential character of purism as "its battle against every species of innovation" and, in focusing his neopurist polemics against "forestierismi" ("foreignisms") in quotidian and scientific usages, denounced the "dictatorship of the literati upon the language" in 1940. It was a matter of course for writers embracing linguistic metamorphosis like Villa and Carlo Emilio Gadda to rebel against such attitudes, arguing as anti-historicist individualists in favor of linguistic creation.[94] Villa's 1952 riposte against the purists was composed in Portuguese directly under an anonymous editorial headnote specifying that "at times the texts of *Habitat* will not be written in the purest [purissimo] Portuguese." Here Villa rejects the fetishism of the pure and beautiful word under which "the harmful seeds of Nazi and racial rhetoric will nest."[95]

The piece opens by describing the rich novelty and amalgamative quality of Brazilian Portuguese as superior to that of Portugal as a consequence of the fact that "great human currents shift, are superimposed, conjugated, intertwined, collide, repel one another" in an "epoch of great transplantations," making this language far richer than a "Baroque-colonial patrimony."[96] Villa's supple approach to language and culture summarizes, "A lingua é um grande teatro, a imensa ribalta em que se concretiza a realidade documenta-se, transforma-se em poesia, e reflete as grandes correntes de humanidade que para ela confluem": "Language is a great theater, the immense stage on which reality is concretized, documented, transformed into poetry, and reflects the great currents of humanity that converge in it. Every living being that has something to say must say its part, whether great or small. The only ones who have nothing to say, and who will remain behind the scenes, biting their nails, lowering the curtain and eating the dust, will be precisely the purists, that is, the firefighters on duty, always ready to extinguish the fire that never happens." He embraces a syntactical and semantic freedom as championed by the historical avant-gardes but with grounding in deep time, recognizing that "no language, as a cultural expression, can suffocate its elements with a caged vocabulary or caged syntax"; he points out that historically, "the . . . three most elevated exemplars of human poetry developed, or better, deflagrated [deflagram] precisely at the apex of the most confused linguistic mixtures, in the critical punctums of cosmopolitanism"—using the language of fire against the firefighters. His first exemplar is Homer, writing in "four strata of dialect, and, in great part, overflows of barbarous, that is to say, not Greek, vocabulary"; his second is Dante, writing in a mixture of Tuscan, French, and Provençal, "with entire tercets [of the *Commedia*] written in Provençal, in French, in Latin, in Hebrew." As the third great paragon of poetry, Villa highlights the "barbarian" (bárbara), "Yankee" (iaunqui) literature of the United States, from Poe to Melville to Faulkner to Eliot, representing an "outbreak of energies so fresh and violent" that he attributes precisely to an admixture of heterogeneous cultural influences, Indigenous, diasporic, and immigrant, placing European literature in crisis: this barbarous writing is driven forward by "the stimulus of heterogeneous forces, such as those of black people: but also the free activity of indigenous people, who repelled the dictates of English 'linguistic legality.' And also the conversion, to that land, of a number of such disparate stimuli (from the Irish to the Spanish, from the Germans to the Italians, from the Japanese to the French)." Villa goes on to call for a new philology that he announces will be proposed within the pages of *Habitat*: a researched and historically rooted Brazilian dictionary and etymological dictionary that can do justice to the complex lexical materials of that language, "as large and wild as the Brazilian forests themselves, which still remain unfathomable."[97] Such a rage to inventory, haunted by that unfathomability, will drive Villa's projects for the rest of his life.

Tagliaferri claims that Villa traveled not only to Rio but also to Bahia and the southern Amazon (home of the Karajá peoples), following the lead of his friend Gastone Novelli, though documentation of these travels has not been confirmed.[98] Both published and unpublished writings attest that Villa would follow Indigenous aesthetics, and include it, rather remarkably by comparison with his peers, in various classifications of contemporary tendencies for the remainder of his career. Tagliaferri also notes that Villa read James Joyce's *Ulysses* in French following the 1948 appearance of the French translation and carried it with him throughout this phase of his vocation, the so-called Brazilian parenthesis. The coalescence of these experiences in Brazil, combined with Villa's exposure to currents in the modernist art of the Americas, leaves a permanent imprint on his poetry.

The shapes of Villa's texts change considerably upon his stay in São Paulo. The open field and syntax of his diagrammatic tableaus and eventual gyres in the vein of "pluri-sense" and "dis-sense" permit a continual linguistic fracture and addition: his stanzas become engines of sonic and semantic variation that must have been informed by what Villa later identified as Joyce's "broken, split, upset, visceral word"[99] and very probably by the deconstructive word variations of the Noigandres group of concrete poets, formed in São Paulo in 1952. That said, the effusive, barbarous mess of Villa's poetry (which late in his career was often published as a facsimile of his handwritten notes as a result of both the fetishism of the artifact on the part of the publishers and the difficulty of typesetting his "stanzas") contrasts starkly with concretism's clean, minimalist, constructivist aesthetic; moreover, concretism was more accessibly internationalist, more willfully transmitted and transmittable, with its plurilingual creations frequently accompanied by a glossary.[100] Rather than registering as cosmopolitan or internationalist, Villa's "polyvernacular" and translinguistic stanzas accommodate language that acts as xenos, both guest and host: language whose characteristics and aspirations invoke a use of natural languages of which one has no "native" possession. Ashon Crawley's critique of xenoglossia converges on the supposition that those who practice it conceive of language as "pure, coherent, stable in its enunciation, such that each language maintains purity."[101] Villa's poetry is intent on generating exactly the forms of barbarism that would most repel the purists.

A case in point is Villa's unpublished "Et ab hic et ab hoc" (figure 2.3)—translatable from Latin as "A little of this & a little of that," echoing a twelve-volume work of *Literary Strangenesses, Oddities, Jokes, and Squabbles* by Carlo Mascaretti, librarian at the Biblioteca Nazionale in Rome (1855–1928), and composed on the title page of ethnologist Jean Guiart's *Les Religions de l'Océanie* (1962).[102] In this and akin pieces Villa exiles himself in Latin, which as an obsolete roving lingua

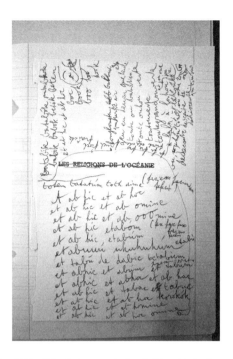

FIGURE 2.3 Emilio Villa, "Et ab hic et ab hoc." Unpublished manuscript. Photograph by Jennifer Scappettone. Copyright Estate of Emilio Villa. Courtesy of Archivio Emilio Villa, Biblioteca Panizzi di Reggio Emilia.

franca ironically offers more room for play than a national or global language in the information age. Here, as elsewhere in Villa's oeuvre, the structuralist grid that is meant to expose deep configurations common to linguistic systems and that prevailed as a substrate through much postwar abstraction (including that of concrete art and poetry) instead ends up testing the distance between linguistic cantons as it puns across "totem," "tatatúm," "toth" and "aime," "omine" and "ooo mine," "hoc," "fax," "fux," "tabac," "book," "korokók," and Indigenous words that could have been inspired by Guiart's study, including "betók" (New Palauan for "many")—hovering between the respective translucency of xenoglossia and an expressive onomatopoeia heading toward glossolalia ("abúm," "whuhuhúm," "boo hoo"). The word subject to Villa's serial permutations becomes a font of associations and dissociations across clefts of space and time, liberated in tables and centrifugal trajectories from the governance of any one domineering logos.

Villa delights in the disgregation and cross-contamination of languages, creating an "abisso/disgregate/stanza" (abyss/*disgregate*/stanza) at the crossroads of "essenza" (essence) and "assenza" (absence), "costanza" (constancy) and "distanza" (distance), as an unpublished diagram/poem on "natural measure" from his archives indicates—the corners of the battered page punning on the Italian word for "corners" (angoli) through carnal and bawdy inscriptions in French (drifting from "angolo" to "strangled" and "screwed in the ass") (figure 2.4). These pieces stage the proliferation of tongues and at the same time the desire to pare language down toward the din of the abyss (תְּהוֹם tehom) or primordial waters of Genesis. Villa's planetary range of reference aspired ultimately to "a return to the primeval

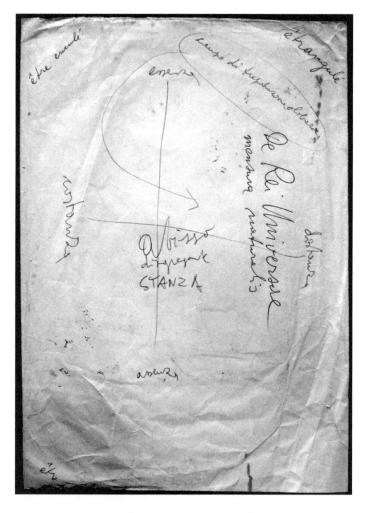

FIGURE 2.4 Emilio Villa, "De Rei Universae: mensura naturalis," circa 1965–1980. Unpublished manuscript. Photograph by Jennifer Scappettone. Copyright Estate of Emilio Villa. Courtesy of Archivio Emilio Villa, Biblioteca Panizzi di Reggio Emilia. Diagram/poem/note in Latin, French, English, and Italian rife with assonance and puns.

sign-symbols from which historic and technological man has become fatally estranged"—a return he saw manifest spatially in the "Scrittura / germinante" (germinating / writing) of Cy Twombly.[103] Rethinking the domain and nature of the Italian language and of Italy itself also evinces utopian dreams of what Villa identifies, in a book first published in collaboration with Alberto Burri, as "a pure phonetic ideology."[104] Although the aspiration toward a supra- or protonational language may drive these experiments, the poetic result is anything but an Esperanto.

ETYMOLOGY AS ROGUE ARCHAEOLOGY: CUNEIFORMISM AS A MEDIUM FOR POETRY

This amalgam of aesthetic and scholarly endeavors would lead Villa, from the 1950s forward, to the wayward translation of the Hebrew Bible that emphasized the text's bawdy elements and Italian's own Eastern roots—undertaken "without university legitimacies or licenses," making up what Giulio Busi calls "almost the samizdat of an illegal philology" that emphasizes the "discontinuous, convulsive, nearly animate, and gasping" nature of biblical prose.[105] It would have drawn Villa's interest that Hebrew, a "dead" literary language, was being revived as a language of the present in Israel, although no documents recording his thoughts about Zionism remain, as far as I have been able to detect, and it is impossible to imagine his embracing any nationalist language or cultural revival that would eclipse other vernaculars on the ground.

By the time Villa began translating Genesis in the 1950s, he had worked extensively on translation of prebiblical texts, from the Ugaritic Legend of Keret (excavated by French archaeologists in Syria in 1930–1931 and regarded as presaging the story of Helen of Troy and paralleling that of Abraham) to the *Odyssey*, throwing himself into the search for continuity across the Mediterranean and Middle Eastern worlds. Having begun to translate Homer in 1942, he would only publish his *Odissea* in 1964, then again in 1972—surely bolstered in the process by reading Joyce's *Ulysses* in French. His work on Genesis unfolded in tandem with a resurgence of interest in origins evident in postwar art movements such as the Gruppo and Fondazione Origine with which Villa collaborated in the 1950s (founded by Alberto Burri, Ettore Colla, Giuseppe Capogrossi, and Mario Ballocco)—but also by Abstract Expressionists such as Rothko and Pollock, whom Villa followed closely. This obsession with origins was propelled by developments such as the 1940 discovery of the monumental cave at Lascaux (which Villa visited in 1961) and the formation of the Collège de Sociologie in the late 1930s in

Paris by intellectuals in the vein of "ethnographic surrealism" like Roger Caillois and Georges Bataille, although Villa was simultaneously conscious of the research into Indigenous aesthetics active in the Americas, in Brazilian modernism, and in North American ethnopoetics, as registered in his published writings and notebooks.[106] The most prominent document of Villa's awareness of Indigenous influence on hemispheric modernism is his *22 cause + 1*, a translingual 1953 artist's book that contains glimmers of Brazilian Portuguese, with drawings by Roberto Sambonet, and riffs on the Indigenous coastal tribe denomination "tupì" recalling Oswald de Andrade's canonical 1928 anticolonial modernist "Manifesto Antropófago," with its punning on Hamlet's "to be, or not to be":

il cuore del cuore **tupì**
conosce il cuore delle erbe,
l'occhio dell'occhio **tupì**
investe il riverbero
delle acque segrete nell'erba,
la pianta del piede **tupì**
calca i delicati labirinti delle erbe,
e io registro il vento
che carezza le erbe **tupì**[107]

the heart of the heart **tupì**
knows the heart of the grasses,
the eye of the eye **tupì**
invests the reverberation
of the secret waters in the grass,
the sole of the foot **tupì**
treads the delicate labyrinths of the grasses,
and I record the wind
that caresses the grasses **tupì**

At the same time, Villa explicitly rejects Romantic exoticism and the facile research into "confused dreams and clippings of unpublished purity" implicit in much of European Orientalism and modernist primitivism, from Modigliani to Picasso to Klee to Conrad; these inclinations, he points out, are effectively appropriations, undertaken in a search for a new European pictorial and literary heritage.[108]

Throughout these endeavors of scholarship and translation, by contrast, Villa manifests a desire to "deflagrate" not merely Italy but Europe—and to expose a spatiotemporal continuum that bucks prevailing myths of progress, as well as of nations and races. As articulated in a 1953 article/manifesto for the Fondazione Origine's journal *Arti visive* titled "What Is Primitive," he seeks to trace the continuity of culture across "East" and "West," across canonical Occidental cultures and their primordial origins, being interested in the "human," against humanism, as no less than "all that which has root and expressive document in the terrain of all peoples in time and in the structural unity of variations and comparisons."[109] This work stages an implicit rebuke to the arid sociological formulas of official culture and "preachers of aesthetics" (predicatori dell'estetica).[110] Villa repudiates the late idealist historicism upon which the notion of the "prehistoric" is based, embracing instead the term "primordial," as manifest in his *L'arte dell'uomo primordiale*, datable to the mid-1960s. On the one hand, he insists, divisions of time are irrelevant in an existence that prevailed prior to the "landslides" (frane) of modern consciousness, an existence in which "the one is everything [L'uno è il tutto]," in which time and its actors are not subdivided and analyzed but flow organically, and naming is unnecessary because "the name/noun [il nome] is the universal voice, the murmur chained to silence, the wind in its matrix."[111] Here we recall the ruach turbine of Villa's Genesis, pitted against the Word of John. On the other hand, Villa treats cave art such as that of the Lascaux grottos not only as coherent and meaningful but also as connected with writing itself, referring to figurations such as a man with the head of a bird as "ideograms" and to symbols and forms considered "enigmatic" at the time as working together in modes that he decodes in terms of "etymology."[112] So although Tagliaferri distinguishes Villa's interest in the "sign" as opposed to the "representation," in accord with the irruptive vein of the Collège de Sociologie, there exists a productive tension in this poetics between the sign's intelligibility as a kind of language and as a Dionysian punctum of chaos.

As the spine that runs throughout the Bible's first five books, Villa identifies a "systematic research into sacred and organic etymology (especially paraetymology)," or what is known to academics as false etymology, in line with the principle of "the creativity of the word." Villa aims, in turn, to highlight this (slightly scandalous) principle in his translation by signaling "the principal motions of etymologizing, etiological or demonological procedures."[113] Whether working on sacralized religious texts or those identified as pagan, the philosophy and methodology are the same. As he puts it in an essay glossing the motivations behind his translation of the *Odyssey*, for instance, "Behind the Homeric verse of Ionic and Aeolian epic poetry, there is the entire exterminated linguistic area of the Mycenaean civilization, of archaic Greek, and of the Mesopotamian languages. Thus my translation accounts above all for the linguistic distress [travaglio] through which the Odyssey was formed."[114] This postscript to Villa's Homer emphasizes etymological play intended to simultaneously reforge a Mediterranean continuity among Semitic, Greek, and Romance languages and restore to the European imaginary the "sorcerers of Mesopotamian origin" that he posits to have continuously inhabited the crowded Mediterranean centers. In the process, of course, he undercuts any ideologically entrenched narrative of the "Greek miracle" that would regard this culture as the origin of Western civilization as we know it.

Villa comes to reformulate modern philology in a subversive and semiutopian key across a range of interminable projects. His radical etymological dictionary of Italian, a project encompassing decades of work on every possible scrap of paper available yet never brought to fruition as a bound volume, set out to trace the relations of his native language to ancient languages outside of Europe—Mesopotamian, Syro-Palestinian, Paleo-Mediterranean—while including all upstart "neoformations" in technology and other areas of contemporary life that represent "a semantic event" as well.[115] This formidable commitment to the national tongue for which he harbored a hatred, a refusal, a blockage—and that he had gradually abandoned as a language of composition—represents a moving struggle to remake that tongue from within through meticulous deconstruction, according to principles diametrically opposed to those of a purist (and residual postwar fascist) national philology. As articulated in a proposal dated to 1973, the etymological dictionary sought ultimately to expose the myth of Romance languages as an ideological attempt to shore up a purely European identity in the context of a reality that in fact extended eastward and traversed all sectors of the Mediterranean, correcting prior volumes composed by "positivist linguistics," "victims of the 'romance' fervor."[116] The project can be generatively cast into the words of Ezra Pound describing Ernest Fenollosa in 1918: "he cannot be looked upon as a mere searcher after exotics. His mind was constantly filled with parallels and comparisons between eastern and western art." Fenollosa was trying to account, in rather more apprehensive terms than Villa—terms recalling those of Henry James in a Manhattan of migrants—for what he regarded as "another and a startling chapter" in the book of the world at the start of the twentieth century: "Vistas of strange futures unfold for man, of world-embracing cultures half weaned from Europe, of hitherto undreamed responsibilities for nations and races."[117] Villa embraced these "strange futures"—and their pasts—wholeheartedly.

It is evident from his language, as well as his persistence across the decades, that Villa (likely mistakenly) regarded his etymological dictionary of Italian, to be titled *Origin and Nature of All Italian Words*, not as an arcane endeavor but as a resource responding to a felt "public urgency," something "necessary," while also satisfying "the great curiosity of readers."[118] Although the project remains unpublished except in bits and pieces, the effort to find alternative roots for European words in the languages of ancient Mesopotamia was finally to be realized in four volumes published between 1984 and 1994 by Giovanni Semerano (Ostuni 1911– Avezzano 2005), an Italian linguist and philologist; Semerano controversially rejected the Indo-European theory and set out to trace a protohistoric unity of Europe and the Middle East, identifying Akkadian and Sumerian origins for Ancient Greek, Latin, and modern European languages.[119]

Regardless of projects we might erroneously regard as competing with Villa's in the scholastic sense, it is clear that the poet was driven by a different kind of impulse, not that of convincing philological authorities but of blasting open barely thinkable possibilities to an avid public, in the vein of art. In a drafted letter to a correspondent who was likewise "invading classical philology" through etymological play undocumented by scholarship, Villa vaunts his audacious methods, proclaiming himself to be "not only a dilettante, but a reprobate; (I am just barely turned toward 'cuneiformist,' from Sumer to Ugarit, an exile from dogmatic, haughty, and arid fields) [non solo dilettante, ma proprio reprobo (io sono soltanto abbastanza versato 'cuneiformista,' da Sumer a Ugarit, esule dai campi dogmatici, altezzosi e aridi)]"—thus playing on the rhyme between "cuneiformist" and "conformist," embracing the powers of formation. Villa declares that it is exactly his correspondent's anxiety—that one can demonstrate almost *anything and everything* through undocumented etymological play—that he is attempting to achieve in his labors: "to demonstrate almost everything, without caesuras, without censorship, with the aim of elasticizing, spiraling, excavating the organism of the prodigious given text, and amidst the rubble to find something else, another prodigious thing." He admits, "it is the textus in every sense receptus that I've permitted myself (recklessly, adventurously) the luxury of shoplifting, bewildering, undermining [è il textus in ogni senso receptus che mi son permesso (avventatamente, avventurosamente) il lusso di taccheggiare, di frastornare, di insidiare]," yet he insists that he believes himself to be working on behalf of a higher reason ("proprio in ragione di più alta (credo) ragione"). Finally, he insists in frank humility that he "won't be the one who uproots Milan [non sarò io a spiantare Milano]," alluding to a passage in Alessandro Manzoni's 1827 historical romance *I promessi sposi*—the novel set to unite Italy through not only its plot but also the author's studied choice to use a bourgeois Florentine vernacular as national tongue. In playing on the famed Manzoni passage ("povero untorello, non sarai tu che spianti Milano"), Villa creates a parallel between the "untorello," a poor protagonist contaminated with the plague, and himself as contaminant of Milan and, by extension, of Italy as nation-state.[120] Painstaking urges to expose the stew of cultures, syllable by syllable, sign by sign, without even positing the possibility of mastery and without leveling the irreconcilable differences between peoples, will become hallmarks of Villa's rollicking xenoglossic poetics, operating in literary-anthropological key with unmistakable political implications. So although Feltrinelli rejected his translation of Genesis in 1975, in the same year, the magazine *Uomini e idee* devoted an issue to Villa's poetics—the first critical exegesis of his oeuvre.

Villa ultimately embraces etymology as a means of breaking the word into parts that then conjoin across unimaginable distances, seeking origins never reachable phoneme by phoneme. One example is his unpublished series of notes on the term PARADISO at the Biblioteca Panizzi (figure 2.5); whereas the accepted etymological explanation attributes the Greek word para-deisos (walled/royal park) to an original Persian word, para-deiza, or walled garden, Villa asks himself, on

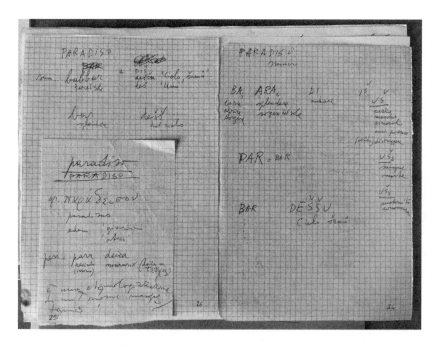

FIGURE 2.5 Emilio Villa, unpublished manuscript fragment from project for an etymological dictionary, seeking to chart alternative Sumerian roots for the word "PARADISO," undated. Photograph by Jennifer Scappettone. Copyright Estate of Emilio Villa. Courtesy of Archivio Emilio Villa, Biblioteca Panizzi di Reggio Emilia.

the note paper, whether both terms are an "etymologization" (i.e., a retrofitting rationalization) of what is actually a Mesopotamian noun possessing a similar set of sounds. On the right, we have his proposals for a possible Sumerian origin, breaking the word into phonetic syllables, BA-ARA-DI-[IS]-US, which leads to something like "carriage for the rising of the sun" (with many outtakes) or else BAR ("splendor") and DESSU ("sky").[121] Villa's copy of his teacher Anton Diemel's 1934 Sumerian-Akkadian vocabulary reveals some traces of research in this vein. Another sheet contains notes on the Egyptian phonemes PR and DT, speculating on a series of meanings and seeming to land on "locus" + "eternity." At the Museo della Carale, a group of unpublished notes titled "Banchetto etimologico della visione del profeta Daniele" ("Etymological banquet of the prophet Daniel's vision") appears to apply a similar procedure to the mysterious inscription written by the hand on the wall in Chapter 5 of Daniel.

This fragmentation and recombination of meanings, read with Villa's references to prehistoric cave paintings as "ideograms" in mind, recalls Fenollosa's *Chinese Written Character as a Medium for Poetry*, edited by Ezra Pound, with its (highly controversial, rejected, and then partially recuperated) speculations on "ideographic" meanings deriving from the combinations of radicals immanent in Chinese characters. Fenollosa views the radicals as "shorthand pictures of actions or processes" (so that "to see," for instance, is made up of the radical for "eye" plus that for "moving through space," "to speak," two words and a mouth with an emerging flame).[122] Fenollosa makes a case for the concrete poetic value of words that are not, ultimately, abstractions, and for translations that retain these concrete meanings—a call famously taken up by Pound in forging Imagism and the Cantos that followed, although Villa tarries in the realm of etymology proper far longer than Pound ever did: "Abstract terms," Fenollosa wrote, "pressed by etymology, reveal their ancient roots still embedded in direct action." Fenollosa claims that strata of metaphor making up language, forgotten in modern "Aryan" languages, can be contrasted with the putative immediacy of Chinese ideograms: "Our ancestors built the accumulations of metaphor into structures of language.... Languages today are thin and cold because we think less and less into them. We are forced, for the sake of quickness . . ., to file down each word to its narrowest edge of meaning. Nature would seem to have become less like a paradise and more and more like a factory." Yet this poetic richness, this paradise of sorts, can be recuperated in the postlapsarian period via study or translation: "It is only when the difficulty of placing some odd term arises or when we are forced to translate into some very different language, that we attain for a moment the inner heat of thought, a heat which melts down the parts of speech to recast them at will."[123] Although Villa studiously destroyed many traces of his influences and hardly could have embraced the anti-Semitic Fascist Italophile Pound without major qualifications, we can assume that he was well aware of this fundamental set of papers in the history of modern poetry. Villa applied the basic structure of deconstruction and composition characterizing these experiments to a different set of "Eastern" materials—for the sake not of romanticizing, comprehending, or deencrypting the East but of quashing the distance between East and West.

AN IDEAL NATIONALITY: ON TWOMBLY

Villa's glosses of the abstract artist Cy Twombly, who came to settle in Rome, first appeared in Italian prose under the heading "Cy Twombly: Talento bianco" ("Cy Twombly: White [or Blank] Talent"); Villa chose to feature Twombly in the inaugural 1959 issue of his magazine *Appia Antica*, described in the editor's note as a "magazine of poetic selection and ideological qualification surrounding artistic production that testifies to being in some sense active or current [attuale]."[124] Two years later, Villa published an open-field poetic "paraphrase for Cy Twombly" that assumed the genre of paraphrase literally, being a free mirroring of Twombly's 1960 wax crayon, pencil, and ballpoint pen drawing *Ode to Psyche*, published across the spine of an exhibition catalog for Rome's Galleria La Tartaruga (figure 2.6).[125] Rather than any "heresy of paraphrase" (à la Cleanth Brooks), Villa's poem may be considered the equivalent of musical interpretation, in which polyphony is achieved via the copresence of distinct tongues: precipitous "parenthèses . . . / dévorées migratrices" (devouring migratory / parentheses) in French, Italian, and English. Broken into irregular columns, the gestural lines of the poem echo the artist's dispersive marks, forging typographical curves and junctions where corners aren't expected: the French words just quoted appear at a crossroads of verse in the upper left-hand corner of the page forged by the vertical English or French word "interpolation," whose "p" is borrowed from "parenthèses."

Twombly had studied at the Art Students League of New York and at Black Mountain College in the early 1950s, where Charles Olson, Robert Motherwell, and Ben Shahn were in residence. His *Ode to Psyche* takes its name from the first of Keats's 1819 odes, an expansion of the sonnet form. In this lyric, the belated Romantic imagines creating a sanctuary to the forsaken goddess Psyche (from the Greek ψυχή, breath) in the mind, even though it is "too late for antique vows, / Too, too late for the fond believing lyre." "In the midst of this wide quietness,"

 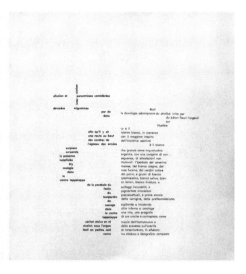

FIGURE 2.6 Emilio Villa, "una parafrasi per Cy Twombly," from *Cy Twombly: e una parafrasi per Cy Twombly*, Catalogo della mostra alla Galleria La Tartaruga (Edizioni della Tartaruga, 1961). © Cy Twombly Foundation and Estate of Emilio Villa. Image courtesy of Menil Library, The Menil Collection, Houston. The verso features Twombly's 1960 drawing *Ode to Psyche*, wax crayon, pencil, and ballpoint pen, private collection, 1960, whereas the recto features Villa's verbovisual "paraphrase."

Keats will dress a floral bower "with the wreath'd trellis of a working brain," embellishing it with décor before or beyond language and its taxonomies: "With buds, and bells, and stars without a name."[126] It is as if the poem could dodge language altogether and be wrought of the pure psuché, or breath, that it wishes to worship in personified or deified form.[127] Twombly's piece seems constructed around a bower of sorts. Within the inset at upper left marked "(detail)," sitting below a semi-illegible line containing the title "Ode to Psyche," Twombly has cited Keats's lines about the love between Cupid and Psyche that is past yet still being readied, exceeding tense and measure: "And ready still past [illegible] kisses to outnumber / [glade] / At tender eye-dawn of Aurorean Love." We hover in a white field of plenitude beyond calculation, imagery, and language—or after their cancellation.

We are called upon to ponder what Twombly's apparently Romantic aesthetic seems to offer the literary arts in political terms and explicitly after Fascism; for Villa makes striking claims for the way "cy"—uncapitalized as if to emphasize the name's relationship to "cipher" and "sigh"—cleaves him or itself away from ideological conscription:

cy si separa
dal codice, dalla tribù, dal
connubio, dalla confederazione, dal
vento, dal frutto, e si
inscrive nell'ira unica del polso, come
in una nazionalità ideale

cy separates himself
from the code, from the tribe, from the
alliance, from the confederation, from the
wind, from the fruit, and inscribes
himself in the singular ire of the pulse, as in
an ideal nationality[128]

Although Twombly's *Ode* might appear suspended in purely formal, intellectual, and aesthetic concerns, its work on language registers in postwar Rome as steeped in the search for a language stripped of ideology, freed from what Pound called "the tale of the tribe" as unifying myth.[129] Villa's assertions were published nearly two decades before Roland Barthes's now obsessively cited reflections on the way that, in Twombly's hand, "the letters that are formed no longer belong to any graphic code, just as the grand phrases of Mallarmé no longer belong to any rhetorical code—not even to the code of destruction"[130]—a statement that, however, disavows their taking place in identifiable natural languages. The graphically explosive polylingual output generated by Villa seeks to emulate what he praises in postwar painterly abstraction: a trouncing of the provincial limits of national or tribal languages. Villa's transgenre linguistic vortices demand that we apprehend the visual articulation of an "ideal nationality" as an unsettled cross section of pulses, as exemplified in the lines of Twombly— whose work cannot be fully appreciated outside of the painter's service year, from 1953 to 1954, as a drafted US Army cryptographer in Washington, DC.[131] Mary Jacobus provides the sobering reminder that Twombly was part of a tremendous Cold War effort on the part of the US military to build a cadre of cryptographic experts.[132]

Villa's revisions for the 1961 version of his remarks on Twombly burst into a polyglot verse matrix and cast response to Twombly's "writing" in more explicitly political terms. The linguistic marks that Villa describes as hovering between the syllabic and ideographic ("tra sillabico e ideografico") in the earlier Italian prose inscribe "a life" ("si incide una vita"), whereas in the revised text, the life inscribed is set into civic space and subject to official authority, and the "sillabico" (syllabic) becomes "sigillando" (coding): "coding and engraving / infernal ciphers it homologates / a life, a civil registry / of unique opposed hours [sigillando e incidendo / cifre inferne si omologa / una vita, una anagrafe / di ore uniche contrastate]."[133] In the original text, Villa writes that Twombly's work cannot be read in the conventional sense because as "germinal writing," it "responds to the calls of a germinal lexicon, struggles free and settles along a dumbfounded [esterrefatta] and purely expanded [estesa] page"; the resulting language "sibilates in a reed-grove of uniform graphemes [sibila in un canneto di grafemi uniformi]."[134] The revised text removes itself from both the antique Sibylline context and the pastoral scene recalling Horus or Moses, placing Twombly's writing squarely in the context of political contestation: in its closing stanza, Villa hails the way cy's scrawling rests "on the juridical page [posa sulla pagina giuridica]" and "whistles / in the fasces of uniform graphemes [fischia / nel fascio di grafemi uniformi]," playing on the assonance between "fischia" and "fascio."[135] Meditating on Twombly's germinal writing, Villa articulates a barbed desire for communicative marks and phonetics to hoot and jeer within the bonds of uniformed letters, sabotaging the reeds bound together as fascio, the basis and unifying symbol of the term Fascism.

Demotic linguistic convocations, "surplace" and "surparole" (the latter term recasting the former's meaning of "standstill" so that it reads as *above place, rank, or square*, and echoes the English "surplus") will be tortured and wriggle their way past ideological inscription in resonance with Twombly's "fischiare." We witness these convocations in the left-hand column of Villa's "paraphrase":

> surplace
> surparole
> la présence
> suppliciée
> éty
> mologie
> dans
> le
> ventre   lappelappe[136]

How does one read this flux of "overspeech" in the shape of a cataract that swamps categories—this apparent semi-French and sporadic English that Villa improperly occupies? Villa presents etymology at work, study of the ἔτυμος (true)—supreme presence hovering over geography and "parole," in the belly, or womb, burrowed by verse at the core of multiple processes by means of the word "of": this "ventre" becomes the womb of the parable, or parabola, of the feast of losing-all of the sacking of the womb, or lap.[137] Like Twombly's fitful homage to Keats's "tuneless numbers, wrung / By sweet enforcement," but in insurrectionary relation to mother tongues and patrie, or fatherlands, Villa's xenoglossia—whistling from beyond the Populus/populace with its overweening bundle of punitive rods—also voices the barbarism of writing lyric in the wake of Fascism.[138]

A SPHERE WITHOUT STRANGERS

Disco Muto (*Mute Record*, figure 2.7), an explicitly choral object-poem that Villa produced with the collaboration of artist Silvio Craia and poet Giorgio Cegna between 1967 and 1972, was designed to mimic the proportions and format of a phonographic record: in an edition of one hundred printed for the Carnevale Internazionale degli Artisti di Rieti, the artists silkscreened vertiginous verses over uniquely colored backgrounds mounted to cardboard discs the size of an LP, providing each "album" with a sleeve silkscreened repeatedly in unique constellations of brightly saturated colors and fonts (including a reproduction of Villa's handwriting) for a richly layered effect. The fact that silkscreening is a popular medium, used on posters and the like, and one that was being mobilized by Andy Warhol earlier in the 1960s, conditions the reading of these objects that hover between high art and ephemera. The poem, whose language remains constant in all versions and thus seems to have been cut as a single stencil frame, is ascribed to the "Coro della Scola Cantorum," with Craia and Cegna listed as "soloists," although it contains textual fragments that we can see Villa working out in other manuscripts (such as in the corners of the text in figure 2.4). "Schola Cantorum" was a generic name being used for the choral ensembles that were proliferating as part of the resurgence of early music in this period, yet given Villa's historical interests, this nomination, using "scola" or the ancient form of the Italian word for school, yokes this verse experiment to the tradition of the Schola Cantorum of Rome, the male liturgical choir whose first iteration is said to have been founded by Pope Sylvester in the year 314. That institution evolved in its function over the centuries from performance of simple unison chants, to plainchant, to highly orchestrated polyphonies by singers whose breath training led to sophisticated vocal renderings of the divine office. *Disco Muto* is choral in

FIGURE 2.7 *Disco Muto (Mute Record) (con il coro della scola cantorum di Macerata solisti Craia e Cegna)*, Emilio Villa, Silvio Craia, and Giorgio Cegna, silkscreen on cardboard, edition of 100, diameter 30 cm, 1967. Photograph by Jennifer Scappettone. Copyright Estate of Emilio Villa. Collection of Biblioteca Nazionale di Firenze.

a concrete sense, insofar as it is translingual and collaborative—a collaboration taking place not only between languages, particularly Italian and French, and between three male "singers" of this xenoglossic "school" but also between the disc and its readers or, to obey the terms the work sets out, its virtual "listeners." The imagination or actual triggering, via record player, of this disc's spinning and the attempt to read what is printed upon it are a Byzantine and deeply embodied affair that could never remain constant from reading to reading—in paradoxical contrast to an album that might have fixed the sound of this chorus in a single moment and would therefore be static, if unmute.

The whorled poem that appears on all editions of *Disco Muto*, exceeding the boundaries of the circle in each version as if it were centrifugally driven outside of its round "frame," is made up of a series of permutations of the same or similar phonemes, such as we witnessed in Villa's "et ab hic": syllables unleashed as if within

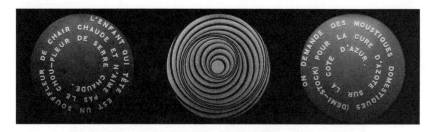

FIGURE 2.8 Three stills from Marcel Duchamp with Man Ray and Marc Allégret, *ANÉMIC CINÉMA*, 1926.

a cyclotron and set to rest in reshuffled semantic tableaus. As such, this work reads as a direct homage to Marcel Duchamp, to whom Villa devoted various writings; in personal correspondence with Villa, Duchamp himself had referred to Villa as "Villadrome" (after "velodrome"), an oft-cited encomium Villa sacralized as a "parabaptism."[139] Villa's discs represent an extension of Duchamp's texts for *ANÉMIC-CINÉMA*, a film produced with Man Ray and Marc Allégret in 1925–1926 and ascribed to Rrose Sélavy (figure 2.8). Interspersed between optically dizzying "rotoreliefs" in subversive play against the diegetic and clarifying function of intertitles, Duchamp's nine spiral texts, viewed in rotation for thirty seconds at a time, employed cross-lingual puns to wrest highly polyvalent works of apparent nonsense. With this work, Duchamp radically reoriented the linear forward motion of reading—beginning with the title, which invites one to read backward in search of a palindrome, only to be short-circuited. As Katrina Martin puts it, "In the tightly wound phrases, horizontal consonance and vertical dissonance create a unique set of linguistic chords which move upon each other in time like the motion of the spiral. Each component part of the work is so thoroughly exploited that its linearity explodes and it is freed to operate dynamically to create a multi-dimensionality within which reverberates an elusive infinity."[140] The notion of "linguistic chords," if understood in the context of Duchamp's work across linguistic systems, presents an apparent contradiction with the modernist's interest in creating a new, wholly abstract language, expressed in the following notes: "*Conditions of a language:* / The search for '*prime words*' ('divisible' only by themselves and by unity). / Take a Larousse dict. and copy all the so-called 'abstract' words, i.e., those which have no concrete reference / Compose a schematic sign designating each of these words. (this sign can be composed with the standard stops). / These signs must be thought of as the letters of the new alphabet."[141] Although such abstraction seems to divest language of its semantic value, leading viewers of the film to liminal innuendoes of a sexual order, Duchamp's cross-lingual puns necessarily invoke cultural ideologies that ground the work in social realities, beginning with the image of a suckling child veering toward subversive queer implications—"L'enfant qui tète est un souffleur de chair chaude [The suckling child is a hot-flesh blower]"—and moving on to vaguely violent implications of incest ("passion de famille") and extermination by gas—"On demande des moustiques domestiques (demi-stock) pour la cure d'azote sur la Côte d'Azur [Domestic mosquitoes (half-stock) are sought for nitrogen treatment on the Côte d'Azur]"—that chill in the context of the recent (and coming) world conflicts (figure 2.8).

Villa's extrapolation of Duchamp's cinematic text, while retaining the sexual overtones, possesses a more pointed relationship to the social barriers that build national languages, even as it confuses them. His text for the spinning silent record forms sonic and conceptual "chords" around a verbal template that hovers at the core of all its variations, yet paradoxically never appears: the word *l'étranger*, the stranger or foreigner. The centrifugal forces of disgregation also lead to repeated plays on the countervailing French term *entre* and Italian term *tra*, both meaning "between." Instead of confronting "l'étranger" directly, virtual listeners become witness to a vast number of its permutations and puns crossing between French, Italian, and overtones of dialects through the record's conceptual spin, wheeling sporadically into neologisms. One edition of the record jacket housed in the Villa archives of the Museo della Carale (figure 2.9) prints many, if not all, movements of the spiral poem in linear form upon a chaotic layering of found textual fragments, seemingly hailing from university documents, Villa's handwritten notes, and other unidentifiable sources screenprinted in orange, maroon, khaki green, and pale lime-yellow strata, ascribing the text to "Emilio Villa, 1968," and thus enabling us to disentangle these linguistic relations in a way that the "oggetti di poesia" (object poems) within the jackets do not.[142]

I will attempt a translation here of a work that is only partially translatable. The first stanza is more or less French and presents a couple of neologisms within bawdy and otherwise audacious syllables:

-BETWEEN BUGGERS
-THE BETWEEN ANGLE
-THE STRONGLES
-THE ENTRANGLE
-BEING ENGLISH
-THE STRANGLE

FIGURE 2.9 Sleeve for *Disco Muto* (*Mute Record*) at 33 RPM (*con il coro della scola cantorum di Macerata solisti Craia e Cegna*), Emilio Villa, with Silvio Craia and Giorgio Cegna, silkscreen on cardboard, edition of 100, diameter 30 cm, 1967. Photograph by Jennifer Scappettone. Copyright Estate of Emilio Villa. Collection of Museo della Carale, Ivrea.

The second stanza introduces a K and some Italian terms and neologisms:

>   -THE STRANKASS
>   -THE SUMMER ALSO
>   -THE SUPERCOOLCALM E
>   -BEING IN TRANCE
>   -BEING IN SLICES

The third stanza introduces further neologisms, as well as a Norman term for "ounces":

>   -THE STRANGE
>   -THE ETRENCHE
>   -THE BETWEEN THREE

-THE ESTRANGLE
-THE ESLICE
-THE BEING OUNCES . . . NAIL

And the fourth stanza seems to delve further into the realms of dialect and spoken language, with the softening of consonants and overall aural elision of terms:

-ESSO OOFLÉ
-ESSO BREFF
-INNA DA ASS
-THE ENTRANCE
-THE BEINGENGLISH
-ESSO OOFLÉED

The first line plays on the terms Esso, for the oil brand or for "it" in Italian, and
probably on the French words soufflé and souffle (breath), as well as, perhaps,
the Italian exclamation "uffa!," meaning "what a drag!," and onomatopoetically
mimicking the sound of sighing, grumbling, or huffing and puffing. The second
line continues this play. Overall, we see the poem generating relations within the
all-male Schola Cantorum in overtly sexual, playfully homoerotic modes, plying
the improper—and overtly heretical—fusion and fission of both bodies and languages, parole and langue, individual singer and reputedly contained collective.
Throughout, the work pokes fun at the notion of "being English" in a poem that
contains no appreciable English (and perhaps, by extension, of "being Italian"
or "being French," as the lines repeatedly lead one to question which language
system is dominating the reading at any given moment). At the same time, the
words for "strangle" or "choke" and "breath" seem to vie with one another for
domination of the choral domain.

   Turning from this individual jacket, which in my experience with several versions of the work appears to be an erratic instance, to behold the vortex of the poem
inside, we grapple with an even more disorienting reading experience. Beholders/
listeners, whether reading still or in motion, may try to track the progression
of phrases from the relatively straightforward "l'être anglais" and "leʒanglais" to
"l'être en trance" or "en tranche" through "l'être anche, l'être onche," through the
passive, "bottom" condition of "le tre enculé" (recalling with a difference the corner pun of figure 2.4) and the more condensed "l'etrankulé" (the line "le tratran-
quille e" seems to uplift the feminine "e"). In translational terms, this progression
brings us from "being English" to "the three English," through "being in a trance"
or "being in edges/a spine/a group/a slice," to "being also" (between French and

Italian) and "being ounces" (using an unfamiliar Norman term from Jersey) to "being" or "the three" "screwed in the ass" and a Maltese expression for "the tranquil." Throughout, *lettre* or *letter* confuses itself with *l'être* or *to be*, and with *le tre*, or *the three*, as well as with *trés*, or *very*, and *tra*, or *between*: this quashing leads to more or less liminal phrasings, such as "l'être en trenche/l'étrangler/l'entrangle" ("to be in a trench"/"the choking"/"the entr-strangle").

To add to the anarchy, in the context of so many visual and sonic disturbances of the same syllables, readers may well begin adding or subtracting consonants and changing vowels on their own, creating new permutations not inscribed into the work itself. This object-poem makes language itself a force of nature or errant machine, reproducing itself in the space *tra*, or "between," letters and languages: being English/being in a trance/being in a trench/the estriangle/being "anche" (also)—whirled for the duration of the experience into lettres étranges, or "foreign letters."

The circular form of *Disco Muto*, which induces a vertigo of reading, was later expanded into a third and more carnal dimension in Villa's collaboration on sculptural *Idrologie*, a collaboration with the same artists, for which Craia created transparent or translucent plastic spheres filled with water, upon which texts and other found textures are screen-printed in multiple colors (figure 2.10). These objects were exhibited in a show for Napoli's Galleria Il Centro in February

FIGURE 2.10 Emilio Villa, with Silvio Craia and Giorgio Cegna, page spread from *Idrologie, con 6 serigrafie* (Edar, 1969). Copyright Estates of Emilio Villa, Renzo Tortelli, and Roberto Gaetani. Courtesy of Museo di Arte Moderna e Contemporanea di Trento e Rovereto.

1970 and accompanied by a screen-printed manifesto signed by all three artists, reading in wriggling, palimpsestic lines in all caps: "The Hydrologies or critical spheres we have thought up, executed, and launched are to be considered pedagogical apertures that can start the maneuvering of an ideological transplant/complaint [*TRAPIANTOCOMPIANTO*] to carry out upon the sterility of lingual mechanisms, vehicles (glutens, pollens), if not sources of frustration and stupidity."[143] Fragments of this text appear on the spheres themselves, along with other bits of linguistic and nonlinguistic detritus, such as found texts of headlines and school textbooks. But once again and in a more extreme way than in *Disco Muto*, the virtual process of reading, because it is subject to the ball's virtual or literal rolling, trumps any careful tracing of letters. The "pedagogical aperture" effected by this xenoglossic teaching text constitutes a lesson in unlearning the ABCs, reshuffling sterile "lingual mechanisms" and ideology, and transplanting hydrology in their place.

In an unusual catalog produced with Rome's Edar Press in 1969, the *Idrologie* were reproduced as color photographs picturing the artists in playful, affectionately homosocial or amorously queer poses around the plastic spheres and occasional hourglass shapes (figure 2.11). Each printing features a unique silkscreened cover apparently reusing the manifesto stencils, six silkscreened prints, fifteen color photographs of the sculptures, and a dense theoretical text by Villa. This

FIGURE 2.11 Emilio Villa, with Silvio Craia and Giorgio Cegna, page spread from *Idrologie, con 6 serigrafie* (Edar, 1969). Copyright Estates of Emilio Villa, Renzo Tortelli, and Roberto Gaetani. Photograph by Jennifer Scappettone. Courtesy of Museo della Carale.

preface is printed in black and on select spreads in offset blues and oranges, the complementary colors' superimposition inducing a sense of dizziness.[144] Villa's barely penetrable Italian is riddled with neologisms and scientific jargon, altered citations in Latin, dialect terms, and comic asides. The artist's book *Idrologie: palle giranti strutture idrologiche* (1968) was also published with unique silk-screened covers, a black and white interior, and additional images in an edition of two hundred copies by the Casa editrice d'arte Foglio OG in Macerata, with which Villa frequently collaborated and which hosted many of Villa's most experimental works.[145]

We might translate the title of this work as *Hydrologies: balls reeling hydrological structures* (although this translation does not reproduce the "anti strutture" [antistructures] embedded across distinct lexemes in Villa's ludic title). Villa's text begins,

> Inventing the sphere (right, not the sphere of the Euclidean fog, but the parthenogenetic, amoeboidizable, planktic sphere, in sum an ex sphere), the sphere of lexical torment, I thought of balls (yeah, when one says balls, the balls that spin, that wobble, everyone laughs; however the pornophysiological layer is not wholly absent) as strike and counterstrike (the kytographic, and ryptological, anaphantic [kytographica, e ryptologale, anaphantica] extremities, mesophonic centers splayed, juxtaposed, amalgamated), yes, as salient and homologously descendant orbit, the hybrid to see as sequence and arrest, as discord and annulment, as marriage [connubio] (con/nubes) and separation; and, yeah, come on, as demiurgic tableware:[146]

By choosing the sphere as poetic form—the corporeal "palle che girano, che dondolano" (balls that spin, that sway)—Villa proposes "an intransigent and militant threat to visual equilibrium, to the static," an entire orbit in which water within contributes to continual motion and disorientation, "assaulted by the flagellum of the unpreyable transverbal." Instead of Euclidean geometry, we behold a sphere recalling drifting primary and primordial monocellular organisms, recalling plankton or amoeboids, recalling glutens and fertile grains of pollen. Instead of ideology, we get hydrology or spinning balls—with the corporeal association and link to a slew of vulgar expressions being deliberate.

Translating work with the circle and spiral of the "record album" into the three dimensions of a sphere, these sculptures embody a form far more elemental. Despite the obvious association with testicles in the "palle" that appear everywhere in day-to-day vernacular Italian speech and that in antiquity signaled uncontrolled male passion, this sphere is described as "parthenogenetic" (from the Greek for "of virgin birth"), referring to reproduction not requiring male fertilization (and inviting contrast with Marinetti's *Mafarka le Futuriste: Romain Africain*, which fantasized reproduction without women). As embodied in the image of the men embracing the ball from both sides, however, the work strongly recalls Aristophanes's speech on the origins of Eros in Plato's *Symposium*. According to this myth, there were originally three genders ruled by the sun, earth, and moon; each human being was round like their celestial parent and could roll powerfully over and over. In a story much like that of Babel, two of these men, Otys and Ephialtes, dared to scale heaven, causing Zeus's division of each human being into two merely walking parts, and their subsequent carnal longing for one another.

The form of the globe as a political as well as planetary construct, so often used in school and newly apprehended as a lonely marble since the 1969 Apollo landing, presides over these sculptures, whereas the intimacy of the balls tinted a fleshy orange refuses to resolve itself into geopolitics. In fact, that the spheres are filled with water alters our understanding of the sculpture, causing the "globe" to recall, instead, the chaotic primeval "waters" of Babylonian myth from which earth was divided in Enūma Eliš and Genesis; once solid land is established, the primordial ooze is vanquished, and Occidental origin stories become those of an anthropocentric, patriarchal, territorialized realm of the Word reinforced by the opening of the Book of John. Thereafter, such a sphere of ooze, such watery chaos, egglike, becomes regarded as "dissolute" and is "suffocated in every moment of its unrolling and seminating itself"—the latter verb harboring a distinct echo of the "seedbed" where Villa was first trained in Latin, the "seminary" ("ad ogni attimo o punto del suo svolgersi e seminarsi, soffocato"). Still, the rolling, innocently "rotund" spheres undercut this authority, in "prosecuted, ready, re-volution, upheaval-unfolding [re-voluzione, rivolgimento-svolgimento perseguito, pronto]," so that, Villa proclaims, "it's enough to roll together with the spheres to feel free, delivered from the obstacles of public persuasion and public drivel."[147]

While Villa's description of the spheres as "demiurgic tableware" may verge on joke ("e, te, va, stoviglie demiurgiche"), the work this artist wishes to perform on language constitutes no less than geopoetics, or creation of an alternative world. Harboring the grunt work of the belly in rumbling, equalizing without being bound to units of measure, the balls are described as "global phono-graphic shelters of nervous borborygms and sectors of equalization not bound to units of measurement: liberation, torn release from the laws and public intimidations of the reigning language [ricoveri fonico-grafici globali di borborigmi nervosi e settori di perequazioni non vincolate a unità di misura: liberazione, strappo svincolo dalle leggi e dalle intimidazioni pubbliche del linguaggio imperante]."[148]

They mold indeed the sort of literary future transgressing measure that James espied or predicted in the abracadabrant word.

Villa routes both the caustic disillusionment and the utopianism experienced in the immediate aftermath of Fascism into poetic receptacles capable of hosting xenoglossic instances of ideological dislodging. His stanzas reflect the welter of cultures inherent within the institution of any national or transnational postwar modernism—dramatizing that syncretism can only truthfully come to fruition in tumult. Such poetic environments render to the senses the synthesis and ecstatic dispersion of cantons, those political and linguistic subdivisions of nations, and redraft as spiral the geometry of corners that, imposed on language and sound, form "cantos," or songs.

3

Amelia Rosselli's Disintegrating Canto(n)s and the Holy Ghost of Parental Tongues

SONGS OF THE STATE VERSUS THE IDIOLECT OF PANMUSIC

In December 1945, Amelia Pincherle Rosselli (Venice 1870–Florence 1954), an acclaimed dramaturge, translator, political activist, feminist, and writer of children's literature, was preparing to return to her home in Florence from Larchmont, New York. She had endured eight years of exile across four countries, during which she served as matriarchal compass for the widows and children of her assassinated sons. Hailing from a family of secular bourgeois Jewish Venetians with a distinguished history of involvement in the independence and creation of the Italian nation-state—encompassing ties to Daniele Manin's 1848 revolution against Austrian colonization in Venice, to the preeminent exiled republican activist/politician Giuseppe Mazzini in London, and to the establishment of a national legal code in Rome—Amelia, separated from her husband since the turn of the twentieth century, had raised three sons. The first, Aldo, died young fighting in the Great War; her second and third sons were murdered in 1937 for militating against the Fascist state at home and abroad. Carlo, a political economist, and Nello, a historian, were also journalists and practitioners of what Carlo theorized as liberal socialism in his only book printed during his lifetime (written in secret on the prison island of Lipari, hidden in an old piano and smuggled out by his wife Marion, then published in 1930 from exile in France).[1] Before their assassination, they spearheaded essential open and clandestine actions to promote a revolution toward a modernized democracy. Both brothers had been arrested and sent into confinement (confino, or the Fascist practice of deporting enemies of the state to remote outposts in southern Italy). Nello was released; Carlo escaped and, from Paris, helped found Giustizia e Libertà (Justice and Liberty),

FIGURE 3.1 Front page of *Giustizia e Libertà*, vol. 5, no. 2 (January 14, 1938), published from Paris. Courtesy of the Fondazione Circolo Rosselli, Florence.

the most influential non-Marxist movement of the Italian Resistance (figure 3.1). Carlo also organized and fought in a brigade against Franco in Spain, disseminating the slogan "Oggi qui, domani in Italia" (Today in Spain, tomorrow in Italy) through a November 1936 broadcast on Barcelona Radio that may have triggered the brothers' murder. The Fratelli Rosselli were killed in Normandy at the hands of a French Fascist cell of terrorists (the Cagoule, or Organisation secrète d'action révolutionnaire nationale, compared by American journalists of the time to the Ku Klux Klan) in conjunction with the Italian Fascist secret service.

Meditating upon the imminent return to her Florentine home after the war, the mother of Carlo and Nello composed a letter to her friend Piero Calamandrei—an author, jurist, professor, and politician who had cofounded the center-left Action Party clandestinely in 1942 as an extension of the Rosselli brothers' tragically disrupted activism. Calamandrei would eventually compose the facade plaque for Amelia's home in Via Giusti memorializing her sons' sacrifice (though not her own; see figure 3.2). In 1941, Calamandrei had printed several hundred copies of his memoir *Inventario della casa di campagna* (*Inventory of the Country House*) as a

FIGURE 3.2 Plaque, with text by Piero Calamandrei, in memory of Carlo and Nello Rosselli at the house of Amelia Pincherle Rosselli, Florence. Photograph by Jennifer Scappettone.

private gift for friends. From the horror of war and the Pact of Steel with Nazi Germany, in lyrical prose, the book describes his childhood memories of the Tuscan countryside. The work closes with an extended reflection on this region as a more appropriate fatherland: "Paese dove ogni sorriso sfuma in mestizia... gli ipogei e i fiori che si nutrono delle loro ceneri, i nostri lutti, il nostro amore, il passato e l'avvenire, le nostre speranze, la nostra libertà: Toscana, dolce patria nostra [Country where every smile dissipates into mournfulness... the hypogeums and the flowers nourished upon their ashes, our cycles of mourning, our love, the past and the future, our hopes, our liberty: Tuscany, our sweet fatherland]."[2] Reading this work incited Amelia to express her longing for her native landscape and language: "You cannot imagine what it means for those living far away from their own country, from their own language, to hear it resound like this, as a song of ineffable sweetness. 'It's like a music [È come una musica],' said one of my young granddaughters yesterday, whom I made read aloud a bit of your *Inventory* to make her more sure of her Italian which is—alas—vacillating. And it seemed to me the most exacting and summarizing judgment.... This thirst for Italian is truly painful."[3]

The granddaughter made to read aloud could potentially have been Silvia Rosselli, daughter of Nello, who was born in 1928 in Rome. Yet the girl's exclamation in response to the Italian text accords perfectly instead with the experience of Amelia's namesake: the daughter of Carlo, liberal socialism's primary theorist and frontline fighter, who was in the womb during his storied escape from Lipari and by consequence born in Paris in 1930. The granddaughter in question must have been the fifteen-year-old Amelia Rosselli, for whom, as a refugee between France, Switzerland, England, and the United States for the first seven years of life, the Italian language emerged as "vacillating" (vacillante) or wavering between experiences: something of a foreign tongue, closer to the abstraction of lyricism, demanding practice in reading out loud. The younger Amelia's lifelong penchant for music would formalize itself shortly thereafter through study, but she routed musical passion and research increasingly through language in the practice of poetry, becoming in the process one of the most searing voices of the twentieth century. The same instinct that could have enabled the young Amelia (or Melina, as she was called at home)—the future musician, musicologist, and poet—to proclaim a passage of Italian prose to be like music also encapsulated the reason for which she would never be able to express a sentiment such as her grandmother's, wherein the privilege of ownership can be applied to the Italian state of citizenship and language, or that of any other nation, such that the exile can measure the distance "from their own country, from their own language." Being born into a state of flight made that impossible.

The younger Amelia Rosselli became a poet, translator, and cultural critic, her writing invoking the literary traditions of distinct epochs and continents with a liberty modeled by modernist US poetry (which she read in her early twenties in the original language[s]), although without recourse to the heavily citational collage effects of an Eliot or Pound. Composed chiefly in Italian and English but also, early on, in French, her poetry incarnates fascination with early Florentine vernacular lyrics and metaphysical verse, simultaneously striking up colloquy with Hopkins, Lautréamont, Rimbaud, Joyce, Campana, Montale, Pasternak, Ingeborg Bachmann, confessionalism from Lowell through Plath and Berryman, the Black Mountain school, the Beat poets, and postwar leftist investigations of the subaltern cultures of the South by key literary colleagues such as Pier Paolo Pasolini, Carlo Levi, and Rocco Scotellaro. But Rosselli's poetics were shaped equally by her training as a musician and years of musicological study, manifesting explicit structural and conceptual wellsprings in Bach through Chopin; Bartók; post-Webernism; various strains of emergent subaltern studies spanning literature, anthropology, and ethnomusicology; and concrete and electronic music.[4] Her musical education was effectively more formal and advanced than her literary education, although somewhat belated in beginning. Jumpstarted in the late 1940s during her matriculation at St. Paul's Girls' School in London, it evolved through private studies with Luigi Dallapiccola and Guido Turchi; workshops with Karlheinz Stockhausen, David Tudor, György Ligeti, Henri Pousseur, and Luciano Berio at the Darmstadt International Summer Courses for New Music and Dartington College of the Arts; and research at the RAI Phonology Studio founded by Berio and Bruno Madera, where works such as John Cage's "Fontana Mix" and Berio and Cathy Berberian's "Thema (Omaggio a Joyce)" were created, all leading to her eventual "substructuralist" studies of pre- and nontempered music of the East and the Global South. Although Rosselli claimed, in a 1981 interview, to have left music for poetry around 1965, we have archival documents attesting to the fact that in the same period she was sending her essay on the harmonic series to Gérald Bennett at the Centre Pompidou and professors Vladimir Ibler and Branko Soucek in Dubrovnik, hoping (without satisfaction), as she described it, to disseminate this work in a more socialist, more experimental, and less "anthropological" context than was possible in contemporary Italy.[5]

In 1965, Rosselli, well into both musical and poetic study and having just published her first collection of verse accompanied by a tractate on meter, made a bold claim for the music that she was seeking: "Io aspiro alla panmusica, alla musica di tutti, della terra e dell'universo, in cui non ci sia più una mano individuale che la regoli [I aspire to panmusic, to the music of everyone, of the earth and of the universe, in which there is no longer an individual hand that governs it]."[6] The intervention speaks to her extensive readings in musicology undertaken as a young woman—resonating with the ideals of world harmony expressed in Alain Danielou's work on tuning and vibration, which must have influenced her lifelong interest in the harmonic series.[7] This ideal of arriving at the music of everyone, echoing antique notions of a universal musicality of the spheres, would find itself in constant battle, however, with the dissonance of her aesthetics in the aftermath of a totalitarian culture and what turned out to be Rosselli's irreparable status of outsider in every country and city—particularly given that her musicality ended up settling in the realm of language, a medium scored against panlyricism with geopolitical divisions. The paradox is registered in an Italian-language entry from her "Diario in tre lingue," in which notes on her evolving practice are woven through her other "native" tongues, English and French, as well.[8] The passage seems at first to be playing on, practicing, or parodying through rhyme the way that inverting the syntax of subject and verb and placing postverbal subjects in different places in a phrase produce a slightly different tone or emphasis in Italian in a manner that is impossible in English: "si dimette dal consiglio municipale la flottiglia navale / si dimette la flottiglia navale dal consiglio municipale [the naval flotilla resigns/steps down from the municipal council / it is the naval flotilla that resigns from the municipal council]." The word "municipal" hails from "municipium," the Latin for a free town governed by its own laws, and "municeps," or a citizen of Rome. The notion that a naval flotilla would be part of a municipal council in the first place skewers any ideal of a city without the need for military defense. Rosselli goes on to produce a provocative parallel between the naval flotilla's (parodic because inappropriate to the context) "resignation" from civic life and that of the speaker: "Ed io che mi dimetto ogni giorno dal consiglio municipale, «mi domando se non sia possibile, in un assurdo sforzo, dimenticare quanto è intorno a me per rinchiudermi nelle alchimie di un linguaggio buono a ogni latitudine» [And I who resign/step down/ discharge myself from the municipal council every day, 'ask myself if it wouldn't be possible, in an absurd effort, to forget how much is around me in order to enclose myself in the alchemies of a language good at every latitude'"] (*LP*, 141).

This fragment, whose final phrase is quoted often, but out of context, articulates the dream of a transnational language. Yet the passage also voices the persecuting history of tension between active citizenship such as that of her family and the militant retribution of the state that was to harrow Rosselli's oeuvre, charging and tormenting its political concerns and the nonnational languages in which they become uncomfortably lodged. It is a history that influenced her stepping away (or "stepping down," "resigning") from the sphere of realpolitik and the compromised solutions of policy.

The tension between the idyll of universal communication and the distressed poetic languages that arise from engagement with geopolitical fracture too intimately experienced to idealize led me to write this book. The endeavor was born on the heels of a dozen years of work researching Rosselli's poetics in the service of an act of editing and translation that was published in March 2012 under the title *Locomotrix: Selected Poetry and Prose of Amelia Rosselli*. Such tension lent itself poorly, if at all, to any "definitive" edition of translations of Rosselli's "Italian" writings into "English" ones, although the pressure to be definitive haunted me as an editor of an early critical anthology of Rosselli's selected poetry and prose, technically the first to be published.[9] Any labor of translation aiming at a so-called general public is assumed to transport the poem from one national language to another, but Rosselli's work properly resides in the lexical, syntactical, and sonic spaces in between. Such a socioaesthetic space, a limbo or vertigo between tongues, is one that is increasingly occupied by our contemporaries in poetry. Such "vacillation" was not welcomed, however, by prior generations of publishers or readers; in fact, the work of Rosselli and Villa appeared to inspire repulsion in both mainstream publishers and nonspecialist readers and listeners at the time I began studying and translating this work twenty-five years ago.

The piece of Rosselli's final sentence above that names the "absurd effort" of enclosing oneself in the oblivion of removal from actual conditions and in the plural "alchemies" of a language that would work at any point of the Global North or South is anomalously lodged within quotation marks, as if to distance it from the speaking subject and from reality. The conjectured alchemy was to be undertaken through the poetry Rosselli would develop over the course of decades of research and experimentation: a transformation of the fell matter of language into the (would-be) universal elixir of a lyricism lacking—or, to be more accurate, exceeding—an I.

In "Metrical Spaces," Rosselli identifies a musical, logical, and associative current beneath the seemingly singular language in which she writes, which brings all peoples together. If the poet's "sonorous logical and associative experience is ... that of all peoples, and reflectable in all languages," then this shared experience can be captured by a poetic stanza conceived as a capacious cube or square, permitting it to fill with the prosody of all languages, culling "all possible imaginable rhythms" within the space simultaneously (*OP*, 184, 187). The dream of a poetry shot through with the rhythms of languages the world over—a dream suspended, hovering over her poetic compositions—gave rise to the theoretical question at the heart of this book.

The ideal of a language good at every latitude comes constantly into conflict with the actual lived experience of politically defined languages, their shibboleths and severances. The subjects of Rosselli's poetry cannot "forget" all that is around them, although their political surroundings might be reflected with extreme obliquity within the art of a unique sensibility galvanized and scarred by history. Still, the utopian search for a universal language remains staunchly articulated. Rosselli's work taught me early on that xenoglossia doesn't have to represent an inspired speaking of the languages of others in the service of domination; it can constitute inspired use of dominant language from the perspective of a refugee, turning the power dynamic assumed by evangelist interpretations of Pentecostal communication across cultural boundaries on its head. This chapter explores Rosselli's tortured Pentecost as a confrontation with the holy ghosts of the tongues she inherited, although never to the point that she expressed being 100 percent at home with them. The difficulty of her idiolect has led the political aspirations of her poetry to be left aside in historical discourse surrounding the Rosselli family's renowned political commitments. But if we understand those commitments in an expanded field, we can grasp their continuum in terms of her war on monolithic language and reparative advocacy for "the music of everyone."

Amelia Pincherle Rosselli, her English daughter-in-law Marion Cave Rosselli (London 1896–London 1949), and Marion and Carlo's daughter Melina

FIGURE 3.3 From left, women pictured are Amelia Pincherle Rosselli, Marion Cave, Amelia ("Melina") Rosselli, Maria Rosselli, and Tullia Zevi in Paterson, New Jersey, June 11, 1944. Male figures and photographer unidentified by archivists. Photograph by Jennifer Scappettone. Courtesy of the Italian Ministry of Culture and the Archivio di Stato di Firenze. Poster behind the group reads "AMERICAN RELIEF FOR ITALY / RECEIVING STATION."

(Paris 1930—Rome 1996) were brilliant, committed women whose contributions to twentieth-century political and literary culture have been overshadowed by the illustrious men in their lives (figure 3.3). Isabelle Richet has highlighted through dedicated study of Marion Cave how anti-Fascist activist women "had to devise new forms of intervention in the public spheres marked by a great fluidity of structure and a free movement across European frontiers," given that existing political organizations did not accept them as equal partners. Seeking to map the "new political space" created by these interventions, she demonstrates how women played a crucial role in the work of counterinformation against Fascism overseas, for instance, where Mussolini was cast in a positive light as a domesticator of labor and bulwark against Bolshevism.[10] Cave, who arrived in Florence in 1919 on scholarship for a master's degree and who taught English literature at the University of Florence in the 1920s, emerges as a militant and passionate figure whose work against Fascism should not be erased by the more canonical interventions on the part of her husband to which they were linked. Hailing from a humble Irish Quaker upbringing, with a father whose political tendencies mixed

Labour and anarchist sympathies, Cave emerges upon reflection as a chief force in Carlo Rosselli's turn away from the academy and from the bourgeois upbringing of his youth toward full-time political activism (in contrast with Nello, who remained an academic historian and whose family—including Aldo and Silvia, two of Amelia's cousins who became writers—therefore enjoyed a modicum of peace and stability by comparison). Cave's commitment encompassed prominent participation in Gaetano Salvemini's democratic debating club Circolo di Cultura, a leading role in the semilegal protests in Florence against the 1924 murder of the Socialist opposition MP Giacomo Matteotti, and work as secretary and general factotum for the first anti-Fascist clandestine paper in Italy, *Non Mollare! (Do Not Yield!)*. "I typed all the handwritten copy and always sat near the stove, so I could throw the sheets into the fire if there was a police raid," she remembered in a 1944 interview conducted in Larchmont; "When the sheets were typed I carried them away concealed in my clothing."[11] Cave would end up as a key mediator in the war of information across national boundaries, training other women in the use of invisible ink and developing a code that used ordinary books and newspapers to communicate with political dissidents who were sentenced to confinement on the islands of the south. Ruth Nattermann has worked with the unpublished private documents of the Rosselli family to reconstruct their extraordinary lives in and out of exile, building upon the work of feminist historians such as Patrizia Gabrielli, who contest the view of anti-Fascism as a "temple of virility" established by historiography.[12] Together with Richet, Nattermann builds a context in which we can understand the power of writing in contouring a new transnational political space of contestation against Fascism.

Resituating the work of the Rosselli women in relation to one another, we are able to continue piecing together the mosaic of an exceptionally committed family's counterproposals to tyranny over several generations of conflict, supplementing the standing historical record with persuasive testimony of the way that artistic and affective labor drive political change—although often on different and more easily obscured spatial and temporal scales. This is work that can already be grasped in reading Melina's youthful letters in Italian to her grandmother, where we witness her, for instance, asking for and mediating the publication of Carlo's autobiographical and economic writings, celebrating the return of her father's body to Italy from Paris's Père Lachaise Cemetery in 1951, and reasoning through her incipient affiliation with the Communist Party as she reads colossal literary classics such as Amelia the elder's copy of *Guerra e pace*.

Disciplinary rigidity, truisms about poetry's aloofness from collective life, and the seeming anomalousness of Rosselli's poetic voice, from its content to the literal sound of her accent, have led to the fact that the verse of Melina is routinely siloed away from discussions of the family's political influence. As a writer who believes in the social value of language work—its ability to move us through social ills and routes beyond that exceed the pragmatic strictures of policy and political programs—I consider this an opportunity gravely missed. It has been well established that the life of the younger Amelia Rosselli was profoundly influenced by the motion engendered by Carlo and Nello's activism and their 1937 assassination: the family's movements between France, Switzerland, England, Italy, and Westchester County, New York, the locus of the family's ultimate wartime shelter thanks to the intervention of First Lady Eleanor Roosevelt, the Mazzini Society, and Max Ascoli of the New School for Social Research. The younger Amelia Rosselli was both the embodiment of and the exception to the postwar panorama in Italy and beyond. She was in the womb when Marion Cave was arrested for organizing Carlo's sensational escape from Lipari in 1929. Feminist and activist groups in England rallied for the release of Cave and her unborn child, leading to their quick release.[13] Nevertheless, Amelia spent the greater part of her first two decades in a continual displacement triggered by the terrorist act of the French Cagoulards when she was seven years old. She was brought up in three tongues and educated in as many (and more) literary traditions; she began writing in each before settling primarily in Italian upon the untimely death of her companion Rocco Scotellaro. One of the lasting monuments to the Rosselli family's experience is a prismatic, polyglot poetry of resistance that challenges us with truculence to continue seeking and redefining the language, the shape and sound, of belonging.

The career of the younger Amelia deviates from that of her more liberal and patriotic elders, however, in expressing a jarring suspicion surrounding projects of nation-building. This outcome is hardly surprising considering the excesses of nationalism that led to the Rosselli family tragedy; it will persist, in forms transmogrifying with the times, all her life, to be encapsulated in her later years by her paranoia about being persecuted by the CIA. In an unpublished 1952 letter written to her brother John in English (the language of nearly all their correspondence with one another), the twenty-two-year-old Amelia reveals herself to be markedly tormented by the question of political action:

> Its [sic] all very well to live as nobly as one can—but in certain matters this proves too thin: how am I to act, politically? . . . I know that in every manner one acts one does harm and good together. Nothing stops me from believing that one may even kill, remorseless, though I know that he who kills will in turn be killed; tooth for tooth. What's more, politically speaking, I will not sacrifice the hopes of tomorrow for the comforts of today. . . . Am I also to stand still and wait? I know I am <u>made</u> for action—how can I do so without vision, and on such a basis?

This visionary yet perforce realist young woman refuses "to sacrifice the hopes of tomorrow for the comforts of today," yet recognizes that every act entails doing both good and ill at once, so that her longings to live "nobly" fail to coalesce in a single vision like that of the Fratelli Rosselli's liberal socialism: "no 'vision' at all has come in comfort—nothing!"[14] This blend of political resolve and skepticism, although persistent, does not lead the eventual poet to withdraw into the private spheres of confession typical of mid- to late twentieth-century poetry. Rosselli explicitly rejected such withdrawal, expressing a wish to compose an objective poetry "where the I is the public."[15] In the place of the nation and in concert with the committed communist intellectuals of her generation, the harmonic I of Rosselli's poetry will forge solidarity with communities of narrowing and dilating scales, from the regional—that of the canton, in minoritarian folk cultures of the Global South witnessing an upwelling of attention from the first wave of subaltern studies—to the international, following culture and politics abroad with acuity for the remainder of her life.[16] Ultimately dodging the need for an all-encompassing "vision" through the tactics of music and verse, Rosselli conceived of the poem as a "total" environment (one might generatively employ the term utopia) hosting a staunchly transregional polyphony—and polyrhythm.[17]

Rather than viewing Rosselli's poetic practice as a withdrawal from political life, we must see in it a contestation of the means by which political life was being fabricated in her time—contrasting not merely the immediate past of Fascist domination but also the compromising oblivion of centrist Christian Democrats that led the Italian government from 1946 through 1981 and that largely chose not to punish war crimes or to expunge Fascist monuments from the national landscape. Piero Calamandrei's lapidary memorial to the Rosselli brothers on Via Giusti, mounted in 1947, contributes to (selective) memory of the Italian Resistance through inspirational imagery of a rare eloquence, presenting a picture of unequivocal victory against the "Fascist ambush" (figure 3.2):

> But the oppressors duped themselves in vain
> to have brought night upon those two brows
> when dawn arose
> upon every summit of Italy
> thousands and thousands of voluntary fighters
> for the Rosselli brigades were seen armed
> with [the Rosselli brothers'] very face
> which bore engraved upon the flame
> a cry launched by a people to the future
> JUSTICE AND LIBERTY

Calamandrei's tablet, as a fragment of "civil religion," has been described as "a political pedagogy for the new Italy," contrasting the reactionary forces that were extinguishing the energies of the left in the service of sundry interests, from the mafia to the Marshall Plan.[18] The tablet articulates the aspirational heroic context in which Amelia Rosselli would choose to live in Italy, unlike her brothers John and Andrea, who settled in England and Indiana, respectively, as the siblings' choice of "homeland" was anything but obvious. The political situation was in actuality rather more ambiguous than rendered by the inscription, despite strong sentiments on all sides.[19] No one in Italy paid for the assassination of the Rosselli brothers: prosecution of those responsible "degenerated into absurdity," in the words of Carlo's biographer Stanislao Pugliese.[20] Minister of Justice and Communist Party leader Palmiro Togliatti issued a general amnesty for the crimes of Fascism in June 1946 as part of a widespread effort of reconciliation aimed at integrating rank-and-file Fascists into a democratic state, and many Fascist government functionaries continued to serve, after the war, in high-ranking roles equivalent to those of their past. Meanwhile, the overwhelming influence of the United States in postoccupation Italy brought the interests of transnational capital to exercise a new, less appreciably authoritarian form of hegemony over Italian culture in a Cold War phenomenon that Pasolini, a communist and close comrade to Rosselli responsible for her first poetic publication opportunities, viewed as the new fascism.[21]

It was not only party politicians who were responsible for domestication of the historical record on a conflict that, as Claudio Pavone has argued, encompassed three conflicts in one within Italy: a patriotic war, a class war, and a civil war.[22] Works of theater, film, and literature took part in evening out a picture of suffering and resistance devoid of complicity that ended up reinforcing a myth of Italians as good people (known through the formulation "italiani, brava gente") and depicted Germans as invading barbarians rather than yesterday's allies. Historian Rosario Forlenza offers a useful synthesis of the fabrication of cultural memory in Italy after the war—a memory that encompasses forgetting, or a "process of oblivion," so as to portray Italians as victims rather than creators of and collaborators with Fascism and Nazism; in building this thesis, he cites literary works such as Salvatore Quasimodo's 1944 poem "Alle fronde dei salici" ("On the Willow Boughs"), which was instantly canonized as part of the grade-school curriculum, becoming part of a narrative of martyrdom.[23] A brief pause to note the difference between this poetry and those of the present study is instructive:

> E come potevamo noi cantare
> con il piede straniero sopra il cuore,
> fra i morti abbandonati nelle piazze

...al lamento
d'agnello dei fanciulli, all'urlo nero
della madre che andava incontro al figlio
crocifisso sul palo del telegrafo?
Alle fronde dei salici, per voto,
anche le nostre cetre erano appese,
oscillavano lievi al triste vento[24]

And how could we sing
with that foreign foot upon our heart,
among the dead abandoned in the squares,
...to the lamb cry
of the children, to the black howl
of the mother running after her son
crucified on a telegraph pole?
On the willow boughs, as ex voto,
even our lyres were hanged,
softly wavering in the sad wind

The poem reworks Psalm 137 to take up the trope of Jewish exile in Babylon that we have previously encountered in Villa's poetry—in very different clothing. Beyond the romantic lyricism of these lines, their ease of accessibility to a generalized Italian public, and their nostalgia even in light of the irruptive "modern" image of the telegraph pole as gallows, we note the intactness of the third person plural here—and its coherent innocence in contradistinction to the "foreign foot" of the invader.

Rosselli's poetry, which was not at all accommodating to uptake by regimes of cultural memory—and far from mimetic of national outcomes in its lexical density and about-face on narrative—emerges as more accurately expressive than either canonized lyric or lapidary tablet of the reality of political language as a tool of collective aggression. For a brutally direct picture of the latter, we can turn to political scientist and journalist Sergio Romano, an exact contemporary of Rosselli who became a member of the bureaucratic class. Romano reflects on the reality of diplomatic language from the point of view of an Italian representative to NATO and ambassador to Moscow in the final years of the USSR—from the point of view, that is, of one who witnessed at first hand the transition between a geopolitical sphere dominated by Fascism and one dominated by the agons of the Cold War. Romano points out that diplomatic language is inherently aggressive, "because it is the instrument a nation uses to affirm, vindicate, contest, refute. Every diplomatic expression is implicitly threatening . . . because it relates to affairs which may at any time call for the use of force: even the most courteous of formulas reveals, beneath it, a potential hostility."[25] We witness this hostility unveiled and transmuted at work in the theater of Rosselli's verse, which transmutes the lapidary tablet imaginatively into a "matchstick" capable of setting history and the present moment afire: "La lapide un fiammifero" (*LP*, 491).

Rosselli's first verse and prose experiments across English, French, and Italian constitute a mirror, an oppositional locus, for the idiom of a pragmatic and ultimately collaborationist late twentieth-century politics that, in the words of the eminent conservative Romano, "must resolve its own aggressiveness within a praetorium where words try to kill one another." The title of her first published collection, the Italian *Variazioni belliche* (translatable as *Bellic Variations* or *Bellicose Variations* [1964]), makes this antagonism explicit. Romano refers to NATO, a diplomatic sphere effectively governed through American English, as a "great linguistic laboratory" wherein one is "constantly subjected to a sort of lexical bombardment coming from America," so that diplomats must use "terms like: dual track decision, first use, dual capable aircraft, first strike, hard target kill." Diplomatic "heteroglottism," by which Romano means the assumption of US English in addition to that of one's native national tongue, must compromise with US English's upstart bequest: "Bellicose, but constrained by its own nature to wage war in the realm of words, it can register only partial victories or, if you prefer, compromises."[26] Rosselli's bellicosity in all three languages but beginning, as we shall see, with an English not confinable to any particular nation-state disputes the straitjacketing and neutralizing language of compromise as well as the hegemonic postwar tongue of diplomatic violence in favor of a teeming hybridity: herein, ideals like that of the nation or of a universal language are haunted by their inevitable debts to other cultures and their inevitable harm.

Rosselli's poetry, that is, plies its way between discursive systems in a manner distinct from dominant cosmopolitan forms of heteroglottism in both twentieth-century politics and twentieth-century literature—the latter typified by the delirious multinational pastiches of her contemporaries in the neoavanguardia and the multilingual montages of their touted modernist predecessors. Her poetry stages the roiling of one linguistic system *within* another, which is more alarming than if it were to allow languages to cohabit without contaminating one another. It makes them unheimlich, unhome-ly spaces, wherein the "home" language of any given poem can become, in Rosselli's handling, a "homicile," in her own coinage from *Sleep: Poems in English*—a hostile fusion of domicile and homicide.[27] Conforming to the linguist's sense of an "idiolect" in its singularity, this idiom is radically inclusive—one is tempted to deploy the term "catholic"—at the level of conception. But it registers as "barbarous" in practice, as it calls out the geopolitical center for its barbarism: "Vissuta in Italia, paese barbaro," she writes in a rare autobiographical line of *Bellic Variations*; "Experienced in Italy, barbarous country" (*OP*, 45).

In 1944, the renegade Swiss linguist Frederick Bodmer proposed in a volume housed in Rosselli's personal library—an aid to her autodidactic studies of languages such as German titled *The Loom of Language: A Guide to Foreign Languages for the Home Student*—that "the constructive task of devising . . . an *auxiliary* medium to *supplement* existing national languages is . . . one of the foremost needs of our time," a prerequisite to keeping the world's peace.[28] One of Bodmer's epigraphs, from H. G. Wells's *Travels of a Republican Radical in Search of Hot Water* (1939), accuses the "old-type historians" of glossing over how "imposition of a language or a blending of languages gives a new twist and often a new power to the community's mental processes."[29] Yet this contortion is hardly a smooth or painless process. Wells goes on: "A language is an implement quite as much as an implement of stone or steel; its use involves social consequences; it does things to you just as a metal or a machine does things to you. It makes new precision and also new errors possible." Novelty makes such precision and errantry difficult to digest. So although Rosselli may speculate about universal understanding in a pentecostal key, the language of her poems, fraught with mordant truths and errancies too estranging to "follow," was for decades met with chastened approbation and deemed arcane or oracular at best—that of a Cassandra at the threshold of the unrepresentable.

It is particularly valuable to read, and reread, this poetry now; for reimagining the contours of so-called national languages and the possibility of shoring up a collective from the tenuous threshold of citizenship and "respingimento," from the point of view of a refugee, is a crucial task in a moment in which, according to the United Nations Refugee Agency, forced displacement has arrived at a record 139.3 million lives.[30] A three-word poem from *Variazioni belliche* portends what a battle this can be and accounts for its author being perpetually misunderstood or underestimated: "Cercatemi e fuoriuscite," the poem as terse command that, by situating us on a grammatical tightrope between transitive and intransitive states, activity and passivity, places us being hailed in a paradoxical state of banishing at large, without any named object, and of being exiled (*LP*, 421). The articulation, "Seek me & banish," or "Seek me & exile," shelters a ghost of the intransitive expression: *Seek me & be banished/exiled*. Essere fuoriusciti, to be exiled, is not an action one can be commanded to realize as a free agent, however, and as such, the poem feels unfinished, aslant, agrammatical, or "out of tune" (stonato), to use a term that editor Elio Vittorini, himself an anti-Fascist modernist writer and translator, deployed to try getting Amelia to "correct" moments like these. The three-word poem nevertheless bodies forth the *possibility* of inhabiting this verb as a free agent. (Her faith in the power of the "grammar of the poor" was trenchant.)[31] The destination of the exiling action is illocatable, to use a word Rosselli forged when translating Emily Dickinson's lyric 963.[32] Locus, place, hails the poet attuned to sonic kinship whose experimentation takes place in locution, or speech. Here we have an illocution—a poem as speech act that itself achieves the order of placing us at sea, ill at ease, between states of mind and citizenship. The poem harbors additional implications of its commandant as excessive, too much, boundless ("illimitato," to return to Rosselli's translation from Dickinson): "Seek me & leak," "Seek me & erupt," and "Seek me & exceed" (all possible translations of the brief lyric) all imply the chimera and the fear of a transnation of language as well as of the poem's first person, their too-muchness for any given locus (*LP*, 421). By contrast, however sought after through literature, the isolated parental tongues (and the parental figures) of this poet come up short.

An early poem from "October Elizabethans" (dated by Rosselli to 1956) imagines the subjecthood of its protagonist as threefold, each soul a fish scattered overseas: "O were I one in Three! Just like the Holy Ghost, / the Father and the Son, I'd reunite my scattered souls / and string them in from all the seas abroad."[33] We know why it was difficult for Rosselli as neither father nor son, but daughter, to fuse, to fish integrity out of the would-be linguistic trinity of her experience. She chooses to live in Italy in a moment of high optimism toward the building of a new society but lacks the opportunity to fight off a Fascist enemy in heroic key: that enemy, although still latent, has assumed new, ambiguous vestments. Moreover, she is a young woman alone in Italy, a simple yet strikingly unusual aspect of her decision about which the family frets. And she registers both on paper and audibly as a foreigner, early on and enduringly, in spite of yet paradoxically because of her family's distinguished national legacy.

Even in the most immediate of terms, belonging will never be straightforward for a woman who experienced being orphaned early on—losing her father at age seven and her mother at nineteen (to be followed shortly thereafter by her companion Rocco Scotellaro at age twenty-three and her grandmother at twenty-four). Rosselli remembered her mother as "un po' sfuggente, preoccupata" (a bit elusive, worried) and described the sense of disembodiedness that lingered in the memory of her more affectionate father; she characterized the relationship that she and her younger brother Andrea had with both their parents as "un po' evanescenti" (a bit evanescent).[34] Rosselli's verse Pentecost, as it were, is conducted without a stable parental tongue as origin, and it is governed by a secularized, para- holy ghost: there is a distinctly phantasmatic quality to its bestowing of

FIGURE 1.6 F. T. Marinetti and Bruno Munari, *Il poema del vestito di latte: Parole in libertà futuriste*, ed. Ufficio Propaganda SNIA Viscosa (Officina Grafica Esperia, 1937), first page spread depicting combat in Ethiopia alongside a graphic of lungs and a can of milk. Copyright 1937 Bruno Munari. All rights reserved to Maurizio Corraini s.r.l. Published with the permission of The Wolfsonian—Florida International University (Miami, Florida). © 2024 Artists Rights Society (ARS), New York

FIGURE 1.7 F. T. Marinetti and Bruno Munari, *Il poema del vestito di latte: Parole in libertà futuriste*, ed. Ufficio Propaganda SNIA Viscosa (Officina Grafica Esperia, 1937), fourth page spread montaging a scene of milking alongside a factory scene. Copyright 1937 Bruno Munari. All rights reserved to Maurizio Corraini s.r.l. Published with the permission of The Wolfsonian—Florida International University (Miami, Florida). © 2024 Artists Rights Society (ARS), New York

FIGURE 2.7 *Disco Muto (Mute Record) (con il coro della scola cantorum di Macerata solisti Craia e Cegna)*, Emilio Villa, Silvio Craia, and Giorgio Cegna, silkscreen on cardboard, edition of 100, diameter 30 cm, 1967. Photograph by Jennifer Scappettone. Copyright Estate of Emilio Villa. Collection of Biblioteca Nazionale di Firenze.

FIGURE 2.9 Sleeve for *Disco Muto (Mute Record)* at 33 RPM (*con il coro della scola cantorum di Macerata solisti Craia e Cegna*), Emilio Villa, with Silvio Craia and Giorgio Cegna, silkscreen on cardboard, edition of 100, diameter 30 cm, 1967. Photograph by Jennifer Scappettone. Copyright Estate of Emilio Villa. Collection of Museo della Carale, Ivrea.

nata e a completa autonomia o quota di disorientamento. l'obliquo totale, investito dal flagello dell'oltre-verbo non predabile; orbite compatte e disunite della sottocoscienza operata; e motivante su fasci di tensioni disorientate, orripilate, su parabole de-torte del lustro del liscio del lubrico, sul volubile assorbente e che fa sparire.

rale; a ribaltare le superfici caotiche, molli del giudizio; a cercare sbocchi per i riflussi delle spinte problematiche, per le emersioni del dilatabile; a individuare l'oltranza minima-massima delle apparenze generali (i dogmi del così detto visuale inerzialmente subìti, esaltati, patiti), l'aldilà dei procedimenti prevedibili e scontati; a distruggere i residui

FIGURE 2.10 Emilio Villa, with Silvio Craia and Giorgio Cegna, page spread from *Idrologie, con 6 serigrafie* (Edar, 1969). Copyright Estates of Emilio Villa, Renzo Tortelli, and Roberto Gaetani. Courtesy of Mart, Archivio del 900, Fondo Librario Stelio Maria Martini, Rovereto.

Così rivendicare la scena il teatro lo stadium del Libero, evocare spessori geniali, spessori critici dell'empito dinamico su tavole nude e libere.

Così, nel piccolo teatro proposto, cominciare (almeno attestare la volontà) a travolgere il potere della induzione spaziale e tempo-

FIGURE 2.11 Emilio Villa, with Silvio Craia and Giorgio Cegna, page spread from *Idrologie, con 6 serigrafie* (Edar, 1969). Copyright Estates of Emilio Villa, Renzo Tortelli, and Roberto Gaetani. Photograph by Jennifer Scappettone. Courtesy of Museo della Carale, Ivrea.

FIGURE 4.1 Etel Adnan, *Al-Sayyab, Mother and Lost Daughter*, 1970. Ink and watercolor on a Japanese book. Signed, dated, and titled by the artist. Closed, 33 × 25.2 cm × 24 pages. Open, 33 × 612 cm. Copyright Estate of Etel Adnan, Paris. Photograph by Jennifer Scappettone. Courtesy of Donation Claude & France Lemand, Institut du monde arabe, Paris.

FIGURE 4.2 Etel Adnan, *Al-Sayyab, Mother and Lost Daughter*, 1970. Ink and watercolor on a Japanese book. Signed, dated, and titled by the artist. Closed, 33 × 25.2 cm × 24 pages. Open, 33 × 612 cm. Photograph by Jennifer Scappettone. Copyright Estate of Etel Adnan, Paris. Courtesy of Donation Claude & France Lemand, Institut du monde arabe, Paris.

FIGURE 4.4 Etel Adnan, *Al-Sayyab, Mother and Lost Daughter*, 1970. Ink and watercolor on a Japanese book. Signed, dated, and titled by the artist. Closed, 33 × 25.2 cm × 24 pages. Open, 33 × 612 cm. Copyright Estate of Etel Adnan, Paris. Courtesy of Donation Claude & France Lemand, Institut du monde arabe, Paris.

FIGURE 4.5 Etel Adnan, *Allah*, 1987, mixed media on paper (leporello). Copyright Estate of Etel Adnan, Paris. Jordan National Gallery of Fine Arts.

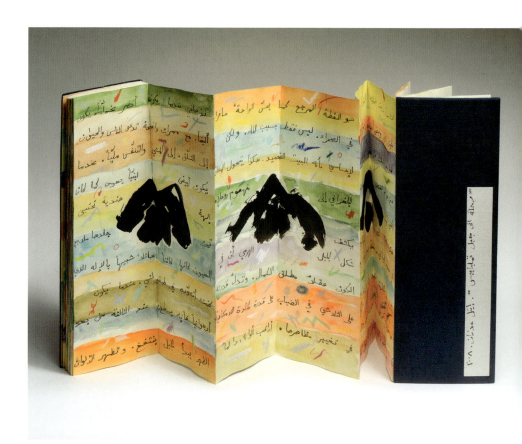

FIGURE 4.9   Etel Adnan, *Rihla ila Jabal Tamalpais* (*Journey to Mount Tamalpais*), 2008. Watercolor and Indian ink on Japanese book, 30 × 10.5 cm × 54 pages: 30 × 567 cm. Copyright Estate of Etel Adnan, Paris. Courtesy of Donation Claude & France Lemand, Institut du monde arabe, Paris.

linguistic competence, hailing from an otherwhere that can never be nailed down. This ghosting proves to be the source of its infinite richness—its harmonics—as well as its scattering of any would-be all-embracing linguistic frame of reference.

"NOT FOR I, NOT FOR ME, THE QUESIT AND THE FULL BOSOM": MOTHER AS VOID

In 1951, we have the first news about Rosselli's exercises in writing—in correspondence with her brother John (in English) and grandmother (in Italian).[35] She is living in Rome, earning a modest income by working part time for the visionary engineer and politician Adriano Olivetti—translating and making editorial suggestions for Edizioni di Comunità, a publishing organ for Olivetti's center-left political movement Movimento Comunità that would make a significant imprint on Italian postwar culture. Rosselli is experimenting with poetic prose in English. This choice of language would be natural, given her high school experiences in two Anglophone contexts (Westchester County and London), but the young Amelia has been reading T. S. Eliot and James Joyce's *Ulysses* alongside her father's *Socialismo liberale*, Gramsci's *Literature and National Life*, André Breton, Benedetto Croce's *Aesthetics*, and Rousseau's *Confessions*—all in the original languages. A letter from November 1950 to her grandmother provides a sample of the wide scope of this twenty-year-old's orbit: it contains updates about the publication of her essay devoted to the harmonic series (to which we will return below); alludes cryptically to the end of her romance with Carlo Levi, friend of her father, painter, and author of the renowned memoir of imposed exile under Fascism, *Christ Stopped at Eboli* (1945); and includes a photograph picturing her in the Piazza del Popolo with her new friend Rocco Scotellaro, a socialist politician from the province of Matera, as well as poet and writer of the intimate sociological study *Peasants of the South*, whom she had met that spring at the national conference on the Italian Resistance and Italian culture in Venice. In this letter, Melina reports to Amelia the elder that she feels *Ulysses* "supersedes all that has been written in these 50 years, for its universalism, and its style, so animated and musical [movimentato e musicale]."[36] However subterranean, the early influence of the Irish writer who had worked on *Dubliners, Chamber Music, Giacomo Joyce, Exiles,* and *Ulysses* in the border city of Trieste must have been profound. We have records of Amelia's interest in her ancestral heritage on both sides of the family and her excitement upon learning in 1953 that "the name Cave is probably not English but Irish, or perhaps Skottish [sic]? It would really please me—an Irish background. Could swallow only Irish history at school."[37] Amelia's notes on Joyce underscore his transmission of the experience of exile and attend meticulously to the musicality of the various languages in which he was experimenting. In 1956, she considers translating Gilbert's *Key to Finnegans Wake* and collecting Joyce's letters. Years later, she will ask John for help remembering what it was that Joyce said he needed in order to write and liberate himself from Ireland: "cunning, exile, silence?"[38] She was correct and mistook only the order of Stephen Dedalus's tactics for freeing himself from home, fatherland, and church.[39] That said, Rosselli's English prose reveals itself to be as much about tethering oneself to home, fatherland, and church as it is about freeing oneself; this push-pull between freedom and affiliation will typify Rosselli's dynamic with regard to languages of relation (familial, political, and spiritual) as well. As in the case of Ingeborg Bachmann, whom she admired, language will become difficultly legible, in many ways singular—an idiolect remarkable for its putative opacity, entirely her own despite yearnings toward collectivity: "we have learned that aphasia and silence are our . . . purest condition," wrote Bachmann. "And we have returned from the land of no one communicating a language whose duration cannot help but coincide with that of our life."[40]

After the war, Amelia had to remain in the United States as a result of her mother's heart condition, which afflicted Cave until the end of her life. In 1946, when they were finally able to depart for Europe, the family found that Amelia's degree from Mamaroneck High School would not be recognized in Italy, and she was obliged to take up a second diploma in England, studying at St. Paul's School for Girls in London, where her mother had graduated. Both women resided in the English capital, yet Amelia lived alone, apparently because of her mother's ill health; we have Amelia's letters to Cave from Hammersmith, soliciting news about her condition and recounting details of her studies and the music she has been listening to on the radio. Amelia was also able to get to know her maternal grandfather during this period.[41] A letter attributed by archivists to June 1948 is written in Italian from Florence (a conscious choice: Cave had reportedly stopped speaking to the children in that language after a stroke that followed her husband's assassination). This letter constitutes a follow-up note to a recent missive from her grandmother communicating the news that Melina wishes to remain in Italy: the young Amelia reassures Cave defensively that it isn't a hasty decision but that she feels much better on the whole in Italy, and she asks forgiveness for being so nervous when with her mother in England. Marion Cave died when Melina was visiting her grandmother in Florence in October of 1949, and it triggered a serious breakdown because this loss was experienced as an adult, as she later explained, whereas that of her father was more abstract.

The English prose poem "My Clothes to the Wind," dated to 1952 and first published in *Primi scritti* (*Early Writings*, 1980), orbits directly around the relationships with her late parents but most concretely and carnally with her mother. It must be the work that she calls "a bit too personal" in a 1951 letter to her grandmother and is in fact rather straightforwardly autobiographical, unlike her mature writing, although it is anything but straightforward in narrative or linguistic terms. Caterina Venturini draws upon this first work in a brief but acute essay to argue for the "mute presence" of the maternal in Rosselli's poetry, "the unnameable taboo of non-love," whereas the paternal "is made eternal in a political martyrdom that . . . is accepted as the martyrdom of Christ for the salvation of men."[42] Venturini briefly notes the piece's work with the Junghian archetype of the orphan and cites Rosselli's testimony that she "didn't open her mouth" for two to three years after her mother's death (a claim that appears impossible to take at face value, at least literally, given the contents of the poet's correspondence). In this section, I examine the piece more closely to understand what Rosselli does say—or to be more precise, write—concerning the maternal and, above all, to characterize the poetry's work on her mother's tongue.

Silvia Mondardini has argued convincingly that Rosselli's English was acquired by proxy through literature: "an English not subsumed with maternal milk but 'sucked' from books."[43] This argument is particularly compelling, although slightly overstated, because Amelia had lived experiences in England and the United States that would have immersed her in spoken Englishes of all sorts. Mondardini proposes that Rosselli's English is oriented (unsuccessfully) toward recuperating the "languelait" (milktongue) theorized by Hélène Cixous[44]: "the maternal song-tongue, the agrammatical tongue that surfaces in the grammaticality of the written language, a language that flows freely and becomes material, narrating body" and that emerges in Rosselli's work instead as the "*corpus* of tradition." Seeking to differentiate Rosselli's poetic uses of English from her metrically constrained Italian and the surrealism of her French, Mondardini ascribes to Rosselli's tongue of reputedly more "maternal" cast, however aspirational, a freer use of sound that outruns sense: "Amelia, who as her cousin Silvia remembers didn't speak any language well and maintained a marked foreign accent (foreign in every language), uses English by choice, throws herself in the Babel of her polypolite unconscious, seeking out that first contact with the Self."[45]

This schema, although anchored in acute insights, ultimately breaks down. Sound outruns sense across Rosselli's languages of composition; she had to seek her father out through reading in libraries as much as her mother; and her constructivist intellectualism lends itself poorly to reliance on the unconscious, as she explicitly sought to set her Junghian analytical experiences aside from her art and frequently corrected truisms surrounding the notion of unconscious inspiration: "chosen style, being apparently only self-expression, or all 'natural,' is the fruit of long reasoning, of research."[46] In fact, she writes to John and to Amelia Pincherle in this period about an essay she is composing about music in response to Breton and the other surrealists, proposing a way forward in the opposite direction: "It's about what comes next after language has been thoroughly hatched up!—about our own incapacity of translating visions, dreams, sensations, emotional behaviour, into language in any manner other than interpretative, indirect."[47] Music offered a way out of this inherently hermeneutic and semantically fraught sphere of language. Argumentation that narrows the field of this prose poetry to the precincts of the early self also glosses over the sociopolitical ambition and import of Rosselli's verse in each idiom, placing emphasis on the drives of an unconscious babble (aligned with Babel) that eclipses the post-Fascist Pentecost Rosselli consciously acted to construct. Finally, as I argue in the final movement of this chapter, falling back on accent as a marker of the "foreign" and on the extended family's testimony of Rosselli's "not speaking well" ostracizes by reflex, positing a neutral accent as the basis of a phantasmatic national identity. Rosselli's brother does speak of Melina's reserved character and difficulty in adjusting to displacements; in a 1946 letter from England to Marion in Italy, he also attests to the well-founded basis of this difficulty, asking if "it's our fate to always be jolted about here and there" and ironizing about how "Questo essere 'cittadini del mondo' e una gran bella cosa in teoria [This being 'citizens of the world' is a really beautiful thing in theory]."[48]

Moreover, the original 1976 Cixous text upon which Mondardini's argument is based, *Coming to Writing*, theorizes encounters with language that are inherently political and colonial—encounters more complex than critical operations that reduce this writing to gender and sexuality studies in isolation allow. Cixous's languelait is, like Dante's vernacular, orally transmitted and lacks written grammar, yet Cixous (born to Jewish parents in Oran, French Algeria in 1937) complicates the seemingly utopian communion represented by languelait when she declares a debt to the tongue of her mother, a German-speaking midwife, for the status it concedes upon her daughter as outsider: "for never having had a rapport of mastery, of ownership with any language; for always having been in the wrong." This xenoglossic relation to languages leads Cixous to "approach every language delicately, never as my own, in order to lick it, to breathe it in, to adore its differences, respect its gifts." Writing in French, Cixous aspires above all to keep her mother tongue "in the elsewhere that carries it along, to leave its foreignness intact, not bring it back to here"[49]—a "here" clearly marked by the imperial center of this notoriously grammatically regulated language. The Jewish

Algerian writer whose mother's tongue was German presents herself as a discrepancy, a gap, a margin, a balancing act (écart), to whom nothing or else everything "falls by right" [Rien ne me revient]:

—I have no roots: from what sources could I take in enough to nourish a text. Diaspora effect.

—I have no legitimate tongue. In German I sing; in English I disguise myself; in French I fly, I thieve, where would I base a text?

—I am already so much the inscription of a discrepancy [écart] that a further discrepancy [écart] is impossible. They teach me the following lesson: you, stranger/foreigner/outsider [l'étrangère], fit in. Take on the nationality of the country that tolerates you. Be good, return to the ranks, the ordinary, the imperceptible, the domestic.[50]

Rosselli's castings out in language to a phantasmatic Anglophone readership, however haunted by the ghost of her mother, however intimate, still address themselves to a community to come, a community being theorized by her friends and associates in postwar Italy—even if, like Cixous's eventual writings, Rosselli's poetics are launched through her status of exception to every preexisting political community. Yet Rosselli's works also divulge a more problematic relationship to the mother tongue itself, far from that naturalized relation allegorized by milk and celebrated by the movement of écriture féminine—one that sends us back to the concept of the nurse's tongue. The voice of Cixous's grammarless languelait is illiterate, yet sings, and has "the right accent."[51] Rosselli, marked as outsider to each tongue from the first by her voice, connects to her mother's native tongue in distinctly literary fashion—writing in a mannered, archaic English from Rome in order to tether herself to that "mother tongue," rather than conserving its moorings in any reputed elsewhere of orality. Rosselli's aspiration toward a language good at every latitude is in short far more harrowed than that of Cixous, another Jewish exile, who posits a mother tongue that is less language than music, the German mother "in my mouth, in my larynx" that "rhythms me": "a language that I speak or that speaks (to) me in all tongues. A language at once unique and universal that resounds in each national tongue when a poet speaks it. In each tongue, there flows milk and honey. And this language I know, I don't need to enter it, it surges from me, it flows, it is the milk of love. . . . The language that women speak when no one is there to correct them."[52] This idyll of an uncorrected spoken woman's language posits a verbal medium that nourishes psychically and physically, hailing from a utopian space and mode of relationality that is nowhere to be found in Rosselli's poetry. This tongue of milk and honey and of love surges from inside the writer's body, having been transmitted directly by the body of the mother, and it generates a pentecostal resonance within each national language as if automatically when spoken by a poet. Rosselli's poetry, by contrast, arises through mediation, "interpretative, indirect," from highly self-conscious, hard-won conceptual constraints, and makes each tongue with which it comes into contact difficultly national, changing several national literatures in the process. As in many critical encounters with difficult poetry, particularly that which emerges out of a polyglot matrix, interpreters resorting to Babel in explication skip too quickly over the labored grammaticality, the tortuous sense, the belonging-by-travail of Rosselli's writings. Xenoglossia thus becomes a crucial interpretive framework for following Rosselli along the tightrope between sound and sense, carnality and writing, intimacy and the (inter)national as it inheres in the nurse's tongue.

"My Clothes to the Wind" begins with the speaker's departure from a mother in London who is nearing death. I quote at length to impart a sense of the prose's texture, with its unexpected displacements of expected terms with others that riddle, while the iconography of the mother, here empty, is constantly filled by proxy.

> The disagreement heavy and unpleasant, I blundered away and left my mother nearly dead sitting pretty on the bed, she had dropsy. . . . we weren't so fierce on leaving her, we scouffled up and poured a kiss upon her scournful. The street out was damp and barely sunny and the thousands of little milk bottles on the red wagon clinked away for the plastered trees and the chummy neighbors but not for I, not for me, the quesit and the full bosom. I gummed up to the tube-station and killed the imbecile amour which anyway had never been an amour, but a pin, a fastener, a substitute for the empty city and the empty mother and the sniggling brother and the toady maid. Biscuit-makers all, and I a crumb who'd not coagulate.
>
> Now we're varnished we call it a fluke, a mother dead is any body dead, porridge is as good as a kiss. An indifferent number of spirits, not she alone, will haunt and wisp about in the quiet. (*LP*, 27)

The opening "disagreement" may concern Amelia's choice of residence, which is soon afterward cited but is not resolved; the heart of the matter is the void that pervades: "the empty city and the empty mother" versus the "sniggling brother," a nod to Rosselli's younger brother Andrea, and the maid routinely hired to care for them in childhood, whereas the more mature John remained in a privileged position alongside Marion. Departure from the mother is scored by emotional wounds, a kiss inappropriately "poured . . . upon her scournful," making it unclear whether the scorn pertains to the mother or daughter. Shortly thereafter, the

AMELIA ROSSELLI'S DISINTEGRATING CANTO(N)S　　177

mother will be dead, the kiss forever to be replaced by porridge; the daughter will protest too much against the pain of this loss, insisting that the loss of the maternal body could be the loss of any body.

The cloudy damp English weather in this vignette contrasts the thousands of milk bottles on the wagon that clink, an abundance of pure white nourishment to be delivered to the neighbors, and even to the bandaged trees, but never to the speaker. The speaker, in other words, lacks mother's milk, so that the third sentence in this mother's tongue resounds with a strange, because archaic and overly formal, literary authority: "not for I, not for me, the quesit and the full bosom." Situated as parallel to the empty bosom by this phrase is the speaker's lack of "quesit"—seemingly a calque of the Italian "quesito," which in juridical language pertains to rights that make up the patrimony of a subject, to which new laws are thus not applied. So mother's milk is missing and care contracted out to an obsequious maid of artificial affect, while the speaker lacks the patrimony of some unidentified right (possibly that of citizenship in her martyred father's country, given the themes that will soon emerge).

We understand from the correspondence that Amelia the elder, also a writer, had critiqued this first paragraph on terms of cause and effect, but Melina respectfully defends herself by explaining that the opening intends only to elicit a poetic pretext from the complex of situations. The poetic pretext seems to be that of a void, both emotional and physical—of, within, and outside bodies. Even the mirror, referred to later as "this patronless show," is characterized as "that secret fantastical hole," so that the speaker's reflection becomes a rabbit hole and, ultimately, a grave that must be abandoned since "one look down its bottom set me gibbering for motherly and brotherly and fatherly comfort" (*LP*, 34). To gibber, an early seventeenth-century term, is to speak rapidly and unintelligibly, often out of fear or shock, and this somewhat unlikely term could well characterize how Rosselli's poems are received, whereas the eloquence of the articulation and the piece's richly allusive texture (harboring echoes of Shakespeare's Hamlet and of Carroll's Alice) make it impossible to read and call this testimony "unintelligible." It is merely more demanding, both in its dark content and in its difficulty, than most readers (including native speakers of English) would have patience for, and the speaker knows it: "this saying of grime is not transparent enough, I cannot do as I desired and make the thing more plain" (*LP*, 29).

Paradoxically and painfully, the first person "gibbers" even for her immediate family—violating reigning truisms about the nearly sacral intimacy of the household and its language, reputed to be transparent to those within even when those outside the home do not understand. The comfortless speaker has thus taken on an "imbecile amour" to fill the overarching void of city, mother, and supporting

178   AMELIA ROSSELLI'S DISINTEGRATING CANTO(N)S

family parts; realizing this folly, she kills the surrogate love as well. Rejecting the deputy sweetness of maid, contracted love, and cookies—retaining her status as individual, a "crumb who'd not coagulate"—the first person resonates with the character of the young Melina, testified to as being a difficult, fiercely independent presence (Marion Cave wrote to John in 1946, "Melina is such a fine-spirited girl, with a sense of independence which is at times rather overpowering!").[53] Later in the piece, the mother will have "gone marketing" and feeds the speaker meager coins, but this "me" will add up to being in excess: "She has fed me senseless small change, brought me to the bank, had me counted and found the sum surplus" (*LP*, 33). The speaker is everywhere inassimilable, surplus, even in relation to the sacrosanct realm of the familial and maternal.

The prose of "My Clothes to the Wind" shifts back and forth into an odd voice, that of the royal we, so that "we're varnished" seems to indicate the embalming and glossing over of death not only of Marion but of Melina and incalculable others. This trope of plurality appears throughout Rosselli's English writing, as in the "One in Three" lyric from 1956. The reference is not only cultural but also immediately psychic: for years following her mother's death, Amelia had people call her Marion, and she even signed her early musicological publications in her mother's name. The phenomenon of being both empty and too many, fragmented and multiplied, pervades the piece: "After coying with my grandmother I sent a flat letter to England the two weeks' holiday must wheeze into permanent residence. Our eighteen years had a will which smelt of ambition and pride so we cut with our grandmother and gathered our selves to the country. . . . Here the light is molten lead yet would not melt the void, kept under key. Our soul coughed in private" (*LP*, 28).

The will of this teenager, or rather (given the phrasing above) of "our eighteen years" themselves, to leave the mother for the country of the father is applicable to a phenomenon of splintering, triggered by guilt that haunts Melina's correspondence with John. The trauma of the loss of a mother while away remains, so that even the heat of the light of the south that molts lead, contrasting leaden England, cannot melt the void, which is kept locked out of reach. Still the speaker insists on the nonspecificity of this loss: "a mother dead is any body dead," and "an indifferent number of spirits, not she alone, will haunt." We know from letters that Melina, in need of money, had some of her mother's clothes tailored to fit her and sold other pieces of Marion's clothing to buy decent things for herself in this period. In this first published work, we behold the textile "clothes" of the self sold to an uncontainable wind, or spirit, by the immaterial father: "he sold my clothes to the wind" (*LP*, 32–33). The speaker calls upon the father's ghost, rendered fleshly sexual at points as if to yank him down to earth, to abet her in release from the mother's ailing body: "Glib mother! Melt, my father, through her bosomed crevice, and dry the ink within her, tell her soft she's wrong to have me chained to rest her pumping heart, so I'll not stir to conquer hungered flesh of father" (*LP*, 32). Rather than milk or even blood, the mother elsewhere described as void is herein filled with ink—an ink the speaker longs to stop from flowing in order to "conquer" the language of the heroic father, while she longs to escape the carnal reality of her mother's failing heart.[54] In an astute analysis, Gian Maria Annovi links the mother's ink to that of a squid, "sign of writing but at the same time black milk, negative food, the same that opens the Paul Celan collection *Deathfugue*. If the language of women is *languelait*, that of Amelia Rosselli is a lingualatte-in-lutto [*languagemilk*-in-mourning]."[55]

The tug of war between mother and father tongues and between flesh and spirit will not end here. It will play itself out at the intersection of languages. Even Cixous registers problems transmuting the "flesh of breath" that was her oral German into literature, as writing necessarily fashions an object corseted, sheathed; "I spit it out, I vomited. I threw myself into *languelait* at the intersection of the other languages, so as not to see how the letters . . . extort, excoriate, reappropriate the blood of the tongues between . . . their teeth."[56] Cixous's writing thus takes place at the crossroads of her nonmother languages, in a process amounting to spitting out the originary nourishment—recalling Spivak's articulation about Beckett's relation to colonial English (and Bergvall's reanimation of the concept).

A calque of the English term "psalm" in Italian haunts a key moment of Rosselli's first work. It is the feminine term "salma" or corpse, whereas the masculine "salmo," like many masculine forms in Romance languages, denotes the abstract concept of sacred song: "Now I live grey fleshed until the psalms grow sound" (*LP*, 33). This duality of salmo and salma within the "psalm," articulating the ambition of "My Clothes to the Wind" to transmute all-too-dead body into intangible, and perhaps even sacred, song manifests one of the subterranean, or rather spectral, forms of xenoglossia in Rosselli's oeuvre to come. In this melancholic prose of mourning prevailed over by ghosts made holy, the dual psalms/corpses are one with the soil—a breeding ground for harmonically haunted sound, if not for readily canonizable lyric. Rosselli will continue to play on the generative confusion between masculine and feminine forms, in concert with her playing—without any showy heteroglot signaling—on the dissonant meanings of translingual homophones (known colloquially as false friends) across her several languages: a poem from *Serie ospedaliera* vacillates in punning between the masculine "labbro," abstracted lips of a wound, and the feminine "labbra," lips of a mouth.[57] The corpses, the bodies of Rosselli's mother and father, must both be confronted with literary effort: they lend themselves only from the distance of xenoglossia, of the one who has not mastered the father tongue or inherited the mother tongue, to the production of poetic sound.

This reading in direct biographical key is particular to this early moment of Amelia's vocation as a writer. Even within this first piece, she suggests that it would have been better to be less personal. Regardless, here the personal is painfully political: "on the whole perhaps it would have been far more heroical to describe the general atmosphere, as a sign of an only nonchalant interest in your own affairs, which anyway some say spring directly from . . . the progress of politically tactical advances of which you are also said to be participant though holding only a moist news sheet in hand" (*LP*, 30). The speaker is herein identified as a reputed participant in political advances by way of proximity but, in actuality, rendered a mere onlooker to the news as a worn material artifact dampened by tears, rain, or rot. With the political heroism of her parents mediated through forms of print, from journalism to encrypted communication to political tractate, one can well understand why Rosselli turned to literature to continue the battle against Fascism and the newer reactionary forces of the Cold War era— even if her "saying of grime" ended up being far too estranging for the political context to digest and therefore to heed.

"CANTONIDISINTEGRATIDELLA/MIAVITA": CLOSURE AND IMPLOSION OF THE CANTO(N)

> 'Tis this
> *I calculate: I must My Self set free, by*
> *Strong Set High Prison Walls*
> —"Blocks of Granite do lead me up to God," from "October Elizabethans," *LP*, 95

In October 1963, the thirty-three-year-old Rosselli (now recognizable as a musician, musicologist, and poet) attended a series of lectures and conversations in Palermo convened by a cell of the Italian neo-avant-garde whose powerful cohort included Nanni Balestrini, Eduardo Sanguineti, Alfredo Giuliani, Elio Pagliarani, and Antonio Porta, all of whom had been included in the anthology *I Novissimi: Poesie per gli anni '60* published two years prior. The conference was organized in conjunction with the "Settimana Internazionale di Nuova Musica" curated by Francesco Agnello, a festival of contemporary "Neue Musik" informed by poststructuralist and Marxist theory, and it continued the search on the part of the Novissimi to revitalize language by critiquing traditional academic and literary culture, as well as the logic of the consumer capitalism that had invaded Italy via the United States—but at a superstructural level.[58] Other prominent cultural actors present were Luciano Anceschi, aesthetic philosopher and editor-in-chief of the journal *Il verri*, and Umberto Eco, author of the 1962 treatise *Opera aperta* (*The Open Work*). The year of this conference was to become part of the group's name: the Gruppo 63, commemorating a series of tumultuous political and social events. It was the year of Dr. Martin Luther King's "I Have a Dream" speech in Washington, DC, of John F. Kennedy's assassination, and in Italy, of both Fellini's *8½* and the censoring of Pier Paolo Pasolini's Christological allegory of labor, *La ricotta*, for blasphemy.

Although she was embraced by the Gruppo 63, one of few women invited to the gatherings in Sicily and Reggio Emilia, Rosselli would characterize the tactics of the Novissimi as "superatissime" (extremely dated, overcome)—belatedly hearkening to modernist authors like Joyce and Pound whom she had read extensively in the original English years before.[59] In 1952, she sold her copies of *Finnegans Wake* and *The Cantos*, considering the latter "interesting, but a bit of a montatura" (hoax, exaggeration).[60] She would clarify in a later interview that she regarded each "linguistic order" as a distinct "discipline of the mind," adding that "the multilingual work that has been fashionable from Pound forward does not in fact interest me."[61] More than polylingual, we might describe Rosselli's language in practice as "minor," staging microdisplacements of so-called national languages from the position of the outsider, through a micropolitics imploding the boundaries of Italian from within—though it is "total" in conception, as we shall see, making the pentecostal key a generative interpretative framework with much to add to the Babel-driven discourse as it stands.[62]

Although it was never published, Rosselli sent to Pier Paolo Pasolini, an outspoken critic of the neoavanguardia, a polemical report on the Gruppo 63 conference that she authored under the pseudonym "Xenaxis"—presumably to echo the exiled Greek avant-garde composer and architect Iannis Xenakis, who had been sentenced *in absentia* to death and then imprisonment as a former member of the National Liberation Front's armed resistance against the Axis powers.[63] Rosselli's essay casts a skeptical eye on the aims of the neo-avant-garde, with their implicit division between experimental style and content-based realism: for a refugee, after all, multilingualism is not a stylistic choice but an embattled reality, part of the content of everyday living; the refugee is always xenos—guest, enemy, stranger.[64] Although Rosselli pushed language to far more extreme degrees of experimentation than Pasolini did, she shared Pasolini's contention that language is never a matter of form alone. Impatience with the antagonism of

182 ❧ AMELIA ROSSELLI'S DISINTEGRATING CANTO(N)S

form and content sheds light on her response to a 1977 interview question soliciting her formula for writing: "Post-neorealist or, better, post-realist."[65] This self-characterization distances her from contemporary literary trends, placing her instead in the company of recent filmmakers, from Rossellini to Pasolini, and more distantly, of the realist novelists of the late nineteenth century. This "post-neorealist" and postrealist poetry represents a unique contribution to the emerging development of conceptualist art across the disciplines in the late 1950s and 1960s, inflected by the invention of subaltern studies among her immediate Italian peers.

Using the notes she had taken at the now mythical founding conference, Rosselli also composed "Palermo '63," a series of lyrics polemical and parodic by turns that were eventually published in *Il verri* with the subtitle "Eight poem-collages written during the first meeting of the Gruppo '63" (1970) and later in *Primi scritti* (1980). All of the poems' titles are directed toward particular members of the movement, except one "To myself" and one titled simply "Chiesa" ("Church"), which is addressed ardently to "Jesusinthelimbs." The invocation of Christ in the third stanza of "Chiesa" leads to a tactic unique within the series—the elimination of the spaces between words:

> Inventa parole e
> perdoni io t'amo Gesùnellemembra.
>
> Rovinainfinitasimuove
> romanzochiarificatoreunisce
> Jesùnellemembratotali
> Combinalarimanuovaiopregoilluminare
>
> iquattromondi
>
> Invent words and
> pardon I love you Jesusinthelimbs.
>
> Infiniteruinmoves
> Romanceclarifierunites
> Jesusinthetotallimbs
> CombinethenewrhymeIpraytoilluminate
>
> thefourworlds (*LP*, 194–95)

Rosselli's representation of prayer amid a group of polemics against men of the avant-garde is anomalous on several counts, and it is not surprising that despite the recent explosion of interest in her work, little analysis of this poem has appeared.[66] Yet from her correspondence, we know that Rosselli was an impassioned organist, making arrangements throughout the 1950s to play the organs of several churches in Rome. The mingling of stylistic novelty with the expression, or trope, of eroticized religious candor is also abundant through the interpolations of neologism and anachronism in the mock-metaphysical English sequence "October Elizabethans" (1956, also collected in *Primi scritti*) and indeed throughout her oeuvre, particularly in *Variazioni belliche* (composed 1959–1961, published 1964) and *Sleep: Poesie in inglese* (composed 1953–1966, published with translations by Antonio Porta and Emmanuela Tandello in 1989 and 1992, respectively). "Chiesa" occupies the conceit of an address to Jesus, rendering this figure identified in her oeuvre with the political savior and the father a complicit agent of "the new rhyme"—of poeisis.[67]

The outmoded stances of ravished mystical poetry and prayer that appear without spaces distinguishing words in "Chiesa" might seem a nod to the "motsfondus" (fusedwords) of Futurism.[68] The other poems in the series, in fact, mimic a neo-avant-garde "destruction of syntax," with their fragmentary and highly paratactic constructions distinguished only by periods, hyphens, dashes, and plus and minus signs, with only the very rare comma. However, the word fusion in "Chiesa" can more generatively be read as an anachronism nodding to ancient manuscripts that lack spaces between words: a tradition of scriptio continua. In a workshop on meter, Rosselli referred to scriptio continua as a sign of the association between visual and sonic registers in archaic writing forms, pointing out that spaces between written words are an invention: "At one time sound was so close to the graphic text that one wrote absolutely without spaces between one word and the other." She added that the interruptions of punctuation in modern discourse are "psychological."[69] As a score, the fused syllables of "Chiesa" evoke the lived collective space of a church through the chanting that takes place within, evening out the rhythmic whims of individual expression and linking the printed poem to the continuum of oral utterance. Confusing antiquated with experimental poetic trappings takes the nod backward in time to *stilnovismo* embedded in the name "Novissimi" (Utterly New) to a more drastic extent—just as, when performing with David Tudor and Merce Cunningham at the Teatro Sistina in 1960, Rosselli's less minimalist aleatory impulses reputedly led her to break into a Gregorian chant (to John Cage's distaste).[70] "A me stessa" explicitly embraces anachronism as opposed to the avant-garde as it declares, "I will die in the old style still worrying about the future" (*LP*, 196).

Yet the continuum of letters and accompanying paratactic syntax of "Chiesa" paradoxically permit an atmosphere of fracture to dominate the poem. At the beginning of the section of fused words, "Infiniteruin" stirs and "romanzochiarificatoreunisce"—a line that trips up reading because it can be read as "romanzo-chiarificato-reunisce" (clarified romance, in the literary sense, reunites) or as "romanzo-chiarificatore-unisce" (clarifier romance unites). The verses "Preghieradisperatarimuove / passionedisperataangoscia" introduce syntactical disturbances; "angoscia" may be read as a noun or a verb paralleling the structure of the prior line, making the relation between the two lines difficult to parse. The designation "Jesusinthetotallimbs" begs the further question: Whose limbs? Without the psychological scoring of punctuation, it becomes difficult to imagine the poem's syllables yoked to the fits and starts of any integrated speaker or these "limbs" belonging to any one individual body, regardless of the avowed presence of an I. The limbs are identified as "total," distinguishing them from the property of an isolated speaker and creating a potential paradox, given that membra are necessarily just appendages of a totality.

The Christ presence that renders these conceptually dismembered limbs entire is entreated to forge or, to use the closest English term, "combine" a new rhyme that will also syncretize traditions or "cantons" both jurisdictional and mystical. In the infinitive, the speaker invokes this poetry's illumination of "thefourworlds," recalling of course the quadriform cross, with its dual axes pointing in four directions.[71] However, we might well read these "worlds" as the France, England, United States, and Italy of Rosselli's geography or as the four heavenly realms of Emanation, Creation, Formation, and Action laid out in the Kabbalah. The poem ultimately estranges prayer a step further, calling on hell to synthesize the collapsed cantons of the speaker's experience:

> Preghieradisperatarimuove
> passionedisperataangoscia
> Infernoimmobilesintetizza
> Cantonidisintegratidella
> miavita.[72]

> Prayerdesperateremoves
> Passiondesperateanguishes
> Immobileinfernosynthesize
> Disintegratedcantonsof
> mylife.

The literally "disintegratedcantons" of this poem, building blocks subject to "infiniteruin," mark as disintegral the cultural and linguistic subdivisions of nations in the speaker's life—as well as the four corners that, once imposed on language and sound, form cantos, or songs. Although the etymological link between the two terms remains uncertain, "cantoni" harbors a distinct echo of "canzoni" (songs), one that Rosselli elsewhere taps in serial variations: the first poem of "Variations (1960–1961)" in her debut collection, *Variazioni belliche*, introduces a play among "la canzonetta / del bar vicino" ("the little song / of the nearby bar"), "etmisfero cangiante" ("changeful hetmisphere [sic]"), "canzoni" ("songs"), and "cantonate" ("street corners") and also introduces a bitter skepticism about the indifference of Christ within a landscape scored by the weapons and combatants of war:

> se dalle lacrime che sgorgavano
> diramavo missile e pedate inconscie agli amici che mal
> tenevano le loro parti di soldati amorosi, se dalle finezze
> del mio spirito nascevano battaglie e contraddizioni,—
> allora moriva in me la noia, scombinava l'allegria il mio
> malanno insoddisfatto; continuava l'aria fine e le canzoni
> attorno attorno svolgevano attività febbrili, cantonate
> disperse, ultime lacrime di cristo che non si muoveva per
> sì picciol cosa, piccolo parte della notte nella mia prigionia.[73]

> if from the tears that were disgorging
> I issued missles and unconscious footfalls to the friends that
> poorly kept up their parts as amorous soldiers, if from the finenesses
> of my spirit battles and contradictions were being born,
> well then tedium was dying in me, my dissatisfied damage
> was wreaking havoc on [literally "uncombining"] happiness; the fine aria
>   continued and the songs
> around and around unwound febrile activities, dispersed
> cantons, final tears of christ who did not move for
> such a tiny thing, tiniest part in the night of my imprisonment.

"Cantons" in the modern and the obsolete senses are linked, and indeed, Rosselli's musicological studies throughout the 1950s were a result of the disintegrated tonal system, based on the need to erect new musical systems to "save art from incommunicability due to the lack of a common and shareable language."[74] Prayer as song or enchantment based on what she will later call "Christemblems"[75] is represented in "Variations (1960–1961)" as forging a dubious sense of integrity; its imperatives are accompanied by critical revelations such as "Retta combinavo / preghiere assurde e tutto il mondo crollava [Upright I composed / absurd prayers and the whole world crumbled]," in a poem whose closure is explosion: "Contro della spia / notturna non è chiaro perché cada la bomba [Against (of) the nocturnal / spy it isn't clear why the bomb should fall (or: so that the bomb falls)]."[76] In her final dialectical movement away from Jesus in the limbs, the displaced speaker of "Chiesa" recalls the hell that synthesized the Italian vernacular—the inferno of Dante, its magisterial architecture of cantos rationalizing the ethical and intellectual sphere of a poet in exile—to synthesize these cantons again. But Rosselli's own efforts of linguistic and architectonic synthesis will rupture and recombine from within, rather than consolidating, the Italian "national" language; they will stage the ecstatic and violent disintegration of cantons.

Grappling with Amelia Rosselli's poetics of "Cantonidisintegrati" requires grappling with phantom instances of polyglotism more discomposing than those of the storied experiments of the organized avant-garde, in texts in which language improperly acquired and/or deployed is estranged. The shapes of the poems in her first full-length collection, *Variazioni belliche*, which eschew the free-verse line in favor of deterministic spatial constraints, accommodate language that is doubly insider and outsider, xenos, both guest and host: language whose utopian and defamiliarizing characteristics and aspirations invite the term xenoglossia. The xenoglossic strategies of this "Xenaxis" lyricist must be read vis-à-vis a sociopolitical context alienated by political trauma from the revolutions of the historical avant-garde, from the capital of a nation and nucleus of a personal-political tragedy where the anarchic liberties of modernist "mots-en-liberté" ultimately served an imperial project of autarky. In *The Loom of Language*, Frederick Bodmer recognizes the limitations of language reform in the face of war, colonialism, and finance, suggesting that only a "new instrument" will suffice to make planetary cooperation possible:

> We cannot hope to reach a remedy for the language obstacles to international co-operation on a democratic footing, while predatory finance capital, intrigues or armament manufacturers, and the vested interest of a rentier class in the misery of colonial peoples continue to stifle the impulse to a world-wide enterprise for the common wealth of mankind. No language reform can abolish war, while social agencies far more powerful than mere linguistic misunderstandings furnish fresh occasion for it. What intelligent language planning can do is to forge a new instrument for human collaboration on a planetary scale.[77]

One such example of a new instrument that would hardly fall under the term "language planning" is enactment of the barbarism of writing lyric after Auschwitz (to which we should add various other crimes in the name of the state, including Hiroshima and Nagasaki) from within a country that Rosselli, in a rare autobiographical verse tableau, called "barbaro" (barbarian, barbarous).[78] Rosselli created a new form to capture totality while referring back to the sacred architecture of devotional lyric whose draw is embedded in poems like "o dio che ciangelli" ("oh god who chancels"), which makes a verb of the chancel, or the space around an altar reserved for the clergy and choir. Rosselli's god "attract[s] so as then to repulse [or repulsate] the joys of the barbarian": "tu attiri / per poi ripulsare le gioie barbare."[79] She reformulated modernist tactics in a subversive and semiutopian key, inventing a "closed" but immersive form in which to capture a nonmastered, deterritorialized idiom. In her "cubic" forms and collapsed cantons, syntax is not so much "destroyed" as dislocated or floating. It lodges us in the space of a clamorous choir to come, a discomfortable space between or beyond sanctioned geopolitical spaces and linguistic systems.

Glossing the imperatives of "Chiesa" demands comprehension of what it means to be a poet of disintegrated cantons: one who never possessed a mother tongue but instead referred to herself as a "child of the Second World War"— simultaneously dismissing the label of cosmopolitanism, with its implications of entitlement, for the term refugee, as we shall see. This tortuous upbringing comes through poignantly in Rosselli's language, whether composing in the French, English, or Italian linguistic "cantons" of her life. She embraced Italy for reasons of affection, paternal and otherwise, and chose to compose the majority of her poetry in a defamiliarizing Italian that traffics in the grammars, lexical associations, and sound systems of dialects living and dead, English, and French: dis- and reintegrating canto(n)s.

In introducing Rosselli's poetry to the Italian literary public in 1963, Pier Paolo Pasolini confronted the problematic of limits triggered by her upcoming debut volume *Variazioni belliche* through deployment of an astonishing metaphor: that of the mushroom cloud. "The avant-gardist revival . . . has found in this sort of stateless person from the great familial traditions of Cosmopolis, a terrain in which to explode with the fatal and marvelous fecundity of mushroom clouds in the act of their becoming forms," he wrote, before affirming, "I will not go beyond the limits of the flyleaf"—admitting that his analysis will be truncated somewhat arbitrarily by the dictates of space, without attempting a comprehensive account of this emerging body of work.[80] The agent of Pasolini's anxious metaphor is difficult to locate: Is the explosiveness Rosselli's or that of the pointedly Anglicized "revival" of the neo-avant-garde, "so gloomy amidst the eternal apprentices of Milan and Turin," which occupies the "stateless" poet's "terrain"? The question is left unresolved; ultimately, this inaugural analysis of Rosselli's work by her mentor of sorts ascribes an agency to the poetry that surpasses that of its author. "A Note on Amelia Rosselli" opens by comparing Rosselli's linguistically inventive idiom to "an emulsion that takes form of its own accord, nonmastered [imposseduta], as one imagines coming about through the most terrible laboratory experiments, tumors, atomic blasts."[81] Pasolini's recourse to the term *imposseduta* (nonmastered, or even impossessed) in this passage suggests that one is obliged to exceed the limits of the vocabulary to characterize the way that Rosselli's language evades ownership and control—even that of its author.

Rosselli's poetry cultivates an explosive relation to limits, not only in linguistic and aesthetic senses but also in geopolitical and sociohistorical terms, and Pasolini distinguishes her explosive experimentalism from that of formalists by describing it as consciously conducted out in the open, in what he paradoxically calls "a public laboratory"—as if the most classified and arcane procedures were being tested amid the social tumult that they address. Pasolini calls the resultant verse "a luxuriant oasis blooming with the stupefying and random violence of the fait accompli," but he traces its origins to "The Myth of Irrationality," in capital letters. In a 1963 letter to John, Rosselli takes issue with this terminology, describing her poems as "quite and unexpectedly rational"; she resolves to publish her tractate on meter separately "so as to clear the mystery."[82] Although it is appropriate to speak of the fait accompli in commenting on this collection of poems, Pasolini ultimately obscures the nature of the determination in play—as Rosselli's postrealist or neorealist determinism is anything but "casuale" (random).

Rosselli may have provoked the atomic metaphor by characterizing one strain of linguistic invention in *Variazioni belliche* as that of "forme miste—fuse—e pseudoarcaiche" (mixed—fused—and pseudoarchaic forms).[83] However, Pasolini's ultimate inscription of her linguistic fusions/fissions under the sign of irrationality and the brutal uncontainability of the atomic blast disavows Rosselli's researched development of an explicitly "closed" poetic of transcultural convergence, whose development was outlined in Rosselli's essay "Spazi Metrici" ("Metrical Spaces") upon Pasolini's very suggestion the prior year. This poetic tractate, eventually published as a postface to *Variazioni belliche*—and which has continued to inspire and mystify readers—describes her strategy for composing, from roughly 1958 forward, within a "cube-form," wherein a spontaneously dictated regularity of line length, in spatial and durational terms, would permit the reception of myriad rhythms and neutralize the energies roiling in each stanza.[84] "By chance, I resolved to reread the sonnets of the first Italian schools; fascinated by regularity, I resolved to reattempt the impossible."[85]

Rosselli's literal deployment of the word "metrica" (metrics) reunites the term's applications in poetic meter and measurement: indeed, the typescript for her second book, *Serie ospedaliera* (*Hospital Series*), housed at the University of Pavia's Fondo Rosselli, contains penciled-in measurements for the poems' first and longest lines. She composed at the typewriter to make use of the monospaced typeface, which enabled the production of clearer poetic lines subtly to signal the metrical rule that lay behind their composition; in another literal deployment of language, which borrows from English and transgresses Italian usage, "Spazi Metrici" uses the term *rigo* (line) as well as the traditional *verso* (line of verse) in describing her process (*OP*, 187). Rosselli's development of a measured, "systematic closed metric"[86] for the twentieth century was designed to resist the instinctual, romantic—in a word, "irrational"—fits and starts of free verse, a formal tendency that she considered "unhinged, without historical justification, and above all, exhausted."[87] The poetic chambers produced within a literally and conceptually "squared" or "cubic" form were designed to house the ideal of an objective, total language unrestricted by the whims of an individual subject or hand (though Rosselli insisted that she did not write "graphic poetry," by which she must mean concrete or visual poetry—that the measurement applied to the sound and conceptual system of the verse rather than its visible geometry).[88]

Rosselli's accounts of her writing process suggest that she considered it a performance, as if typing were akin to playing an instrument.[89] Like many poets of her generation, Rosselli favored the typewriter because through this instrument she could work at high speed, without second-guessing an image: "with the typewriter I can for a little while follow a thought perhaps faster than light" (*OP*, 189). She described this process as "thinking with eyes closed as if at the piano," as if attempting to produce antirhetorical receptacles of sound and perception, yet she refused to call such thinking "illogical."[90] Rosselli's process reveals the influence of Charles Olson's 1950 manifesto "Projective Verse," which inaugurated the new, improvisational technique of open-field composition enabled by the typewriter and the "stance toward reality" that gave rise to it.[91] Olson's essay, first published in *Poetry New York*, was translated into Italian and published in *Il verri* in 1961, where Rosselli would have seen it, although she soon had a copy of Donald Allen's seminal volume *The New American Poetry, 1945–1960*, which presents Olson as a leading figure of the Black Mountain school and "Projective Verse" as "the dominant new double concept" of the era.[92] Scholars of Rosselli have been quick to gesture to affinities but have done less to elucidate the differences between these writers. Olson aimed through projective verse to establish the laws of "the breathing of the man who writes as well as of his listenings," and highlighted the typewriter's use in scoring reading: "due to its rigidity and its space precisions, it can, for a poet, indicate exactly the breath, the pauses, the suspensions even of syllables, the juxtapositions even of parts of phrases, which he intends. For the first time the poet has the stave and the bar a musician has had."[93] Rosselli's analysis of her American male elder, however, constitutes a characteristically creative act of hermeneutic syncretism: it emphasizes the utility of Olson's "composition by field" for *displacing* the poetic subject, in line with the objectivist compositional parameters of post-Webernism, and the nonintentional writing practices of figures like John Cage (who taught at Black Mountain College during the summers of 1948, 1952, and 1953 until embarking on a European tour with David Tudor that would eventually bring him to Darmstadt). Rosselli elicits from Olson's spatial focus a tactic for dodging tendencies of privatization and egotism abundant in the Anglo-American confessional school of poetry and in certain European exponents of l'écriture féminine.[94] This revisionist interest in Olson becomes clear in the 1975 script for a radio broadcast on American poets of the elite, in which she describes his "conception of metric spatiality" in her own terms: "in an attempt to abolish the I of the poet, he projects surrounding space, the totality of chaos, into the page; considering the poem as 'transported energy' and the line as a vectorial unity in the field of the page.... Metaphors and images generate a sort of animated grid [reticolo animato]; the poetry in itself is not a space of separation from reality, but itself becomes a reality in which the world 'narrates itself' and 'enacts itself' ['si racconta' e 'si agisce']."[95] Although projective verse opens the poem to contingencies beyond the poet's purview, the expressivist project and gestural liberation of Olson's open field—inflected by the rhetoric of abstract expressionism—could not be further from the constraining of the ego manifest in Rosselli's use of the enclosing square and cube. "Spazi Metrici" clarifies her aim to rein in the fits and starts of subjective judgment that are accommodated too "gentilmente" (courteously) by free verse:[96] enabled by the typewriter, which renders the page a grid of equivalently spaced characters, and approximated when taking notes in the city by writing on graph paper, the cube-form dictates line length and necessitates the total replenishment of space.

Reading "Spazi Metrici" thus makes clear that although the apparent spontaneity of Rosselli's compositional process at the typewriter seduces comparison with the surrealists and "itinerant mystics" that Pasolini invokes in his commentary, any impromptu compositional performance exists within a dialectic.[97] The "new geometrism" of her mature poetic, with its tubular and squared forms, has more in common with the radically objective wing of modernist and postmodern art practices based on the meeting of constraint and nonintentionality than it does with irrationalism or the infinite possibilities of the open work. It casts the square or cubic frame to which she subjects letters, syllables, words, phrases, and sentences as an "absolute time-space": "I framed them [Le inquadrai] in an absolute time-space. My poetics could no longer escape [scampare] the universality of the unified space [dello spazio unico]: the lengths and tempos of poetic lines were pre-established, my organizational unity was definable, my rhythms adapted themselves not to my will alone, but to the space that had already been determined, and this space was wholly covered by experiences, realities, objects, and sensations."[98] In an apparent paradox, the "reality" of the poem is to become more expansive through her geometric constraint, no longer "soggettivamente limitata" (subjectively limited) (*OP*, 186). Rosselli thus declares to John in her letter on Pasolini's "Notizia," "As to 'Mystery' & 'neurosis' & 'Mito dell'Irrazionale'—some type of objection—I would have spoken rather of the 'Mito del Razionale'!"[99] Analyzing the conceptual implications of framing devices in Rosselli's poetic that denaturalize the voicing of the individual ego can clarify the transdisciplinary modernist underpinnings of her poetic enterprise and the way her work tussles with the assumptions of expressivist lyric to achieve a more objective and culturally capacious xenoglossic verse.[100]

Although a modernist fascination with pure geometry and structuralist fixation on the grid were developing in the two- and three-dimensional visual arts of her day, Rosselli's metrical strategy is most directly an outgrowth of her musical training. Rosselli's synthesis of spontaneity and measure, rationality and "thinking with the eyes closed" invites comparison above all with its points of contact in the calculated nonintentional practices of the musical and literary avant-garde. Her studies in dodecaphonic music with Luigi Dallapiccola and Guido Turchi in Rome were bolstered by her acceptance to the Darmstadt summer courses in new music from 1959 to 1961, where post-Webernism was being developed (although a psychological breakdown prevented her from participating in 1960); these courses exposed her to key debates and dialogue with the principal actors of the postwar avant-garde such as Stockhausen, Boulez, and Cage.[101] She also attended classes in contemporary electronic music with Luciano Berio at the Dartington College of Arts in 1962 and, in the same period, worked at the RAI Phonology Studio founded by Berio and Bruno Maderna, the best-equipped forum for electronic music production in its day, where she explored the harmonic series, concrete music, and, importantly for a poet, phoneme analysis.

Rosselli's early musicological study of "La serie degli armonici" ("The Harmonic Series," appearing in its most robust form in *Civiltà delle macchine 2* [1954]), to which she returned throughout her life and which she translated into

French and English for international dissemination, reflects her early search for "an *a priori* or ideal form" to be found within the scales, rhythms, and harmonic solutions of folk music existing outside of the tempered scale—a posited organic state "to be found in non-'educated' song."[102] In this moment, Rosselli's leftist intellectual comrades in Italy, from Scotellaro to Levi to Pasolini, were reinventing Fascist populism's bid to "go towards the people." In a moment when figures like Max Horkheimer dismissed irrational aspects of folk culture such as magic, Neapolitan anthropologist and member of the Rosselli-affiliated Action Party Ernesto de Martino (1908–1965) and Calabrian ethnomusicologist Diego Carpitella (1924–1990) were conducting ethnographies surrounding tarantism and gathering the raw musics of a "subaltern popular world" seemingly untouched by capitalist modernity, with its forces of rationalization; they read these traditions as subjugated forms of knowledge harboring the seeds of revolution.[103] In the process, they were inventing branches of subaltern studies that would counter the reactionary bourgeois manipulation of the masses as worshippers in "the tribal mysticism of race and blood"—anticipating "the cultural barbarization that accompanies the subaltern popular world's irruption into history" theorized by the late Gramsci. Beginning in 1950, Rosselli will collaborate with Carpitella on the study, transcription, and analysis of folk songs of the South.[104]

The relation of Rosselli's ethnomusicological work to the broader context of subaltern studies was long eclipsed for a host of reasons but closer study of these dispersed "transpositions" is evolving. Rosselli's aim to study and create "panmusic" tapped into this "larger global movement, a moment in a long liberatory process," as de Martino put it.[105] "A great deal of the world's music, including Oriental music, certain types of folk music, and many traditions of tempered music, is inspired and instinctively based on the harmonic series," Rosselli wrote; "It has been proved that the voice, when singing freely, follows this scale more closely than the tempered scale or the Pythagorean scales."[106] This interest in non-rationalized song paralleled her readings in poetics—"la musique savante ne suffit pas," she quotes of Rimbaud's *Illuminations* in a 1952 letter to John—but it also manifests her early attention to Bartók's experimental notation of folk song and use of harmonics and her research into theories of tuning and harmony. These were first reflected in her 1950 review of Roberto Lupi's 1946 book *Harmony of Gravitation*, which speculates on the limitations of (Western) music theory in heeding the tacit functions of "relations between different harmonic atmospheres."[107] In an interview with Giuseppe Salviati, Rosselli identified this search for the untranscribed "substructures" of popular music through meter as "structuralist or poststructuralist"; such "substructures" hold out the promise of what Peleggi calls "the mirage of logic, of the perfect natural form translated into music."[108] Rosselli elsewhere asserted, succinctly yet without ample assistance to

AMELIA ROSSELLI'S DISINTEGRATING CANTO(N)S — 193

her future interpreters, "That my research in the field of 'folk,' or ethnomusicology, influenced the search for a stricter, more severe, and geometrically formulated versification is obvious."[109]

That Rosselli's musicological research had been spurred by her desire "to find a synthesis of the rational written music of the West, and the oral instinctual music of the East" alerts us to an additional dream lodged within her theory of metrical spaces. Pressing beyond an escape from the self, this practice extends to a search for a more capacious poetic, unfettered by the metrics of any given language[110]:

> Transposing the rhythmic complexity of language spoken and thought but unscanned, through an abundant variation of timbral and rhythmic particles within a single [unico] and delimited typical space, my meter, if not regular, was at least total: all possible imaginable rhythms filled my square [quadrato] meticulously..., my rhythmics were musical in the sense developed by the latest experiments of post-Webernism; my regularity, when it existed, was contrasted by a swarming of rhythms translatable not into feet or into long or short measures, but into microscopic durations that were only just annotatable... with pencil on graph paper in millimeter rule. (*OP*, 186–87)

This metric is "total"; it contains "all possible imaginable rhythms" in a single, "absolute" space.

In the essay "Documento," which appeared in *La fiera letteraria* in July 1968 under the title "Alla ricerca dell'adolescenza" (the personalism of which spurred Rosselli's objections), she described the dialectic between the initial drafting of her long poem *La libellula* as a fluid "canto" (song) in 1958—spontaneous but based on a decade of research into formulating metrical, philosophical, and "historically 'necessary,' inevitable" systems—and its extensive reworking to eliminate excesses four years later: "I believe that the non-intentionality of the text, and the consequent severity in revising and correcting it, contributed in rendering it a work superior to my other, more calculated and suffered works" (*USP*, 283–84). The language of this statement resonates with the work of John Cage, who began working with nonintentional practices using the magic square and then the *I Ching*, or *Book of Changes*, in the early 1950s, having been introduced to the ancient divination text by Christian Wolff (whose father published the first complete English translation for Pantheon Books in 1950).[111] Cage used the Chinese text to free sounds from his will as composer for practically the rest of his career in composition; his *Music of Changes*, one of the first fruits of this practice, was written for David Tudor, with whom Rosselli studied and had a relationship in the early 1960s. Rosselli was, for her part, introduced to the *I Ching* through her Junghian psychoanalyst Ernst Bernhard, whose "Psiche e Coscienza" series for Astrolabio brought out an Italian translation of the work with a preface by Carl Jung in 1950; she testifies to her use of the text in daily life, and the fact that the divination text consists of sixty-four hexagrams roughly resembling squares suggests some additional link to the importance of that form.[112] Other prominent teachers at Darmstadt such as Boulez and Stockhausen were opposed to Cage's use of chance, and Rosselli's relationship to Cage would be as complicated and polemical as many of her ties to the avant-garde. However, in a letter to her brother John, the musicologist, from September 1961, she reports hearing "a really light & amusing piece by Cage (against whom I had many prejudices) for 'prepared' piano," and in a bio of 1981 or later accompanying "La serie degli armonici" to musicologists in Dubrovnik at the Fondo Rosselli in Pavia, we find Rosselli characterizing her 1961 studies with Tudor at Darmstadt as "attempting a deterministic approach to the non-deterministic puzzles and graph-suggestions of Mr. John Cage."[113] Rosselli's self-characterization emphasizes a materialist species of determinism, one in which constraint enables the liberation of the isolated subject/idiom into a matrix of collective meaning experientially and linguistically. The constraint of the forma-cubo constitutes a means of "sprigionamento"—literally, a release from the imprisonment of personal experience in encountering the totality of space and time.[114] In a 1988 lesson on metrics, she notes that "it's the material to offer this disimprisonment [sprigionamento] from the space of experience, the encounter of space-time with personal experience."[115]

In the space provoked by transcription of a reality filled with innumerable rhythms, Rosselli aspires to not only exceed the egotism of the individual voice but also that of a given language's rhythmic capacities, for writing into squares or conceptual "cubes" permits the copresence of multiple metrics, which in turn disclose the embedded traces of foreign rhythmic substructures.[116] She notes in "Metrical Spaces" that "the language in which I write . . . is only one, while my sonic, logical, and associative experience is certainly that of all peoples, and reflectable in all languages."[117] As we recall, she elsewhere admits to the absurdly utopian character of her effort to "seek universal forms"; the Italian passage in "Diario in tre lingue" quoted above confesses, "And I who discharge myself/resign [mi dimetto] from the municipal council every day, 'ask myself if it wouldn't be possible, in an absurd effort, to forget how much is around me in order to enclose myself in the alchemies of a language good at every latitude.' "[118] The passage, with its ambiguous passive or reflexive voice and unattributed quotation, bespeaks an ambivalence about its avowed desire, oscillating between the need constantly to discharge oneself from the workings of the state and the need to disavow the reality of Rome in order to forge this alchemical enclosure in a more capacious language of citizenship.

Rosselli was not alone in seeking a "total" language through a geometric ideal. In the experimentation with rectilinear geometry spanning the visual, musical, and literary abstraction of the twentieth century—from the "universal plastic means" of De Stijl (to which Rosselli refers in the *Diario)* through the postwar abstraction of Pietro Dorazio and Agnes Martin, the magic squares of post-Webernism, and the grids of conceptualism—we find parallel aspirations to recover basic universal forms through abstraction.[119] It was in a 1965 roundtable surrounding the abstract painter Piero Dorazio that Rosselli declared, "I aspire to panmusic, to the music of everyone, of the earth and of the universe, in which an individual hand no longer governs"; the event included figures such as Vittorio Gelmetti, composer of electronic music/musique concrète for Michelangelo Antonioni's 1964 film *Il deserto rosso*. Adriano Spatola, to whom Rosselli dedicates a poem in "Palermo '63," summarizes this global, cross-media phenomenon with breathtaking range in *Verso la poesia totale;* written in the late 1960s and published in 1978, Spatola's book traces the response to a postwar situation in which "culture increasingly assumes the connotations of a phenomenon disconnected from strictly national spheres and endowed with laws valid almost everywhere," as well as an effort to "overcome personalistic impediments" in a "total" poetry.[120] But even these formulations begin to elicit an inherent tension between "universal" language and the more discomfiting species of xenoglossia that we find in Rosselli's verse, one haunted by political persecution and the policing of national identity.

As Paolo Cairoli and Valentina Peleggi have argued, Rosselli's work must be distinguished from the ahistorical species of utopian formalism found in the majority of Webern's followers. In the canonical reading by György Ligeti of Pierre Boulez's *Structure 1a*—written in 1958, the year before Rosselli enrolled in Ligeti's course on problems in Webern—Ligeti warns that the automatism of serialism should not tempt one to "regard the serial mode of working as a dialectic between freedom and mechanical compulsion." Instead, in serial work, "you build your own prison as you please, and once safely inside you are again free to do as you please": "the vital thing is how far, and in what way, one can tug at one's chains."[121] In his metaphorical treatment of imprisonment as a formal exercise, the composer insists on the freedom within constraint, opening up a space for play. But in the same period, other writers and composers who had had firsthand experience with resistance movements were grappling with imprisonment in more than formal terms. Antonio Gramsci's prison letters and notebooks were first published posthumously by Einaudi in the late 1940s and seized public consciousness in Italy. In the footsteps of the compositions *Canti di prigionia* (*Songs of Imprisonment*, 1938–1941) and *Il prigioniero* (*The Prisoner*, 1944–1949) by Rosselli's teacher Dallapiccola, composers Maderna and Vittorio

Fellegara both chose to set excerpts from an anthology of letters from the Italian Resistance almost as soon as it was published. It was in the period of Rosselli's most intense involvement with this scene, from 1958 to 1960, that the crucial debate between Stockhausen and Luigi Nono was unfolding at Darmstadt over the fragmentation of textual material charged by the recent devastation of war. The debate was triggered by Nono's 1956 cantata composition *Il canto sospeso* (*The Song Suspended* [or *Interrupted*]), which drew on the texts of Resistance prisoners from around the world sentenced to death.[122]

Nono's use of prison letters from across Bulgaria, Greece, Poland, the Soviet Union, Italy, and Germany montaged and fractured the devastation of the voices it contained; textual spatializations created by *Sospeso*'s text setting generated various levels of what scholars have called "delinearization," rearranging words' internal components or weaving several words together through juxtaposition. For instance, here I cite number 3, hailing from a fourteen-year-old student in Greece:

Soprano	Mi portano a Kessarianì		*a*	
Contralto	*o o a a i*		*a*	Oggi
Tenore	*a a i* M'impiccheranno			

Soprano	*i i e a* insieme ad altri sette		
Contralto	ci fucileranno . *e e*		*e*
Tenore			perché sono

Soprano	*a i*		*a*	*a*
Contralto	a moriamo da uomini per la pa - - tria. (ecc.)			
Tenore	patriota	*a a a*	*a*	

I will include a translation of the three parts, with the proviso that the broken-off vowels that echo semantic sections would need to be altered to match the English-language soundscape:

They will bring me to Kessarianì   *a*

   o   *o*   *a a i*   *a* Today

                 a a i They will hang me

      i   *i e a*   together with seven others

     they will fire at us   *e e*   *e*

                       because I am a

  a   *i*   *a*   *a*

  a   we will die as men for the fa - - therland. (etc.)

     patriot   *a a a*   *a*

Stockhausen questioned the appropriateness of Nono's approach to highly volatile material, proposing that the semantic meaning of the testimonials was jettisoned in linguistic disintegration—reduced to sheer formalism: "Nono composes the text as if he wanted to withdraw its meaning from a public view, in which it does not belong. . . . [H]e makes sounds, or noises, from language. He does not allow the texts to be declaimed, but rather places them in such an indiscriminately strict and dense musical form that one can no longer understand anything of them when listening."[123] Nono justified himself by hearkening to Schönberg's 1912 statement about the relationship between text and music. According to Schönberg, the meaning of words written "in the ecstasy of composition" was better derived when hearing them in a purely musical interpretation than when adhering to "the surface of the pure and simple thoughts expressed by the words."[124] Nono goes on to draw out a theory of musical composition as a multidimensional ensemble of constellations of words and phonemes, which calls for repetitions and manipulations of the text, and insists that the "scomposizione," or decomposition, of phonetic material has always had the capacity to intensify rather than deplete a text's semantic values. Above all, Nono insisted on the revolutionary aim of his work, which was to break the individual voices of the prisoners away from their atomized death sentences. In Part III of *Canto sospeso*, he notes, a new text is created by way of interpolation: the juxtaposition of three texts written in the moments before the victims' execution. By spatializing the language of these letters from prison and rendering them choral, his music strives to tear these voices away from the master narrative of Fascism—to preserve the words' meaning but in liberated form. Nono's method thereby underscores the political efficacy of what is legible by travail in his composition as he distinguishes it from the non-semantic glossolalia of which Stockhausen accused him.

Rosselli's choice of cover art for *Serie ospedaliera* (*Hospital Series*, with distinct overtones of "hospes," guest/host, published in 1969), a series of receding squares, white on white, spurs the vertigo of infinite regress, which can also be experienced as imprisonment (figure 3.4). The image uncannily resembles the 1952 *Monument to the Unknown Political Prisoner* by Max Bill, champion of concrete poets. Asked about the walls constantly appearing so as only to be undermined in her verse, Rosselli responded, "I detained the explosions that gathered in me. If I alternate, I mean to demonstrate the duality of the demonstration."[125] Fracture, arson, even urination and ejaculation versus ubiquitous walls: the revolt against persecution suffered by a person imprisoned before exiting the womb persists in her poetry's paradoxical collusions of formal liberty and semantic incarceration. Revising poetic hermeticism, these metrical spaces host alarming semantic vagrancy—tropological shifts and paronomasia—within a prevailing environment of semantic enclosure that alternates in its effect between suffocation and *ristoro*, or reprieve.

FIGURE 3.4 Cover of Rosselli's second volume, *Serie ospedaliera* (Mondadori, Il Saggiatore, 1969), featuring artwork by Anita Klintz and Peter Gogel.

Although the cube-form is the matrix of "an absolute time-space" capable of hosting the associative logic of all languages, Rosselli's dense aural texture encourages, accommodates, and naturalizes linguistic anomalies through repetition and assonance and generates syntactical ambiguities. The resultant texts possess the ambient quality of a meditative chant, although they stray from the candid mysticism of "Chiesa" into an ironized sacrality of political utterance, articulated in an unhomely speech:

Ma in me coinvenivano montagne. Nella cella di tutte
le solitudini preparavano bistecche e insalate riccamente
condite. Nella cella delle pulchritudini attendevo
l'ordine di partire, insalata mista, per il tempo
che massacrava: ma nessun ordine attendeva fuori la
porta delle silenziose immagini. Il choc alla nuca
ruppe violento entro la porta—la scalata alla montagna
preparò la discesa precipitosa. Vietate al sole d'entrare,
vietata alla porta d'aprirsi vietata all'ira di soddisfarsi
fuori delle finestre dei poveri. Vietate alla noia
d'allontanarsi vietate. Nelle castelle di tutte le
bellezze moriva un vecchio sagace.
Condizionata ad una presa di potere che non era il
mio entravo in piazza e vedevo il sole bruciare, le
donne stagliare erbe su della piazza che ardeva di
malizia: la milizia.

Il sol fa mi do di tutte le tue battaglie. (*LP*, 315)

But in me mountains coinvened. In the cell of all
solitudes they prepared steaks and salads richly
seasoned. In the cell of pulchritudes I awaited
the order to depart, mixed salad, for time
which slaughtered: but no order awaited out the
portal of silent images. *Shock* to the nape
broke violent within the portal—the climb to the mountain
prepared the headlong descent. Prohibit the sun to enter,
the portal prohibited to open the ire prohibited to satisfy itself
outside the windows of the poor. Prohibit bother
to distance itself prohibit. In the castelles of all
beauties an elderly sage was dying.

Conditioned to a power seizure that wasn't my
own I entered the square and saw the sun burning, the
women hacking grasses upon the square that blazed with
malice: the militia.

The sol fa mi do of all of your battles.

Composed from a point where landscapes and tongues *co-invengono* or "co-invene," her language charges the limits of the terms "mother tongue" and "fatherland" with its ruptures of propriety. We have alien systems informing word choice from just outside the portal, *fuori la porta* instead of *della porta*, breaking *entro la porta, within* the portal—subtle yet disquieting deviations from the norm. In the first glossary provided to Garzanti upon Pasolini's suggestion, Rosselli explains anomalous prepositional additions in her poems such as "*contro* del *magazziniere*" ("against *of* the store-keeper") as "preferable" because of the poetic context, where each rhythmic or intensifying addition of a word is "licit": she notes that such elements of the poem are unchangeable as a result of her metrical rule because "broken and incorrect language is born along with its squared form."[126] Rosselli thereby requires a new species of reading, one committed to unlearning the caprices of an only apparently rational national grammar. It is a form of reading less insistent on the linear unfolding of narration and more akin to absorption within each strategically imprisoned environment/instance; as she states in the "Debate on Dorazio," contemporary poems in squared form recall the rationalist painting of the day in their desire "to cover the entire space of their *quadri* [squares, frames, picture] with a geometric confusion of colors, vocalic timbres, without clarifying a central sense to the poem, but letting the ensemble speak for itself."[127]

Rosselli also explains in her glossary that the gender of certain terms is inverted throughout *Variazioni belliche* for ironic or sonic effects: here, the norm for castles, *i castelli*, becomes *le castelle*. Yet we accept these deviations and their conceptual effects because the poem builds its own digressive logic through assonance—*nelle castelle* rhymes with *nella cella*, as *malizia* does with *milizia*, and narrative rhetoric gives way to the proliferation of staccato terms beginning with "p" and what Rosselli would in her theoretical work call "phonetic nodes": *pre* and *po*. Repetition produces a proliferation of cells, acts of waiting, prohibitions, and fires. The sixteen-line poem itself, as a shape and set of more or less regular lines, also resembles a ruptured cell and, more familiarly, a sonnet that has erupted, the form's summation—just like the denationalized language in which it appears, and the denationalized author—surplus. The sonnet is, after all, "una cosa barbara" (a barbarian thing), according to a poem from *Serie ospedaliera* (*Hospital Series*, 1963–1965)—literally an index of the communication of peoples, musics, and mathematics in the thirteenth-century Sicilian court of the Hohenstaufen Emperor Frederick II, a generative storm of Arab and northern "barbarian" influence.[128]

We can imagine that by breaking "tutte le tue battaglie"—"all of your battles"—down into a constituent sol, fa, mi, do, Rosselli is liberating these sounds as noise, releasing them into new rhythmic, harmonic, communicative, and political possibilities in natural but denaturalized languages. The poetic error of this "strange[r] of Rome, Je[w] and proselyt[e]" (as named in the King James version of the Pentecost narrative) within her cubic constraint alienates the linguistic makeup of Rome from itself, so that readers of this canto find themselves outside the jurisdiction of any canton, or nation.[129]

Although Pasolini's "Notizia su Amelia Rosselli" notoriously, and misleadingly, characterizes Rosselli's linguistic errancies through the Freudian category of the unconscious *lapsus*, or slip, his nuclear metaphor at once accounts for the poems' consciously researched compositional method and captures their discomposing effect, literalizing the term "experimentation" with a terrible historical inflection that again calls for being barbarian to the barbarous. Pasolini concedes that there is a dialectic at play in these stanzas, noting that in Rosselli's "laboratory," the tumors and atomic blasts are "dominated" but "only scientifically"—"So that the magma— the terribleness—is fixed in strophic forms that are the more closed and absolute the more arbitrary they are."[130] Pasolini's deployment of the mushroom cloud figure expresses something of a truth to the experience of reading Rosselli's poetry that evades every painstaking analysis of her demanding poetic tractate in isolation. For however cultivated and strategic her "new geometrism" may be, however controlled the length of the strophē (turning), in reading, her lines vaunt anything but that coolness of composition we might associate with cubism, suprematism, De Stijl, or even their reverberation in postwar abstraction, concretism, and the antihumanist turn in 1960s and 1970s conceptualism. Rosselli's geometric compressions serve to host a mutation of "organic" uses of language that bespeaks the anxiety and the destructive radiance of the atomic age.[131] Her cube-form occupies the verge of a painfully historicized postmodern poetic: the mushroom-cloud metaphor indexes the implosion of the supposed rationalism of modernity via the murderous atomic force that is its apotheosis. Rosselli's metrical spaces represent the transition from a modernist aspiration to produce a "total" poetic of "panmusic" to a granular postwar aesthetic in which such totality is exposed as possible only through the most violent means. A sensibility we might call atomic makes itself felt through the morphing of words in her "cantons" disgregated into granular bits, so that in "Le tue acquerelle scomponevano la mia mente" ("Your acquarelles discomposed my mind"), for example, the "scomporre" (discomposing) of the speaker's mind and of the light is echoed in the "scompiglio" (mess) of spring, the "scostarsi" (straying) from the train, the "accostarsi" (veering) of the train, and even the "stornare" (warding off) of swallows in the final stanza (*LP*, 461–62).

The bellicosity of Pasolini's metaphor compels because it hails from beyond the domestic landscape of Italian Fascism with which Rosselli's work would reflexively come to be associated, a fact conditioned by the nationality of her famous father—and a nationality that pertained to herself only through travail. The "scoppi atomici" resonate from beyond the strictly national tragedy of the Second World War, calling to mind the *fungo* (mushroom) tower that appears in the opening sequence of Antonioni's 1962 *L'eclisse:* an apparition of violent alterity in the stark Fascist-modernist geometry of the Esposizione Universale Roma (EUR), revealing the transnational violence of the near past visible when the curtain is drawn from the picture windows of the bourgeoisie. The mushroom cloud figure was ostensibly chosen by the older poet to designate an alien phenomenon in a world of nuclear bombs become violently one—a figure with global reach but deterritorialized from its origin and destination in a European context.

The geographical alterity of the mushroom cloud, which immediately invokes the United States or Japan rather than the war-torn landscape of Fascist Italy, builds on the ambiguous nationality of "questa specie di apolide dalle grandi tradizioni famigliari di Cosmopolis" (this sort of stateless person hailing from the great family traditions of Cosmopolis), as Pasolini had characterized his object of criticism. Rosselli occupied an implosive cultural state but rejected this characterization: "The designation 'cosmopolitan' goes back to an essay by Pasolini . . ., but I reject that epithet for us: we are children of the Second World War. . . . The cosmopolite is a person who chooses to be so. We were not cosmopolitans; we were refugees" (*USP*, 35). Although the intellectuals of the twenty-first century have labored to distance cosmopolitanism from the privileged universal category that Rosselli rejects, bringing the concept into line with a minoritarian modernity bespeaking as much victimization as privilege, we need to honor her distinction while attempting to account for the utopian—and dystopian—aspects of her poetic.[132] The dissonance between linguistic, sonic, and cognitive orders obliged to cohabit Rosselli's stanzas constitutes an extension of being a "child of the Second World War"—with obvious implications for the undertheorized category of "self-expression." In "Ed hanno soffici manti quei ragazzi," a later poem from *Documento*, we find Rosselli identifying with a feminized Pacific metaphor that happens to constitute the apex of conflict between the United States and Japan, undecidably placed between nation-states and between the roles of victim and aggressor:

> Nella Pearl Harbor che sono io esprimersi
> mai ebbe a miglior sorte altro che
> vanagloriosa espulsione dei resti (*OP*, 390)

In the Pearl Harbor that I am self-expression
never had a better fate than
vainglorious expulsion of remains

Such stanzas, which never permit us to forget the human substance that remains in the wake of victory or defeat, reveal Rosselli's generative oasis to be the domain of post-Enlightenment poetics,[133] wherein the violent unreason stemming from the programmatic disenchantment of history is radiantly disclosed by an I become harrowingly public.

HARMONICS OF THE TRANSLINGUAL VOICE: FROM UNA LINGUA VACILLANTE TO OVERTONE AS HOLY GHOST

We are now poised to understand Rosselli's aspiration to trigger what is fundamentally a revolution in listening. As indicated in earlier sections of this chapter, preceding and in tandem with her studies in poetics, Amelia Rosselli harbored a lifelong obsession with the harmonic series, or the sequence of natural overtones that resonate when plucking a string or blowing through a column of air (including the one shared by the vocal cords). These overtones (also known as upper harmonics or partials) are an organic outcome of the physics of vibration (wherein all vibrations are accompanied by faster oscillations) and the basis of all musical scales and tuning systems.[134] Every tone or fixed pitch (called in music theory a "fundamental") in a string or wind instrument is actually a composite: the sum of the dominant pitch that we hear and a series of higher pitches that become gradually less perceptible as they increase in distance from the fundamental. The harmonic series can therefore be thought of as a chord embedded within any resonant musical note or speech event. It is a key factor in our differentiation of "noise" (wherein overtones are so dense or fluctuating that we cannot perceive pitch) from less dissonant sound.

The majority of overtones are harmonics, or simple fractional vibrations of the fundamental; the first three intervals created by this series of overtones are an octave, a perfect fifth, and a perfect fourth, which grant them a harmonious feel, whereas the later intervals are narrower and, when heard, create increasing senses of dissonance. Sound "color" and the timbre of different voices and musical instruments derive from the differences in audibility of the various overtones. Human perception of these overtones is routinely edited out, however, by adult brains that have learned to distinguish coherent chunks of content, such as phonemes and words, or fixed pitches and musical phrases. Contemporary ethnomusicologist and vocalist Mark Van Tongeren argues in a 2023 study for expanded listening practices that incite awareness of these hidden yet omnipresent harmonies: "Becoming aware of the overtones resounding through your mouth every time you speak is something like learning that your body is 90 percent water: hard to believe, but true."[135]

Rosselli, who began studying piano and violin in London, became interested in exploring tuning and harmonics outside of the tempered scale in the early 1950s—influenced by her recent exposure to Bartók's modal or "primitive" scales and to the notion, writ large, that traditional Western harmonic systems and sonorities that had reigned since the Cinquecento had collapsed. As attested in her first published essay, a review of the Florence-based composer/theorist Roberto Lupi's 1946 *Harmony of Gravitation* for the first issue of *Diapason* (itself named after the term for a swelling burst of harmony), new research in acoustics pointed to a way forward for both music and musicology: to develop one's musical ear as an artist so as to "intuit the natural scales and their vertical relations," thus apprehending new musical possibilities organically rather than through the imposition of artificial systems and, as a theorist, to "universalize the new material through exacting studies of psychology and musical acoustics."[136] This is what she would try to achieve as a musicologist and composer, although for political, personal, and disciplinary reasons, her ideas ultimately failed to receive their due, as noted above. Rosselli ultimately proposes a scheme of ampler musical apprehension and experimental composition derived from the overtones and intervals of the harmonic series.[137] In the debate on music and painting, Rosselli compares the analysis of sonic spectra (which, she points out, can prove that vowels constitute noise rather than sound) to the potential analysis of the light spectrum; she is clearly interested in the sound of poetic shimmer.[138]

Another element of Rosselli's bibliography on this subject housed at the Fondo Rosselli in Pavia is the writing on tuning and scale of the French Indologist/musicologist Alain Danielou, who argued for the creative power of the sounded word from Genesis through the Vedas, contouring ways in which the laws of music, bridging physics and metaphysics, reflect the natural attunement of the world. Danielou quotes early on in *Music and the Power of Sound: The Influence of Tuning and Interval on Consciousness* and its precursors from a passage of the *Book of Rites* edited by Confucius that would have appealed to the idealistic young artist: "music is intimately connected with the essential relations between beings." He also invokes the second-century BCE writings of Dong Zhongzu: "The fact of harmony between heaven and earth and humankind does not come from a physical union . . .; it comes from a tuning on the same note producing vibrations in unison."[139] This ideal of relationality through attunement recalls the aspirations of Rosselli's "panmusic." It also resonates with that of more immediate literary elders, influenced by high modernism yet occupying a more interrogative relation to hegemonic languages, like second-generation Lithuanian Jewish modernist poet Louis Zukosfky. Zukofsky maintained in a 1950 "Statement for Poetry" that the "upper limit" of musicality enabled poetry, as acoustic material, to transcend the divisions of communicability that find their apotheosis in grammar books: "it is possible in imagination to divorce speech of all graphic elements, to let it become a movement of sounds. It is this musical horizon of poetry (which incidentally poems perhaps never reach) that permits anybody who does not know Greek to listen and get something out of the poetry of Homer: to 'tune in' to the human tradition, to its voice which has developed among the sounds of natural things, and thus escape the confines of a time and place, as one hardly ever escapes them in studying Homer's grammar. In this sense poetry is international." And it persists in the work of contemporaries like the Black internationalist artist Will Alexander (born in Los Angeles in 1948), who writes "as if the words are translated from another language": "It's not that I know these other languages,. . . but I can feel their rhythms, although I'm writing in English. Writing a foreign language within your own language creates another language. . . . I can hear words that don't exist."[140]

Despite the exalted ideals of thinkers pressed to surpass the nationalism of the first half of the twentieth century, we have seen that the language of poetry continues to be wielded as a mechanism of division as well as of attunement. Poetries resounding as dissonant—such as Rosselli's, on the page and off—remain subject to the whims of nationalist ideological conditioning. Her voice was received as foreign because of the arbitrary, learned identification of certain tendencies in her accent (such as the sliding R) as anathema, inadmissible deviations from the presumed standard of the culture. Even the assessment of her grandmother with which we began the chapter, of her Italian as "ahimé—vacillante," expresses a close relative's incapacity to hear the young reader's wavering between sonic and semantic systems—the vibration—as harmonic enrichment and, moreover, part and parcel of the history of Italy rather than the singular fate of an individual tragically severed from the sociopolitical collective. From her first publication, Rosselli is aware of the caprices and ignorance behind charges of dissonance, noting that an ear unattuned to superior harmonies can dismiss them as discordant, "off-key": "Lupi confirms what Schoenberg has often revealed—that is, how imprecise the notion of dissonance is, exactly because it is generated by a more or less sensitive perception or interior awareness of superior harmonics."[141] At the dawn of her career as a poet in June 1962, Rosselli would report to Pasolini that Elio Vittorini, editor of the journal *Il Menabò*, "seemed so embarrassed by my linguistic 'ductility' or anarchy ('fused,' invented or deformed, or archaizing words) that... he asked me to correct the 'out-of-tune notes' [stonature] as much as possible."[142] (She added, "I wrote to him communicating my decision (and your advice) not to change that vernacular language, at times resonating as working-class [popolare], or distorted [storpiata], at all.")[143] The poetic manipulation of a confounding range of sociolects always ends up being received as idiolect, as irreparably singular in Rosselli's case.

Finding that current musical instruments based on the tempered scale "cannot express this still-unknown species of acoustic 'halo' ['alone'] that we seek," as she put it in her review of *Harmony of Gravitation*, a twenty-one-year-old Rosselli undertook the design of an experimental keyboard that reproduced the first sixty-four harmonics, collaborating on its fabrication with an Ancona firm of musical engineers, Farfisa (Fabbriche Riunite di Fisarmoniche) (figure 3.5).[144] In June 1952, Amelia wrote to her grandmother that in her most visionary moments, she believes that such instruments will come to replace those based on the tempered scale and

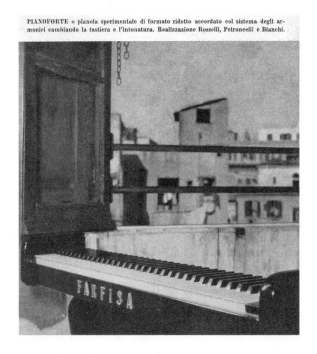

FIGURE 3.5 Image of Rosselli's experimental keyboard from Marion (Amelia) Rosselli, "La serie degli armonici," *Civiltà delle macchine* II, no. 2 (1954): 43. Courtesy of Centro per gli Studi sulla Tradizione Manoscritta di Autori Moderni e Contemporanei, Università di Pavia.

those with fixed keys—and that the ear will come to adapt itself "to a subtler conception of melodic relations, [and] will more precisely mirror this series, this species of fixed scale that we carry within us, and outside of us, invisible, for years, or rather from the time that music was born."[145] She asserts in the English manuscript of "The Harmonic Series" that her system of research and practice will cause "the analytical, disintegrative interpretation of music" predominant in the West for the last four hundred years, "with its arbitrary sub-divisions of rhythm, and artificial formations of chords," to give way to "a scheme which reproduces four dimensions in space-time": "intensity, pitch, rhythm, and timbre . . . all derived from the harmonic series, each a product of the other."[146] Unfortunately, she was only able to produce the one keyboard model, and further attempts to publish "The Harmonic Series" outside of Italy did not bear fruit. Commentators on Rosselli's writing have generally been more befuddled than enlightened by this seemingly arcane musicological passion, so that a precise analytic for reading it alongside her poetry is lacking. In this concluding section, I propose that harmonics can help us attune more perspicuously to the ghostings or, in Lupi's terminology, the sonorous "halos" of tongues foreign to the linguistic fundamentals of Rosselli's writings, thereby helping us become new sorts of listeners. These hauntings of languages beyond the mother- or fatherland for which she composed at any given time are apprehensible not only through diction and syntax, but through sonic channels of rhythm and accent, such as in Caroline Bergvall's animal-inhabited, trafficked, "autographic" throat: "Cat is the tone in my speech, its accentedness, its autography. . . . So what if I were to decide to talk with a cat in the throat?"[147] They are the linguistic analog to the nontempered folk songs collected by Carpitella and others, in whose strains one more easily perceives harmonics that become toned down in disciplined musics. Although listeners and readers of Rosselli's poetry in distinct national languages have been conditioned to treat these lingual sculptings as anathema and heralds of the stranger, I propose that we understand them in harmonic terms, as chords. Whereas Fascism trains you to stand as a being of the national language alone, against whom all other languages are a threat (think of Depero's "State of Mind in New York"), in Rosselli's most utopian aspiration, you can become a being listening for harmonics, who apprehends all languages as overtones clustered around each tongue, resistant to Fascism's hailing.

A comment on the displacing effect of Rosselli's language by Alfonso Berardinelli in an RAI broadcast is symptomatic of her lasting marginality within Italian literary circles as it registers the way her voice hovers between the phonetic norms of nation-states: "non si capisce bene da dove venga" (one does not understand very well where it comes from).[148] In the seemingly homogeneous population of Italy, Rosselli's spoken accent, with its notable guttural R and other traces of alterity with respect to the faulty notion of a "standard" Italian, is the source of ample fascination, as well as some measure of provincial literary condescension; despite the fact that native speakers of several northern Italian regions are known for the guttural R, I have heard Rosselli's pronunciation characterized as other to Italian, French, and English colleagues alike.[149] Recent writings on accent have begun to transform understanding of this all too readily naturalized concept of lingual difference. As we recall, Caroline Bergvall advocated for embracing the "cat" signaled by the accented autography of speech, normally marked as inarticulate: "the animal, the pure physiology of sound" can be invoked strategically to address "questions of cultural and linguistic dominance, and attending issues of language policy and language erasure," as in Bergvall's installation "Say: Parsley" surrounding the massacre of Creole Haitians at the border of the Dominican Republic in 1937, based on their pronunciation of the R sound in the shibboleth "perejíl."[150] Recent theorizations emphasize that the supposedly neutral accent of any locus or state—think the Queen's English or an Albion voice—is actually "a particular masquerading as a universal—a mechanism for redrawing false binaries (people with accents / people without accents) based on the sounds of ethnic, regional, and/or class difference."[151]

Rosselli's xenoglossic poetics asks for us to swell received geopolitical frameworks as it tests well-worn demarcations of nation, region, dialect, and even diaspora, distinguishing its own transnational sphere of political aspiration while disbelonging in ways that reigning academic categories in Europe and the United States cannot easily classify. "Accent does not demarcate mappable social or regional locations; rather, accented speech and listening muddy and proliferate geopolitical space," write Pooja Rangan, Akshya Saxena, Ragini Tharoor Srinivasan, and Pavitra Sundar in the introduction to their 2023 collection *Thinking with an Accent*.[152] Building on Jordan-born Lebanese-English artist Lawrence Abu Hamden's audio documentaries surrounding the politics of listening, the editors describe accent as "an irregular and itinerant concoction of contagiously accumulated voices."[153] The pertinence of this descriptor to Rosselli's midcentury poetics shows how germane her oeuvre is to the contemporary textual soundscape. Rosselli's rejection of the lyric of the confessional first person, her striving to express collective experience in its stead at a scale that defied the provincialism of her day, must ultimately be judged as successful by careful readers, given the fertile muddying of geographies and proliferation of tonalities that her "saying of grime" achieves; her poetry extends the work of her anti-Fascist women elders in troubling geopolitical boundaries through transgressions of nationalist communication channels.

The voice of Rosselli itself places us between loci through what Antonella Anedda has called a "scivolamento," or sliding.[154] Her poetry as read, or ideally as heard, in the very voice of spaesamento, displacement, characteristic of her recitations attunes us immediately to sound. A RAI transmission that included her reading of "Faro," a poem bearing an Italian title from her English-language collection *Sleep: Poesie in inglese*, helps expand our understanding of the place Rosselli occupied in the literary and geopolitical landscape sonically.[155] The voice of the transmission, whose Rs slide into L sounds, whose "all" slides into "awl," estranges English from itself, highlighting musicality and making the poem impossible to experience as transparently semantic and yet, in a manner consistent with the xenoglossic poetics explored in this book, impossible to consign to the category of "glossolalia" or "Babel." The verse's I declares itself as only "fit to say" a series of seemingly random, yet rhyming, iambic nouns paired with their definite articles, although a cycling through iambic pentameter, quadrimeter, and hexameter emphasized by assonance and a hammering delivery ensures an estrangingly musical experience:

> be kind be kind be kind I hear this phrase
> screaming in my ear each day, be sweet
> be sweet be sweet be sweet this is all
> I can say (or seem to say). Alas the phrase the
> flare the open door the glare the blare the fan
> the flight the high tower reaching up towards glaze
> are all I am fit to say, to see to hear to feel
> to sway.[156]

The peculiar poetic logic of kinship, of "kind," haunts the I and the kindness we are at first inclined to read in this poem, as kinship is tangled in line with the arbitrary classifications of rhyme. Amid the hammering off-rhymes of iambs, semantic association skids, though the whole tends toward an improvised coherence through images of stupefaction: the sentence or "phrase" slides into visual flare, glare, glaze, and sonic "blare." The message in saying caves to the carnal senses of language's transmission: seeing, hearing, feeling, and finally swaying ("the swaying of the hill"), which displaces saying, are overloaded—fraught in the etymological sense, as with a ship's cargo. The final couplet's promise of illumination instead delivers utter disorientation. "So that's what they're for, the lighthouse watching / anxiously": the lighthouse hovers at the poem's close, an anxious onlooker rather than a true piloting core. The image of the lighthouse or lantern appears constantly in Rosselli's work as an inoperative figure for navigation. In "Faro," land itself barrels, sways—another image of vacillation from a person who considers herself, as she wrote to John in 1956, "a wild bussola," or compass gone awry.[157]

In early 2014, after fourteen years of reading, researching, and translating Amelia Rosselli, I found myself faced, in terms more immediate than ever, with the task of transmitting her voice to an English-speaking audience. Invited to give a reading at a salon in a colleague's home in Madison, Wisconsin, I decided to present a section of a work from *Locomotrix*, my recently published collection of translations. The title of that collection followed Rosselli's unexpected use of the term locomotrix, a feminine locomotion: "tuo motivo non urlare, dinnanzi alla / cattedrale; esilio o *chance* non ti perdonano / la locomotrice [your motive not to howl, facing the / cathedral; exile or *chance* don't pardon you / the locomotrix]."[158] The original poem hosts the English word *chance* within an Italian poetic ecology, an unusual move for this poet that nevertheless represents a "traditional" modernist multilingual insertion, italicized to mark it off from the seemingly native fabric. In the subsequent line, however, instead of using the more common "locomotiva," or locomotive, to echo the "motive" both musical and psychic that begins this poem, Rosselli drifts to the more challenging sound of locomotrice (technically indicating an electric train). This unexpected drift in the soundscape of a train of thought forces us to slow down and apprehend that the term "locomotive" hails from the notion of a "locus," or luogo, sent into motion, whereas "locomotrice" calls to mind simultaneously the distinctly feminine "matrice," or classical Latin "matrix," uterus, or mold—from "mater," mother, now altered in its ending with the suffix -trix, perhaps, as the *Oxford English Dictionary* indicates, after "nutrix," or nurse/wet nurse. "Locomotrix" defamiliarizes as it feminizes the locomotive, forcing association with this matrix as well as Rosselli's spatial "metrics."

Yet although I could try to echo such aspects of Rosselli's lexical choices with English parallels, lacking access to a sound system in Madison, I was forced to confront the heresy of relaying the "voice" of the Italian text with my own. I was faced with the limits not only of the usual semantic equivalents but also of phonemes and beats detached from their sonorous manifestation via Rosselli's person, tuned by exile between four nations and three languages. A performer of organ, piano, violin, percussion, and voice for theater as well as concert settings in the heady postwar years of interarts experimentation, Rosselli evolved a powerful practice of reciting her own poems—one noted for having struck a rowdy crowd dead silent during an epoch-defining poetry festival at Castelporziano in 1979. The performative aspect of her work is one with which strictly literary criticism and translation have proved unable to contend adequately, particularly insofar as it reaches beyond musicological conception into modes of recitation or even *canto* (song).[159] Yet performance was a central element of both poetic composition and presentation for her, pervading her own exegeses in terms of linguistic rhythm, vocal timbre, and breath.[160] Although critics have mounted various studies of Rosselli's multilingualism, including two monographs devoted to the subject, the sonic elements of Rosselli's xenoglossia have been largely overlooked or naturalized.[161] This seemingly peripheral issue is in fact crucial because accent, the sound of language perceived to be within or outside the domain of one's "mother tongue," continues to be one of the most blatant ways in which belonging is policed—one of the most trenchantly embedded signs of who is "us" and who is other.

Wishing to convey these crucial aesthetic, historical, and psychological contexts for a difficult body of verse in the bare intimacy of a Midwestern living room, I found myself feeling obliged to *reperform* as opposed to merely reading the original and translated texts of the polyglot poet/musicologist. The work in question was a poemetto, or long poem in thirteen sections titled "Impromptu," composed in a single morning in December 1979—according to a now-legendary narrative based on Rosselli's attestations—in a sort of rapture or "colpo d'ispirazione" (bout of inspiration) following a crippling seven-year interval in which she was unable to produce new work.[162] First published in 1981, "Impromptu" was reissued in 1993 in an edition for which Rosselli proposed a companion cassette of recitations with commentary. Although only the recording of "Impromptu" itself materialized, it forms a precious testament to the text's musical aspirations—one that has received little attention in the critical record.[163]

Rosselli's performances have a vacillating linguistic quality, which is to say a vibrational quality, creating halos of sound, of experience, and of meaning. The way that Rosselli recites the third section of "Impromptu" in particular (audible in the recording I have archived at Pennsound|Italiana) estranges listeners from the messages it bears. It is as if the melody, the accentuation, the pulsation of the text, of the recitative—"a musical declamation . . . sung in the rhythm of ordinary speech with many words on the same note," according to the *American Heritage Dictionary*—exists on a plane above and beyond its semantic value as an autonomous complex of assonant or dissonant phonemes. Rosselli's reading, like her compositions, follows a musical and perceptual as opposed to narrative trajectory of association. It is inherently polyphonous, wherein melody and rhythm drift from expected standards of spoken stress, manifesting independent agency. There's something nearly liturgical in the way that she chants the poem, recalling "Chiesa" and the anecdote surrounding the 1960 performance with Tudor and Cunningham at the Teatro Sistina, generating dissonance through the clash of sonic and narrative contexts.[164] The re-pulsing of inspiration by a poetic outsider recalls her early "O dio che ciangelli" ("Oh god who chancels"), in which god, addressed as tu, "attract[s] / so as then to repulsate [or, repulse/repalpitate/rethrob/revibrate] barbarian joys [tu attiri / per poi ripulsare le gioie barbare]" (*LP*, 268).

Chiara Carpita points out that Rosselli's personal library contains a meticulously annotated edition of Curt Sachs's *Le sorgenti della musica* (*The Wellsprings of Music*).[165] In his section on "Rhythm and Form," the two organizing principles of melody, Sachs writes that despite poetry's penchant for regulating rhythm, "all versification depends on irrational respiration with a meaningful lengthening and shortening of individual syllables. As a spoken art, it requires a freedom in which both the stresses and the meters are little more than merely suggested."[166] By establishing spatial and durational rather than traditional metrical constraints, Rosselli sought a dialectic of control and rhythmic freedom that cannot be understood strictly in written terms; it requires analysis of rhythmic dilation and contraction out loud of the sort modeled in this recitation.

One example will have to suffice to give a sense of how this studied dilation might manifest in performance. A coinage via the present participle that rhymes with, while transmuting, the musical direction *andante* ends the third section of "Impromptu": "della mia stralunante morte" ("of my moonstriking death," in my translation, for reasons that will become clear). In the definitive Meridiano edition of Rosselli's works, as well as the recent trilingual version published by Guernica, the editors duly note that in cleaned-up manuscripts of this text, the word *stralunante* (dazzling, stunning) is "corrected" in favor of the term *stralunata* (dazed).[167] It is therefore more compelling that when Rosselli performs this text for the recording included in the 1993 edition, she not only retains the original term, *stralunante*, but also emphasizes it by drawing out the action of bedazzlement vocally. The death in question is not an object moonstruck but an agent that keeps dazzling: it is aurally and visually moonstriking.[168]

The point of Rosselli's performance (and my translation of it) was to defamiliarize through studious lyrical transgressions, and yet when I reperformed this work in/as translation at a conference at the American Academy in Rome thereafter, an excitable fan in the audience relayed to me that the arrangement was "perfetto, perché lei era strainera, e tu sei straniera!" This guileless trumping of all musicality and definition of two very different species of Italian citizens as "straniere" epitomize how tightly regulated Italianness continues to be, even within the putatively enlightened circles of the literary world. All of the artistry and research Rosselli devoted to tethering herself to that state—not to mention the family's sacrifice in the name of fighting Fascism—collapse under the overweening category of "accent," eclipsing every other feature of belonging or unbelonging. Rather than measuring Rosselli's divergence from the phonetic norms of standard Italian, which were famously difficult to impose along the regionally divisive Italian peninsula, much less through its diaspora in a century of emigration and exile, it would be more accurate to think of Rosselli's poetic and actual "voice," artifact of a singular fusion of world-historical and personal circumstances, as itself plural: comprising reputedly separate cantons of expression that come together in a harmonic that "native" speakers of Italian, English, and French have been trained to recognize as dissonant.

The Rosselli family's expulsed geography is extraordinary but more exemplary, more emblematic of the global future, than most readers would have projected or hoped; it is the outcome of political and psychic trauma that found its tragic end in a suicide eerily foreshadowed by Amelia Pincherle Rosselli's 1906 play *L'idea fissa*, or *The Fixed Idea*, in which a protagonist with a dual personality commits suicide by throwing himself from a window.[169] I don't normally foreground Rosselli's disability (mental illness never diagnosed with stability but thought to be paranoid schizophrenia, accompanied by visions of inner persecution by the CIA) or her suicide, but I am drawn to do so in this political moment, in which amped-up fantasies of "invasion" by non-nationals continue to fortress and weaponize the United States while, on the shores of the Mediterranean, a neofascist government resists refugees in the name of investment, both brokering deals with offshore detention sites that weaken or negate the rights of asylum seekers. Nationalism, sexism, ableism, and racism didn't directly prompt Rosselli's suicide, and yet the status of perpetual outsider plagued Rosselli throughout her life. We can see her grappling with accent and citizenship on an intimate scale, by spending her last lire in the 1950s on pronunciation lessons for Rs that struck her would-be fellow citizens as too French or too English and in her formal bid for "double nationality" in the country of her father as well as of her mother ("not a word of this to nonna!" she pleads to John in a letter of February 1951—as the adults exchanged anxious notes about her difficulty in adapting to new contexts or her unpragmatic passion for her estranged grandfather Joe's realm of "musical rages").[170] Her work's belligerent alterity continues to plague its reception: I have argued with powerful yet timorous editors for the exceptional relevance of Rosselli from a global perspective, noting her importance for emerging twenty-first-century Italian poets and an older generation of renowned American authors: John Ashbery, the first to publish Rosselli's English poetry outside of Italy; Jerome Rothenberg, founder of the Ethnopoetics movement; and Jackson Mac Low, renowned experimentalist and comrade of John Cage, to name only a few of her own contemporaries; there will be others.[171]

Rosselli's is a Pentecost taking place on a vibrational level—never the ideological reworking of the psalm for the complicit nation-state, but each psalm haunted by its material echoes, its laboriously embodied transmission, its gravitational pull in other languages. This is what makes it so richly barbarous—anticipating Lyn Hejinian's eventual call for a barbarian poetry after Fascism: "Poetry after Auschwitz must indeed be barbarian; it must be foreign to the cultures that produce atrocities. As a result, the poet must assume a barbarian position, taking a creative, analytic, and often oppositional stance, occupying (and being occupied by) foreignness—by the barbarism of strangeness."[172] Rosselli's harmonics help us to hear the seeming dystopia of accented speech, its branding of the outsider, as a utopia of bridged cultures and experiences. Rosselli stands as a central protagonist of twentieth-century arts precisely because of her disintegration of cantons from the margins. Heedless of cultural propriety, the new cantos that result refract the conflicts inherent in the institution of any national literature—and elicit that the nation is itself a fundamentally clamorous form.

4

"Fog Is My Land"

Etel Adnan's Painting in Arabic and the
Reinvention of Belonging

LEPORELLO AS GEOPOETICS

The book opens in an accordion continuum from right to left, each page more than four times the size of my hand (figure 4.1). A panorama unfolds page by page and scene by scene in brilliant royal blue, ochre, carmine, gray, and viridian watercolor and ink, twenty-four squares in total. Stretching to several widths of a long table in the gray storerooms of the Institut du Monde Arabe, it makes for a 612-centimeter-vast landscape of text I have been trying to behold in person for seven years, yet whose monumental scale I somehow never anticipated from the one image available through my screen. Handwritten in irregularly inked Arabic script across six of these pages is the poem"الأم والطفلةُ الضائعة" ("Al-Umm wa al-Ibnat al-Da'i 'la," or "The Mother and the Lost Daughter") by Badr Shakir al-Sayyab (Jaykur 1926–Kuwait City 1964)—the exiled Iraqi communist writer and translator from a village at the confluence of the Tigris and Euphrates who revolutionized Arab poetry by employing free verse. But the hand of the artist's book is that of Etel Adnan, the poet, essayist, and visual artist (Beirut 1925–Paris 2021); Adnan chose this poem to form part of an intimate pantheon of poet-kith to transcribe in accordion books, leporellos as she called them, made precious through illumination. This leporello dates to 1970; al-Sayyab had been the first poet Adnan chose to pay homage to in this form, shortly after his death in 1964. In one of the interior monologues of her best-known work in the Arab world, *Sitt Marie-Rose*, first published from Paris in French in 1978, and from Sausalito in English by Post-Apollo four years later, al-Sayyab is compared with Che Guevara as inimitable: "It is always the next phase, the next poem or the next march through the jungle that shapes them."[1] Theirs is the work of potentiality, shaped by the

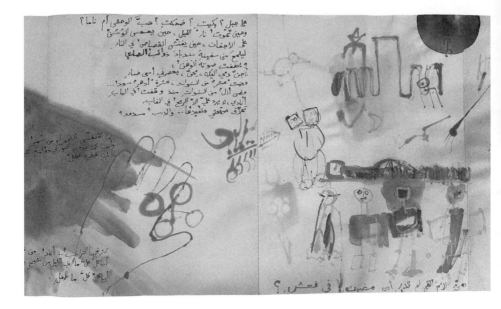

FIGURE 4.1 Etel Adnan, *Al-Sayyab, Mother and Lost Daughter*, 1970. Ink and watercolor on a Japanese book. Signed, dated, and titled by the artist. Closed, 33 × 25.2 cm × 24 pages. Open, 33 × 612 cm. Copyright Estate of Etel Adnan, Paris. Courtesy of Donation Claude & France Lemand, Institut du monde arabe, Paris.

ungiven future; al-Sayyab can't be imitated, but can be transcribed and therefore somatically, visually, verbally incorporated as elective kin in a community to come.

I wrote "landscape of text," but "landscape" suggests a unified field. Instead, what opens to vision is a series of abstract vignettes not cohering in any single geography. I understand why, to date, the book hasn't been easy to find reproduced in its entirety: it isn't as coherent as variations on a theme of inkwells or as easy to hold in the mind as the panorama of a skyline. In fact, looking more closely, this illuminated manuscript simultaneously possesses the quality of a sketchbook—holding free color washes as well as quick-painted sketches: of a frog or rat and a palm tree, of a bird and futuristic-looking figures or Kachina dolls, of a car and a cannon, of an eye and a cross-legged figure wearing a cloak. The work possesses the quality of an experimental, monumentally proportioned composition book where, surrounding the formal al-Sayyab poem, traces of languages or half-languages that are not mother tongues to the text reside: readily recognizable symbols such as arrows, fish, those of the two genders combined into one glyph, and the crescent facing left that artist/writer/publisher/life partner Simone Fattal adopted as the emblem of Post-Apollo Press; potential alchemical or celestial alphabets; potential Chinese characters for earth, eye, and mouth, or simply geometry; abstract signs recalling Indigenous American petroglyphs; and above all, possible riffs on alphabets of the eastern Mediterranean, such as Arabic, Phoenician, Greek, Demotic, and Sumerian. The signs are impossible to pin to any given linguistic system; these lines wrought with the freedom of the brush reside in the borderlands between languages ancient, contemporary, and future. The outlines of hands appear on this palette of sorts as well, as in prehistoric cave paintings; one is reminded of Emilio Villa's obsession with "the primeval sign-symbols from which historic and technological man has become fatally estranged."[2] These hands also prefigure the choral chapters of *Sitt Marie-Rose* that represent the voices of deaf and speech-impaired Palestinian students, chapters that begin with the children's reaching for a language that will enable them to communicate: "We're here to learn the special languages that will help us communicate with others. We read words on lips whose sounds don't reach us. We utter sounds that make people shudder it seems. We can't hear them. We can use our fingers for an alphabet."[3]

Two inscriptions in Arabic stand out as clear: the al-Sayyab lyric and a separate vow inscribed in red and bisected by one of the accordion folds, constituting the beginning of the Shahadah, or the oath and first pillar of Islam: "لَا إِلَٰهَ إِلَّا ٱللَّٰه"(there is no god but God—markedly missing the second half that names Muhammed as God's messenger, thereby remaining in a space both more interstitial and more universal) (figure 4.2). This first half of the oath, highly recognizable and sacred for the literate, almost hides in plain view along the fold line, as if about to be closed and kept secret—written in red superimposed with washes of yellow gold and rust, yet as if in invisible ink for those who do not read Arabic. It is as though Adnan is practicing to generate new glyphs while casting out in the language of one ideal community—a community that begins with the late poet al-Sayyab, who cohabited with her the pages of the Beirut-based poetry journal *Shi'r* founded by Adonis and Yusuf al-Khal to modernize Arabic poetry without merely mimicking Western modernism. Omar Berrada writes of her leporellos that "in their very loyalty to Arab contemporaneity," they "depict a tension constantly being renewed between the duty to remember and the desire for rupture."[4]

I properly encountered Adnan's work for the first time in 2004, at "Poetry and Its Arts: Bay Area Interactions, 1954–2004," an exhibition hosted by the California Historical Society.[5] I was seized in the face of two concertina books within

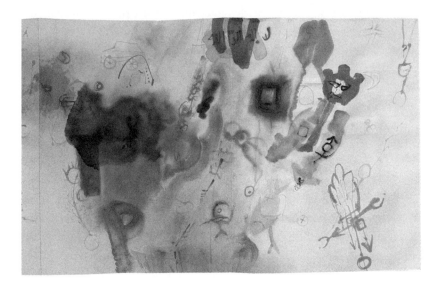

FIGURE 4.2 Etel Adnan, *Al-Sayyab, Mother and Lost Daughter*, 1970. Ink and watercolor on a Japanese book. Signed, dated, and titled by the artist. Closed, 33 × 25.2 cm × 24 pages. Open, 33 × 612 cm. Photograph by Jennifer Scappettone. Copyright Estate of Etel Adnan, Paris. Courtesy of Donation Claude & France Lemand, Institut du monde arabe, Paris.

whose accordion folds Adnan had transcribed and illuminated other authors' poems. I recognized the folds, the form: the matrix of these compact yet panoramic books was identical to that of orihon, a type of Japanese codex invented during the Heian era that represents a fundamental transition between the scroll and the modern book. Adnan's painted lines of handwriting-drawing-cryptograms within these zigzag paper spreads defied the distinctions between the three modalities—and indexed infinitude in the form of folds in the compressed space beneath the vitrine glass, where one couldn't possibly take all in at once. The languages of composition were multiple; the leporellos, as Adnan calls them, were "Untitled" yet named the poets and works partly transcribed within: *Homage to Beirut* (an Arabic text by the twice-exiled Kurdish Iraqi poet Buland al-Haidari, devoted "to those in whom Beirut remained, although they left, and to those whom Beirut deserted, although they stayed") and "Black Spoon"(a multilingual 1993 poem by the Bolinas-based poet/publisher Duncan McNaughton).[6] As someone who had plunged into translating Amelia Rosselli—whose geography obliquely mirrored Adnan's from another edge of the Mediterranean and from another vantage onto the Ottoman Empire's collapse—I had grown

"FOG IS MY LAND"

familiar with the experience of not assuming coherence between place of residence, national affiliation, and the language of poetic composition and of having to suss out which languages might be at play in any given stanza. Here that puzzling was happening in a vibratory, multihued visual field whose horizontal bands of wash invoked a musical score.

This initial encounter with Adnan's panoramic writings, coinciding with my exit from graduate school, formed the entryway into the rest of a lifetime of taking in her work. I heard her launch *In the Heart of the Heart of Another Country*—which includes "To Be in a Time of War," a searing indictment of the so-called Global War on Terrorism composed exclusively in the infinitive tense— at City Lights in 2005, recognizing only much later that the antiwar activism in the Bay Area of that moment mirrored the anti-colonial struggles under which Adnan had become an "Arab American poet."[7] I devoured all the books I could, beginning with *Of Cities and Women* and *Sitt Marie-Rose*, and eventually invited Adnan into a book project honoring women elders for Belladonna*; she continued to publish with abundance into her nineties, so that I couldn't keep up, and the art world began to "discover" that she was a distinguished painter.[8] In 2017, lacking complete access to the precious dispersed primary sources yet still enthralled, I began research for an essay about the way the leporellos open up a space of expansive confusion and harmony—or simply of friendship—against geopolitical fracture, reconstituting a political space and identity foreclosed by current circumstances. But the essay wanted to move further than I could answer. I include the still-open question of that essay, in all its discomfort, in this book to ask how zones of unmastery in writing might trouble the inherited frameworks of reception through which we read national and diasporic writings now. Encountering xenoglossic writing and theorizing xenoglossia demands that we ourselves, as readers, move beyond our own spheres of mastery to enter the realm of the beginner, of the autodidact—aware of our ignorance and our place and aware that, as Adnan wrote from Beirut in 1990, "every theory is a burial."[9]

The test of xenoglossia, seeking out the mobility and confines of this book's thesis, necessitates that we shift gears at this juncture to examine the other side of the colonialisms presented in earlier chapters—studying the dynamics at the Eastern edge of the Mediterranean to see how they might be revised in situations wherein languages are not only distanced but forbidden, even if that entails migrating beyond my comfort zone as a scholar. The work of Adnan's leporellos is xenoglossic to a degree more perplexingly literal than that of the previous poetry in this book. Although her Arab father attempted under the forbidding conditions of the French Mandate for Syria and the Lebanon to teach his daughter Arabic, as we shall see, these lessons consisted of transcribing a script she didn't understand in a language that, thereafter, she never claimed fully to know or to read—so that her later attempts to connect to Arabic and its nonconformist poets through painting constitute a practice of xenoglossia in the form of writing. Such writing is inspired, although not in the Christian or, for that matter, any organized religious sense. Grappling with Adnan's leporellos has been an unexpected, unprescribed, yet vital chapter in my study of xenoglossic poetics, born of curiosity, elective affinity, political reverence, and ardor that pressed me to exceed—in the fraught sense of fuoriuscire—the barriers of inherited literary preoccupations. In questioning and in listening, it inked a path toward correction of inherited colonial perspectives as well as the requisite anxiety of the beginner, through which I discovered how much remains to be translated from Arabic to make that path easier to follow with precision. The story of Adnan's leporellos appeared to me, as it clarified itself over the past seven years, to constitute a swan song to the injunction of specialization that commandeers and fractures not only academic but also intellectual life more generally in the Occident—not in the sense that it shirks deep and prolonged study (for any cavalier incorporation would only reproduce the violence of appropriation), but in the sense that it embraces being plunged into the humble stance of apprenticeship, astonishment, and connection to the seemingly unakin.[10] In interpreting Adnan's cross-disciplinary, cross-media, at times "unlettered" and bohemian body of work, I also find helpful Walter Mignolo's assertion that in "posttraditional social orders," the defense of tradition must be combated constantly "at all levels, including the cultures of scholarship and the parochial defense of disciplinarity, even under new paradigms."[11]

Although fascism did not take hold of power in Lebanon, her country of birth, Etel Adnan's work directly rebukes the violence of the tribe that inhered in Lebanese groups such as the Phalanges, a right-wing Christian political party founded in 1936 as a paramilitary youth organization, inspired by the spectacles of Fascist and Spanish Falange parties at that year's summer Olympics in Berlin (and although less explicitly, its Arab equivalent, the Najjadah). Originally a minority, the group came to prominence in the 1970s, constituting the most important force within the Christian camp during the Lebanese Civil War (so-called civil war, although in reality, like many such wars, it represented an international conflict conditioned by French and British colonialism and involving most acutely Palestine, Israel, and Syria). *Sitt Marie-Rose* is based on the life of Marie-Rose Boulos, a Christian Syrian immigrant to Lebanon who transgresses dictated tribal allegiance to provide social services to the Palestinian Resistance and who is tortured and executed by Phalangists as an example for the offense. The bulk of the novel recounts the kidnapping and murder of Marie-Rose from a variety of perspectives, preaching her "love of the Stranger" against the "umbilical cords that bind . . . together" the reactionary Christian youth militia.[12] One among the executioners expresses his will to power, in which all life can be distilled down to a cultural and existential agon: "I am absolute order. I am absolute power. I've reduced all truths to a formula of life and death."[13] In a 1983 interview about the work's translation into English for the radical lesbian feminist periodical *Off Our Backs*, Adnan distills the book's subject to "the tribal mentality of the Middle East," which has been present for a thousand years. Identifying herself as a Christian at this moment (the religion of her Greek mother), she confirms that she is in danger for (like Marie-Rose) being a woman who did not assume the side of her group in the civil war, aligning instead with the displaced Palestinians widely viewed as intruders and, through writing, calling out the manipulation of history and cruel excesses of allegiance to clan inhering in the violence.[14] Along the way, Adnan's work breaks down the mobilizing passions that Robert O. Paxton identifies in his canonical study of the five stages of fascism, correcting for the blinders of intellectual historians who seek philosophical coherence in movements that in reality "despise thought and reason," and that function instead by cultivating feelings of belonging within brotherhoods conceived and patrolled as unified and pure.[15] Adnan describes those who agree with the tribal current as happy in being multiplied and those who disagree as crushed.[16] Yet we can view her painting in Arabic as an attempt to reconstitute community among the dissident, in the process creating a more ideal collectivity.

TO WRITE AND TO PAINT IN A FOREIGN LANGUAGE

In her 1989 essay titled "To Write in a Foreign Language," Etel Adnan describes the trajectory of her relationship to Arabic: a language equated in childhood with shame, backwardness, and sin through her French convent schooling in Beirut during the French Mandate for Syria and Lebanon (1923–1946), which granted Lebanese political supremacy to Maronite Christians. This relationship with the language of the Beirut streets evolved in its political and affective implications in tandem with a series of intercultural wars that directly conditioned her life—World Wars I and II, the Algerian War of Independence, and the Lebanese Civil War. Arabic was the language of her father, Assaf Kadri, a Sunni Muslim from Damascus born to an Albanian mother and a high-ranking officer of the Ottoman Empire, who taught her the alphabet when she was a child.[17] Determined to overcome what he regarded as the propaganda of the French, he had the only child of his second marriage copy pages upon pages from an Arabic-Turkish grammar hailing from his days as a cadet, which she would use to decline verbs but ultimately lacked the discipline to study for comprehension. The child would have needed discipline dearly in a context where she lacked a patient teacher—and where for the students referred to by the nuns as "les indigènes," speaking Arabic in school was forbidden.[18] Those caught doing so would be forced to bear stones in their pockets—a performative form of punishment that transforms heritage into a burden in this colonial context. This literalized metaphor adds burdensome new meaning to Frantz Fanon's statement that "to speak means to be in a position to use a certain syntax, to grasp the morphology of this or that language, but it means above all to assume a culture, to support the weight of a civilization."[19] Adnan's mixed identity would prove consistently challenging even in an independent sectarian Lebanon, whose constitution, as her friend Fawwaz Traboulsi summarizes, "establishes the judicial, civic and political equality of all Lebanese as citizens (*muwatinin*), while at the same time institutionalising their judicial and political inequality as subjects (*ahlin*) belonging to hierarchised religious communities with unequal access to political power and public office."[20] Christians were privileged by this arrangement in a continuation of Western hegemony.

"To be a refugee is not to go away, it's not to be able to come back," Adnan told me in a 2017 interview; hers was a family of refugees.[21] Greek was the language of her mother, an Orthodox Christian who grew up in the Smyrna of the Ottoman Empire—a city burned to the ground during its definitive Turkish occupation in 1922. Although Adnan's father—equally defeated by the fall of the Ottomans, albeit from a more privileged socioeconomic position—saved his second wife's family from poverty and starvation, the fact that he was Muslim led some close relations violently to reject the union; indeed, their marriage would be impossible in the Lebanon of today, where civil unions are not permitted despite activist campaigns to the contrary. They spoke Turkish together, and while on the battle-front, he sent his wife romantic, almost novelistic letters in the language of her primary convent schooling, French, lucidly inscribed in pen and ink. Adnan's parents moved to Beirut at the end of World War I, where her father could continue to operate in an Arab context—although under French occupation, Arabs were effectively demoted to the status of aliens in their own land. The family's common languages were spoken Ottoman Turkish, which held within it a great deal of Arabic and Persian filtered through Qur'anic study; spoken Greek; and increasingly, the French of educational systems occupying the Levant.[22]

The Arabic script itself must have harbored a melancholic charge for Adnan's father, given that upon the founding of the Turkish Republic, Mustafa Kemal Atatürk (his former classmate) launched a series of nationalist linguistic reforms that have been compared to their contemporary Fascist counterparts, despite being part of a modernizing, Westernizing, secular agenda: in 1928, Atatürk replaced the Perso-Arabic script that had been used to convey Ottoman Turkish for a thousand years with the Latin alphabet and campaigned for the replacement of Arabic and Persian loan words with Turkish equivalents. Abandonment of the Arabic writing system would coincide with an immediate boost in literacy rates in a territory where knowledge of the abjad, a consonantal alphabet now cast as ill-suited to conveying Turkish vowels and other phonemes, had been limited to a privileged elite, so that for the vast majority of Turkish speakers in the fallen Ottoman Empire, this script would have been as mysterious as it was for the vanquished officer's five-year-old daughter.

The notion of a native language is thus braided with contradiction for Etel Adnan. Of the Arabic letters she absorbed through a childhood channel more somatic than semantic and to which she would return later in life, she writes, "I did not try to have them translated to me, I was satisfied with the strange understanding of them: bits here and there, sentences where I understood but one key word; it was like seeing through a veil, looking at an extraordinary scenery through a screen."[23] Adnan's lifelong process of upholding this distressed relationship with her father's tongue, for which the streets of Beirut served as her other jeopardized teacher, drafts a maquette of cultural belonging that obliges readers to revise still-prevalent assumptions of immediate claims on cultural heritage—beginning with the essentialist biological trope of the mother tongue, whose naturalization of language acquisition is undermined by ever-shifting geopolitical realities. The protracted practice of copying Arabic poetry that Adnan will later evolve suggests a need for unlearning the cultural education that assumes a West to East direction in the literal act of reading, as in the figurative act of inheriting influence. As in Rosselli, it represents a casting out, through art, for a parental tongue; it performs line by line an apprenticeship in the father tongue that remains unconsummated yet is invested with the passion of perpetual beginning. The practice of copying also connects the poet to centuries-old ritual traditions of cultural transmission and calligraphic practice, undermining avant-garde truisms first hatched by Futurists about the need to destroy the past in order to move forward.

With the onset of World War II, which Adnan described as having parented her city, the English of Anglophone armies occupying Beirut would become more and more prevalent in Lebanese intellectual and commercial life, rivaling or even eclipsing French in an emerging triangulation of cultural forces.[24] Counterintuitively, when Adnan moved to California in 1955, US English would become a vital crucible, offering her a liberation of expression akin to a "rebirth," in her own terms. The disjunctive map of linguistic attachment borne out by Adnan's eventual (but not exclusive) predilection for English and her experimentation with Arabic and other non-Latin writing systems reflect affective landscapes of dislocation and continuity that have evolved over the last century of global conflicts and that reigning discursive categories of cultural nativity, or political binaries of citizenship and statelessness, fail to account for.[25] The complex of these attachments compels us to revise assumptions of a binary struggle inherent in diglossia as well and to reconceive diaspora without recourse to what Yogita Goyal identifies as the flattening accusations of assimilation or cosmopolitanism.[26] To write in Arabic, a language Adnan does not think she can read, which is both her native tongue and not, is freighted in ways that are shared by many others in her country: "we Lebanese were colonized by the French, and in that process we were alienated from the Arabs," she explains to the separatist audience of *Off Our Backs*. "Most of us do not speak one language well. You will find families in which everyone speaks a different language depending on what school they went to."[27]

For Adnan, the screen, the veil, through which she perceives Arabic does not signal blockage alone. Placing herself behind a veil metaphorically locates her inside the Arab world but from the seemingly compromised standpoint of a woman—in what might read as a paradoxical self-Orientalizing move for an outspoken writer who played her part in a social revolution as one of the first generation of Arab girls who went to work.[28] Yet the veil is here transmuted into a mediating force of translucency that intensifies the power of the occluded text, whose mystery can be traced but not comprehended or shelved in the lettered sense. What can such refraction of vision and experience mean for a poet? Might the mediation of the screen function beyond its obvious foreclosure from nationally or ethnically conscripted identity to model the possibility of a more plastic relationship to cultural heritage, activist solidarity, and geopolitical futurity?

Lacking a dominant native tongue, Adnan's work constitutes a rejoinder to both exclusionary colonial nationalism and acritical tribal ethnocentrism, typical of xenoglossic modalities.[29] Charles Richet coined the term xénoglossie to describe the mysterious facility in Greek achieved by one Madame X—a medium who, though lacking a classical education, was able to write long passages from Plato and the New Testament hailing from the Franco-Greek Dictionary of Byzantios while in a trance. This scene of learning without learning secularizes the New Testament Pentecost narrative and hands divine inspiration over to the Byzantine dictionary.[30] In the twentieth-century origins of "xénoglossie" as concept, dictation is being taken from vocabularies and grammars rather than from religious gospel, and it is worthy of note that Adnan's father, already in an unorthodox marriage, did not have her copy the Qur'an but, instead, the text that would have bridged Arab with Turkish identities in the Ottoman Empire. Through manipulation by an artist of Adnan's alternately international and subnational sensibility, the never-quite-mother languages of the father and of the state—and even the seemingly dictatorial pedagogy of transcription—become instruments of buoyancy and resistance. Within painted textscapes capable of accommodating multiple sign systems, including systems that colonialism and "progress" forbade her from experiencing as native, this poet insists upon introducing the marginalized scripts of an embattled linguistic contact zone of global modernity into an anticolonial "wireless imagination." This xenoglossic space flouts the imperialist politics driving the Futurist forebears of the global avant-garde—politics that led Marinetti to draw a crude analogy between those citizens of modernity who make use of transnational communications without awareness of its deeper significance and "*the Arabs who watched with indifference the first airplanes in the skies above Tripoli*" (emphasis in original)—victims of the revolutionary aerial bombardment and seizure of Ottoman Tripolitania Vilayet practiced by Italians during the Italo-Turkish War and later hailed by the Alexandria-raised Marinetti as "the most beautiful aesthetic spectacle of my existence."[31]

In the wake of the world wars and an era of widespread decolonization, tactics of painterly abstraction seemed to offer literary artists across the globe one route to translinguistic communion. Beyond the dream of universal communicability pervading the postwar fervor of internationalism, alphabets infused with the gesticulations of action painting appeared to offer the promise of subversive occupation. The scrawled passages on canvas by Adnan's contemporary Cy Twombly became theorized by Villa, we will recall, as refutations of authoritarianism: as "whistles / in the fasces of uniform graphemes," and the very formation of "an ideal nationality."[32] Mohammed Melehi, a modernist Moroccan artist, professor at the École des Beaux-Arts of Casablanca, and editor of the transregional arts journal *Intégral* (1971–1978) to which Adnan contributed, witnessed such fermentation of painterly abstraction in postwar Rome when he moved there to study in 1957, enjoying what he identified as "la démocratie qui régnait entre les artistes à Rome," unique within Europe.[33] Melehi suggests that in countries where populations are divided by language (such as Morocco's French, Arabic, and Berber/Tamazight), painting has a specific suturing capacity, enjoying a more immediate and universal impact than text—although *Intégral* as a journal of "plastic and literary creation" as well as Melehi's works themselves dissolve any binary opposition between language and visual art, carving out space for sites of their imbrication such as calligraphy and political posters. In a 1967 questionnaire, Melehi characterized Arab art in utopian key as "permanent, présent et accessible à tout individu indépendamment de sa formation ou de sa culture," contrasting it with a Western figurative genealogy that relies on the cultivation of bourgeois taste. He moreover dissolved the line between reading and visual scanning that is blurred in calligraphy, an art of "mobility and vibration," with the statement "*La lecture est la pure identification visuelle d'un message et l'écriture est la pure transmission d'un message visuellement conçu*" (emphasis in original).[34]

Admitting to being haunted by such desires for immediate communicability, Adnan asks what she calls an unanswerable question: "What can I say of the fact that I do not use my native tongue and do not have the most important feeling as a writer I should have, the feeling of direct communication with one's audience?"[35] (We can presume that Adnan is referring here to Arabic and the Arab public.) Her visual art offers a nondiscursive answer to the unanswerable, being intimately tied to her shuttling across languages both under duress and by choice. Although critics mark a topical and tonal dichotomy between her writing (characterized as politicized and dark) and her visual art (depicted as cognitive/metaphysical, sensuous, and bright), studying the interweaving of these practices in her oeuvre draws us away from the facility of such dyads into a more ambiguous sociolyric space. More than a "bridge" between writing and artmaking, which is the metaphor that Adnan's recent biographer uses, Adnan's painting in accordion books underscores that—as she puts it in another piece—"writing is drawing, drawing is writing, writing is drawing…," especially if not exclusively in Eastern contexts: drawing itself is a kind of language.[36] The uncertain signs of her drawn and painted texts complicate presumptions of literate accessibility that go hand in hand with prevailing concepts of national and native languages and, by extension, concepts of citizenship and diaspora. Adnan's painted texts problematize even more rigorously than her printed texts the centuries-old imposition of the monolingual paradigm traceable to the French Revolution, and they register its lasting personal and political impacts. This writing/drawing forges a version of kithship with poets, refugees, and other marginalized subjects across and beyond linguistic affiliation and nation. The resultant linguistic climates propose refuge in mutual unmastery and can be seen to perform decolonization on an intimate scale.

Beyond her teeming corpus of lucid and freely styled works of verse and prose, Adnan has developed a body of writing whose relationship to its adopted languages is more distressed. Adnan herself singles out this aspect of her oeuvre as special, both for its unusual methods and for its historic significance, yet thus far, it has received only cursory critical treatment. In this chapter, I wish to explore the geopolitical implications of this body of work, which veers into the painterly: of poetic texts that toe the line between writing and drawing, xenoglossia and glossolalia. On the one hand, Adnan experiments with a spontaneous, seemingly purely gestural idiom, as in her masterwork *L'apocalypse arabe*. On the other hand, in painting on accordion books, this queer poet tackles the transcription of that father tongue over which she has never assumed perfect control—one that was occluded and that under colonization and new forms of nationalism she was not supposed to know. Adnan excavates a positive valence from this occlusion: "I think that I loved the act of writing things I did not understand, and I pretended that I was learning a language . . . just by writing it down. There must have been something hypnotizing about these exercises because much later, and for different reasons, I ended up doing practically the same thing."[37] Transcription of Arabic texts becomes a method for dwelling in a tongue that is destined by the corrosive undertow of Western influence to remain "foreign," withheld, and yet known on some translinguistic, translettered level. The translucency of Arabic appears to have opened up alternative possibilities of belonging over the course of Adnan's career. Regarded as a generative withdrawal from political ontologies imposed by an occidental worldview, opacity became a form of resistance to demands for colonized peoples' transparency voiced in 1969 by Édouard Glissant in his celebrated groundbreaking statement at the National Autonomous University of Mexico: "Nous réclamons le droit à l'opacité [We demand the right to opacity]."[38] Yet in love with light, Adnan will theorize and practice, in both writing and painting, a luminous strain of (semi-)opacity more akin to the shimmer provoked by a veil or fog. We recall here Deborah Bird Rose's application of the Aboriginal concept for the dynamic interaction of patterns in a performance or painting, which lures the attention as the glint of sun on water tantalizes the eye, and enhances awareness of the bling of encounter and transformation with ancestors, with other species, with others: this "Brilliance [shimmer, or bir'yun] . . . brings you, into the experience of being part of a vibrant and vibrating world."[39]

Adnan presents English, Arabic, and painting as idioms that disclosed routes beyond the imperial language of her education. She had fallen in love with poetry, devouring such French modernists as Baudelaire and Rimbaud, while studying under the diplomat and literary critic Gabriel Bounoure—the brilliant and charismatic founder of an experimental school in Beirut, the École des Lettres. Detecting her genius, Bounoure encouraged Adnan to apply for the scholarship to study in Paris that eventually led her to leave Lebanon for the first time, breaking violently from her now widowed mother's staunchly traditional expectations. She studied aesthetic philosophy at the Sorbonne from 1949 onward with Gaston Bachelard and Étienne Souriau in a context scored by World War II, but while living among Americans in the international house, Adnan became drawn to the unknown territory of the United States, which held out the promise of surpassing mere affirmation of her early formation. She moved to the Bay Area of California in 1955 on a scholarship for graduate studies in philosophy at Berkeley. After two and a half years of classes at Berkeley and Harvard with teachers such as Stanley Cavell and a semester-long break in Mexico between the two, she abandoned her doctoral program: her grasp of English had hardly prepared her for the Anglo-Saxon philosophical schools' intense focus on linguistics and symbolic logic, however enthralling she found the latter's emblems, and in the academic context of analytic philosophy at the time, thinkers she treasured such as Nietzsche were considered to be poets, thereby being disqualified from value as philosophers. She became captivated by the wonder and adventure of the American language, however, and it would lead her more squarely in the direction of poetics. It was at the University of California at Berkeley that Adnan first met Arabs who were not Lebanese or Syrian and became involved with the movement for Arab solidarity in concert with the Algerian War of Independence (1954–1962). As a secular dream of pan-Arab unity evolved, Adnan began to resent her colonial education, having to express herself in French, and to reject a notion of "francophonie" reserved exclusively for the subjects of colonized nations: through a transformative relationship with an artist from Mill Valley, she would eventually decide: "I didn't need to write in French anymore, I was going to paint in Arabic."[40]

QUEER XENOGLOSSIA AND THE REIMAGINATION OF KINSHIP

Adnan's choice to write in the tongue of the father harbors particularly urgent political possibilities, as it did for Amelia Rosselli. Yet the result is neither strictly patrilinear nor monolithic in either case. For Adnan, a staunch critic of the macho brotherhoods that drove the Lebanese Civil War, rejects any form of tribalism or sectarianism tied to what she calls "relative identities," stressing active acceptance over the naturalization of blood kinship.[41] A discussion of the word "son" in an interview with Lynne Tillman, for instance, reveals that Adnan regards this term through its vernacular usage in Semitic languages, which goes back millennia to the Aramaic of the New Testament: "When Jesus said, 'I am the Son, Father,' he meant 'I am accepted, and what I say is agreeable to the Father.'"[42] This conception revises understanding of the most canonical of dogmas through philology in a way that recalls Villa's speculative work on Semitic languages, yet it de-essentializes the structuralist assumptions of origins discourse that Villa's work can appear to take for granted: here it is acceptance and agreement that herald kinship, not blood. Adnan's painted language furthers this possibility of denaturalized affiliation: merging traditions normally rarefied from one another, her calligraphic transcriptions carry Arab culture into global contexts where it may be received unmediated by exogenous myths of the East. We can therefore distinguish in Adnan a queer xenoglossia that manifests belonging otherwise through an embodied practice of writing what is "native" and "foreign" at the same time, enacting the poiesis of kith. Through the "kin-aesthetics" of writing and painting, Adnan brings into being forms of elective and open affiliation that have been imagined and theorized by kinship critiques across queer, feminist, and critical race studies and that inhere in queer theory's reimagining of relationality, without ever disavowing the "intractability of kinship as an ideology, a material relation, an affective structure, and a narrative frame," as the editors of *Queer Kinship* articulate.[43] We will see that the violent policing of performances of tribal affiliation in the neofascist context against which Adnan's most canonical works were composed leaves no space for a fantasy of relationality fully freed from kinship's overdetermining frames.

How exactly does the dream of painting in Arabic constitute itself in Adnan's written works? And how are readers to travel across the competing sign systems in which it takes root? Toward the end of "To Write in a Foreign Language," Adnan characterizes Frantz Fanon's indictment of the French colonial system and the psychological effects of its linguistic policies as "beautifu[l]," while declining to "accus[e] the old colonial system" herself, claiming full responsibility for her language use as an Arab writer and stressing the difference between the Arab condition and that of Black Africans whose native tongues were subject to cultural genocide under colonization.[44] Adnan and Fanon were exact contemporaries, and her reading of his work was clearly formative; yet Adnan chooses to force the languages that circumstance imposed on her into plastic conditions, proposing through writing and what was strategically described in a transcontinental Arab milieu as "arts plastiques" that "international" linguistic systems can be altered or broken from within in poetry—producing politically and aesthetically expansive, even explosive results. By alternating between and merging the mediums of writing and painting, her poetry eludes the antinomies characterizing her contemporaries' critiques of linguistic ideology to propose a paradox or a both/and proposal: "Poets are deeply rooted in language and they transcend language."[45]

Adnan's relationship with drawing and painting, a "language beyond words,"[46] was spurred by a sudden encounter, in concert with learning English, in the period when her alienation from France led her to feel that she was lacking a means of self-expression. Upon finding the analytic philosophy taught in the United States incommensurate with her interests in aesthetics, and in need of money, Adnan took a job teaching aesthetics at Dominican College in San Rafael. (Significantly, she declined to teach French, choosing instead to teach philosophy in English.) Ann O'Hanlon, a progressive product of the Works Progress Administration and Buddhist founder of the college's art department, provoked Adnan into practice in 1959 by suggesting that one couldn't teach philosophy of art without direct experience of the subject. She offered Adnan pastels and narrow scraps of paper left over from her art classes, and the results of Adnan's observations of landscape were immediately compelling. The narrow proportions of the paper scraps (about 3 by 10 inches) would have invited an analogy to writing, prefiguring the leporello format that Adnan would eventually deploy with great originality. In the 1960s, Adnan started using discarded scraps of canvas that O'Hanlon provided for painting with a palette knife. Painting began to parallel poetry as a medium: "Abstract art was the equivalent of poetic expression; I didn't need to use words. . . . I didn't need to belong to a language-oriented culture but to an open form of expression," she recalls of this discovery. She immediately makes a connection between language and geography: "I understood . . . that I moved not on single planes but within a spherical mental world, and that what we consider to be problems can also be tensions, working in more mysterious ways than we understand."[47] Abstraction here offers the possibility of remapping one's relation to language and culture altogether.

Although she had published a book of poetry in Beirut at the age of twenty (*Le livre de la mer*), Adnan felt that it was untranslatable because its founding eroticism between the sea (gendered feminine in French) and sun (masculine in French) is inverted in Arabic. She consistently describes her emergence as a poet as coinciding with her first publication in English, a language that (though she has not commented upon it) would have offered a route out of these gender binaries. Adnan, who was openly queer, had been mocked as a "garçon manqué" (literally, failed boy) as a child, making being a boy "both appealing as a fact and shameful as a desire," and she recalls being happy to have her hair cut "à la garçon" and to be dressed in boys' clothes: "it must have reinforced my identity of being neither just a girl, nor a boy, but a special being with the magical attributes of both."[48] In the United States, she could live out secular pan-Arab commitments while being a queer woman in ways that would be foreclosed in Lebanon itself, where the strictures on identity were more intense. Moreover, to write poetry in the California of the 1960s would bring a dream of mobility and of solidarity across confined identities seemingly within reach. Poetry was itself a "brotherhood," a religion, or an alternative kinship network in which—in pointed contrast to the tribal mentality of lingering fascist energies to be narrated in *Sitt Marie-Rose*— it was possible to dodge gendered roles, religious dogma, state enforcement,

"FOG IS MY LAND"

and capitalist frames of utility, conceiving of the collective as a fellowship that even exceeded the limits of the human species: "That was a time when poetry became . . . the only religion which has no gods and dogmas, no punishments, no threats, no hidden motivations, no commercial use, no police and no Vatican. It was an open brotherhood open to women, men, trees and mountains."[49] Adnan's parents had "disappeared," and she was living at the edge of a different continent and reinventing her language, relations, and world.[50]

At the École des Lettres, Adnan had developed a sense of poetry itself as "a counter-profession," "an expression of personal and mental freedom," and more radically, a "perpetual rebellion" that eventually led her to "cut all ties with home and country."[51] Now in the United States, she entered this utopian fraternity out of shared desperation over war atrocities, publishing her first English-language poems, "The Ballad of the Lonely Knight in Present-Day America" and "The Enemy's Testament," in the *S-B Gazette*, a free pamphlet series opposing the Vietnam War printed covertly by Leon Spiro on the presses of San Francisco City Hall. A torn scrap of paper communicated in 1961 that her writing was "muchly accepted," and "The Enemy's Testament," narrated from the point of view of a murdered Viet Cong soldier, became the second poem in the seminal 1967 anthology *Where Is Vietnam?* edited by Walter Lowenfels. Says Adnan, "I became an American poet that way."[52]

Adnan's strong claim for a citizenship other than one justified by jus sanguinis or jus soli—for a nationality constructed through writing—is remarkable on multiple accounts: "They got me out of my lair / for I was infesting my own land, / and they, the foreigners, came to liberate me, / liberate me of my share."[53] Adnan claims US affiliation through poetry composed in an American idiom rather than through dictates of citizenship. However, she asserts solidarity with a republic of thought more ideal than one that would pledge allegiance to the flag leading troops into atrocity—a republic born of protest. "The Enemy's Testament" ventriloquizes the hypocritical rhetoric of the very nation-becoming-empire to which it asserts belonging through its ironic opposition, through the mouth of the dead that enfleshes its logical repercussions—recalling the strategies of Villa's 1947 "Dichiarazioni del soldato morto." Identification with a Viet Cong soldier signaled solidarity with Asians who were previously subject to French colonialism but was a means of connecting with Adnan's own past as well: her family had taken in an orphaned boy named Pierrot, the son of a French mother and a father from French Indochina, during school holidays.[54] Removal from Lebanon does not constitute abandonment of Lebanon; another of Marie-Rose's Lebanese feminist colleagues, Hala Salaam Maksoud, asserted that living in the United States and working with the United Nations permitted her and her husband to live out their devotion to an Arab secular Lebanon in a more perfect way because from that outpost "we felt we could represent the totality of Lebanon and our Arab commitment much better than in Beirut."[55] That said, the world of diplomats and activists is still conditioned by geopolitical categories that are so dizzied in Adnan's art as to lose their footing (if not their force) as polarities. As Mary Layoun describes the poetic remaking of location and identity in Adnan's prose, "It is not 'real' and it cannot be simply marshaled as a blueprint"—and yet the fragility of that landscape of connection makes it more compelling and provocative.[56]

The fact that Adnan sent her antiwar poetry to Robert Kennedy (and that he responded to it) shows how much optimism Adnan still harbored about the direction of the United States at that time (and of poetry itself).[57] Adnan's self-identification never ended at "American," however, and as she confessed of this period of poetic rebirth, "The old ghosts had not disappeared."[58] Notwithstanding the fact that she could not compose in Arabic, but only spoke the language of the street, Adnan held to her identity as an Arab writer; when pressed for categorization, she agreed that the term "Arab American" applied best, but such combination is deceptively crude because "an identity is not always a geographic territory. My identity was in not wanting to be rejected by Arab poets." She described herself as being integrated into Arab poetry in the mid-1960s by Yusuf al-Khal, the first gallerist of modern painting in Beirut, editor of the crucial little magazine *Shi'r* (*Poetry*, 1957–1970), and translator of such works as *The Waste Land*.[59] Al-Khal supported and published her work in translation by the expatriated Iraqi poet Sargon Boulus, as well as translating Adnan's work himself; Adnan's biographer Wilson-Goldie writes that al-Khal's blessing allowed her to join the so-called Arab republic of letters.[60] Adnan in turn had a part in enabling a transnational "brotherhood" of Arab poetry by connecting the Beirut scene with Abdellatif Laâbi, the Rabat-based editor of the radical tricontinental magazine of "décolonisation culturelle" *Souffles-Anfas* in 1966—recognizing him as a fellow student of Bounoure (figure 4.3).[61] (Adnan was to be the only woman poet published in *Souffles*.) Regardless of these relationships, as Lisa Suhair Majaj and Amal Amireh pointed out in their 2002 anthology devoted to Adnan's work, its literary reception continues to fall through the cracks of the nationally and linguistically siloed traditions that it itself superimposes or blurs, and the fact that Adnan does not compose in Arabic long led her to remain undercanonized in the Arab literary sphere, particularly outside of Lebanon.[62]

When in 1972, after fourteen years in California, Adnan returned to a culturally vibrant Beirut and became the incisive cultural editor of *Al Safa*, a newly founded French-language newspaper, and then of *L'Orient le Jour*, she piqued interest in her

FIGURE 4.3 Mohammed Melehi, covers of the quarterly review *Souffles* 1 (1966), 7–8 (1967), and 13–14 (1969), edited by Abdellatif Laâbi. Courtesy of Abdellatif Laâbi.

provocative editorials by way of their signature alone: her name registers mixed origins and the performative reinvention of kinship through the act of naming. Etel was an ancient Greek name in disuse; Adnan, strictly Muslim and usually a male first name, was only adopted as a family surname by her father upon the 1932 census, when French authorities required all families to register their names as citizens of the republic.[63] It was a name that resonated with the rise in Arab national feeling because, according to a tradition revived in late nineteenth-century Turkey as part of an Ottoman nationalism, 'Adnān was an ancestor of the northern Arabs, the equivalent of a Romulus or Remus.[64] "Adnan" in Turkish and Arabic (عدنان) embeds within it the dual meaning of "pioneer," or "the person who has existence in two parallel worlds." It seems as though Adnan took the performative force of her name to heart; her art harmonizes ever-multiplying sets of parallel worlds in aesthetic, gendered, and geopolitical terms—at times at great personal risk.

Those risks—and the death threats that accompanied the Arabic publication of her novel *Sitt Marie-Rose* in the midst of the Lebanese Civil War—ultimately led her and her partner Fattal to return to the Bay Area in 1977. Marie-Rose's heroic philosophy as represented by Adnan's interior monologue may seem utopian in its appeal to Gilgamesh: "I represent love, new roads, the unknown, the untried. For ten thousand years in this part of the world we've been tribal, tribal, tribal. But Gilgamesh left alone, all ties forever broken."[65] Yet the militarized policing of identity the book narrates was far from fictional and pursued its author as well. Only through art, through poiesis, can the ideal republic be constituted, its signs transgressing hegemonic patriarchal dictates, and perhaps only through poiesis can an immaterial revolt against the conditions of the present engender a threat of such finality. The disabled students of Marie-Rose, lacking access to the signs of hegemonic society, speak an embodied choral language, using their hands and expressing themselves through dance by feeling the vibrations from the radio. In the final sequence, Adnan narrates in a sentence both giddy and grimly determinist, philosophical, and realist that "whether you like it or not, an execution is always a celebration. It is the dance of Signs and their stabilization in Death."[66] Although it is not clear whose celebration this is, Marie-Rose's execution activates her death and life as indomitable martyrdom, multiplying the implications of her example through the dance of signs, and stabilizes as exemplary her fugitive life and sacrifice. Articulated at the core of the canonical novel of the Lebanese Civil War, in a moment when both Palestine and Lebanon are again under siege, this harrowing dance continues to reverberate.

Adnan's construction of identity inheres in dynamic reoccupation and recirculation, rather than being tethered to bounded forms that would isolate certain subjects as extraterritorial; she writes of maps that they "are not about shapes, but about energies flowing in and out of places" yet adds to this a qualification of the cosmopolitan freedom of movement: "They are about directions and obstacles."[67] Her politics unfolds through the battle to achieve solidarities, liberated from while never turning a blind eye to the brutal day-to-day walls and blockades of nation and empire. She speculates that the embattled state of the Arab world is the very foundation of her identification with it. "If the Arab world weren't forever at war, and so much under attack, maybe I wouldn't have been Arab," she says to Hans Ulrich Obrist in an interview, implying that she had taken it on of her own volition: "But the daily politics of it keep me from getting complacent." Later, she returns to the question of writing itself: "I would have had another life if I had written in Arabic."[68]

What difference does it make, then, that Adnan has not written but instead "painted" in Arabic? Experiencing Arabic as a "lost paradise," Adnan forged another way to write into this part of her heritage and contemporary political moment. It unfolded during the reign of Egypt's second president, Gamal Abdel Nasser Hussein, whose iconic status as a champion of Arab independence and unity skyrocketed upon his nationalization of the Suez Canal and subsequent political victory against invading Israel, Britain, and France, in the immediate aftermath of Algeria's wrested independence from France. Having discovered accordion books—in Japanese, "orihon / 折本," or in Italian, "leporelli"—in a North Beach cafe during the early 1960s through Rick Barton, an artist living on the margins of San Francisco, she became enthralled by the way that these long folding scrolls invited reading in time, and she found in them a channel for connecting with Arab writers. She began a practice of copying and illuminating Arabic texts into leporellos found in Japanese shops that endured for the rest of her life—a multivoiced practice of homage that Simone Fattal identifies as a politicized "anthology" of contemporary poets that Adnan knew and loved.[69] It is both a personal pantheon and a claim for a different form of canonization, based on revolutionary aesthetics and affection. Rather than emulating the "codification" of classical calligraphy, Adnan deployed her "extremely imperfect" handwriting to manipulate the inherently plastic Arabic alphabet.[70] The leporellos gesture simultaneously toward East Asian calligraphic traditions—to which the Bay Area arts scene, with its vital exchange among Beat poets, abstract expressionism, and calligraphic abstractionists like Saburo Hasegawa and Bernice Bing, may have accustomed her—through the matrix of the orihon itself and through her fluid, energetic strokes of ink. Although copying may at first glance seem traditionalist and backward-looking, Adnan took on the most radical authors in creating this pantheon of transcription, in that gesture of simultaneous memory and rupture to which Omar Berrada attests; she began with "Madinat al-Sindbad" ("Sinbad's City") by Badr Shakir al-Sayyab, who had just passed away young and penniless. Al-Sayyab was once an avowed communist who was exiled and imprisoned for his political beliefs, and he introduced modernity into Arabic poetics through impassioned and highly personal free-verse experiments.[71] As a creative practice evolved from her father's dictated exercises in copying from a grammar book, Adnan's transcriptions herald, in gestural form, the grammatical detournements of French and English language lessons in Theresa Hak Kyung Cha's *DICTEE*.[72]

Amid the furor of Adnan's rise to the status of a global art-world sensation following her 2012 participation in Documenta 13, which led to much focus on her abstract landscapes on canvas, she began to emphasize the revolutionary significance of these hybrid works on paper, stressing that she was the first Arab painter besides Shaker Hassan al Saïd to use personal, nontraditional handwriting in calligraphic art.[73] Critics have taken note. In a pioneering taxonomy of the globally disseminated "Calligraphic School of Art" (traditionally known as Hurufiyya), Wijdan Ali presents Adnan and Shaker Hassan as pioneers of the "calligraffiti" style, in which personal handwriting by artists not necessarily trained in classical calligraphy becomes a channel of expressive freedom.[74] Yet I would argue that these books still deserve a more protracted critical discourse because they are books and, therefore, demand durational unfolding and literary hermeneutic procedures, rather than exposing themselves to eye, wall, or digital space all at once as visual artworks appear to do. This is partly why—with scholars such as Johanna Drucker and Amaranth Borsuk constituting valuable exceptions—"critical writing about book art and specifically about artist books lags far behind critical writing about other media," as the "New Manifesto for Book Art Criticism" of 2020 articulated.[75] In some of the scarce critical engagements of these works that ponder the demands of their writing, Jean Frémon and Lucy Ives each note that for the Istanbul Biennale of 2015, a wall text for the leporello containing Adnan's illuminated handwritten *Family Memoirs on the End of the Ottoman Empire* was instead transferred to an obscured card, and pages directly addressing the still unacknowledged Armenian genocide (one hundred years prior) were placed on a table to be turned by a white-gloved museum attendant. Frémon ponders whether this constitutes self-censorship on the part of the curators, and one can only imagine that it does.[76] Ironically, Adnan's Post-Apollo and later books circulate relatively freely throughout the world in the same moment of this attempt to quiet the writing's castigatory implications, "hiding in plain sight" as experiments published by small presses in their unrelenting critique of hegemonic violence.

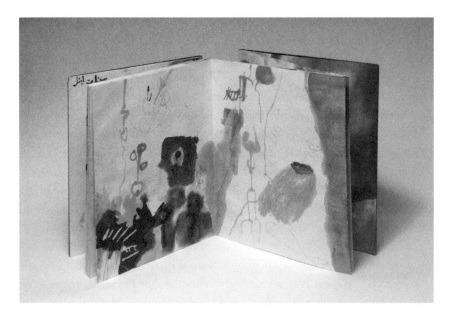

FIGURE 4.4 Etel Adnan, *Al-Sayyab, Mother and Lost Daughter*, 1970. Ink and watercolor on a Japanese book. Signed, dated, and titled by the artist. Closed, 33 × 25.2 cm × 24 pages. Open, 33 × 612 cm. Photograph by Jennifer Scappettone. Copyright Estate of Etel Adnan, Paris. Courtesy of Donation Claude & France Lemand, Institut du monde arabe, Paris.

Al-Sayyab, Mother and Lost Daughter (1970; figure 4.4) is one of Adnan's few early leporellos in homage to Arabic poetry that circulates in museums because she normally gave these artist's books as gifts to the poets transcribed. The piece incorporates al-Sayyab's revolutionary verses against a luminous blue, orange, and yellow ground of washes sporadically becoming salience—with fields of color becoming in places line, umbilicus, language, dissolving the threshold between gesture, scribble, and alphabet. The work obliges a uniquely estranging reading process: a reader who does not know Arabic (such as the author of this study) might be reeled in until opacity becomes intolerable, spurring an effort to discover both the foreign alphabet and the work of a poet still obscured by lack of translation and occidental provincialism; yet literate native speakers experience defamiliarization as well in the face of illuminated portions, struck by the initial impression that there is no language here, yet recovering bits of the alphabet upon closer study. In a 1973 essay, Abdelkebir Khatibi analyzed the "split" and disfiguration of the linguistic sign in calligraphy: "it offers us a text and its usual meaning, then takes it away little by little, disfigures it, recovers it, mirrors it." In "transport[ing] language into another code, another realm of the imaginary," thereby slowing the production of meaning, Khatibi argues, calligraphy is akin to poetry.[77] The humility, or approachability, of Adnan's handwriting and painterly calligraphy jumpstarts a process of exiled reading and (under hospitable conditions) of transcultural understanding that we do not normally associate with untranslated and untranslatable poetry. It makes the process of translation aggressively visible without "giving us" or eclipsing the transcribed original in any way.[78]

Adnan's leporello poses an oblique supra- or subdiscursive dialogue with al-Sayyab's 1961 poem of supplication, which calls on a thirsty child compared with the sun (shams, شمس, which can also be a girl's name) to drink the speaker's blood as water. The page spread in figure 4.4 contains no obvious words, although seeking divulges gestures toward depiction of an explosive alphabet.[79] The first line of al-Sayyab's poem bids the sun to stop and refrain from setting because night brings death and those missing cannot return to family if darkness falls. Although al-Sayyab was invested in breaking the monorhyme of classical Arabic poetry, structure arises in his verse through repetition: the lam, ل ("L") recurs throughout the beginning of the poem.[80] On Adnan's left page, a hook form recalling the ل appears prominently in orange at the top of the right page, and its mirror image appears in black on the left, superimposed over what appears to be an abstract evil eye. Meanwhile, two explosive devices—a thick yellow form resembling a cannon and an outlined phallus on the right (possibly wrought of mīms ["M," م—the abbreviation for male]) and an orange mass shooting out orange rays in the bottom left corner—appear to be expelling the letter ن (nūn; "N") in various orientations and species of perspective (in gold on the right page and in a cluster of red on the left). As nūn ن is the abbreviation used for the feminine, the visual drama of this page spread may bespeak the way that masculine warrior tactics have imploded the (feminine) sun, dispersing the daughter. Ultimately, these signs hover between lettered and unlettered experience: they appear to have been painted with both the curiosity and the pleasure of one who approaches a language from the outside, who is unalphabeted in the strict sense. Such painting/writing must be read for its contribution to the transcontinental discourse surrounding pan-Arabism and radical experimental Arab arts at the time. The sun and explosive marks resonate with the trademark cover of *Souffles-Anfas* (1966–1972) designed by Mohammed Melehi, which was dominated by an explosive sun ringed with electromagnetic radiation in shifting colors, heralding the formation of Arab *arts plastiques*—with the *plastiquer* of this phrase being a militant reference to the revolutionary fervor of that moment of third-worldism: to dynamite, bomb attacks (see figure 4.3).[81] These explosive suns would return as the central icon of Adnan's *Arab Apocalypse*, discussed below.

Not all of Adnan's extant (or accessible) transcriptions display the radical transmogrification of the alphabet suggested by this early leporello. A more recent work pays homage to the Sudanese writer al-Tayyeb Salih, transcribing the first paragraph of his 1971 novel *Bandarshah* into legible Arabic script and naming itself after the author and his subtitle, *Daw al-Bayt* (*The Light of the House*). *Bandarshah* tracks the transformation and redemption of the agricultural village of Wad Hamid on the Nile in northern Sudan in the 1960s, which is being devastated by urbanization. The passage Adnan has chosen to transcribe alongside her watercolor and ink paintings depicts a wizened character addressing his grandson, the book's protagonist who returns to the village after years of exile. The excerpt Adnan illuminates ends with these words: "He said, aiming his words at the sand at the bottom of his cane, 'You have long been absent from home [balad: "our country; homeland; village, town"].' I began to think. What would I say in these circumstances? 'Yes, years.'"[82] That the words are aimed as much at the sand as at the grandson bespeaks a double displacement: not only that of a younger generation that fled to the Global North, as in Salih's celebrated *Season of Migration to the North*, but also that of the ground of this home, the sand itself. We can presume that the elder character's address to the sand would have had powerful resonance for Adnan, who has charged the European notion of "homeland" imposed upon Arab territory with contradiction. In an interview, she asserts (provocatively and perhaps fancifully) that the idea of "the land" doesn't exist in the nomadic Arab world: that "Arab poetry is interested in

"FOG IS MY LAND"

the surface of the planet" because the desert hosts not agriculture, but drought, sandstorms, and cosmic events.[83] Constantly shifting, redistributed sand leveled in this way challenges the conceptual basis not only of "land" but also of the very term *deterritorialization*, doing away with oppositions between territory and statelessness based on the assumption of rooted earth.[84] The sand as evocation of landscape would have dual resonance for Adnan, who in her late years was unable to travel to the coastal places where she felt most at home (her native Beirut or the California where she was "reborn"), residing instead and as if accidentally in the inland metropolis of Paris (where the consummate signifier of 1960s utopianism was the beach to expose below the paving stones). Adnan inscribes the name and date of Salih's original work on her page and concludes by inscribing the leporello with her own signature, the year, and the site of transcription/displacement: Paris, forty years later.

The paintings Adnan paired with these lines from *Bandarshah* exist in a rather oblique relationship to their content; they are not illustrations but simultaneities, perhaps images of the home in which she was reading the novel.[85] True to the word "illuminations," the pages depict homely objects in the tradition of the still life (books, a newspaper, an ink pot, potted plants, fruit) shot through by a searing Mediterranean "light of the house." Adnan conceived of light as "the ultimate material for art," the medium of Muslim mystics and opalescent Syrian glass as well as of the Space Age, with its neon sculptures and "light shows." The envelope of light here assumes a performative force that, one imagines, itself embodies the house, home, and homeland.[86] Adnan's illumination depicts through infusion the binding force of the sun, which puns on the kinship-through-acceptance this artist emphasized in the Arabic or Aramaic terms for "son."

Adnan's process of transcription can be understood as an intimate devotional activity, one reaching back to the scribes, although as embodied practice, it has an affinity with the iterative work of certain conceptual and other contemporary poetries.[87] She describes the ritual preparations with which she would begin each leporello as entry into a sacral rite analogous to that of the painters of icons her Greek mother cherished, upholding a centuries-old tradition while "still carrying on to new shores the inherent possibilities of Arabic writing."[88] Her act of copying and illuminating Arab writings that still, decades later, lack representation in much comparative literary discourse in the West will transport this marginalized work to new audiences in particularly vivid ways while, perhaps paradoxically, remaining illegible except to those who strain to read past the opacity of the abjad. It generates a xenoglossic condition in readers with no literacy in Arabic who push beyond their limits in order to comprehend a ravishing artifact, while simultaneously enhancing the mystic aura surrounding the alphabet whose long

240   "FOG IS MY LAND"

history Johanna Drucker outlines in *The Alphabetic Labyrinth* (a study that, as formidably wide ranging as it is, omits the Arabic tradition because of acknowledged lack of linguistic expertise).[89]

For the lexicographer, cryptographer, historian, and occultist Johannes Trithemius (Trittenheim 1462–Würzburg 1516), writing at the dawn of movable type in Europe that would displace the scribe and render signs like the fricative Þ (thorn) obsolete, "Nothing will draw the monk more closely to active perfection" than the basic channeling of the word. The framing of his *De laude scriptorum* thematizes the humility of being without language, as well as the promise of its assumption through a physical, nearly amorous act that the progress of printing will eclipse: "my whole being is filled with the desire for, and the love of, writing."[90] The anachronistic art of copying reemerges as a negation of subjective authorship in the late twentieth century with translational force, assembling disparate geographies into copresence. In the work of Caroline Bergvall with English translations of the first tercet of Dante's *Inferno* in "Via: 48 Dante Variations," we see an admission of humility accompanied by a longing for a connection with the literal *writing* of one's influences, its incorporation—in a circumstance of emphatic removal from any "original" that brings us back to the de facto mediation of the nurse's tongue. Bergvall describes her labors as scrivener of Dante's translators in the British Library: "My task was mostly and rather simply, or so it seemed at first, to copy each first tercet as it appeared in each published version of the *Inferno*. To copy it accurately. . . . To reproduce each translative gesture. To add my voice to this chorus, to this recitation, only by way of this task."[91] Bergvall's description emphasizes the forging of historical relationships that the somatic act of copying enables, making antique writing actual (in the sense of "actuelle," present). By working with translations of Dante, Bergvall's piece admits to the mediated quality of her experience of the *Commedia* and (as Keats's "On First Looking Into Chapman's Homer" did) heeds the canonical author's collective generation and metamorphosis through translation into English or, to be more precise, what she will later theorize as the "midden," "middling," "middle," and "meddling" of Englishes over time.[92] Such transformation also enriches the given dictates of relationality, deviating from "family line" and "blood routes" through "power lines, wired and electrical, electromagnetic landscapes" and toward "fine lines that crisscross between belonging, adhering, disappearing."[93] Yet the humbling manual labor involved in copying and "Via"'s eventual articulation as voiced performance also make the material one's (s)kin in a way that transcends (or subtends) discursivity. "There are ways of acknowledging influence and models, by ingestion, by assimilation, by one's total absorption in the material. To come to an understanding of it by standing it in it, by becoming it. Very gradually, this

"FOG IS MY LAND" 241

transforms a shoe into a foot, extends copyism into writing, and perhaps writing into being."[94] The shoe assumed as artifact other to oneself metamorphoses into a foot that can move one, in accordance with the poem's own scansion.

Adnan's practice, which unlike traditional transcription focuses on writers of the present moment, opens up a series of related but more complex questions of cultural belonging. What does it mean to "spit out" colonial French and assume somatically a language from which one has been shut out in the lettered sense? Adnan's transcription practice suggests that cultural belonging can and, at times, must perforce be recast from passive inheritance to an active passion. The result is an expression of admiration and fellowship with one's contemporaries even broader than pan-Arabism could have projected (and indeed, she did generously include non-Arab writers in the process of homage, from McNaughton to Lyn Hejinian and the young poets Jonathan Skinner and Sarah Riggs). Adnan has remarked that the continuum between drawing and painting and emphasis on the word unite all of Asian culture, claiming that "writing is seen as the most magical of arts, and the most important of religious arts, because it brings you closer to the Quran, and therefore to the direct word of God. . . . The prestige of the written word unites all of Asia."[95] Her leporellos extend an Arabic literary tradition and revolution at once, marrying it with the physical substrate and gestural energy of an East Asian tradition and translating it consciously into foreign cultural contexts. Appreciating "the flow, the apparent lack of boundaries, the river image of these long unfolding papers" used in Chinese and Japanese literary traditions,[96] Adnan describes the leporello as a musical score on which the mind never rests as it scans and as a visual translation that transports, as the original Greek term for translation suggests. The modular form of the leporello makes for flexible readings whose permutations are infinite because of the variety of juxtapositions enabled by folding the book at different points.[97]

Moreover, modulating lines of letters or images allow each reader to translate the writing into their own "inner language, or languages, into that which we call the understanding."[98] This inner language seems to be a way of indexing consciousness, a site into which, as Adnan has elsewhere described it, inner and outer world, subject and object "melt."[99] This language courses below the workings of "national" languages to transform what we mean by understanding itself. In translating the comprehension of written texts through affinity into figurative and abstract signs, Adnan hopes to present "a vision of reality as a permanently transformed score meant to remain obscure as such but 'heard' or 'seen' through the translatorial powers of our minds."[100] This neologism—translatorial—provides a useful inroads into understanding the transfiguration of the illuminated text as it moves across varieties of sensory experience.

How are we to understand the aesthetic and political work done by these elusive artifacts? The formal operations on the Arabic alphabet achieved by the painters of the Hurufiyya movement must be read in concert with Iftikhar Dadi's politically saturated analysis of the "heroic" phase of "calligraphic modernism," which developed in the decades following decolonization in Asia and Africa (1955–1975). Dadi points out that artists of former colonies were under intense national pressure "to produce nothing less than the development of a new cultural language that would exploit the opening provided by decolonization."[101] While acknowledging the importance of national uplift to the development of these styles, Dadi stresses above all how these works exceed the nation-building project, as diasporic artists exposed to canonical and contemporary Western artworks launched new international affiliations and constellating identities. Dadi also traces, of necessity, the emptying out of the promise of decolonization as freedom in the face of a neocolonial globalization process. Yet in works of calligraphic modernism, he sees a resistance to the media spectacle that determines contemporary occidental imaginations of Islamic culture, invoking Dipesh Chakrabarty in an assertion that they help us conceive "a global Muslim ethics and community that is predicated upon the persistence of a textuality that is not fully translatable within western enlightenment ideals," offering up "a theoretical model with the potential to extend the critical goal of 'provincializing Europe.'" Works of calligraphic modernism testify, in Dadi's analysis, to the fact that "*a threat of opacity* to the western-universal norm exists, aesthetically and ethically."[102]

As I have been arguing, in Adnan's handling, opacity as literal strategy makes for a durational experience of understanding that surpasses blunt blockage or threat; her translucent painting/writing can also be a beckoning, creating ultimately, for readers, an experience of shimmer, of bedazzlement wed to reckoning. In this visual ecology, the image is exposed as an entity encompassing "thickness"—consisting of transit between layers, so that we can read the veil or the screen as enrichment and draw. As Adnan clarifies in conversation with Lisa Robertson, "Images . . . are moving things. They come, they go, they disappear, they approach, they recede, and they are not even visual—ultimately they are pure feeling. They're like something that calls you through a fog or a cloud."[103] Such a description recalls the oil pastels that Adnan scribbles over the inked Arabic for the word "Allah" in a 1987 leporello (figure 4.5), partially obscuring the represented syllables, whereas Adnan's unconventional addition of the diacritic maddah (the tilde-shaped marking over the first letter alif) adds to the beginning of the name of God a glottal stop and long "a" (/a:/), sonically extending the

FIGURE 4.5 Etel Adnan, *Allah*, 1987, mixed media on paper (leporello). Copyright Estate of Etel Adnan, Paris. Jordan National Gallery of Fine Arts.

opening vowel (as in "AAAAAAllah"). We also recall here the washes that overtake possible letters or glyphs in *Al-Sayyab, Mother and Lost Daughter*, including the wash of yellow ochre over cadmium yellow partially obscuring the calligraphy in red ink for the opening of the Shahadah (figure 4.2). A leporello of highly defamiliarizing script like this exists not only as a private conversation between Arab poets across chasms of linguistic and cultural difference but also as a first "translation" of the exiled Iraqi al-Sayyab—in the more literal, Poundian sense of "traduction."[104] It is more appealing, in the sense of address or even accusation, than a so-called literal translation naively claiming to convey the immanent and instantaneous authority of the original text—and truer to the distressed conditions that attend any such cross-cultural transmission.

TONGUES OF FIRE: VEILING AND UNVEILING IN *THE ARAB APOCALYPSE*

Adnan ultimately saw fit to transmute the fugitive gestures of her "calligraffiti" into poetry appearing under the sign of the French and English languages as well. She began her masterwork *L'apocalypse arabe* (1980) in Beirut, two months before the Lebanese Civil War, as "an abstract poem on the sun"; she composed its fifty-nine poems—one for each of the fifty-nine days of the Christian Lebanese Front's siege of the Tall al-Zaʿtar refugee camp for Palestinians within the Christian sector of Beirut—over the course of a year through direct experience. Adnan translated *The Arab Apocalypse* herself into English, at first spontaneously, in performance, reportedly without being aware that she was doing so, and then formally for Simone Fattal's Post-Apollo Press, which Fattal had founded to publish Adnan's work in 1989.[105] It was arguably the urgency of these circumstances of composition that led Adnan to infiltrate the text(s) with a more "immediate" and universal idiom, that of the semi-apprehensible glyph—each example of which appears to be redrafted with each new edition. *The Arab Apocalypse* is thus in part supralinguistic. This epic work confounds the genres of Adnan's production as codified by criticism: in an interview with Claudia Rushkowsky, she defines it against disciplines, in terms of literal and metaphysical vision: "*The Arab Apocalypse* is not philosophy, it's not traditional poetry: it's really an apocalyptic vision."[106] At times, the text is closer to painting than poetry, acting (as in "Poem I") as a literal "palette" upon which languages, named colors, and literal images blend and blur across a page so wide as itself to suggest a landscape. Having finally been given the chance to behold *The Mother and the Lost Daughter* in person, I now regard both its form and its glyphs as foundations of this later, monumental poetic panorama's transmutation of literacy.

Deploying the hegemonic idioms of her education at large, Adnan braids through these imperial tongues of French and English signs inspired by other alphabets, Semitic scripts, Chinese characters, Egyptian hieroglyphs, and glyphs of Indigenous peoples of the Americas, as well as proliferating punctuation marks, the signs of symbolic logic, and the sheer gesture typical of action painting, channeling her decades-long practice in (partial) abstraction (figure 4.6). As gestures, these signs hold out the dream of transparency while in almost every case thwarting definitive decryption. Sonja Mejcher-Atassi reads them merely as emphasizing "the visual aspect of writing," not bringing anything other to the written text; Caroline Seymour-Jorn describes them apprehensively as "enigmatic symbols"; Aditi Machado reads them as idiosyncratically intelligible and points out how much the glyphs change in form from edition to edition, concluding that they "cannot be 'fixed' in the way of linguistic paradigms" and must be recreated.[107] When questioned, Adnan responds that "the signs are my excess of emotions. I cannot say more. I wrote by hand, and, here and there, I put a word, and I made instinctively a little drawing, a sign."[108] Having perused multiple editions to find the glyphs relatively stable, though freshly painted for each volume, I propose that the limits on definitive decryption should not invite us to stop *reading*. Adnan's placement of these pictorial, pictographic, or paralinguistic signs on par with hegemonic colonial languages suggests an equal traffic between them, in a process of presencing and metamorphosis under siege that could be fruitfully compared to what Chadwick Allen and Edgar Garcia have theorized as "trans-Indigenous" world poiesis.[109] Adnan's painted signs invoke ancient and future attempts at codifying experience while falling tactically short

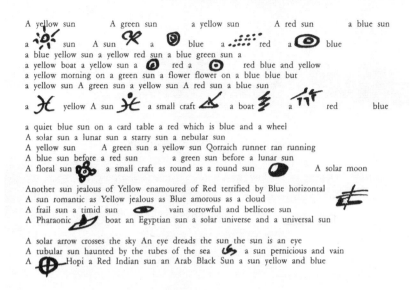

FIGURE 4.6 Etel Adnan, opening of "Poem I" of *The Arab Apocalypse* (Post-Apollo Press, 2006), 7.

of conforming to any single linguistic system, historical regime of "development," or worldview, holding out the potential of transplanetary communication and indeed community from within a nightmare of civil war. In "Poem I," the staggering copresence of colored suns ("A ... Hopi a Red Indian sun an Arab Black Sun a sun yellow and blue") suggests not only the visible light of the sun's electromagnetic spectrum or the explosions crossing party and militia cantons that drive the war, but polycentrism.[110] It at once reveals the absurdity of ascribing race to a heavenly body ("Another sun jealous of Yellow enamored of Red terrified by Blue") and the multiplicity of linguistic, cultural, and political cores around which the text orbits, around which it should be read.[111] The Arabic of the literate withheld from the "indigène" as child in a French convent school has here exploded into these signs, these possible origins and futures of and beyond language: a barrage against the hegemonic narrative framework composed by a poet who has spat out one colonial tongue, assumed another through protest, and now reports on tragic circumstances from beyond the bounds of every canton.

In a foreword to the poem's 2006 English reissue, Jalal Toufic, a writer, film theorist, and artist born to a Palestinian mother and Iraqi father who has resided at length in Beirut, identifies *The Arab Apocalypse* as an "Arab book of poetry in part because it was withdrawn, occulted by the surpassing disasters that have affected the Arab world," and asserts that Adnan's graphic signs are partial translations—possessing the power to "jolt" the substantial fraction of the adult Arab population that is illiterate, "for whom Arabic is as illegible as English and French," to read.[112] Finally translated into Arabic in 1990 by Chawqi Abdel-Amir, the book had long remained out of print until its 2006 English-language "resurrection" amid the violence of the Second Gulf War. This act occupies a rich place in Toufic's own oeuvre, following what he calls a "withdrawal of tradition" in the wake of disaster, Toufic's metric for tragedy that is not captured by the numbers of casualties or by the record of physical destruction and psychological traumas that normally engender attention in the aftermath of disaster—being immaterial, yet of incalculable importance.[113] Making a bold claim for *L'apocalypse arabe/The Arab Apocalypse* as "one of the twentieth century's major Arabic books of poetry" notwithstanding its non-Arabic languages of composition, Toufic simultaneously stresses the "vertiginous extension" of Arabic tradition that takes place in this work of revelation, such that the tradition "comes to include many a bodhisattva as well as many a schizophrenic/psychotic who is not an Arab by descent and/or birthplace but who exclaims in his or her dying before dying: 'Every name in history is I' (Nietzsche)."[114]

Any purist tribalism ultimately fails and falls short in *The Arab Apocalypse*: the tradition that Adnan counts as "Arab" includes within it figures as far-flung as Buddhist saints, Mao, and Shawnee leader Tecumtha, as well as Rimbaud and Artaud. So although the book is doubtless the apocalyptic testament and telegraphic indictment of violence against Arabs in Tell al-Zaatar, it is simultaneously an indictment of all dispossession, including particularly that of Indigenous Americans, who are cast as parallel to the occupied Palestinians. Adnan was one of the first to make the connection between Indigenous peoples of the Americas and Palestinians in her writings, an analogy that has since become key to political struggles for sovereignty on the Gaza Strip and the West Bank.[115] Representative heroes Faysal al-Awwal, champion of pan-Arabism, and the Odawa rebel Pontiac sleep hand in hand in the sunset while the poem expresses, in labored English, that "the last king of the humiliated races remains lain on the horizon" before a horizontal series of dots and dashes seems to project itself across the landscape in a final, syllable-less verse (*AA*, 51). While "fascism dressed in green masturbates its guns" (*AA*, 20), the symbol of the Nazis is eclipsed by "the Hopi's swastika" (*AA*, 29), thereby becoming instead a sign of physical migration and a sacred symbol of sun and earth. Still, poems like "Poem XXXII" refuse to paint black and white pictures of nations in terms of ally and foe, declaring that "there is in every tribe a gold-thirsty traitor" just as "there is in every Arab a traitor thirsting for the west" (*AA*, 51). Against the sectarianism bolstered by Western colonialism, Adnan impugns the tribe as "delirious" (*AA*, 34), a sort of gang taking the sun as its god while storming "with whetted swords to fight the sea" (*AA*, 35). Ultimately, as in this futile exercise of aggression, "the sun unites the Arabs against the Arabs" (*AA*, 40). The "I" defined here, against the explosive suns and tribes it witnesses, is a suffering public so multitudinous and sprawling (think of Rosselli's "the I is the public")[116] as to defy being pinned to a certain identity or "side" in the civil and transnational conflict.

We can extend Toufic's analysis by tracking the way this extension of tradition plays out in the decentralized and proliferating figure of the sun, multiplied so that the book has many explosive nuclei. In Adnan's hands, the condescending French reference to Arabs as "les enfants du soleil" (children of the sun) is charged with explosive meaning, as the technicolor sun of the covers of *Souffles* that radiated blast and rebellion and the sun that would light up Salih's depicted *House* join forces with those of Nietzsche's Apollo, Antonin Artaud's Heliogabalus, and Judge Schreber, whose redemptive transformation from man into woman would be dictated somatically through divine rays (via the anus) in an "unfathomable" Grundsprache, or proto/basic language.[117] Like Schreber, Adnan as queer and perhaps spiritually or performatively trans visionary takes dictation from a grand cosmological scale in haptic fashion, drawing-writing, yoking transmissions of oppositional cultural fragments to one another without suturing over the discursive fault lines in the postapocalyptic tradition the book cobbles together. The plays on the sun and moon recall her early work *Le livre de la mer*, which she deemed unthinkable in Arabic because it would lose the gendered dyad of those celestial bodies' names; here, the interaction between these bodies is more than dyadic, it is dual ("a lunar sun") (*AA*, 7).

For Toufic, himself subject and theorist of exile, to invoke "tradition" in the wake of a disaster requires first resurrecting it, lest one find oneself dueling with its mere counterfeit. In "Credits Included," an essay about the withdrawal of tradition provoked by disasters such as the atomic bomb in the collection *The Withdrawal of Tradition Past a Surpassing Disaster* (which also recollects and contextualizes his preface to *The Arab Apocalypse*), Toufic identifies the removal of Arabic script and Sufi culture from early twentieth-century Turkey as one of the most exemplary cases of such a withdrawal and one that has largely gone unhonored—" 'this question mark so black, so huge it casts a shadow over him [or her] who sets it up' (Nietzsche, *Twilight of the Idols*)."[118] Tapping into this historical drama of withdrawal reflected with precision in her late-Ottoman childhood, Adnan's work with unauthorized languages and Arabic script surely reanimates rather than appropriates them. According to Toufic's logic, her book itself, being occulted from Arab culture by way of the very disaster it recounts, becomes part of Arab tradition by virtue of this withdrawal from view, thereby demanding resurrection.

In the face of neonationalisms such as those stoked in Beirut in 2005—Toufic's otherwise highly allusive foreword explicitly cites the "100 percent Lebanese" banners that attended demonstrations following the assassination of former prime minister Rafîk al Harîrî—Adnan's trans- or intranational calligraphy, paralleling her performative descriptions of a technicolored and multiraced sun, implicitly ridicules anyone who would plant this yellow dwarf like a flag. We witness in "Poem XII," for instance, the sun invoked in the Latin alphabet evolving, between arrows, from a simple round mimetic form to the precursor of its representation as a Chinese character, 日 (the standard account of this evolution draws a progression from a circle containing a dot to a gradually more squared-off form), before it floats both carnally and unbridledly "like a tattoo" over a tree on fire. As soon as the poem's first person plants the sun in terrainless sky, we see Adnan's calligraphic representation take off in favor of quivering motion forward that emanates from the belly of women and that veers toward a counterlinear, horizontal tear (figure 4.7).

Musing on why she used the glyphs in an interview, Adnan suggests, "Maybe it is because I see these apocalypses ... because my first thought is always explosive. It is not cumulative."[119] One is reminded of Pasolini's nuclear terminology to describe Rosselli's experiments. Here the "terrible laboratory experiments" are happening in collisions of imagery both figurative and concrete that mimic the nuclear fusion of the guiding image, making clear it is the nuclear weapon that founds the virulent concept of "race" and not the other way around: "Each nuclear explosion blooms into a sun-brain like a flower ! / Within the sun's atoms we created virulent races STOP" (*AA*, 34). Explosion becomes wedded

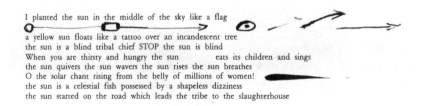

FIGURE 4.7   Etel Adnan, from "Poem XII" of *The Arab Apocalypse* (Post-Apollo Press, 2006), 30.

to painting/drawing as visual transcription, resisting the aggregation of the analytically crafted sentence and accentuating the brutality of experience. "Yes, light is also terror, the ten thousand suns of Hiroshima," Adnan admitted in her 1973 contribution to *Intégral*, stressing its transmission through explosives increasingly more murderous and capable of transnational reach. Still, she insisted on the capacity of artists from North Africa and the Arab East to wrest figurative lightness of illumination as well, at least ephemerally: "If, in the end, it must be our catastrophe, for the moment may it also be our happiness."[120]

Against the aggressive forward velocity of violence apprehended through *The Arab Apocalypse*'s images and signs, we often encounter the word STOP in all caps. Adnan's epic is full of radios, telephones, and computers that transmit the sun and sea's apocalyptic messages, and it cites the same technology that inspired Marinetti and comrades into the forging of a wireless imagination: the telegraph, which became not only convenient but also fundamental to imperial conquest and management and the waging of world war.[121] The convention "STOP" used to end sentences is deployed sporadically as jolt to substitute for standard punctuation, thereby granting the text a simultaneous immediacy and the sense of being transmitted via dictation from afar, across the subterranean and subaqueous cables or via radio waves. In my interview with her, Adnan stressed that this work enabled her own spontaneous, almost unthinking translation into English because it was first composed with a basic syntax that was antithetical to the "analytic" quality of French language and literature—a xenoglossic railing against French that would come more easily to a "barbarian" poet: "STOP   STOP   STOP   STOP   STOP   STOP   STOP   STOP   STOP   STOP//   un avion-soleil un soleil————> avion tout tourne là-haut / il n'y a ni eau   ni plasma   ni air   il y a la radio."[122] It thus falls curiously well into the Futurist call for "destruction of syntax" (avoiding adjectives, abolishing adverbs and conjunctions, using infinitive verbs, and building toward production of a continuous image flow unsubordinated to any I) in favor of a more immediate and globally oriented idiom: "STOP   THE VERB'S CREATION   STOP" (*AA*, 43). Ultimately, though, the STOP is resolutely anti-Futurist in the imperialist and positivistic sense. It is a cry to halt that jolts the reader out of any complacent comportment rightward: a clamorous demand in an unceasing apocalyptic present tense. In a footnote to another essay, Toufic laments that with the contemporary technologies available to modern journalism, "gone is the resonant *displacement* of the *stop* from the horrified reaction to an atrocity to the standard punctuation of the telegraphic medium."[123]

When pressed about what she meant by invoking a "spherical mental world" in "To Write in a Foreign Language," Adnan responded by refuting the notion of one-dimensional ethnic identities through reference to the globe that through the radio infiltrates our being and thinking, linking the solar radiation that pervades her *Apocalypse* to those message-carrying electromagnetic waves: "We all live in a spherical world where things come to us. Every one of us is a radio transmitter that broadcasts and receives."[124] Adnan implicitly cites the theories of fellow queer Bay Area poet Jack Spicer, for whom poets were radios taking dictation from the "Outside."[125] The metaphor of dictation has a history in the avant-garde: Marinetti's "Technical Manifesto of Futurist Literature" was itself, the Futurist claimed, the result of dictation (from a plane's propeller), as we recall.[126] The *Apocalypse's* dictation is rather more anarchic than that of the collaborationist Marinetti, with Adnan's I emerging as a "prophet of a useless nation" (*AA*, 41). Civil war tests the very grounds and containability of nation, and the ambivalence of Adnan's sun—gendered male against a "lunar Beirut," multiplying sadistic acts as it suckles itself [*AA*, 44]—lends a bitterness to the vivid icon of *Souffles/Anfas:* "The Arabs' sun   is a perennial atom bomb drinking milk sadistic tubercular" (*AA*, 52). But in this sphere, no icon is ever one; the sun is simultaneously, for example, a camera that documents the destruction of the Palestinian camp "for the C.I.A.'s archives" (*AA*, 59), a "whale wrapped with electric wire HOU! HOU! HOU!" (*AA*, 44), and the white head of Christ whose will is "A 10 dollars bill posted in New York," as the xenoglossic narration reports (*AA*, 45).

If this "language-circuit" we rely upon has burned in *The Arab Apocalypse* by force of its destructive suns, what might bring us back together would be the manipulation of a dethroned language by poet-herds, its unchaining from the tree of evil that appears to be represented in the right margin of this page (figure 4.8). The painted glyph may stand, alternately, for the ancient wisdom of

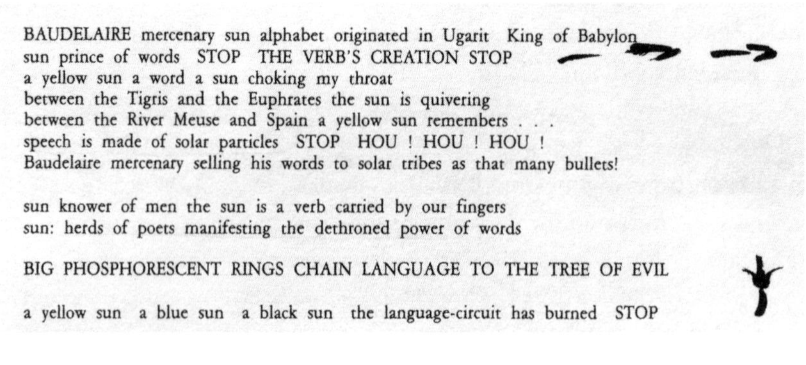

BAUDELAIRE mercenary sun alphabet originated in Ugarit   King of Babylon
sun prince of words   STOP   THE VERB'S CREATION STOP
a yellow sun a word a sun choking my throat
between the Tigris and the Euphrates the sun is quivering
between the River Meuse and Spain a yellow sun remembers . . .
speech is made of solar particles   STOP   HOU ! HOU ! HOU !
Baudelaire mercenary selling his words to solar tribes as that many bullets!

sun knower of men the sun is a verb carried by our fingers
sun: herds of poets manifesting the dethroned power of words

BIG PHOSPHORESCENT RINGS CHAIN LANGUAGE TO THE TREE OF EVIL

a yellow sun   a blue sun   a black sun   the language-circuit has burned   STOP

FIGURE 4.8 Etel Adnan, from "Poem XXIV" of *The Arab Apocalypse* (Post-Apollo Press, 2006), 43.

the cuneiform abjad, the "alphabet originated in Ugarit" (now Ras Shamra, on the Syrian coast) (*AA*, 43) that accompanies Baudelaire's entrance at the beginning of this poem: for the sign also bears some resemblance to the Ugaritic "s," thereby forcing us to read backward to ponder whether the forward-moving signs that began appearing in "Poem II" and at the top of this page were indeed arrows propelled forward into an apocalyptic future or inverted letters of the Ugaritic alphabet compelling us back—or both, in a Benjaminian evocation of the *Angelus Novus* by Paul Klee, one of Adnan's most cherished influences.

Adnan's leporellos have become increasingly exhibited and sought after by galleries in the wake of her rise as a nonagenarian art-world star, yet the forms of circulation and viewership that dominate the visual art market threaten to reify or reduce those that function as texts to mere aesthetic marks. Those who have been reading Adnan's politically saturated writing for decades will long for the resonance between her seemingly distinct oeuvres to be elucidated. Although Adnan may have enjoyed the privilege of relative freedom of movement in her last decades, the political geography of her upbringing remains in violent flux, with refugees hailing from multiple loci. At the time of writing, the Syrian civil war has raged on despite the sabotage of the authoritarian Assad dynasty, and Lebanon, hosting 1.5 million Syrian refugees and the largest overall number of refugees per capita and square kilometer in the world, has remained on the front lines of one of the largest humanitarian crises of our time; 3.2 million refugees have sought shelter in Turkey, and Greece alternately hosts and threatens to eject tens of thousands of asylum seekers in overcrowded camps amid the aftereffects of a government-debt crisis. As I revise, thousands of innocent Palestinian survivors in camps remain under siege, and Lebanon has become a major target of Israeli bombardment, provoking a massive exodus of civilians. Throughout, the language of the tribe shows no sign of abating. Against this backdrop, we are pressed to read Adnan's works of writing that verge on drawing beyond, or through, their entrancing or enthralling power to ascertain how they help us remap political belonging.

Adnan's xenoglossic deployment of so many languages imposed, elected, lost, and imagined—a language use I have called "unauthorized"—resonates with the act of "otherwise belonging," to borrow a term from Ashon Crawley's *Blackpentecostal Breath*. As we recall, Crawley bases his recasting of sociopolitical possibility on the aesthetic praxis of the multiracial, multiclass, transnational Christian sect of Pentecostalism, whose hallmark ecstasis was that of speaking (and writing) in tongues—a practice whose performances by subaltern citizens of Los Angeles prompted debates over whether the mysterious language that resulted was glossolalia (nondiscursive and heavenly language) or xenoglossia (natural language that the speakers had not been taught). Yet Crawley also looks to the cryptic script at the heart of the so-called Ben Ali Diary—an Arabic manuscript by an enslaved African Muslim jurisprudist in the antebellum US South. Raised in the Pentecostal church, Crawley views this manuscript from a subjugated figure other to that church as linguistic matter that disrupts constructs of subjectivity and citizenship as coherent and stable.[127] He refers to such wayward occupations of language as "centrifugitive": performative acts through which submerged "otherwise possibilities" resurface under conditions of radical sociality, disrupting reigning configurations of power.[128]

The Arab Apocalypse ultimately radicalizes a quasi-Pentecostal situation in which "people's tongues will turn into tongues of fire" (*AA*, 77) in a literalization of traditional pictorial representations of the Holy Ghost as flame yet hailing from the mouths of the populace themselves. Adnan's apocalyptic vision foretells that fire will ultimately have a purgative effect, making way for a true language of the collective: "this tongue smoking like roast-lamb will disappear / make tomorrow's men speak in signs collectively" (*AA*, 75)—turning its back on "virulent religions" (*AA*, 32) and any colonial Christian imposition that prompted the twenty-seven days of destructive attacks on the already dispossessed that the poem represents. Adnan's xenoglossic parlance entails traces of language wielded under duress, telegraphically. Throughout, it manifests translingual phrasings that sound "foreign," in lines like the English version's "Amidst a smell of corpses forgotten by the garbage collector sleeps the sun / while perspire the plants" (*AA*, 41), which appear to borrow the syntax and order of perception of French. The poem dramatizes the humiliation of her father's tongue: "They threw the Arabic language to the garbage," so that it necessitates resurrection by another species—"toads took it up" (*AA*, 75). The "besieged Palestinians" are represented as rejecting human language altogether: "And tired of words they begin to bark" (*AA*, 54). In a secular apocalyptic vision in which "throats will choke with gold" (*AA*, 77), deaf people who have a speech impediment are installed upon the Throne of Goodness, recalling the chorus of *Sitt Marie-Rose*'s Palestinian students. Paradoxically, this xenoglossic art discloses the syllables of those without a voice, the language of those deemed to be without a language, without ever *speaking for*. The act of reading Adnan induces one into the channels of knowledges occulted by provincial political self-interest or the will to spiritual monoliths— and itself promises to become a means of generating this new collective through a language previously missing from the books of history and future.

If Pentecost in its colonial vestments aligns with the destruction of Arab refugee camps in the name of the Lebanese Christian "tribe" with which Adnan would have been associated, she chooses instead to practice xenoglossia with a repressed language deemed sinful by her French Christian education—a potentially dangerous act in a context in which those holding power would attempt to preserve the Mandate's colonial design on Lebanon as a safe space for Christianity. Adnan's "drawn" writings constitute experiments in attachment that take up Pentecostal practice from below. They compose homages to a native language that is imperfectly known, forging solidarity with Arab authors and other colonized peoples forced into various forms of flight. In duration—under reading conditions that are not easily enabled by visual art exhibitions—Adnan's leporellos and gestural glyphs performatively alter the act of reading as well, asking us to absorb the imperfectly legible and to seek meaning in expressive forms that transgress the limitations of what we understand to be national languages. Adnan's work ultimately permits us to apprehend the fallout of statelessness across generations and geographies in terms that expose the holes in political definitions of citizenship—in material gestures that bespeak liberation from political constrictions or denial, however fleeting and rarefied the literary utopias created by these works may be. Across a textual field of mutual defamiliarization, Adnan's signs herald unsanctioned, intimate collectivities.[129] Her art thereby offers powerful rejoinders to overweening forces of dispossession that normally determine the discourse surrounding the refugee. In this key, we can reinterpret her apologia for not learning Arabic as an active political deportment: "I did not take time out of everyday life to consecrate all my efforts to acquire Arabic as a full language. When the sun is strong and the sea is blue I can't close my windows and go in and 'study' anything. I am a person of the perpetual present. So I stayed 'outside.' "[130] For Adnan, commitment to daily life comes at the cost of not being literate in her "native" language yet keeps her doubly "outside"—both outside culture in the mastered sense and fully integrated into the landscape of the present moment. Compare this commitment with that of Édouard Glissant's "man of the present":

> Homme du présent, pour ce qu'il revendique, protège et peut-être perpétue l'actuel et, malgré les distances, les enveloppes qui l'excluent, plonge dans la totalité. Dans la totalité rêvée, où frémissent ensemble le contour du paysage et la fraîcheur menacée de son éternel demain. Dans la totalité vécue, où l'opacité s'ouvre peu à peu et le partage s'établit.

> He claims, protects and perhaps perpetuates the present [l'actuel], despite the distances, the sheathings, which exclude him, plunge him into totality. In totality dreamed, where the outline of the landscape and the threatened freshness of its eternal tomorrow shiver together. In totality lived, where opacity opens little by little and sharing is established.[131]

The man of the present stands equally excluded, yet by virtue of this exclusion, he is immersed in totality, depicted as a future-oriented landscape. That opacity, opening bit by bit, in a process rarely analyzed in its minutiae by criticism, becomes the medium of this moment-by-moment propulsion toward new and more open forms of belonging; it resonates with the whole of Adnan's shimmering body of work. Opacity, in this scenario, participation in poetry across a screen or veil, simultaneously preserves the mystery of experience in a way that does not constitute mere obfuscation or orientalization. For in this conception, as Adnan declares to poet Lisa Robertson, "some things are not meant to be clear; obscurity is their clarity. Obscurity is as rich as luminosity." Rather than absence of light, obscurity is comprehended by the poet/painter as "a different manifestation of light."[132]

Adnan's commitment to the present tense ultimately forges a new political comportment and a novel definition of citizenship. "Time is my country, fog is my land," she writes in the 2012 *Sea and Fog*.[133] Metamorphic, transubstantial, a "vertical ocean," Adnan's fog as experienced from the Bay Area of her political and aesthetic rebirth and beyond discloses a geopolitical utopia captured in her painted writing, even if the utopia inheres only in the folds of an artist's book to be shared with aspirational comrades.[134] To live such a landscape fully was to deny herself full entry into the Arab lettered canon, but it did not preclude her from painting her own experience of it into Arabic, as in the paper landscape of *Rihla ila Jabal Tamalpais* (*Journey to Mount Tamalpais*, 2008, figure 4.9). In this leporello, against boldly gestural serial paintings of Tamalpais in opaque black India ink, horizontal bands of watercolor washes in shifting oranges, blues, yellows, greens, and purples host text from her Post-Apollo essay devoted to that mountain of the Coast Miwok, Tamal-Pa, its convulsive spine of the revolutionary Americas appearing as "an oasis, . . . as the very idea of home"—now translated from English into Arabic. It is as though the mountain's ever-altering hues were laid out here as a dazzling color spectrum to become the shimmering scroll upon which her reflections on perception-as-becoming could float within the luminosity they describe, surrounded by traces of her now-signature glyphs and geometry. It could be said of this exalted context, echoing Walter Benjamin, that here "the language of translation envelops its content like a royal robe with ample folds."[135] Here, Adnan's life's work comes full circle through an act of self-transcription and self-illumination as an Arab writer. This folded landscape renders her work part of the Arab pantheon that began with her homages to Al-Sayyab, insisting that, as she wrote in the 1986 volume composed over two decades of reflection in a fulsome first person plural, "Our identity is the series of the mountain's becomings, our peace is its stubborn existence."[136]

FIGURE 4.9 Etel Adnan, *Rihla ila Jabal Tamalpais (Journey to Mount Tamalpais)*, 2008. Watercolor and India ink on Japanese book, 30 × 10.5 cm × 54 pages: 30 × 567 cm. Copyright Estate of Etel Adnan, Paris. Courtesy of Donation Claude & France Lemand, Institut du monde arabe, Paris.

For an inviolate present moment contingent upon readers' engagement and attention, yet beckoned by beauty, the opacity of these painted languages opens a shifting semiotic field of kithship. Against all overweening tribal dispositions and hatreds, Adnan's shimmering scroll enables a political deportment of mutual confoundment and mutual recognition.

CRITICAL PRACTICES OF UNMASTERY: AN ASPIRATIONAL COLLECTIVE

I had to err far from whatever comfort zone I might have pitched to understand how Adnan's work lands in the context of Arabic calligraphy and the literature of pan-Arabism (two subjects I am sure never to be able to master) or what it might mean to collaborate and create within a language Adnan herself had not been permitted to master in the scripted sense. This work plunged me into dialogue with patient colleagues and generous new friends: Ghenwa Hayek, Alexander Key, Omnia El Shakry, Adrien Zakar, Aamer Nazih Ibraheem, M'barek Bouhchichi, and Ghazal Mosadeq, among others. These conversations helped me begin to understand Badr Shakir al-Sayyab's *Mother and Lost Daughter*—both the poem and Adnan's 1970 illumination of it—as a shared bequest that retained its obscurity. The whole effort opened a world, the world, the only one we have, although I'm aware that I'm destined perpetually to be a beginner here, that unignorance is a glacial lifelong process. This process leads me to propose that Adnan's work, having expressed multitudes, affective, cultural, and political, obliges a xenoglossic critical approach—that it obliges a beginner's stance and the effort of collectives of interpretation to dream of comprehension.

Refugees, living divided geographies, suffer for that fact, that loss, rendered so vivid in Adnan's conjuring of Beirut and Tamalpais over and over from the narrow, inland vantage of Paris, unable to go back. But they can simultaneously multiply geography for others through their work, patching together an ideal cartography. What Adnan deserves is not theory as burial or preservation of oeuvre but illumination—infinite as the maps she drew up composed of arrows, infinite as the pleated, recombinable cartographies of her leporellos. Those folds permit not only three-dimensional expansion of the text-as-landscape but also innumerable juxtapositions and reconfigurations: "Thus, although a painted landscape on a traditional canvas freezes, so to speak, its subject matter, a landscape on these accordion-like books can be seen in different manners . . . so that a single landscape becomes many, according to the way the work is folded," as she wrote.[137] If maps govern circulation and blockage, the circulation of the blood of cities, "blood of a Territory," then the ample cartography implied by Adnan's writing and visual art balks the conscriptions of territory and blood, without ever disavowing the bloodshed produced in a geopolitical process of containment and expulsion that—long after the demise of the Fascism of Mussolini and Hitler—continues to attempt its own unrelenting present.

5
Glottal Stop

*Xenoglossic Breathing and Transmutations of the
Mother Tongue in LaTasha N. Nevada Diggs*

"Michael Brown, Tamir Rice, Eric Garner; Palestine, 43 students abducted and found dead in Iguala, Mexico; 219 girls kidnapped in Nigeria; 1,000+ aboriginal women missing or murdered in Canada ... I can't breath[e] ... ana'akot noktiipa ... inau teo aheahe."[1] In an adaptation of the end-of-year "best of" list hosted by the Walker Center for the Arts devoted to 2014, "The Year According to LaTasha N. Nevada Diggs," this polyglot, polytalented poet, performer, and curator schooled her museum readership through a thirteen-entry synopsis of the year's critical events of which these deaths and disappearances, and the galvanizing anthems that emerged from them, form the punctum. Diggs's précis of the year of Michael Brown's murder at the hands of a white police officer in Ferguson, Missouri, reaches to tether this epoch-defining loss to the concurrent work of literary and performance artists: to the passing of Black poetic elders Amiri Baraka and Maya Angelou and to the publication of eleven books of experimental poetry, with pronounced emphasis throughout on work by Indigenous, African diasporan, and South Asian artists. Alongside an homage to a pop-up bookstore and pamphlet press in Diggs's native Harlem by Sharifa Rhodes-Pitts, the author of *Harlem Is Nowhere*, Diggs's transcultural references blast apart the narrow focus of many such inventories produced for US periodicals. Prominent on the list are global Indigenous artworks, as she highlights dance from threatened Pacific islands by the Samoan and New Zealand choreographer Lemi Ponifasio; Martha Redbone's operatic channeling of the voices of her African, Cherokee, Choctaw, Shawnee, and European ancestors; and the need for Indigenous language acknowledgment at the state level highlighted by a documentary on Marie Wilcox, the last fluent native speaker of the Wukchumni language.

The penultimate entry of Diggs's list of touchstones for the year 2014 ends with the words "I can't breath[e] . . . ana'akot noktiipa . . . inau teo aheahe."[2] Although readers can divine that their meaning must index breathlessness, these culminating un-Googleable phrases in unidentified languages mount an implicit challenge: go out and learn. Over the course of trying to determine the meaning and language group of the untranslated phrases, I, as unprepared critic, have been able to divine that aheahe is Hawaiian for a light, gentle breeze, a faint diminishing sound, or a hacking cough. My colleague in Hawaii patiently explains that transcriptions into Hawaiian lack Ts, so the middle quote appears more Māori. I then discover via a *Dictionary and Grammar of the Language of Sa'a and Ulawa, Solomon Islands* published by the Carnegie Institute of Washington in 1918 (which includes a chilling section on "The Lord's Prayer in Twenty Languages as Used in the Diocese of Melanesia in the Islands of the South Pacific") that inau is the first person singular in this language (I, me, my); that teo is to be humble, lowly, helpless; and that ahe is a tide rip. This leaves me in a tidepool of sorts.

Diggs's provocation is no decree to get thee to university, as a host of elders from Franz Fanon to Theresa Hak Kyung Cha to M. NourbeSe Philip have exposed the blindered, blindsiding violence of education's dictates. They have refused to accept the inscription of the self branded as outsider as an "*Accomplice in His Texts*," or to "*Acquiesce, to and for the complot in the Hieratic tongue*," which Cha describes as "*Their tongue, the counterscript*."[3] Diggs's acknowledgments for her debut collection, *TwERK*, include a range of thanks to specific people who taught her different languages: Cherokee, Japanese, Quechua, Māori, and Samoan. The book's section of endnotes, a playful variant on Eliot's derisory footnotes to *The Waste Land* or the modernist academic's trusty *Annotated Index to the Cantos of Ezra Pound*, takes on the heading as if it were a museum placard listing the materials deployed in a mixed-media assemblage and ends with "Lonely Planet phrase books."[4] This constitutes a politics.

Amid her highlights of the year 2014 stands Diggs's starstruck review of a multimedia performance of the 2012 album *Albion Voice* at New York's The Kitchen by the London-born musician of Bengali heritage, Bishi. Diggs praises Bishi's transit across English, Bengali, Bulgarian, and biblical Greek and her range of fabulous costumes. "Not only was there a brown realness in front of you exploring 'personal and national identity' through projected video animation and voice, but also this striking brown buoyancy tracing the evolution of English as the medieval mongrel tongue it once was to what it is today."[5] This praise for a fellow polyglot performer of color—or "fellow sistren," as Diggs puts it, borrowing the Rastafarian term for female comrade—makes great sense to those who know *TwERK*, Diggs's dazzling and bedazzled 2013 collection of poems that hacks into English through sampling from twenty-three languages, or more if you count Pig Latin and dialectal inflections.[6] *Albion Voice* begins with Bishi's recitation of the prologue to the *Tales of Caunterbury* in Middle English, underscoring up front the way that Anglo-Norman infiltration within an emerging London dialect made English the amalgamation it is today (which was also the inspiration for Caroline Bergvall's 2011 *Meddle English*). The implication is that Gram Chara—a reworking of the Bengali song by cosmopolitan and antinationalist bard Rabindranath Tagore that Bishi performs as a moving duet with her mother, herself a classically trained singer, and honors the centenary of Tagore's becoming the first non-European to win the Nobel Prize—might in turn play a part in the kaleidoscopic future of the English language.

What impresses a close reader of Diggs's poetry, however, is how much more culturally illocatable it is when compared with the ludically syncretic claims of Bishi's audiovisual performances. The video for "Albion Voice," directed by longtime collaborator Matthew Hardern, has Bishi wielding a sitar and at times a jeweled bindi while slipping through a range of regalia that perform imperial Englishness with sexy aggression, from a bustier gown wrought of a patchwork of Union Jack, St. George, and Indian flags to kitschy détournements of the iconography of Brittania.[7] Most outrageous (and provoking the most offensive commentary on YouTube) is the video's animation of chipped and worn commemorative dishware featuring Bishi in the place of Queen Elizabeth II (figure 5.1), wearing a bridal nath and singing melancholically of the would-be "joining of hearts, the

FIGURE 5.1 Bishi, screenshot from video for "Albion Voice," directed by Matthew Hardern, Gryphon records, 2012, picturing parodically altered commemorative royal mugs at a thrift shop.

weaving of clans" within England: "let West be a husband and East be a wife." (Because the performer is deeply involved in queer culture, this last line calls to be received as amped-up camp.) Singing in sweet clarity (that of a Londoner histrionically performing Received, or standardized, English Pronunciation), Bishi inhabits the fraught ideal of an "Albion voice"—one lacking local or foreign inflection—within her apparently incommensurable skin: "Bewildering world with no end or start / I am Indian in skin but English of heart / Bewildering world, despair and rejoice / Indian skin, Albion voice."

The juxtapositions are jarring and pointed, with the Royal Bengal tiger at the feet of Bishi-as-Brittania eclipsing the traditional lion and possibly citing Edward Armitage's propagandistic 1858 oil painting *Retribution*, which justified English atrocities against the Indian Rebellion of 1857. Yet the album as a whole offers up a cultural cornucopia holding out for, or at least fantasizing about, the idyll of harmonious racial-ethnic integration within the construct of Englishness, and it was touted promotionally as "an ode to ever-changing England."[8] On the surface across which it ludically skids, Bishi's brand of mash-up feels coeval with, and pop-kin to, the admiring Diggs, yet ultimately less threatening than the poetry of *TwERK*. The contrast between these lyricist/performers, in terms of both textual content and its delivery as enunciated material, is instructive: it can help us sound the difference between a mode of multilingualism that imagines its own incorporation into the state apparatus, however ironically, and a more discomfiting performance of translingualism that upsets the very epistemic categories of inside and outside, colonizer and colonized, West and East, skin and heart—performing statelessness in the break. Diggs's more illocatable version of multilingualism emerges as xenoglossic.

In this chapter, I identify the transmutation of concepts of the mother tongue extended by Diggs's polyglot performances, both written and vocalized, which I view as xenoglossic in the tradition of the Azusa Street Revival, and highlight how they rapturously deploy languages apparently alien to the speaker's experience, lacking either a perceived birthright or institutionally backed mastery. Diggs's work participates in what Ashon Crawley has theorized as the Blackpentecostal tradition—bringing to being "otherwise possibilities" of radical solidarity that are tribe-trouncing in nature—while practicing a form of Pentecostalism very different from the glossolalic tradition of speaking in tongues that dominates Crawley's archive, which is characterized by ecstatic paralinguistic yet unintelligible speech.[9] The xenoglossic mode in which Diggs composes is closer to the mythical reconciliation of Babel, in which the Holy Spirit or Breath's descent upon the apostles of Christ effectively brought the earth back to the condition of common natural language(s) suggested by Diggs's epigraph to *TwERK*: "And the earth was of one language, and of one speech" (Genesis 11:1).

More immediately, Diggs's Pentecostalism calls to mind the utopian moment of the Azusa Street Revival led by African American preachers in early twentieth-century Los Angeles (1906–1915). The primary catalyst for the global spread of Pentecostalism and equally important to Crawley, as we recall, the Revival was characterized by multiracial and multiethnic congregations witnessed being suddenly granted the gift of speaking in languages such as Yiddish, German, and Spanish. Although opacity has been a crucial feature of anti-, post-, and decolonial poetics and the tactics of what Kamau Brathwaite invoked as "nation language," xenoglossic performances like those of the Los Angeles Pentecostalists and of Diggs discomfit and dislodge precisely because they are partially transparent. In line with *TwERK*'s "hyphy dancehall" fabulousness, one could call these xenoglossic performances iridescent: punctuated by glimmers of legibility that yoke the inquisitive reader/listener in, while resisting comprehension, consumption, and subsequent incorporation into extant sociopolitical bodies.[10] In fact, the stress on the ecstatic body of the poet straining athletically to articulate the languages of the planet comes to eclipse any focus on the single body politic in Diggs, producing a form of linguistic translucency in which recognition and alienation spasm, artfully, in concert with the trained muscles of the performer: "what happens when you twerk the language. A flexibility. A tension. A release. A muscle spasm. Thigh buster."[11] This makes somewhat literal Fred Moten's assertion that "your ass is in what you sing. Dedicated to the movement of hips, dedicated by that movement, the harmolodically rhythmic body."[12] The result can be defamiliarizingly erotic; the autodidactic training of body, mind, and voice involved in the xenoglossic process comes in this contemporary poetry to replace more familiar and potentially dangerous valorizations of recapturing any prelapsarian state of the mother tongue.

PERFORMANCE BEYOND CITIZENSHIP, BODIES
BEYOND THE BODY POLITIC

In distinguishing Diggs's work from less threatening forms of multilingualism, it is useful to recall Fred Moten's theoretical project surrounding extraterritorial freedom in *In the Break: The Aesthetics of the Black Radical Tradition* (2003) because Moten sets the stage for an anti-colonial poetics of worldmaking that rejects standard appeals to the nation-state. Moten's classic in the poetics of Black study begins with a critique of subjectivity and, by extension, of community on geopolitical grounds.[13] This critique is routed through Saidiya Hartman's

Scenes of Subjection, which itself bears the traces of Judith Butler's theories of subjection, "wherein the call to subjectivity is understood also as a call to subjection and subjugation and appeals for redress or protection to the state or to the structure or idea of citizenship—as well as modes of radical performativity or subversive impersonation—are always already embedded in the structure they would escape."[14] Moten contours the way performative modes of the Black radical tradition detach themselves from such oppressive structures of citizenship through "elevating disruptions of the verbal that take the rich content of the object's/commodity's aurality outside the confines of meaning" (*ITB*, 7). To do so, Moten adopts a liberatory hermeneutic mode inherited from Frederick Douglass, whose thought is presented as countervailing that of Douglass's "'contemporaries'" Marx, Nietzsche, Freud, and Saussure (the scare quotes are Moten's own). But this hermeneutics, being para- and extralinguistic, really originates from the scream of Douglass's Aunt Hester, stripped and whipped by a plantation master in a grotesquely canonical scene of nineteenth-century US (literary) history. In Moten's handling, the "improper" speech of objectified and commodified persons—from Aunt Hester's scream to the material surplus of performed language, or what is routinely read by hegemonic linguistics as the accent, troubled syntax, and seeming agrammaticality of Black vernaculars—is presented as disrupting the logics of capitalist and state oppression through "cutting" performances of aurality (*ITB*, 14). The phantasm of Received Pronunciation calls to mind Fanon's critique of the colonial's search for the perfect diction of the white Parisian in *Black Skin, White Masks*, a diction bound to be undercut by the "epidermal" character of race.[15] Far from that species of radical conformity, the Black performances at the heart of Moten's project instead give vent to the "inspirited materiality" of speech as breath and sound, "a spirit manifest in its material expense or aspiration" (*ITB*, 11).

For Ferdinand de Saussure, the possibility of a universal language was predicated on the abstraction of speech. Black subjects violently foreclosed from such abstraction and from the "traditional" forms of kinship we have explored critiques of thus far—being bound historically to a dehumanizing circuit of commodity exchange that removed the father's name and power from view and that traumatized the conditions of motherhood—rupture the fiction of universality. Along with it, they undermine the seemingly suprahistorical constructs of nation, race, and family through surplus phonic substance irreducible to any geopolitical entity or tribe: "For Saussure such speech is degraded, say, by accent, a deuniversalizing, material difference; for Chomsky it is degraded by a deuniversalizing agrammaticality, but Glissant knows that 'the [scarred] spoken imposes on the slave its particular syntax.' These material degradations—fissures or invaginations of a foreclosed universality, a heroic but bounded eroticism—are black performances" (*ITB*, 14). For Moten, these "invaginations" are the folds of the flesh disavowed by European theorists in their attempts to siphon off bodily surplus from language; here, Moten deploys Jacques Derrida's sexualized term against itself.[16]

Moten's work adds a new dimension to critiques of the mother tongue explored thus far, as he will keep ever in view "The ongoing stealing away of and from maternal body, maternal shore, maternal language.... away (from) home" in Black performance, "Born not in bondage but in fugitivity, in stolen breath and stolen life" (*ITB*, 305*n*). In these cases, the mother tongue has been subject to severance enforced by property relations under capitalism, by theft—although the lasting musicality detached from language is imbued for Moten with a fugitive power. Moten's poetics of "surplus lyricism," a lyricism that exceeds identity as such, builds upon Hortense Spillers's seminal writing on maternal and paternal dispossession, which in 1987 exposed the seemingly universal abstractions of "mother" and "father" as ahistorical and "kinship" in the biological/genetic sense as starkly contingent, undercut by the stealing and enforced dispersal of both Black and Indigenous communities that gave rise to the so-called New World. Spillers identified in these conditions of trauma an insurgent potential for the African American female subject to reside outside the Law of the Father, operating somehow beyond, although brutally through, the "American Grammar Book."[17] In turn, in experimental Black performance read with an attention to sexual identity, Moten locates the possibility of altering the "exclusionary brotherhoods of criticism" without attempting "a nostalgic and impossible suturing of wounded kinship" (*ITB*, 18). He situates these practices in a contemporary moment "imprecisely characterized as post-cold war . . . or *newly* globalized" ("imprecisely" because European colonialism imposed conditions of globalization long before the late twentieth century), a moment when "a universalization of ritual . . . rears its head in the invocation of roots or of tradition or interculturalism or appropriation, all of which are made possible by the ongoing development of Northern hegemony" (*ITB*, 32). Two decades later, in a contemporary moment increasingly marked by the rise of reactionary and indeed neofascist myths of the tribe, the attention within the discursive lineage of Black study to notions of tradition, ethnicity, and race as frames that can be broken emerges as a crucial corrective.

Moten casts the radical performative practices at the heart of his study as "multiply tongued" (quoting Nathaniel Mackey) and as proximate to glossolalia, as in the work of Artaud: "This music is not only the 'last resort' of 'wounded kinship,' but is also, precisely as that last resort, the emergence from broken matrilinearity of an insistent reproductive *mater*iality."[18] Pivoting from music to poetry in this chapter, we can build upon Moten's theorization across the literary and sonic arts, being convinced that xenoglossia is a more precise descriptor than glossolalia for practices that work with and "twerk" natural languages under conditions of dispossession. LaTasha N. Nevada Diggs emerges as exemplary in bodying forth a form of contemporary Black xenoglossic practice characterized by sensuous surplus—by musical and physical interference—while remaining in a fugitive zone of unauthorized access to foreign natural languages rather than veering into pure sound. The very title of *TwERK* makes literal Moten's point that poetry, singing, and playing an instrument are all choreographic practices fundamentally "dedicated to the movement of hips, . . . the harmologically rhythmic body" (*ITB*, 39–40). In the work of Diggs, it isn't the nonsemantic noise of Aunt Hester's scream that cuts through theoretical discourses; it's the glimmer of meaning in languages beyond the reputed mother tongue of the United States that cuts through deadening New World histories to a potential vector of freedom, or at least of recognition among those who have been subjugated by those histories: of planetary harmonics.

Diggs's biography and some of her prose suggest that the welter of languages within the pages of her debut collection, *TwERK* (2013), can be traced to her native Harlem, with its Black US southern, Caribbean, Cherokee, Korean War vet, and even Valley Girl influences, and more broadly to New York City—a city now, as in Louis Zukofsky's day, reputed to be the most linguistically diverse on earth, harboring approximately eight hundred spoken languages.[19] *TwERK*'s soundscape sparks comparison with the creative transcription of mingling vernaculars in the New York streets that proliferated in works of ethnic modernism, from John Dos Passos's *Manhattan Transfer* (1925), Claude McKay's *Home to Harlem* (1928), Zukofsky's "Poem Beginning 'The'" (published in Pound's journal *The Exile* in 1928), and Henry Roth's *Call It Sleep* (1934), through Ishmael Reed's *Mumbo Jumbo* (1972) and Edwin Torres's explosive contemporary Nuyorican verse scores. However, the range of languages in which Diggs's verse delectates exceeds the author's "proper" linguistic background from the start. She conjures, in their order of indexing, Japanese, Spanish, English, Hindi/Urdu, Welsh, Māori, Hawaiian, Samoan, Malay, Swahili, Runa Simi (Quechua), Vietnamese, Yoruba, Portuguese, Chamorro, Cherokee (Tsa'lāgī'), Barbadian dialect, Kikongo, Tagalog, a pidgin of Port Moresby in Papua New Guinea, Hawaiian Pidgin, and Papiamentu, and includes passages in unindexed Nation language, Pig Latin, and Snoop-Dogg-style shizzling. The author may be as remote from these languages as her readers are.

Like *The Waste Land*, *The Cantos*, and other works of cosmopolitan multilingualism, this is a poetry of discernible reach and research. Yet the conditions of access to multiple languages and cultures in the late twentieth century enabled by advanced forms of globalization—characterized by uneven vectors of time-space compression, economic liberalization, and the information revolution of the internet—have been thrown open in ways that may have perturbed the early twentieth-century guides to "Kulchur" engaged in forging a new "tale of the tribe." *TwERK* samples the languages and lingos of globalization, transnational capitalism, and information overload deliriously and never without critique, moving beyond the surface multiculturalism propounded by neoliberal and authoritarian states and producing a field of difference that challenges the uptake of minor tongues by colonial languages. Fellow traveler and scholar of Nuyorican poetry and performance Urayoán Noel brings out one of the title's more ingenious puns: "In limning the *lingua*, Diggs refracts the *franca* and its franchise, making us aware of the ambient noise of our networked (née-TwERKED) bodies."[20] *TwERK* stages its sampling of cultures in coalition with fellow critics of commodified bodies and globally circulated representations that do harm to their objects. Skirting the more immediate invocations of heritage present in Bishi or in earlier artists like Theresa Hak Kyung Cha, Diggs spirals vertiginously around the erasure of heavily mediated, even branded, histories. Alongside Gary Simmons's *Erasure Drawings* of racially typecast cartoon characters, originally inspired by abandoned blackboards in a schoolhouse studio, *TwERK* asks through the title of a poem, "have you forgotten any personal property?" (*T*, 16).

TwERK nevertheless contains a wealth of references that send us to the note section in the back, once we know it exists. Yet resisting the notion of the glossary or annotation, the author identifies her exegeses as "rhinestones, acrylic on panel, knives, mirror, packing tape, fur, found medical illustration paper on mylar, rubber tires, wood, metal, plastic, porcelain, paper, latex paint, Lonely Planet phrase books" (*T*, 89). Vaunting these unassuming material origins, Diggs lends an immediacy to the least immediate section of her book and resists the forbidding assumption of difficulty attached to multilingual work in a monoglot climate. *TwERK*'s accessibility distances this text from its most canonical modernist precursors, whose elite revisions of the canon simply ended up producing generations of new gatekeepers, by a wide gulf. Nowhere is this accessibility gap more patent than in the last item indexed: "Lonely Planet phrase books." It stresses not only the autodidactic impulse that led to these poems but also Diggs's conversationally oriented, ground-level approach to foreign languages— an approach that Gramsci would likely place halfway between the "spontaneous" and the "normative," as it arises from an interstice between the grammar book and a "direction-giving organic center."[21] In Tyrone Williams's reading (most immediately addressing Harmony Holiday), which subtly de-otherizes English marked as Black, "Black English cannot help but draw on orthodox and heterodox grammars and syntaxes of the American language, understood as a composite of languages from every continent on earth."[22] Diggs's emphasis on communicability and the ambient, although playful and incomplete, presence of translations throughout the text renders these poems approachable. Indeed, the book's popularity surpasses any small-press publisher's expectation for experimental poetry: *TwERK* sold two thousand copies in just over a year and a half and was well into its fourth printing as of 2022.[23] Diggs's reliance on the phrasebook also removes her language play from normative claims to authenticity or accuracy: "I love the tentative landscape of phrasebooks," Diggs says in an interview. "They are never 100 percent accurate."[24]

The self-consciously "multilingo," playfully trochaic poem "metromultilingo-pollonegrocucarachasblahblahblah," written on commission for an event curated by the Nuyorican transdisciplinary artist and "neo-lingualisualist" Edwin Torres, is reminiscent of metropolitan modernist language collages; it samples the linguistic hodgepodges that inhabit various New York subway and train lines, closing with a commute to the World Trade Center and the ticking of a broker's watch.[25] This detail and other images reminiscent of the 1990s, like the "Nihongo in Prada / cross town to Vanderbilt for feudal bukkake"[26]—a picture defined by the consumerist decadence of a soon-to-be-burst Japanese bubble—mark it as a pre-9/11 poem of relatively unperturbed globalization, hailing from a universe long since imploded. Against this poem's domineering capitalist tempo stands the cockroach, or "water bug," as it is called in New York euphemese:

> & while a Pentecostal woman in overtly modernized
> African attire
> fails to notice the water bug running across her ankle boots
>
> la cucaracha es universal
> y todo todo sabe a pollo
>
> (*T*, 48)

Although the broker's time may seem eternal, it's the rhythm of the overlooked cockroach that is universal, coursing through in the uneven cadence of a Spanish, and later Mexican, popular song. In a Cross Cultural Poetics interview with Leonard Schwartz, Diggs remarks that "our ears are only tuned to the language of commerce in the city, which is oftentimes English (unless you're in Jackson Heights)."[27] In a lyric essay on polycultural Harlem, Diggs builds on this observation, noting of 111th Street, "In this assumed English-only neighborhood, if you turn down the volume of the Queen's chatter, other mother tongues are heard."[28] Founders of the language justice collaborative Antena Aire, Jen/Eleana

GLOTTAL STOP   267

Hofer and JD Pluecker, argue in their manifestos that English-only expectations are a logical outcome of capitalist networks designed to avoid all forms of friction and feedback under globalization: "Capital is not interested in reminding us that there is more to learn; in fact, capital colludes to soothe us into thinking we already know everything, to produce a sense of normality, expectedness, regularity in a world that is anything but."[29] Antena Aire, which also stages interpretation events in which each participant is invited to speak in the language that makes them most comfortable, proposes "discomfortable" writing, which resists transparency, as a corrective to the arrogance of capital: "To make us strangers in a place we thought was home. To find spaces for listening inside strangeness."[30] Diggs's subway poem constitutes a buoyant example of the discomfortable, estranging the contemporary soundscape of metropolitan transit and exposing a plurilingual, polyrhythmic measure that is routinely stifled or, as the poem suggests, "castrated by humdrum": if one listens carefully, Diggs explains to Schwartz on Cross Cultural Poetics, urban spaces host a "clusterfuck of tongues" that can at times only be understood through the physicality of the language being performed.[31] The poem rewards those who do not understand Spanish with the musicality of the easily voiceable refrain "todo todo sabe a pollo" and enables those who do—or who take the time to translate the simple phrase via a dictionary, a neighbor, or (most likely) the internet—to ask further questions.

As "metromultilingopollonegrocucarachasblahblahblah" closes, those who grasp the final Spanish phrase are left wondering whether this chicken that lends its generic flavor to everything is a signifier for the homogeneity of production under capitalism or the commonality of the lowly. The Pentecostal woman whose feet are crossed by the water bug provides the cultural and linguistic key to this scene and, to some extent, to *TwERK* itself. For the epigraph to *TwERK* invokes the story of Pentecost as told through its precursor in Genesis 11:1: "And the earth was of one language, and of one speech." The genius of this citation resides in the fact that it, too, hovers as a double-edged sword; the sentence may refer both to the dystopian, difference-trouncing, English-only ideology of US-driven late capitalism *and* to a future utopia—modeled by this poetic work, or skillful *wERK*—in which imperfect xenoglossic accessibility to a range of languages makes communication and sisterhood among subaltern subjects possible. Diggs's willingness to tarry with the discomfortable in speaking languages beyond the prescribed—what she described in a conversation with my students, responding to their questions about appropriating foreign tongues, as "just wanting to dance with you"—is a part of quotidian practice for the multilingual person, although rarely reflected in literary study.[32] As Doris Sommer narrates of the decision-making involved, "Do I risk addressing a stranger in Spanish? Will it be

268   GLOTTAL STOP

an invitation to intimacy, an aggressive unmasking, or a ridiculously wrong channel? The question may sound irrelevant to people who don't make these decisions daily and may not worry about the risk. Perhaps they'll counsel us to get over the complication and simply speak English, as if worrying about which language to use were not an exercise in the interpersonal delicacy and caution that amount to civic behavior."[33] Diggs's poems oblige immersion in this interpersonal delicacy and caution, and by extension they model a future-oriented civic behavior.

THE VOICE AS A WIND INSTRUMENT

However antielitist and approachable, Diggs's xenoglossia provokes unease as it defamiliarizes both the seeming "mother tongue" out of which it flees and the process of linguistic articulation itself. Consider a poem like Diggs's open-field lyric "border universe," in which lines brusquely mingling colonial Spanish and Runa Simi alternate with their interlinear translation into largely italicized (and thereby marginalized) English. The poem begins,

> ñoqa chutarayani.
> *I lie.*
> ñoqa kani llulla qhapaq de uno *sueño*
> *I am a noble liar*   from a dream
> y ñoqanchis tiyanchis chinkakunapi hatun ch'aki.
> *and we live in a large dry labyrinth.*

(*T*, 33)

The speaker of this poem is unidentified and unidentifiable and warns us from the start that it is unreliable, a liar hailing from a dream; resisting conflation with the author or even with the human, it seems to give voice to a landscape of precipitous edges, of border-quashing landslides like those of the Andes—its abode a "large dry labyrinth," suggestive of colonized and depopulated Inca sites. Diggs suspends us in a state of confusion appropriate to the vague and perhaps impossible image of a "border universe," one rife with borders and yet lacking identifiable shape, resisting geopolitical containment; perhaps it is a universe of "boarders" rather than settled inhabitants. Countervailing the seemingly straightforward alternation between italicized and unitalicized verse characteristic of bilingual editions or code-switching texts, readers encounter tripwires in seeking parallels between the two, discovering that they need to work to determine whether this

GLOTTAL STOP   269

is in fact a bilingual text that translates itself with fidelity or a more recalcitrant species of translingual environment. A minimum of interpretive work enables us to apprehend that from the first line, we are being set adrift among possibilities of meaning: "ñoqa chutarayani" means "I lie down" in Quechua, yet is apparently "translated" as "I lie," a slightly ambiguous phrase whose swing toward untruth rather than corporeal horizontality is reinforced by the "false rich man" or "noble liar" of the next line.

In performance, Diggs reads the entire two-and-a-half-page poem in mongrel Spanish and Runa Simi first and then the English translation, without providing any preliminary explanations for easy listening such as have become customary in the banter of the "poetry reading" as a US American form. This renders more extreme the already defamiliarizing experience of reading it on the page, through which multiple signifying systems accrue to "t'akarinchis q'atapa verdad / en qasi wasiy / *spill the muddy truth / in my vacant home*" (note the inversion of orthographic expectations of italicized "foreign" terms).[34] The muddiness and homelessness of the poem's truth are shared by poem and receiver: as Diggs writes elsewhere, "In search of somewhere, in this stew, I am at home here."[35] The piece forms a provocative contrast with Tagore's much-loved song "Gram Chara," the song covered by Bishi with her mother for *Albion Voice*, which imagines an earthen road leading away from the speaker's home village, beckoning the landed toward the unknown. Listeners to Diggs are likely to find themselves awash in syllables, only occasionally to be gratified by a recognizable colonial Spanish term such as "verdad." They are likely to detect the more radical foreignness of the Quechua in phrases such as "t'akarinchis q'atapa" through Diggs's halting articulation of the glottal stop: a consonant formed by release of the airstream through pumping of the glottis following its total closure.

In the poem "daggering kanji," this glottal stop becomes a sovereign feature of Diggs's lyricism, one that organizes by frenzied replication, slicing through an otherwise unruly semantic field of words from languages alien to one another, devoid of syntactical linkages—devoid of any linkage, in fact, other than their initial letter k and their disruption by the glottal stop itself (figure 5.2). The poem assaults all of its initial k sounds with the k-apostrophe symbol that stands for the velar ejective stop in the International Phonetic Alphabet, producing an effect of ostranenie or defamiliarization in every case. Readers are encouraged to listen to a performance from the poem's beginning in conjunction with reading.

Diggs specifies in *TwERK*'s endnotes that "daggering kanji" is composed in Hawaiian (as in kumu, to make a start, create), Tagalog (kulisap, a swarming, as of insects), Japanese (kabuki, the dance-drama form), Māori (kare, a friend), Cherokee (kanoheda, personal story), and English (as in khakis, kabob, kamikaze, all

k'k'kumu	kk'kk'khakis	k'k'kare	kk'kk'amikazae
k'k'ku'ulala	*k'k'ku'ulala*	*k'k'ku'ulala*	*k'k'ku'ulala*
k'k'kazoo	kk'kk'kūlolo	k'k'kahuna	kk'k'kabob
k'k'ku'ulala	*k'k'ku'ulala*	*k'k'ku'ulala*	*k'k'ku'ulala*
k'k'kali	kk'k'kulisap	k'k'kabuki	k'k'kk'kumala
k'k'ku'ulala	*k'k'ku'ulala*	*k'k'ku'ulala*	*k'k'ku'ulala*

FIGURE 5.2 LaTasha N. Nevada Diggs, opening of "daggering kanji," from *TwERK*, 64.

borrowings from other languages). Additional languages, such as Sanskrit and Urdu, are present here yet uninventoried. Diggs also lists Quechua as a language of composition, but from my research, this seems to be a slyly oblique indication of the velar ejective's irruption of all of the poem's other lexicons. This form of glottal stop appears in the Cuzco dialects, but glottal occlusion is a feature of other Indigenous languages, such as, prominently, the glottalized click consonants of sub-Saharan African languages like Khosa, rendered performatively fabulous by Miriam Makeba.

Seemingly borrowing from the glottalized stop of Quechua dialects and placing it after the initial k of a swarm of words that are less and more familiar, Diggs imposes the breath stoppage as a stuttering spasm between initial consonant and vowels, lopping off detonated word starts. This renders the terms virtually unrecognizable in performance: the relatively friendly onomatopoeic term "kazoo," for instance, becomes a swallowed series of cutting clicks followed by a breathless "azoo." A different effect occurs when Diggs performs the piece's italicized grayscale chorus, made up entirely of the Hawaiian term ku'ulala, "wild," which has its own glottal stop, its diacritical mark the 'okina (note the opposing direction), yet is enhanced with two extra opening velar ejective k's. Following each breathtaking barrage of glottal stops, Diggs draws out and raises the pitch of the "oo" sound, enhancing the rhyme with the French expression of surprise or concern, "oh là là," and its erotically inflected English adaptation, "ooh-la la!"

Diggs's seemingly random choice of a single definition in her notes—that "kinkajou" means a honeybear—highlights how arbitrary the selection of annotations can be and suggests that semantic assignments are not the key to grasping the poem's meaning. At the same time, although the piece announces itself explicitly as being written "*after Christian Bök*," renowned for his epic interpretations of Kurt Schwitters's Dada sound poem "Ursonate," "daggering kanji" would be best described as a xenoglossic, as opposed to glossolalic, sound poem. It is the cutting of meaning by sound that emerges as the poem's substantive contribution/play.

Registered by a single closed quotation mark ('), the glottal stoppage appears to the eye as a series of lacerations in the air, irrupting the disturbingly near appearance of the acronym kkk. To the ear, the stop registers as a virtuosic variation on beatboxing, a studied ability to freeze and force air backward and forward in the lungs over and over—but one whose viral insistence on shutting off oxygen to the vocal cords before allowing it to rush back inflicts both awe and disquiet. Multiplied exponentially and placed in relation to the plural k, this glottal stop's very incorporation into the poet-performer's repertoire seems to channel harm. It executes what Nathaniel Mackey identifies in his essay "Breath and Precarity" as a "radical pneumaticism" that pervades Black music and especially that of wind instruments, "in which the involuntary is rendered deliberate, labored, in which breath is belabored, made strange."[36] Through such performances, Diggs transmits that what Gerard Manley Hopkins called "world-mothering air," this "nursing element," does not "nestl[e] ... everywhere" for everyone: "This air, which, by life's law, / My lung must draw and draw" is also subject to the capriciousness of interpretation of state law and its recognized (or unrecognized) citizens; as such, it tragically does not hold that, as Hopkins claimed, "It does no prejudice."[37] Diggs's virtuosity makes it clear that the human voice is itself a wind instrument, and that the vocal cords are a site through which skill may be channeled toward expression of a deeply incorporated panic.

CHOREOGRAPHY OF CUTS

Diggs's sound poem takes the phrase "clusterfuck of tongues" literally—or rather, makes this concept literal. "Daggering" is a provocative Jamaican dance form accompanying dancehall music that moves so intensely into the spheres of wrestling and dry sex that it has spurred censorship on the part of the Jamaican government. It involves variants on twerking, the polyrhythmic, muscular booty twist and jerk that reputedly hails from New Orleans's bounce music in the 1990s, but with roots in African culture. Although twerking abounds in contemporary media culture, Diggs contests a merely presentist reading of her book's title by pointing out that this gesture appears throughout the African diaspora—and points to the range of linguistic innovations that accompany it: "There's *gouye/gouyad* in Haiti and *El Mapale* in Colombia. In Senegal there is the *ventilateur*. The *vacunao* is from Cuba, and the *mapouka* is from Cote d'Ivoire. There is the Cameroonian *zingué* and the Zimbabwean *kwassa kwassa*. Somalia has *niiko*. The Afro-Arab communities in Oman, Saudi Arabia, and the United Arab Emirates can get a shy bootylicious with their *malaya*. And *dutty whine* or *winin'* you can find in Jamaica. So maybe [twerking] is not so much about muscle memory than it is about blood memory."[38] While resisting the notion that this dance move is innately Black, Diggs—who worked as a dancer at major Manhattan clubs in the 1990s—explains that her poetry seeks to "activate" and "twerk" all "these layers of blackness, these modes of code-switching, vernaculars, and otherness."[39]

The appropriation of racialized dance moves like twerking (widely associated with women of color) led to controversy in the year *TwERK* was published, when Miley Cyrus performed at the MTV Video Music Awards show, both twerking and fondling her Black female backup singers as if they were props, prompting accusations of "cultural appropriation at its worst," even minstrelsy, as well as the accusation of appropriating female liberation (but also, arguably, contributing to the term's celebrated entry into the Oxford Dictionaries Online).[40] Pairing "daggering" with "kanji" (the Japanese term for Han Chinese characters, imported in the fifth century CE and now fully incorporated into written Japanese) continues the book's extended dialogue with the Japanese language and culture, as well as its appropriations. *TwERK*'s opening section, "anime," inaugurates the book's engagement with what Mike Ladd calls "Black-American Orientalism," which Diggs "does not absolve—yet joyfully disarms."[41] Neither does *TwERK* absolve the racist caricatures of Blackness embedded in the decadent fascinations of 1990s-era Japan: manga and videogame franchises like Dragon Ball and Pokémon or the contemporary blackface trend of ganguro girls (ガ ン グ ロ). The gerund in "daggering kanji" enables us to visualize the Chinese written character as a medium for poetry that can be twerked and itself twerks—or cuts.[42]

Daggering has been described as so violent a dance that it makes twerking look like child's play. The term can also refer to violent sex, with obvious phallic implications, and Diggs's poem therefore harbors a possible joke on the epidemic of broken penises that has accompanied this Jamaican trend. An earlier version of the poem appeared in *Black Scholar* in 2008, under the title "kanji gnu glue," as a series of apprehensible quatrains and couplets, with a visual effect very different from the revision's ambient expanse of syllables; "kanji gnu glue" was almost narrative, although circling around a group of cutting consonants, as its sexual references were more explicit. It contained the only slightly encoded refrain, "come canyons

/   kaja cuckoo coos cribs cushy cashews /   come canals / cocky canker crackerjacks cool corkscrew."[43] The major difference between the initial poem and its revision as "daggering kanji," however, is the addition of the glottal k before a spreading panorama of k words, from the familiar "king" and "khakis" (an Urdu word of Persian origins for "soil-colored," introduced into English via colonizing military campaigns in India and Africa) to the Hawaiian-derived "kahuna" (priest, sorcerer, expert) and Sanskrit "kali" (the fierce Hindu goddess associated with empowerment) and the refrain "*k'k'ku'ulala*," repeated forty times. The term *ku'ulala* is Hawaiian for wild. Merging this term, with its 'okina—the Hawaiian word for the symbol that represents the glottal stop, which literally means "cutting" (*'oki* "cut" + *-na* "-ing")—with the velar ejective k' of the Aymara and Cuzco dialects of Quechua is a form of daggering indeed: erotic, cunning, and cutting. This move invites charges of appropriation (to which we will return) and a confusion of the Hawaiian and Quechua glottal stops (marked as ' and ', respectively), yet accusations such as these misunderstand the spirit of this poem and volume, which aims at honoring and "dancing with" what lies beyond one's own property and mastery through sampling, accompaniment, and riffs, as in musical improvisation. Diggs has performed with musicians such as Sunny Jain, Guillermo E. Brown, Carl Hancock Rux, the Nuyorican Soul Orchestra, Vernon Reid, Ryuichi Sakamoto, Kaoru Watanabe, and artist collective GENG PTP, and *TwERK* seems to take the multitextured global polyrhythms of M.I.A. as presiding genius. The terms that fill the poem are themselves borrowings and appropriations: the slang term "kudos," from the Greek; the Arabic, Persian, and Urdu "kabob"; the Cantonese-mimicking "kumquat"; and the Yiddish "klutzy," from German "klotz" (wooden block). Others are of indefinite origin: "kazoo," a U.S. term, is apparently onomatopoeic. There are puns: "kitíkití" is Tagalog for mosquito larva, or a pun on calling to kitty, and the Japanese term "kiru" is particularly dual-edged because it can mean either "cut, slice, carve" (if written as kanji, as 切る) and "kill" (if written as katakana, キル, in a Japanese approximation of English pronunciation). And there are words whose trajectories bespeak racist associations: "kinky," from curly, as applied especially to hair, and then to crookedness and unconventional sexual behavior.

The trajectory of this text is undoubtedly sexual: it moves from "k'k'kumu" (*kumu* being Hawaiian for begin or for reason or teacher) to close on "cc'cc'cum," in its sole shift from "k" to the rounder "c." The intervening forty *k'k'ku'ulala*s punctuate the text with their only apparently glossolalic "clusterfucks": they preface the Hawaiian word for wild or crazy with the potential Quechua glottal stop while embedding within them a more immediately apprehensible "ooh la la!" (used in French as a signal of negative surprise or shock but in anglophone contexts as an exoticizing, francophiliac expression of pleasure). In performance, this trajectory becomes intensely corporeal: the four *k'k'ku'ulala*s between each set of four k words provide a rare space of reprieve in which the poet can audibly inhale following the plosive pressures of the ks and glottal stop, and Diggs's *ooh*s gradually build toward the orgasmic possibilities of the text's "clusterfuck of tongues."[44] In a brief but astute review, Amaranth Borsuk alludes to the eroticism of this poem in terms of oral sex: the text "simultaneously swallows and spits as the glottal hits the back of the throat and the velar flicks off the soft palate."[45] Oral sex may be a useful metaphor, given the dance happening in the throat, but I want to call on the notion of hegemony as a dance between coercion and consent. Dance may be the consummate way to describe the kind of oppression and empowerment taking place in dance forms as apparently harmless as salsa and milonga and as intense as twerking and daggering.

Moten's language of the "cut" becomes useful in thinking Diggs's vocal tactics through. The poet/theorist recovers a "freedom drive" in Black performances that disrupts any linguistic universalism based on abstracting the sign from its enunciation, a trend he traces as reaching from the early modern search for a universal language through the late modern science of linguistics: "This disruption of the Enlightenment linguistic project is of fundamental importance. . . . More specifically, the emergence from political, economic, and sexual objection of the radical materiality and syntax that animates black performances indicates a freedom drive" (*ITB*, 7). Moten's project assumes a liberatory approach to deviation from throttling standards of accent, syntax, and vocabulary that normally herald one's successful integration into a state apparatus. This reading of the subversive potential in accentuating the voice's materiality (which entails ample attention to the workings of breath) permits us to understand Diggs's virtuosic translinguistic performances in a geopolitically liberatory key. Yet Diggs's planetary aesthetic moves beyond Moten's theorization, given that he assumes a performance of English or of languagelessness—not a xenoglossic aesthetic that subjects colonial tongues to breathing skills learned from the study of Indigenous tongues.

At the same time that it melds tongues in the sexual ecstasy of *ulala*, the text gives voice to rifts. Each "k'k'k-" registers as a stutter, a refusal to disavow the disjunction between the words and their self-consciously nonnative speaker. "This is why some people insist that I do not sound like a New Yorker," Diggs underscores: "I have never been fluent."[46] The "k'k'" or, at times, "kk'kk" or "kk'k" preceding these k words simultaneously estranges them from themselves—and a reader who is looking can hardly fail to notice the sinister "kkk" embedded within each cluster, although performance defamiliarizes this formation

GLOTTAL STOP   ❦   275

through incorporation: having first swallowed it, it cuts and rejects it. Diggs's virtuosic performance of the glottal stop from Quechua—one of the Indigenous languages she has formally studied, along with Cherokee, traveling to Peru for the purpose—cleaves these words away from our comprehension, leaving the lopped-away, now guttural vowels to begin "-abuki," "-arma," "-ung-fu," and so on.

Linguistic borrowings often embed within themselves the residue of conflict and domination—a daggering that is both decreative and catastrophic. This makes Gramsci's work with the hybrid linguistic substratum carried within each of us, often in an incoherent, disintegral form, relevant to such a text: "one's personality is bizarrely composite: it contains . . . prejudices from all historical phases at the narrow-minded local level and intuitions of a future philosophy which will be that of a human race united the world over. . . . The starting-point of critical elaboration is . . . 'knowing thyself' as a product of the historical process that has unwound to date, which has deposited in you an infinity of traces, without the aid of an inventory."[47] Gramsci's concept of "knowing thyself" requires linkage with cultural memory that has been foreclosed. When the inventory of this substratum has been harmed, even devastated by cultural genocide, its recovery becomes an imperative that requires a planetary imaginary. Moreover, with a historical view of "kin" that Black study bolsters, we are aware that cultural memory is inherited in surplus of biological ties. Such an imaginary and Diggs's clear interest in Caribbean vernaculars immediately call to mind M. NourbeSe Philip's *Zong!*, which excavates Indigenous African and colonial European words and syllables from the language of a pernicious English legal text. Philip's own exegesis, "Wor(l) ds Interrupted: The Unhistory of the Kari Basin," proposes "kinopoesis" as an addition to Pound's phanopoeia, melopoeia, and logopoeia (the play of image, music, and meaning, respectively), a physical movement of the melancholic formulation "*nolanguageofourown*": "*nolanguageofourown*   moves   is restless   is kinetic   . . . // . . . wherever european and african tongues have faced off against each other   wherever the european has attempted to impose his tongue on the african   the outcome has been a kinetic language drumming a beat with the bone of memory against the gun metal skin of the sea   scatting soughing coughing laughing into vividity   patwa nation language creole pidgin vernacular demotic an ting an ting."[48] In Diggs, we have two endangered Indigenous languages coming together in alliance as refrain and one attempt to impose the Quechua tongue upon a global expanse—with equally kinetic effects of twerking.

The sporadic references to knives and weaponry in *TwERK*—with "knives," we recall, being one of the sources cited in its glossary of sorts—thus bespeak not only street smarts and the aggressive aesthetics of hip-hop and collage, linking this work to that of Krista Franklin in poetry and collage and Wangechi Mutu in the visual arts, but also defiance in the face of cultural disappearance and amnesia.[49] The convocation of languages that takes place in these pages is closer to Ernesto Laclau and Chantal Mouffe's concept of articulation than to a classical notion of representation, with articulation emphasizing the recombination of collective identities as the poet ushers subaltern tongues into alliance with one another.[50] But Diggs's pastings of sampled sources are never without their residual slits, placing this work in generative proximity to the field of translation theory and resisting the domesticating label of multiculturalism. As Sarah Dowling argues, unlike the images of multinational melting pots that now ornament advertisements for Coke and the like, "in Diggs's poetry—as in so much multilingual work—it is precisely through the sonic qualities of rhythm and rhyme that we're forced to confront difference as difference."[51] Beyond these more traditionally studied features of rhythm and rhyme, Diggs achieves radical results in the very choreography of breath. Twisting a medium riddled with hazards into collaboration through labored virtuosity, the breath of the performer achieves what Nathaniel Mackey describes with his own athletic density in "Breath and Precarity" as a "recension," or critical revision of a text: here breath "becomes tactical, tactile, textile, even textual, a haptic recension whose jagged disbursements augur duress" (that is, duress as defined by restraint, restriction, or compulsion by threat, specifically unlawful constraint).[52]

Refusing to blunt the effects of hauling words over geography and time, resisting the forging of seamless translations, and forcing readers to dwell in a state of nonunderstanding can have an expansively seductive effect on English-only Americanism. As the founders of the interpretive collaborative Antena Aire, Hofer and Pluecker, put it in "A Manifesto for Ultratranslation," "If reading work in translation makes us wish we knew two or ten or thirty more languages, that's a good thing. Rather than running away from the untranslatable, scorning it or eyeing it suspiciously, or lamenting the loss it represents, we experience the untranslatable as invitation to further immersion, further closeness. A hint of light knifing through a door slightly ajar. Always the light slivering through, the door impossible to close because the foundation has shifted imperceptibly, the threshold askew."[53] This becomes an argument for the place of experimental poetry in a plurilingual world. Although it has become customary and even respectable in the United States to lament one's lack of formal training in certain foreign languages which one therefore cannot engage, as well as the lack of a truly international language, there are benefits to the preservation of linguistic difference and translucency. This is why, in 1918,

Gramsci criticized the fabrication of Esperanto as a bourgeois cosmopolitan endeavor, as opposed to a truly international one: "The advocates of a single language are worried by the fact that . . . there is an endless number of different languages which restrict the ability to communicate. This is a *cosmopolitan*, not an international anxiety, that of the bourgeois who travels for business or pleasure."[54] From early on, Gramsci argued that language can only be created from the ground up, through continuous molecular processes of contact with the masses, not as the result of a fabrication such as Esperanto—a term that comes to stand in his oeuvre for positivist science in general. He did, however, advocate for the creation of "verbal complexes" that could forge solidarity: "Esperanto, although it . . . has more to do with bourgeois cosmopolitanism than with proletarian internationalism, shows nevertheless . . . that there is a desire for and a historical push towards the formation of verbal complexes that transcend national limits and in relation to which current national languages will have the same role as dialects now have."[55] We see, hear, and feel this formation occurring in the pages of *TwERK* and are forced to participate in it as we attempt, stuttering, to voice and dance these words aloud or in our underprepared heads. *TwERK* is a formation whose constitutive lacerations might have both frightened and allured Henry James, as did the idiom of the cafés on Manhattan's Lower East Side, which "showed to my inner sense, beneath their bedizement, as torture-rooms of the living idiom; the piteous gasp of which at the portent of lacerations to come could reach me in any drop of the surrounding Accent of the Future. The accent of the very ultimate future, in the States, may be destined to become the most beautiful on the globe and the very music of humanity (here the 'ethnic' synthesis shrouds itself thicker than ever); but whatever we shall know it for, certainly, we shall not know it for English—in any sense for which there is an existing literary measure."[56] Diggs's erudite yet approachable polyglot space of communion is the twenty-first-century version of this proto-modernist zone: a space of future communicability and of a muscular alteration of measure.

AN ORPHANED TONGUE: IDENTITY AND/AS LONGING

Diggs's seemingly playful use of so many colonial and Indigenous languages brings with it the harrowing age-old yet contemporary question: Who has the right to compose in languages that are not theirs by birthright? Is it possible to learn and indulge in lyrical play with an Indigenous language without recolonizing

278 GLOTTAL STOP

it? Thinking in 2014 about what it means to perform Blackness, ever responding implicitly to the charge about which tongues are hers to utilize, Diggs says,

> Most people reading my work won't be able to figure out my race. The most they can say is, "This person is obviously not white, but I don't know what this person is." . . . It is also asking: What is American-ness to me? If we're talking about the conversation of language or mother tongue—I speak English because I was born here in North America, but I still don't feel it's my mother tongue. What is my mother tongue? American history has complicated any opportunity for me to find out what my mother tongue would be. There are so many tongues that have their place here. Some still exist. Some are extinct. So which one? Tsalagi (Cherokee)? I know a little and would love to improve, but I have no direct ties to the environment where it would be spoken to me daily. What if I were born in Puerto Rico? Is Spanish then my mother tongue? I'm not sure—Spanish is, like English, a colonial language. . . . What if I was born in the Philippines? If my father was a US Navy man and my mother Pinay by birth but with an ancestry that's Malaysian, Spanish, and Ati. In that case and in my case, what is the definitive root of me? I believe, like these histories, it is a mixture of tongues, a mash-up of rule and conquer, assimilation and adaptation. And in the States, my tongue is kind of an orphaned one. I'm trying to locate the cousins and aunties to my tongue, if that makes sense.[57]

She does not feel English to be her mother tongue, but because "American history has complicated any opportunity for [her] to find out what [her] mother tongue would be," xenoglossic procedures in the refuge or laboratory of poetry enable Diggs to draw on and forge an amalgamative language that feels more adequate to her experience, although she remains "outside."

In more recent presentations, Diggs is more forthright about her limited access to international languages and her claims to Native heritage, describing herself as "a reluctant monolingual who knows at least three or more words in some 10+ different languages, many of which are not Romance languages aka European tongues aka colonial tongues aka imperial tongues (that includes Japanese) / A child of a Black and Native woman from the South fed on commodity aka welfare cheese, Depeche Mode, Video Music Box, Kung Fu Theater on Channel 5, Godzilla marathons on Channel 9 & U68."[58] She identifies her work as reaching beyond her proper identities, which are presented in the plural, to address subjugated transcultural histories: "my personal identities as well as intersectionality, translingualism, intercultural histories, histories that are often taught separate from predominant histories—who 'won' and who didn't—thus maintaining that layered narratives & traumas are always presented in one terribly basic binary (Black vs. White, Native vs. White, . . . & so on)."[59] (On Instagram, the artist's signature hashtag is #neverbasic.) Diggs's current project, "Global Studies," is written partly in the voice of an "Indian interpreter," and she now specifies that her "ninth great grandfather was apparently an Indian interpreter."[60] The figure of the interpreter is a fascinating one, irreducible to one side or the other of a cultural chasm.

In conversation with the 92nd Street Y about her 2023 collection *Village*, Diggs describes the prominence of Tsalagi (Cherokee) and (Brazilian) Portuguese within the work as registering "a kind of longing," foregrounding outright that "in certain communities, to be a descendant is not enough. I am of that ancestry and I need to know my place."[61] Alongside the need to "know her place," she performs the intersectional consciousness of the land acknowledgment in performance and in writing. A poem about the domestic abuse to which her mother was subjected, about the pain of hearing "momma muddle moan" a "raw babble," for instance, is titled "jesus children of DᎣᏢᏚ[america]" (alluding to the 1973 Stevie Wonder song as filtered by Cherokee); this move inserts in the privileged place of the English term for the continent the Tsalagi syllabary for the sounds D "a"- Ꮻ -"me"- Ꮅ "li"- Ꮝ "ga," if not the actual Cherokee word "DᎣᏢᏏ" (phonetically written as "amelige").[62] Defensiveness around identity in conversation and explication—and in institutionally oriented justifications of this art, which punctuate the volume with irony—turns sporadically, within the poetry, into performative invocation of a parallel universe in the place of this "American" one. Rather than reaching outward to the "foreign," Diggs activates the language of one nation of Indigenous peoples concentrated in her mother's native Carolinas to which she has access. However, it is a nation to which she knows she can't belong. Placing Cherokee in the place where English would normally reign represents the dream of citizenship within a different sort of world. This act of conjuring may be considered wake work, and it is far from naive. It is rather one of the "self-taught hymns in high water" that accompanies both mother and daughter in *Village* through the process of envisioning a better society than the one in which her mother was "muffled" and died, one that might, temporarily, "rescue me :: rescue my mauled momma" (*V*, 26).

This intersectional poetics can be considered part of underrepresented yet mounting movements to strategically align Black and Indigenous resistance to cultural genocide, including reparative action surrounding the endangerment or annihilation of Indigenous languages and creoles. In insisting on these ties, however distressed, Diggs's poetry aligns with recent scholarship by figures like Tiya Miles, Malinda Maynor Lowery, David A. Chang, and Joyce Pualani Warren, who study literary and historical genealogies that (as Pualani Warren puts it) "impel us to think about how blackness and indigeneity have deep, nuanced, and mutually constitutive roots that belie settler colonialism's recent construction of the two as mutually exclusive."[63] The bridging of cultures in the languages of Diggs's poetry takes place on yet another level in the sampling of her hybrid spoken-word and musical performances, both individual and collaborative, which deploy live-recorded sample loops and delays to create layered vocals (including vocals sung) and percussive sound as a thick texture over which recited poems course.[64]

None of the Black poets and aestheticians discussed in this chapter—not Moten, Mackey, Philip, or Diggs—turns a blind eye to the violence opened up by kinship as a construct. Their work on transgenerational trauma and the genealogy of Black study writ large introduces a further critique of the concept of the mother tongue as wielded by European nationalist movements and their violent apotheosis in fascism. We may now return to Moten's rewriting of Derridean "invagination" (a feature of texts that fold in on themselves, denying both inside and outside/other a stable identity) with Diggs's nonpulmonic consonants in mind. Moten identifies a double hermeneutic movement to be elicited from Frederick Douglass's narrative surrounding his Aunt Hester's sexualized torture and scream at the hands of the boy's first "master": "The first element is the transference of a radically exterior aurality that disrupts and resists certain formations of identity and interpretation by challenging the reducibility of phonic matter to verbal meaning or conventional musical form. The second is the assertion of what Nathaniel Mackey calls ' "broken" claim(s) to connection' between Africa and African America that seek to suture corollary, asymptotically divergent ruptures—maternal estrangement and the thwarted romance of the sexes—that [Mackey] refers to as 'wounded kinship' . . . and 'the sexual "cut." ' "[65]

The glottal stop as performed by Diggs constitutes neither semantic content nor strictly musical riff, but sonic matter exterior to the "national" languages any traditional literary-critical interpreter might seek to classify. This translingual feature of her performances may be recognized as a cutting revision of the duress of kinship resulting from centuries of historical theft, but from a feminist perspective that manifests, somatically, the violence of this "cut." It constitutes a studied "haptic recension," to echo Mackey, that should also reassess the mission to identify what kind of "native" the poet and her words might be in classic geopolitical terms. Diggs's second collection of poetry takes on the challenge of pinning down her mother tongue explicitly and grounds what some readers might have taken to be a purely ludic translingual delirium of her debut collection in the day-to-day violence and hardship experienced by generations of Black "daughters of men" on the North American continent.[66]

EXTENSIONS OF THE MOTHER/TONGUE: NURSES, FOSTER PARENTS, BIRTH AND ADOPTIVE MAMAS IN *VILLAGE*

LaTasha N. Nevada Diggs's *Village* (2023) signals through its title a different scale of community appropriate to understanding her work: neither the nation nor the family in the strictest sense but a division in between comprising more ambiguous social ties, ostensibly less yoked to blood and milk. Against the backdrop of globalization, the scale of the village as opposed to the metropolis strikes us as saturated in nostalgia for a simpler time. "There's this proverb that Hillary Clinton borrowed: 'It takes a village to raise a child.' It also takes a village to destroy a child. Punto," asserts the author in conversation with longtime interlocutor Uruyoán Noel.[67] The book, begun in 2006 as a master's thesis at California College of the Arts in the immediate wake of her mother's passing, was set aside for years while she was working on *TwERK* and other projects (implicitly because of the emotional difficulty of the task). It was completed during the pandemic, while Diggs was living through the demolition of her neighbors' adjoining apartment units in a gentrifying Harlem. The relationship of the title to the proverb (and to its invocation by a Democrat associated with swapping a New Deal social contract for neoliberalism) cuts in various directions. Clinton's book on *Lessons Children Teach Us* about the impact individuals and groups beyond the family have on a child incited rebuttals from US conservatives, including Senator Rick Santorum's overt reinstallation of the family in the place of the broader social context: *It Takes a Family: Conservatism and the Common Good* (2005). Diggs's village is most immediately Harlem—the Harlem of Langston Hughes's exploded "dream deferred," seen through the eyes of women, and now replete with a trigger warning. It is also a rural township in the Pee Dee region of North Carolina where her mother was born, named after historic Indigenous tribes whose descendants have been recognized by the state of South Carolina but not the federal government. (The line for "Village" appears blank in the mother's birth certificate reproduced here.)[68]

Lacking a definitive cartographic address, Diggs's village is, intermittently, surrogate mother and a scourge that destroys mother and child. The book constitutes a self-conscious monument to a "blitzed" single mother's struggles, herein rendered "*historic struggles*," as well as to the haggard individuals, among them war veterans and heroin addicts, who served as foster parents: "to honor the nameless, representing saviors & teachers to a pocket of youth, often the 'black sheep' or 'oddballs,' who were w/out functioning family units."[69] It also contains "The Last Days of Pompeii: *An Installation*," a counter-memorial to an abusive estranged father figure identified as Albert Goldstein, a veteran of the Korean and Vietnam Wars. With a mordant sarcasm that appropriates the language of the institutional artist's statement for (literally) purgative purposes, "The Last Days of Pompeii" lays out in verse the blueprint for an installation consisting most prominently of the substances of Goldstein's abuse and of a plastic bucket for the bloody feces and vomit of which the battered mother was tasked to dispose—cruel substitutes for the force of milk and blood in idealized invocations of maternal care from both the Left and the Right.[70]

The leakage of bodily fluids, their purgation, appears throughout the collection in scenes of aborted and surrogate domestic care and violence. Spilt blood appears in "some sort of alchemy," which recounts in flashes of oral history and ancestral vision the grandmother's murder by her jealous husband for being a "*ge7ba*" (a term glossed in the book's "selective glossary" as *Quehbaor, Kehba*, "the Arabic (or Aribaci [presumably Arabizi, the Arabic chat alphabet]) equivalent to the word 'Ho' or 'Whore'") (*V*, 127). Spilt nursing milk appears in a poem called "fantasma #2" conjuring the ghost of a "miss moccasin" (ostensibly Indigenous, given her name) who tries to act as surrogate nurse for the speaker's mommy (accentuating the ties between Indigenous and Black communities) while the great-grandmother fishes for food (the grandmother having been killed, as we realize only later, and the grandfather officially "Unknown," as Margie Diggs's birth certificate reproduced in a documentary appendix testifies).[71] The murder surfaces through the mother's stories, which defamiliarize while citing the emphatically national and international touchstones that have defined midcentury history with a capital H: "my mommy says 1945. Pearl Harbor. was 1941. My mommy says again Pearl Harbor. 1945 . . . whatever year that was. . . . the kamikazes. aim & die."[72] Although the events of this poem involving farm hands in Jim Crow–era North Carolina seem worlds away in experience from the geopolitics of the Second World War, Diggs uses this poetry to excavate routinely eclipsed relations between the "domestic" and the international, moments like the abusive Goldstein's "mutterings in Korean" (*V*, 65), which sound the far-reaching consequences of postwar occupation by Western powers, as Adnan's writing had, down to the day-to-day violence of those on its front lines and their "loved" ones.

The book's jacket copy for Coffee House Press announces succinctly that "Diggs examines how trauma reshapes lineage, language, and choice, disrupting attempts at reconciliation across generations." The relation of choice to lineage and language in positive as well as negative terms is key. The early poem "tending to drunk mothers" redefines kinship as it recognizes the work of "all chosen mamas": "kin not kin likely kin but always kindred" (*V*, 9). The transgenerational trauma depicted here is close, much closer in time and space than the conditions of "wounded kinship" during enslavement appear to be, so that the task of critical fabulation might seem less daunting than the one Saidiya Hartman

GLOTTAL STOP   283

first theorized. Yet the archival traces of these individuals are scarce: they reside not in family albums (as Diggs specifies that photographs lay beyond reach for her mother because of cost)[73] but in documents from Mt. Sinai Hospital and the City of New York's Human Resources Administration that testify without ulterior captioning to the damage that war, poverty, and alcohol (as well as the legacy of slavery and unremitting anti-Black racism) can wreak on the immediate family. Both the author's and her mother's photos emerge as framed by identification cards for food stamps and public assistance prior to the title page, and a tenderness unfolds as document after document attests to "the failure of the United / States" that the mother represents, although the totality of this archive is aired in implicit disobedience to the "mother's famous quote, 'Latasha, why do you always have to open up your damn mouth?' "[74]

In her seminal study *In the Wake: On Blackness and Being*, Christina Sharpe sets out "to declare that we are Black peoples in the wake with no state or nation to protect us, with no citizenship bound to be respected, and to position us in the modalities of Black life lived in, as, under, despite Black death."[75] Statelessness and death are the brutal frames for the poetry of *Village*, which nevertheless rejects the naturalized notion that the family—the "domestic"—ought to be capable of standing in for the state, in situations where the home may morph into a scene of assault and mothering is perforce replaced by "a worrying" (*V*, 9). Diggs sets out to confront "what is / impossible w/out resources w/in a stable, safe, & sober village" (*V*, 32). The collection opens with a piece called "Performance" threaded serially throughout the first section that constitutes instructions for the author/ speaker's funeral:

> i desire that "my peoples,"
> of flighty species—two legged, winged, w/ domestic
> & international country codes &/or zip codes—
> be contacted immediately in order to offer assistance
> & relief for any milonga thrown by surviving
> estranged blood relatives.
>
> (*V*, 4)

Estrangement of blood relatives pervades this writing, composed as a paraofficial act of disinheritance as well as a claim to inheritance: "My mother's death made familial estrangement official," she says to Noel,[76] and in "Performance," the poet issues a range of performatives in the sense of speech acts: "i disinherit all trifling estranged blood relatives" (*V*, 4). In their stead, plural "peoples" are adopted, yet not without the scare quotes of distance: peoples in various species

284 GLOTTAL STOP

of flight, human, winged and nonwinged, "w/ capricious international country codes" (*V*, 5), speaking a range of domestic, international, and more-than-human tongues. The xenoglossic moves of *Village* are nevertheless less "capricious" and more focused than those of *TwERK*, being dominated by the Tsalagi (ᏣᎳᎩ in the Cherokee syllabary) and Brazilian Portuguese tongues that harbor particular affective charge for Diggs; each was encountered in her late teens and represents a "failed dream" of learning and forgetting but, above all, of belonging.[77] The poet now contends frontally with these "failures," explicitly setting aside the ideal of fluency, the desirability or even validity of the blood metaphor (one that is colonial freight, as many Indigenous activists note), and the mirage of fulsome citizenship, in a realist and antisentimental vein. In dialogue with Noel, Diggs expresses the paradoxical state of knowing and not knowing, of community and isolation, that emerges from this nonfluency: "To belong. To not belong. To mind my place."[78]

Having set out to memorialize as "'chosen' family" people of "nonconforming identities," such as the kind veteran/addicts Cowboy and Billy and otherwise nameless saviors also described as "outsider/insider people" (in a poem whose title is lifted verbatim from a Creative Capital Award application question), the book ends with two poems that make it clear that the author, too, considers herself to be of nonconforming identity—outsider/insider.[79] Implicitly responding to charges of linguistic and cultural "capriciousness" that charge the author with not being "_____ enough," the poem "items of confectionery" declares the first person to be lacking:

> am not   Black enough
> am not   an enrolled tribal member
> . . .
> am not   Native enough
> . . .
> am not   White passing
>   or White presenting
>
> (*V*, 111)

The poem then announces the speaker's lack of fluency in both Spanish and what might appear to be her native tongue:

> am not   Caribbean
> am not   fluent in Spanish
> am not   fluent in English
>
> (*V*, 111)

These states of lack are presented as parallels to a state of effective if not technical orphanhood and a failure to mother:

am	w/o a mother
am not	an orphan
am not	a single mother
am not	a mother

(*V*, 111)

Such reputed failures to realize full subjecthood (and by extension, citizenship) in terms aligned with cultural authenticity in the United States are historicized by the next and final poem, which twists the language of a public service announcement on US television hailing from the late 1960s through 1980s, following the introduction of curfews for minors in cities, to bring out the frayed relations between mother and child implicit in it: "the time is ____. Do you know where your children are?" Such frayed relations seem to be determined already at the time of birth for certain people, across the generations:

the time is 12:37 A.M., the mother's race is Colored

the time is 4:49 A.M., the name for the child will be decided by a nurse
as the mother is high on Twilight
as the mother's grandfather died in a sanatorium somewhere near Pee Dee

the time is 7:49 A.M., the name for the child will be decided by a nurse
as the mother was under the influence of alcohol at the time of her arrival

(*V*, 112)

The poem is effectively a concrete visual work scrambling the order of perception; crossing over these verses in diagonal grayscale are riffs on the public service announcement's question: "do you know? / do you know where your children are? / do you know where your children been?" In the absence of this knowledge, nurses of various genders and geographies will be called upon to name, to suckle, to take up the work of care.

In conversation with Claudia Rankine, who asks her what one learns from the mother in thinking about generational literacy, Diggs describes the village as an entity in evolution that produces a pluriform literacy, through conversation with those beyond one's blood, in a way that implicitly recasts, without refusing, the process of mother-tongue literacy: "In the shaping and re-shaping of what could be seen as a village, . . . felt as a village, that literacy comes in different shapes and forms. It comes from random conversations with elders who may not be related to you, it comes from random conversations in Costco, it comes from random conversations in the street. . . . I become shaped by all those conversations, taking bits and pieces."[80] Those "conversations" also involve the archive; the "kack-aLack" refrain that pervades the "magic garden" section of *Village*, for instance, channels Zora Neale Hurston's fieldwork in Lakeland, Florida, with railroad lining songs, replacing lack with echo and, by extension, survival.[81] Still, rather than a feel-good reconciliation with history, Diggs aims to leave the reader with many sorts of lack. A poem about the lack of space for dead bodies in New York City, implicitly addressing the death of the mother, ends with the words "the orphan is becoming a refugee" (*V*, 103). Asked by the 92nd Street Y what she hopes listeners will learn from her performance of *Village*, Diggs states, "I hope they are introduced or reacquainted with all of the different types of erasures that can take place in the life of one person."[82]

MOTHER BREATH AND PENTECOSTAL INSURGENCE

Fred Moten's blurb, itself a poem and essay, for the US reedition of the classic work of anticolonial poetics by the Tobagonian Canadian poet and theorist M. NourbeSe Philip, *She Tries Her Tongue, Her Silence Softly Breaks* (originally printed in Cuba in 1988), synthesizes in nuce how the "expense" of air in the form of poetry is capable of transforming territorialized earth and sea into a regenerative "expanse": "Tried and errant, reordering with every expense of air every expanse of earth and sea, . . . Philip's tragic transport, as a curate of the impure word, the degeneration and regeneration of grammar, their rupture and their fullness—bears the black history of romance."[83] The term "romance" here is barbed because exposing the "linguistic rape and subsequent forced marriage between African and English tongues" inflicted by Atlantic chattel slavery is part of the project, as Philip herself underscores.[84] However, Philip inaugurates an embodied feminist attempt to confrontationally contest the marriage of "Queenglish and Kinglish—the anguish that is english in colonial societies" by digging into the space between languages so as to "engender by some alchemical practice a metamorphosis within the language from father tongue to mother tongue."[85] ("Alchemy" hails etymologically, as Philip reminds us, from the Arabic "*al kim-iya*, the art of the black and Egypt" that "succeeded in transforming the leavings and detritus of a language.")[86] Philip's work resounds forcefully in the poetry of younger generations, finding one likely tribute in Diggs's "some kind of alchemy" about her murdered yet visionary grandmother and, indeed, in Diggs's project of deterritorializing grammar at large. In counter-catechistic lyric, Philip protests the struggles resulting from cultural genocide in being "verbal or linguistic squatters, possessing adversely what is truly ours."[87]

Philip's "Discourse on the Logic of Language" is another example of a genre to which we have returned throughout this book: a détournement of the grammar lesson such as practiced by Theresa Hak Kyung Cha in *DICTEE*. In manipulating exercises of dictation, such texts tweak Fanon's point in *Black Skin, White Masks* that to enter another language is to be interpellated into its ideological strictures: strategically unfaithful translations and nonstandardized uses of colonial languages refuse compliance with what is dictated in cultural and theological terms or acceptance of the self's inscription as an "*Accomplice in His Texts*" within a tongue Cha renders as other, as "*Their tongue, the counterscript.*"[88] Quotation, erasure, collage, parody, sampling, and the deployment of languages not "proper" to texts in this lineage of counter-grammar all swerve from dictation and occupy and transform cited hegemonic languages from subaltern stances.

Xenoglossic writings in this lineage hold out the promise of pentecostal communion across linguistic divisions that were enforced through chattel slavery in a pointed strategy to deter insurgence. "Discourse on the Logic of Language" rebukes the ideological presumptions of the received concept it names: four-column page spreads place science and education texts that expose the white supremacist matrix of speech biology under colonialism alongside the genocidal edicts that divided ethnolinguistic groups among the enslaved in order to provoke a Babel stymying revolutionary impulses: "If they cannot speak to each other, they cannot then foment rebellion and revolution."[89] Such edicts aimed to prevent communication among the captive by establishing punishment via unspeakable tortures for speaking native languages, even to the point of extracting the offending tongue from the mouth. One bitterly invective stanza of "Discourse" mimics a multiple-choice exam to cast the production of intelligible speech—speech intelligible, that is, to the colonizer and slaveholder and therefore, in this case, English speech—as a brutally enforced choreography of imposed breath: "Air is forced out of the lungs up the throat to the larynx where it causes the vocal cords to vibrate and create sound. The metamorphosis from sound to intelligible word requires / (a) the lip, tongue and jaw all working together. / (b) a mother tongue. / (c) the overseer's whip. /(d) all of the above or none."[90] Lyric variations on the "l/anguish / anguish /—a foreign anguish" extracted by English as a father tongue that strives "to articulate the non-being of the African" are countervailed by Philip's hungering descriptions of mothers blowing the language of their mothers and mother's mothers into their babies' mouths.[91]

Dialectically generated between the columns of this text reside theses about breath as a common and potentially insurgent substance, passed on by the care work of women. These theses are carried on through the creation of literal breathing spaces between linguistic fragments within Philip's monumental xenoglossic and open-field work *Zong!* (titled after an ironic historical derangement of the slave ship originally named *Zorg*, or Dutch for "care"; "that exclamation point breaks the word into song/moan/chant/shout/breath," notes Christina Sharpe).[92] Philip's insertion of gaps into the language of a legal document that treated enslaved and murdered Africans as lost "cargo" enables the language of that lawless law to be broken and redistributed into all colonial and Indigenous languages of the world, now working in concert through her poem as a reanimating wake. These breathing spaces and their function are glossed and extended by Philip's more recent essay, "The Ga(s)p."[93] Produced as a response to Nathaniel Mackey's "Breath and Precarity" and emerging from the way linguistic fragments are "driven pneumatically by the energy of the breath" in *Zong!*, "The Ga(s)p" also articulates the necessity of breathing for those who could not and cannot breathe, from those drowned in the Middle Passage to the victims of contemporary anti-Black violence.[94] Implicitly correcting the focus on heroic performances of breath control and circular breathing coded as male and conceived as monadic in Mackey's text (from Charles Olson through Horace Silver), Philip situates breathing in the Black female imaginary as a shared process, contingent and relational. Her essay begins with the tender observation that life begins in the vulnerability of another's breath, with the mother's breathing on behalf of the child: "We begin life in a prepositional relationship with breath: someone breathes for us."[95] The entry into breathing for oneself—the emergence of the individual subject—is then marked by a shock of air, a gasp.[96] Against any biological essentialism of relations through the scene of birth and through critique of Hannah Arendt's universalizing conception of natality through the lens of chattel slavery, Philip extends the act of "radical hospitality" represented by a mother's breathing for her child to call on this breath "memory that is a blueprint for community and interdependency" before adding a brutal reminder of the conditions of forced motherhood for enslaved women: "Despite the forced couplings."[97] The breath Philip conceives is a melancholic breath, in Sharpe's terms, which is about moving grief and love, their charge, through the body; this is an "aspiration" of wake work: to put breath back into bodies from which it has been stolen.[98] Philip glosses this task of performances of her work: "When I perform *Zong!*, I allow the words and word clusters to breathe for I 'n I—for the we in us that epigenetically we carry within the memory of our cells. When I invite the audience to read with me, we collectively engage in breathing for the Other—for those who couldn't breathe—then / can't now."[99] In an unanticipated move that complicates hospitality, breath, and belonging, Philip invokes the singing of the Black female a cappella group Sweet Honey in the Rock, whose setting of Lebanese American poet Kahlil Gibran's "On Children" carried the author through the unspeakable pain of labor, to shift the verses' meaning, now articulating the vocation of mothering, or nursing, despite the pervasive violence of conception under enslavement: "'Your children are not your children,' they sing. Yet we house them, I reply . . .; 'they come through you but not from you,' and yet we breathe for them; 'though they are with you, yet they belong not to you.'"[100]

With Philip's anticolonial poetics of counter-essentialism and care in mind, we can return to Diggs on the mother tongue—or rather, the seeking out and questioning of such a tongue through exploration of a body that is not essence, but "worn" like the "tight chemise" of Zora Neale Hurston's relationship to her racialization.[101] In a statement on her poetics, Diggs expresses her history and current moment as an act of research:

> My love for the mishaps when at play with multiple languages is obvious. Even when one questions why I do what I do how dare I, this dance through sound, place and memory is where I naturally tweet like Tweet. Won't stop. Oops. Can't stop. What is not always obvious is my personal questioning of self, of this body my essence wears, of a past and present that is searching. It is how I teach myself the histories of those who may or may not have been the victor. Call it Hip-Hop. Or when a cassette gets chewed up in the player. Or what happens when I question the rue. Like any mess of beans with salt thrown in too quickly, the risk of getting it wrong eventually gets it right. . . . What and who I am, my origins and ancestries, are always underneath/above the blanket being woven. I respond and explore the sonic, visual, and textual vocabularies I am drawn to. And what I often dream, learn, forget, mourn, celebrate. In search of somewhere, in this stew, I am at home here.[102]

This stew recalls not only the melting pot metaphor but also the "general queer sauce of New York" composed by those Henry James rejects as "alien."[103] To claim the stew as home is not to seize it as static abode but to adopt the stewing, the immersive steeping in what is other to oneself as well as what is immanent, as a familiar verb.

In the process, Diggs draws her audience away from what is familiar, making a new and sometimes unaccommodating home of the in-between. In her 2023 book launch for *Village* at Joe's Pub, Diggs built her way up vocally from recitations of her own poetry to (shyly, she declared) belting out an edition of "Arrieros somos y en el camino andamos" (Cuco Sanchez's song taken from the proverb, "we are all mule-drivers," i.e., we are all humans making our way through life). In the middle of this piece, she addresses a jubilant audience in a typical nonrhotic New York accent (i.e., one that drops the "r" in "artist"), saying, "You're gonna go home and say, this Black Native girl sang a ranchero with a Japanese musician and a Chinese laptop hip-hop artist, and I didn't see that coming."[104] "Si todo el mundo, salimos de la nada / Y a la nada, por Dios que volveremos / Me río del mundo, que al fin ni el es eterno": the ranchera's reflection on existential communality and suffering, which ends with a laugh, seems a consummate lyrical and nonessentialist expression of Diggs's playfulness, which still manages to do justice to the place of this musical form within the nationalist consciousness of a country south of the US border. Diggs is never fully at home or at ease with the discrete language cultures she touches, never without an accent, and the politics of her expression through these tongues is always vexed; yet xenoglossia opens up a channel for being shyly willing to sing and dance with and through them. I have adopted such a process throughout this extended fourteen-year act of criticism, making a tenuous home of the more or less alien sauce of my New York ancestors and beyond while remaining cognizant of my limits—periodically shifting perspective to glimpse the potential blindnesses of my adopted discourse to make of the inevitable mishaps an open tutorial.

The work of ingestion and purgation, inhalation and gasp, within Diggs's xenoglossic writings and performances, both written and vocalized, leaves the original ingredients in the syllables of geopolitical domination forever altered. What if we heeded Diggs's example of linguistic risk, of potentially getting it wrong in an act of learning? What if care were more commonly routed through an interest in, even a speaking of, languages other to one's apprehensible, geopolitically identifiable flesh and blood? What if we sang with the tongues of the nurses? How would breath need to be wielded differently? What sorts of subversive, rageful, yet reparative breathlessness might result?

Coda

A Xenoglossic Community to Come: Belonging by Rogue Translation in Sawako Nakayasu and Sagawa Chika's Mouth: Eats Color

The work of Sawako Nakayasu, a Yokohama-born, US-educated and -raised poet and translator, on the once-neglected modernist poet and translator Chika Sagawa (Sagawa Chika according to Japanese naming conventions) assumed two starkly different forms in the early twenty-first century, with seemingly antithetical reading publics in mind. *The Collected Poems of Chika Sagawa* was published by Canarium Books in 2015 and went on to win the PEN Award for Poetry in Translation.[1] This accessible volume, which Nakayasu characterizes with a wink as corresponding to "the classical ballet version of translation,"[2] brought to a broad public the oeuvre of a radical woman artist who had been neglected by a patriarchal literary sphere that retreated inward, to focus on traditional Japanese forms, in the buildup to and aftermath of the Second World War and who was neglected again by feminist studies because of that movement's stress on confessional watashi-gatari, or the direct first-person expression of womanly experience.[3] Reissued by the Modern Library in 2020, *The Collected Poems* canonized a valuable corrective to anglophone provincialism surrounding global modernism; indeed, a 2021 article suggested that Nakayasu had rendered Sagawa's work more accessible in the English-dominated world than it was in Japan, although a Japanese edition of her poems, translations, written prose, journal entries, and letters published the next year was a rousing success, selling seven thousand copies in a mere five months.[4]

In line with conventions of the literary mainstream, *The Collected Poems* gathers Sagawa's oeuvre as composed in "Japanese" and translated into "English," in a graceful, portable monolingual edition where the only kanji are those that appear within Sagawa's birth name, Kawasaki Chika (also pronounceable as Ai)

川崎愛. Yet Nakayasu's introduction to this volume testifies narratively to the poetry's "dislocated, tenuous ground" straddling East and West, urban and rural, modernizing and archaic realities in the Tokyo of the early Showa period: a metropolis aggressively reconstructing itself from the devastating Great Kantō Earthquake, to which Sagawa moved in 1928.[5] The precocious Sagawa quickly integrated herself into the avant-garde literary circle teeming around Kitasono Katue's Arcueil Club and the *esprit nouveau* poets publishing in the journal *Shi to Shiron* (*Poetry and Poetics*). Her first publications were translations, and she tackled an ambitious range of figures, including James Joyce, Virginia Woolf, Charles Reznikoff, and the Hungarian writer Ferenc Molnár. Nakayasu and others have traced how Sagawa's poetry borrows freely from foreign lexicons and adapts modernist gestures from Cubism to Surrealism to Objectivism, while transferring fundamental energies of waka, such as attention to seasonal change, into the contemporary internationalist welter. In an analysis that compares Sagawa's work with that of Japanese Futurist Hirato Renkichi, Alys Moody describes the pooling of influences as a burrowing: "She finds the point where Objectivism and *waka* meet, and burrows in until both become irrevocably strange—until the clarity becomes hazy."[6] This haziness is an apt parallel to the translucency we have been tracking throughout the xenoglossic poetics of the twentieth century.

Tragically, Sagawa developed stomach cancer in 1935 to which she succumbed at age twenty-five; her poems were collected and published posthumously by Ito Sei the next year. Her premature death meant that Sagawa was spared the danger and ensuing ideological accommodations of her circle triggered by the nationalist Tokubetsu Kōtō Keisatsu or "Thought Police," echoed in the rise of authoritarianism and various strands of modernist capitulation or complicity from Berlin to Rome—in Marinetti's participation in a program of linguistic autarky, to cite a single Axis example.[7] The coming years were to consolidate what Naoki Sakai calls "the regime of homolingual address," which serves "to repress the awareness of this disparity between the invocation of 'we' and its representation."[8] A late diary entry from Sagawa's hospital deathbed reads, "Lying in bed staring at the sky, the things to come and the things that have passed all blend into one, and I do not like it. One of the clouds looks like Mussolini's face, and that was strange [をかしかった]."[9] The hallucination recalls Fortunato Depero's icon of Mussolini/Marinetti as Mind/Mediator with which we began modeling the imperious face of Pentecost, visualizing the literally fascistized binding of linguistic cacophony into a unitary, "FIRM," state of mind. The leveling of historical difference and the nightmare of a cloud assuming a human dictator's visage foretell, wittingly or not, a history subsumed by a jingoistic, autarchic futurism. Nakayasu's exhumation of Sagawa transports us to a modanizumu (modernism) that

CODA   293

flourished immediately prior to the full-blown consummation of Fascism, its alliances, and its dubious retribution—to an internationalist exuberance devastatingly, but somewhat mercifully, preserved for this poet by a premature death.

In 2011, the centenary year of Sagawa's birth in the far north of Yoichi, Hokkaido—and while working toward *The Collected Poems*—Nakayasu invented her own press as a harbor for wildly translingual *Sagawa Chika Translations, Anti-Translations, and Originals*, provocatively naming the solo venture Rogue Factorial. The collection, *Mouth: Eats Color*, was produced on a kind of dare from fellow poet/translator Jen/Eleana Hofer of Antena Aire via a comment stream on Facebook, following Nakayasu's proposal to "go rogue" and produce a collection of self-published antitranslations: "Can you do this in a month so I can teach it?" A young mother with numerous constraints on her time for art, Nakayasu embraced the challenge by vowing to compose, lay out, request permissions for, and produce the Print on Demand work in a single month; she regarded the effort as a performance, infused with the lived sensation of writing that courses through journalism, all with a lucid feminist bent.[10] The self-published result conjures a very different picture of translation, not as what Sakai has described as the "transfer of a message from one clearly circumscribed language community into another distinctively enclosed language community," but a risky, disorienting venture for both writers and readers.[11] To read this work is to parse and piece together the work's nondomesticated constitutive relations as if poetic language and its community were a puzzle drawing on sources beyond those of the authorized box—a puzzle of affiliation subject to constant addition, erosion, leakage, and kaleidoscopic shift. The book aggressively lacks an index, and "originals" normally appear long trailing their plural "translations"— scrambling utterly the source/target metaphor for translation and producing in its place a choose-your-own-adventure "traduction," to hearken to the English coinage via French by way of Ezra Pound.

Disordering, in turn, the portraits of both "Sagawa Chika" and "Japanese modernism," Nakayasu exposes the performative nature of pronomial invocation, of the "we," to borrow Sakai's terms and those of Jean-Luc Nancy; the puzzle pieces settle in a belonging to come whose relation to desire is front and center (quodlibet or whatever being, in Agamben's terms, belonging, always libidinal).[12] In the process, Nakayasu concocts a very different genre of literary historiography and future for ten of Sagawa's poems, destabilizing their authorship and the idea of authorship writ large in favor of an ephemeral hive mind bearing the traces not only of Sagawa's influence—or confluences—but of one particular month of the following millennium in time, all the while reconstituting the language and, I will argue, the citizenry of both the poems' compositional origins and their readership. The book convokes a community aspiring toward the delirious (inter)species of "we" that forms the matrix of Sagawa's own poetry and translation, generating through rogue translation a counterfactual Japanese that ecstatically exceeds its orthodox borders, while baring again and again the language's immanent hybridity. This ravenous "we" is constantly in the (re)making as readers approach the work (and are compelled or repelled): a hive overseen by a "rogue queen" like the performance artist to whom Nakayasu dedicates the volume. The insect metaphor is deliberate because Nakayasu is devoted to the study of nonhuman communities, a fact that distinguishes her from many of the writers we've become acquainted with thus far.[13]

If Sagawa was spared from witnessing the horrors of the late 1930s and 1940s by mortal illness, Nakayasu picks up on the prior moment of ebullient Japanese internationalism and recruits it into the present moment. She does so by fusing these histories through poetic language, disobeying norms of translation that dictate that "source" and "target" grammars and times should be dyadically siphoned off from one another. That is, she counterfactually creates a speculative history and present, one lacking the dreadful (and Sagawa-less) final chapter of Japanese imperial Axis authoritarianism behind it and thereby altering everything that came afterward, including the postwar literary-critical attention narrowed to that which passed muster as authentically Japanese. For those who are literate in Japanese, *Mouth* jumpstarts a xenoglossic process of unlearning the hierarchies of inside and outside within this conglomerate signification system, with its syllabaries and logographic kanji. Unraveling the textile of Japanese before our ears and eyes, Nakayasu also bids us to learn, so as to unlearn, both Japanese and English and (perhaps forevermore) to alter our ways of reading for the foreign and familiar in the process.

Nakayasu attributes the authorship of *Mouth: Eats Color* to herself "with" Sagawa, yet the slim volume also includes poems by feminist modernist Mina Loy ("Widow's Jazz," 38) and by the Bostonian expatriate in Paris, Lost Generation poet, and Black Sun Press publisher Harry Crosby ("White Fire," 48; "Animal Magnetism," 54). Both poets are retranslated into English, taking Sagawa's translations into Japanese as "originals." Nakayasu goes further and provokes a transhistorical and transethnic, pan-Asian diasporic kinship network by roguishly including two poems by the New York School Chinese American poet Frances Chung (1950–1990), author of *Crazy Melon and Chinese Apple*, originally published posthumously under the direction of Walter Lew for Wesleyan in the year 2000. Chung, like Sagawa and Nakayasu, writes multilingual poetry, although in a different key from the heady aspirational modernist internationalism of the *esprit nouveau*; Chung convokes in almost documentary fashion the street-level crossing of languages and therefore of "villages" and cultures in Chinatown, Little Italy, and Latinx communities on New York's Lower East Side. She begins *Crazy Melon*, dedicated "to the Chinatown people," provocatively with Spanish lines and their English translation: "Yo vivo en el barrio chino / de Nueva York . . . I live in / New York's Chinatown. Some / call it a ghetto, some call / it a slum, some call it home. Little Italy or Northern / Chinatown, to my mind, the / boundaries have become fluid."[14] These writing practices share the cultural approach of being "nonbinary"—a form of translation Nakayasu called for in a 2020 talk titled "Translation Is a Genre."[15]

Nakayasu re-culls Chung's "scenes gathered from a Chinese-English dictionary," the title of a poem by the New York poet that appears to present, line by line, the English translations of dictionary definitions for which the Chinese terms have been withheld.[16] We realize retrospectively that Chung's poem may have functioned as a partial blueprint for a Nakayasu "translation" (72–73) that plucks the Chinese characters (kanji) from Sagawa's poem "波" ("Waves") and translates the radicals that constitute them literally and liberally (in counter-Orientalist echo of the experimental literalism of Ernest Fenollosa and Ezra Pound). She then splices these "character"-actors into the standard translation of another poem.

In the new poem, "Waves—A List of Characters, and Backside," the characters for sailor 水夫 (suifu) from the first line of "波" are translated literally into the persona "Husband of Water," and 笑う (warau or laugh), comprising the radicals for "bamboo" over "heaven," becomes the Fenollosa-style "ideogrammatic" rendering "Fresh Looking Bamboo That Lives Fast and Dies Young," an improperly painterly, associative translation of the character, perhaps oriented toward a portrait of Sagawa herself (figure C.1). In an additional twist for the weave, Nakayasu gathers the "scenes" for these now embodied, theatrical "characters" from Sagawa's poem "Backside," grafting the lines onto the "characters" with a colon, in reverse order, from the poem's bottom, "And then the people," backward. Sagawa's final character in "Waves," 口 (mouth), thus becomes paired with "eats color" from the first line of "Backside," displacing Sagawa's original agent, "Night." The altered line becomes the title of the 2011 collection, enabling fresh reflections on the mouth's confluence of communicative and digestive functions that we recall threatening a dumbstruck James in the "hot pot" of Mannahatta. The change also pushes color from being a disembodied phenomenon to one that can be ingested in fleshly terms, implying along the way that the "color" associated with skin/nation/ethnos, as a fiction or metaphor, is still concrete, yet can be "eaten" as well, recalling the anthropophagic modernism of de Andrade.

On page 61, Nakayasu presents a more straightforward translation of "Waves." The laughter of sailors in Sagawa's poem becomes part of a strangely physicalized

| 波 | WAVES—A LIST OF CHARACTERS, AND BACKSIDE | BACKSIDE |

水夫が笑つてゐる。
歯をむきだして
そこらぢゆうのたうちまはつてゐる
バルバリイの風琴のやうに。
倦むこともなく
彼らは全身で蛇腹を押しつつ
笑ひは岸辺から岸辺へとつたはつてゆく。

我々が今日もつてゐる笑ひは
永劫のとりこになり
沈黙は深まるばかりである。
舌は拍子木のやうに単純であるために。
いまでは人々は
あくびをした時のやうに
ただ口をあけてゐる。

Husband of Water: and then the people.

Fresh-Looking Bamboo That Lives Fast and Dies Young: moves forward.

That Which Halts Rice From Growing in the Mouth: caress the writhing darkness.

Harp of Wind: tar from cigarettes.

Person After Handling a Forest Fire: fingers stained.

Skin of Man Who Goes: tickle.

Kingly Human Flesh: these are weeds.

Belly of the Snake: by its feet.

Hand on Armour: and the space beneath

Fresh-Looking Bamboo That Lives Fast and Dies Young: that was chopped down.

Night eats color
Flower bouquets lose their fake ornaments.
Day falls into the leaves like sparkling fish
The shapeless dreams and trees
Struggle like the lowly mud
Nurtured outside this shriveled, deridable despair.
And the space that was chopped down
Tickles the weeds by its feet.
Fingers stained with cigarette tar
Caress the writhing darkness.
And the people move forward.

FIGURE C.1 Comparative view of the versions of Sagawa Chika's "波" and Sawako Nakayasu's "Backside" that are spliced into "Waves—A List of Characters, and Backside," *Mouth: Eats Color*, pages 65, partial view of 72, and 68.

yet deterritorialized performance of the barrel organ, Orgue de Barbarie, or Barbary organ (a term based on the exonym "Berber" applied to the Amazigh from across a cultural divide—deriving from the Arabic, or else the Greek, term suggesting "barbaric," from the nonsense *bar bar bar*): "Unflaggingly / They press the bellows with their entire bodies / While laughter passes from shore to shore." Here the pressing of entire bodies renders the barbarous playing of the organ grinder fleshly and choral, whereas laughter becomes extraterritorial, roving from shore to shore. The poem's second and final stanza goes on to describe the silence of the contemporary moment:

> The laughter we have today
> Is captive to the eternal
> And silence only grows deeper still.
> Because the tongue is simple, like a pair of clappers.
> Now, people
> Simply open their mouths
> As when yawning.

(MEC, 61)

The translations of *Mouth* make for a tongue whose polyphonic complexity contrasts the simplistically percussive two-part clapper—as well as the depths of muteness corraled in the mouths of contemporary people open not to sing but rather as if to yawn, expressing somnolence, saying nothing. The tongue protruding from the self-published Rogue Factorial volume's back cover, in a ludically cropped portrait by Said Karlsson, suggests a refusal of quietism. What's more, when the book is opened, this cover image places on display the willingness of the open human mouth on the back to approach and possibly kiss the forked tongue of the bearded dragon on the front in an insistence on interspecies tenderness.

A more perplexing gesture within *Mouth: Eats Color*, although fully in line with the overall play of late-pentecostal impropriety, is Nakayasu's inclusion of a heavily punning, seemingly homophonic translingual poem crossing Spanish or para-Spanish with French, titled "Flanky Pongo (Urla) #8" (perhaps a pun on hanky-panky?) by the San Diego–based contemporary poet Steve Willard, author of the 2007 collection *Harm* (*MEC*, 67). A collaborative occasional "confluence" of English and Japanese by Nakayasu and her friend, the writer Miwako Ozawa, also appears in *Mouth: Eats Color* (75–77). To round out the volume is "Conversation," by the fictional poet Masako Hiraizumi, whom Nakayasu was invited to invent by Lytton Smith for an Open Letter anthology, perhaps in response to the controversy surrounding Kent Johnson's forging of the literary hoax, Araki Yasusada (a supposed poet-hibakusha, or survivor of the atomic bombing of Hiroshima).[17] Adopting as method the modernist citational practice of Sagawa's "Gate of Snow" ("雪の門" or Yuki no Mon), which liberally incorporates adapted lines from Charles Reznikoff's *Jerusalem the Golden* to make them her own,[18] "Conversation" borrows amply from Sagawa's store of images in "Backside." Additional "foreign" characters populate *Mouth: Eats Color*—"the rogue queen Violet Juno," John Cage, Yoko Ono, and "my friend Morton"—mimicking Sagawa's transgression of literary propriety in weaving Harry Crosby's verse sailors and Reznikoff's Queen in May into her own poems.

All this impropriety serves to affirm that the authorship of neither "source" nor "destination" is singular. Instead, authorship becomes a convocation; it requires attribution to a widening hive or swarm, transgressing the boundaries of coteries, literary-historical categories, and languages. Nakayasu's notes contain a theorization of these curatorial and compositional choices in the guise of a prose poem called "So You See Now if You Push Through This Idea," which again replicates Sagawa's methods in drawing on key terms from the modernist's work (sailor, carpet, beard, petal, embroidery).[19] The piece suggests that the "ideal brilliant order" for the book's community or commonwealth is a beehive, overseen

298 CODA

by this alternative species of queen, herself a force not of unification but of "loosening." Yet it irrepressibly mixes metaphors for the provisional kinship to come (shifting to figures that are textile, floral, and lucent), showing off how we can as ebulliently fabricate metaphors of kinship (such as through blood, soil, or milk) as we can cast them off. In the prose's subjunctive voice, this communal order shall be "emitted, rocked, and constructed" among extraterritorial "sailor bee[s]" until "it all gets modified, crushed, loosened by the whiskery introduction of the miracle new, . . . young and nubile queen, distant and intimate, hopelessly among them." The process requires constant readjustment of "relations, proportions, and values" toward the whole, in motions of "rainbow conformity." Nakayasu's playful tractate proposes that the accepting witness admit how "this unprotected order" allows what is now a tapestry to "bloom profusely." It finally leaps to the conclusion that "the past should be altered by the present as much as the present is directed by the past," thereby making explicit the outcome of altering poetry and history in the process.

Mouth: Eats Color opens on one of Nakayasu's seventeen versions of Sagawa's lyric "Promenade" to be peppered throughout. The disobedient translator will withhold the "original" until page 57, and the one seemingly conventional "definitive" translation will appear on page 40 as "Promenade (A)," with the mistaken kanji for "report" rather than "pavement" intact, as it is in this opening errant version (figure C.2). In confrontation with this opening-field poem, this reader, who is (as I'll reveal below) only half-prepared for the daunting task, becomes aware of floating among language systems: seeking a hook to bridge English and Japanese, unsure whether to move forward or backward, up or down in the

PROMENADE (A)   PROMENADE (Pろめなで)   PROMENADE (露命撫で)

Seasons change their gloves   背亜損lsちゃんドテェイrgろヴぇs   背亜損(せあそん) 銭(ちゃん) ド(した) 手醉ひ(てえい)が辺
A three o'clock   アthレエおℓ'cろck   (ろべ) 吾(あ) 令(れい) 惡露(おろ)
Trace of sun   Tら背尾fすn   羅(ら) 脊尾(せお) 押(おす)
Of flower petals which bury their report オffロウェrベタlsウィch部ryテェイれぽrt 小呂(おろ) 上(うえ) ベタ(べた) 浮い(うい) 部(ぶ) 手醉ひ(て
A black and white screen   アbらck案dウィテscれえn   えい) レボ(れぼ)
Eyes covered by clouds   アbらck案dウィテscれえn   あら 浮いて(ういて) 列絵(れえ)
Some promise-less day comes to an end エイェスコヴェレdbycろうds   永(えい) 子べ(にべ) 老(ろう)
                                 染めp路店—レッs打y混めsとあんえんd   染め(そめ) 露天(ろてん) 列(れつ)打(うつ) 混め(こめ) と(と)、
                                                                 案緑(あんえん)

FIGURE C.2 Comparative view of versions of Sagawa's "Promenade," *Mouth: Eats Color*, pages 40, 47, and 49.

CODA   299

groping, it dawns on her that the tether is frayed. Indeed, Nakayasu emphasizes that breakneck translation and borrowing from English and French were key conditions of production for Sagawa's poetic language and that of her comrades (her pen surname 左川 meaning "left river," presumably an allusion to the Left Bank)—until Japanese militarization shut such activity down in the 1930s.

The language of *Mouth* appears to waver among English, Japanese, French, Chinese, and Spanish, but for anyone with access to the four scripts used in Japanese (kanji, hiragana, katakana, and romaji), a more complex picture emerges in the experience of reading (or attempting to read). The rules for applying logograms, syllabic kana, and the Latin alphabet to words and word endings of different ancestries are repeatedly transgressed, exposing and inverting through this unorthodoxy the presumptions of origin, nativity, and foreignness, as well as gender, embedded in Japanese orthographic hierarchies. (The same transgressions of orthographic convention were anticipated by the xenoglossic modernism of Yi Sang, whose poetry was written on the nether side of a violently charged colonial divide, in the Japanese-occupied Korea of the 1930s, and whose translation Nakayasu later undertook in a collaborative effort with Jack Jung, Don Mee Choi, and Joyelle McSweeney.)[20] In the middle column of figure C.2, we can see Nakayasu's rascally transcription of the English translation of "Promenade," from the poem on page 40 titled "Promenade (A)," while using a keyboard set to Japanese. The clue to this operation emerges in the poem's title. Rather than deploying Sagawa's original transcription of the French or English word "Promenade" via the "standard" Japanese pronunciation, reading in katakana (the Japanese syllabary for foreign words), "プロムナアド" (PU-RO-ME-NA-A-DO, page 57), this new poem is titled "Pろめなで" (P-RO-ME-NA-DE, page 47) in an amalgamation of romaji (Roman lettering for the initial P) and the privileged native Japanese syllabary of hiragana (ろ for RO, め for ME, な for NA, and で for DE). The conceptual gesture generates a glitching that is nevertheless "faithful" to Sagawa on transmuted terms, insofar as the source text has been somatized—transcribed, but through the mediation of a 2011 Japanese keyboard rather than the hand of a Bergvall or Adnan. This mediation is not apolitical but reflects the "state" of mind of its programmer: said keyboard appears arbitrarily to have dictated which phonemes are to be marked as "foreign" and which are "native" but, as a result, quashes barriers between languages to create mongrel words and lines. So in the second line, for instance, "アthレエお'cろck" (from "A three o'clock"), the first phoneme for "A" is katakana, whereas the "three" is divided between roman "th" and katakana "レエ" (re-e); the "o'clock" arbitrarily contains two "native" Japanese hiragana (for "o'" and "ro") interposed amid the roman letters c and k. Next, in the third column, Nakayasu reuses the glitch text as a source for new hiragana (in parentheses), and she assigns new Chinese characters to the resulting phonetic poem (*MEC*, 49). She subsequently translates this more plausibly "Japanese" (yet not) text back into English: the three Chinese characters in the title that emerged from typing English into a Japanese keyboard (beginning with 露 for "ro," or "Dew") become the basis of a new poem and its translation into English: "Promenade (Pass the Hand Over a Life as Fleeting as The Dew)," with a distinct echo of Issa Kobayashi's iconic haiku about the world of dew ("露の世は/露の世ながら/さりながら") (*MEC*, 51).

I want to pause in closing to expand upon the use of the term xenoglossic in Nakayasu's case. As we know, the term "translingualism" arising out of sociolinguistics stresses contact and collision rather than dialectics or code switching, invoking movement not only between and across but also beyond discrete languages, with the *trans-* meaning to reflect an epistemic upheaval of the categories traversed.[21] Nakayasu's work pursues this epistemic upheaval in linguistic and cultural terms. Indeed, the final gloss to *Mouth: Eats Color* asks and declares, in the key of Gertrude Stein's questions-as-declarations and declarations-as-questions, that the translations of "Puromenaado" using strictly Chinese characters (without the conventional addition of hiragana to integrate these characters into a "Japanese" language system) are or are not written in Chinese: "Are 'プロムナ アド (Puromunaado 2)' and 'プロムナアド (Puromunaado 4)' in Chinese or are they not" (*MEC*, n.p.). The key of unknowing and the embrace of the stonato ("off-key") are so barbarously pursued in this work that one is destined to be forever 外人 within its poetic ecology—gaijin, the derogatory Japanese term for a foreigner lacking the interposition of "国" or "country," made up more frankly of the kanji for outside + person—as both reader and (co-)composer.

The process of deciphering the mongrel language of *Mouth: Eats Color* has proven stunningly similar to the way in which translating Amelia Rosselli put me in touch with the technical foundations of my family's own idiolect, a mongrel English containing scraps of hundred-year-old Neapolitan and Sicilian preserved by immigrant usages and deformations, and the Yiddish with which these signifiers cohabited Manhattan and the Bronx, all eroded over time by error and trial. Moving beyond translation, Nakayasu renders both putative insider and outsider to these texts an italicized *xenos*. In fact, the more Japanese one knows, the more difficult *Mouth* is to read because the more estranging are the operations of sign systems uprooted from convention as one attempts to parse the verse's turns and twists.

In the 2020 chapbook *Say Translation Is Art*, Nakayasu produces a manifesto for such procedures: "Say partial translation, half-assed translation, abandoned translation, mediocre translation, . . . // Say unmarketable translation, say unremarkable translation, say unsellable translation, say unlikable translation. / Say rescue the translation from belligerent capitalism translation, from imperialist takeover translation, well-meaning neoliberal multicultural translation, from too much love is suspicious translation."[22] The resulting work, with its errors, incompletions, polemics, and desires, becomes an oddly generative teaching tool, as corroborated by the swarm of responses published online by students of the poet/editor/translator Johannes Göransson.[23] When reading these poems, my own students who are native readers of Chinese described a woozy, dreamlike experience reminiscent of early language learning, bespeaking the connection and alienation between Chinese and Japanese language systems: a reverie of excavation and burial of kinship lines.

Though I studied Japanese intensely for two years several decades ago—a starry-eyed twentysomething inspired by a copy of *The Chinese Written Character as a Medium for Poetry* in an Umbrian library to read 松尾 芭蕉 (Matsuo Bashō) and 小林 一茶 (Kobayashi Issa) in the original language—this is the first time that I am addressing Japanese materials in my public scholarship; for as part of a working army sponsored by 文部省 (the Japanese Ministry of Education) to teach English in Japanese public high schools (and as a person dependent upon that salary to pursue said immersion), I never attained the literate fluency of which I'd dreamt (though I did serve as English-language editor of a collection of hibakusha testimonials, clinching my permanent distrust of nationalist frames for war exploits).[24] Burrowing my way out of extreme disorientation, accompanied by other artists in the founding of a one-off literary journal and various experiments in installation as translation, I found in the end that my approach to language would never be the same; it had for two years been turned inside out, with subjectivity differently accented, hierarchy freshly embedded, syntax inverted, quantification reclassified, and the totality of signification conventions rendered 外. I became fascinated along the way by the proverb "門前の小僧習わぬ経を読む," which can roughly be translated as "The apprentice before the temple gate will recite the sutras without being taught"—its invocation of how the recitation and singing of poetry and scripture can derive from staying close to the unknown, without "learning" it in the strictest sense. The fate of cropping half-knowledges of languages from the frame of my reflections on poetry, language, and culture was seemingly sealed by the apparent incommensurability of my sundry literary interests in disciplinary terms. Perhaps this monograph—with its illicit cartography evolving across rabbit holes of scholarly research, poetry, and translation since 2010, and in some ways since my days as an assistant English teacher and explicit cultural ambassador to the United States—is an attempt to make amends for having personally advanced the hegemony of

English in mid-1990s Aichi Prefecture, contributing to a naturalized situation in which Minae Mizumura must ask, "What will become of all the national languages that are not English?"[25] Perhaps it is an argument for approaching one's own national and nonnational languages as a student, as 外, in the way these poets have—and for approaching the 外 as perpetual teacher, as possible dance partner, kith, and ally.

Works like Nakayasu's *Mouth: Eats Color* inhabit the intoxicating internationalist imaginings of the historical avant-gardes from Paris to New York to Tokyo from within the lines of the surviving artifacts and therefore channel or transduce the fever for translingual expression into an electric collaboration with poets across languages and times. These poems invite us into a disorienting yet libidinously jubilant and politically vital mode of reading as a way of being together in rogue commonwealth that I name xenoglossic. Although taboo within both the academic culture of specialization and prevailing US discourse surrounding cultural propriety, such modes of reading are becoming more visible within a culture of comparativism in crisis. In his address at the 2021 American Comparative Literature Association (ACLA) meeting, Waïl Hassan, a theorist of translational literature, ventured beyond his identifiable realm of mastery to recast the geopolitics of comparison via the Italian-language volumes of Juan Andres, a Spanish Jesuit, "On the Origins, Progress and Current State of Each Literature," written in the late eighteenth century, so as to elicit from them a different world picture wherein Arabic plays a fundamental role in the formation of European literature.[26] And in "Speaking of Babel," delivered to the ACLA conference two years prior, Amitav Ghosh challenged the audience to support linguistic heterogeneity, within and without ourselves, when he glossed the duplicitous rhetoric of globalization that "frames diversity both as an aspirational ideal as well as a legitimizing charter" even as it erases the forms of human flourishing represented by linguistic proliferation. In linguistically diverse places, Ghosh argued, in the place of the arrogance of mastery embodied by European notions of cosmopolitanism, there reside "streams" of language that flow through each individual, that "bleed into and mingle with each other in such intricate ways that everyone becomes individuated by their own, idiosyncratic conjunctions of language."[27] As a scholar, poet, and translator who has worked primarily across anglophone and Romance-language literary contexts, I have found myself enthralled enough by this poetry to press beyond that realm of reputed expertise, with its constitutive myth of kinship, toward the frayed edges of the imperfectly known. I embrace the thinking of Naoki Sakai and of these poets as Virgils through the half-veiled traversal of work that does not presuppose a homolingual address, but pointedly performs the generation and erosion of an "'us' for whom neither reciprocal apprehension nor transparent communication [is] guaranteed"—and that does so in an ecstatic mode of co-inspiration.[28]

"The so-called language barrier is permeable." So wrote the Antena Aire collaborators in opening their *Manifiesto para la interpretación como instigación/ Manifesto for Interpretation as Instigation*.[29] The artists congregated here have devoted their lives to that too-often occulted territory between divisible languages, cultures, and states. They have made that vital permeability of the skin between expressive systems apprehensible, manifesting that the zone between languages is a lived continuum. It's a zone where a pink seesaw might be installed, transforming a violent barrier into a shared site of play, even if the infrastructure of a heavily militarized border ensures that the encounter will be fleeting—a performance lasting as livable reality for only forty minutes, destined to the condition of a viral provocation.[30] In envisioning a colloquium between these texts, I identified an illumination from the fifteenth-century Rohan Book of Hours as paradigm: the arrogant Tower of Babel struck down, smiting its architects—and the detail of a figure who from within the rays of the heavens seems to turn the notorious Fall into difference into a dive (figure C.3). The image suggests that there are many ways to fall: a fall can be multidirectional, a dance. These artists propose that we do less erecting of defensive and ivory towers and more diving, with respect for the gravity of what we touch and in the awareness that it might go wrong. Through their books, sculptures, paintings, and performances, these poets have altered the shape and sound of belonging, breaking free of the paradigms of paranoid privatized culture against privatized culture that somehow still reign, despite the mirrored realities of multilingualism and supranationalist emergency that we are living at present—realities that call for "nonbinary" translation. They have transfigured comprehension in harmonic response to George Steiner's address to poets—"Which is to say to anyone who makes the language live and who knows that the affair at Babel was both a disaster and—this being the etymology of the word 'disaster'—a rain of stars upon man."[31]

"I have become intrigued with displaced things," said Don Mee Choi in a 2012 interview—"things that are wrong. And translation is in a perpetual state of being wrong."[32] Antena Aire took this utterance as epigraph for their *Manifesto for Ultratranslation*.[33] "We do so many wrong things out of the fear of doing the wrong thing," said Nakayasu in a 2020 talk.[34] These assertions suggest that the state of risking being wrong, of waywardness, may be the very state where we most fruitfully come together. The authors within these pages have transmuted the polyglot spaces that induce so much discomfort, so much disciplinary,

FIGURE C.3 Detail from anonymous master, *Grandes Heures de Rohan*, fifteenth century. Folio page 23, verso. Bibliothèque nationale de France, Département des Manuscrits, Latin 9471. Source: gallica.bnf.fr.

egocentric, and xenophobic anxiety, into "great theaters" of Brechtian encounter, but the risk therein also leads to reverie. The act of generating *Mouth: Eats Color* (and its press) in a month became itself a performance, inducing with each reading a promenade through the arcades of tongues that is resolutely dreamlike, perhaps tracking a fallen version of Benjamin's messianism ("For if the sentence is the wall before the language of the original, literalness is the arcade").[35] As utopian as this may sound, it approximates the experiences I've had in teaching this work and in learning from it over and over—a defamiliarizing enterprise wherein, at least for the time of reading, we are not chanceled: "In reality, we are all angels," writes Don Mee Choi in *DMZ Colony*, her lyrical reckoning with the barrier dividing the Korean peninsula; "We are all orphans, orphans who aren't orphans. Angels who aren't angels."[36]

Mouth: Eats Color demands more than a reader fluent in Japanese, English, Chinese, Spanish, and French; it does not merely invoke the cosmopolitan. The xenoglossic poetics of this work eats national languages and their presuppositions for breakfast, impelling the reader to piece together a quavering continuum of apprehension, destined never to arrive at total comprehension. In the process, this poetry provides the blueprint for a community both past—dampened if not fully damned by fascism—and to come, in which poetic expression models heterolingual forms of recognition rather than transmission of impermeable, self-same, and state-sanctioned "content." Over the course of grasping at understanding such work, the first-person plural may become an index not of the commonness among us, but of the humbling, tender effort to come together in the accents of the very ultimate future despite our incommensurability.

Notes

INTRODUCTION: FROM BABEL TO A POSSIBLE PENTECOST: THE ABRACADABRANT WORD AND THE INVENTION OF "XENOGLOSSIA"

1. Howard Morphy, "From Dull to Brilliant: The Aesthetics of Spiritual Power Among the Yolngu," *Man* 24, no. 1 (1989): 21–40, https://doi.org/10.2307/2802545; Deborah Bird Rose, "Shimmer: When All You Love Is Being Trashed," in *Arts of Living on a Damaged Planet*, ed. Anna Lowenhaupt Tsing, Elaine Gan, and Nils Bubandt (University of Minnesota Press, 2017), 51–63. The concept of "reciprocal capture" was developed by the philosopher Isabelle Stengers, and I am indebted to Bird Rose for having first introduced me to her work; see Isabelle Stengers, *Cosmopolitics*, trans. Robert Bononno (University of Minnesota Press, 2010), which specifies early on that "cosmopolitics" does not mean to invoke the Kantian form of cosmopolitan civility, but Deleuze's idiot, that speaker of the idiolect who slows things down.

    A note on standards of transcription: I do not italicize terms hailing from languages other than English in this book unless italicized in my source texts, out of respect for the continuum out of which all languages hail. For an argument against italicization, see, for instance, Divya Victor, *Kith* (Fence Books, 2017), which deitalicizes terms from the languages of India as part of a dismantling of Orientalist stances that insists on the ambivalence of belonging, of "writing what I know alongside what I don't yet know" (189): "I have refused to remain foreign in a language that is as much mine as it is yours" (187), Victor asserts, "& so I began this manuscript. & so I made of poetry something / *other* than an explanation / —of an 'us' you couldn't know / —of kith unitalicized" (188).

2. Adolf Hitler, *Mein Kampf (My Battle)*, trans. E. T. S. Dugdale (Riverside Press Cambridge, 1933), 47, 26–27; Victor Klemperer, *The Language of the Third Reich: LTI, Lingua Tertii Imperii: A Philologist's Notebook*, trans. Martin Brady (Athlone Press, 2000), 20–21.

3. See Gabriella Klein, "L'italianità della lingua e l'Accademia d'Italia. Sulla politica linguistica fascista," *Quaderni Storici* 16, no. 47 (2) (August 1981): 639–75, for this comparison and for the thorough analysis of Italian linguistic purism and Fascist neopurism relied upon in the above summary.

4. George Orwell, "Politics and the English Language," *Horizon* 13, no. 76 (April 1946): 265, 257–58, 264.

5. See for instance Brett Samuels, "Trump Escalates Anti-Migrant Rhetoric Ahead of Biden Match-Up," *The Hill*, March 10, 2024, https://thehill.com/homenews/campaign/4519783-trump-immigration -rhetoric-biden-matchup/.

6. Jacques Derrida, *Monolingualism of the Other, or, the Prosthesis of Origin*, trans. Patrick Mensah (Stanford University Press, 1998), 23. The quote from Pierre Joris, theorist of "nomad poetics," hails from his *Justifying the Margins* (Salt, 2009), 7.
7. Édouard Glissant, *Le Discours antillais* (Seuil, 1981), 231.
8. "The critique of culture is confronted with the last stage in the dialectic of culture and barbarism: to write poetry after Auschwitz is barbaric, and that corrodes also the knowledge which expresses why it has become impossible to write poetry today." Theodor W. Adorno, *Prisms*, Studies in Contemporary German Social Thought, trans. Samuel and Shierry Weber (MIT Press, 1981), 34. The original 1949 text (published in 1955) reads, "Kulturkritik findet sich der letzten Stufe der Dialektik von Kultur und Barbarei gegenüber: nach Auschwitz ein Gedicht zu schreiben, ist barbarisch, und das frißt auch die Erkenntnis an, die ausspricht, warum es unmöglich ward, heute Gedichte zu schreiben."
9. Amelia Rosselli, *Le poesie*, ed. Emmanuela Tandello (Garzanti, 2016), 111. This volume will hereafter be cited as *LP*, and I will refer to it principally in citing her poetry due to its availability in the Anglophone world.
10. In *Locomotrix*, I translated the title of this book as *Bellicose Variations*, though I could have retained Rosselli's more Latinate and warlike *Bellic*. This poem appears in Amelia Rosselli, *Locomotrix: Selected Poetry and Prose of Amelia Rosselli*, ed. and trans. Jennifer Scappettone (University of Chicago Press, 2012), 73.
11. Umberto Eco, "Ur-Fascism, Adapted from a Speech Delivered at Columbia University in Commemoration of the Liberation of Europe," *New York Review of Books* 42, no. 11 (June 22, 1995): 15.
12. Max Horkheimer and Theodor W. Adorno, *Dialectic of Enlightenment: Philosophical Fragments*, ed. Gunzelin Schmid Noerr, trans. Edmund Jephcott (Stanford University Press, 2002), xvii.
13. Horkheimer and Adorno, 1969 preface to *Dialectic of Enlightenment*, xi.
14. Carlo Rosselli, "Primo maggio," in *Giustizia e libertà*, April 30, 1937, reprinted in Carlo Rosselli, *Scritti dell'esilio: Dallo scioglimento della concentrazione antifascista alla guerra di Spagna (1934– 1937)*, 2 vols. (Einaudi, 1992), 2:512.
15. These impressions were collected soon thereafter in *The American Scene* (1907). "New York and the Hudson: A Spring Impression," in Henry James, *Collected Travel Writings: Great Britain and America*, ed. Richard Howard (Library of America/Random House, 1993), 453, 458.
16. James, "New York and the Hudson," 456.
17. See, for instance, C. K. Ogden and I. A. Richards, *The Meaning of Meaning: A Study of the Influence of Language Upon Thought and of the Science of Symbolism*, 5 vols., ed. W. Terrence Gordon (Routledge/Thoemmes, 1994), 1:86. Ernest Weekeley, *An Etymological Dictionary of Modern English* (John Murray, 1921), 6, identifies it as cabalistic, from Greek, composed of letters whose numerical values equal 365.
18. James, "New York and the Hudson," 452, 453.
19. A *Ford Times* reporter from November 1916 narrated: "In contrast to the shabby rags they wore when they were unloaded . . ., all wore neat suits. . . . And ask anyone of them what nationality he is, and the reply will come quickly, 'American!' 'Polish-American?' you might ask. 'No, American,' would be the answer. For they are taught in the Ford school that the hyphen is a minus sign." Quoted in Werner Sollors, *Beyond Ethnicity: Consent and Descent in American Culture* (Oxford University Press, 1986), 91.
20. Gilles Deleuze and Félix Guattari, *Kafka: Toward a Minor Literature*, trans. Dana Polan (University of Minnesota Press, 1986), 19.
21. Walt Whitman, "Crossing Brooklyn Ferry," in *Leaves of Grass* (D. McKay, 1900), 181.
22. James, "New York and the Hudson," 454, 461, 454.
23. James, "New York and the Hudson," 461, 455.
24. James, "New York and the Hudson," 453, 457, 460, 455.
25. James, "New York and the Hudson," 456, 452. It would be fruitful to compare James's reflections with other literature of muckraking journalism, such as Hutchins Hapgood, *Types from City Streets*

INTRODUCTION ❧ 309

(Funk & Wagnalls, 1910). Such passages make it clear why the future Fascist Ezra Pound would admire James's representations of "race against race, immutable," forces that far from being transient "are the forces of race temperaments, are major forces and are . . . great protagonists." Ezra Pound, *Literary Essays of Ezra Pound* (New Directions, 1968), 298, 301.

26. On the "global village," see Marshall McLuhan, *The Gutenberg Galaxy: The Making of Typographic Man* (University of Toronto Press, 1962).

27. Theodore Roosevelt, *Works* (Scribner's, 1926), vol. 24, 554. Despite a long history of multilingual American literature, which was suppressed by World War I–era propaganda against foreign languages that endures, the consequence of what Joshua L. Miller calls "English-only Americanism" has been the unquestioned dominance of a cloudy overweening construct known as American English (often taking forms as mild as those of suspicion or indifference). See Joshua Miller, *Accented America: The Cultural Politics of Multilingual Modernism* (Oxford University Press, 2011). The result for poetic expression that spans multiple languages has been an alternating rarefaction and marginalization. Werner Sollors discusses the history and diversity of multilingual publications in *Ethnic Modernism* (Harvard University Press, 2008); see especially "American Languages," 85–91.

28. James, "New York and the Hudson," 471.

29. James, "New York and the Hudson," 464.

30. James, "New York and the Hudson," 464; Louis Zukofsky, " 'A'-18," in *A* (Johns Hopkins University Press, 1993), 397.

31. Charles Richet, "Xénoglossie: l'écriture automatique en langues étrangères," *Proceedings of the Society for Psychical Research* 19 (1905–7): 162–266.

32. For another example of this term being used as breath, see Genesis 2:7: "And the Lord God formed man of the dust of the ground, and breathed into his nostrils the *breath of life*; and man became a living soul."

33. Acts of the Apostles 2:9–11, King James version cited here as elsewhere. My reading here relies on Darrell L. Bock, *Acts* (Baker Academic, 2007), 101–4. Bock cites Virgil's *Aeneid* and Pliny the Elder's list of conquests as examples of the Roman claim to universal rule.

34. Jing Tsu, *Sound and Script in Chinese Diaspora* (Harvard University Press, 2010), 12.

35. This term is glossed throughout Roger Griffin, *The Nature of Fascism* (St. Martin's, 1991).

36. See the deservedly famous and still pertinent Eco, "Ur-Fascism."

37. For an overview of the incipient internationalist language and vision sparked by the Movement for Black Lives, see Adom Getachew, "The New Black Internationalism," *Dissent*, Fall 2021, https://www.dissentmagazine.org/article/the-new-black-internationalism/. On errantry as a formation of identity opposing the monolithic "rooted" form (already critiqued by Deleuze and Guattari in *A Thousand Plateaus* but opposing the invasive or determinist nomadism potentially implicit in their work), see Édouard Glissant, *Poetics of Relation*, trans. Betsy Wing (University of Michigan Press, 1997), 11–22.

38. See for instance Agamben's conflation of the two and reduction of both to heralds of the death of language: "Glossolalia and xenoglossia are the ciphers of the death of language: they represent language's departure from its semantic dimension and its return to the original sphere of the pure intention to signify." I cited this moment from *Categorie italiane* in my first writing on this topic: Roland Greene et al., eds., "Xenoglossia," in *The Princeton Encyclopedia of Poetry and Poetics* (Princeton University Press, 2012), 1543–44. A recent example is Daniel Tiffany, "Speaking in Tongues: Poetry and the Residues of Shared Language," ed. Kristina Marie Darling, *Tupelo Quarterly*, March 14, 2020, https://www.tupeloquarterly.com/prose/speaking-in-tongues-poetry-and-the-residues-of-shared-language/. The forum contains various incisive commentaries on multilingualism by writers such as Edgar Garcia and Eugene Ostashevsky, departing from Tiffany's own fine attention to the diction of what Julian Talamantez Brolaski has called "mongrelitude." For an empirical, analytical, and theoretical study of glossolalia as a sociolinguistic fact drawing on Korean Christian practices of tongues, see Nicholas Harkness, *Glossolalia and the Problem of Language* (University of Chicago

INTRODUCTION

Press, 2021). For a succinct working bibliography on glossolalia, see Watson E. Mills, ed., *Speaking in Tongues: A Guide to Research on Glossolalia* (W. B. Eerdmans, 1986), 13–31; or simply Watson E. Mills, *Glossolalia: A Bibliography* (E. Mellen, 1985). In a fascinating divergence from the standard idioms of multilingual criticism, Harris Feinsod echoes "xenoglossia" in his looser use of the term "xenoglossary" to refer to the deployment of foreign words by Wallace Stevens, Jorge Luis Borges, and José Lezama Lima in a postwar period of Anglophone supranational provincialism wherein foreign terms in poems "amplify or confirm geopolitical divisions, but they cumulatively construct . . . a shared auxiliary lexicon open to poets across the Americas." Harris Feinsod, *The Poetry of the Americas: From Good Neighbors to Countercultures* (Oxford University Press, 2017), 98. His use of the term and the poets he studies provide a fascinating contrast with the more opaque and awkward work within this book.

39. See these critiques recapitulated in Marshall Sahlins, *What Kinship Is—and Is Not* (University of Chicago Press, 2014). These poets propose a different form of the "sym-poesis" advocated for by Donna J. Haraway in *Staying with the Trouble: Making Kin in the Chthulucene* (Duke University Press, 2016).

40. I cite the poet-theorist's form of resistance to demands for colonized peoples' transparency voiced in 1969 by Édouard Glissant: "Nous réclamons le droit à l'opacité." Édouard Glissant, *Le discours antillais* (Éditions du Seuil, 1981), 11; Édouard Glissant, *Caribbean Discourse: Selected Essays*, trans. and intro. J. Michael Dash (University of Virginia Press, 1989), 1.

41. See Waïl S. Hassan, "Agency and Translational Literature: Ahdaf Soueif's 'The Map of Love,' " *PMLA* 121, no. 3 (May 2006): 753–68, and "Translational Literature and the Pleasures of Exile," *PMLA* 131, no. 5 (October 2016): 1435–43.

42. From biblical times, "[t]he movement breaches the walls of the largest cities, even Rome, the capital of the empire; today, Pentecostalism breaks down rigid traditional ecclesiastic structures and joins the secular, modern world, reaching out in all languages to all peoples and nations." See Waldo César, "From Babel to Pentecost: A Social-Historical-Theological Study of the Growth of Pentecostalism," in *Between Babel and Pentecost: Transnational Pentecostalism in Africa and Latin America*, ed. André Corten and Ruth Marshall-Fratani (Indiana University Press, 2001), 32. See also André Droogers, "Globalisation and Pentecostal Success," in *Between Babel and Pentecost: Transnational Pentecostalism in Africa and Latin America*, ed. André Corten and Ruth Marshall-Fratani (Indiana University Press, 2001).

43. Quoted in Cecilia Rasmussen, "Vision of a Colorblind Faith Gave Birth to Pentecostalism," *Los Angeles Times*, June 14, 1998. Headline and breathing quote hail from a front-page article of *Los Angeles Daily Times*, April 18, 1906. See also Gary B. McGee, "Shortcut to Language Preparation?: Radical Evangelicals, Missions, and the Gift of Tongues," *International Bulletin of Missionary Research* 25, no. 3 (July 2001): 118–23, which narrates precursors at Bethel College in Topeka, Kansas, as well, adding the following to the mix of languages reputedly gifted to participants: Zulu, Swahili, Tibetan, Bengali, "Esquimaux," and sign language, among others.

44. Jenny Evans Moore, who would go on to marry William J. Seymour, "Music from Heaven," *The Apostolic Faith* 1, no. 8 (May 1907): 3, archived at https://pentecostalarchives.org/?a=d&d=AFL19070705-01.1.3.

45. Republished as Frank Bartleman, *Azusa Street* (Whitaker House, 2000), 51.

46. James, "New York and the Hudson," 454.

47. William J. Seymour, in the widely distributed Pentecostal journal *The Apostolic Faith*, quoted in Paul Harvey, *Freedom's Coming: Religious Culture and the Shaping of the South from the Civil War Through the Civil Rights Era* (University of North Carolina Press, 2005), 133. See also Cecil M. Robeck Jr. and Amos Yong, eds., *The Cambridge Companion to Pentecostalism* (Cambridge University Press, 2014). Charles Fox Partham, Seymour's teacher, is credited with developing the practice of tongues through a belief in xenolalia and founding the Pentecostal church; regardless, the Azusa Street mission is credited with launching its global mission. See Amos Young and Tony Richie, "Missiology and the Interreligious Encounter," in *Studying Global Pentecostalism: Theories and Methods* (University of California Press, 2010), https://www.jstor.org/stable/10.1525/j.ctt1ppt8r. See also Murray W.

INTRODUCTION   311

Dempster, Byron D. Klaus, and Douglas Peterson, *The Globalization of Pentecostalism: A Religion Made to Travel* (Regnum, 1999); David Martin, *Pentecostalism: The World Their Parish* (Blackwell, 2002); and Sturla J. Stålsett, ed., *Spirits of Globalization: The Growth of Pentecostalism and Experiential Spiritualities in a Global Age* (SCM, 2006).

48. Ashon T. Crawley, *Blackpentecostal Breath: The Aesthetics of Possibility* (Fordham University Press, 2016), 6–7, 38.

49. Crawley, *Blackpentecostal Breath*, 37. Another example of tongues as resistance appears in James K. A. Smith's "Tongues as Resistance Discourse," in *Speaking in Tongues: Multi-Disciplinary Perspectives*, ed. Mark J. Cartledge (Paternoster, 2006), 81–110.

50. Crawley, *Blackpentecostal Breath*, 227.

51. Macchia writes, "the scattering of Babel also held out a promise that humanity might rediscover a unity that does not dissolve but rather embraces the diversity of idioms, backgrounds and stories that God willed to providentially release in history. The unity of Pentecost is thus not . . . abstract and absolute but rather concrete and pluralistic." See Frank Macchia, "Baptized in the Spirit: A Global Pentecostal Theology" in *Speaking in Tongues: Multi-Disciplinary Perspectives*, ed. Mark J. Cartledge (Paternoster, 2006), 45.

52. Christine F. Cooper-Rompato, *The Gift of Tongues: Women's Xenoglossia in the Later Middle Ages* (Penn State Press, 2010), 15, 16. Cooper-Rompato uses medieval accounts of women's miraculous translation capacities to illuminate the gendered anxieties and dreams surrounding an upwelling of literary and scriptural translation from Latin to emerging vernaculars as well as between European vernaculars.

53. Gloria Anzaldúa, "Speaking in Tongues: A Letter to Third World Women Writers," in *The Gloria Anzaldúa Reader*, ed. AnaLouise Keating (Duke University Press, 2009), 26, 34.

54. Emilio Villa, "Cy Twombly: Talento bianco," *Appia Antica* 1 (July 1959): 36. Reproduced in Emilio Villa, *Attributi dell'arte odierna: 1947–1967*, Vol. 1, ed. Aldo Tagliaferri (Le Lettere, 2008), 127. All translations in this text are my own unless otherwise noted.

55. Jhumpa Lahiri, *In Other Words*, trans. Ann Goldstein (Alfred A. Knopf, 2016), 84–85, retranslated by me. Lahiri identifies her impulse to write in Italian as "born from my realization that I am a writer without a true mother tongue; from feeling, in some sense, linguistically orphaned." See Jhumpa Lahiri, *Translating Myself and Others* (Princeton University Press, 2022), 10.

56. Dante Alighieri, *De vulgari eloquentia*, trans. Steven Botterill (Cambridge University Press, 1996), 3.

57. Gary P. Cestaro, *Dante and the Grammar of the Nursing Body* (University of Notre Dame Press, 2003), 18.

58. Kamau Brathwaite, *History of the Voice: The Development of Nation Language in Anglophone Caribbean Poetry* (New Beacon, 1984), 14, 10.

59. The literature on ethnic modernisms and diasporic avant-gardes is voluminous, uncontainable even within a telegraphic footnote. See, for example, Carrie Noland and Barrett Watten, eds., *Diasporic Avant-Gardes: Experimental Poetics and Cultural Displacement* (Palgrave Macmillan, 2009) and other volumes on multilingual literature concentrated below.

60. Lisa Robertson, *Nilling: Prose Essays on Noise, Pornography, the Codex, Melancholy, Lucretius, Folds, Cities and Related Aporias* (BookThug, 2012), 76, 80.

61. Robertson, *Nilling*, 84. Robertson is fascinated by the polylingual and polycultural origins of European lyric, including its Arabic influences, and cites within this "Untitled Essay" María Rosa Menocal's *Shards of Love: Exile and the Origins of the Lyric* (Duke University Press, 1993).

62. Robertson, *Nilling*, 83–84, 87. The term "geopoetics" appears to hail from Meschonnic but can also be traced to Daniel Maximin, *Les fruits du cyclone: Une géopoétique de la Caraïbe* (Seuil, 2006). See Lyn Hejinian, *The Beginner* (Tuumba Press, 2002).

63. Marianne Shapiro, *De Vulgari Eloquentia: Dante's Book of Exile* (University of Nebraska Press, 1990), 9.

64. "The weak *child*, who is so aptly called a child-without-any-say [Unmündige], does it not have to accept language, since it consumes the milk of its mother and the spirit of its father with language?" Johann Gottfried Herder, "Treatise on the Origin of Language," in *Sourcebook in the History of Philosophy of Language: Primary Source Texts from the Pre-Socratics to Mill*, ed. Margaret Cameron, Benjamin Hill, and Robert J. Stainton (Springer, 2016), 942. This is not to say that Herder had simplistic monoglot ideals, as suggested by the literature in sociolinguistics; see Charles L. Briggs and Richard Bauman, "Language, Poetry, and Volk in Eighteenth-Century Germany: Johann Gottfried Herder's Construction of Tradition," in *Voices of Modernity: Language Ideologies and the Politics of Inequality* (Cambridge University Press, 2003); see, for instance, Herder's 1764 essay "On Diligence in the Study of Several Learned Languages," in Johann Gottfried Herder, *Johann Gottfried Herder: Selected Early Works, 1764–1767*, ed. Ernest A. Menze and Karl Menges (Penn State Press, 2010). "The nursling hears the first words at his mother's breast spoken to him from the soft and gentle maternal voice, and they cling to his virgin memory, before he yet has power over his own speech organs." Jakob Karl Ludwig Grimm, *On the Origin of Language*, trans. Raymond A. Wiley (Brill Archive, 1984), 13.

65. Yasemin Yildiz, *Beyond the Mother Tongue: The Postmonolingual Condition* (Fordham University Press, 2012).

66. *Sangiuliano: «Dante è Il Fondatore del Pensiero di destra italiano»*, from a video recording hosted at the *Corriere della Sera*'s YouTube channel, January 14, 2023, https://www.youtube.com/watch?v=UrcPb-kzXKg.

67. Mikhail Bakhtin, *Rabelais and His World*, trans. Helene Iswolsky (Indiana University Press, 1984), 470–71.

68. Shapiro, *De Vulgari Eloquentia*, 8.

69. Emily Apter, *Against World Literature: On the Politics of Untranslatability* (Verso, 2013), 4, 2.

70. On the rich topic of universal languages, see, for example, Umberto Eco, *The Search for the Perfect Language*, trans. James Fentress (Blackwell, 1995).

71. Barbara Cassin, ed., *Vocabulaire européen des philosophies: Dictionnaire des intraduisibles* (Le Robert, 2004); and Barbara Cassin et al., eds., *Dictionary of Untranslatables: A Philosophical Lexicon* (Princeton University Press, 2014), 1223.

72. Gayatri Chakravorty Spivak, *Death of a Discipline* (Columbia University Press, 2003), 73.

73. Gayatri Chakravorty Spivak, "The Politics of Translation," in *The Translation Studies Reader*, ed. Lawrence Venuti (Routledge, 2000), 407.

74. To those who would charge that these poets are not widely known or taught, I would offer, with Spivak, "I cannot see why the publishers' convenience or classroom convenience or time convenience for people who do not have the time to learn should organize the construction of the rest of the world." Spivak, "The Politics of Translation," 404. Spivak's translation practice lends nuance to the dyad of self and other that pervades so much criticism in the West; for a useful corrective of learning "to think about some others' others," I suggest Haun Saussy, *The Making of Barbarians: Chinese Literature and Multilingual Asia* (Princeton University Press, 2022).

75. See Victor, *KITH*.

76. Spivak, "The Politics of Translation," 397, 398. See Mahasweta Devi, *Breast Stories*, trans. Gayatri Chakravorty Spivak (Seagull, 1997), http://archive.org/details/breast-stories-by-mahasweta-devi-mahasveta-debi-gayatri-chakravorty-spivak. Spivak reads the protagonist of this short story, Jashoda, not only as a mythical "suckler of the world" (75) but also as an allegory of postcolonial India.

77. Spivak, "The Politics of Translation," 397–99.

78. J. M. Coetzee, *Doubling the Point: Essays and Interviews* (Harvard University Press, 1992), 342; Gayatri Chakravorty Spivak, "Bonding in Difference: Interview with Alfred Arteaga," in *The Spivak Reader: Selected Works of Gayatri Chakravorty Spivak*, ed. Donna Landry and Gerald M. MacLean (Routledge, 1996), 22. Spivak is quoting from Coetzee's linguistic autobiography in J. M. Coetzee, *Doubling the Point: Essays and Interviews* (Harvard University Press, 1992), 342.

INTRODUCTION   313

79. Caroline Bergvall, "A Cat in the Throat: On Bilingual Occupants," *Jacket* 37 (Early 2009), http://jacketmagazine.com/37/bergvall-cat-throat.shtml.

80. Later version of the text published in *Meddle English* and at Academy of American Poets, "Cat in the Throat," text, Poets.org, accessed March 31, 2024, https://poets.org/text/cat-throat.

81. Bergvall, "A Cat in the Throat." For further critique of the voice as a naturalized concept and praise for works that highlight the separation of body and voice, see Yoko Tawada, "The Art of Being Non-synchronoous," trans. Susan Bernofsky, in *The Sound of Poetry, the Poetry of Sound*, ed. Marjorie Perloff and Craig Douglas Dworkin (University of Chicago Press, 2009), 184–95. For a critical overview of "voice" in lyric poetry, see Jonathan Culler, *Theory of the Lyric* (Harvard University Press, 2017).

82. Later version of the text published in *Meddle English* and at Academy of American Poets, "Cat in the Throat."

83. Caroline Bergvall, *Meddle English: New and Selected Texts* (Nightboat, 2011), 17.

84. Peter Ives, *Gramsci's Politics of Language: Engaging the Bakhtin Circle and the Frankfurt School* (University of Toronto Press, 2004) provides a valuable account of the relation of the "language question" (as it was referred to in Italy at the time) to Gramsci's conceptions of hegemony and subalternity—a relation largely overlooked in Anglophone criticism.

85. Antonio Gramsci, *Selections from Cultural Writings*, ed. David Forgacs and Geoffrey Nowell-Smith, trans. William Boelhower (Harvard University Press, 1985), 27.

86. Louis Zukofsky, "Basic," in *Prepositions: The Collected Critical Essays of Louis Zukofsky* (Horizon, 1968), 147, 155.

87. Eugene Jolas, *Man from Babel* (Yale University Press, 1998), 272–73. See also Marjorie Perloff, " 'Logocinema of the Frontiersman': Eugene Jolas's Multilingual Poetics and Its Legacies," in *Differentials: Poetry, Poetics, Pedagogy* (University of Alabama Press, 2004), 83–102.

88. Preface to Eugène Jolas, *Words from the Deluge* (Gotham Book Mart, 1941), reprinted in Eugène Jolas, *Eugene Jolas: Critical Writings, 1924–1951*, ed. Klaus H. Kiefer and Rainer Rumold (Northwestern University Press, 2009), 178.

89. Eugène Jolas, "From Jabberwocky to Lettrism," ed. George Duthuit, *Transition* 1 (January 1948): 104. On Jolas's "amerigrating" Atlantica and his move to a vertical language beyond translation as "an ideal of universal utterance that can only be realized through futuristic fantasy," see Emily Apter, *The Translation Zone: A New Comparative Literature* (Princeton University Press, 2006), 52–58.

90. Michael North, *Reading 1922: A Return to the Scene of the Modern* (Oxford University Press, 1999), 58–64.

91. Indeed, as Jolas narrates, *Pearson's* rejected his poems in the 1920s with a dismissal quite interesting for—because diametrically opposed to—our argument: " 'There is, in fact', Harris remarked, 'no example in history of a poet who abandoned his native language in adolescence, and later succeeded in penetrating the mysteries of a new one. There are so many grammatical pitfalls that can never be overcome, unless the words have been felt in childhood." See *Man from Babel*, 49.

92. See Ezra Pound, *The Cantos of Ezra Pound* (New Directions, 1996), 706, 708. Readers such as Yunte Huang take a rather more playful approach, and I offer his chapter on Pound's "translational" writing in *Chinese Whispers: Toward a Transpacific Poetics* (University of Chicago Press, 2022), 66–80, as one example of how the practices of translation and poetry in combination with scholarly research can lead to less stultifying interpretative trajectories.

93. See Pier Paolo Pasolini, *Volgar' eloquio*, ed. Antonio Piromalli e Domenico Scafoglio (Athena-Materiali e strumenti, 1976). For a reading of how Pound's expression also eulogizes Wang Youpu's translation of the imperial Sacred Edict into vernacular Chinese, or baihua/guanhua, see Haoming Liu, "Pharmaka and Volgar'Eloquio: Speech and Ideogrammic Writing in Ezra Pound's Canto XCVIII," *Asia Major* 22, no. 2 (2009): 179–214.

94. Konstantin Balmont, *Poetry as Sorcery*, quoted in Gerald Janecek, *Zaum: The Transrational Poetry of Russian Futurism* (San Diego State University Press, 1996), 212; Rosselli, *LP*, 141.

314   INTRODUCTION

95. Taking the experiments of Marinetti and his cohort further by displacing the letter with images or non-semantic signs, lithographed works of Russian *zaum* or "transense" and Dada collages formulated modernist fantasies of nonrationalized communication capable of incorporating the fragmented tongues of Babel and transgressing the codes of the nation-state. Although I would largely distinguish the more appreciably xenoglossic poetics from the glossolalia of zaum, traces of intelligibility haunt these languages of laughter, birds, and gods. Zaum founders Velimir Khlebnikov, who was of mixed Russian, Armenian, and Zaporozhian Cossack descent, and Aleksei Kruchenykh, born to a Ukrainian peasant family, were working in an empire that had just completed a bloody two-hundred-year expansionist project to form the largest contiguous country in the world. Although the new subjects were obliged to speak Russian, their native tongues ranged from Finnish in the north to Georgian in the south, Mongolian in the east, and Polish in the west. Russian native speakers, too, encountered hundreds of languages unknown to them in the streets and beyond, and these sounds were invoked, albeit in floating bits and pieces, in zaum. Gerald Jarecek draws out the fragments of Georgian and Armenian that Kruchonykh would have heard on the street in Tiflis (now Tbilisi), for example, amid the "Russian" zaum, coinages, onomatopoeia, and pure nonsense in his 1917 book *1918*. See Gerald Jarecek, *Zaum: The Transrational Poetry of Russian Futurism* (San Diego State University Press, 1996), 223–25. Harsha Ram describes Khlebnikov's experiments with verbal roots and neologisms to "the intuition of a specifically Russian and Slavic linguistic continuum that was folk-romantic, philological as well as Pan-Slavic in inspiration," whereas his later work was Pan-Asianist, "stretching to and beyond the limits of the Russian empire to project alliances between Asiatic states." In this way, it anticipates the philological strivings we will study in Emilio Villa. See Harsha Ram, "Futurist Geographies: Uneven Modernities and the Struggle for Aesthetic Autonomy: Paris, Italy, Russia, 1909–1914," in *The Oxford Handbook of Global Modernisms*, ed. Mark Wollaeger and Matt Eatough (Oxford University Press, 2012), 11. For a thorough overview of sound poetry, see Perloff and Dworkin, eds., *The Sound of Poetry, the Poetry of Sound*.

96. George Steiner, *After Babel: Aspects of Language and Translation* (Oxford University Press, 1975), as summarized by Lydia He Liu, *Translingual Practice: Literature, National Culture, and Translated Modernity—China, 1900–1937* (Stanford University Press, 1995), 13.

97. Mikhail M. Bakhtin, *The Dialogic Imagination: Four Essays*, ed. Michael Holquist, trans. Michael Holquist and Caryl Emerson (University of Texas Press, 1981), 270.

98. Bakhtin, *The Dialogic Imagination*, 287; Mikhail M. Bakhtin, *Problems of Dostoevsky's Poetics*, ed. Caryl Emerson (University of Minnesota Press, 1984), 200.

99. Emilio Villa, "Os puristas são enfadonhos e inúteis" ("Purists Are Irksome and Futile"), *Habitat* 7 (July 1952): 2. Original text in Portuguese; translation mine. See also Bakhtin, *The Dialogic Imagination*, 278. Even Khlebnikov's dream of creating a new artificial language is reduced to a "utopian philosopheme of poetic discourse" expressing a Ptolemaic (rather than Galilean) conception of the world. Bakhtin, *The Dialogic Imagination*, 288. Jahan Ramazani is one of those critics who endeavors across many pointed works to correct the assumption that "poetry is far more nationally or locally rooted than the novel." Ramazani makes a case for poetry that is rather weaker and more defensive than what I will propose here, possibly because the stylistic gambit of his analyses is narrower: "Despite Bakhtin's privileging of the novel as the ultimate cross-generic genre, postcolonial poetry—while perhaps neither as rich in sociohistorical mimesis as the postcolonial novel nor as analytically astute as postcolonial theory, neither as enforceable as law, nor as musically and orally resonant as song, nor as devotionally pitched as liturgy—borrows from its generic others to create fresh formal amalgamations that make it new." See "Poetry and Postcolonialism," in *The Cambridge History of Postcolonial Literature*, ed. Ato Quayson (Cambridge University Press, 2012), 946, 978.

100. Critics of modernism devoted to an analysis of polyglossic diction, such as Michael North, began to question the association of modernism strictly with canonical authorities whose multilingual texts could be argued to resolve themselves in unitary tableaus in the late 1990s. See *Reading 1922: A Return to the Scene of the Modern* (Oxford University Press, 1999), 12. In recent work, Marjorie

Perloff outlines a distinction between high modernist multilingual collage and contemporary writing of migration. See "Language in Migration: Multilingualism and Exophonic Writing in the New Poetics," *Textual Practice*, 24, no. 4 (2010): 725–48. My colleague Chicu Reddy built on Perloff's theorization of "exophony" to feature poets mixing languages in his recent edited issue of *Poetry* magazine; see Srikanth Reddy, "Editor's Note," *Poetry*, April 2022, https://www.poetryfoundation .org/poetrymagazine/articles/157567/editors-note-621f7691b7bc1. On modernist multilingualism as kitsch, see Daniel Tiffany, *My Silver Planet: A Secret History of Poetry and Kitsch* (Johns Hopkins University Press, 2014). Canonical works of ethnic studies such as Gloria Anzaldúa, *Borderlands / La Frontera: The New Mestiza* (Aunt Lute, 1987), while stressing *la mezcla* (hybridity), assume an expressive use of language grounded in the proper lived experience of ethnic identities in conflict. The critical record tends to follow this premise. See, for example, *Code-Switching in Conversation: Language, Interaction and Identity*, ed. Peter Auer (Routledge, 1998); and Penelope Gardner-Chloros, *Code-Switching* (Cambridge University Press, 2009). This tendency began to be challenged in the attention to disidentification with existing structures and the "breathtaking vulnerability" of speaking one's other language in Doris Sommer, ed., *Bilingual Games: Some Literary Investigations* (Palgrave Macmillan, 2003); quoted here from page 9.

101. See Édouard Glissant, *L'intention poétique*, trans. Nathanaël Stephens (Nightboat, 2010) and *Philosophie de la relation: poésie en étendue* (Gallimard, 2009) and Brathwaite, *History of the Voice*.

102. See, for example, "Discorso futurista di Marinetti ai veneziani," in F. T. Marinetti, *Teoria e invenzione futurista*, ed. Luciano De Maria (Mondadori, 1983), 37, hereafter *TIF*. For a thorough reading of the phenomenon, see Lucia Re, "Barbari Civilizzatissimi: Marinetti and the Futurist Myth of Barbarism," *Journal of Modern Italian Studies* 17, no. 3 (2012): 350–68.

103. Lyn Hejinian, *The Language of Inquiry* (University of California Press, 2000), 326.

104. See Daniel Maximin, *Les fruits du cyclone: Une géopoétique de la Caraïbe* (Seuil, 2006); Henri Meschonnic, *Politique du rythme: Politique du sujet* (Verdier, 1995); and Angela Last, "Fruit of the Cyclone: Undoing Geopolitics Through Geopoetics," *Geoforum* 64 (August 1, 2015): 56–64, https://doi.org/10.1016/j.geoforum.2015.05.019. Last advocates for a reimagining of global community fueled by cultural practices that eschew the "fantasies of mastery, stability, and control" that shape classical Western geography and geopolitics.

105. See, for instance, Jodi Melamed, *Represent and Destroy: Rationalizing Violence in the New Racial Capitalism* (University of Minnesota Press, 2011).

106. See Kwame Anthony Appiah, *Cosmopolitanism: Ethics in a World of Strangers* (Norton, 2006); and Homi Bhabha, Carol Breckenridge, Dipesh Chakrabarty, and Sheldon Pollock, "Cosmopolitanisms," *Public Culture* 12, no. 3 (2000): 577–89.

107. See David Damrosch, *What Is World Literature?* (Princeton University Press, 2003), and *How to Read World Literature* (Wiley-Blackwell, 2009); Franco Moretti, *Distant Reading* (Verso, 2013); Pascale Casanova, *The World Republic of Letters*, trans. M. B. DeBevoise (Harvard University Press, 2004); Rebecca L. Walkowitz, *Cosmopolitan Style: Modernism beyond the Nation* (Columbia University Press, 2006), and *Born Translated: The Contemporary Novel in an Age of World Literature* (Columbia University Press, 2015).

108. See, for instance, Rey Chow, *The Age of the World Target: Self-Referentiality in War, Theory, and Comparative Work* (Duke University Press, 2006) on the violent self-referentiality of Western discourse, and James Clifford on "discrepant cosmopolitanisms" in "Mixed Feelings," in Pheng Cheah and Bruce Robbins, eds., *Cosmopolitics: Thinking and Feeling Beyond the Nation* (University of Minnesota Press, 1998), 362–70.

109. See David Palumbo-Liu, *The Deliverance of Others: Reading Literature in a Global Age* (Duke University Press, 2012).

110. Wai Chee Dimock, "Genre as World System: Epic and Novel on Four Continents," *Narrative* 14, no. 1 (2006): 85–101.

INTRODUCTION

111. Spivak, "The Politics of Translation"; Lawrence Venuti, *The Scandals of Translation: Towards an Ethics of Difference* (Routledge, 1998).

112. See Cassin, ed., *Vocabulaire européen des philosophies*; and Apter, *Against World Literature*.

113. See Steven G. Kellman, *The Translingual Imagination* (University of Nebraska Press, 2014).

114. For a start, see Steven G. Kellman and Natasha Lvovich, eds., *The Routledge Handbook of Literary Translingualism* (Routledge, 2021). Some leading scholars in this trend still place surprising emphasis on "the plurality of Englishes worldwide" rather than the play between national languages. See Jerry Won Lee, *The Politics of Translingualism: After Englishes* (Routledge, 2017), 6. See also, for instance, A. Suresh Canagarajah, *Translingual Practice: Global Englishes and Cosmopolitan Relations* (Routledge, 2013); Sender Dovchin and Jerry Won Lee, eds., *Translinguistics: Negotiating Innovation and Ordinariness* (Routledge, 2020); and Jerry Won Lee, *Locating Translingualism* (Cambridge University Press, 2022).

115. Lydia He Liu, *Translingual Practice*, 26.

116. Rosselli, *LP*, 141. I will explore this phrase further in chapter 3.

117. Jahan Ramazani, *A Transnational Poetics* (University of Chicago Press, 2009), and *Poetry in a Global Age* (University of Chicago Press, 2020).

118. See Amitav Ghosh, "Speaking of Babel: The Risks and Rewards of Writing About Polyglot Societies," *Comparative Literature (University of Oregon)* 72, no. 3 (September 9, 2020): 292.

119. Ghosh, "Speaking of Babel," 294.

120. Sarah Dowling, *Translingual Poetics: Writing Personhood Under Settler Colonialism* (University of Iowa Press, 2018). See Werner Sollors, ed., *Multilingual America: Transnationalism, Ethnicity, and the Languages of American Literature* (New York University Press, 1998), and *Ethnic Modernism* (Harvard University Press, 2008); see also Lawrence Alan Rosenwald, *Multilingual America: Language and the Making of American Literature* (Cambridge University Press, 2008); Miller, *Accented America*; and Maria Lauret, *Wanderwords: Language Migration in American Literature* (Bloomsbury, 2014). Charles Bernstein's contributions to this literature consist of decades of translations, curation, and teaching as well as criticism, but for a representative essay on the dismantling of petrified collective and individual identities through "idiolectical" poetry, see "Poetics of the Americas," in *My Way: Speeches and Poems* (University of Chicago Press, 1999), 113–37. Juliana Spahr, an early student of Bernstein, was an early influence on this project in her placement of multilingual US poetry as central rather than marginal to her reading and teaching, and I am grateful for the PDFs she sent me nearly twenty years ago, when Glissant, Brathwaite, and creole and pidgin poets were less readily available than they are now. See Juliana Spahr, "Multilingualism in Contemporary American Poetry," in *The Cambridge History of American Poetry*, ed. Alfred Bendixen and Stephanie Burt (Cambridge University Press, 2014), 1123–43, https://doi.org/10.1017/CHO9780511762284.054, for a syncretic account. In her latest monograph, Spahr adds needed historiographical nuance to questions opened up by both Benedict Anderson and Pascale Casanova about the formation of nationalist and transnational literary communities. Spahr follows these questions through three moments: avant-garde modernism in a global English, reading its mongrel language use as a reflection of colonialism that yet points a capacious and critical way forward for the English language; a range of short-lived movement literatures flourishing in minority communities of the post–World War II period that were largely ignored by the literary establishment; and the state- and institutionally sponsored policies of multiculturalism at the turn of the twenty-first century, which threatened to absorb any potential literature of opposition. See Juliana Spahr, *Du Bois's Telegram: Literary Resistance and State Containment* (Harvard University Press, 2018). The phrase between quotation marks is from an editorial statement for *XCP: Cross-Cultural Poetics*, whose complete run is archived at Mark Nowak, ed., "XCP: Cross Cultural Poetics," *XCP: Cross Cultural Poetics*, 2010, 1997, https://opendoor.northwestern.edu/archive/collections/show/21. The radio broadcast "Cross-Cultural Poetics" by Leonard Schwartz also deals routinely with translingual work; see Leonard Schwartz, "Cross Cultural Poetics," audio archive of radio show, Pennsound, 2018, 2003, https://writing

INTRODUCTION · 317

121. .upenn.edu/pennsound/x/XCP.php. Other touchstones include the works of Yunte Huang, especially his most recent volume devoted to transpacific multilingual poetics under globalization, *Chinese Whispers*, and the early experimental *Shi: A Radical Reading of Chinese Poetry* (Roof Books, 1997), and Erín Mouré, *My Beloved Wager: Essays from a Writing Practice* (NeWest Press, 2009).

121. See Eugene Ostashevsky, "Translingualism: A Poetics of Language Mixing and Estrangement," *Boundary 2* 50, no. 4 (2023): 171–94, https://doi.org/10.1215/01903659-10694267; Johannes Göransson, *Transgressive Circulation: Essays on Translation* (Noemi, 2018); Johannes Göransson, "The Beautiful Betrayal: Translingual Poetry as Counterfeit Voice," *Action Books* (blog), May 21, 2020, https://actionbooks.org/2020/05/the-beautiful-betrayal-translingual-poetry-as-counterfeit -voice-by-johannes-goransson/; and for a substantial selection of both poetry and prose in English that are the product of years of thinking through translation and translingualism, Uljana Wolf, *Subsisters: Selected Poems*, trans. Sophie Seita (Belladonna*, 2017).

122. Steiner, *After Babel*, 228.

123. While the efforts of the historical avant-garde to implode the poetic stanza have given rise to essential studies by scholars such as Mary Ellen Solt, Willard Bohn, Johanna Drucker, Marjorie Perloff, and Steve McCaffery, analysis of the works' graphic demands tends to be relegated to specialized discussions of visual poetry and artists' books, and the revivification of Futurism by later generations of the avant-garde has yet to be adequately recognized. Beppe Cavatorta provides one exception; see his "Back to Futurism: The Ill-Digested Legacies," in *Carte italiane* 2, no. 6 (2010): 23–48.

124. Minae Mizumura, *The Fall of Language in the Age of English*, trans. Mari Yoshihara and Juliet Winters Carpenter (Columbia University Press, 2015), 175.

125. See the concluding reflections of Walter Benjamin, "The Work of Art in the Age of Mechanical Reproduction," in *Illuminations*, ed. Hannah Arendt (Shocken, 1969), 244; for authoritative readings of the meaning of this phrase, see Martin Jay, "'The Aesthetic Ideology' as Ideology; Or, What Does It Mean to Aestheticize Politics?," *Cultural Critique*, no. 21 (1992): 41–61, https://doi .org/10.2307/1354116; and Roger Griffin, *Modernism and Fascism: The Sense of a Beginning Under Mussolini and Hitler* (Palgrave Macmillan, 2007), from which I cite here a passage on page 24.

126. Emilio Villa, *17 variazioni su temi proposti per una pura ideologia fonetica*, with plates by Alberto Burri (Edizioni d'Origine, 1955), in Emilio Villa, *L'opera poetica*, ed. Cecilia Bello Minciacchi (L'Orma, 2014), 199–228.

127. See Charles Olson, "Projective Verse," in *The New American Poetry, 1945–1960*, ed. Donald Allen (Evergreen, 1960), 386.

128. Naoki Sakai, *Translation and Subjectivity: On Japan and Cultural Nationalism* (University of Minnesota Press, 1997).

129. For exhaustive accounts of Depero's stay in New York, see Fortunato Depero, *Un futurista a New York*, ed. Claudia Salaris (Del Grifo, 1990); Maurizio Scudiero and David Leiber, *Depero futurista e New York* (Longo, 1986); Gabriela Belli's catalogue, *Depero futurista: Rome—Paris—New York, 1915–1932* (Skira, 1999); Laura Chiesa, "Transnational Multimedia: Fortunato Depero's Impressions of New York City (1928–1930)," *California Italian Studies* 1:2 (2010): 1–33; and Raffaele Bedarida, "'Bombs Against the Skyscrapers': Depero's Strange Love Affair with New York, 1928–194," *International Yearbook of Futurism* (2016): 43–70. Chiesa disagrees with Günther Berghaus's interpretation of Depero's aesthetic of "steel," which the elder scholar regards as less Futurist and more Fascist in *Futurism and Politics: Between Anarchist Rebellion and Fascist Reaction, 1909–1944* (Berghahn Books, 1996); she interprets it as parodic, as subversive, but I have a hard time reading it in such a strongly parodic light. In a different narrative trajectory, Depero could be generatively compared and contrasted with Francesco Cangiullo, the Futurist whose work also traversed media and languages yet relied on the richness of local Neapolitan idioms—and who broke appreciably with the group in 1924 and never signed on to Fascism through a party *tessera*.

130. Fortunato Depero, *Depero Futurista, 1913–27* (Edizioni della Dinamo, 1927), 224–25.

131. See Bedarida, "'Bombs Against the Skyscrapers,'" 45, 53. See also Emilio Gentile, "Impending Modernity: Fascism and the Ambivalent Image of the United States," *Journal of Contemporary History* 28, no. 1 (January 1993): 7–29. Gentile argues that Fascist culture of the late 1930s perceived Americanism ambivalently both as a fascinating metaphor of youth and candor to emulate and as terrifying.

132. Fortunato Depero, *Fortunato Depero nelle opere e nella vita* (Trento, 1940), 292–93; later edited as Fortunato Depero, *Un futurista a New York*, ed. Claudia Salaris (Editori del Grifo, 1990), 88.

133. On this symbol, see T. Corey Brennan, *The Fasces: A History of Ancient Rome's Most Dangerous Political Symbol* (Oxford University Press, 2022).

134. From Gramsci's notebook 29, in Antonio Gramsci, *Quaderni del carcere*, 4 vols. (Einaudi, 2014), 3:2343, 2350, translation mine. For an English translation, see David Forgacs, ed., *The Gramsci Reader: Selected Writings 1916–1935* (New York University Press, 2000), 354, 355.

135. This date hails to Emmanuela Tandello's research and notes on *Sleep: Poesie in inglese* within Amelia Rosselli, *L'opera poetica*, ed. Stefano Giovannuzzi (Mondadori, 2012), 1495. This volume will be referred to as *OP*.

136. Amelia Rosselli, *Locomotrix: Selected Poetry and Prose of Amelia Rosselli*, ed. and trans. Jennifer Scappettone (University of Chicago Press, 2012), 233. Hereafter *Locomotrix*.

137. "La poesia è un piacere privato," a 1977 interview with Gabriella Sica, in Monica Venturini and Silvia De March, eds., *È vostra la vita che ho perso: Conversazioni e Interviste, 1964–1995* (Le Lettere, 2010), 15. This volume will hereafter be referred to as *CI*.

138. Rosselli, *Locomotrix*, 233.

139. See Gilles Deleuze and Félix Guattari, *What Is Philosophy?*, trans. Hugh Tomlinson and Graham Burchell (Columbia University Press, 1994). They refer in turn to Dostoyevsky and to Nicholas of Cusa, *The Idiot* (trans. of *Idiota* [1450]) (London, 1650).

140. Rosselli, *Locomotrix*, 234. For the date of composition, see *OP*, 1490.

141. Rosselli, *Locomotrix*, 78–79. See also Amelia Rosselli, *Lettere a Pasolini, 1962–1969* (San Marco dei Giustiniani, 2008), 25.

142. 12:09 at "Con l'ascia dietro le spalle: 10 anni senza Amelia Rosselli," ed. Andrea Cortellessa, *La musica, la metrica* (RAI 3, February 9, 2006), https://media.sas.upenn.edu/pennsound/groups/Italiana/Amelia-Rosselli/Amelia-Rosselli_03_Con-l-Ascia-Dietro-le-Spalle_February-09-2006.mp3.

143. *Ellis Island*, directed by Meredith Monk (Greenwich Film Associates and ZDF Germany, 1981),: 28, https://vimeo.com/ondemand/ellisisland1981.

144. See Krista Tippett, "Meredith Monk—Archaeologist of the Human Voice," *On Being*, accessed May 3, 2019, https://onbeing.org/programs/meredith-monk-archaeologist-of-the-human-voice/.

1. WIRELESS IMAGINATION: FUTURIST DELUSIONS OF AUTARKY AND THE DREAM (OR NIGHTMARE) OF A TRANSNATIONAL LANGUAGE

1. Baker & Godwin, Printers, "The Laying of the Cable—John and Jonathan Joining Hands," c. 1858, woodcut with letterpress, 42.5 × 56.5 cm, Prints and Photographs Division, Library of Congress, http://www.loc.gov/pictures/item/2004665357/.

2. "The Telegraphic Messages of Queen Victoria and President Buchanan," August 28, 1858, wood engraving; illustration in *Frank Leslie's Illustrated Newspaper*, p. 191, August 28, 1858, Prints and Photographs Division, Library of Congress, http://www.loc.gov/pictures/item/2005694829/.

3. William Clark, ed., *Empire Club Speeches; Being Addresses Delivered Before the Empire Club of Canada during Its Session of 1903–04* (William Briggs, 1904), 94. Fleming's baldly imperialist "girdle" brings out the way that contemporary networks, as extensions of historical cabling infrastructure,

I. WIRELESS IMAGINATION ❧ 319

manifest what Tung Hui-Hu identifies as "a *reemergence* of sovereign power within the realm of data," despite their decentralized and apparently ethereal and democratic nature (emphasis in original). Tung-Hui Hu, *A Prehistory of the Cloud* (MIT Press, 2015), xiii.

4. For an argument that much of the global media system was in place before the high tide of imperialism, pointing to other factors that drove their proliferation, including corporate cartels and international law, see Dwayne R. Winseck and Robert M. Pike, *Communication and Empire: Media, Markets, and Globalization, 1860–1930* (Duke University Press, 2007).

5. For a perspicuous discussion of the distinction between the wireless and radio, see Timothy C. Campbell, *Wireless Writing in the Age of Marconi* (University of Minnesota Press, 2006).

6. The dominance of Anglo-American media infrastructure in the process of globalization and its befitting prominence in critiques of cultural and media imperialism from Herbert I. Schiller forward have had the effect of flattening the discourse somewhat, obscuring contributions to the understanding of these technologies by authors from cultures on the margins or "semiperiphery" (about which see below). For a pioneering study of cultural imperialism, see Herbert I. Schiller, *Mass Communications and American Empire* (A. M. Kelley, 1969).

7. For a classic analysis in English of Futurist ideals, see Marjorie Perloff, *The Futurist Moment: Avant-Garde, Avant Guerre, and the Language of Rupture* (University of Chicago Press, 1986).

8. For the helpful details about the French and English translations, which make it clear that the manifesto spurred discussion in both French and English and in prominent newspapers and journals, further disseminating the buzz about the Futurist movement, see Lawrence Rainey, Christine Poggi, and Laura Wittman, eds., *Futurism: An Anthology* (Yale University Press, 2009), 540*n*. Marinetti also delivered the manifesto as a lecture at the Galérie La Boëtie in June of 1913.

9. F. T. Marinetti, "Distruzione della sintassi—Immaginazione senza fili—Parole in libertà," in *Teoria e invenzione futurista*, ed. Luciano De Maria (Mondadori, 1968), 65–80. Hereafter, this volume will be referred to as *TIF*. For lengthy passages I am relying on the translation from Rainey et al., eds., *Futurism*, 143–51; here 143. However, I have made certain key changes, most obviously to their substitution of "radio" for "wireless" (senza fili), and use my own translations from the Italian for short phrases.

10. Rainey et al., eds., *Futurism*, 143.

11. *TIF*, 68. On time-space compression, see David Harvey, *The Condition of Postmodernity: An Enquiry Into the Origins of Cultural Change* (Blackwell, 1989), particularly 201–83.

12. *TIF*, 69.

13. *TIF*, 303.

14. *TIF*, 69, 72; Marinetti quotes the "Technical Manifesto" in the later manifesto, as he was wont to do; *TIF*, 48. Though it is not within the bounds of my argument to dwell on this, the Futurist approach to the lyric anticipates many quarrels with that genre as omnivorous and pedantically the expression of "overheard" "speech." Such issues, although long preceded by a substantial literature among avant-garde practitioners themselves, were critically canonized for the broader Anglophone academy in historical poetics; see Virginia Jackson and Yopie Prins, eds., *The Lyric Theory Reader: A Critical Anthology* (Johns Hopkins University Press, 2014).

15. Nikola Tesla, "When Woman Is Boss: An Interview with Nikola Tesla," *Collier's Weekly* 70, no. 5 (January 30, 1926): 17.

16. "Distruzione della sintassi," in *TIF*, 69, 66, 68.

17. As Peter Bürger wrote in a follow-up to his *Theory of the Avant-Garde*, the paradox of the avant-garde's failure is that it was so successful in being integrated by institutions. See Peter Bürger, "Avant-Garde and Neo-Avant-Garde: An Attempt to Answer Certain Critics of Theory of the Avant-Garde," trans. Bettina Brandt, *New Literary History* 41 (2010): 695–715. Puzzlingly, Bürger mentions Fascism only once in *Theory of the Avant-Garde* as an extreme example of the liquidation of art's autonomy as claimed by bourgeois cultural movements of the nineteenth century. See Peter Bürger, *Theory of the Avant-Garde*, trans. Michael Shaw (University of Minnesota Press, 1984), 24–25.

1. WIRELESS IMAGINATION

18. Claudio Fogu, *The Fishing Net and the Spider Web: Mediterranean Imaginaries and the Making of Italians* (Palgrave Macmillan, 2020), 167–68, http://link.library.eui.eu/portal/The-Fishing-Net-and-the-Spider-Web-/uOJcNoNhy98/.

19. Roger Griffin, *Modernism and Fascism: The Sense of a Beginning Under Mussolini and Hitler* (Palgrave Macmillan, 2007), 196.

20. For a discussion of this watershed moment in curating the memory of Fascism, see the introduction to Sharon Hecker and Raffaele Bedarida, eds., *Curating Fascism: Exhibitions and Memory from the Fall of Mussolini to Today* (Bloomsbury, 2022), 1–4.

21. Harsha Ram, "Futurist Geographies: Uneven Modernities and the Struggle for Aesthetic Autonomy: Paris, Italy, Russia, 1909–1914," in *The Oxford Handbook of Global Modernisms*, ed. Mark Wollaeger and Matt Eatough (Oxford University Press, 2012), 2. Ram shows how the cases of Italy and the Russian Empire, identified as "semiperipheral," resist early readings of the geography of the avant-garde based on center and periphery, from Bürger to Poggioli to Perloff, as well as more recent analyses of the republic of letters by Pascale Casanova and world-systems theory.

22. I refer of course to Pascale Casanova, *The World Republic of Letters*, trans. M. B. DeBevoise (Harvard University Press, 2004).

23. See Ashon T. Crawley, *Blackpentecostal Breath: The Aesthetics of Possibility* (Fordham University Press, 2016), 207–42. Crawley claims that xenolalia (also known as xenoglossia), in its urge to translate the other, represents "a settler colonial claim on language whereas glossolalia is a disruption of—because it is the grounds for, the flesh of—language" (227).

24. Recall the Divine Electric Light hailed in the "Against Passéist Venice" manifesto; Marinetti produced overtly heretical works in this period, such as *Le monoplan du pape: Roman politique en vers libre* (*The Pope's Monoplane: Political Novel in Free Verse*, 1912, with an Italian edition published in 1914 bearing the subtitle *Romanzo profetico*, or *Prophetic Novel*), which, following a trip to the underworld, casts the pope into the Adriatic Sea. Schnapp and others have noted "how thoroughly the already secularized romantic language of transcendence and sublimity was grafted onto the technology of flight during these early years, even within the domains of aeronautic science and engineering." See Jeffrey T. Schnapp, "Propeller Talk," *Modernism/Modernity* 1, no. 3 (September 1, 1994): 162, https://doi.org/10.1353/mod.1994.0063. Campbell continues to elucidate the modernizing of a Romantic trope of dictation via the mechanical transcriptions of *marconisti;* however, as a result, he tends to lay heavy emphasis on the role of the aural in a manifesto that is resolutely transsensory and that necessitated the revolutionizing of the visual field. See Campbell, *Wireless Writing in the Age of Marconi*, 79–96. Marinetti's dictation narrative was published two years after he enjoyed one of Italy's earliest passenger flights at the Milan International Air Week in September 1910.

25. See "Technical Manifesto of Futurist Literature," in *TIF*, 50. Schnapp discusses this signature antihumanism in "Propeller Talk," 161.

26. This program appears in the "Technical Manifesto of Futurist Literature," in *TIF*, 46–54; the quotes hail from *TIF*, 74, 78.

27. *TIF*, 77. When Stéphane Mallarmé's poetic constellation *Un coup de dés* (*A Throw of the Dice*) was published in the British journal *Cosmopolis* in 1897, it signaled the opening of new routes through which verse could address the disintegrating borders of geography and language in contexts of unprecedented circulation and migration. Although Mallarmé's work is understood to have exploded verse's formal horizons, the sociopolitical valences of the traditional poetic stanza's eruption on (and beyond) the page have yet to be adequately sounded. The Futurist "destruction of syntax" and of orthographic decorum enabled by *Un coup de dés*, with works of "words-in-freedom" breaking down the linear, hieratic logic of hypotaxis, opened up a newly anarchic—and potentially expansionist—landscape of linguistic collision and recombination. In the far more frequently discussed "Lettre-Ocean," Apollinaire simultaneously explored the possibilities of a "wireless" polyglot composition reflecting the trajectory of a letter crossing the Atlantic to his brother in Mexico.

I. WIRELESS IMAGINATION   321

28. *TIF*, 80.

29. *TIF*, 78–79.

30. *TIF*, 146, 145.

31. See Luca Cottini, *The Art of Objects: The Birth of Italian Industrial Culture, 1878–1928* (University of Toronto Press, 2018), who quotes from Pietro Gargano, *Una vita, una leggenda: Enrico Caruso, il più grande tenore del mondo* (Mondadori, 1997), 54.

32. Cottini, *The Art of Objects*, 103–4.

33. "Wireless Imagination," Rainey et al., eds., *Futurism*, 143.

34. See "The Founding and Manifesto of Futurism," the notorious and oft-repeated bullet point 9 of the manifesto, reprinted and translated in Rainey et al., eds., *Futurism*, 51. As James Leveque puts it, the Futurists "militariz[ed] the aesthetic, whose independence was taken for granted, rather than aestheticizing the martial." James Leveque, "Futurism's First War: Apocalyptic Space in F.T. Marinetti's Writings from Tripoli," *Romance Notes* 55, no. 3 (2015): 427.

35. These campaigns resulted in Italy's seizure of the coastal Ottoman Tripolitania Vilayet. Jeffrey Schnapp points out that since 1910, wireless telegraphy and aviation were indissociably linked not only through journalism's love affair with flight but also in the science of air-to-ground reconnaissance. See Schnapp, "Propeller Talk," 167. For the ways in which these events fueled World War I, see Christopher M. Clark, *The Sleepwalkers: How Europe Went to War in 1914* (Allen Lane, 2012), especially "Air Strikes on Libya," 242–50. For Marinetti's boasts to Aldo Palazzeschi and narration of his having killed three Arabs with his own hands, constituting "the most beautiful two months of my life," see Marinetti to Palazzeschi, letter of January 1912, in *F. T. Marinetti-Aldo Palazzeschi: Carteggio*, ed. Paolo Prestigiacomo (Mondadori, 1978), 61.

36. Filippo Tommaso Marinetti, *La Bataille de Tripoli, 26 Octobre 1911, vécue et chantée par F. T. Marinetti* (Edizioni futuriste di "Poesia," 1912), 59, and F. T. Marinetti, *La battaglia di Tripoli (26 Ottobre 1911) vissuta e cantata da F. T. Marinetti* (Edizioni Futuriste di "Poesia," 1912), 61. My translation.

37. Rainey et al., *Futurism*, 146.

38. Rainey et al., *Futurism*, 146.

39. "Risposto alle obiezioni" to the Technical Manifesto, dated August 11, 1912, in *TIF*, 58. "La distruzione del periodo tradizionale, l'abolizione dell'aggettivo, dell'avverbio e della punteggiatura determineranno necessariamente il fallimento della troppo famosa armonia dello stile, cosicché il poeta futurista potrà utilizzare finalmente tutte le onomatopee, anche le più cacofoniche, che riproducono gl'innumerevoli rumori della materia in movimento."

40. Rainey et al., *Futurism*, 129. I have substantially altered the translation.

41. Christine Poggi, "The Futurist Noise Machine," *The European Legacy* 14, no. 7 (December 1, 2009): 824, https://doi.org/10.1080/10848770903363912.

42. F. T. Marinetti, *Zang Tumb Tumb: Adrianopoli Ottobre 1912. Parole in libertà* (Edizioni futuriste di "Poesia," 1914), 36. A section of the poem was translated into English in *The World Magazine*, August 9, 1914.

43. "I am at war with the precious, ornamental aesthetics of Mallarmé and his quest for the rare word." "Distruzione della sintassi," *TIF*, 77.

44. For a recent, careful analysis of the possible influence of Marinetti's journeys to Moscow and St. Petersburg in the winter of 1914 upon Russian Cubofuturists (especially Vasily Kamensky's groundbreaking typographic visual poems), incorporating information about the Russian translation of manifestos between 1913 and 1914 (including precepts from "Destruction of Syntax"), see Eugene Ostashevsky, "Vasily Kamensky and F. T. Marinetti: Italian Words-in-Freedom and Russian Typographic Visual Poetry," in *International Yearbook of Futurism Studies*, ed. Günter Berghaus (De Gruyter, 2022), 190–223, https://doi.org/10.1515/9783110800920-007. Ostashevsky concludes that these writers drew imaginatively on the main principles of the manifestos surrounding *parole in libertà* but would not have had access to much of the poetry and, ultimately, appropriated the precepts that had reached them for their own needs.

322 ·◈ I. WIRELESS IMAGINATION

45. Roman Jakobson, *My Futurist Years*, ed. Bengt Jangfeldt, trans. Stephen Rudy (Marsilio, 1997), 177.

46. Campbell, *Wireless Writing in the Age of Marconi*, 94.

47. For the *serata* proclamation, see "Discorso ai triestini," in *TIF*, 249.

48. Tullio Pànteo, *Il poeta Marinetti* (Società Editoriale Milanese, 1908), 115. It has been suggested that apart from a quick biographical sketch, the majority of Pànteo's book was ghostwritten by Marinetti. See Domenico Cammarota, *Filippo Tommaso Marinetti, Bibliografia* (Skira, 2002), 49–50. On the history of "Fatta l'Italia . . ." and its appropriation by Gabriele D'Annunzio and the Fascist regime, see Stephanie Malia Hom, "On the Origins of Making Italy: Massimo D'Azeglio and 'Fatta l'Italia, Bisogna Fare Gli Italiani,'" *Italian Culture* 31, no. 1 (March 1, 2013): 1–16, https://doi.org/10.1179/0161462212Z.00000000012.

49. See Giovanni Lista, "Gli anni trenta: l'aeropittura," in *Futurismo 1909–2009. Velocità + Arte + Azione*, ed. Giovanni Lista and Ada Masoero (Palazzo Reale di Milano, 2009), 237–72.

50. F. T. Marinetti, "Prefazione," in Adelmo Cicogna, *Autarchia della lingua: Contributo ideale e pratico alla santa battaglia* (Edizioni dell' autore brossura, 1940), 7.

51. See Tullio De Mauro, *Storia linguistica dell'Italia unita* (Laterza e Figli, 1970), 135. For pre-Fascist actions against multilingualism, see Gabriella Klein, *La politica linguistica del fascismo* (Il Mulino, 1986), 69. Roger Griffin provides an eloquent synthesis of the grounds that enabled ultranationalism to take root in Italy, many of which have to do with the clash of cultures within the peninsula and the weakness of the education system: "the diverse histories, traditions, cultures, and dialects of Italy's component regions; its deeply entrenched social divisions; the acute poverty, anarchy, and feudal conditions of large areas of the South; the rapid and poorly planned industrialization and wild capitalism of the North West corner of the country (the 'industrial triangle'), out of step with economic conditions elsewhere; the comparative weakness of the technocratic, industrial classes and 'new bourgeoisie' within the political class; the widespread illiteracy; the rudimentary educational system, and inadequate social infrastructure in much of the peninsula and especially in the islands; the arch-conservatism of the Catholic Church . . ., and its alienation from the new state; the endemic egoism and corruption of a 'political class' out of touch with the living conditions and needs of the growing masses; the state's repressive use of the police and the military to quell public disorder. . . . The cumulative effect was a yawning gap between the 'legal' and 'real' Italy which hampered the nationalization and democratization necessary to make the 'actually existing' nation an effective source of personal and collective identity." Roger Griffin, *Modernism and Fascism*, 196.

52. For an early expression of the need for "defense" of the language, see Tommaso Tittoni, "La difesa della lingua italiana," *Nuova Antologia* 61 (1926): 377–87. For an early grammar, see Ciro Trabalza and Ettore Allodoli, *La grammatica degl'italiani* (Le Monnier, 1933). For contemporary studies, see Enzo Golino, *Parola di Duce: Il linguaggio totalitario del fascismo* (Rizzoli, 1994); Laura Ricci, *La Lingua dell'impero. Comunicazione, letteratura e propaganda nell'età del colonialismo italiano* (Carrocci, 2005); and Sergio Raffaeli, "'Si dispone che . . .': Direttive fasciste sulla lingua: antiregionalismo e xenofobia," *Lingua Nostra* 58 (1997): 30–45.

53. For statistics on illiteracy, see De Mauro, *Storia linguistica dell'Italia unita*, 91. Once Gentile was removed from his cabinet position as Minister of Public Instruction the next year, the schools aimed more straightforwardly at fascistizing the population from childhood on. For a contemporary account of these developments, including Gentile's "Faustian compact" with the regime and his demotion to the position of editor-in-chief of a national encyclopedia, see the address to the New School of Social Research by emigré Max Ascoli, friend and host to the Rosselli family. Max Ascoli, "Education in Fascist Italy," *Social Research* 4, no. 3 (September 1937): 338–47. For an account of Gentile's importance in providing action-oriented and thus modernist philosophical rationalizations of Fascism, see Claudio Fogu, *The Historic Imaginary: Politics of History in Fascist Italy* (University of Toronto Press, 2003).

54. Klein, *La politica linguistica del fascismo*, 38; Fabio Foresti, ed., *Credere, obbedire, combattere: Il regime linguistico nel ventennio* (Edizioni Pendragon, 2003), 32–48.

1. WIRELESS IMAGINATION   323

55. See Foresti, *Credere, obbedire, combattere*, 17.

56. From a 1929 conference in Pesaro on "Il Futurismo e il Novecento," quoted in Giordano Bruno Guerri, *Filippo Tommaso Marinetti: Invenzioni, avventure e passioni di un rivoluzionario* (Mondadori, 2017), 226. For the inaugural address, see 227.

57. The term "deterritorialized cosmopolitanism" is Harsha Ram's. See Ram, "Futurist Geographies," 6.

58. Quoted in Pànteo, *Il poeta Marinetti*, 186–87. I am grateful to Silvia Guslandi for first bringing my attention to this passage.

59. Milena Contini, *Le Afriche di Marinetti: Viaggio nelle pagine africane del "barbaro" futurista* (Aracne editrice, 2020), 19.

60. See F. T. Marinetti, *Critical Writings*, ed. Günter Berghaus, trans. Doug Thompson (Farrar, Straus, and Giroux, 2006), xix.

61. *TIF*, 9.

62. From "Autoritratto," in Filippo Tommaso Marinetti, *Scatole d'amore in conserva* (Edizioni d'arte Fauno, 1927), 8, http://archive.org/details/scatole_images.

63. *TIF*, 7. The figure of the nurse will recur in his last work, *Venezianella e Studentaccio* (*Venezianella and the Punk Student*) (1943–1944, published posthumously), where the protagonist, the daughter of Venice, has returned from volunteering for the Red Cross at the battle of Tobruk against the Allies. See the volume edited by Paolo Valesio and Patrizio Ceccagnoli: Filippo Tommaso Marinetti, *Venezianella e studentaccio* (Oscar Mondadori, 2013). I write extensively about this work in *Killing the Moonlight: Modernism in Venice* (Columbia University Press, 2014), 171–91.

64. Antonio Gramsci, *Quaderni del carcere*, vol. 3, ed. Valentino Gerratana (G. Einaudi, 1975), 2021–22. Translation mine.

65. Gary P. Cestaro, *Dante and the Grammar of the Nursing Body* (University of Notre Dame Press, 2003), 48. See also Barbara Spackman, "Fascist Puerility," *Qui Parle* 13, no. 1 (2001): 13–28.

66. Cestaro, *Dante and the Grammar of the Nursing Body*, 48.

67. *TIF* 37. For more on Marinetti's self-identification with the barbarian see Lucia Re, " 'Barbari Civilizzatissimi': Marinetti and the Futurist Myth of Barbarism," *Journal of Modern Italian Studies* 17, no. 3 (2012): 350–68.

68. See Julia Kristeva, *La révolution du langage poétique: L'avant-garde à la fin du XIXe siècle, Lautréamont et Mallarmé* (Éditions du Seuil, 1974).

69. In his critique of the naturalization of concepts of "mother tongue" and "native speaker" within contemporary formal and sociological linguistics, which seeks to restore the forgotten history of their status within organicist ideology and radical/nationalist identity politics, Christopher Hutton outlines the struggles within the National Socialist period to fix the link between the mother tongue and *Volk* in the face of colonization and the new states of Central and Eastern Europe created in 1917–1918: "German linguists were struggling with a sense of cultural insecurity and a perception that they were being submerged by more powerful cultural forces, the universalizing 'West' on one side, the Slavic hordes on the other and, most insidious of all, the Jews within. These Jews, who were 'more German than the Germans', threatened the link between mother-tongue and race, for they came . . . heralding the dissolution of language and thought (since each nation could no longer be seen as having its own thought expressed in its own unique language), the end of the Herder–Humboldt dream of a world of autonomous authentic national essences living side by side but preserving their distinctiveness." Hutton reminds us that "the rise of mother-tongues reflects a particular set of historical circumstances, not a transhistorical law of human identity formation." Christopher Hutton, *Linguistics and the Third Reich: Mother-Tongue Fascism, Race and the Science of Language* (Routledge, 1999).

70. From "Autoritratto," in Filippo Tommaso Marinetti, *Scatole d'amore in conserva. Illustrazioni di Pannaggi; coperta e fregi di Carlo A. Petrucci* (Edizioni d'arte Fauno, 1927), 8. Translation mine. To translate the word for Black in the Italian of the time always poses a problem; because it is not necessarily derogatory, I have chosen to use contemporary standards.

71. Cestaro, *Dante and the Grammar of the Nursing Body*, 18.

72. Quintilian, *Institutio Oratoria, Book I*, ed. Harold Edgeworth Butler (Harvard University Press, 1920), 22.

73. For a brief reading, see Emilia Campagna, "Il rumore della musica, la musica dei rumori. Percorsi interdisciplinari tra suono, parola e disegno alla scoperta del futurismo," *Musicheria.Net: Bottega dell'educazione musicale*, November 25, 2011, https://www.musicheria.net/2011/11/25/il-rumore-della-musica-la-musica-dei-rumori/. The performance is reported on in " 'Inaugurazione dell'Esposizione Libera Futurista,' " *Lacerba* 2, no. 9 (May 1914): 143.

74. For a complication of the March on Rome as Fascist origin myth, see, for example, Chapter 4 of Robert O. Paxton, *The Anatomy of Fascism* (Knopf, 2004), 87–118.

75. See Lucia Re, "Italians and the Invention of Race: The Poetics and Politics of Difference in the Struggle Over Libya, 1890–1913," *California Italian Studies* 1, no. 1 (2010): 6, 7, https://escholarship.org/uc/item/96k3w5kn.

76. For an influential study of the avant-garde producing this equivocation, see Marjorie Perloff's pioneering study *The Futurist Moment*, xviii. Renato Poggioli, from whom Perloff draws her title, was explicit in arguing that the conflation of radical aesthetics with radical politics was both theoretically and historically erroneous and points out that Italian Futurism was always equal to nationalism, whereas Russian Futurism *became* nationalist; Poggioli posits that the relationship between aesthetics and politics is coincidental, capable of swinging right or left (as in the case of Italian Futurism's alliance with Fascism and Russian Futurism's alliance with Communism). Renato Poggioli, *The Theory of the Avant-Garde*, trans. Gerard Fitzgerald (Belknap, 1968), 95–96. My study of two different faces of "Pentecostal" poetics is meant to underscore this dual potential.

77. Re, "Italians and the Invention of Race," 11. The literature on racialization is too enormous to cite here, and Re produces a robust survey in "Race Studies and the Literary Construction of Race in Liberal and Giolittian Italy," in the same essay, pp. 20–29.

78. See W. E. B. Du Bois, "Inter-Racial Implications of the Ethiopian Crisis: A Negro View," *Foreign Affairs* 14, no. 1 (1935): 89. For South Asian solidarity with Ethiopia, see Arlena Buelli, "The Hands Off Ethiopia Campaign, Racial Solidarities and Intercolonial Antifascism in South Asia (1935–36)," *Journal of Global History* 1, no. 1 (February 21, 2022): 1–21, https://doi.org/10.1017/S1740022822000092.

79. For a general account of these efforts and of the importance of the invasion of Ethiopia to the African Diaspora, see Cedric J. Robinson, "The African Diaspora and the Italo-Ethiopian Crisis," *Race and Class* 27, no. 2 (01 1985): 51–65, https://doi.org/10.1177/030639688502700204; and Mohammed Elnaiem, "The Defense of Ethiopia from Fascism," *Black Radicals* (blog), April 22, 2020, https://daily.jstor.org/the-defense-of-ethiopia-from-fascism/.

80. Ruth Ben-Ghiat, "When Harlem and Little Italy Clashed Over Ethiopia," *Lucid* (blog), June 8, 2021, https://lucid.substack.com/p/when-harlem-and-little-italy-clashed?s=r. Robeson would soon star in *Jericho* (1937), the story of a medical student who is drafted into the US Army during World War I but deserts when he is unjustly accused of murder. Jericho escapes to the Sahara Desert where he joins a group of Tuaregs.

81. See Derrick M. Nault, "Haile Selassie, the League of Nations, and Human Rights Diplomacy," in *Africa and the Shaping of International Human Rights*, ed. Derrick M. Nault (Oxford University Press, 2020), https://doi.org/10.1093/oso/9780198859628.003.0004.

82. For more context, see Alberto Sbacchi, "Poison Gas and Atrocities in the Italo-Ethiopian War (1935–1936)," in *Italian Colonialism*, ed. Ruth Ben-Ghiat and Mia Fuller (Palgrave Macmillan, 2005), 47–56; Angelo Del Boca, *I gas di Mussolini. Il fascismo e la guerra d'Etiopia* (Editori Riuniti, 1996); Neve Gordon and Nicola Perugini, *Human Shields: A History of People in the Line of Fire* (University of California Press, 2020), 60–70; and Paolo Borruso, *Debre Libanos 1937: Il più grave crimine di guerra dell'Italia* (Laterza, 2020), 202.

I. WIRELESS IMAGINATION 325

83. Simon Tisdall, "The United Nations Has the Power to Punish Putin. This Is How It Can Be Done," *The Guardian*, April 6, 2022, sec. Opinion.

84. See his preface in Cicogna, *Autarchia della lingua*, 7.

85. Filippo Tommaso Marinetti, "Contro l'esterofilia. Manifesto futurista alle signore e agli intellettuali," *Gazzetta Del Popolo*, September 24, 1931, https://collections.library.yale.edu/catalog /10660837.

86. F. T. Marinetti and Bruno Munari, *Il poema del vestito di latte: parole in libertà futuriste*, ed. Ufficio Propaganda SNIA Viscosa (Officina Grafica Esperia, 1937). Hereafter *PVL*.

87. For the 1942 Einaudi-issued abecedarian for children containing the entry "hitleriano" for the letter H (bowdlerized without comment in later editions), see Luigi Mascheroni, "Quando Munari scelse la 'H' di Hitler," *ilGiornale.it*, June 10, 2021. On Munari's forging of a career split aimed at avoiding being regarded as a derivative Futurist, see Marco Meneguzzo, *Bruno Munari: Opere 1930–1995* (Fumagalli, 1995), 7. For an argument that helpfully excavates Munari's relationship to Futurism despite the artist's disavowals, while absolving him of political responsibility for the affiliation, see Pierpaolo Antonello, "Beyond Futurism: Bruno Munari's Useless Machines," in *Futurism and the Technological Imagination*, ed. Günter Berghaus (Rodopi, 2009), 315–36: "Although he played lip-service to Futurism and, above all, to Fascism in some of his writing of the period, there were no ideological motivations behind Munari's artistic activities" (317). Ironically, Antonello provides a brief exegesis of *Il poema del vestito di latte* in the same essay.

88. Balla's manifesto was first published as an independent leaflet in Italian on May 20, 1914, and then as independent leaflet in French, also in May 1914. "Manifesto della moda femminile futurista" was first published in the journal *Roma futurista* (February 29, 1920). Both manifestos are reproduced in Rainey et al., eds., *Futurism*, 254.

89. Dante Alighieri, *De vulgari eloquentia*, trans. Steven Botterill (Cambridge University Press, 1996), 3.

90. For more on the way the regime fetishized artificial fabrics, see Karen Pinkus, *Bodily Regimes: Italian Advertising Under Fascism* (University of Minnesota Press, 1995).

91. See Jeffrey T. Schnapp's work tracing Marinetti's correspondence at the Beinecke, published in "The Fabric of Modern Times," *Critical Inquiry* 24, no. 1 (October 1997): 196, 197, https://doi.org /10.1086/448872.

92. *PVL*, unpaginated. For an analysis of the puerile in relation to Fascist rhetorics of virility, see Spackman, "Fascist Puerility."

93. *PVL*, closing verse.

94. *PVL*.

95. For an early analysis of aeropoetry in English by one of Futurism's most consistent commentators, see Willard Bohn, "The Poetics of Flight: Futurist 'Aeropoesia,'" *MLN* 121, no. 1 (2006): 207–24.

96. See Antonello, "Beyond Futurism," 321.

97. *PVL*.

98. *PVL*.

99. See Schnapp, "The Fabric of Modern Times," 237.

100. *PVL*. Quicklime was likely used in ancient naval warfare as a blinding agent; on the other hand, quicklime was used to plaster the hair in nineteenth-century Somalia.

101. *PVL*.

102. See Klaus Theweleit, *Male Fantasies, Volume 1* (University of Minnesota Press, 1987).

103. *PVL*.

104. Schnapp, "The Fabric of Modern Times," 238.

105. In the 1918 poem "Love—Chemical Relationship," the Baroness cast the two "characters," the young Marcel Duchamp as "A Futurist" and herself as "A Future Futurist." See Elsa von Freytag-Loringhoven, *Body Sweats: The Uncensored Writings of Elsa von Freytag-Loringhoven*, ed. Irene Gammel and Suzanne Zelazo (MIT Press, 2011), 253, hereafter *BS*.

1. WIRELESS IMAGINATION

106. See Amelia Jones, *Irrational Modernism: A Neurasthenic History of New York Dada* (MIT Press, 2004), for this proposition and an avant-garde inclusive of "the messy, subjective, and disorderly practices identified in some way with irrationality, often . . . by proximity to the creative bodies of women, queers, colored, and/or otherwise 'grotesque' subjects" (25–26).

107. Irene Gammel, *Baroness Elsa: Gender, Dada, and Everyday Modernity: A Cultural Biography* (MIT Press, 2003), 108.

108. Quoted in Gammel, *Baroness Elsa*, 156.

109. Gammel, *Baroness Elsa*, 8, 3, 6, 10.

110. Quoted in Gammel, *Baroness Elsa*, 351.

111. Quoted in Gammel, *Baroness Elsa*, 350.

112. *BS*, 270.

113. *BS*, 91–2.

114. See *BS*, 350n.

115. See the chapter on the Mostra Augustea della Romanità in Joshua Arthurs, *Excavating Modernity: The Roman Past in Fascist Italy* (Cornell University Press, 2012), 91–124.

116. "Logos," *transition* 16–17 (June 1929): 25–27. Reprinted in Eugène Jolas, *Eugene Jolas: Critical Writings, 1924–1951* (Northwestern University Press, 2009). See also Gammel, *Baroness Elsa*, 388.

117. Manuscript housed at the Beinecke quoted in Kelbert, "Eugene Jolas: A Poet of Multilingualism," *L2 Journal* 7, no. 1 (2015): 51.

118. For the "Pentecostal word" and for an extended discussion of the differing modes of multilingualism proposed by Jolas's poetry, see Eugenia Kelbert, who cites from the Eugene and Maria Jolas Papers at the Beinecke Library: "Eugene Jolas: A Poet of Multilingualism," 52. For the description of Atlantica, see Jolas, *Eugene Jolas*, 284.

119. Eugéne Jolas, "Super-Occident," *transition* 15 (February 1929): 15.

120. C. K. Ogden, *Debabelization: With a Survey of Contemporary Opinion on the Problem of a Universal Language* (Kegan Paul, Trench, 1931). For relations between Joyce and Jolas, see Jean-Michel Rabaté, "Joyce and Jolas: Late Modernism and Early Babelism," *Journal of Modern Literature* 22, no. 2 (Winter 1998–1999): 245–52.

121. Emily Apter, *The Translation Zone: A New Comparative Literature* (Princeton University Press, 2006), 52.

122. "Technical Manifesto of Futurist Literature," in *TIF*, 50.

123. The published version of the poem appears in *BS*, 195.

124. Had Elsa von Freytag-Loringhoven and her agent, literary executor, friend, and lover Djuna Barnes succeeded in pulling together a collection of her poetry before her untimely 1927 death at age fifty-three, we might have some definitive idea of the Baroness's ultimate intention for what would appear fixed on the page. Regardless, her life's work in restless, revisionary manuscript, readymades, ephemeral assemblages, and shock-costumed spontaneities at every imaginable locus—from the offices of the *Little Review* to Broadway subway stations and the French Consulate in Berlin—suggests that fixing was contrary to her nature. So does the poem itself. For the "mother of Dada" reference, see Robert Reiss, "'My Baroness'": Elsa von Freytag-Loringhoven," in *New York Dada*, ed. Rudolf E. Kuenzli (Willis Locker & Owens, 1986), 81. In the case of "X-RAY," I have paid attention to the variants housed at Elsa Von Freytag-Loringhoven, "Xray—The Versioning Machine 5.0," accessed April 9, 2024, https://digitalmitford.org/v-machine/samples/xray.html.

125. See Gammel, *Baroness Elsa*, 161. She gave the work to her friends, the Chicagoan pianist Allen Tanner and Russian painter Pavel Tchelitchew, while living in Berlin in 1923 in gratitude for their financial support. See Gammel, *Baroness Elsa*, 323.

126. Daniel Headrick, *The Invisible Weapon: Telecommunications and International Politics, 1851–1945* (Oxford University Press, 1991), 116.

127. *BS*, 49–50.

128. Quoted in Gammel, *Baroness Elsa*, 351.

129. Quoted in Gammel, *Baroness Elsa*, 352.

130. From "A Dozen Cocktails—Please," in von Freytag-Loringhoven, *BS*, 50.

131. *BS*, 270.

132. *BS*, 270–71.

133. *BS*, 271. The translation is by the editors of the volume and appears on p. 388n but has been altered by me to reflect the English term and to imagine a defamiliarized English in which the Baroness herself might translate.

134. *BS*, 271–72.

135. Quoted in *BS*, 388n.

136. Kenneth Rexroth remembered asking Duchamp whether he considered the Baroness a Futurist or a Dadaist, and his response was: "She is not a Futurist. She is the future." See Kenneth Rexroth, *American Poetry in the Twentieth Century* (Herder & Herder, 1971), 77.

137. *BS*, 225.

2. ANTIFASCIST PHILOLOGY AND THE REJECTION OF LINGUISTIC PURITY IN EMILIO VILLA

1. Emilio Villa, "Sulla traduzione dei testi biblici," *Il verri* 43, nos. 7–8 (November 1998): 13. Translations from this piece, as with all other unattributed translations in the book, are mine.

2. See Villa's commentary on 1:2 in Emilio Villa, "Genesi [Traduzione e note di commento]," circa 1953–1985, Archivio Emilio Villa, Biblioteca Panizzi.

3. Villa, "Sulla traduzione dei testi biblici," 13.

4. Notes to typescript prepared for Feltrinelli, Archivio Emilio Villa, Biblioteca Panizzi.

5. Adriana Cavarero, *For More Than One Voice: Toward a Philosophy of Vocal Expression*, trans. Paul A. Kottman (Stanford University Press, 2005), 20. *Qol*, signifier of the acoustic sphere, is present in the Psalms, Cavarero explains. Note that I have re-translated the title to reflect the polyphonic implications of Cavarero's original title.

6. Cavarero, *For More Than One Voice*, 20. For another example of ruach's interpretation through the ages, see James Arthur Diamond, "Maimonides, Spinoza, and Buber Read the Hebrew Bible: The Hermeneutical Keys of Divine 'Fire' and 'Spirit' (Ruach)," *The Journal of Religion* 91, no. 3 (2011): 320–43, https://doi.org/10.1086/659772.

7. Villa, "Genesi [Traduzione e note di commento]." I have left out the Italian here only because translating it was relatively straightforward.

8. Villa, "Genesi [Traduzione e note di commento]."

9. My understanding of the Hebrew text and its exegesis is indebted to readings from and conversations with Rachel Havrelock, author of *River Jordan: The Mythology of a Dividing Line* (University of Chicago Press, 2011) and *The Joshua Generation: Israeli Occupation and the Bible* (Princeton University Press, 2020), and Ilana Pardes, author of *Countertraditions in the Bible: A Feminist Approach* (Harvard University Press, 1992).

10. Villa, "Genesi [Traduzione e note di commento]." Notes to unpublished typescript prepared for Feltrinelli, Archivio Emilio Villa, Biblioteca Panizzi.

11. Cecilia Bello Minciacchi, editor of his *Proverbi e Cantico*, insists on the "absolute secularity" of Villa's work with those biblical texts. Cecilia Bello Minciacchi, ed., *Proverbi e Cantico: Traduzioni dalla Bibbia*, trans. Emilio Villa (Bibliopolis, 2004), 9.

12. Villa, notes to "Genesi" not included in *Il verri*'s printing of "Sulla traduzione dei testi biblici," "Genesi [Traduzione e note di commento]," Archivio Emilio Villa, Biblioteca Panizzi.

13. Villa, "Sulla traduzione dei testi biblici," 13.

14. Resonance of this story in the story of Zipporah ("bird" in Hebrew) is brought out in Pardes, *Countertraditions in the Bible*, 79–97.

15. Emilio Villa, "L'Enuma Eliš (Tavola I)," *Letteratura* 3, no. 3 (July 1939): 24n.

16. See for instance Carolyn Valone, "The Pentecost: Image and Experience in Late Sixteenth-Century Rome," *The Sixteenth Century Journal* 24, no. 4 (1993): 801–28, https://doi.org/10.2307/2541602. Valone's intention is to trace the work of the popes to unite the churches of East and West and to practice conversion in the East and the so-called New World.

17. Ashon T. Crawley, *Blackpentecostal Breath: The Aesthetics of Possibility* (Fordham University Press, 2016), 212, 216, 217.

18. Emilio Villa, "Sopra il ritorno al canto," *Il Frontespizio* (1937).

19. "Note sul concetto di senso," unpublished manuscript, circa 1960–1970, Archivio Emilio Villa, Biblioteca Panizzi.

20. Unpublished manuscript, Archivio Emilio Villa, Biblioteca Panizzi.

21. Andrea Zanzotto, "Come sta Villa?," *Il verri* 43, nos. 7–8 (November 1998): 60. For a thorough treatment of the relation between the two writers, see Chiara Portesine, "Un 'Orfeo robot.' Zanzotto a contatto con lo sperimentalismo laterale di Villa," in *Emilio Villa e i suoi tempi: Finestre per la monade*, ed. Aldo Tagliaferri and Chiara Portesine (Mimesis, 2016), 43–174.

22. Zanzotto, "Come sta Villa?," 61.

23. See Emilio Villa, trans., *Antico teatro ebraico: Giobbe, Cantico dei Cantici, a cura di Emilio Villa* (Poligono Società Editrice, 1947), and Minciacchi, ed., *Proverbi e Cantico*, as well as the notes and fragment of Genesis 3 within a dossier dedicated to Villa and edited by Aldo Tagliaferri, *Il verri* 43, nos. 7–8 (November 1998): 8–25.

24. Villa, "Sulla traduzione dei testi biblici," 18, 19.

25. Villa, "Genesi [Traduzione e note di commento]," Archivio Emilio Villa, Biblioteca Panizzi.

26. Robert Alter, *Genesis* (W.W. Norton, 1997).

27. Villa, "Sulla traduzione dei testi biblici," 12.

28. Villa, "Sulla traduzione dei testi biblici," 14n.

29. Villa, "Genesi [Traduzione e note di commento]," typescript.

30. Villa, "L'Enuma Eliš (Tavola I)," 3.

31. Villa, "Genesi [Traduzione e note di commento]."

32. Rachel Havrelock argues that this separation narrative is part of a priestly myth that establishes the need to maintain social dualities between human and divine, Israel and other nations, holy and profane, and pure and impure. See Havrelock, *River Jordan*, 8.

33. For Villa's 1974 petition to Milanese friends in the editorial world aimed at publishing the project, see the manuscript in the Archivio Villa at the Biblioteca Panizzi, cited in Aldo Tagliaferri, in his headnote to Villa's "Sulla traduzione dei testi biblici," 9.

34. Tagliaferri, headnote to Villa's "Sulla traduzione dei testi biblici," 9.

35. Villa, "Genesi [Traduzione e note di commento]."

36. Villa, "Sulla traduzione dei testi biblici," 13.

37. For English-language treatments of this genealogy, see Stefan Arvidsson, *Aryan Idols: Indo-European Mythology as Ideology and Science* (University of Chicago Press, 2006); Bruce Lincoln, *Theorizing Myth: Narrative, Ideology, and Scholarship* (University of Chicago Press, 2000); George L. Mosse, *Toward the Final Solution: A History of European Racism* (University of Wisconsin Press, 1985); Maurice Olender, *The Languages of Paradise: Aryans and Semites, a Match Made in Heaven*, rev. and augm. ed. (Other Press, 2002); Martin Bernal, *Black Athena: The Afroasiatic Roots of Classical Civilization* (Rutgers University Press, 1987); and Léon Poliakov, *The Aryan Myth: A History of Racist and Nationalist Ideas in Europe* (New American Library, 1977).

2. ANTIFASCIST PHILOLOGY ❧ 329

38. See Alfredo Trombetti, *L'unità d'origine del linguaggio* (Libreria Treves di Luigi Beltrami, 1905). Aldo Tagliaferri notes that Villa had begun an essay on Trombetti in *Il clandestino: Vita e opere di Emilio Villa* (Mimesis, 2016), 31.

39. James B. Pritchard, *Ancient Near Eastern Texts Relating to the Old Testament with Supplement* (Princeton University Press, 2016).

40. For a particularly sensitive treatment of the continuum between poetry and criticism in Villa's oeuvre, see Chiara Portesine, "Un sistema di rischi e possibilità: Emilio Villa e la sfida oracolare alla prosa critica," *L'Ulisse* 21 (October 10, 2018): 97–109.

41. Cecilia Bello Minciacchi, "Emilio Villa, l'esilio nella lingua," *Avanguardia* 25, no. 74 (January 2020): 124. Villa's journal explicitly refused the label "avant-garde," calling the tendency out as "drowning in a boring confusion of superficiality, exhibitionism, and forgeries"; see Emilio Villa, *Appia antica. Atlante di arte nuova* 1 (July 1959), headnote.

42. Zanzotto, "Come sta Villa?," 60. Chiara Portesine rightly points out, however, that in excessively accentuating the figure of the "clandestine" artist, Villa scholarship has lost opportunities to trace connections with his contemporaries—a labor she begins to take up. See Chiara Portesine, "The Flippant Ball-Feel e l' «armonia dinamica»," *Diaforia* 18 (March 2017): 163–64.

43. See Anton Deimel, *Šumerisch—Akkadisches glossar* [1934] (Verlag des Päpstl. Bibelinstituts, 1962), with annotated copy in the Archivio Emilio Villa at the Biblioteca Panizzi.

44. See Ernesto Buonaiuti, *Storia del cristianesimo* (Corbaccio, 1943), as well as the anonymous works he later claimed credit for: *Lettere di un prete modernista* (Libreria editrice Romana, 1908) and Ernesto Buonaiuti, *The Programme of Modernism: A Reply to the Encyclical of Pius X, Pascendi Dominici Gregis* (T. Fisher Unwin, 1908). For information on Villa's work devoted to "Trombetti (teorista monogenista del linguaggio)," see the most complete biographical account of his life to date: that of Tagliaferri, in *Il clandestino*, 31—this biography unfortunately lacks notes.

45. For this episode, see Tagliaferri, *Il clandestino*, 50.

46. This article of December 1941 is quoted in Tagliaferri, *Il clandestino*, 29–30.

47. The Biblioteca Panizzi keeps the most complete bibliography of these writings in their inventory for the Archivio Emilio Villa.

48. For this precious narrative of his life during the war, see Tagliaferri, *Il clandestino*, 39–41.

49. A telling statement of Villa's lasting ties to the modernist spirit of the autonomy of art appears in a text titled "Essential notes on poetics": "in the face of the imposing coercive communications media, of the vastness of bourgeois exhibitionism, of the visceral search for public consensus, of the stockpiling of (a-expressive) cultural consumption of the masses (class-men) on the part of current economic and political powers, poetic writing, originary Writing demands the freedom of being for itself and against, of not collaborating, of not communicating, of being . . . nature and condition of its own self-constitution." Quoted in Portesine, "Un 'Orfeo robot,'" 88. Translation here, as elsewhere, is my own.

50. Emilio Villa, *Conferenza* [1984], with a preface by Aldo Tagliaferri (Coliseum, 1997), 44.

51. See Tommaso Tittoni, "La difesa della lingua italiana," *Nuova Antologia* 61 (1926): 377–87, as well as Gabriella Klein, "L'italianità della lingua e l'Accademia d'Italia. Sulla politica linguistica fascista," *Quaderni Storici* 16, no. 47 (2) (August 1981): 639–75. See also Ruth Ben-Ghiat, "Language and the Construction of National Identity in Fascist Italy," *The European Legacy, Toward New Paradigms* 2, no. 3 (1997): 438–43, https://doi.org/10.1080/10848779708579754.

52. Ben-Ghiat, "Language and the Construction of National Identity in Fascist Italy," 440.

53. See Fabio Zinelli, "Una «lamentosa cosmogonia supposta con la semplice innocenza di materiali usuali». Emilio Villa Lombardo," in *Letteratura e filologia tra Svizzera e Italia: Studi in onore di Guglielmo Gorni* (Edizioni di Storia e Letteratura, 2010), 249–71.

54. Emilio Villa, *L'opera poetica*, ed. Cecilia Bello Minciacchi (L'Orma, 2014), 115. This volume will be referred to as *OP*.

2. ANTIFASCIST PHILOLOGY

55. *OP*, 115.

56. Cover of Emilio Villa, *Green* (La nuova foglio, 1971).

57. Tagliaferri, *Il clandestino*, 211.

58. Emilio Villa, *Brunt H: Options: 17 Eschatological Madrigals Captured by a Sweetromatic Cyberne-togamig Vampire, by Villadrome* (Foglio editrice d'arte, 1968). Various page spreads may be found online.

59. Villa, *Brunt H*, unpaginated.

60. See "La Tenzone" (1948), in *OP*, 309.

61. Manzoni was elected president of a commission of the young government of Italy aimed at pro-pounding the Florentine dialect as national tongue (which had little success in a country with an 80 percent illiteracy rate). He would be challenged by, among others, Graziadio Isaia Ascoli, founder of the journal *Archivio glottologico italiano*, who believed that the national language needed to be disseminated through school, where dialects would need to be a starting point for instruction.

62. Gramsci criticized the laissez-faire attitude toward subaltern populations implicit in Gentile's subtraction of grammar from school curricula, seeing in grammar a route toward betterment. See "Questa tavola rotonda è quadrata," in Antonio Gramsci, *Quaderni del carcere*, vol. 3 (Einaudi, 2014), 2349.

63. For an exhaustive English-language analysis of the role of language and of the relation of Grams-ci's background in linguistics to his political philosophy, see Peter Ives, *Language and Hegemony in Gramsci* (Pluto, 2004).

64. Gramsci, *Quaderni del carcere*, vol. 3, 2345. See also Antonio Gramsci, *Selections from Cultural Writings*, ed. David Forgacs and Geoffrey Nowell-Smith, trans. William Boelhower (Harvard University Press, 1985), 27.

65. Gramsci, *Quaderni del carcere*, vol. 3, 2343, 2350.

66. Gramsci, *Quaderni del carcere*, vol. 2, 1376–78.

67. Gramsci, *Quaderni del carcere*, vol. 3, 2344.

68. Gramsci, *Quaderni del carcere*, vol. 2, 1376.

69. Gramsci, *Quaderni del carcere*, vol. 3, 2345.

70. Gabriele D'Annunzio, *Italia o Morte. La Pentecoste d'Italia* (La Fionda, 1919), 46.

71. These two articles were republished, with Villa's preceding Marinetti's and a jocose editorial state-ment, in a limited-edition chapbook of two hundred copies by Luciano Caruso and Stelio Maria Martini as Emilio Villa and F. T. Marinetti, *Dannunziana* (Visual Art Center, 1974). For these cita-tions, see pp. 21, 17, and 24. Original texts published in *Letteratura* 3, no. 4 (October 1939).

72. Villa and Marinetti, *Dannunziana*, 10.

73. Stefan Arvidsson, *Aryan Idols*, 179.

74. Villa and Marinetti, *Dannunziana*, 16.

75. Villa and Marinetti, *Dannunziana*, 3.

76. See the text *Poesia è, quaderni del Fondo Moravia*, no. 1 (2002): 23–4. It was later collected in Emilio Villa, *The Selected Poetry of Emilio Villa*, ed. Dominic Edward Siracusa (Contra Mundum Press, 2014), 579–92.

77. *OP*, 85, 88. Minciacchi compares Villa to the soldier in his verse, but I would emphasize the rebel-lious poet's heavily ironic stance toward this dead and servile soldier, which refuses identification. See Cecilia Bello Minciacchi, "Emilio Villa, l'esilio nella lingua," accessed July 13, 2022, https://iris.uniroma1.it/handle/11573/1544842.

78. See Aldo Tagliaferri, *Presentimenti del mondo senza tempo: Scritti su Emilio Villa*, ed. Gian Paolo Renello (Argolibri, 2022), for instance, 45, and Gian Paolo Renello's preface, 20.

79. Andrea Cortellessa, "Poesia informe?," in *Emilio Villa: Poeta e scrittore*, ed. Claudio Parmiggiani (Mazzotta, 2008), 46.

80. Quoted in *OP*, 307.

2. ANTIFASCIST PHILOLOGY ☙ 331

81. Instituto Lina Bo e P. M. Bardi, Casa de Vidro, Pietro M. Bardi, Arquivo Documental, poem included in undated letter from Villa to Bardi.

82. Villa, poem included in undated letter to Bardi.

83. Although I have lectured on this topic, this is not the place to delve into Bardi's spotty history of complicity within the regime, as he did sign on to the Fascist Party and advocated vociferously—to the point of falling into disgrace with the authorities—for Rationalist architecture and modernist ideals; Bardi had had a gallery in Milan and founded the Studio d'Arte Palma in Rome in 1944, a few months before the city's liberation by the Allies. For a thorough reflection on this, see Adrian Anagnost, "Limitless Museum: P. M. Bardi's Aesthetic Reeducation," *Modernism/Modernity Print Plus*, December 27, 2019, https://modernismmodernity.org/articles/anagnost-limitless-museum.

84. Brazil's place in the geopolitical context was complex, to say the least. At the outbreak of the war, the only overseas nations hosting flights to Brazil were Italy and Germany, and they were coaxed to allow these flights to operate until American air fields were put into place; nonetheless, Brazil was coaxed to enter the war on the side of the Allies in 1944 and was the only South American nation to send troops overseas.

85. Pietro Maria Bardi, "Para uma nova cultura do omem," *Habitat* 2 (November): 1–2, translation mine.

86. Bardi, "Para uma nova cultura do omem," 2.

87. S. M. Caffey, and G. Campagnol, "Dis/Solution: Lina Bo Bardi's Museu de Arte de São Paulo," *Journal of Conservation and Museum Studies* 13, no. 1 (2015): 5, http://dx.doi.org/10.5334/jcms.1021221.

88. This may be a developing field. Following the international conference on Emilio Villa and Brazil (O Continente Involuntário) of November 2024 in which I presented fragments of this chapter, there is an edited collection in press placing Emilio Villa in a transatlantic context: Gianluca Rizzo, ed., *Emilio Villa visto da entrambe le sponde dell'Atlantico* (Editrice ZONA, 2024).

89. See Adriano Spatola, *Toward Total Poetry*, trans. Guy Bennett and Brendan W. Hennessey (Otis/ Seismicity Editions, 2008), 19. On the relationship between typographically innovative modernist poetry and structuralist linguistics, see Johanna Drucker, *The Visible Word: Experimental Typography and Modern Art* (University of Chicago Press, 1994). For an art-historical treatment of the postwar turn in the visual arts toward language and informational representative strategies, see Eve Meltzer, "The Dream of the Information World," *Oxford Art Journal* 29, no. 1 (2006): 115–35; the broader argument has since been published in Eve Meltzer, *Systems We Have Loved: Conceptual Art, Affect, and The Antihumanist Turn* (University of Chicago Press, 2013).

90. See Villa's letters to Bardi at the Bardi Foundation, São Paulo, April 19, 1949, and October 5, 1951.

91. Villa, *Green*, cover.

92. Theory of Tables and Figures, for the "1ST MEDITERRANEAN CULTURES after 1000 A.C." panels, Acervo do Centro de Pesquisa do Museu de Arte de São Paulo Assis Chateaubriand. Translation from Italian text mine.

93. See Bruno Migliorini, *Storia della lingua italiana* (Sansoni, 1960) and Bruno Migliorini, *Manuale di Esperanto* [1922], ed. Renato Corsetti (Cooperativa Editoriale Esperanto, 1995), https://www .esperanto.it/wp-content/uploads/2019/08/Bruno-Migliorini-MANUALE-ESPERANTO.pdf

94. Klein, "L'italianità della lingua," 643–44.

95. Emilio Villa, "Os puristas são enfadonhos e inúteis (Purists Are Irksome and Futile)," *Habitat* 7 (July 1952): 1, 2. Original text in Portuguese; translation mine.

96. Villa, "Os puristas são enfadonhos e inúteis," 1, 2.

97. Villa, "Os puristas são enfadonhos e inúteis," 2.

98. Tagliaferri, *Il clandestino*, 85.

99. Villa, *Conferenza*, 46.

100. I have some confidence that the experiments of Noigandres would have had an absorptive influence on Villa, though in an email message of July 26, 2019, Augusto de Campos assured me that the only member of that group with whom Villa had direct contact was the Roman-born Waldemar Cordeiro, and my conclusion is simply that more research needs to be done in this vein.

101. Crawley, *Blackpentecostal Breath*, 212, 216, 217.

102. Carlo Mascaretti, *Et ab hic et ab hoc: Stranezze, bizzarrie, scherzi e bisticci letterari*, 12 vols. (Unione Tipografico-Editrice Torinese, 1915–1934). See also Jean Guiart, *Les religions de l'Oceanie* (Presses Universitaires de France, 1962).

103. Aldo Tagliaferri, "Su E. Villa," *Il verri* 43, nos. 7–8 (November 1998). The "Scrittura / germinante" quote is from *Attributi dell'arte odierna*, 127.

104. Emilio Villa, *17 variazioni su temi proposti per una pura ideologia fonetica*, with plates by Alberto Burri (Edizioni d'Origine, 1955).

105. Giulio Busi, "Datene notizia ad Abramo il Bandito. Il laboratorio biblico di Emilio Villa," in *Emilio Villa: Poeta e scrittore*, 17. See also Giancarlo Lacerenza, "Villa traduttore della *Bibbia* ebraica," in *Segnare un secolo. Emilio Villa: La parola, l'immagine* (DeriveApprodi, 2007), 49–70. Lacerenza notes that a certain "Emilio Villa" contributed twice on "Aryan, or Indo-European" languages to the outwardly Fascist journal *La difesa della razza* in 1938–1939 and sporadically contributed on ancient languages to the Fascist journal *Il Meridiano di Roma* in 1937–1938. Tagliaferri attests that these texts were by another scholar, unrelated to Villa.

106. Active between Milan and Rome from 1950 to 1958, Gruppo Origine dissolved after one group show at the Galleria Origine in Rome but transmuted quickly into the Fondazione Origine, with its related journal, *Arti visive*. The group, embracing the nonfigurative, opposed what they viewed as the decorative tendencies in abstraction, as well as the progressivist utopia of the Fronte Nuovo delle Arti. For an account of the postwar interest in Genesis on the part of Abstract Expressionists, see Robert Rosenblum, "The Abstract Sublime," *Art News* 59, no. 10 (February 1961), 350–359. For more background on Villa's interest in origins, see Tagliaferri's afterword to Emilio Villa, "Il Testo e il contesto," in *L'arte dell'uomo primordiale* (Abscondita, 2005), 107–23.

107. Reprinted in *OP*, 153.

108. See "Ciò che è primitivo," in Villa, *L'arte dell'uomo primordiale*, 90, and 89–92, first published in May 1953 in Fondazione Origine's journal, *Arte visiva*.

109. Villa, *L'arte dell'uomo primordiale*, 90.

110. Villa, *L'arte dell'uomo primordiale*, 92.

111. Villa, *L'arte dell'uomo primordiale*, 57; see also 60–61.

112. Villa, *L'arte dell'uomo primordiale*, 15–19.

113. Villa, "Sulla traduzione dei testi biblici," 19.

114. From a January 1973 article in the weekly *Tempo*, Emilio Villa, quoted by Aldo Tagliaferri in his introduction to *Odissea* (1964), trans. Emilio Villa (Derive Approdi, 2005), 8.

115. Emilio Villa, "Progetto per un nuovo Dizionario etimologico," in *Emilio Villa: Poeta e scrittore*, 388.

116. Villa, "Progetto per un nuovo Dizionario etimologico," 385.

117. Ernest Fenollosa et al., *The Chinese Written Character as a Medium for Poetry* (Fordham University Press, 2010), 41, 42.

118. Villa, "Progetto per un nuovo Dizionario etimologico," 385.

119. Giovanni Semerano, *Le origini della cultura europea: Rivelazioni della linguistica storica* (Leo S. Olschki, 1984); and in English translation, Giovanni Semerano, *The Origins of European Culture: English Translation of the Introduction to the Second Volume: Etymological Dictionaries*, trans. Eleanor Daunt (Leo S. Olschki, 1996).

120. Quoted in Tagliaferri, *Il clandestino*, 57. See Alessandro Manzoni, *I promessi sposi. Storia Milanese del secolo XVII scoperta e rifatta da Alessandro Manzoni*, vol. 3 (Baudry, 1828), 260.

121. I am grateful to Claudio Sansone for conversations surrounding the accuracy (or lack thereof) and intrigue of these interpretations.

122. See Fenollosa's first examples, in Fenollosa et al., *The Chinese Written Character as a Medium for Poetry*, 44–46.

123. Fenollosa et al., *The Chinese Written Character as a Medium for Poetry*, 54, 55, 51.

2. ANTIFASCIST PHILOLOGY   333

124. Emilio Villa, editor's note signed "e.v.," *Appia Antica* 1 (July 1959): 15.

125. This text was eventually republished with the date 1957 as "allusion et," part of the translingual *Heurarium / Emilio Villa 1947–1961* (Edizioni Ex, 1961), 38–39.

126. John Keats, "Ode to Psyche," in *The Odes of John Keats*, ed. Helen Vendler (Harvard University Press, 1985), 45.

127. As such, it seems to answer Mallarmé's nostalgia in "The Crisis of Verse" for "the primacy of the perceptible rhythm of respiration or the classic lyric breath." Stéphane Mallarmé, "Crisis of Verse," in *Divagations* [1897], trans. Barbara Johnson (Belknap, 2007), 208. Jacobus discusses the implications of Twombly's 1957 assertion that he had been reading Mallarmé. See Mary Jacobus, *Reading Cy Twombly: Poetry in Paint* (Princeton University Press, 2016), 82–87.

128. Emilio Villa, "Cy Twombly: Talento bianco," *Appia Antica* 1 (July 1959): 36. Reproduced in Emilio Villa, *Attributi dell'arte odierna: 1947–1967*, vol. 1, 127. All translations in this text are my own unless otherwise noted.

129. This phrase is Ezra Pound's: he described the Cantos as needing to be integrated "as reading matter, singing matter, shouting matter, the tale of the tribe." Pound borrowed the formulation from Rudyard Kipling, who at an address to the Royal Academy Dinner of 1906 described the poet's role in producing the "Record of the Tribe," describing a people's common beliefs, values, and unifying myths. For a thorough analysis of this phenomenon and how it relates to Pound's forging of a new epic, see Michael André Bernstein, *The Tale of the Tribe: Ezra Pound and the Modern Verse Epic* (Princeton University Press, 2014).

130. Roland Barthes, "Cy Twombly: Works on Paper," in *The Responsibility of Forms: Critical Essays on Music, Art, and Representation*, trans. Richard Howard (University of California Press, 1985), 161. This essay hails from 1979.

131. In a now famed anecdote, "Twombly recalls . . . that [while still in the army as a cryptographer] he often drew at night, with lights out, perfecting a kind of meandering and imprecise graphology for which he would shortly be esteemed." See Robert Pincus-Witten, "Learning to Write," in *Cy Twombly: Paintings and Drawings* (Milwaukee Art Center, 1968), n.p. Reprinted in *Eye to Eye: Twenty Years of Art Criticism* (UMI Research Press, 1984), 87–91.

132. Jacobus sets out to read Twombly through cryptography, but given the methodological difficulties of knowing exactly what Twombly did in the US Army, her chapter falls back on a discussion of blankness and the signature/gesture in general. Mary Jacobus, *Reading Cy Twombly: Poetry in Paint* (Princeton University Press, 2016), 81–102.

133. Villa, "Cy Twombly," 36; Villa, *Attributi dell'arte odierna*, 125.

134. Emilio Villa, "Cy Twombly: Talento bianco," *Appia Antica* 1 (July 1959): 36.

135. This part of the text was first published in *Cy Twombly, e una parafrasi per Cy Twombly di Emilio Villa* (Galleria La Tartaruga, 1961) and is reprinted in Aldo Tagliaferri, ed., *Attributi dell'arte odierna: 1947–1967, Nuova edizione ampliata*, vol. 1 (Le Lettere, 2008), 127, where the date 1957 is given without explanation and is possibly incorrect because it differs from the date given in the notes to the text in vol. 2, 384. *Attributi* was originally published in 1970, and the selections and edits are chiefly Villa's own.

136. Villa, revised poem as printed in Tagliaferri, ed., *Attributi*, 124, 126.

137. Villa, revised poem as printed in Tagliaferri, ed., *Attributi*, 127.

138. Keats, "Ode to Psyche," 44.

139. See the reproduction of Duchamp's postcard of June 3, 1963, to Villa from Etna, and "Marcel Duchamp: In Memoriam," in *Emilio Villa: Poeta e scrittore*, 186–87.

140. Katrina Martin, "Marcel Duchamp's *Anémic Cinéma*," *Studio International* 189, no. 973 (January–February 1975): 53–60. Martin performs a thorough reading of each roto-relief in a way I cannot do justice to in this space.

141. Marcel Duchamp, *The Writings of Marcel Duchamp*, ed. Michael Sanouillet and Elmer Peterson (Da Capo, 1989), 31.

334 ~~ 2. ANTIFASCIST PHILOLOGY

142. Another version in hot pink, orange, yellow, and black exists at the Fondazione Bonotto, but I have not been able to see it in person.

143. From a 1970 manifesto broadside by Emilio Villa, Silvio Craia, and Giorgio Cegna, Galleria Il Centro, Napoli, held at the Fondazione Caruso, Florence.

144. Emilio Villa, Silvio Craia, and Giorgio Cegna, *Idrologie, con 6 serigrafie: Galleria Il Centro, Napoli, 16 Febbraio 1970* (Edar, 1969).

145. Emilio Villa, Silvio Craia, and Giorgio Cegna, *Le Idrologie* (Foglio OG, 1968).

146. Villa's text, unpaginated, is the same in both Edar and Foglio OG editions, although in the former, it is partly redoubled in the dizzying two-tone type.

147. Villa, text for *Idrologie*, both editions.

148. Villa, text for *Idrologie*, both editions.

3. AMELIA ROSSELLI'S DISINTEGRATING CANTO(N)S AND THE HOLY GHOST OF PARENTAL TONGUES

1. See Carlo Rosselli, *Socialismo liberale* (Edizioni U, 1945), 5. Carlo Rosselli's political thought is encapsulated in this 1930 volume calling for a reformed socialism inspired by the Risorgimento of Mazzini, English Labourism, and Scandinavian social democracies.

2. Piero Calamandrei, *Inventario della casa di campagna* (Le Monnier, 1941), 258.

3. Istituto Storico della Resistenza in Toscana (ISRT), Firenze, Fondo Piero Calamandrei, Amelia Rosselli a Piero Calamandrei, Larchmont, December 12, 1945. Translation from Italian here and throughout my own unless otherwise indicated.

4. On these relationships to the latest developments in musicology, see for example Valentina Peleggi, "Amelia Rosselli: Musica in poesia," *Quaderni del Circolo Rosselli* 30, no. 107 (2010): 67–104; Chiara Carpita, "'Spazi metrici' tra post-webernismo, etnomusicologia, gestalttheorie ed astrattismo. Sulle fonti extra-letterarie del 'nuovo geometrismo' di Amelia Rosselli," *Moderna* 15, no. 2 (2013): 61–105; and Laura Barile, "'Trasposizioni': I due mestieri di Amelia Rosselli," *California Italian Studies* 8, no. 1 (2018), https://doi.org/10.5070/C381038273. Barile does a thorough job of laying out the postwar interest in subaltern cultures by intellectuals frequented by Rosselli. I previously published in English on Rosselli's relation to musicology in "'Cantonidisintegratidella / miavita': Closure and Implosion of the Canto(n) in Amelia Rosselli, and the Dream (or Nightmare) of a Transnational Language," *Moderna* 15, no. 2 (2013): 131–54. Since this publication, a more extensive bibliography on Rosselli and musicology has appeared in Emmanuela Tandello's introduction to Amelia Rosselli, *Due parole per chiederti notizie: Lettere (inedite) a David Tudor*, ed. Roberto Gigliucci (Fondazione Giorgio e Lilli Devoto, 2015), 12–14.

5. Amelia Rosselli in Adele Cambria, "Un armadio tutto per sé," in Amelia Rosselli, *È vostra la vita che ho perso. Conversazioni e interviste 1963–1995*, ed. Monica Venturini and Silvia De March, preface by Laura Barile (Le Lettere, 2010), 61. Hereafter, this volume will be referred to as *CI*. Rosselli later claimed that she left music around 1965. See also the correspondence, biography, and bibliography surrounding "La serie degli armonici" at the Fondo Rosselli in Pavia.

6. Amelia Rosselli, "Musica e poesia: Dibattito su Dorazio," in *Una scrittura plurale: Saggi e interventi critici*, ed. Francesca Caputo (Interlinea, 2004), 38. Hereafter, this volume will be referred to as *USP*.

7. See Alain Danielou, *Music and the Power of Sound: The Influence of Tuning and Interval on Consciousness* (Simon and Schuster, 1995)—first published in 1946 in English and then in 1959 in French.

8. She dated this "Diary in Three Tongues" to the mid-1950s, although it was only published belatedly with her other early writings in 1980. For an analysis of the difficulty of dating Rosselli's works and the reasoning behind the Meridiano edition's chronology of her career, see Stefano Giovannuzzi,

"Bilanci di un curatore tra filologia e pratica editoriale," *Prassi ecdotiche della modernità letteraria*, no. 2 (August 1, 2017): 143–67. In *Locomotrix*, which was published shortly before the collective Meridiano edition, the product of a team based in Italy and the United Kingdom with easier access to archives, I followed the chronology of Emmanuela Tandello's edition of Rosselli's collected poetry for Garzanti, which took the author at her word—an approach that can be justified, in my opinion, against all literary-historical positivism because the author's understanding and narrative of her development are itself essential factors in literary history. See Amelia Rosselli, *Le poesie*, ed. Emmanuela Tandello (Garzanti, 2016), hereafter *LP*. Because this remains the most accessible and nearly complete edition of Rosselli's poetry, available in more compact, economical, and digital editions for an international readership that will be reading this book, I will refer chiefly to it in this chapter despite its relative lack of philological attention, reserving the Meridiano edition of complete writings (*L'opera poetica*) for the rich scholarly apparatus and the additional texts that it restored to the public. Because *Locomotrix* is the one critical edition of Rosselli's selected works in English, containing a scholarly apparatus and a biography that can lead interested readers to new material, I will refer to it as English-language default rather than to the now numerous editions of individual Rosselli volumes that have arisen since by translators such as Gian Maria Annovi and Diana Thow, Deborah Woodward, and Giuseppe Leporace—a reception history that began with Amelia Rosselli, *War Variations*, trans. Lucia Re and Paul Vangelisti (Green Integer, 2005).

9. See Amelia Rosselli, *Locomotrix: Selected Poetry and Prose of Amelia Rosselli*, ed. and trans. Jennifer Scappettone (University of Chicago Press, 2012). Months after my anthology was published in the United States, the monumental Meridiano edition of Rosselli's poetry was finally issued in Italy: Amelia Rosselli, *L'opera poetica*, ed. Stefano Giovannuzzi (Mondadori, 2012), with crucial critical apparatuses from Francesco Carbognin, Chiara Carpita, Silvia De March, Gabriella Palli Baroni, and Emmanuela Tandello. That essential volume will hereafter be referred to as *OP* when its documentary contexts are most needed.

10. Isabelle Richet, "Marion Cave Rosselli and the Transnational Women's Antifascist Networks," *Journal of Women's History* 24, no. 3 (2012): 119, https://doi.org/10.1353/jowh.2012.0033. This work has been expanded as the full-scale biography, Isabelle Richet, *Women, Antifascism and Mussolini's Italy: The Life of Marion Cave Rosselli* (I.B. Tauris, 2018).

11. A 1944 interview with a daily paper in Larchmont, New York, quoted in Richet, "Marion Cave Rosselli and the Transnational Women's Antifascist Networks," 121.

12. See Ruth Nattermann, "The Female Side of War: The Experience and Memory of the Great War in Italian-Jewish Women's Ego-Documents," in *The Jewish Experience of the First World War*, ed. Edward Madigan and Gideon Reuveni (Palgrave Macmillan, 2018), 233–54. See also Patrizia Gabrielli, *Tempio di virilità: L'antifascismo, il genere, la storia* (FrancoAngeli, 2008) as well as Patrizia Gabrielli, *Col freddo nel cuore: Uomini e donne nell'emigrazione antifascista* (Donzelli, 2004).

13. See Isabelle Richet, "Marion Cave Rosselli and the Transnational Women's Antifascist Networks."

14. Letter to John Rosselli, November 13, 1952, Fondo Rosselli, Centro di ricerca sulla tradizione manoscritta di autori moderni e contemporanei, Università degli Studi di Pavia; hereafter Fondo Rosselli.

15. From a 1992 radio transmission with Gabriella Caramore and Emmanuella Tandello, printed in *CI*, 276.

16. For a study of the tendency by "upside-down intellectuals" from Pier Paolo Pasolini to Rocco Scotellaro to Danilo Dolci to reoccupy Mussolini's dictate to "go towards the people," see David Gutherz, "Towards the People: The Search for Subjugated Knowledges in Post-Fascist Italy" (PhD diss., University of Chicago, 2019).

17. In stressing the importance of the aural dimension as a harbor for totalizing possibilities, I am drawing a contrast with the "non meglio precisato visioni" that probably appeared to Rosselli for the first time in 1954, which in the first instance led to her recovery in a Swiss clinic—psychic disturbances that plagued her to the point of her suicide in 1996 and interrupted (rather than driving) her writing

practice. See for example Silvia De March, *Amelia Rosselli tra poesia e storia* (L'Ancora del Mediterraneo, 2006), 88.

18. Marta Baiardi, "Le tavole del ricordo. Shoah e guerre nelle lapidi ebraiche a Firenze e dintorni, Part II: Guerre mondiali, persecuzioni e Shoah: La presenza ebraica nelle epigrafi fiorentine," *Margini* 12 (2018), https://www.margini.unibas.ch/web/rivista/numero_12/saggi/articolo2/baiardi.html.

19. For a narrative of the continuities and ruptures between Fascist and democratic Italy that argues for the value of literary works as a key source of dissent in the immediate postwar period, see Franco Baldasso, *Against Redemption: Democracy, Memory, and Literature in Post-Fascist Italy* (Fordham University Press, 2022).

20. Stanislao G. Pugliese, *Carlo Rosselli: Socialist Heretic and Antifascist Exile* (Harvard University Press, 1999), 223.

21. Rosselli's story is particularly haunted by the Cold War in ways that this chapter will not have space to explore. She was an avowed communist, turning away from the revolutionary liberal socialism of her father; in paranoid schizophrenic episodes that lasted through the end of her life, she swore that the Central Intelligence Agency (CIA) was inhabiting her brain—a torment about which she wrote in the essay "History of an Illness," published implausibly in the leading literary journal *Nuovi Argomenti* in 1977. While my requests to the US government have not turned up a CIA file devoted to Rosselli's family, her fears were well grounded.

22. Claudio Pavone, *Una guerra civile: Saggio storico sulla moralità nella Resistenza* (Bollati Boringhieri, 1991).

23. Rosario Forlenza, "Sacrificial Memory and Political Legitimacy in Postwar Italy: Reliving and Remembering World War II," *History and Memory* 24, no. 2 (2012): 89. A different picture of literary resistance arises in Baldasso, *Against Redemption*.

24. Salvatore Quasimodo, *Giorno dopo giorno* (1947), with an introduction by Carlo Bo (Mondadori, 1965), 41. Translation here and unless otherwise indicated is my own.

25. Sergio Romano, "The Heteroglottism of European Diplomacy," in *The Fairest Flower: The Emergence of Linguistic National Consciousness in Renaissance Europe* (University of California Los Angeles Center for Medieval and Renaissance Studies and Accademia della Crusca, 1985), 195. While Romano's underscoring of the bellicosity of American English is well taken, it must be noted that he was complicit in and even responsible for the deification of right-wing figures such as guerrilla fighter Amedeo Guillet. See for instance Bastian Matteo Scianna, "Forging an Italian Hero? The Late Commemoration of Amedeo Guillet (1909–2010)," *European Review of History / Revue Européenne d'histoire* 26, no. 3 (May 4, 2019): 369–85.

26. Romano, "The Heteroglottism of European Diplomacy," 197, 195–96.

27. The word "homicile" appears in "Ashore's the great servility," from *Sleep*: "A soldier wooden he / staked by the running homicile / flash-deep"; *OP*, 884. For an introduction in English to "Metrical Spaces" and an extended discussion of the "homicile" as key concept, see my introduction to *Locomotrix*, 1–47.

28. Frederick Bodmer, *The Loom of Language*, ed. Lancelot Thomas Hogben (George Allen, 1944). Citation is from the 1985 Norton edition, 3. Amelia Rosselli worked with the 1944 edition, a copy of which is preserved in the Fondo Rosselli at the University of Viterbo.

29. H. G. Wells, *Travels of a Republican Radical in Search of Hot Water*, taken as epigraph for Bodmer, *The Loom of Language*.

30. See United Nations High Commissioner for Refugees (UNHCR), "Global Appeal 2025: Executive Summary," UNHCR Operations Worldwide, accessed May 9, 2025, https://reporting.unhcr.org /global-appeal-2025-executive-summary. See also "UNHCR: Number of Humanitarian Emergencies in 2023 the Highest in a Decade," UNHCR US, accessed January 22, 2024, https://www .unhcr.org/us/news/press-releases/unhcr-number-humanitarian-emergencies-in-2023-highest-in -decade.

3. AMELIA ROSSELLI'S DISINTEGRATING CANTO(N)S ❦ 337

31. For the note on "stonature," see the letter to Pasolini of June 21, 1962, included in *Locomotrix*, 275. I have translated the poem from *Variazioni belliche* naming the "grammar of the poor" in *Locomotrix*; see p. 77.

32. This translation formed the epigraph to *Locomotrix*.

33. Amelia Rosselli, "October Elizabethans" (1956) in *OP*, 571.

34. *USP*, 293. I translated the entirety of this crucial interview with Giacinto Spagnoletti for *Locomotrix*, 253–66.

35. The correspondence with Amelia Pincherle Rosselli, which I studied extensively in Florence and which is (as I will argue here) central to the story of "My Clothes to the Wind" and to the eventual volume of early writings collected as *Primi scritti* (published in 1980), is missing from the valuable etiology outlined by Chiara Carpita in *OP*, 1382.

36. Letter of September 23, 1950, from Melina Rosselli in Rome to Amelia Rosselli in Bagno a Ripoli, Archivio Rosselli, Archivio di Stato, Firenze.

37. Letter written in English to John Rosselli, September 28, 1953, Fondo Rosselli.

38. Letter written in English to John Rosselli, March 21, 1959(?), Fondo Rosselli.

39. "I will not serve that in which I no longer believe, whether it calls itself my home, my fatherland, or my church: and I will try to express myself in some mode of life or art as freely as I can and as wholly as I can, using for my defense the only arms I allow myself to use—silence, exile, and cunning." James Joyce, *A Portrait of the Artist as a Young Man* (Wordsworth Editions, 1992), 191.

40. See Tandello's reading of this Bachmann fragment from Rosselli's papers in Pavia: Emmanuela Tandello, "Amelia Rosselli. Cortocircuiti del senso," in *Poeti della malinconia*, ed. Biancamaria Frabotta (Donzelli, 2001), 179–90.

41. For accessible details of Rosselli's biography such as these, see "Extreme Facts: An Interview with Giacinto Spagnoletti," in *Locomotrix*, 253–66.

42. Caterina Venturini, "'A mother dead is any body dead.' Madre e materno in Amelia Rosselli," *Nuovi Argomenti*, no. 74 (June 2016): 45.

43. Silvia Mondardini, "Amelia fu Marion: «I me you the others». Appunti per il recupero degli scritti inglesi di Amelia Rosselli," *Cahiers d'études italiennes*, no. 16 (June 30, 2013): 282. This essay is an excellent study of a terrain less explored by criticism. All quotations are my own translations of Mondardini.

44. See the 1976 essay "La venue à l'écriture" in Hélène Cixous, *Entre l'écriture* (Des Femmes, 1986), 9–69. Hereafter I will often cite the translation in English, while occasionally retranslating. Hélène Cixous, *"Coming to Writing" and Other Essays*, ed. Deborah Jenson (Harvard University Press, 1991).

45. Mondardini, "Amelia fu Marion," 286, 285, 286–87.

46. Interview with Giacinto Spagnoletti translated in *Locomotrix*, 259. For her reconstruction of her father through literature, see the same piece, 266.

47. Letter in English from Amelia Rosselli to John Rosselli, January 14, 1952, Fondo Rosselli.

48. Letter in Italian from John to Marion Rosselli, July 15, 1946, Fondo Rosselli.

49. For an English version, see Cixous, *"Coming to Writing" and Other Essays*, 22.

50. Hélène Cixous, *Entre l'écriture* (Des Femmes, 1986), 24, or Cixous, *"Coming to Writing,"* 15. I have changed the translation.

51. Cixous, *"Coming to Writing,"* 22. My retranslation.

52. Cixous, *Entre l'écriture*, 31, 30; Cixous, *"Coming to Writing,"* 22, 21.

53. Letter of September 26, 1946, to John Rosselli from Marion Cave Rosselli, Fondo Rosselli.

54. This may be read as an Oedipal complex in reverse, a fairly classic Electra complex, yet Rosselli's transgression of heteronormative gender roles makes it unwise to shoehorn readings into any antique Freudian or Junghian frameworks.

55. Gian Maria Annovi, *Altri corpi: Poesia e corporalità negli anni sessanta* (Gedit, 2008), 106–7.

56. Cixous, *"Coming to Writing,"* 22.

338   3. AMELIA ROSSELLI'S DISINTEGRATING CANTO(N)S

57.	Se

    questa tetra verginità non può
    rimuovere dal cuore i suoi salmi
    allora non v'è nessuna pace per
    chi scuce, notte e dì, trite cose
    dai suoi labbri.

    If

    this tetric virginity cannot
    remove its psalms from the heart
    then there prevails no peace at all for
    she who unstitches, night and day, trite things
    from the lips.

    See *LP*, 555; *Locomotrix*, 130–31.

58.	See Eco's 1971 critical eulogy, "The Death of the Gruppo 63," now reprinted in Umberto Eco, *The Open Work. With an Introduction by David Robey*, trans. Anna Cancogni (Harvard University Press, 1989), 236–49. Eco's concept of the open work was itself inspired both by the theorization of space in architecture by Bruno Zevi and by the new music coursing through Italy. See Bruno Zevi, *Saper vedere l'architettura* (Einaudi, 1948), translated as *Architecture as Space: How to Look at Architecture* (Horizon Press, 1957). Eco first delivered his lecture "The Open Work" at the Twelfth International Philosophy Conference in Venice in 1958, shortly before John Cage performed "Sounds of Venice" on a Radio Audizioni Italiane (RAI) quiz show.

59.	See "Scienza e istinto," an interview with Elio Pecora, in *CI*, 21, and "Il dolore in una stanza," on p. 65 of the same volume. On the problematic gender dynamics at play in this movement, see Lucia Re, "Language, Gender, and Sexuality in the *Neoavanguardia*," in *Neoavanguardia: Italian Experimental Literature and Arts in the 1960s*, ed. Mario Moroni, Luca Somigli, and Paolo Chirumbolo (University of Toronto Press, 2010), 171–211.

60.	Letter from Amelia Rosselli to John Rosselli, June 9, 1952, Fondo Rosselli.

61.	"La poesia è un piacere privato," a 1977 interview with Gabriella Sica, in *CI*, 15.

62.	See Gilles Deleuze and Félix Guattari, *Kafka: Toward a Minor Literature* (University of Minnesota Press, 1986).

63.	For an extended treatment of Pasolini's rejection of the avant-garde in English, see Ara H. Merjian, *Against the Avant-Garde: Pier Paolo Pasolini, Contemporary Art, and Neocapitalism* (University of Chicago Press, 2019).

64.	See Amelia Rosselli, *Lettere a Pasolini, 1962–1969*, ed. Stefano Giovannuzzi (San Marco dei Giustiniani, 2008), 78.

65.	Rosselli, "La poesia è un piacere privato," *CI*, 14.

66.	An exception appears in Chiara Carpita's thorough commentary on *Primi scritti* as a whole in the Meridiano edition, which devotes several sentences to "Chiesa," reading it as a parodic invocation of the experiments of the Gruppo 63. See *OP*, 1413.

67.	Rosaria Lo Russo offers a compelling argument for the way that Rosselli's "glorious and violent mystical-erotic inspiration" occupies the tradition of feminine mystic "oral writing"—particularly the trope of the mystic marriage to Christ—in order to "seduce the Father-God into a 'parity' of communication." This argument stresses the way that phonic dissolution of the poems in *La libellula, Variazioni belliche*, and *Serie ospedaliera* enacts a parodic de- and resemanticization of the paternalistic canon. See "I santi padri e la figlia dal cuore devastato," in *La furia dei venti contrari: Variazioni Amelia Rosselli, con testi inediti e dispersi dell'autrice*, ed. Andrea Cortellessa (Le Lettere, 2007), esp. 69–74. Hereafter, this volume will be cited as *FVC*.

68. For "fusedwords-in-freedom," see, for example, Filippo Tommaso Marinetti, *Selected Poems and Related Prose. With an Essay by Paolo Valesio*, ed. Luce Marinetti, trans. Elizabeth R. Napier and Barbara R. Studholme (Yale University Press, 2002), 244.
69. "Laboratorio di Poesia," in *CI*, 237. An English translation of this talk and a re-translation of "Metrical Spaces" is in press as Amelia Rosselli, *Delirious Verse: A Talk on "Metrical Spaces,"* ed. and trans. Andrea di Serego Alighieri, with "Metrical Spaces," trans. Jennifer Scappettone, The Yellow Papers 7 (The Last Books, 2025).
70. See "Partitura in versi," in *CI*, 145.
71. "Il Cristo trainava," in *OP*, 117.
72. Alessandro Baldacci writes of Rosselli's answer to the "santi padri" (holy fathers) in *La libellula* taking the form of a "preghiera spaesata, con i modi di un 'incanto vuoto'" (displaced prayer, with the means of an "empty enchantment"). See Alessandro Baldacci, *Amelia Rosselli* (Laterza, 2007), 53.
73. *OP*, 41, and my translation.
74. See Peleggi, "Amelia Rosselli," 68.
75. "Dialogo con i poeti," in *OP*, 265.
76. *LP*, 407. Cesare Catà provides a useful description in arguing against the "Brétonian" wing of Rosselli criticism (poetry as madness, as the irrational) in favor of a "Celanian" method: "la poesia di Amelia Rosselli è un linguaggio che nasce a partire da un'assenza esplosiva della lingua italiana, laddove essa è chiamata oltre se stessa." Cesare Catà, "'Il lapsus' della critica italiana Novecentesca: Il caso letterario 'Amelia Rosselli,'" *Italianistica: Rivista di letteratura italiana* 38, no. 1 (2009): 161.
77. Bodmer, *The Loom of Language*, 518.
78. "Contiamo infiniti morti!" in *LP*, 281. "The critique of culture is confronted with the last stage in the dialectic of culture and barbarism: to write poetry after Auschwitz is barbaric, and that corrodes also the knowledge which expresses why it has become impossible to write poetry today." Theodor W. Adorno, *Prisms*, trans. Samuel and Shierry Weber (MIT Press, 1981), 34.
79. *LP*, 268; *Locomotrix*, 78–79.
80. "Notizia su Amelia Rosselli," *Il menabò* 6 (1963): 66–69. My translation of the full essay appears in *Locomotrix*, 283. All unattributed translations in this piece are my own.
81. *Locomotrix*, 281. For a thorough analysis of the nuclear imagination in postwar Italy, see Maria Anna Mariani, *Italian Literature in the Nuclear Age: A Poetics of the Bystander* (Oxford University Press, 2023).
82. Letter to John Rosselli, October 25, 1963, Fondo Rosselli. Original text is in English. For more on this theme, see Emmanuela Tandello, "Amelia Rosselli o la geometria della passione," in *Amelia Rosselli. Un'apolide alla ricerca del linguaggio universale*, ed. Stefano Giovannuzzi, *Quaderni del Circolo Rosselli*, no. 17 (1999): 7–18.
83. This quote hails from "Glossarietto esplicativo," in *USP*, 69. Rosselli's glossary for Pasolini refers to individual incidences of words that are "fused"; see Amelia Rosselli, *Lettere a Pasolini*, 21, 25, 28, 30, 32, 33, 34, 36.
84. "Spazi Metrici," first published as an appendix to *Variazioni belliche*, was reprinted most recently in the Meridiano edition of her collected works: see *OP*, 181–89. Among the crucial analyses of "Spazi metrici," which are multiplying steadily, are Chiara Carpita, "La metrica tridimensionale di Amelia Rosselli," *Soglie: Rivista quadrimestrale di poesia e critica letteraria* 2 (August 2004); Paolo Cairoli, "Spazio metrico e serialismo musicale. L'azione dell'avanguardia postweberniana sulle concezioni poetiche di Amelia Rosselli," *Trasparenze*, Supplemento non periodico a *Quaderni di poesia* 17–19 (2003), ed. Giorgio Devoto and Emmanuela Tandello: 289–300; "La poetica" in the introduction to Tatiana Bisanti, *L'opera plurilingue di Amelia Rosselli: Un distorto, inesperto, espertissimo linguaggio* (ETS, 2007), 28–55; and Francesco Carbognin, *Le armoniose dissonanze: "Spazio Metrico" e intertestualità nella poesia di Amelia Rosselli* (Gedit, 2008), 15–44. Following the considerable challenges of ordering the Meridiano edition of Rosselli's collected works, and in the process of critiquing the

"ideal" chronology created by Tandello for the Garzanti edition, Stefano Giovannuzzi lays out the complexity of yoking the "cubic" or "squared" system delineated in "Spazi Metrici" (published as a companion to *Variazioni belliche*) to the entirety of Rosselli's career in publishing, highly skeptical of the author's pronouncements never to have abandoned it. The trouble with this skepticism is that it takes "Spazi Metrici" too literally, setting aside its transdisciplinary and conceptual implications, or the attested relations of this system to an interest in the harmonic series that lasted for the rest of her life. See Giovannuzzi, "Bilanci di un curatore tra filologia e pratica editoriale." With all due respect to a leading scholar in the field, the grip that this complex of inventions had on Rosselli—even when the poems she is writing are no longer appreciably (visibly) "cubic"—compels us to continue plumbing the relation of "Metrical Spaces" to her life's work, because its presiding ideals continue to haunt.

85. My translation of "Metrical Spaces" appears in *Locomotrix*; here I am citing from p. 250.

86. Interview with Ambrogio Dolce, "Amelia Rosselli: Poesia non necessariamente ascientifica," *Idea* XLIV (1988), now quoted in *USP*, 329n.

87. "Introduzione a 'Spazi Metrici,'" in *USP*, 59. I translated this text for *Locomotrix*, 245–46.

88. Rosselli and Gabriella Sica, "La poesia è un piacere privato," *CI*, 17.

89. In describing the early series "Poesie '59," for example, she notes that for some poems "it was enough for me to play a prelude of Bach or Chopin to reinterpret it, almost immediately afterward, in poetic form." See "Fatti estremi," her 1987 interview with Giacinto Spagnoletti, in *CI*, 84.

90. "Incontro con Amelia Rosselli sulla metrica," in *OP*, 1254; Rosselli, *Delirious Verse*, 25.

91. We have yet to comprehend the connotations of what Charles Olson in 1950 called "COMPOSITION BY FIELD" and the transnational exchanges that stimulated it as sociopolitical provocations. Charles Olson, "Projective Verse," in *The New American Poetry, 1945–1960*, ed. Donald Allen (Evergreen, 1960), 386. In Rosselli's personal copy at the Fondo Rosselli in Viterbo, marked "Rosselli '66" on the title page, this essay is heavily annotated.

92. Stefano Giovannuzzi takes note of the 1961 translation in his commentary on *Variazioni belliche* in *OP*, 1283, 1299. See Allen, *The New American Poetry*, xiv.

93. Olson, "Projective Verse," in *The New American Poetry*, 386, 393.

94. Rosselli rues this tendency of confessional writing in, for example, her 1979 interview with Mariella Bettarini. See *CI*, 32–33.

95. The Olson discussion appears in "Poesia d'elite nell'America di oggi," in *USP*, 160.

96. "Spazi Metrici," in *OP*, 186.

97. "Notizia su Amelia Rosselli," in *La libellula*, 103, was also translated for *Locomotrix*, 281–83.

98. "Spazi metrici," in *OP*, 186.

99. Letter to John Rosselli, January 25, 1952, Fondo Rosselli.

100. The modern definition of lyric, a notoriously contradictory and controversial task, is broached in a plurality of ways in Virginia Jackson and Yopie Prins, eds., *The Lyric Theory Reader: A Critical Anthology* (Johns Hopkins University Press, 2014). In their overview, Jackson and Prins note that despite critical differences, lyric has come to signify the domain of personal expression in modern and contemporary scholarship. Rosselli complicates such a view because she is well aware of critiques of the lyric launched by the historical avant-garde that were overlooked by a broad swath of Anglophone critics focused on the mainstream until recently; moreover, she has her own communist critique of bourgeois confessionalism. She needs, of course, to be seen as responding both to the European tradition of lyric and to the Anglo-American context in which she received her primary education.

101. In a 1992 interview, Rosselli relates a telling anecdote about her 1960 performance with Merce Cunningham and David Tudor, during which her less minimalist aleatory impulses led her to break into the anachronism of a Gregorian chant until an audience member screamed "Amen!"—to Cage's distaste. See "Partitura in versi," in *CI*, 145.

102. See "Paesaggio con figure," in *CI*, 284, and "Introduzione a Spazi Metrici," in *USP*, 59. Rosselli's musicological studies are reflected in the following publications, the first signed under her mother's name

3. AMELIA ROSSELLI'S DISINTEGRATING CANTO(N)S   ❧   341

Marion: Marion Rosselli, "Armonia di gravitazione," *Il Diapason* 1, nos. 8–9 (August–September 1950): 24–29; Marion Rosselli, "Nuovi esperimenti musicali con un nuovo strumento," *Il Diapason* 4, nos. 11–12 (1953): 12–14; Marion Rosselli, "La serie degli armonici," *Civiltà delle macchine* 2, no. 2 (1954): 43–44; and Amelia Rosselli, "La serie degli armonici (1953–1977)," *Il verri* 8, nos. 1–2 (1987): 166–83. "Armonia di Gravitazione" and "The Harmonic Series" are reprinted in *USP*, 27–33 and 45–58.

103. See Max Horkheimer, "Preface," in Theodor Adorno et al., *The Authoritarian Personality* (Norton, 1993), ix–x.

104. Ernesto de Martino, "Towards a History of the Subaltern Popular World," trans. David Gutherz and Daniela Licandro, *Chicago Review* 60, no. 4/61, no. 1 (Winter 2017): 67. See also Barile, " 'Trasposizioni': I due mestieri di Amelia Rosselli."

105. De Martino, "Towards a History of the Subaltern Popular World," 70.

106. See "La serie degli armonici" files, Fondo Rosselli. Citation hails from Rosselli's own English text.

107. Amelia Rosselli to John Rosselli, January 25, 1952, Fondo Rosselli, and Rosselli, "Armonia di gravitazione," in *USP*, 29.

108. Giuseppe Salviati, "Nel linguaggio dinamico della realtà. Conversazione con Amelia Rosselli," *Clandestino* no. 1 (1997): 12; Peleggi, "Amelia Rosselli," 69.

109. "Introduzione a 'Spazi Metrici,' " in *USP*, 60.

110. "La serie degli armonici," in *USP*, 48–51.

111. See Richard Kostelanetz, ed., *Conversing with Cage* (Routledge, 2003), 67–68. For an initial discussion of Rosselli's relation to Cage, see Cairoli, "Spazio metrico e serialismo musicale," 295–98.

112. See Ulderico Pesce, "La donna che vola," *Quaderni del Circolo Rosselli* 19 (1999): 44, and Chiara Carpita's analysis of the figure of the mandala and use of the *I Ching*, "Amelia Rosselli e il processo di individuazione: alcuni inediti," in *CI*, 136–51.

113. See "La serie degli armonici" correspondence to professors Vladimir Ibler and Branko Soucek, dated to post-1981, Fondo Rosselli.

114. For more on metaphorical freedom and imprisonment as form and antiform, see Ambra Zorat, "Intorno a libertà e prigionia: Alcune riflessioni su *Variazioni belliche* di Amelia Rosselli," *RiLUnE* no. 2 (2005): 1–11.

115. "Incontro con Amelia Rosselli sulla metrica," in *OP*, 1258; or *Delirious Verse*, 29, for a different translation by Andrea di Serego Alighieri.

116. Here I build upon the insights of Meredith Martin's *The Rise and Fall of Meter: Poetry and English National Culture, 1860–1930* (Princeton University Press, 2012), an innovative approach to the "military metrical complex" of nationalist poetics. Martin's argument highlights the way that prosody ensconced in the literary traditions of "national" languages tends to obscure the presence of metrics from other languages embedded within the dominant tongue.

117. "Spazi Metrici," in *OP*, 184.

118. *OP*, 184, 625.

119. Piet Mondrian, "Neoplasticism in Painting," in *Manifesto: A Century of Isms*, ed. Mary Ann Caws (University of Nebraska Press, 2001), 426.

120. Adriano Spatola, *Toward Total Poetry. With an Afterword by Guy Bennett*, trans. Brendan W. Hennessey and Guy Bennett (Otis/Seismicity Editions, 2008), 19, 38.

121. György Ligeti, "Pierre Boulez: Decision and Automatism in Structure Ia.," *Die Reihe* no. 4 ("Young Composers") (1960): 36; 53.

122. Piero Malvezzi and Giovanni Pirelli, ed., *Lettere di condannati a morte della Resistenza europea*, 3rd ed. (Einaudi, 1956).

123. Quoted in Martin Iddon, *New Music at Darmstadt: Nono, Stockhausen, Cage, and Boulez* (Cambridge University Press, 2013), 150.

124. Quoted in the 1960 essay "Testo—musica—canto," in Luigi Nono, *La nostalgia del futuro: Scritti scelti, 1948–1986*, ed. Angela Ida De Benedictis and Veniero Rizzardi (Il Saggiatore, 2007), 64.

125. "La poesia è un piacere privato," in *CI*, 16.

126. Rosselli, *Lettere a Pasolini, 1962–1969*, 29.

127. Rosselli, "Musica e pittura: Dibattito su Dorazio," in *USP*, 35.

128. "L'ironia un ginocchio ancora più duro," in *LP*, 491.

129. See Acts of the Apostles 2:10–11.

130. Translated in *Locomotrix*, 281. For a revision of the Freudian slip through aphasia and the play on "slip" and "sleep," see Tandello, "Amelia Rosselli. Cortocircuiti del senso."

131. The atomic aesthetic is skillfully sketched and historicized, although in the context of the United States, in Brooke Kamin Rapaport and Kevin Stayton, eds., *Vital Forms: American Art and Design in the Atomic Age, 1940–1960* (Brooklyn Museum of Art in association with Harry N. Abrams, 2001).

132. See Pheng Cheah and Bruce Robbins, eds., *Cosmopolitics: Thinking and Feeling Beyond the Nation* (University of Minnesota Press, 1998); Homi Bhabha, Carol Breckenridge, Dipesh Chakrabarty, and Sheldon Pollock, "Cosmopolitanisms," *Public Culture* 12, no. 3 (2000): 577–89; and Kwame Anthony Appiah, *Cosmopolitanism: Ethics in a World of Strangers* (Norton, 2006).

133. I have in mind the terms of Enlightenment established by the classic study by Theodor W. Adorno and Max Horkheimer, *Dialectic of Enlightenment*, trans. John Cumming (Continuum, 1999).

134. For a basic introduction to the harmonic series including graphs and audio samples, see overtone singer Wolfgang Saus's website devoted to the concept: Wolfgang Saus, "Harmonic Series—Structure, Application and Background," accessed February 19, 2024, https://www.oberton.org/en/overtone -singing/harmonic-series/.

135. Mark Van Tongeren, "Introduction: Where Art Meets Science and Contemplation," in *Overtone Singing: Harmonic Dimensions of the Human Voice* (Terra Nova, 2023).

136. See Rosselli, "Armonia di Gravitazione," in *USP*, 27.

137. See "La serie degli armonici" files, Fondo Rosselli.

138. "Musica e pittura," in *USP*, 39.

139. Quoted in Alain Daniélou, *Introduction to the Study of Musical Scales* (India Society, 1943), 6–7, http://archive.org/details/in.ernet.dli.2015.234279.

140. Louis Zukofsky, *Prepositions: The Collected Critical Essays of Louis Zukofsky* (Horizon Press, 1968), 26–27. See Harryette Mullen and Will Alexander, "Hauling up Gold from the Abyss: An Interview with Will Alexander," *Callaloo* 22, no. 2 (1999): 401.

141. Rosselli, "Armonia di Gravitazione," in *USP*, 29.

142. See letter of Amelia Rosselli to Pier Paolo Pasolini, June 21, 1962, translated in *Locomotrix*, 275.

143. The Italian original passage appears in *OP*, 1287.

144. Rosselli, "Armonia di Gravitazione," in *USP*, 27.

145. Amelia Rosselli to her grandmother Amelia Pincherle Rosselli, June 27, 1952, Archivio Rosselli, Archivio di Stato di Firenze.

146. Rosselli, "The Harmonic Series," Fondo Rosselli.

147. Caroline Bergvall, "A Cat in the Throat: On Bilingual Occupants," *Jacket* 37 (Early 2009), http:// jacketmagazine.com/37/bergvall-cat-throat.shtml.

148. Listen to Andrea Cortellessa, ed., "I libri, la poesia," February 6, 2006, Broadcast 1 of the series "Con l'ascia dietro le spalle: 10 anni senza Amelia Rosselli," RAI Radio 3, https://media.sas.upenn .edu/pennsound/groups/Italiana/Amelia-Rosselli/Amelia-Rosselli_01_Con-l-Ascia-Dietro-le-Spalle _February-06-2006.mp3. Archived at PennSound | Italiana, ed. Jennifer Scappettone, http://writing .upenn.edu/pennsound/x/Italiana.php. For astute remarks on Rosselli's pronunciation as sign of a "lingua-corpo" (body-language), see Niva Lorenzini, *La poesia: Tecniche di ascolto: Ungaretti, Rosselli, Sereni, Porta, Zanzotto, Sanguineti* (Manni, 2003), 98–99.

149. Both criticism and translation—especially that of poetry—would benefit from contending directly with the challenge to the disembodied universal claims of logocentrism posed by Adriana Cavarero's *A più voci: Per una filosofia dell'espressione vocale* (Castelvecchi, 2003; translated to lose the title's

"Polyphony" as *For More than One Voice: Toward a Philosophy of Vocal Expression*), which builds on Hannah Arendt's political theory to distinguish an embodied and relational ontology of acoustic emission. Recuperating the channels of reciprocal communication between singular voices, whether semantically laden or not, from Western philosophical abstractions of logos, Cavarero then moves discussions of voice from ontology into the sphere of politics by emphasizing the resonance, music, and acoustic correspondence *a più voci* (in plural voices; in polyphony).

150. Bergvall, "A Cat in the Throat." See Caroline Bergvall and Ciárán Maher, *Say: 'Parsley,'* Sound and language installation, 2004, with reprise in 2019, https://carolinebergvall.com/work/say-parsley/, textual features represented in the book *Fig*, 49–60.

151. Pooja Rangan et al., eds., *Thinking with an Accent: Toward a New Object, Method, and Practice* (University of California Press, 2023), 4.

152. Rangan et al., eds., *Thinking with an Accent*, 7.

153. Rangan et al., eds., *Thinking with an Accent*, 5.

154. Anedda is building on the discourse of the "lapsus" and likely on the "Cortocircuiti" essay surrounding "slips of the tongue" and "sleep" by Tandello cited above. Listen to Amelia Rosselli, Andrea Cortellessa, and Antonella Anedda, *Le lingue, la voce*, vol. 2, 5 vols., *Con l'ascia dietro le spalle: 10 anni senza Amelia Rosselli* (RAI 3, 2006), digitized for Pennsound | Italiana by Jennifer Scappettone, https://media.sas.upenn.edu/pennsound/groups/Italiana/Amelia-Rosselli/Amelia-Rosselli_02_Con-l-Ascia-Dietro-le-Spalle_February-08-2006.mp3.

155. Rosselli et al., *Le lingue, la voce*.

156. Despite her attempts to get these poems to English-language readers, City Lights never responded, and the collection ended up in editions published in Rome (Rossi & Spera, 1989), a slim volume with translations by Antonio Porta, and in Milan, with translations by Rosselli and Emmanuela Tandello (Garzanti, 1992). This poem first appeared in the latter and was republished in *OP*, 1006. "Faro" also appears on p. 238 of *Locomotrix*, the first collection in the Anglophone world to include selections from *Sleep*.

157. Letter to John Rosselli of June 10, 1956, from Lungotevere Sanzio 5, Rome, Fondo Rosselli.

158. *Locomotrix*, 126–27.

159. A new generation of scholars and performers like Rosaria Lo Russo is in the process of changing this. Lo Russo performs an homage to Rosselli included in the CD included with *La furia dei venti contrari*.

160. See, for example, her interview for *Videor: Videorivista di poesia diretta da Elio Pagliarini* no. 1 (1989), archived at https://www.youtube.com/watch?v=GYitmH0E-W0&list=PLE1E11A737881A1C4, accessed December 1, 2015; it has since been rendered private, and one hopes for a future publication of a more formal sort. In this interview, Rosselli also notes that Joyce, Montale, Musil, Pasternak, and even Dante all received some form of musical education.

161. See Tatiana Bisanti, *L'opera plurilingue di Amelia Rosselli: Un Distorto, inesperto, espertissimo linguaggio* (ETS, 2007); and Sara Di Gianvito, *Nell'officina poetica di Amelia Rosselli: Il plurilinguismo dei Primi scritti e il ruolo del Diario in tre lingue* (Franco Cesati, 2022). See also Daniela La Penna, *"La promessa d'un semplice linguaggio": Lingua e stile nella poesia di Amelia Rosselli* (Roma: Carocci editore, 2013).

162. Citation is from "Non si può diventare poeti forzati," a 1991 interview with Maria Pia Ammirati, in *CI*, 157.

163. "Impromptu" appears in *LP*, 817–35 and its publication history is recounted in *OP*, 1415–27. The first editions were published by San Marco dei Giustiniani and Carlo Mancosu in 1981/2003 and 1993. A trilingual edition edited by Gian Maria Annovi containing translations into English and French in collaboration with Diana Thow and Jean-Paul Vegliante was issued shortly after this episode (Guernica Editions, 2014). To continue, it's imperative to listen to the recording of Rosselli's recitation, which I have cross-posted via PennSound | Italiana at http://writing.upenn.edu/pennsound/x/Italiana.php.

164. See "Partitura in versi," in *CI*, 145.
165. Chiara Carpita, "Amelia Rosselli, *Impromptu. A Trilingual Edition*," *Nuovi argomenti*, October 21, 2015, http://www.nuoviargomenti.net/poesie/nota-introduttiva-a-a-rosselli-impromptu-a-trilingual-edition/.
166. Curt Sachs, *The Wellsprings of Music* (Springer, 1961), 112.
167. Compare *LP*, 822, with *OP*, 676, which both retain "stralunante."
168. I have written more extensively about this poem and my reperformance as a translation strategy in "Chloris in Plural Voices: Performing Translation of 'A Moonstriking Death,'" *Translation Review* 95 (July 2016): 25–40. The piece was translated with Silvia Guslandi as "Chlori a più voci: La performance della traduzione di una 'stralunante morte,'" *Nuovi argomenti* 74 (May 2016): 92–102.
169. Amelia Pincherle Rosselli, *Illusione, Commedia in tre atti; L'idea fissa [e] L'amica: Scene* (Casa Editrice Nazionale, 1906).
170. Amelia Rosselli to John Rosselli, February 12, 1951, reproduced in *Locomotrix*, 270. Aldo Rosselli, *La famiglia Rosselli: Una tragedia italiana. With a Foreword by Sandro Pertini and Preface by Alberto Moravia* (Leonardo, 1992), 19.
171. I first established Rosselli's ties to the Anglo-American literary world, including the tie to Ashbery, in the introduction to *Locomotrix*.
172. Lyn Hejinian, *The Language of Inquiry* (University of California Press, 2000), 326.

4. "FOG IS MY LAND": THE LUMINOUS OPACITY OF ETEL ADNAN'S PAINTING IN ARABIC AND THE REINVENTION OF BELONGING

1. Etel Adnan, *Sitt Marie-Rose: A Novel*, trans. Georgina Kleege, 3rd ed. (Post-Apollo Press, 1992), 76.
2. Emilio Villa, *Attributi dell'arte odierna: 1947–1967*, ed. Aldo Tagliaferri (Le Lettere, 2008), 127.
3. Adnan, *Sitt Marie-Rose*, 29.
4. Omar Berrada, "J'ai suivi des lignes que je n'ai mais vues: Motif du lien et de la séparation dans l'oeuvre d'Etel Adnan," in *Écrire, c'est dessiner: d'après une idée d'Etel Adnan*, ed. Jean-Marie Gallais (Centre Pompidou-Metz, 2021), 59. Translation here, as throughout the book, is mine unless otherwise cited.
5. This show was curated by Steve Dickison and staff at the San Francisco State University Poetry Center; sadly, no catalog exists.
6. Buland Ḥaydarī, *Ilá Bayrūt ma'a taḥīyātī* (Dār al-Sāqī, 1989). Duncan McNaughton, *Valparaíso* (Listening Chamber, 1995).
7. Etel Adnan, *In the Heart of the Heart of Another Country* (City Lights Books, 2005).
8. Jennifer Scappettone, Etel Adnan, and Lyn Hejinian, *Belladonna Elders Series 5: Poetry, Landscape, Apocalypse*, ed. Jennifer Scappettone (Belladonna*, 2009). See also Cuguoglu Cacekli Naz, "An Analysis of the Discovery Narrative: The Case of Etel Adnan" (Curatorial Practice MA Program, San Francisco, California College of the Arts, 2020), https://vault.cca.edu/items/f030b30d-1453-469f-9326-be26c3a57817/2/.
9. Etel Adnan, *Of Cities and Women: Letters to Fawwaz* (Post-Apollo Press, 1993), 81.
10. I am using the terminology of Lyn Hejinian in invoking the beginner and senses of astonishment. I met Adnan through Hejinian and invited the two of them into my Belladonna* book honoring women elders. See Lyn Hejinian, *The Beginner* (Tuumba Press, 2002) and Lyn Hejinian, *My Life and My Life in the Nineties* (Wesleyan University Press, 2013).
11. See Walter Mignolo, *Local Histories/Global Designs: Coloniality, Subaltern Knowledges, and Border Thinking* (Princeton University Press, 2012), 203.

4. "FOG IS MY LAND"

12. Adnan, *Sitt Marie-Rose*, 95.

13. From Fouad's monologue, Adnan, *Sitt Marie-Rose*, 37.

14. Inez Reider and Etel Adnan, "Tribal Mentality," *Off Our Backs* 13, no. 8 (September 1983): 32.

15. Robert O. Paxton, "The Five Stages of Fascism," *The Journal of Modern History* 70, no. 1 (1998): 1–23, https://doi.org/10.1086/235001.

16. Reider and Adnan, "Tribal Mentality," 32.

17. See Etel Adnan, *Voyage, War, Exile: Three Essays* (Litmus Press, 2025), 11–32, first published as Etel Adnan, "To Write in a Foreign Language," *Electronic Poetry Review* 1 (1996), http://www.epoetry .org/issues/issue1/alltext/esadn.htm. For useful detailed biographical notes on Adnan, see Lisa Suhair Majaj and Amal Amireh, eds., *Etel Adnan: Critical Essays on the Arab-American Writer and Artist* (McFarland, 2002), 15–24; and Kaelen Wilson-Goldie, *Etel Adnan* (Lund Humphries, 2018). In Lynne Tillman and Etel Adnan, "Etel Adnan: Children of the Sun," *Bidoun*, no. 18: Interviews (Summer 2009), https://bidoun.org/articles/etel-adnan, we learn that Assaf Kadri first married a woman from Damascus, with whom he had three children. Adnan hypothesizes that he found her mother, a beautiful yet destitute woman of sixteen (twenty years his junior), "in the street" of Smyrna during World War I when he was its governor and that she might have been reduced to prostitution had she not married him. It is not clear when Adnan's mother learned about Kadri's earlier wife and children.

18. This reference to Arab students as "les indigènes" hails from an interview that I conducted with Adnan in her Paris home on September 23 and 24, 2017, a lightly edited video recording of which is published at her new author page at PennSound, the University of Pennsylvania's audiovisual archive of contemporary experimental poetry: http://writing.upenn.edu/pennsound/x/Adnan.php. Much of the biographical information that I lay out here, when not otherwise cited, derives from this set of interviews.

19. See Frantz Fanon. *Black Skin, White Masks*, trans. Charles Lamb Markmann (Pluto, 2008), 8 (17–18 in French edition).

20. Fawwaz Traboulsi, *A History of Modern Lebanon* (Pluto Press, 2012), 110, https://doi.org/10.2307/j .ctt183p4f5. Traboulsi is the "Fawwaz" to whom the letters of *Of Cities and Women* are addressed.

21. Interview with Jennifer Scappettone, http://writing.upenn.edu/pennsound/x/Adnan.php.

22. I use this term (Levant) as the nearest English, and thus relatively accessible, equivalent to the term al-Mashriq, which is Etel Adnan's preferred term for the region commonly referred to as the Middle East. In both its French (Levant) and Arabic permutations, it refers to a "land where the sun rises." Says Adnan, "'Mashriq' means 'the place where the sun rises'; it also means the rays of light. . . . Historically, the Mashriq is the Eastern Arab world. So we can say 'the Mashriq and Iran.' Arabs themselves say 'the Mashriq,' but also make the mistake of saying 'the Middle East,' which is a name that comes from Britain calling it 'halfway down the spice route to the Indies.' It's a colonial notion." See Hans Ulrich Obrist and Etel Adnan, "Conversations with Etel Adnan," in *Etel Adnan in All Her Dimensions = Ītil ʿAdnān bi-kulli abʿādihā*, ed. Hans Ulrich Obrist (Mathaf, 2014), 31.

23. Adnan, "To Write in a Foreign Language," 28.

24. Adnan calls Beirut "a child of WWII": "In 1920 we had refugees from Armenia. WWII brought foreign armies, not bloodshed. Beirut profited, because when armies are around, there's money." Tillman and Adnan, "Etel Adnan: Children of the Sun."

25. As with Rosselli's siblings, those of Adnan's mother ended up in Alexandria, Genova, Limassol, and Thessaloniki, as Serhan Ada notes in "The Impossible Homecoming," a text for the exhibition *Etel Adnan: Impossible Homecoming* held at the Pera Museum in Istanbul in 2020.

26. Yogita Goyal, "We Need New Diasporas," *American Literary History* 29, no. 4 (December 2017): 640–63, https://doi.org/10.1093/alh/ajx030.

27. Reider and Adnan, "Tribal Mentality," 32.

28. Adnan explains that by the time she was sixteen, Beirut had become a boom town due to the Second World War and offices had multiplied; the French needed help, inflation was on the rise, and it

became acceptable that girls find jobs as secretaries. Adnan took an exciting and politically intense job at the French Information Bureau. See Etel Adnan, "Growing Up to Be a Woman Writer in Lebanon (1986)," in *Voyage, War, Exile*, 53–55.

29. By "acritical ethnocentrism," I mean to distinguish this habit from forms of ethnocentrism that were mobilized toward political progressivism in the twentieth century, invoking Ernesto De Martino's concept of "critical ethnocentrism." For a gloss, see George R. Saunders, " 'Critical Ethnocentrism' and the Ethnology of Ernesto De Martino," *American Anthropologist* 95, no. 4 (1993): 875–93.

30. See Acts of the Apostles 2:1–13, and Charles Richet, "Xénoglossie: l'écriture automatique en langues étrangères," *Proceedings of the Society for Psychical Research* 19 (1905): 162–266. Richet is better known for having won the Nobel Prize for his research into anaphylaxis.

31. Xenoglossia resonates with the "minor," in the sense developed in Deleuze and Guattari's analysis of the deterritorialization of a major language deployed from a marginal position; see Gilles Deleuze and Félix Guattari, *Kafka: Toward a Minor Literature* (University of Minnesota Press, 1986). I am interested in a host of propositions staked out by this seminal work while being aware of its limits, which lead me to adopt the language of xenoglossia instead. For the purposes of this chapter, I am particularly interested in the assertion that minor literature has no subjects but only "*collective assemblages of enunciation*" (italics in original, 18). The assumption of the collective voice is distressed in this case both by Adnan's status as a queer woman writer and her status as perpetual outsider. To read her is to presume the critiques of subalternization present in Edward W. Said, *Culture and Imperialism* (Knopf, 1993), 79, who stresses the need for a "contrapuntal" reading of imperialism and resistance to it as interrelated processes, and in Gayatri Chakravorty Spivak, *A Critique of Postcolonial Reason: Toward a History of the Vanishing Present* (Harvard University Press, 1999), which underscores the constitutive place of gender in constituting the subject of language and power. See also, for example, the legacy of Spivak's canonical 1988 essay registered in Gayatri Chakravorty Spivak, *Can the Subaltern Speak? Reflections on the History of an Idea*, ed. Rosalind C. Morris (Columbia University Press, 2010).

32. Emilio Villa, "Cy Twombly: Talento bianco," *Appia Antica* 1 (July 1959): 36. Translation mine.

33. Mohammed Melehi, "Questionnaire," *Souffles*, special issue on "Situation arts plastiques Maroc," 7–8 (1967): 56–68.

34. Melehi, "Questionnaire," 62: "mobilité et vibration restent les seules intrigues pour le spectateur où se manifestent un message et une éducation visuels. C'est un art qui ne fait pas appel dans sa communication à une culture littéraire ou historique." See Salwa Mikdadi Nashashibi, *Forces of Change: Artists of the Arab World* (International Council for Women in the Arts; National Museum of Women in the Arts, 1994), 36. See also Abdelkebir Khatibi, "A Note on the Calligraphic Sign," originally published in *Intégral* 2 nos. 3/4 (January 1973), now published in translation by Teresa Villa-Ignacio in Anneka Lennsen, Sarah Rogers, and Nada Shabout, eds., *Modern Art in the Arab World* (Museum of Modern Art, 2018), 352–54.

35. Adnan, "To Write in a Foreign Language," 31. Both Ammiel Alcalay and Cole Swensen have built on Adnan's intimations that she turned to painting as a rejection of her French linguistic indoctrination. See their contributions to *To Look at the Sea Is to Become What One Is: An Etel Adnan Reader*, ed. Thom Donovan and Brandon Shimoda (Nightboat Books, 2014), vol. 1, i–xv, and vol. 2, 377–83.

36. See Obrist and Adnan, "Conversations with Etel Adnan," 73.

37. Adnan, "To Write in a Foreign Language," 17.

38. Édouard Glissant, *Le discours antillais* (Éditions du Seuil, 1981), 11; Édouard Glissant, *Caribbean Discourse: Selected Essays*, trans. and intro. J. Michael Dash (University of Virginia Press, 1989), 1.

39. Bird Rose, "Shimmer: When All You Love Is Being Trashed," in *Arts of Living on a Damaged Planet*, ed. Anna Lowenhaupt Tsing, Elaine Gan, and Nils Bubandt (University of Minnesota Press, 2017), G53.

40. Adnan, "To Write in a Foreign Language," 25.

41. Daniel Kurjaković and Etel Adnan, "Etel Adnan: Every One of Us Is a Radio Transmitter," trans. Patrick Gillot, *ArtAsiaPacific*, no. 101 (December 2016): 91.

4. "FOG IS MY LAND"   347

42. Tillman and Adnan, "Etel Adnan: Children of the Sun." The pun between sun and son recurs throughout her work.

43. See Tyler Bradway and Elizabeth Freeman, eds., *Queer Kinship: Race, Sex, Belonging, Form* (Duke University Press, 2022), here quoting from pages 4 and 2.

44. Adnan, "To Write in a Foreign Language," 32. Adnan invokes the first chapter of Fanon's *Peau noire, masques blancs* (Seuil, 1952); she also notes that Arab writers have not seen their languages eradicated by colonization as Black African writers have. She uses the term "international" to refer to languages like English in scare quotes within "To Write in a Foreign Language," 31.

45. Adnan, "To Write in a Foreign Language," 32.

46. Obrist and Adnan, "Conversations with Etel Adnan," 42.

47. Adnan, "To Write in a Foreign Language," 25.

48. Adnan, "Growing Up to Be a Woman Writer in Lebanon," 43.

49. Adnan, "To Write in a Foreign Language," 27.

50. Etel Adnan and Lisa Robertson, "Etel Adnan by Lisa Robertson," *BOMB Magazine*, no. 127 (April 1, 2014), https://bombmagazine.org/articles/etel-adnan/.

51. Adnan, "Growing Up to Be a Woman Writer in Lebanon (1986)," 60.

52. Adnan's narrative is consistent throughout her written work and interviews, but this statement appears recently in Obrist and Adnan, "Conversations with Etel Adnan," 40.

53. "The Enemy's Testament," in Walter Lowenfels, ed., *Where Is Vietnam? American Poets Respond: An Anthology of Contemporary Poems* (Anchor, 1967), 3.

54. Adnan recalls learning about sexual difference through innocent play with this boy. See Adnan, "Growing Up to Be a Woman Writer in Lebanon," 36–37.

55. This "we" refers to Maksoud and her husband Clovis Maksoud, ambassador of the Arab League to the United Nations and the United States from 1979 through 1990, who worked with presidents from Kennedy through George W. Bush. "We were committed to the Palestinian cause but we could not identify with many of the practices of individual Palestinians in Beirut. We were committed to an Arab secular Lebanon and we saw our slogans being misused and old friends jumping on the bandwagon of the new emerging sectarian movements in our midst." Hala Salaam Maksoud, *Hala: Hala Salaam Maksoud: A Life Dedicated to Social Progress and Human Dignity* (Foundation for Arab Policy Studies, 2003), available at https://www.abu-omar-hanna.info/?article73&lang=ar.

56. Mary N. Layoun, "Mobile Belonging? The Global 'Given' in the Work of Etel Adnan," in *The Edinburgh Companion to the Arab Novel in English: The Politics of Anglo Arab and Arab American Literature and Culture*, ed. Nouri Gana (Edinburgh University Press, 2013), 131.

57. See Adnan, "To Write in a Foreign Language," 26–27.

58. Adnan, "To Write in a Foreign Language," 28.

59. "Yusuf integrated me into Arabic poetry. Before even reading a line. It changed my life." Obrist and Adnan, "Conversations with Etel Adnan," 79. See also my PennSound interview with Adnan at https://media.sas.upenn.edu/app/public/watch.php?file_id=223293.

60. Al-Khal's translation from the English was published as *Khams Hawas Li Mouten Wahed* (Gallery One, 1973). See also Wilson-Goldie, *Etel Adnan*, 93, which is likely citing Muhsin al-Musawi, "The Republic of Letters: Arab Modernity?," *Cambridge Journal of Postcolonial Literary Inquiry* 1, no. 2 (September 2014): 265–80.

61. Etel Adnan, "On Small Magazines," *Bidoun*, September 22, 2015, https://bidoun.org/news/etel-adnan-collection. Issandr El Amrani notes that the journal's trademark cover (which was designed by Mohammed Melehi), "emblazoned with an intense black sun, radiated rebellion"; see his "In the Beginning There Was *Souffles*: Reconsidering Morocco's Most Radical Literary Quarterly," *Bidoun* 13: Glory (Winter 2008), https://bidoun.org/articles/in-the-beginning-there-was-souffles. See also Abdellatif Laâbi, "La culture nationale, donée et exigence historique," *Souffles* 4 (1966): 5.

62. Majaj and Amireh, eds., *Etel Adnan: Critical Essays*.

4. "FOG IS MY LAND"

63. On the strangeness of Adnan's name, see Simone Fattal, "A Few Years in Journalism," Etel Adnan, accessed October 22, 2017, http://www.eteladnan.com/journalism/. On the adoption of the family surname, see Wilson-Goldie, *Etel Adnan*, 50.

64. I am indebted to my Stanford colleague Alexander Key for this connection. See the entry for Adnan in H. A. R. Gibb, *The Encyclopaedia of Islam* (Brill, 1960), http://pi.lib.uchicago.edu/1001/cat/bib/260038.

65. Adnan, *Sitt Marie Rose*, 58.

66. Adnan, *Sitt Marie Rose*, 104–5. This novel was published in French and banned in the Christian sector of East Beirut.

67. She continues, "The circulation of the blood. The blood of cities. The blood of a territory." Hans-Ulrich Obrist, ed., *Mapping It Out: An Alternative Atlas of Contemporary Cartographies* (Thames & Hudson, 2014), 182.

68. Obrist and Adnan, "Conversations with Etel Adnan," 30.

69. Simone Fattal's essay "On Perception: Etel Adnan's Visual Art," a pioneering and intimate contribution to the expanding literature on the topic, stresses that "these books are [Adnan's] greatest contribution to the contemporary visual arts." See Majaj and Amireh, eds., *Etel Adnan: Critical Essays*, 101.

70. For this quote and narration of her discovery, see Etel Adnan, "The Unfolding of an Artist's Book," *Discourse: Journal for Theoretical Studies in Media and Culture* 20, no. 1 (March 2013): 12, 20.

71. See Obrist and Adnan, "Conversations with Etel Adnan," 73. Al-Sayyab esteemed the writing of T. S. Eliot notwithstanding the latter's condition as "the poet of death, feudalism, and world imperialism." Quoted in Elliott Colla, "Badr Shakir Al-Sayyab, Cold War Poet," *Middle Eastern Literatures* 18, no. 3 (2015): 257. Colla illuminates the political contradictions in this poet's oeuvre and his eventual work with the CIA front organization, the Congress for Cultural Freedom. Colla underscores the way al-Sayyab's "pan-Arab ideologies could be married with blatantly pro-American positions, and do so in the name of anti-imperialism, art and modernity" (259).

72. Theresa Hak Kyung Cha, *DICTEE* (Third Woman Press, 1995).

73. Etel Adnan, "Writing Mountains," *Ab Print* 4 (Fall/Winter 2014): 57.

74. See Wijdan Ali, *Modern Islamic Art: Development and Continuity* (University Press of Florida, 1997), 163–68.

75. Megan N. Liberty, David Solo, and Corina Reynolds, "A New Manifesto for Book Art Criticism," *Book Art Review*, 2020, https://centerforbookarts.org/bar/about. See for instance Johanna Drucker, *The Visible Word: Experimental Typography and Modern Art, 1909–1923* (University of Chicago Press, 1994); Johanna Drucker, *Figuring the Word: Essays on Books, Writing, and Visual Poetics* (Granary Books, 1998); Johanna Drucker, *The Century of Artists' Books* (Granary Books, 2004); and Amaranth Borsuk, *The Book*, MIT Press Essential Knowledge Series (MIT Press, 2018). The book on Adnan's leporellos contains an essay by Anne Moeglin-Delcroix about accordion books that situates this form at the nexus of music, visual art, and sculpture (though without specific reference to Adnan); see "Pli sur pli," Etel Adnan, *Leporellos: Etel Adnan* (Galerie Lelong, 2020), 86–99.

76. See "Leporellos," in Adnan, *Leporellos*, 28–29. Lucy Ives also refers to the stifling arrangement in "Of Light & Folds," *ARTnews.Com* (blog), August 10, 2021, https://www.artnews.com/art-in-america/features/etel-adnan-painting-poetry-artist-books-1234601190/.

77. See Abdelkebir Khatibi, "A Note on the Calligraphic Sign," in Lennsen, Rogers, and Shabout, eds., *Modern Art in the Arab World*, 354. These ideas were fully developed in *The Wound of the Proper Name*: see Abdelkebir Khatibi, *La blessure du nom propre* (Les Lettres nouvelles, 1974).

78. Such acts stand in sharp contrast to the tradition outlined in Lawrence Venuti, *The Translator's Invisibility: A History of Translation* (Routledge, 2008).

79. For this and all other readings of the Arabic texts, I am immensely indebted to Ghenwa Hayek and Adrien Zakar.

80. In a lecture, Huda Fakhreddine described Adnan's 2001 leporello devoted to al-Sayyab's "Unshudat al-Matar" held at the Ramzi and Saeda Dalloul Art Foundation in Beirut as an "eloquent and

4. "FOG IS MY LAND"

critically insightful visual translation," in which the repeating squares of the leporello reveal the form subtending al-Sayyab's free verse. Huda Fakhreddine, "Everyone Lives in Time and Poetry Begins at STOP: Etel Adnan and Arabic" (Etel Adnan: In the Rhythms of the World, Giorno Poetry Systems, New York City, 2025).

81. For more on the adoption of the term "arts plastiques" or "al-funun at-tashkiliyya" in the little maga-zine *Souffles* as a reference to explosives and its relation to armed anticolonial struggles throughout the third world, see Clare Davies, *Decolonizing Culture: Third World, Moroccan, and Arab Art in Souffles/Anfas, 1966–1972*, Essays of the Forum Transregionale Studien 2 (Forum Transregionale Studien, 2015), 24–26. For more on *Souffles-Anfas*, see Olivia C. Harrison and Teresa Villa-Ignacio, *Souffles-Anfas: A Critical Anthology from the Moroccan Journal of Culture and Politics* (Stanford University Press, 2015).

82. Al-Tayyib Salih, *Bandarshah*, trans. Denys Johnson-Davies (Kegan Paul, 1996), 3. I have cited my colleague Ghenwa Hayek's translation rather than that of Johnson-Davies but provide the latter for reference. On the way colonizing reading practices have distorted and undermined *Bandarshah's* reception, see هيفاء سعود الفيصل / Haifa Saud Alfaisal, "World Reading Strategies: Border Reading Ban-darshah / « بندرشاه » استراتيجيات القراءة العالمية: قراءة حدودية لـ," *Alif: Journal of Comparative Poetics*, no. 34 (2014): 199–224.

83. Obrist and Adnan, "Conversations with Etel Adnan," 30.

84. Teresa Villa-Ignacio reads Adnan's *There: In the Light and the Darkness of the Self and of the Other* as imagination of a "postnationalist, post-terrorist, entirely deterritorialized planet on which national boundaries and global networks are unmade by the resurgence of natural environments. Recognizing the historical finitude of the nation-state structure, *There* envisions a deterritorialized future in order to begin that deterritorialization in the present." Teresa Villa-Ignacio, "Apocalypse and Poethical Daring in Etel Adnan's There: In the Light and the Darkness of the Self and of the Other," *Contemporary Literature* 55, no. 2 (2014): 304–35.

85. Adnan calls the visual parts of the leporellos an "equivalence," both response and counterpoint as opposed to illustration or analysis, and embraces the term "Illuminations." See Adnan, "The Unfold-ing of an Artist's Book," 22, 25.

86. See Etel Adnan, "Light: The Ultimate Material for Art" (1973), translated from French by Teresa Villa-Ignacio, in Lennsen, Rogers, and Shabout, eds., *Modern Art in the Arab World*, 355–56.

87. Adnan develops this process in an age when the developments in new media described by Jacob Edmond in *Make It the Same: Poetry in the Age of Global Media* (Columbia University Press, 2019) generate a culture of iteration and sampling. That said, working in a staunchly analog medium with the intimacy of the painted book as form causes this act of copying from the so-called periphery to produce very different effects.

88. Adnan, "The Unfolding of an Artist's Book," 25.

89. Johanna Drucker, *The Alphabetic Labyrinth: The Letters in History and Imagination* (Thames and Hudson, 1995).

90. Johannes Trithemius, *In Praise of Scribes: De Laude Scriptorum* (Coronado Press, 1974), 472.

91. Caroline Bergvall, *Fig* (Salt, 2005), 65.

92. See "Middling English," in Caroline Bergvall, *Meddle English: New and Selected Texts* (Nightboat Books, 2011), 5–19.

93. Bergvall, "Middling English," 5.

94. Bergvall, *Fig*, 65.

95. Obrist and Adnan, "Conversations with Etel Adnan," 31.

96. Etel Adnan, *Journey to Mount Tamalpais: An Essay* (Post-Apollo Press, 1986), 32.

97. For an argument that "the leporello opens a horizontal space that enables possibilities of being, of thinking, and of acting that are at once historical and new," see Rozen Whitworth, "The Unfolding of an Artist's Book: Etel Adnan, Relationality, and the Fold," *Journal of Middle East Women's Studies* 20, no. 1 (March 1, 2024): 141–48, https://doi.org/10.1215/15525864-10961873.

98. Adnan, "The Unfolding of an Artist's Book," 22.

99. Adnan and Robertson, "Etel Adnan by Lisa Robertson."

100. Adnan, "The Unfolding of an Artist's Book," 24.

101. Iftikhar Dadi, "Rethinking Calligraphic Modernism," in *Discrepant Abstraction*, ed. Kobena Mercer (MIT Press, 2006), 98. Treichl characterizes the artists of the Hurufiyya movement as modernizing Islamic calligraphy while enacting an evacuation of meaning: "The characters become pure signs, and temporarily emptied of their referential meaning, they become available for new meanings." See Christiane Treichl, *Art and Language: Explorations in (Post) Modern Thought and Visual Culture* (Kassel University Press, 2017), 3. Naef further contextualizes Adnan's place within this pan-Arab art movement, the only one of its kind, as she points out; see Silvia Naef, " 'Painting in Arabic': Etel Adnan and the Invention of a New Language," *Manazir Journal* 1 (2019): 14–22.

102. Dadi, "Rethinking Calligraphic Modernism," 111. See also Dipesh Chakrabarty, *Provincializing Europe* (Princeton University Press, 2007).

103. Adnan and Robertson, "Etel Adnan by Lisa Robertson."

104. I have made a related argument regarding the first "English" translation of Ezra Pound's Fascist Italian *Cantos* in Jennifer Scappettone, " 'Più MOndo i: / TUtti!': Traffics of Historicism in Jackson Mac Low's Contemporary Lyricism," *Modern Philology* 105, no. 1 (2007): 185–212, https://doi.org/10.1086/587207.

105. On the performed self-translation, see my dialogue with Adnan from September 2017 at https://media.sas.upenn.edu/app/public/watch.php?file_id=223293.

106. Etel Adnan, "Woman Between Cultures: Interview with Etel Adnan," by Allen Douglas and Fedwa Malti-Douglas, January 8, 1987, quoted in Lisa Suhair Majaj and Amal Amireh, introduction to *Etel Adnan: Critical Essays*, 18. Interview with Rushkowsky appears on page 52.

107. See Sonja Mejcher-Atassi, "Breaking the Silence: Etel Adnan's *Sitt Marie-Rose* and *The Arab Apocalypse*," in *Poetry's Voice—Society's Norms: Forms of Interaction between Middle Eastern Writers and their Societies*, ed. Andreas Pflitsch and Barbara Winckler (Reichert, 2006), 208; Caroline Seymour-Jorn, "*The Arab Apocalypse* as a Critique of Colonialism and Imperialism," in Majaj and Amireh, eds., *Etel Adnan: Critical Essays*, 43; and Aditi Machado, "On Etel Adnan's 'The Arab Apocalypse,' " *Jacket2*, November 30, 2016, https://jacket2.org/article/etel-adnans-arab-apocalypse.

108. Obrist and Adnan, "Conversations with Etel Adnan," 81.

109. See Chadwick Allen, *Trans-Indigenous: Methodologies for Global Native Literary Studies* (University of Minnesota Press, 2012), and Edgar Garcia's application of this methodology toward world poetry in *Signs of the Americas: A Poetics of Pictography, Hieroglyphs, and Khipu* (University of Chicago Press, 2020).

110. Etel Adnan, *The Arab Apocalypse* (Post-Apollo Press, 1989), 7. This volume will hereafter be referred to as *AA*.

111. *AA*, 7.

112. Toufic cites the figure of 38.7 percent tallied in 1999 when hailing the illiterate fraction of adult Arabs. See *AA*; Toufic's foreword has no pagination but is reproduced in Jalal Toufic, *The Withdrawal of Tradition Past a Surpassing Disaster* (Forthcoming Books, 2009), http://www.jalaltoufic.com/downloads/Jalal_Toufic,_The_Withdrawal_of_Tradition_Past_a_Surpassing_Disaster.pdf.

113. See "Credits Included," in Toufic, *The Withdrawal of Tradition Past a Surpassing Disaster*, 11–12.

114. Toufic, *The Withdrawal of Tradition Past a Surpassing Disaster*, 12.

115. See Ammiel Alcalay, *To Look at the Sea Is to Become What One Is: An Etel Adnan Reader*, ed. Thom Donovan and Brandon Shimoda, vol. 1 (Nightboat Books, 2014), viii. For more on global solidarity with Palestine, see Olivia C. Harrison, "Cross-Colonial Poetics: *Souffles-Anfas* and the Figure of Palestine," *PMLA* 128, no. 2 (March 2013): 353–69. For a treatment of the place of Palestine in antiracist activism and anticolonial solidarity in France, see Olivia C. Harrison, *Natives Against Nativism: Antiracism and Indigenous Critique in Postcolonial France* (University of Minnesota Press, 2023).

4. "FOG IS MY LAND"   351

116. Amelia Rosselli, "Paesaggio con figure," in *CI* 276.

117. Tillman and Adnan, "Etel Adnan: Children of the Sun." Schreber's *Grundsprache* has been translated as basic language or as "fundamental" language, emphasizing the fundament. See Daniel Paul Schreber, *Memoirs of My Nervous Illness* [1903], trans. Ida Macalpine and Richard A. Hunter (Harvard University Press, 1988), 119. To enumerate the many analyses of Schreber's work here, from Freud to Deleuze and Guattari's *Anti-Oedipus*, would be superfluous.

118. Toufic, *The Withdrawal of Tradition Past a Surpassing Disaster*, 29–30.

119. Obrist and Adnan, "Conversations with Etel Adnan," 81.

120. Adnan, "Light: The Ultimate Material for Art," 356.

121. See for instance Katherine Hayles, *How We Think: Digital Media and Contemporary Technogenesis* (University of Chicago Press, 2012).

122. Etel Adnan, *L'apocalypse arabe* (Galerie Lelong, 2021), 58. See Scappettone and Adnan, interview on PennSound, Part 7 on Cultural Identity, Multilingualism, and Translation, https://media.sas.upenn .edu/app/public/watch.php?file_id=223293

123. Toufic, *The Withdrawal of Tradition Past a Surpassing Disaster*, 86n.

124. Kurjaković and Adnan, "Etel Adnan: Every One of Us Is a Radio Transmitter," 91.

125. See "Dictation and 'A Textbook of Poetry,'" in Jack Spicer, *The House That Jack Built: The Collected Lectures of Jack Spicer*, ed. Peter Gizzi (Wesleyan University Press, 2010), 1–48.

126. For an analysis of Marinetti's claim in the manifesto opening, see Jeffrey T. Schnapp, "Propeller Talk," *Modernism/Modernity* 1, no. 3 (September 1, 1994): 153–78.

127. Ashon T. Crawley, *Blackpentecostal Breath: The Aesthetics of Possibility* (Fordham University Press, 2016), 201. Crawley is building on the analysis of the Arabic heterography and authorial ambiguity offered by Ronald A. T. Judy, *(Dis)Forming the American Canon: African-Arabic Slave Narratives and the Vernacular* (University of Minnesota Press, 1993). In my reading, xenoglossia would have been more scandalous to cultural commentators, who were unprepared to believe that Black congregants of multiple classes would find themselves able to read or speak natural languages in which they lacked training.

128. Crawley, *Blackpentecostal Breath*, 3. Others have read the irregularities of Bilali's manuscript not as cryptic but as innovations deriving from African vernacular usage and oral transcription. See Yusef Progler, "Ben Ali and His Arabic Diary: Encountering an African Muslim in Antebellum America," *Muslim and Arab Perspectives*, no. 5–11 (2004): 19–60. Pentecostalism has evolved practices in which, in Fred Moten's terms, the personal becomes much larger, insofar as "We're sent to one another": "to be sent, to be transported out of yourself, it's an ecstatic experience. . . . It's not an experience of interiority, it's an experience of *exteriority*, it's an *exteriorization*." See Adam Fitzgerald, "An Interview with Fred Moten, Part 1," *Literary Hub* (blog), August 5, 2015, https://lithub.com/an -interview-with-fred-moten-pt-i/.

129. My argument thus resonates with Teresa Villa Ignacio's ultimate conclusion that "By . . . commemorating the future of the *you* and the *I* in its present tense, [Adnan] dares the impossibility of community into its tense present." See Villa-Ignacio, "Apocalypse and Poethical Daring in Etel Adnan's *There*," 333.

130. Adnan, "To Write in a Foreign Language," 32.

131. Édouard Glissant, *Poetic Intention*, trans. Nathanaël, with Anne Malena (Nightboat Books, 2010), 79–80; Édouard Glissant, *L'intention poétique: Poétique II* (Gallimard, 1997), 85.

132. Adnan and Robertson, "Etel Adnan by Lisa Robertson."

133. Etel Adnan, *Sea and Fog* (Nightboat Books, 2012), 101.

134. Obrist and Adnan, "Conversations with Etel Adnan," 50.

135. See Adnan, *Journey to Mount Tamalpais*, 10. Walter Benjamin, "The Task of the Translator," in *Selected Writings*, ed. Marcus Paul Bullock and Michael William Jennings, vol. 1 (Belknap, 1996), 258.

136. Adnan, *Journey to Mount Tamalpais*, 63.

137. Adnan, "The Unfolding of an Artist's Book," 24.

5. GLOTTAL STOP: XENOGLOSSIC BREATHING AND TRANSMUTATIONS OF THE MOTHER TONGUE IN LATASHA N. NEVADA DIGGS

1. Latasha N. Nevada Diggs, "2014: The Year According to LaTasha N. Nevada Diggs," Walker Art Center, *Guest List* (blog), December 23, 2014, https://walkerart.org/magazine/2014-the-year-according -to-latasha-n-nevada-diggs.

2. Diggs, "2014." Amid this litany, Diggs inserts the comment, "Something seems to be happening where, in social media, local concerns are becoming global matters and where we are witnessing and participating in mobilization more than we have in a dang long time."

3. Theresa Hak Kyung Cha, *DICTEE* (Berkeley: University of California Press, 2001), 17, 18.

4. LaTasha N. Nevada Diggs, *TwERK* (Belladonna, 2013), 89. Hereafter *T*.

5. Diggs, "2014." The embedded quotation is from the promotional material for the show, archived at https://thekitchen.org/event/bishi-albion-voice.

6. Diggs, "2014."

7. Matthew Hardern, director, *Albion Voice*, Digitized music video (Gryphon Records, 2012), https:// www.youtube.com/watch?v=QEWhVmzWjIc.

8. Bishi, *Albion Voice*, Album (Gryphon, 2012). A more thorough analysis of this album on the musicological front appears in Simon Keegan-Phipps and Trish Winter, "*Albion Voice*: The Englishness of Bishi," in *Mad Dogs and Englishness: Popular Music and English Identities*, ed. Lee Brooks, Mark Donnelly, and Richard Mills (Bloomsbury, 2017), 193–210. Keegan-Phipps and Winter present Bishi as an example of cosmopolitanism that problematizes the dualism of elite and discrepant hybridity, arguing that her voice is characterized by Received Pronunciation (RP) more than the regional or working-class accents of British pop: "Bishi's RP represents a thoroughly standardized English voice, which not only disrupts common perceptions of vocal authenticity (as inalienable from the local, regional, working class voice) but also throws into sharp relief the extensive heterophony of other sounds and images from which the album is created" (204).

9. Ashon T. Crawley, *Blackpentecostal Breath: The Aesthetics of Possibility* (Fordham University Press, 2016), 2.

10. *T*, 5. For the generative dialogue across our projects and his thinking on metaphors of opacity versus iridescence, I wish to thank my colleague Edgar Garcia, author of *Signs of the Americas*.

11. LaTasha N. Nevada Diggs, Morgan Parker, and Virginia McLure, "LaTasha N. Nevada Diggs & Morgan Parker by Virginia McLure," *BOMB Magazine*, March 26, 2014, https://bombmagazine.org /articles/latasha-n-nevada-diggs-morgan-parker/.

12. Fred Moten, *In the Break: The Aesthetics of the Black Radical Tradition* (University of Minnesota Press, 2003), 39–40; hereafter *ITB*.

13. For a recent rereading of global Black anglophone decolonial projects as acts of "worldmaking" rather than anticolonial nationalism, see Adom Getachew, *Worldmaking After Empire: The Rise and Fall of Self-Determination* (Princeton University Press, 2019).

14. *ITB*, 2. See Saidiya V. Hartman, *Scenes of Subjection: Terror, Slavery, and Self-Making in Nineteenth-Century America*, Race and American Culture (Oxford University Press, 1997); and Judith Butler, *The Psychic Life of Power: Theories in Subjection* (Stanford University Press, 1997).

15. Frantz Fanon, *Black Skin, White Masks*, trans. Charles Lamb Markmann (Pluto, 2008).

16. See Jacques Derrida, "The Law of Genre," trans. Avital Ronell, *Glyph* 7 (1980): 202–32. See also the precursor to Derrida in Merleau-Ponty's description of the "flesh" as "folding-back, invagination, or padding." Maurice Merleau-Ponty, *The Visible and the Invisible*, ed. Claude Left (Northwestern University Press, 1968), 152. Although Moten cites a host of women theorists, the bulk of his artistic references in this early work are male jazz musicians and writers (including queer men); it will be productive to see how they might apply or necessitate reworking in light of performances by women.

5. GLOTTAL STOP   353

17. For "surplus lyricism," see *ITB*, 26. The seminal text is Hortense Spillers, "Mama's Baby, Papa's Maybe: An American Grammar Book," *Diacritics* 17, no. 2 (1987): 65–81.

18. *ITB*, 38–39. "Wounded kinship" is Nathaniel Mackey's phrase, with reference to the horn of Eric Dolphy, in *Paracritical Hinge: Essays, Talks, Notes, Interviews* (University of Wisconsin Press, 2005), 224.

19. See especially Latasha N. Nevada Diggs, "The Liquor Store Opens at 10 am," *Quaderna* 2 (2014), https://quaderna.org/wp-content/uploads/2014/05/the-liquor-store-opens-at-10-am.pdf.

20. Review of *TwERK* by Urayoán Noel, *Lana Turner* 7 (2014), 392.

21. Antonio Gramsci, quoted in Alessandro Carlucci, "Alfredo Panzini: La faciloneria di un linguista," in *Il nostro Gramsci: Antonio Gramsci a colloquio con i protagonisti della storia d'Italia*, ed. Angelo D'Orsi (Viella, 2011), 263–69. Translation mine.

22. Tyrone Williams, "Poetic Language and the Outside (a Response to Daniel Tiffany)," *Tupelo Quarterly*, March 14, 2020, https://www.tupeloquarterly.com/prose/tyrone-williams/.

23. Private email correspondence with Belladonna founder and director Rachel Levitsky, April 16, 2015, and with Belladonna staff, July 13, 2022.

24. "The FPP Interview: LaTasha N. Nevada Diggs," *First Person Plural*, accessed April 1, 2015, http://www.firstpersonpluralharlem.com/2013/10/13/the-fpp-interview-latasha-n-nevada-diggs/.

25. "Edwin Torres (Bio Page)," *The Brooklyn Rail*, accessed April 15, 2024, https://brooklynrail.org/people/edwin-torres/.

26. *T*, 48.

27. LaTasha N. Nevada Diggs, Cross Cultural Poetics interview with Leonard Schwartz, January 16, 2014, accessed March 1, 2015, https://media.sas.upenn.edu/pennsound/groups/XCP/XCP_290_Diggs_1-16-14.mp3.

28. Diggs, "The Liquor Store Opens at 10 am," p. 1 of pdf.

29. Antena, "A Manifesto for Discomfortable Writing" (Antena Pamphlets: Manifestoes and How-To Guides, 2013), accessed March 15, 2015, http://antenaantena.org/wp-content/uploads/2012/06/discomfortable_eng.pdf, p. 2 of pdf. See also Antena, "A Manifesto for Ultratranslation" (Antena Pamphlets: Manifestoes and How-To Guides, 2013), accessed April 15, 2015, http://antenaantena.org/wp-content/uploads/2012/06/ultratranslation_eng.pdf, p. 2 of pdf. Antena Aire's public engagements include live reciprocal interpretation of panels like the one I attended at the &NOW festival in 2014 at the University of Colorado at Boulder, where Diggs presented "The Liquor Store Opens at 10 am" alongside Antena, Mónica de la Torre, and Jai Arun Ravine.

30. Antena, "A Manifesto for Discomfortable Writing," p. 1 of pdf.

31. *T*, 45; Diggs, Cross Cultural Poetics interview with Leonard Schwartz.

32. LaTasha N. Nevada Diggs, Skype conversation with Jennifer Scappettone's course in "Poetry of and off the Page," University of Chicago, February 12, 2014.

33. Doris Sommer, ed., *Bilingual Games: Some Literary Investigations* (Palgrave Macmillan, 2003), 9.

34. *T*, 34. See for instance LaTasha N. Nevada Diggs, "Poem Present Reading" (Poem Present Series, University of Chicago, November 6, 2014), https://www.youtube.com/watch?v=SP6aOmMyoME. Diggs's compatriot in poesy, Douglas Kearney, credited for crucial dialogue and the design of *TwERK*'s cover, has deconstructed this tendency of banter to domesticate experience of poetic material: "Possibly you suspect your poem is 'difficult' and you seek—via anecdote, explanation, or prolepsis—to make it 'easier,' lest you die up there, rictus slick with flop sweat." See Douglas Kearney, "I Killed, I Died: Banter, Self-Destruction, and the Poetry Reading" (Lecture, The Poetry Project, Bagley Wright Lecture Series on Poetry, May 20, 2021), https://doi.org/Transcription at https://yalereview.org/article/i-killed-i-died.

35. LaTasha N. Nevada Diggs, "LaTasha N. Nevada Diggs: Artist's Profile and Statement," Foundation for Contemporary Arts, *C.D. Wright Award for Poetry* (award announcement), 2020, https://www.foundationforcontemporaryarts.org/recipients/latasha-n-nevada-diggs/.

36. Nathaniel Mackey, "Breath and Precarity," in *Poetics and Precarity*, ed. Myung Mi Kim and Cristanne Miller (State University of New York Press, 2018), 8.

37. Gerard Manley Hopkins, "The Blessed Virgin Compared to the Air We Breathe," in *Poems and Prose* (Penguin, 1985), 54.

38. Shannon Gibney and LaTasha N. Nevada Diggs, "Muscle Memory/Blood Memory," accessed October 30, 2024, https://walkerart.org/magazine/latasha-diggs-twerk-poetry/. It seems important to note here that critics have resisted the popular cultural absorption of twerking as essentially African, although it may be an "oral-kinetic étude" that is part of a network of diasporic expression. See Kyra D. Gaunt, *The Games Black Girls Play: Learning the Ropes from Double-Dutch to Hip-Hop* (NYU Press, 2006); and Kyra D. Gaunt, "Is Twerking African? Dancing and Diaspora as Embodied Knowledge on YouTube," in *The Routledge Companion to Black Women's Cultural Histories* (Routledge, 2021), 310–20.

39. Ginny and Diggs, "Muscle Memory/Blood Memory." On Diggs's trajectory as a dancer, see her autobiographical essay "Shake Your Money Maker," at Harriet, Poetry Foundation, December 3, 2013, accessed April 1, 2015, http://www.poetryfoundation.org/harriet/2013/12/shake-your-money-maker/.

40. See, for example, Hadley Freeman, "Miley Cyrus's Twerking Routine Was Cultural Appropriation at Its Worst," *UK Guardian*, August 27, 2013. On the media storm surrounding twerk's (non)entry into the Oxford English Dictionary, see Maddie Crum, "Was 'Twerk' Actually Added to the Dictionary?", *Huffington Post*, May 22, 2014, accessed April 1, 2015, http://www.huffingtonpost.com/2014/05/22/new-dictionary-words_n_5366127.html.

41. "Advance Praise for *TwERK*," in *TwERK* front matter, n.p.

42. On the Chinese written character as a medium for poetry, see Ernest Fenollosa, *The Chinese Written Character as a Medium for Poetry*, ed. Ezra Pound, Haun Saussy, Jonathan Stalling, and Lucas Klein (Fordham University Press, 2008).

43. LaTasha N. Nevada Diggs, "kanji gnu glue," *Black Scholar* 38, nos. 2–3 (Summer–Fall 2008): 35.

44. Diggs, Poem Present performance at the University of Chicago.

45. Amaranth Borsuk, Review of *TwERK*, *Poetry Project Newsletter* (Fall 2013), https://www.2009-2019.poetryproject.org/wp-content/uploads/n237.pdf.

46. Diggs, "The Liquor Store Opens at 10 am," p. 6 of pdf.

47. Antonio Gramsci, *Quaderni del carcere*, ed. Valentino Gerratana, vol. 2 (Einaudi, 2014), 1376. My translation.

48. M. NourbeSe Philip, "Wor(l)ds Interrupted: The Unhistory of the Kari Basin," ed. Janet Neigh, *Jacket2*, September 17, 2013, https://jacket2.org/article/worlds-interrupted.

49. Diggs describes her interest in pidgin as "this 'collage' of words, sounds, histories, natural forces that conjoined, [to] create this new language." See "DWYCK: a Cipher on Hip Hop Poetics Part 1," Harriet, Poetry Foundation, December 18, 2013, accessed April 1, 2015, http://www.poetryfoundation.org/harriet/2013/12/dwyck-a-cpher-on-hip-hop-poetics-part-1/.

50. See Ernesto Laclau and Chantal Mouffe, *Hegemony and Socialist Strategy* (Verso, 1985).

51. Sarah Dowling, "Multilingual Sounds: Coca-Cola's 'It's Beautiful' vs. LaTasha N. Nevada Diggs's *TwERK*," *Jacket2*, October 19, 2014, accessed April 10, 2015, http://jacket2.org/commentary/multilingual-sounds.

52. Mackey, "Breath and Precarity," 8.

53. Antena, "A Manifesto for Ultratranslation," p. 3 of pdf.

54. Antonio Gramsci, *Selections from Cultural Writings*, ed. David Forgacs (University Press, 1985), 27.

55. Antonio Gramsci, *Selections from Critical Writings*, 43.

56. "New York and the Hudson: A Spring Impression," in Henry James, *Collected Travel Writings: Great Britain and America*, ed. Richard Howard (Library of America/Random House, 1993), 471.

57. Diggs, Parker, and McLure, "LaTasha N. Nevada Diggs & Morgan Parker by Virginia McLure."

58. LaTasha N. Nevada Diggs, "LaTasha N. Nevada Diggs Presents at the 2019 Creative Capital Artist Retreat," YouTube, September 30, 2019, https://www.youtube.com/.

5. GLOTTAL STOP ☙ 355

59. Diggs, "LaTasha N. Nevada Diggs Presents at the 2019 Creative Capital Artist Retreat."

60. LaTasha Diggs, "LaTasha N. Nevada Diggs: Global Studies," Creative Capital, 2016, https://creative-capital.org/artists/latasha-n-nevada-diggs/.

61. LaTasha N. Nevada Diggs, "Subverting the Obvious with LaTasha N. Nevada Diggs | 92NY Insider," 92NY, accessed March 24, 2024, https://www.92ny.org/insider/latasha-n-nevada-diggs.

62. LaTasha N. Nevada Diggs, *Village* (Coffee House Press, 2023), 26. Hereafter, this volume will be cited as *V*.

63. See Alaina E. Roberts, *I've Been Here All the While: Black Freedom on Native Land* (University of Pennsylvania Press, 2021); Anya Montiel, "Together We Lift The Sky: yəhaẃ and Black-Indigenous Artists Advance Social Justice," *National Museum of the American Indian Magazine* 21, no. 4 (Winter 2020), https://www.americanindianmagazine.org/story/together-we-lift-the-sky; Tiya Miles, *Ties That Bind: The Story of an Afro-Cherokee Family in Slavery and Freedom* (University of California Press, 2015); Malinda Maynor Lowery, *Lumbee Indians in the Jim Crow South: Race, Identity, and the Making of a Nation* (University of North Carolina Press, 2010); David A. Chang, *The Color of the Land: Race, Nation, and the Politics of Landownership in Oklahoma, 1832–1929* (University of North Carolina Press, 2010); Gabrielle Tayac, ed., *IndiVisible: African-Native American Lives in the Americas* (Smithsonian Institution's National Museum of the American Indian, in association with the National Museum of African American History and Culture and the Smithsonian Institution Traveling Exhibition Service, 2009); and Joyce Pualani Warren, "Reading Bodies, Writing Blackness: Anti-/Blackness and Nineteenth-Century Kanaka Maoli Literary Nationalism," *American Indian Culture and Research Journal* 43, no. 2 (May 1, 2019): 51, https://doi.org/10.17953/aicrj.43.2.warren. See also the online exhibition curated by Anya Montiel, "Ancestors Know Who We Are: Black-Indigenous Women Artists Address Race, Gender, Multiracial Identity, and Intergenerational Knowledge," Ancestors Know Who We Are | Smithsonian National Museum of the American Indian, 2022, https://americanindian.si.edu/; and Eve Tuck's podcast with graduate students at the University of Toronto devoted to Black and Indigenous peoples on Turtle Island: "The Henceforward," http://www.thehenceforward.com. Intersectionality is also an important framework for understanding this more playfully worded "clusterfuck"; the classic text is Kimberlé Crenshaw, "Mapping the Margins: Intersectionality, Identity Politics, and Violence Against Women of Color," *Stanford Law Review* 43, no. 6 (1991): 1241–99, https://doi.org/10.2307/1229039.

64. See for instance *World Poetry Day Special: LaTasha N. Nevada Diggs*, Ocean Archive (Venice, Italy, 2019), https://ocean-archive.org/view/602. In an article that follows upon her coediting of the *Cambridge History of American Poetry*, Stephanie Burt identifies *TwERK* as an example of the process-based definition of American poetry: "At once inventive and brilliantly symptomatic, Diggs's work draws together many of the ways in which a poem can insist that it is not a thing, not stable, but a transformative performance, a rival to other performances: pop stars' celebrity, correspondents' privacy, instrumental music, educational testing, freestyle rapping." Stephanie Burt, "Is American Poetry Still a Thing?," *American Literary History* 28, no. 2 (April 1, 2016): 271–87, https://doi.org/10.1093/alh/ajw009.

65. *ITB*, 6. The "sexual 'cut'" is a phrase from Nathaniel Mackey's *Bedouin Hornbook* (University of Kentucky, 1987).

66. *V*, 107.

67. Urayoán Noel and LaTasha N. Nevada Diggs, "LaTasha N. Nevada Diggs by Urayoán Noel: Making Visible the Muted Disasters," *BOMB Magazine*, February 7, 2023, https://bombmagazine.org/articles/latasha-n-nevada-diggs-by-urayoán-noel/. Diggs is referring to Hillary Rodham Clinton, *It Takes a Village: And Other Lessons Children Teach Us* (Simon & Schuster, 1996).

68. *V*, 48–49.

69. *V*, 10, 32, 68.

5. GLOTTAL STOP

70. *V*, 62–66.

71. *V*, 92, 117.

72. *V*, 48–49.

73. Noel and Diggs, "LaTasha N. Nevada Diggs by Urayoán Noel." On critical fabulation, see Saidiya Hartman, "Venus in Two Acts," *Small Axe* 12, no. 2 (July 17, 2008): 1–14.

74. *V*, 33, 32.

75. Christina Elizabeth Sharpe, *In the Wake: On Blackness and Being* (Duke University Press, 2016), 30.

76. Noel and Diggs, "LaTasha N. Nevada Diggs by Urayoán Noel."

77. Noel and Diggs, "LaTasha N. Nevada Diggs by Urayoán Noel."

78. Noel and Diggs, "LaTasha N. Nevada Diggs by Urayoán Noel."

79. Diggs, "What kind of impact—artistic, intellectual, communal, civic, social, political, environmental, etc.—do you hope your project will have? (200 words)," in *V*, 68.

80. Schomburg Center, "Poetry for Our Time: Latasha N. Nevada Diggs & Claudia Rankine | Schomburg Center Literary Festival," June 17, 2023, https://www.youtube.com/watch?v=4LXAH_r2iHU.

81. See Hurston's 1933 recorded reperformance of "Shove It Over": Zora Neale Hurston, "Florida Memory • Zora Neale Hurston, the WPA in Florida, and the Cross City Turpentine Camp," State Library and Archives of Florida, Florida Memory, accessed March 23, 2024, https://www.floridamemory.com/learn/classroom/learning-units/zora-neale-hurston/documents/audio/.

82. Diggs, "Subverting the Obvious."

83. Fred Moten, blurb for M. NourbeSe Philip, *She Tries Her Tongue, Her Silence Softly Breaks* (Wesleyan University Press, 2015). Now published by the author's own Poui Publications in Toronto.

84. Philip, *She Tries Her Tongue, Her Silence Softly Breaks*, 89.

85. Philip, *She Tries Her Tongue, Her Silence Softly Breaks*, 77, 90.

86. Philip, *She Tries Her Tongue, Her Silence Softly Breaks*, 85.

87. Philip, *She Tries Her Tongue, Her Silence Softly Breaks*, 87.

88. Cha, *DICTEE*, 17, 18.

89. Philip, *She Tries Her Tongue, Her Silence Softly Breaks*, 30.

90. Philip, *She Tries Her Tongue, Her Silence Softly Breaks*, 33.

91. Philip, *She Tries Her Tongue, Her Silence Softly Breaks*, 30, 32.

92. M. NourbeSe Philip, *Zong!* (Wesleyan University Press, 2008). See Sharpe, *In the Wake*, 108. There is no space here to do justice to this essential work. Many critics have thought about its multilingual character, including Eva Karpinski, who writes of how "philip mobilizes multilingual plasticity and polysemy through strategies that include breaking down larger units of language into smaller molecules, to the level of syllables, phonemes, plosives, labials, and vowels; reducing language to a prelinguistic, preliteracy state of grunts, moans, and gasps, where no distinction between languages is marked." Eva C. Karpinski, "Moving the Bones: Multilingual Plasticity in Marlene NourbeSe Philip's Zong!," *Canadian Review of Comparative Literature / Revue Canadienne de Littérature Comparée* 45, no. 4 (2018): 639. Eventually, Karpinski argues, "West African patois is . . . allowed to take over the entire page (e.g. 168), where African languages are speaking to/through each other" (641).

93. M. NourbeSe Philip, "The Ga(s)p," in *Poetics and Precarity*, 31–40.

94. Philip, "The Ga(s)p," 39.

95. Philip, "The Ga(s)p," 31.

96. Philip, "The Ga(s)p," 32.

97. Philip, "The Ga(s)p," 38.

98. Sharpe, *In the Wake*.

99. Philip, "The Ga(s)p," 39.

100. Philip, "The Ga(s)p," 38.

101. Zora Neale Hurston, *Mules and Men* (Harper Perennial, 2008), 1.

102. LaTasha N. Nevada Diggs, "LaTasha N. Nevada Diggs-Artist's Profile and Statement," Foundation for Contemporary Arts, C.D. Wright Award for Poetry (award announcement), 2020, https://www.foundationforcontemporaryarts.org/recipients/latasha-n-nevada-diggs/.

103. James, "New York and the Hudson," 452, 453.

104. LaTasha N. Nevada Diggs, "Village" (Joe's Pub, New York City, May 25, 2023), https://www.youtube.com/watch?v=Ozegd_7yvcA.

CODA: A XENOGLOSSIC COMMUNITY TO COME: BELONGING BY ROGUE TRANSLATION IN SAWAKO NAKAYASU AND SAGAWA CHIKA'S *MOUTH: EATS COLOR*

1. Chika Sagawa, *The Collected Poems of Chika Sagawa*, trans. Sawako Nakayasu (Canarium Books, 2015).

2. Sawako Nakayasu, "Translation Is a Genre" (Poem Present, University of Chicago, March 2, 2020).

3. For an account of this double marginalization, see Rina Kikuchi and Carol Hayes, "Selected Translations of Sagawa Chika's poems (I)," *Shiga daigaku keizai keiei kenkyūsho (Institute for Business and Economics Research, Shiga University) Working Papers Online Journal* 192 (June 2013), http://mokuroku.biwako.shiga-u.ac.jp/WP/No192.pdf.

4. Irina Holca, "Sawako Nakayasu Eats Sagawa Chika: Translation, Poetry, and (Post)Modernism," *Japanese Studies* 41, no. 3 (September 2, 2021): 379–94, https://doi.org/10.1080/10371397.2021.2008236. See Sagawa Chika, *Sagawa Chika zenshū*, ed. Ryū Shimada (Shoshi Kankanbō, 2022).

5. See Nakayasu's introduction to Sagawa, *The Collected Poems of Chika Sagawa*, xvi.

6. Alys Moody, "The Imagination of a New Era: New Translations of Japanese Modernism," *Sydney Review of Books*, February 6, 2018, https://sydneyreviewofbooks.com/review/chika-sagawa-hirato-renkichi-collected-poems/.

7. For an account of the jingoistic verse trends into which avant-garde and proletarian poets were forced during the Pacific War, see John Solt, *Shredding the Tapestry of Meaning: The Poetry and Poetics of Kitasono Katue (1902–1978)* (Harvard University Press, 1999), 136–211.

8. Naoki Sakai, *Translation and Subjectivity: On Japan and Cultural Nationalism* (University of Minnesota Press, 1997), 5.

9. Sagawa, *The Collected Poems of Chika Sagawa*, 133.

10. This narrative is recounted in Nakayasu, "Translation Is a Genre." The book was published as Sawako Nakayasu with Chika Sagawa, *Mouth: Eats Color: Sagawa Chika Translations, Anti-Translations & Originals* (Rogue Factorial, 2011), hereafter cited as *MEC*.

11. Sakai, *Translation and Subjectivity*, 6.

12. Giorgio Agamben, *The Coming Community*, trans. Michael Hardt (University of Minnesota Press, 1993).

13. See "Insects," in *MEC*, 53, and Sawako Nakayasu, *The Ants* (Les Figues Press, 2014), as well as the metareflections on bees below.

14. Frances Chung, *Crazy Melon and Chinese Apple: The Poems of Frances Chung*, ed. Walter K. Lew (Wesleyan University Press, University Press of New England, 2000), 4.

15. Nakayasu, "Translation Is a Genre."

16. Chung, *Crazy Melon and Chinese Apple*, 134.

17. *MEC*, 71. For a synthesis of this hoax and a reading of its operations against the literary marketplace, see Marjorie Perloff, "In Search of the Authentic Other," *Boston Review*, April 2, 1997, https://www.bostonreview.net/forum/in-search-of-the-authentic-other/.

18. For a close reading of these changes, see Holca, "Sawako Nakayasu Eats Sagawa Chika," 383–84.

358   CODA

19. All the quotations from the rest of the paragraph hail from the cited piece in *MEC*, "Notes," n.p.

20. See Sawako Nakayasu, "Introduction to the Japanese Poems of Yi Sang," in Sang Yi, *Yi Sang: Selected Works*, trans. Don Mee Choi et al. (Wave Books, 2020), 84–85.

21. See for instance Lydia He Liu, *Translingual Practice: Literature, National Culture, and Translated Modernity—China, 1900–1937* (Stanford University Press, 1995); A. Suresh Canagarajah, *Translingual Practice: Global Englishes and Cosmopolitan Relations* (Routledge, 2013); Jerry Lee, *The Politics of Translingualism: After Englishes* (Taylor & Francis, 2017); and Sender Dovchin and Jerry Won Lee, eds., *Translinguistics: Negotiating Innovation and Ordinariness* (Routledge, 2020).

22. Sawako Nakayasu, *Say Translation Is Art* (Ugly Duckling Presse, 2020), 10.

23. Johannes Göransson, "Mouth: Eats Color and the Devoration of Languages," selections from University of Notre Dame graduate poetry workshop blog, January 12, 2015 (blog url unavailable for citation).

24. Miyuki Kamezawa, ed., *The Unforgettable Day: Cries of "Hibakusha" from Hiroshima and Nagasaki* (Group for Spreading Out "The Unforgettable Day," 1995).

25. Minae Mizumura, *The Fall of Language in the Age of English*, trans. Mari Yoshihara and Juliet Winters Carpenter (Columbia University Press, 2015), 175.

26. *Dell'origine, progressi e stato attuale d'ogni letteratura* was published in seven volumes in Parma (1782–1799) before it was translated into Spanish and published in Madrid. See Waïl S. Hassan, "Geopolitics of Comparison: World Literature Avant La Lettre," *Comparative Literature* 73, no. 3 (September 9, 2021): 255–69, https://doi.org/10.1215/00104124-8993912.

27. Amitav Ghosh, "Speaking of Babel: The Risks and Rewards of Writing About Polyglot Societies," *Comparative Literature* 72, no. 3 (September 9, 2020): 286, 287.

28. Sakai, *Translation and Subjectivity*, 4.

29. Antena (JD Pleucker and Jen/Eleana Hofer), *Manifesto for Interpretation as Instigation/Manifiesto para la interpretación como instigación* (Libros Antena•Antena Books, 2013), http://antenaantena .org/wp-content/uploads/2012/06/interpasinstig.pdf.

30. I refer to Rael San Fratello (Ron Raél and Virginia San Fratello), *Teeter-Totter Wall*, installed across the border of El Paso and Ciudad Juárez for 40 minutes on January 18, 2017; see https:// www.rael-sanfratello.com/made/teetertotter-wall; there are many other such provocations.

31. George Steiner, *After Babel: Aspects of Language and Translation*, 2nd ed. (Oxford University Press, 1992), xviii.

32. Don Mee Choi, "A Conversation with Don Mee Choi—Lantern Review Blog," December 5, 2012, https://www.lanternreview.com/blog/2012/12/05/a-conversation-with-don-mee-choi/.

33. Antena, *A Manifesto for Ultratranslation / Un manifiesto para la ultratraducción* (Antena Pamphlets: Manifestoes and How-To Guides, 2013), accessed April 15, 2024. I cite the English-language text for the convenience of the reader, aware that this move is in itself problematic and contrary to the spirit of the collective itself.

34. Nakayasu, "Translation Is a Genre."

35. Walter Benjamin, "The Task of the Translator," in *Selected Writings*, ed. Marcus Paul Bullock and Michael William Jennings, vol. 1 (Belknap Press, 1996), 260.

36. Don Mee Choi, *DMZ Colony* (Wave Books, 2020), 115.

Selected Bibliography

Adnan, Etel. *Journey to Mount Tamalpais: An Essay*. Post-Apollo Press, 1986.

——. *Sitt Marie-Rose: A Novel*. Post-Apollo Press, 1998.

——. *The Arab Apocalypse*. Post-Apollo Press, 1989.

——.*Voyage, War, Exile: Three Essays*. Litmus, 2025.

Adnan, Etel, and Hans-Ulrich Obrist, eds. *Etel Adnan in All Her Dimensions = Ītil ʿAdnān bi-kulli abʿādihā*. Mathaf, 2014.

Adorno, Theodor W. *Notes to Literature*. Ed. Rolf Tiedemann. Trans. Shierry Weber Nicholsen. Columbia University Press, 1991.

——. *Prisms*. Trans. Samuel Weber and Sherry Weber. MIT Press, 1981.

Agamben, Giorgio. *Categorie italiane: Studi di poetica*. Marsilio, 1996.

——. *The Coming Community*. Trans. Michael Hardt. University of Minnesota Press, 1993.

Alighieri, Dante. *De vulgari eloquentia*. Ed. Pier Vincenzo Mengaldo. Antenore, 1968.

——. *De vulgari eloquentia*. Trans. Steven Botterill. Cambridge University Press, 1996.

Anderson, Benedict R. *Imagined Communities: Reflections on the Origin and Spread of Nationalism*. Verso, 2006.

Aneesh, A. *Neutral Accent: How Language, Labor, and Life Become Global*. Duke University Press, 2015.

Annovi, Gian Maria. *Altri corpi: Poesia e corporalità negli anni sessanta*. Gedit, 2008.

Anzaldúa, Gloria. *Borderlands: The New Mestiza = La Frontera*. Spinsters/Aunt Lute, 1987.

Appiah, Kwame Anthony. *Cosmopolitanism: Ethics in a World of Strangers*. Norton, 2006.

Apter, Emily S. *Against World Literature: On the Politics of Untranslatability*. Verso, 2013.

——. *The Translation Zone: A New Comparative Literature*. Princeton University Press, 2006.

Arsanios, Mirene. *Notes on Mother Tongues: Colonialism, Class, and Giving What You Don't Have*. Ugly Duckling, 2020.

Arvidsson, Stefan. *Aryan Idols: Indo-European Mythology as Ideology and Science*. University of Chicago Press, 2006.

Attanasio, Daniela, and Emmanuela Tandello. *Amelia Rosselli*. S. Sciascia, 1997.

Auer, Peter. *Code-Switching in Conversation: Language, Interaction and Identity*. Routledge, 1998.

Bakhtin, Mikhail M. *The Dialogic Imagination: Four Essays*. Ed. Michael Holquist. Trans. Michael Holquist and Caryl Emerson. University of Texas Press, 1981.

——. *Rabelais and His World*. Trans. Helene Iswolsky. Indiana University Press, 2009.

Baldacci, Alessandro. *Amelia Rosselli*. Laterza, 2007.

Baldasso, Franco. *Against Redemption: Democracy, Memory, and Literature in Post-Fascist Italy*. Fordham University Press, 2022.

Bartleman, Frank. *Azusa Street*. Whitaker House, 2000.

Bauman, Richard. *Voices of Modernity: Language Ideologies and the Politics of Inequality*. Cambridge University Press, 2003.

Bello Minciacchi, Cecilia. "Emilio Villa, l'esilio nella lingua." *Avanguardia* 25, no. 74 (2020): 123–45.

Ben-Ghiat, Ruth. *Fascist Modernities: Italy, 1922–1945*. University of California Press, 2001.

——. "Language and the Construction of National Identity in Fascist Italy." *The European Legacy, toward New Paradigms* 2, no. 3 (1997): 438–43. https://doi.org/10.1080/10848779708579754.

Benjamin, Walter. *Selected Writings*. Ed. Marcus Paul Bullock and Michael William Jennings. 4 vols. Belknap, 1996.

Berghaus, Günter. *Futurism and Politics: Between Anarchist Rebellion and Fascist Reaction, 1909–1944*. Berghahn, 1996.

Bergvall, Caroline. "A Cat in the Throat—on Bilingual Occupants." *Jacket* 37 (Early 2009). http://jacketmagazine.com/37/bergvall-cat-throat.shtml.

——. *Meddle English: New and Selected Texts*. Nightboat, 2011.

Bernstein, Charles. *My Way: Speeches and Poems*. University of Chicago Press, 1999.

Bernstein, Michael André. *The Tale of the Tribe: Ezra Pound and the Modern Verse Epic*. Princeton University Press, 2014.

Bevilacqua, Alexander. *The Republic of Arabic Letters*. Harvard University Press, 2018.

Bhabha, Homi, Carol A. Breckenridge, Dipesh Chakrabarty, and Sheldon Pollock. "Cosmopolitanisms." *Public Culture* 12, no. 3 (2000): 577–89.

Bird Rose, Deborah. "Shimmer: When All You Love Is Being Trashed." In *Arts of Living on a Damaged Planet*. Ed. Anna Lowenhaupt Tsing, Elaine Gan, and Nils Bubandt. University of Minnesota Press, 2017.

Bisanti, Tatiana. *L'opera plurilingue di Amelia Rosselli: Un distorto, inesperto, espertissimo linguaggio*. ETS, 2007.

Bishi. *Albion Voice*. Album. Gryphon, 2012.

Bodmer, Frederick. *The Loom of Language*. Ed. Lancelot Thomas Hogben. George Allen, 1944.

Boon, Marcus. *The Politics of Vibration: Music as a Cosmopolitical Practice*. Duke University Press, 2022.

Borsuk, Amaranth. *The Book*. MIT Press, 2018.

Bradway, Tyler, and Elizabeth Freeman, eds. *Queer Kinship: Race, Sex, Belonging, Form*. Duke University Press, 2022.

Brathwaite, Kamau. *History of the Voice: The Development of Nation Language in Anglophone Caribbean Poetry*. New Beacon, 1984.

Briggs, Charles L., and Richard Bauman. "Language, Poetry, and Volk in Eighteenth-Century Germany: Johann Gottfried Herder's Construction of Tradition." In *Voices of Modernity: Language Ideologies and the Politics of Inequality*. Cambridge University Press, 2003. https://doi.org/10.1017/CBO9780511486647.006.

Campbell, Timothy C. *Wireless Writing in the Age of Marconi*. University of Minnesota Press, 2006.

Campos, Augusto de, Décio Pignatari, and Haroldo de Campos. *Teoria da poesia concreta: Textos críticos e manifestos, 1950–1960*. Edições Invenção, 1965.

Canagarajah, A. Suresh. *Translingual Practice: Global Englishes and Cosmopolitan Relations*. Routledge, 2013.

Carbognin, Francesco. *Le armoniose dissonanze: "Spazio metrico" e intertestualità nella poesia di Amelia Rosselli*. Gedit, 2008. http://www.loc.gov/catdir/toc/casalini07/08271402.pdf.

Cartledge, Mark J. *Speaking in Tongues: Multi-disciplinary Perspectives*. Wipf & Stock, 2012.

Casanova, Pascale. *The World Republic of Letters*. Trans. M. B. DeBevoise. Harvard University Press, 2004.

Cassin, Barbara, ed. *Vocabulaire européen des philosophies: dictionnaire des intraduisibles*. Le Robert, 2004.

Cassin, Barbara, Emily Apter, Jacques Lezra, and Michael Wood, eds. *Dictionary of Untranslatables: A Philosophical Lexicon*. Princeton University Press, 2014.

Cassirer, Ernst. *The Myth of the State*. Yale University Press, 1946.

SELECTED BIBLIOGRAPHY 361

Cavarero, Adriana. *For More Than One Voice: Toward a Philosophy of Vocal Expression*. Trans. Paul A. Kottman. Stanford University Press, 2005.

Cestaro, Gary P. *Dante and the Grammar of the Nursing Body*. University of Notre Dame Press, 2003.

Chakrabarty, Dipesh. *Provincializing Europe; with a New Preface by the Author*. Princeton University Press, 2007.

Cheah, Pheng, and Bruce Robbins, eds. *Cosmopolitics: Thinking and Feeling Beyond the Nation*. University of Minnesota Press, 1998.

Chow, Rey. *The Age of the World Target: Self-Referentiality in War, Theory, and Comparative Work*. Duke University Press, 2006.

Cixous, Hélène. *Entre l'écriture*. Des Femmes, 1986.

Cooper-Rompato, Christine F. *The Gift of Tongues: Women's Xenoglossia in the Later Middle Ages*. Penn State Press, 2010.

Cortellessa, Andrea, ed. *La furia dei venti contrari: Variazioni Amelia Rosselli, con testi inediti e dispersi dell'autrice*. Le Lettere, 2007.

Crawley, Ashon T. *Blackpentecostal Breath: The Aesthetics of Possibility*. Fordham University Press, 2017.

Damrosch, David. *How to Read World Literature*. Wiley-Blackwell, 2009.

——. *What Is World Literature?* Princeton University Press, 2003.

Daniélou, Alain. *Music and the Power of Sound: The Influence of Tuning and Interval on Consciousness*. Simon and Schuster, 1995.

D'Annunzio, Gabriele. *Italia o morte. La Pentecoste d'Italia*. La Fionda, 1919.

De Certeau, Michel. "Vocal Utopias: Glossolalias." *Representations*, no. 56 (1996): 29–47.

De March, Silvia. *Amelia Rosselli tra poesia e storia*. L'Ancora del Mediterraneo, 2006.

De Mauro, Tullio. *Storia linguistica dell'Italia unita*. Laterza e Figli, 1970.

Deleuze, Gilles, and Félix Guattari. *Kafka: Toward a Minor Literature*. Trans. Dana Polan. University of Minnesota Press, 1986.

——. *What Is Philosophy?* Trans. Hugh Tomlinson and Graham Burchell. Columbia University Press, 1994.

Depero, Fortunato. *Liriche Radiofoniche*. G. Morreale, 1934.

Derrida, Jacques. *Monolingualism of the Other, or, the Prosthesis of Origin*. Trans. Patrick Mensah. Stanford University Press, 1998.

——. *Sovereignties in Question: The Poetics of Paul Celan*. Ed. Thomas Dutoit and Outi Pasanen. Fordham University Press, 2005.

Devi, Mahasweta. *Breast Stories*. Trans. Gayatri Chakravorty Spivak. Seagull, 1997.

Diggs, LaTasha N. Nevada. "The Liquor Store Opens at 10 Am." *Quaderna* 2 (2014). https://quaderna.org/wp-content/uploads/2014/05/the-liquor-store-opens-at-10-am.pdf.

——. *TwERK*. Belladonna*, 2013.

——. *Village*. Coffee House, 2023.

Di Gianvito, Sara. *Nell'officina poetica di Amelia Rosselli: Il plurilinguismo dei Primi scritti e il ruolo del Diario in tre lingue*. Franco Cesati editore, 2022.

Dovchin, Sender, and Jerry Won Lee, eds. *Translinguistics: Negotiating Innovation and Ordinariness*. Routledge, 2020.

Dowling, Sarah. *Translingual Poetics: Writing Personhood under Settler Colonialism*. University of Iowa Press, 2018.

Drucker, Johanna. *Figuring the Word: Essays on Books, Writing, and Visual Poetics*. Granary, 1998.

Eco, Umberto. *La ricerca della lingua perfetta nella cultura europea*. Editori Laterza, 1993.

——. "Ur-Fascism, Adapted from a Speech Delivered at Columbia University in Commemoration of the Liberation of Europe." *New York Review of Books* 42, no. 11 (June 22, 1995): 12–15.

Edmond, Jacob. *Make It the Same: Poetry in the Age of Global Media*. Columbia University Press, 2019.

Fanon, Frantz. *Black Skin, White Masks; Forewords by Ziauddin Sardar and Homi K. Bhabha*. Trans. Charles Lamb Markmann. Pluto, 2008.

Feinsod, Harris. *The Poetry of the Americas: From Good Neighbors to Countercultures.* Oxford University Press, 2017.

Fenollosa, Ernest, Ezra Pound, Haun Saussy, Jonathan Stalling, and Lucas Klein, eds. *The Chinese Written Character as a Medium for Poetry.* Fordham University Press, 2010.

Fogu, Claudio. *The Fishing Net and the Spider Web: Mediterranean Imaginaries and the Making of Italians.* Palgrave Macmillan, 2020.

——. *The Historic Imaginary: Politics of History in Fascist Italy.* University of Toronto Press, 2003.

Foresti, Fabio, ed. *Credere, obbedire, combattere: Il regime linguistico nel ventennio.* Edizioni Pendragon, 2003.

Freytag-Loringhoven, Elsa von. *Body Sweats: The Uncensored Writings of Elsa von Freytag-Loringhoven.* Ed. Irene Gammel and Suzanne Zelazo. MIT Press, 2011.

Fusco, Florinda. *Amelia Rosselli.* Palumbo, 2007. http://www.ilibri.casalini.it/toc/08906519.pdf.

Gambarota, Paola. *Irresistible Signs: The Genius of Language and Italian National Identity.* University of Toronto Press, 2011.

Gammel, Irene. *Baroness Elsa: Gender, Dada, and Everyday Modernity: A Cultural Biography.* MIT Press, 2003.

Garcia, Edgar. *Signs of the Americas: A Poetics of Pictography, Hieroglyphs, and Khipu.* University of Chicago Press, 2020.

Gentile, Emilio. *The Struggle for Modernity: Nationalism, Futurism, and Fascism.* Praeger, 2003.

Ghosh, Amitav. "Speaking of Babel: The Risks and Rewards of Writing About Polyglot Societies." *Comparative Literature* 72, no. 3 (September 9, 2020): 283–98.

Glissant, Édouard. *Le Discours antillais.* Seuil, 1981.

——. *Philosophie de la relation: poésie en étendue.* Gallimard, 2009.

——. *Poetic Intention.* Trans. Nathanaël. Nightboat, 2010.

——. *Poetics of Relation.* Trans. Betsy Wing. University of Michigan Press, 1997.

Golino, Enzo. *Parola di duce: Il linguaggio totalitario del fascismo.* Rizzoli, 1994.

Göransson, Johannes. "The Beautiful Betrayal: Translingual Poetry as Counterfeit Voice." *Action Books* (blog). May 21, 2020. https://actionbooks.org/2020/05/the-beautiful-betrayal-translingual-poetry-as-counterfeit-voice-by-johannes-goransson/.

Gramsci, Antonio. *La questione meridionale.* Editori riuniti, 2005.

——. *Letteratura e vita nazionale.* Ed. Valentino Gerratana. Editori riuniti, 1996.

——. *Quaderni del carcere.* Ed. Valentino Gerratana. 4 vols. Einaudi, 2014.

——. *Selections from Cultural Writings.* Ed. David Forgacs. Harvard University Press, 1985.

Griffin, Roger. *Modernism and Fascism: The Sense of a Beginning Under Mussolini and Hitler.* Palgrave Macmillan, 2007.

——. *The Nature of Fascism.* St. Martin's, 1991.

Grimm, Jakob Karl Ludwig. *On the Origin of Language.* Trans. Raymond A. Wiley. Brill Archive, 1984.

Haraway, Donna Jeanne. *Staying with the Trouble: Making Kin in the Chthulucene.* Duke University Press, 2016.

Harkness, Nicholas. *Glossolalia and the Problem of Language.* University of Chicago Press, 2021.

Harrison, Olivia C. *Natives Against Nativism: Antiracism and Indigenous Critique in Postcolonial France.* University of Minnesota Press, 2023.

Hartman, Saidiya. *Lose Your Mother: A Journey Along the Atlantic Slave Route.* Farrar, Straus and Giroux, 2007.

——. *Scenes of Subjection: Terror, Slavery, and Self-Making in Nineteenth-Century America.* Race and American Culture. Oxford University Press, 1997.

——. "Venus in Two Acts." *Small Axe* 12, no. 2 (June 2008): 1–14.

Hassan, Waïl S. "Agency and Translational Literature: Ahdaf Soueif's 'The Map of Love.' " *PMLA* 121, no. 3 (May 2006): 753–68.

——. "Geopolitics of Comparison: World Literature Avant La Lettre." *Comparative Literature (University of Oregon)* 73, no. 3 (September 9, 2021): 255–69.

——. "Translational Literature and the Pleasures of Exile." *PMLA* 131, no. 5 (October 2016): 1435–43.

Hejinian, Lyn. *The Beginner.* Tuumba Press, 2002.

SELECTED BIBLIOGRAPHY 363

——. *The Language of Inquiry*. University of California Press, 2000.

Herder, Johann Gottfried. *Johann Gottfried Herder: Selected Early Works, 1764–1767: Addresses, Essays, and Drafts; Fragments on Recent German Literature*. Ed. Ernest A. Menze and Karl Menges. Penn State Press, 2010.

Hiddleston, Jane, and Wen-chin Ouyang, eds. *Multilingual Literature as World Literature*. Bloomsbury Academic, 2021.

Horkheimer, Max, and Theodor W. Adorno. *Dialectic of Enlightenment: Philosophical Fragments*. Ed. Gunzelin Schmid Noerr. Trans. Edmund Jephcott. Stanford University Press, 2002.

Huang, Yunte. *Chinese Whispers: Toward a Transpacific Poetics*. University of Chicago Press, 2022.

Hutton, Christopher. *Linguistics and the Third Reich: Mother-Tongue Fascism, Race and the Science of Language*. Routledge, 1999.

Ives, Peter. "Global English, Hegemony and Education: Lessons from Gramsci." *Educational Philosophy and Theory* 41, no. 6 (January 2009): 661–83. https://doi.org/10.1111/j.1469-5812.2008.00498.x.

——. *Gramsci's Politics of Language: Engaging the Bakhtin Circle and the Frankfurt School*. University of Toronto Press, 2004.

——. *Language and Hegemony in Gramsci*. Reading Gramsci. Pluto, 2004.

Jacobus, Mary. *Reading Cy Twombly: Poetry in Paint*. Princeton University Press, 2016.

Jakobson, Roman, and Linda R. Waugh. *The Sound Shape of Language*. Mouton de Gruyter, 1987.

James, Henry. *Collected Travel Writings: Great Britain and America*. Ed. Richard Howard. Library of America/Random House, 1993.

Janecek, Gerald. *Zaum: The Transrational Poetry of Russian Futurism*. San Diego State University Press, 1996.

Jing Tsu. *Sound and Script in Chinese Diaspora*. Harvard University Press, 2010.

Jolas, Eugène. *Eugene Jolas: Critical Writings, 1924–1951*. Ed. Klaus H. Kiefer and Rainer Rumold. Northwestern University Press, 2009.

——. "From Jabberwocky to Lettrism." *Transition* 1 (January 1948): 104–20.

——. *Man from Babel*. Yale University Press, 1998.

——. *Words from the Deluge*. Gotham Book Mart, 1941.

Joris, Pierre. *A Nomad Poetics: Essays*. Wesleyan University Press, 2003.

Kelbert, Eugenia. "Eugene Jolas: A Poet of Multilingualism." *L2 Journal* 7, no. 1 (2015).

Kellman, Steven G. *The Translingual Imagination*. University of Nebraska Press, 2014.

Kellman, Steven G., and Natasha Lvovich, eds. *The Routledge Handbook of Literary Translingualism*. Routledge, 2021.

Klein, Gabriella. *La politica linguistica del fascismo*. Il Mulino, 1986.

Klemperer, Victor. *The Language of the Third Reich: LTI, Lingua Tertii Imperii: A Philologist's Notebook*. Trans. Martin Brady. Athlone Press, 2000.

Kristeva, Julia. *Revolution in Poetic Language*. Columbia University Press, 1984.

——. *Strangers to Ourselves*. Columbia University Press, 1991.

Lahiri, Jhumpa. *Dove mi trovo*. Ugo Guanda Editore, 2018.

——. *In altre parole*. Ugo Guanda Editore, 2015.

——. *Translating Myself and Others*. Princeton University Press, 2022.

Last, Angela. "Fruit of the Cyclone: Undoing Geopolitics Through Geopoetics." *Geoforum* 64 (August 1, 2015): 56–64. https://doi.org/10.1016/j.geoforum.2015.05.019.

Lauret, Maria. *Wanderwords: Language Migration in American Literature*. Bloomsbury, 2014.

Lee, Jerry. *Locating Translingualism*. Cambridge University Press, 2022.

——. *The Politics of Translingualism: After Englishes*. Taylor & Francis, 2017.

Lincoln, Bruce. *Theorizing Myth: Narrative, Ideology, and Scholarship*. University of Chicago Press, 2000.

Liu, Lydia He. *Translingual Practice: Literature, National Culture, and Translated Modernity—China, 1900–1937*. Stanford University Press, 1995.

Marinetti, Filippo Tommaso. "Contro l'esterofilia. Manifesto futurista alle signore e agli intellettuali." *Gazzetta Del Popolo*, September 24, 1931. https://collections.library.yale.edu/catalog/10660837.

——. *Critical Writings*. Ed. Günter Berghaus. Trans. Doug Thompson. Farrar, Straus, and Giroux, 2006.

——. *Teoria e invenzione futurista*. Ed. Luciano De Maria. Mondadori, 1983.

——. *Zang Tumb Tumb: Adrianopoli Ottobre 1912: Parole in libertà*. Edizioni futuriste di "Poesia," 1914.

Marinetti, Filippo Tommaso, and Emilio Villa. *Dannunziana*. Ed. Luciano Caruso and Stelio Maria Martini. Visual Art Center, 1974.

Maximin, Daniel. *Les fruits du cyclone: Une géopoétique de la Caraïbe*. Seuil, 2006.

Mejcher-Atassi, Sonja. *Reading Across Modern Arabic Literature and Art*. Reichert, 2012.

Meschonnic, Henri. *Politique du rythme: Politique du sujet*. Verdier, 1995.

Mignolo, Walter. *Local Histories/Global Designs: Coloniality, Subaltern Knowledges, and Border Thinking*. Princeton University Press, 2012.

Miller, Joshua. *Accented America: The Cultural Politics of Multilingual Modernism*. Oxford University Press, 2011.

Mills, Watson E. *Glossolalia: A Bibliography*. E. Mellen, 1985.

——, ed. *Speaking in Tongues: A Guide to Research on Glossolalia*. W.B. Eerdmans, 1986.

Mizumura, Minae. *The Fall of Language in the Age of English*. Trans. Mari Yoshihara and Juliet Winters Carpenter. Columbia University Press, 2015.

Moe, Nelson. "At the Margins of Dominion: The Poetry of Amelia Rosselli." *Italica* 69, no. 2 (1992): 177–97.

Mondardini, Silvia. "Amelia fu Marion: «I me you the others». Appunti per il recupero degli scritti inglesi di Amelia Rosselli." *Cahiers d'études italiennes* no. 16 (June 30, 2013): 281–302. https://doi.org/10.4000/cei.1285.

Morphy, H. "From Dull to Brilliant: The Aesthetics of Spiritual Power Among the Yolngu." *Man* 24, no. 1 (1989): 21–40. https://doi.org/10.2307/2802545.

Moten, Fred. *In the Break: The Aesthetics of the Black Radical Tradition*. University of Minnesota Press, 2003.

Nakayasu, Sawako. *Say Translation Is Art*. Ugly Duckling, 2020.

Nakayasu, Sawako, and Chika Sagawa. *Mouth: Eats Color: Sagawa Chika Translations, Anti-Translations and Originals*. Rogue Factorial, 2011.

Noland, Carrie, and Barrett Watten, eds. *Diasporic Avant-Gardes: Experimental Poetics and Cultural Displacement*. Palgrave Macmillan, 2009.

North, Michael. *Reading 1922: A Return to the Scene of the Modern*. Oxford University Press, 1999.

Nosthoff, Anna-Verena. "Barbarism: Notes on the Thought of Theodor W. Adorno." *Critical Legal Thinking*: Law and the Political, October 15, 2014. https://criticallegalthinking.com/2014/10/15/barbarism-notes-thought-theodor-w-adorno/.

Obrist, Hans-Ulrich, ed. *Mapping It Out: An Alternative Atlas of Contemporary Cartographies*. Thames & Hudson, 2014.

Ogden, C. K. *Debabelization: With a Survey of Contemporary Opinion on the Problem of a Universal Language*. Kegan Paul, Trench, 1931.

Orwell, George. "Politics and the English Language." *Horizon* 13, no. 76 (April 1946): 252–65.

O'Reilly, Andrea. *Maternal Theory: Essential Readings*. Demeter Press, 2007.

Ostashevsky, Eugene. "Translingualism: A Poetics of Language Mixing and Estrangement." *Boundary 2* 50, no. 4 (2023): 171–94. https://doi.org/10.1215/01903659-10694267.

Palumbo-Liu, David. *The Deliverance of Others: Reading Literature in a Global Age*. Duke University Press, 2012.

Pardes, Ilana. *Countertraditions in the Bible: A Feminist Approach*. Harvard University Press, 1992.

Parmiggiani, Claudio. *Alfabeto in sogno: Dal carme figurato alla poesia concreta*. Mazzotta, 2002.

Pasolini, Pier Paolo. "Notizia su Amelia Rosselli." *Il Menabò* 6 (1963): 66–69.

——. *Saggi sulla letteratura e sull'arte*. Mondadori, 1999.

——. *Volgar' eloquio*. Ed. Antonio Piromalli and Domenico Scafoglio. Athena—Materiali e strumenti, 1976.

Paxton, Robert O. "I've Hesitated to Call Donald Trump a Fascist. Until Now." *Newsweek*, January 11, 2011. https://www.newsweek.com/robert-paxton-trump-fascist-1560652.

——. *The Anatomy of Fascism*. Knopf, 2004.

Peleggi, Valentina. "Amelia Rosselli: Musica in poesia." *Quaderni Del Circolo Rosselli* 30, no. 107 (2010): 67–104.

Perloff, Marjorie. "Eugene Jolas's Multilingual Poetics and Its Legacies." In *Differentials: Poetry, Poetics, Pedagogy*. University of Alabama Press, 2004.

——. *The Futurist Moment: Avant-Garde, Avant Guerre, and the Language of Rupture*. University of Chicago Press, 1986.

——. "Language in Migration: Multilingualism and Exophonic Writing in the New Poetics." *Textual Practice* 24, no. 4 (August 2010): 725–48. https://doi.org/10.1080/0950236X.2010.499660.

Perloff, Marjorie, and Craig Douglas Dworkin, eds. *The Sound of Poetry, the Poetry of Sound*. University of Chicago Press, 2009.

Philip, M. NourbeSe. "The Ga(s)p." In *Poetics and Precarity*. Ed. Myung Mi Kim and Cristanne Miller. State University of New York Press, 2018.

——. *She Tries Her Tongue, Her Silence Softly Breaks*. Wesleyan University Press, 2015.

——. "Wor(l)Ds Interrupted: The Unhistory of the Kari Basin." Ed. Janet Neigh. *Jacket2*, September 17, 2013. https://jacket2.org/article/worlds-interrupted.

——. *Zong!* Wesleyan University Press, 2008.

Pound, Ezra. *The Cantos of Ezra Pound*. New Directions, 1996.

Pugliese, Stanislao G. *Carlo Rosselli: Socialist Heretic and Antifascist Exile*. Harvard University Press, 1999.

Rabaté, Jean-Michel. "Joyce and Jolas: Late Modernism and Early Babelism." *Journal of Modern Literature* 22, no. 2 (Winter 1998): 245–52.

Raffaeli, Sergio. "«Si dispone che...»: Direttive fasciste sulla lingua: Antiregionalismo e xenofobia." *Lingua Nostra* 58 (1997): 30–45.

Rainey, Lawrence, Christine Poggi, and Laura Wittman, eds. *Futurism: An Anthology*. Yale University Press, 2009.

Ramazani, Jahan. *The Cambridge Companion to Postcolonial Poetry*. Cambridge Companions to Literature. Cambridge University Press, 2017.

——. *Poetry in a Global Age*. University of Chicago Press, 2020.

——. *A Transnational Poetics*. University of Chicago Press, 2009.

Rangan, Pooja, Akshya Saxena, Ragini Srinivasan, and Pavitra Sundar, eds. *Thinking with an Accent: Toward a New Object, Method, and Practice*. University of California Press, 2023.

Re, Lucia. "'Barbari Civilizzatissimi': Marinetti and the Futurist Myth of Barbarism." *Journal of Modern Italian Studies* 17, no. 3 (June 1, 2012): 350–68. https://doi.org/10.1080/1354571X.2012.667228.

——. "Italians and the Invention of Race: The Poetics and Politics of Difference in the Struggle Over Libya, 1890–1913." *California Italian Studies* 1, no. 1 (2010). https://escholarship.org/uc/item/96k3w5kn.

——. "Variazioni su Amelia Rosselli." *Il verri* 11, no. 3–4 (December 1993): 131–50.

Richet, Charles. "Xenoglossie: L'écriture automatique en langues étrangères." *Proceedings of the Society for Psychical Research*, no. 19 (July 1905): 162–266.

Richet, Isabelle. "Marion Cave Rosselli and the Transnational Women's Antifascist Networks." *Journal of Women's History* 24, no. 3 (2012): 117–39, https://doi.org/10.1353/jowh.2012.0033.

——. *Women, Antifascism and Mussolini's Italy: The Life of Marion Cave Rosselli*. I.B. Tauris, 2018.

Robertson, Lisa. *Nilling: Prose Essays on Noise, Pornography, the Codex, Melancholy, Lucretius, Folds, Cities and Related Aporias*. BookThug, 2012.

Rosselli, Amelia. *Delirious Verse: A Talk on 'Metrical Spaces'*, Ed. and trans. Andrea di Serego Alighieri and Phil Baber, including 'Metrical Spaces', trans. Jennifer Scappettone. The Yellow Papers, no. 7. The Last Books, 2025.

——. *È vostra la vita che ho perso. Conversazioni e interviste 1963–1995*, ed. Monica Venturini and Silvia De March (Le Lettere, 2010).

——. *La furia dei venti contrari. Variazioni Amelia Rosselli, con testi inediti e dispersi dell'autrice*, ed. Andrea Cortellessa (Le Lettere, 2007).

——. *Le poesie*. Ed. Emanuela Tandello. Garzanti, 2016.

——. *Lettere a Pasolini, 1962–1969*. San Marco dei Giustiniani, 2008.

——. *Locomotrix: Selected Poetry and Prose of Amelia Rosselli*. Ed. and trans. Jennifer Scappettone. University of Chicago Press, 2012.

——. *L'opera poetica*. Ed. Stefano Giovannuzzi, with contributions by Emmanuela Tandello, Francesco Carbognin, Chiara Carpita, Silvia De March, and Gabriella Palli Baroni. Mondadori, 2012.

——. *Una scrittura plurale: Saggi e interventi critici*. Ed. Francesca Caputo. Interlinea, 2004.

Rosselli, Carlo. *Scritti dell'esilio: Dallo scioglimento della concentrazione antifascista alla guerra di spagna (1934–1937)*. 2 vols. Einaudi, 1992.

Sagawa, Chika. *The Collected Poems of Chika Sagawa*. Trans. Sawako Nakayasu. Canarium, 2015.

——. *Sagawa Chika zenshū*. Ed. Ryū Shimada. Shoshi Kankanbō, 2022.

Sahlins, Marshall. *What Kinship Is—and Is Not*. University of Chicago Press, 2014.

Sakai, Naoki. *Translation and Subjectivity: On Japan and Cultural Nationalism*. University of Minnesota Press, 1997.

Sakai, Naoki, Brett de Bary, and Toshio Iyotani, eds. *Deconstructing Nationality*. East Asia Program, Cornell University, 2005.

Saussy, Haun, ed. *Comparative Literature in an Age of Globalization*. Johns Hopkins University Press, 2006.

——. *The Making of Barbarians: Chinese Literature and Multilingual Asia*. Princeton University Press, 2022.

Scappettone, Jennifer. "Xenoglossia." In *The Princeton Encyclopedia of Poetry and Poetics*. Ed. Roland Greene, Stephen Cushman, Clare Cavanagh, and Jahan Ramazani. Princeton University Press, 2012.

Semerano, Giovanni. *Le origini della cultura europea*. L.S. Olschki, 1984.

——. *L'infinito: un equivoco millennario: le antiche civiltà del Vicino Oriente e le origini del pensiero greco*. Bruno Mondadori, 2001.

Shapiro, Marianne. *De vulgari eloquentia: Dante's Book of Exile*. University of Nebraska Press, 1990.

Sharpe, Christina Elizabeth. *In the Wake: On Blackness and Being*. Duke University Press, 2016.

Snodgrass, Ann. *Knowing Noise: The English Poems of Amelia Rosselli*. Peter Lang, 2001.

Sollors, Werner. *Beyond Ethnicity: Consent and Descent in American Culture*. Oxford University Press, 1986.

——. *Ethnic Modernism*. Harvard University Press, 2008.

——, ed. *Multilingual America: Transnationalism, Ethnicity, and the Languages of American Literature*. New York University Press, 1998.

Sommer, Doris. *Bilingual Aesthetics: A New Sentimental Education*. Duke University Press, 2004.

——, ed. *Bilingual Games: Some Literary Investigations*. Palgrave Macmillan, 2003.

Spahr, Juliana. *Du Bois's Telegram: Literary Resistance and State Containment*. Harvard University Press, 2018.

——. *Everybody's Autonomy: Connective Reading and Collective Identity*. University of Alabama Press, 2015.

——. "Multilingualism in Contemporary American Poetry." In *The Cambridge History of American Poetry*. Ed. Alfred Bendixen and Stephen Burt. Cambridge University Press, 2014.

Spatola, Adriano. *Verso la poesia totale*. G. B. Paravia, 1978.

Spatola, Adriano, and Brendan W. Hennessey. *Toward Total Poetry. With an Afterword by Guy Bennett*. Trans. Guy Bennett. Otis/Seismicity Editions, 2008.

Spillers, Hortense. "Mama's Baby, Papa's Maybe: An American Grammar Book." *Diacritics* 17, no. 2 (1987): 65–81.

Spivak, Gayatri Chakravorty. *Can the Subaltern Speak?: Reflections on the History of an Idea*. Ed. Rosalind C. Morris. Columbia University Press, 2010.

——. *Death of a Discipline*. Columbia University Press, 2003.

Stanley, Jason. *How Fascism Works: The Politics of Us and Them. With a New Preface*. Random House, 2020.

Steiner, George. *After Babel: Aspects of Language and Translation*, 2nd ed. Oxford University Press, 1992.

Stengers, Isabelle. *Cosmopolitics*. Trans. Robert Bononno. University of Minnesota Press, 2010.

Stewart-Steinberg, Suzanne. *The Pinocchio Effect: On Making Italians, 1860–1920*. University of Chicago Press, 2008.

SELECTED BIBLIOGRAPHY

Tagliaferri, Aldo, ed. *Emilio Villa: Opere e documenti*. Skira, 1996.

——. *Il clandestino: Vita e opere di Emilio Villa*. Mimesis, 2016.

——. *Presentimenti del mondo senza tempo: Scritti su Emilio Villa*. Ed. Gian Paolo Renello. Argolibri, 2022.

Tagliaferri, Aldo, and Chiara Portesine, eds. *Emilio Villa e i suoi tempi: Finestre per la monade*. Mimesis, 2016.

Tandello, Emmanuela. *Amelia Rosselli: La fanciulla e l'infinito*. Donzelli, 2007.

——. "Doing the Splits: Languages(s) in the Poetry of Amelia Rosselli." *Journal of the Institute of Romance Studies* 1 (1992): 363–73.

Theweleit, Klaus. *Male Fantasies*. University of Minnesota Press, 1987.

Tiffany, Daniel. "Speaking in Tongues: Poetry and the Residues of Shared Language." Ed. Kristina Marie Darling. *Tupelo Quarterly*, March 14, 2020. https://www.tupeloquarterly.com/prose/speaking-in-tongues -poetry-and-the-residues-of-shared-language/.

Toufic, Jalal. *The Withdrawal of Tradition Past a Surpassing Disaster*. Forthcoming Books, 2009. http:// www.jalaltoufic.com/downloads/Jalal_Toufic,_The_Withdrawal_of_Tradition_Past_a_Surpassing _Disaster.pdf.

Trombetti, Alfredo. *L'unita d'origine del linguaggio*. Libreria Treves di Luigi Beltrami, 1905.

Van Dyck, Karen. "Migration, Translingualism, Translation." In *The Translation Studies Reader*, ed. Lawrence Venuti, 466–85. Routledge, 2012.

Venturini, Caterina. "«A mother dead is any body dead». Madre e materno in Amelia Rosselli." *Nuovi Argomenti*, no. 74 (June 2016): 45–55.

Venuti, Lawrence. *The Scandals of Translation: Towards an Ethics of Difference*. Routledge, 1998.

——. *The Translation Studies Reader*. Routledge, 2012.

——. *The Translator's Invisibility: A History of Translation*. Routledge, 2008.

Victor, Divya. *Kith*. Fence, 2017.

Villa, Emilio. *Attributi dell'arte odierna, 1947/1967*. Ed. Aldo Tagliaferri. Le Lettere, 2008.

——. *Brunt H: Options: 17 eschatological madrigals captured by a sweetromatic cybernetogamig vampire, by Villadrome*. Foglio Editrice d'Arte, 1968.

——. *Conferenza*. Ed. Aldo Tagliaferri. Coliseum, 1997.

——. "Cy Twombly: Talento bianco." *Appia Antica*, no. 1 (July 1959): 36.

——. *Emilio Villa: Poeta e scrittore*. Ed. Claudio Parmiggiani. Mazzotta, 2008.

——. *L'arte dell'uomo primordiale*. Abscondita, 2005.

——. *L'opera poetica*. Ed. Cecilia Bello Minciacchi. L'Orma, 2014.

——, ed. and trans. *Odissea*. DeriveApprodi, 2005.

——. "Os puristas são enfadonhos e inúteis." *Habitat*, no. 7 (July 1952).

——. *The Selected Poetry of Emilio Villa*. Ed. Dominic Edward Siracusa. Contra Mundum, 2014.

Villa, Emilio, Silvio Craia, and Giorgio Cegna. *Idrologie con 6 serigrafie, Galleria Il Centro, Napoli, 16 febbraio 1970*. Edar, 1969.

——. *Le idrologie*. Foglio OG, 1968.

Walkowitz, Rebecca L. *Born Translated: The Contemporary Novel in an Age of World Literature*. Columbia University Press, 2015.

——. *Cosmopolitan Style: Modernism Beyond the Nation*. Columbia University Press, 2006.

Wolf, Uljana. *Subsisters: Selected Poems*. Trans. Sophie Seita. Belladonna*, 2017.

Yi, Sang. *Yi Sang: Selected Works*. Trans. Don Mee Choi, Jack Jung, Sawako Nakayasu, and Joyelle McSweeney. Wave Books, 2020.

Yildiz, Yasemin. *Beyond the Mother Tongue: The Postmonolingual Condition*. Fordham University Press, 2012.

Zanzotto, Andrea. *Scritti sulla letteratura*. Mondadori, 2001.

Zukofsky, Louis. "*A*." New Directions, 2011.

——. *Prepositions: The Collected Critical Essays of Louis Zukofsky*. Horizon, 1968.

Index

Note: page numbers followed by *f* refer to figures.

abjad, 223, 239, 251

abracadabrant word, 9, 12, 17, 19, 154

abstraction, 146, 195, 230, 244, 332n106; language and, 24; of lyricism, 158; modernist, 125; painterly, 142, 225; postwar, 99, 131, 195, 201; of speech, 262

Accademia della Crusca, 128, 336n25

accent, 12, 26, 173–75, 207–8, 262, 274, 290; of the future, 277; performing, 40; Rosselli and, 49, 163, 205, 207, 211–13

accessibility, 88, 167; literate, 226; *TwERK*'s, 265; xenoglossic, 267

Adnan, Etel, 8, 32–33, 36, 38, 40, 215–39, 241–56, 299, 345n18, 347n52, 348nn69–70; al-Mashriq and, 345n22; *L'apocalypse arabe/The Arab Apocalypse*, 227, 238, 243–50, 252; Beirut and, 33, 345n24, 345n28; collective voice and, 346n31; community and, 351n129; copying and, 349n87; Fanon and 346n44; Hejinian and, 344n10; leporellos of, 215, 217–20, 234–39, 241–43, 251, 253–54, 256, 348n75, 348n80, 349n85, 349n97; mother of, 344–45n17, 345n25; occupation and, 282; painting and, 346n35; pan-Arab art movement and, 350n101; sexual difference and, 347n54; *Sitt Marie-Rose*, 215, 217, 219–21, 230, 233–34, 252, 347n66; strangeness of name of, 347n63; *There: In the Light and the Darkness of the Self and of the Other*, 349n84. *See also* Al-Sayyab, Badr Shakir; Fattal, Simone

Adorno, Theodor, 5, 7–8, 32, 40, 342n133

aesthetic revolution, 31, 36

Africa, 18, 38, 68–69, 75, 79, 85, 117, 273, 280; decolonization in, 242; East, 69; Horn of, 74, 78; North, 74, 249

Agamben, Giorgio, 293, 309n38

alchemy, 1, 34, 161, 282, 286

Alexander, Will, 33, 205

Alexandria, 16, 33, 37, 52, 58, 67–68, 72, 225, 345n25; Jewish community of, 99

Algeria, 174, 234

Algerian War of Independence, 40, 221, 228

Al-Khal, Yusuf, 217, 232, 347n60

alphabets, 146, 217, 221, 223, 225, 237–39, 244; Arabic, 235, 241; Arabic chat, 282; International Phonetic, 269; Latin, 223, 248, 299; Ugaritic, 251. *See also* abjad

Al-Sayyab, Badr Shakir, 218–17, 235–37, 243, 254, 348n71, 348n80; *Mother and Lost Daughter*, 215, 255

Alter, Robert, 105

alterity, 17, 25, 102, 207, 213; geographical, 202; linguistic, 20; temporal, 114

Alto Adige, 42, 66

anachronism, 113, 183, 340n101

Andrade, Oswald de, 134, 295

Anedda, Antonella, 208, 342n154

Annovi, Gian Maria, 179, 335n8, 343n163

Antena Aire, 266–67, 276, 293, 303, 353n29

370 INDEX

anti-Semitism, 3, 39, 117

Antonioni, Michelangelo, 195, 202

anxiety, 1, 12, 54, 137; of the atomic age, 201;
of the beginner, 220; elite, 116; international,
27, 277; xenophobic, 303

Anzaldúa, Gloria, 20, 314n100

Apter, Emily, 24, 91, 313n89

Arabic, 18, 225, 273, 282, 286, 296, 302, 345n22,
351n127; Adnan and, 40, 215, 217–24, 226–30,
232–39, 241–42, 245–47, 252–55, 347n59;
alphabet, 241; European lyric and, 311n61;
Libyan, 60; Ottoman script of, 3; Villa
and, 108

archives, 86, 92, 109, 283, 286, 334n8, 345n18;
Brazilian, 124; C. I. A.'s, 250; Crawley's, 260;
deficient, 2; Villa's, 132, 147

Arendt, Hannah, 288, 342n149

art, 124–26, 137, 190, 236, 337n39, 348n71; Adnan's,
226, 230, 232–33, 235, 239, 253; autonomy
of, 329n49; cave, 135; conceptualist, 182; of
copying, 240; Freytag-Loringhoven and, 96;
Futurist, 53–55; high, 144; history, 36, 39,
125–26; incommunicability and, 185; Jolas and,
91; Nakayasu and, 293; New York and, 43;
pan-Arab movement in, 350n101; performance,
89; planetary, 39; postwar movements in, 133;
Rosselli's, 174, 223; scene, 86; Villa and, 108,
117, 130–31; visual, 225–26, 251, 253, 256,
348n75; western, 136; world, 219, 235, 251;
xenoglossic, 252

Artaud, Antonin, 115, 246–47, 263

Arteaga, Alfred, 25–26

artist's books, 63, 348n75; Adnan and, 215, 236, 254;
Il poema del vestito di latte (*The Poem of the
Milk Dress*, Marinetti and Munari), 38, 62–63,
78; Villa and, 38, 114, 127, 134, 152

Ascoli, Graziadio Isaia, 116, 329n61

Ascoli, Max, 164, 322n53

Ashbery, John, 48, 213, 344n171

assemblages, 86–89, 256, 326n124; of enunciation,
346n31. *See also* Freytag-Loringhoven, Elsa von

Atatürk, Mustafa Kemal, 3, 40, 222–23

Autarchia della lingua (Cigona), 65*f*, 77

autarky, 38, 67, 78, 97, 112, 117, 186; Italian, 77; of
language, 37, 65, 292

authoritarianism, 36, 225, 292, 294

authorship, 127, 293–94, 297; subjective, 240

autodidacticism, 24, 108, 124; criticism and, 219;
Diggs and, 261, 265; Rosselli and, 169

automatism, 195; Surrealist, 30

Azusa Street Revival, 17–18, 260–61, 310n47

Babel, 12–14, 18–21, 23, 27–28, 35, 153, 174, 181, 303,
313n95; curse of, 90; Dante and, 37, 70; Depero
and, 42–44, 46, 49; New, 42–44, 46; Ogden
and, 91; poetry and, 176; reconciliation of, 260;
scattering of, 311n51; Tower of, 14, 30, 104, 113,
303; Villa and, 104, 107, 113; xenoglossic poetics
and, 209

Bach, Johann Sebastian, 158, 340n89

Bachmann, Ingeborg, 158, 172

Bakhtin, Mikhail, 23, 30, 35, 314n99

Balestrini, Nanni, 125, 180

Balla, Giacomo, 56, 72–73; "Futurist Manifesto
of Men's Clothing," 78, 325n88

barbarian, 5, 7, 17, 20, 26, 67, 166, 187, 201; literature,
129; Marinetti and, 71; poetry and, 32, 213, 249;
sonnet as, 200; south of Italy and, 74

Bardi, Pietro Maria, 124–28, 330n83

Barnes, Djuna, 88, 94, 326n124

Bartók, Béla Viktor János, 158, 192, 204

Bartoli, Matteo, 115–16

Beat poets, 158, 235

Beckett, Samuel, 25–26, 109, 179

Bello Minciacchi, Cecilia, 109, 330n77

belonging, 16, 164, 170, 212, 215, 240, 254, 284,
289, 303; alternative possibilities of, 227;
ambivalence of, 307n1; anxiety of, 1; belonging-
by-travail, 176; cultural, 223, 241; fascism and,
221; linguistic, 26; margins of, 20; narratives
of, 102; otherwise, 229, 251; policing of, 211;
political, 89, 251; to come, 293

Bengali language, 20, 25, 258–59, 310n43;
devotional poetry, 35

Ben-Ghiat, Ruth, 75, 112

Benjamin, Walter, 37, 254, 303, 317n124

Benveniste, Émile, 22

Bergvall, Caroline, 26–27, 31, 179, 207–8, 240,
259, 299

Berrada, Omar, 217, 235

Berio, Luciano, 159, 191

Bernstein, Charles, 35, 316n120

Bird Rose, Deborah, 2, 227

bir'yun/shimmer, 2, 204, 227, 242

Bishi, 258–60, 265, 269, 352n8

Black Mountain College, 140, 158, 189–90

blood, 6–7, 22, 48, 80, 97, 121, 179, 237, 281–85;
belonging and, 16; care and, 290; of Christ, 19;

common, 3; kinship and, 228–29, 298; memory, 272; nation and, 16; purist stances on, 117; race and, 192; relation, 1; routes, 240; sociobiology of, 17; territory and, 256, 347n67

Bo Bardi, Lina, 124–25

borders, 17–18, 88, 208, 268, 290, 320n27, 358n30; crisis of, 16; cultural, 29; geopolitical, 56; inscription of, 70; Joyce and, 171; militarized, 303; national, 18, 37; open, 50

Borsuk, Amaranth, 235, 274

Boulez, Pierre, 191, 194–95

Bounoure, Gabriel, 227, 232

Brathwaite, Kamau, 21, 31, 261, 316n120

Brazil, 28, 104, 124, 130, 330n84, 331n88

breath, 41, 57, 149, 190, 210, 271, 288–90; choreography of, 276, 287; divine, 1, 107; flesh of, 179; in free verse, 58; of history, 109; imposed, 287; lyric, 332n127; as psuché, 140–41; as ruach, 98–99; speech as, 262; stolen, 263; stoppage, 270; training, 144; voice and, 274; wind as, 14, 309n32

breathing, 41, 57, 85, 189, 288, 310n43; melancholic, 288; skills, 274; spaces, 288; techniques, 40

breathlessness, 40, 258, 290

Breton, André, 171, 174

Brolaski, Julian Talamantez, 33, 309n38

Brown, Michael, 257

Bürger, Peter, 55, 319n17, 319n21

Burri, Alberto, 99, 113–14, 125, 133

Cage, John, 159, 190, 193–94, 213, 297, 338n58; Rosselli and, 183, 191, 194, 340n101, 341n111

Calamandrei, Piero, 156, 157f, 165–66

calligraphy, 225–26, 235, 237, 241–43, 248–49; Hurufiyya movement and, 235, 242, 350n101

Campana, Dino, 111, 158

Campbell, Timothy C., 64, 318n5, 320n24

Cangiullo, Francesco, 64, 73, 317n128

cantons, 154, 184–87, 201, 214; of expression, 212; linguistic, 131, 187; party and militia, 245

capitalism, 91, 263, 267, 322n51; consumer, 181; translation and, 301; transnational, 265

Carpita, Chiara, 211, 335n9, 336n35, 338n66, 339n84, 341n112

Carpitella, Diego, 192, 207

Caruso, Enrico, 54, 58

Caruso, Luciano, 119, 125, 330n71

Casanova, Pascale, 34, 316n120, 319–20nn21–22

Cavarero, Adriana, 99, 327n5, 342n149

Cave Rosselli, Marion, 161–64, 171–72, 178, 228

Cegna, Giorgio, 144, 145f, 148f, 150f-51f

Celan, Paul, 36, 179

Cestaro, Gary, 21, 70, 72

Cha, Theresa Hak Kyung, 235, 258, 265, 287

chancel (verb), 48, 187, 212, 305

Cherokee language ('Tsa'lāgĭ'), 258, 264, 269, 275, 278–79; syllabary, 284

Chinese language, 139, 193, 217, 295, 313n93, 354n42; in Adnan's work, 244, 248; kanji, 272, 295; in *Mouth: Eats Color* (Sagawa), 299–301, 305

Choi, Don Mee, 33, 41, 299, 303, 305

Chopin, Frédéric François, 158, 340n89

chorality, 50, 105, 144–45

Christ, 14, 182, 184–85, 250; apostles of, 260; blood of, 19; death of, 123; disciples of, 104; martyrdom of, 173; mystic marriage to, 338n67, 343n164; Passion of, 121

Chung, Frances, 294–95

citizenship, 29, 40, 160, 169–70, 177, 254, 262, 279, 284–85; accent and, 213; Adnan and, 231; Black people and, 283; English and, 10; language and, 1, 4, 22, 158, 226, 252; language of, 96, 194; margins of, 32; political definitions of, 253; statelessness and, 224

City Lights, 219, 343n156

Cixous, Hélène, 173–75, 179

clarity, 8, 254, 260, 292

code switching, 1, 16, 31, 34, 268, 272, 300

Coetzee, J. M., 25–26, 312n78

Cold War, 123, 142, 166–67, 180, 335n21

Collège de Sociologie, 133, 135

colonialism, 71, 186, 219, 225; British, 36, 220; European, 40, 263; French, 220, 231; national languages of, 21; mongrel languages and, 316n120; settler, 41, 280; speech biology and, 287; Western, 247

common sense, 102–3

communication, 25, 53, 225–26, 346; among captives, 287; economizing drives of, 29; encrypted, 180; foundering, 49; immediate, 37; mass, 55, 58; nationalist channels of, 208; nonrationalized, 313n95; parity of, 338n67, 343n164; Pentecostal, 161; radio, 73; reciprocal, 342n149; simplified, 90; sonnet and, 200; subaltern, 267; telecommunications, 13, 29, 37, 51, 57; telegraph, 52; transparent, 36, 303; transplanetary, 245; universal, 24, 51, 160; wireless, 58

community, 1–2, 20, 102, 111, 175, 281, 284;
Alexandria's Jewish, 99; breath and, 288; to
come, 216; critique of, 261; dissident, 221;
imagined, 24; European expatriate artist, 88;
global, 315n104; impossibility of, 351n129;
Italian, 43; language, 293; language of, 217;
mental processes of, 169; of *Mouth: Eats Color*,
294, 297, 305; Muslim, 242; political, 22; nurse's
tongue and, 23; of speakers, 15; terms of, 96;
transplanetary, 245; xenoglossic poetry and, 41
concrete poetry, 38; Brazilian, 125
conquest, 83, 85; of Albania, 27; chivalric, 123; of
Ethiopia, 74; imperial, 79, 249
Conrad, Joseph, 34, 134
Cooper-Rompato, Christine, 20, 89, 311n52
copying, 221–23, 225, 235, 239–41
cosmopolitanism, 12, 31, 34, 85, 129, 187, 202, 259,
305, 307n1, 315nn106–7, 352n8; bourgeois, 27,
277; deterritorialized, 67, 322n57; diaspora and,
224; discrepant, 315n108; European notions
of, 302; global Englishes and, 316n114, 352n8;
modernist, 28–29, 31; multilingualism and,
19, 264, 358n21; vs. xenoglossia, 1, 16; women
and, 89
Craia, Silvio, 144, 145f, 148f, 150, 151f
Crawley, Ashon T., 19, 41, 57, 102, 130, 251–52,
260–61, 320n23, 351n127
creole, 21, 275, 279; poets, 316n120
criticism, 35, 39, 41, 263, 290, 312n74, 337n43;
Adnan and, 244, 254; Anglophone, 313n84;
cultural, 33; Freytag-Loringhoven and, 88;
literary, 14, 210; Pasolini's, 202; of poetry,
342n149; Rosselli, 339n76; Villa's, 108,
328n40; xenoglossic, 29, 42, 219, 256
Croce, Benedetto, 115, 171
Crosby, Harry, 294, 297
cube-form/forma-cubo, 5, 39, 188, 190, 194,
198, 201
cultural divisions, 16, 104
cuneiform, 111, 137, 251
Cunningham, Merce, 183, 211, 340n101

Dada, 30, 88, 94, 96, 271; collages, 313n95; Freytag-
Loringhoven as mother of, 86, 326n124,
327n136
Dadi, Iftikhar, 241–42
Dallapiccola, Luigi, 159, 191, 195
dance, 90, 234, 267, 289, 290, 302, 303, 354n39;
daggering, 271–75; twerking, 271–272, 354n38

Danielou, Alain, 159, 204
D'Annunzio, Gabriele, 67, 73, 117–18, 321n48
Dante Alighieri, 21–24, 31, 65f, 124; *Commedia*,
129; *De vulgari eloquentia*, 21, 23, 29, 70, 116,
122; *Inferno*, 240; literary Italian and, 37;
musical education and, 343n160; vernacular
of, 22, 174, 186
Darmstadt School of New Music, 38, 159, 190–91,
194, 196
Dartington College of the Arts, 159, 191
decolonization, 225–26, 242
deconstruction, 19, 104, 136, 140
Deleuze, Gilles, 11, 48, 107, 307n1, 309n37, 318n138,
346n31, 351n117
Depero, Fortunato, 33, 42–46, 49, 64, 292,
317n128; "State of Mind in New York," 44,
46, 207
Derrida, Jacques, 4, 263, 352n16
De Stijl, 195, 201
dialects, 58, 66, 95, 111, 111–14, 149, 152, 187;
Barbadian, 264; centrifugal influence of,
67; Cuzco, 270, 273; Duchamp and, 147;
Florentine, 329; Homer and, 31, 129; as integral
languages, 116; in Italy, 122, 322n51, 329n61;
Lombard, 109, 113, 122; London, 259; Milanese,
111–12, 114; Neapolitan, 58, 300; Nones, 42;
Pasolini and, 29; Quechua, 270, 273; regional,
37, 112; role of, 277; Rosselli's poetics and, 208;
Sicilian, 123, 300; writing in, 35
diaspora, 170, 208, 212, 224, 226; African, 257, 272;
Black, 16; Black African, 40; Jewish, 14
Dickinson, Emily, 170
dictation, 49, 57–59, 64, 224, 247, 249–50, 287,
320n24
Diemel, Anton, 110, 139
Diggs, LaTasha N. Nevada, 8, 32–33, 40–41, 257–61,
264–87, 289–90, 352–57; "daggering kanji,"
269–73; *TwERK*, 258, 260–61, 264–77,
281, 284, 353n54, 355n64; *Village*, 279, 281,
283–84, 286
Dillingham Commission, 12, 43
Diodati, Giovanni, 99, 105
disaster, 246–48, 303
dissonance, 49–51, 119, 146, 159, 202–3, 205, 211
distance, 54, 132, 138, 158, 253; scare quotes of, 283;
of xenoglossia, 179
dolce stil novo, 6, 122
Donne, John, 6–7
Dorazio, Pietro, 195

INDEX

Douglass, Frederick, 262, 280

Dowling, Sarah, 35, 276

Drucker, Johanna, 235, 239, 316n122, 331n89

Duchamp, Marcel, 87, 96, 325n105, 327n136;
Anémic Cinéma, 146–47; *The Horse*, 126

Eco, Umberto, 7, 16, 37, 181, 309n36, 312n70, 338n58

education, 1, 20, 66–68, 110, 287; Adnan's, 40,
219–220, 227–28, 244, 252; classical, 224;
collective, 2; colonial, 222, 228, 258, 286–87;
cultural, 223; hegemonic systems of, 36; Fascist,
7–8, 66, 110, 111–12, 115, 322n51, 322n53, 330n62;
language and, 90; literary, 158; Marinetti's,
58; musical, 158, 343n160; Nakayasu's, 291;
Pentecostalism and, 14, 18; public, 115, 301;
Rosselli's, 47, 158–59, 164, 169, 340n100;
system, 322n51; Villa's, 110–12; women and, 89

Eliot, T. S., 28, 111, 114, 129, 158, 171, 348n71;
The Waste Land, 31, 232, 258, 264

elite, 190, 223; anxiety, 116; canon and, 265;
cosmopolitanism and, 202, 352n8; culture, 31;
Florentine, 116; nationalist, 124

English, 3–4, 10–13, 25–26, 28, 37, 39, 149, 316n121,
326n133; Adnan and, 223–24, 227–31, 235,
243–46, 249, 252; American, 88–89, 309n27,
336n25; avant-garde modernism and, 316n120;
BASIC, 27, 91; Bishi and, 258–60; Black, 265;
Cixous and, 175; creole and, 21; Depero and,
43–44; Diggs and, 264–66, 278; Freytag-
Loringhoven and, 88–89, 95–96; Futurist
manifesto in, 319n8; Genesis in, 98–99; as
international language, 29, 346n44; Jolas and,
90; Lahiri and, 20; *Mouth: Eats Color* and,
297–302, 305; Nono and, 196; only, 266–67,
309n27; paralanguages and, 36; Received
Pronunciation (RP), 262, 352n8; Rosselli and,
6, 47–49, 158–60, 164, 168, 171–73, 177–79,
181, 183, 187, 189, 192, 206–10, 213, 334–45n8,
343n146; Sagawa's work and, 291, 294; speech,
287; translation of Pound's Fascist Italian,
350n104; in *TwERK* (Diggs), 268–70, 273–74,
277; Villa and, 102–3, 109, 114, 117, 119, 129,
140, 143; in *Village* (Diggs), 279, 284; in *Zong!*
(Philip), 275

Enlightenment, 7, 274

Enūma Eliš, 104, 106, 111, 153

epic poetry, 80, 135, 244, 249, 333n129

Eritrea, 59, 75–76

errantry, 16, 169, 309n37

Esperanto, 13, 17, 24, 27–28, 90, 133; Gramsci on,
115–16, 277

Esposizione Universale Roma (EUR), 126, 202

Ethiopia, 37, 73–76, 80*f*, 82; Italian/Fascist invasion
of, 38, 73–76, 112, 324n79; South Asian
solidarity with, 324n78

etymology, 90, 116, 135–39, 143; folk, 9, 107

exile, 22–23, 38, 70, 88, 186, 210, 238; Jewish, 167;
Joyce and, 337n39; linguistic, 111; Rosselli
and, 39, 46, 155, 163, 171–72, 202, 212; Toufic
and, 247

Exodus, 72, 124

experimental poetry, 4, 36, 107, 110, 257, 266,
276, 245n18

Fanon, Frantz, 34, 222, 229, 258, 262, 287, 246n44

fasces, 45–46, 121–22, 143, 225; auto-fasces, 45;
Italian, 47

fascist populism, 16, 192

Fattal, Simone, 217, 233, 235, 244, 347n63, 348n69.
See also Post-Apollo Press

Fenollosa, Ernest, 136, 139, 295, 332n122, 354n42

First World War/World War I/ Great War, 55, 73,
86, 117, 155, 221–22, 321n35, 324n80, 345n17;
censorship during, 309n27; Italian occupation
of Somalia and Eritrea, 59; mass graves of, 92;
outbreak of, 11; veterans of, 95

fluency, 1–2, 16, 26, 274, 284, 301; bilingual, 34;
disfluency, 16, 89, 91; linguistic, 114

Fogu, Claudio, 55, 322n53

Fondazione Origine, 133, 135, 332n106, 332n108

Frémon, Jean, 236

Freud, Sigmund, 262, 351n117

Freytag-Loringhoven, Elsa von (Baroness), 8, 31,
33, 38, 86–97, 326n124; Duchamp and, 96,
325n105, 327n136. *See also* Barnes, Djuna;
Dada; Jolas, Eugene

friction, 2, 26, 30, 54, 116, 267

future, 69, 124, 157, 165, 183, 216, 351n129; accents
of, 50, 277; apocalyptic, 251; deterritorialized,
349n84; of English language, 259; Freytag-
Loringhoven as, 96, 327n136; global, 213;
language of, 28, 114, 217; literary, 154, 293;
of poiesis, 128

Futurism, 55–57, 66, 78–79, 84, 183, 317n122;
avant-guerre, 73, 90; colonial, 42; Fascist,
46, 55; Italian, 324n76; Japanese, 292; Munari
and, 325n87; nationalism and, 38; Russian, 64,
324n76. *See also* Marinetti, Filippo Tommaso

INDEX

Garcia, Edgar, 244, 309n38, 350n109
Genesis, 14, 39, 153, 204, 267, 309n32, 328n23;
   milk and, 84; Villa's translation of, 98–101,
   104–8, 132–33, 135, 138
geopolitics, 1, 24, 33, 153, 282; of comparison, 302;
   Western, 315n104
German, 3, 5, 18, 42, 89, 261, 273; Cixous and,
   174–75, 179; Freytag-Loringhoven and, 90, 95;
   Rosselli and, 169; Villa and, 108
gesture, 5, 102, 104, 237, 299, 333n132; action
   painting as, 244; cosmogonic, 105; material,
   253; modernist, 292; translative, 240;
   xenoglossia as, 19, 40
Ghosh, Amitav, 35, 302
Gentile, Giovanni, 66, 115, 322n53, 330n62
Glissant, Édouard, 17, 31, 253, 262, 309n37, 316n120;
   Le Discours antillais, 4; "Nous reclamons le
   droit à l'opacité," 227, 310n40; poetics of, 21
globalization, 36, 40, 52, 264–66, 281, 318n6;
   communication under, 29; decolonization and,
   242; European colonialism and, 263; rhetoric
   of, 302; Suez Canal and, 68; verse and, 35
Global North, 161, 238
Global South, 19, 24, 70, 85, 159, 161, 165
glossolalia, 13, 16, 20, 131, 197, 209, 227, 251, 263–64,
   309–10n38; Blackpentecostal practice and, 102;
   language and, 309n38, 320n34; Pentecostalism
   and, 18; of zaum, 313n95. *See also* xenoglossia
glottal stop, 41, 242, 269–71, 273–75, 280
grammar, 2, 22, 25, 205, 235, 265, 286; Arabic-
   Turkish, 40, 222; Cixous and, 174–75;
   deterritorializing, 287; early, 322n52;
   fragmented, 27; Gramsci on, 47, 116, 330n62;
   Homer's, 205; Marinetti and, 70; national,
   200; Phoenician, 110; of the poor, 170, 336n31;
   vernacular, 48; written, 174
grammars, 24, 66, 187, 224, 294; Black English
   and, 265; national, 5, 17; normative, 27, 47;
   subaltern, 27
Gramsci, Antonio, 8, 31, 47, 69, 116–17, 192, 195,
   265, 275; on Esperanto, 27, 115–16, 277; Gentile
   and, 330n62; hegemony, 27, 313n84; linguistics
   and, 330n63, 353, 354; *Literature and National
   Life*, 171; subalternity, 313n84
Greek, 5, 138, 140, 153, 205, 224, 241, 273, 296,
   308n17; Adnan and, 217, 222; ancient, 9, 137;
   archaic, 136; biblical, 258; Bishi and, 258;
   Genesis and, 98–99; Homer and, 31, 129;
   Madame X and, 13; Villa and, 109

Griffin, Roger, 15, 55, 309n35, 322n51
grime: saying of, 177, 180, 208
Gruppo 63, 181, 338n66
Gruppo Origine, 133, 332n106
Guattari, Félix, 11, 48, 107, 309n37, 318n138,
   346n31, 351n117
Guiart, Jean, 130–31

handwriting, 109, 114, 130, 144, 147, 214–18,
   235, 237
Harlem, 33, 73, 75, 257, 264, 266, 281
harmony, 39, 192, 204, 219; disharmony, 91;
   typographical, 57; world, 159
harmonics, 34, 171, 203–7; Bartók's use of, 192;
   planetary, 264; Rosselli's, 214; upper, 203
harmonic series, 159, 171, 191–92, 203–4, 207,
   339n84, 342n134
Hartman, Saidiya, 40, 261, 282, 356n73
Hassan, Waïl S., 34, 302
Hassan al Said, Shakir, 235
Hawaiian language, 258, 264, 269–70, 273;
   Pidgin, 264
Hebrew Bible, 39, 98, 104, 110, 133, 327n9
Hebrew language, 9, 18, 31, 39, 98–100, 104–7,
   129, 327n14
Hejinian, Lyn, 22, 213, 241, 344n10
Herder, Johann Gottfried, 23, 108, 311–12n64, 323n69
hermeneutics, 16, 262
historical avant-garde, 30–31, 36, 52, 129, 186, 302;
   critiques of the lyric, 340n100; European, 126;
   language and, 64, 85, 117; poetic stanza and,
   316n122. *See also* Futurism; Marinetti, Filippo
   Tommaso
historicism, 33; exploded, 33; institutional, 100;
   late idealist, 135; Villa and, 117
history, 37, 49, 56, 66, 75, 89, 100, 118–19, 124,
   252, 298, 311n51; American, 278; of American
   literature, 309n27; of Arabic alphabet, 239; art,
   36, 39, 125–26; of the avant-garde, 88; black,
   286; breath of, 109; Diggs and, 286, 289; of
   exploitation, 69; Fascist, 119; of "Fatta l'Italia,"
   321n48; hysteria and, 6; Irish, 172; of Italian, 128;
   of Italy, 205; of language question, 115; literary,
   262, 334n8; manipulation of, 221; media, 52;
   of modern poetry, 140; Nietzsche on, 246;
   oral, 282; of rebellion as nature, 108; reception,
   335n8; repetition of, 2; Rosselli's poetry and, 161,
   168, 203; speculative, 294; subaltern and, 192;
   Villa on, 111; violent, 85; world, 95

INDEX

Hitler, Adolf, 3, 117, 256
Hofer, Jen/Elena, 267, 276, 293. *See also* Antena Aire
Holy Spirit/Holy Ghost, 17, 57, 99, 102, 106, 170, 260; absence of, 36; Christian, 46; of Pentecost, 14, 101; representations of, 15*f*, 252
Homer, 31, 57, 129, 133, 136, 205
Hopkins, Gerard Manley, 158, 271
Horkheimer, Max, 7–8, 192, 342n133
Horus, 100, 143
humanity, 108, 311n51; inhumanity, 4; music of, 12, 277; poetry and, 129; real, 8
Humboldt, Wilhelm von, 23, 323n69
Hurston, Zora Neale, 286, 289, 356n81
Hutton, Christopher, 71, 323n69
hybridity, 168, 314n100; dualism of, 352n8; linguistic, 39, 294

identity, 25, 71, 224, 329, 351, 355; Adnan's, 222, 230, 232, 234, 247, 254; collective, 33, 322n51; containment of, 22; defensiveness around, 279; errantry as formation of, 309; European, 136; geopolitical, 4; invagination and, 280; language and, 4, 23; of liberal Italy, 74; lyricism and, 263; national, 76, 115, 195, 258; nonconforming, 284; oppression of, 26; policing of, 23, 195, 229, 233; political, 219; politics of, 323n69; sexual, 263; visual, 12
ideograms, 135, 139; Chinese, 139, 295
ideology, 39, 51, 57, 91, 151–52; of clarity, 8; English-only, 267; of fascism, 16; high, 23; kinship as, 229; of language, 25, 39, 119, 142, 229; of mother tongue, 14, 78, 211, 223; of official academics and grammars, 24; organicist, 323n69; phonetic, 38, 133
idiolect, 16, 20, 28, 39, 47–48, 168, 172, 300; of Deleuze's idiot, 307n1; Rosselli's, 161; sociolect and, 206
illiteracy, 27, 64, 66, 117, 175, 246, 322n51, 322n53, 330n61, 350n112
immigrants, 8–9, 18, 28, 41, 49–51, 89, 129, 300, 307n5
immigration: mass, 4, 50; US, 12, 42–43
imperium, 55, 121; Roman, 46
imprisonment, 95, 155, 185, 194–97, 235, 341n114; of Xenakis, 181
industrialization, 79, 322n51
inscription: border, 70; ideological, 126, 143; of the self, 287; social, 35

inspiration, 18, 37, 54, 57, 211; co-inspiration, 303; divine, 224; Rosselli's, 338n67, 343n164; unconscious, 174; von Freytag-Loringhoven and, 97
insurrection, 102–3
internationalism, 26, 130, 225, 292–93; Black, 16, 74, 205, 309n37; Japanese, 294; modernist, 294, 302; pan-Arab, 228, 230, 238, 241, 246, 348n71; proletarian, 27, 277; tongues and, 18
invention, 1, 28, 34, 183; linguistic, 188
iridescence, 2, 261, 352n10
Israel, 101, 133, 220, 234, 251, 328n32
Italianity/italianità, 16, 37, 77–78, 118
Italianness, 88, 115, 212
Italian, 6–7, 18, 29, 37, 40, 42, 44, 48, 126, 213, 234; autarky and, 78; defense of, 3, 65; Genesis in, 99, 107; history of, 128; Lahiri and, 20, 311n55; linguistic purism and, 307n3; Marinetti and, 52, 59–60, 62, 66–67, 72; paralanguages and, 36; Rosselli and, 39, 47, 157–60, 164, 168, 171–73, 177, 179, 181, 186–87, 189, 194, 205, 207–8, 210; standard, 27, 111, 115–16, 207, 212; unified, 23, 70; vernacular, 152, 186; Villa and, 39, 98, 109, 112, 114, 119–20, 122–23, 132–33, 136, 140, 143–45, 147–50, 152
Italo-Turkish War, 59, 225
Ives, Peter, 115, 236, 330n63

Jacobus, Mary, 142, 332n127, 333n132
Jakobson, Roman, 64
James, Henry, 8–14, 17, 19, 22, 154, 308–9n25; New York and, 8–9, 12, 43, 49, 51, 89, 136, 277, 289, 295; xenophobia of, 9, 13. *See also* abracadabrant word; immigrants
Japanese language, 129, 258, 264, 269, 272–73, 278, 294, 297, 299–301, 305; counterfactual, 291, 294; English and, 298; keyboards, 299–300
Jim Crow, 19, 282
Jolas, Eugene, 28, 90–92, 313n89, 313n91, 326n118, 326n120
journalism, 180, 293; flight and, 321n35; modern, 249; muckraking, 308n25
Joyce, James, 28, 109, 115, 158, 181; *Anna Livia Plurabelle*, 91; *Finnegans Wake*, 28, 47, 90, 172, 181; Jolas and, 326n120; Rosselli on, 172, 343n160; Sagawa and, 292; *Ulysses*, 130, 133, 171

Kadri, Assaf, 221, 345n17
Keats, John, 140–41, 144, 240

Kennedy, John F., 181, 347n55

kinship, 17, 23, 52, 71, 209, 229, 301–2; blood, 228; contingency of, 263; diasporic, 294; elective, 24, 216, 229 (*see also* kith); kinship-through-acceptance, 239; of orphans, 5, 278, 305; performative, 41, 233; poetry and, 230; provisional, 298; queer, 27, 229; sonic, 170; traditional forms of, 262; violence and, 280; wounded, 263, 280, 282, 353n18

Khatibi, Abdelkebir, 237

Khlebnikov, Velimir, 64, 313–14n95, 314n99

kith, 1, 24–25, 215, 302, 307n1; poiesis of, 229

kithship, 25, 226, 255

Klee, Paul, 134, 251

Lahiri, Jhumpa, 20, 311n55

language, 17, 24–27, 30, 34, 43–44, 49–50, 89–91, 129–33, 141–44, 186, 217, 237–38, 240–41, 252, 315n100, 356n92; abstract art and, 230; acquisition, 20, 24, 72, 223; artificial, 314n99; assimilation and, 10–11, 29, 224, 278; autarky of, 37–38, 65–66, 77–78, 112, 117; barrier, 303; beyond, 104, 141, 245; body, 342n148; borders of, 320n27; children and, 311n64; choral, 234; circuit, 250; Cixous on, 174–76; colonizing, 21; colonial, 40, 244, 265, 278, 287; common, 13, 185; community, 293; of composition, 26, 86, 96, 136, 219; continuum of, 20, 104, 183, 303, 305, 307n1, 314n95; cultural, 242; cultures, 290; death of, 257, 309n38; debate on, 128; Diggs and, 257–68, 270, 277–79, 282, 354n49; diplomatic, 167; dissolution of, 323n69; drawing as, 226, 241; Duchamp and, 146–47; erasure, 4, 208; exchange, 15; Fascist ideologies of, 2–3; fascistization of, 66, 73, 112; foreign, 4, 17, 56, 265, 276, 309n27; foundations of, 99; future of, 9; of the future, 12, 28, 114; Gramsci on, 115–16, 277, 330n63; household, 22, 177; identity and, 23; ideology of, 119; imperial, 227; Indigenous, 257, 277; international, 28, 276; internationalist, 309n37; juridical, 177; learning, 24, 224, 227, 253, 284, 290, 301; magical, 29; major, 346n31; Marinetti and, 62, 70–73; metaphor and, 139; modernization of, 52; mongrel, 316n120; nation, 21, 261, 264, 275; native, 3, 14, 26, 41, 136, 157, 223, 253, 287; 313n91; natural, 13, 23, 251; Nono and, 197; of the Other, 102; performative kinship and, 41; performed, 262; poetic, 1, 22, 32, 64, 85, 102,

205, 293–94, 299; poets and, 229; policy, 208; politics, 36; postwar avant-gardes and, 126; proto/basic, 247, 350n117; question, 115–16, 313n84; received ideologies of, 29; revitalization of, 41, 181; Rosselli and, 157–61, 164, 169–75, 181, 187–89, 193–95, 200–201, 207; Semitic, 39, 104, 228; settler colonial claim on, 19, 320n23; state, 3–4; street, 223, 232, 264, 266, 275, 286, 295, 314n95; systems, 16–17, 149, 298, 300–301; threadbare, 8; of translation, 25, 254; of the tribe, 251; Turkish, 3, 40, 222–23, 233; unitary, 116; universal, 5, 17, 24, 34, 161, 168, 195, 262, 274, 326n70; unsanctioned use of, 89; vertical, 313n89; Villa and, 104–7, 110–12, 114–15, 124, 135–36, 147, 149–50, 153–54; visual art and, 225, 237, 331n89; of women, 179. *See also* Arabic; creole; dialects; education; English; Esperanto; German; grammars; Hawaiian; Italian; mother tongue; national language; native tongues; Persian; Portuguese; Sanskrit; Tagalog; Urdu; vernaculars; Yiddish

Lanital, 79–80, 82

Last, Angela, 33, 315n104

Latin, 5, 22, 57, 66, 98–99, 109, 137, 160, 210, 311n52; alphabet, 223, 248, 299; Dante and, 21, 31, 129; species of, 23; Villa and, 111–12, 117, 130, 152–53

League of Nations, 38, 74–76

Lebanese Civil War, 220–21, 228, 233–34, 243

Lebanon, 40, 219–22, 227, 230–32, 234, 251, 253; secular, 232, 347n55

Levi, Carlo, 158, 171, 192

Libya, 14, 37, 59, 69, 76; Libyan war, 74; Ottoman, 59, 73

Ligeti, György, 159, 195

linguistics, 274, 300, 323n69; analytic philosophy and, 228; Ascoli and, 116; comparative, 108; glottology, 116; Gramsci and, 27, 330n63; hegemonic, 262; historical, 107, 115–16; positivist, 136; sociolinguistics, 34, 300, 311n64; structuralist, 331n89

literary discourse, 36; comparative, 239

literary measure, 13, 22, 277

literary movements, 31, 88

literary tradition, 158, 164; Arabic, 241; Japanese, 241; national, 88, 341n116

literature, 108, 117, 155, 158, 166, 170, 337n46; children's, 129; Cixous and, 179; dialect, 66; English, 162, 173; ethnic, 32; European, 129, 302; French, 249; global, 24, 32; Hebrew,

98, 104; minor, 107, 346n31; modernization of, 52; of muckraking journalism, 308n25; multilingual, 1, 34–35, 47, 309n27, 311n59; national, 214; of opposition, 316n120; of pan-Arabism, 255; Rosselli and, 180; translational, 34, 302; twentieth-century, 2, 168; Western, 14; Western experimental, 114; world, 20, 24, 34; Yankee, 129

Locomotrix: Selected Poetry and Prose of Amelia Rosselli, 5, 7, 160, 210, 308n10, 334n8, 336n27, 336n31, 340n97, 343n156, 344n171

Lupi, Roberto, 192, 204–5, 207

Macchia, Frank, 19, 311n51

Mackey, Nathaniel, 31, 40, 263, 280, 353n18, 355n65; "Breath and Precarity," 271, 276, 288. *See also* kinship: wounded

McNaughton, Duncan, 218, 241

Maderna, Bruno, 159, 191, 195

Maksoud, Hala Salaam, 231, 347n55

Manzoni, Alessandro, 115–16, 137, 329n61

Māori, 258, 264, 269

Marconi, Guglielmo, 52, 53*f*, 58–59

Marinetti, Benedetta, 55, 126

Marinetti, Filippo Tommaso, 16, 24, 37–38, 42, 45, 52–58, 65–73, 83–85, 117–19, 225, 313n95, 320n24, 321n35, 330n71; Alexandria and, 33, 37, 58, 67–68; barbarian and, 323n67; *La Bataille de Tripoli*, 59–61; Beinecke and, 325n91; "Destruction of Syntax—Wireless Imagination—Words-in-Freedom," 52, 57–58, 62, 321n44; "The Founding and Manifesto of Futurism," 68, 320n34, 351n126; Freytag-Loringhoven and, 90–91, 95–96; fusedwords-in-freedom and, 338n68; Italianness of, 88; linguistic autarky and, 292; *Mafarka le Futuriste: Roman Africain*, 68, 153; nationalism of, 86; Pànteo and, 321n48; *The Poem of the Milk Dress*, 78–80, 82*f*, 90; polyglossy of, 32; in Russia, 321n44; "Self-Portrait," 72; "Technical Manifesto of Futurist Literature," 54, 57, 60, 62, 250, 319n14, 320nn25–26; wireless imagination and, 249; *Zang Tumb Tumb: Adrianopoli ottobre 1912*, 62–64. *See also Autarchia della lingua*; Munari, Bruno

Marshall Plan, 122, 166

Martin, Katrina, 146, 333n140

Martini, Stelio Maria, 119, 330n71

Martino, Ernesto de, 192, 345n29

MASP (Museu de Arte de São Paulo), 124–28

Maximin, Daniel, 21–22, 33, 311n62

mediation, 176, 299; of the nurse's tongue, 240; of the screen, 223–24

Mediterranean, the, 40, 59, 133, 136, 213, 217–19; cultures of, 127; telegraph lines and, 52

Melehi, Mohammed, 225, 233*f*, 238, 347n61

memory, 235, 289, 312n64; blood, 272; breath, 288; cultural, 166–67, 275; of Fascism, 319n20; muscle, 272; nationalist, 113; selective, 165

Meschonnic, Henri, 22, 33, 311n62

metamorphosis, 244; of language, 30, 128, 286; of sound, 287

metaphysical verse, 6, 158

metrical spaces/spazi metrici, 188–91, 193, 197, 201, 339n84

Migliorini, Bruno, 128

migration, 13, 34; mass, 15; physical, 246; writing of, 314n100

Milan, 137–38, 187, 343n156; Bardi and, 125, 330n83; Gruppo Origine and, 332n106; Marinetti and, 57, 59, 67–68, 320n24; Villa and, 33, 110–11

Milanese dialect, 111–12, 114, 117

milk, 61–62, 69–73, 79–85, 117, 175–77, 250; blood and, 16, 62, 80, 97, 117, 179, 281–82, 298; casein, 79–80, 84; fiber, 78; mother's, 70, 85, 173, 177, 311n64; nationhood and, 16; soil and, 16, 80, 97, 117, 298; spilt nursing, 282

minor languages, 11, 67

minor tongues, 40, 265

Mizumura, Minae, 37, 302

modernism, 28, 55, 292, 314n100; aesthetic, 56; anthropophagic, 295; Brazilian, 134; calligraphic, 242; early, 84; ethnic, 264, 311n59; European, 37; Fascist, 42, 71, 125; global, 291; hemispheric, 134; high, 205; Japanese, 293; postwar, 154; revolutionary, 37; Western, 217; xenoglossic, 299

modernity, 43, 348n71; in Arabic poetics, 235; capitalist, 192; global, 225; minoritarian, 202; rationalism of, 201

Mondardini, Silvia, 173–74

Monk, Meredith, 49–50

montage, 81, 114, 196; geopolitical, 35; mixed-media, 79; multilingual, 168; polyglot, 28; transhistorical, 125

Montale, Eugenio, 158, 343n160

Moten, Fred, 31, 40, 261–64, 274, 280, 286, 351n128, 352n16

378 INDEX

mother tongue, 4–5, 15, 25–26, 31, 70–72; Adnan
and, 223; Cixous and, 174; Dante and, 21, 24;
Diggs and, 260, 264, 268, 278, 280, 285, 289;
Freytag-Loringhoven and, 86, 90, 96; Hutton
on, 323n69; ideology of, 14; Lahiri and, 311n55;
Marinetti and, 71, 78; Moten on, 261, 263;
national language and, 36; Philip on, 286–87;
Rosselli and, 39, 47, 175, 180, 187, 200, 211;
Yildiz on, 23, 70–71
multiculturalism, 34–35, 40, 265, 276, 316n120
multilingualism, 1, 42, 181, 260–61, 303, 309n38;
colonial, 38; cosmopolitan, 122, 264; of
historical avant-garde, 117; Jolas's poetry and,
326n118; modernist, 6, 16, 28–29, 47, 122, 210,
314n100; nationalism and, 4, 12, 85, 226; pre-
Fascist actions against, 322n51; Rosselli's, 47, 210
Munari, Bruno, 38, 78–81, 82f, 325n87
Museo della Carale, 139, 147
music, 5, 18, 36, 157–59, 263, 275, 338n58, 342n149;
accordion books and, 348n75; Black, 271;
choral, 50, 144–45, 196–97, 296; early, 144;
of everyone, 159, 161; of humanity, 12, 277;
performance, 355n64; Rosselli and, 165, 172,
174, 191–93, 195, 204, 206–7, 334n5; theory, 203
Mussolini, Benito, 45, 55–56, 66, 73–77, 83–84, 112,
162, 256, 335n16; face of, 46f, 292; hanging of,
111; imperialist agenda of, 32; March on Rome,
3, 44, 55–56, 73, 118, 323n74; Marinetti and, 65,
118; regime of, 43. See also Ethiopia
musical horizon of poetry, 205
myth, 153, 328n32; Babylonian creation, 104, 106;
Depero and, 43; Fascist regime and, 73, 323n74;
of Futurism's birth, 79; of Italians as good
people, 166; of kinship, 302; Marinetti and, 71;
of Romance languages, 39, 136; Sumerian, 106;
tribal, 4, 142; trinity and, 106; Villa and, 100,
116; Villa as, 108. See also Babel

Nakayasu, Sawako, 8, 41, 291–95, 297–300; Mouth:
Eats Color, 41–42, 293–94, 297–98, 300,
302–3, 305
nationalism, 3–5, 31, 95, 205, 227; anticolonial,
352n13; colonial, 224; excesses of, 164;
expansionist, 55; Futurism and, 38, 96, 324n76;
Italian authoritarian, 39; Marinetti's, 86;
neonationalisms, 248; Ottoman, 233; Rosselli
and, 164, 213
national language, 4, 7, 12, 17, 21, 30, 38, 64–66;
Ascoli and, 329n61; consolidation of, 115;

Fascism and, 207; Gramsci on, 47; imposition
of, 111; mother tongue and, 4, 36; Rosselli and,
48, 160, 176, 186; Villa and, 117, 122
nation language, 21, 261, 264, 275
native tongues, 4, 21, 159, 175, 224, 226, 229,
284, 214n95
Nattermann, Ruth, 163
Nazism, 3, 7–8, 37, 117, 166
negativity, 90–91
neoavanguardia/neo-avant-garde, 109, 114, 168,
180–81, 183, 187
Nietzsche, Friedrich, 228, 246–47
Noel, Urayoán, 265, 281, 283–84
Nono, Luigi, 196–97
norms, 200; grammatical, 31; linguistic, 66;
phonetic, 207, 212; of translation, 294
North, Michael, 28, 314n100
nostalgia, 22, 68, 85, 167, 281, 332n127
novel, 314n99; heteroglossic, 30, 35
nurse's tongue, 23–24, 31, 70, 175–76, 240

Off Our Backs, 221, 224
Ogden, C. K., 27, 91
O'Hanlon, Ann, 230
Olivetti, Adriano, 171
Olson, Charles, 41, 140, 189–90, 288, 340n91
opacity, 2, 17, 36, 172, 227, 237, 253–54, 261;
of abjad, 239; calligraphic modernism and,
242; demi-opacity, 32; metaphors of,
352n10
Orientalism, 134, 272
orihon, 218, 234–35
Ostashevsky, Eugene, 33, 35, 309n38, 321n44
otherwise possibilities, 252, 260
Ottoman Empire, 37, 63, 73, 218, 221–23, 225, 236;
Tripolitania Vilayet, 225, 321n35
overtones, 203–4, 207, 342n134

painting, 5, 204, 232, 238; action, 225, 244; Adnan
and, 38, 40, 220–21, 226–27, 229–30, 241–42,
244, 249, 254, 346n35; calligraphic, 36;
rationalist, 200
Palazzeschi, Aldo, 64, 321n35
Palestine, 220, 234, 257, 350n115
Pànteo, Tullio, 64, 321n48
Pasha, Isma'il, 68
Pasolini, Pier Paolo, 28–29, 48, 187, 205, 335n16,
341, 342; avant-garde and, 338n63; "Notizia su
Amelia Rosselli," 188, 191, 201–2; La ricotta, 181;

Rosselli and, 158, 166, 181–82, 188, 190, 192, 200, 248, 336n31, 339n83

Pasternak, Boris, 158, 343n160

Paxton, Robert O., 221, 323n74

Peleggi, Valentina, 192, 195, 344n4

Pentecost, 14, 21, 35, 39, 57, 89, 252, 311n51; Depero and, 46, 292; Diggs and, 41, 267; inverse, 51; Italian, 118; narrative, 201, 224; Rosselli and, 161, 170, 174, 213; Villa and, 101–2, 104, 113

Pentecostalism, 17–19, 251, 260–61, 310n42, 351n128

performance, 210, 212, 227; Adnan and, 243; art, 89; Black, 263; of breathlessness, 40; deterritorialized, 296; Diggs and, 269–70, 274–75, 279, 283, 286, 355n64; Nakayasu and, 293; Nuyorican, 265; Philip and, 288–89; Rosselli and, 189–90, 340n101; of translingualism, 260; voiced, 240; vocal, 36

Perloff, Marjorie, 73, 314n95, 314n100, 316n122, 319n7, 319n21, 324n76, 357n17

Persian language, 3, 138, 222–23, 273

Philip, M. NourbeSe, 31, 41, 86, 258, 280, 286–89, 356n92; *Zong!*, 275, 288

philology, 3, 101, 129, 228; classical, 137; illegal, 133; modern, 136; national, 136; Sumerian and Akkadian, 110; Villa and, 107, 137, 314n95

philosophy, 275; Adnan and, 230, 233; aesthetic, 227; analytic, 228–29; language and, 115; of language, 23, 70; materialist, 117; political, 330n63; power, 8

pidgin, 264, 275, 316n120, 354n49

Pig Latin, 259, 264

Pluecker, JD, 267, 276. *See also* Antena Aire

Pollock, Jackson, 99, 133

poesis, 1, 70, 101, 103–4, 128; kinopoesis, 275; sym-poesis, 310n39

poetic language, 32, 64, 85, 102, 160, 293–94; citizenship and, 1, 22; Sagawa's, 299

poetics, 29–31, 35–36, 55, 348–50, 353, 354, 356, 357; Adnan and, 228; anticolonial, 261, 286, 289; Arabic, 235; Bergvall's, 26–27; Dante's, 22; Diggs's, 289; ethnopoetics, 134, 213; feminist, 71; future-oriented, 5; Futurist, 64; geopoetics, 22, 33, 153, 311n62; historical, 319n14; intersectional, 279; Marinetti and, 59–60; Moten's, 261, 263; nationalist, 341n116; opacity and, 261; Pentecostal, 324n76; Rosselli's, 6–7, 158, 160, 175, 186, 191–92, 203, 208; transnational, 31, 35; utopian, 21; Villa's, 101–2, 114, 125, 127, 135, 138; xenoglossic, 6,

16–17, 33, 102, 138, 208–9, 220, 292, 305, 313n95; Zanzotto's, 104, 113

Poggi, Christine, 62, 319n8

Poggioli, Renato, 319n21, 324n76

policing: of identity, 23, 195, 233; of performances of tribal affiliation, 229

politics, 55, 258; Adnan's, 234; aestheticization of, 37; cosmopolitics, 307n11; of expression, 290; geopolitics, 1, 24, 33, 153, 282, 302, 315n104; identity, 323n69; imperialist, 62, 225; Jolas and, 91; language, 36; of listening, 208; of milk and honey, 71; of poetics, 29; radical, 324n76; Rosselli and, 165, 168, 181; voice and, 342n149

polyphony, 55, 140, 342n149

populism, 16, 192

Porta, Antonio, 180, 183

Portuguese language, 128, 264; Brazilian, 20, 109, 117, 129, 134, 279, 284

Post-Apollo Press, 33, 217, 236, 244

post-Webernism, 158, 190–91, 193, 195

Pound, Ezra, 28, 31, 47, 114, 142, 275, 293, 313n93; *Cantos*, 31, 47, 139, 181, 258, 264, 333n129, 350n104; collage and, 158; *The Exile* (journal), 264; Fenollosa and, 136, 295, 139; James and, 308–9n25; Pasolini and, 29; Provençal verse and, 122; Rosselli and, 181; Tagliaferri and, 109; Villa and, 140. *See also* traduction

prison, 57, 95, 195; camp, 111; letters, 195–97. *See also* Lipari, 155, 164

propriety, 200; cultural, 214, 302; in language, 72; literary, 297

Provençal language, 31, 109, 129; poetry, 22, 122

punctuation, 84, 183–84, 244, 249

purists, 3, 112, 128–30

Quechua language (Runa Simi), 258, 264, 268–70, 275; dialects, 270, 273

Qur'an, 222, 225, 241

race, 3, 67, 192, 245, 248, 262–63, 309n25; Diggs and, 278, 285; epidermal character of, 262; laws, 110–11; Libyan war and, 74; mother-tongue and, 323n69

racism, 15, 213, 283

Radio Audizioni Italiane (RAI), 207–8, 338n58; Phonology Studio, 159, 191

Ram, Harsha, 56, 314n95, 319n21

Ramazani, Jahan, 30–31, 35, 314n99

Ray, Man, 146

rayon, 79, 81

Re, Lucia, 73–74, 315n102, 323n67, 324n77, 338n59

reading, 146, 151, 200, 237, 252–53, 294, 299, 301, 305; colonizing, 349n82; of poetry, 23, 201, 269, 302; Rosselli's, 211; slow, 7; vertigo of, 150

refugees, 37, 69, 169, 181, 187, 213, 222, 226; Adnan and, 251, 253, 256; Albanian, 27; Armenian, 345n24; cosmopolitans and, 202; refugee camps, 243, 252. *See also* Rosselli, Amelia

refusal, 36, 99, 107, 112, 136, 274, 297

resurrection: of *The Arab Apocalypse* (Toufic), 246, 248; of Arabic, 252; Osiris's canonical, 101; of Pentecost, 21

Reznikoff, Charles, 292, 297

rhythm, 207, 210–12, 266; Chinese, 42; of iambic pentameter, 92; of respiration, 332n127; and rhyme, 276

Richet, Charles, 224, 345n30

Richet, Isabelle, 162–63

Rimbaud, Arthur, 111, 158, 192, 227, 246

Robertson, Lisa, 22, 31, 33, 242, 254, 311n61

Robeson, Paul, 75, 324n80

Romano, Sergio, 167–68, 336n25

Rome, 14, 119, 128, 155, 158, 160, 194, 201, 292; American Academy, 212; Bardi and, 125, 330n83; Biblioteca Nazionale, 130; Gruppo Origine, 332n106; March on, 3, 44, 55–56, 73, 118, 323; Marinetti and, 80, 83; Palazzo Braschi, 46*f*; papal, 102; Pentecostalism and, 310n42; Pontifical Biblical Institute, 110; postwar, 142, 225; Rosselli and, 171, 175, 183, 191; Schola Cantorum, 144; Twombly and, 140; Villa and, 122, 125–26

Roosevelt, Theodore, 12, 58

Rosselli, Amelia ("Melina"), 5–8, 27, 29, 32–33, 36, 38–40, 46–49, 155, 158–98, 200–214, 223, 228, 247, 248, 334n4, 334–35n8, 339n84, 340nn100–101, 343n160, 343n164; "Chiesa," 182–83, 186–87, 198, 211, 338n66; Cold War and, 335–36n21; confessional writing and, 340n94; cube-form, 5, 39, 188, 190, 198, 201; "Diario in tre lingue," 5, 159, 194; gender and, 337n54; oral writing and, 338n67; Pasolini and, 158, 166, 181–82, 188, 190, 192, 200, 248, 336n31, 339n83; "Poesie," 6, 340n89; santi padri and, 338n72; *Serie ospedaliera*, 179, 189, 197–200, 338n67,

343n164; suicide of, 213, 335n17; translating, 218, 300; *Variazioni belliche*, 6, 168–69, 183, 185–88, 200, 308n10, 336n31, 338n67, 339n84, 340n92, 343n164. *See also* accent; Cage, John; English; exile; Italian; language; *Locomotrix: Selected Poetry and Prose of Amelia Rosselli*; mother tongue; music; poetics; voice; writing; xenoglossia

Rosselli, Amelia Pincherle, 155–57, 161–63, 171, 174, 177, 213, 337n35, 342n145, 344n169

Rosselli, Carlo, 8, 46, 155–58, 163–66, 334n1

Rosselli, Nello, 46, 155–58, 163, 165–66

Rothko, Mark, 99, 133

ruach, 98–99, 135, 327n6

Rushkowsky, Claudia, 244, 350n106

Sachs, Curt, 211–12

Sagawa, Chika, 8, 41, 291–99, 357n3; *Mouth: Eats Color*, 41–42, 293–94, 297–98, 300, 302–3, 305

Sakai, Naoki, 41, 292–93, 302

Salih, al-Tayyeb, 238–39, 247

Samoan, 258, 264

Sanskrit, 270, 273

Saussure, Ferdinand de, 262

Schnapp, Jeffrey, 79, 84, 320nn24–25, 321n35, 325n91

Schönberg, Arnold, 197, 205

Schreber, Daniel Paul, 247, 350–51n117

Schwartz, Leonard, 266–67, 316n120

Scotellaro, Rocco, 158, 164, 170–71, 192, 335n16

Second World War, 2, 23, 43, 73, 221; aftermath of, 291; Beirut and, 39, 187, 202, 345n28; geopolitics of, 282

Selassie, Haile, 75

Semerano, Giovanni, 137

sense, 49, 102–4, 176; dis-sense (Villa), 23, 29, 103, 130; images, 61; sound and, 173

Seymour, William J., 17, 19, 244, 310n44, 310n47

Shahadah, 217, 243

Shapiro, Marianne, 23–24

Sharpe, Christina, 40, 283, 288

silence, 49, 117, 135, 172, 296–97, 337n39

Silicon Valley, 114, 117

slavery, 112; chattel, 286–88; language and, 287; legacy of, 283, 289

sociality, 19; radical, 41, 252

solitudes, 54, 90, 199

Somalia, 59, 69, 75–76, 272, 325n100

INDEX

sound, 29, 145, 149, 154, 179, 183–84, 264, 280, 289; accent and, 163; of belonging, 164, 303; color, 203; fasces and, 121–122; of foreign tongues, 32; noise and, 203–4; physiology of, 208; poetic, 180, 204; poetry, 30, 42, 72, 102, 271, 314n95; Rosselli and, 38, 173, 176, 189, 208, 210–11; speech and, 26–27, 262, 287; systems of dialects, 187

Spahr, Juliana, 35, 316n120

Spanish language, 18, 99, 109, 261, 358n26; Chung and, 295; colonial, 268; Diggs and, 264, 266–69, 278, 284; mongrel, 269; Nakayasu and, 297, 299

Spatola, Adriano, 126, 195

speech, 2–3, 26, 262; accented, 208, 214; acts, 170, 283; Babel and, 12, 14, 18; biology, 287; of children, 72; ecstatic, 260; event, 203; impairment, 217; impediment, 252; James and, 11–12; mouth and, 11; national, 70; ordinary, 211; organs, 312n64; overheard, 319n14; of the people, 66; poet and, 170; Russian Futurism and, 64; signifying, 99; sound and, 205; translation and, 139; unhomely, 198; vernacular, 22, 152; of women, 20

Spillers, Hortense, 263, 353n17

Spivak, Gayatri Chakravorty, 24–27, 31, 179, 312n74, 312n76, 312n78, 346n31

statelessness, 4, 31, 40, 224, 239, 253, 260, 283

Steiner, George, 30, 36, 303

Stockhausen, Karlheinz, 159, 191, 194, 196–97

stonature, 205, 336n31

stralunante, 212, 343nn167–68

stranger, 44, 47, 147, 175, 181, 207, 220, 267

structuralism, 126, 131, 191; and substructuralism, 192

subaltern, 24, 27; cultures, 158, 334n4; groups, 115, 251, 330n62; popular world, 192; studies, 158, 165, 182, 192; subjects, 19, 25, 267; tongues, 85, 96, 276

subalternity, 115, 313n84

Sudan, 68–69, 72, 83, 238; Khartoum, 68, 80

Suez Canal, 59, 68, 80, 83, 234

subjectivity, 25, 102, 262, 301; constructs of, 252; critique of, 261

surrealism, 126, 134, 173

Swahili language, 264, 310n43

syntax, 2, 114, 222, 262, 301; Adnan and, 249, 252; of Black English, 265; black performance and, 274; caged, 129; destruction of, 70, 90, 183, 249, 320n27; elementary, 8; Futurism and, 60, 62,

64, 90, 102, 249, 320n27; Homer's, 57; Jolas and, 91; Marinetti and, 60, 70; Rosselli and, 159, 183, 187, 207; Villa and, 130

Syria, 40, 133, 219–21

Tagalog, 264, 269, 273

Tagliaferri, Aldo, 107, 109, 114, 119, 125, 130, 135, 311n54, 328n38, 332n105

technology, 43, 52, 59; Adnan and, 249; communication, 51; European modernism and, 37; of flight, 320n24; Marinetti and, 86; modern, 56; nature and, 81; telegraphic, 64; Villa and, 136

telegraph, 29, 37, 51–53, 55–56, 58–59, 63, 249; infrastructure, 68; pole, 167

telegraphy, 59, 321n35

Tillman, Lynne, 228, 345n17

Torres, Edwin, 33, 264, 266

Toufic, Jalal, 245–49, 350n112

Traboulsi, Fawwaz, 222, 345n20

tradition, 20, 263; Arabic, 239, 246, 248; Arabic literary, 241; Blackpentecostal, 260; of Black Pentecostalism, 19; Black radical, 262; corpus of, 173; defense of, 220; Fascism and, 67; German, 23; human, 205; Jewish community of Alexandria and, 99; of language acquisition, 24; of lyric, 340n100; myths of, 22; national literary, 88; of oral writing, 338n67, 343n164; Ottoman nationalism and, 233; Schola Cantorum, 144; of scriptio continua, 183; vernacular, 122; Villa and, 109, 119; withdrawal of, 246–47

traduction, 243, 293

translation, 16, 20, 22–25, 31, 35–36, 39, 240, 291, 316n121; of Adnan, 232, 237, 249; of al-Sayyab, 243; of Genesis (Villa), 98, 100–101, 104–8, 133, 138; intralinear, 268; Jolas and, 90, 313n89; of Joyce, 130, 133; language of, 254; of Marinetti, 56, 321n44; miraculous, 21, 311n52; Nakayasu and, 298–301; nonbinary, 303; Pentecost and, 14; poetry and, 1, 342n149, 343n168; Pound and, 350n104; of Rosselli, 47–49, 160, 210, 212, 221; of ruach, 99; Sagawa and, 293–95; Spivak and, 25, 312n74; theory, 276; transcription as, 240–41, 243; undomesticated, 34; Villa and, 108, 111, 117, 133, 135, 139; visual, 241, 348n80

translingualism, 1, 7, 34, 117, 260, 278, 300

translucency, 17, 131, 224, 227, 261, 292

transparency, 177, 227, 244, 267, 310n40

382 INDEX

trauma, 120, 263; maternal, 40, 178, 289; political, 186, 213; psychic, 213; transgenerational, 280, 282

tribe, 134, 247, 262; Fascist tales of, 23; of Israel, 101, 104; languages of, 50, 251; Lebanese Christian, 252; myths of, 22, 36, 263; solidarity and, 260; tale of the, 142, 265, 333n129; violence of, 220

Trombetti, Alfredo, 108, 110, 328n38, 329n44

Tudor, David, 159, 183, 190, 193–94, 212, 340n101

tuning, 159, 192, 204; systems, 203

Turchi, Guido, 159, 191

Turkey, 40, 59, 233, 247, 251

Turkish Republic, 3, 222

Twombly, Cy, 99, 122, 133, 140–44, 225, 332n127, 333nn131–32

universal forms, 126, 194–95

universal language, 5, 24, 34, 161, 168, 195; artificial, 17

unlearning, 16–17, 27, 29, 36, 42; Adnan and, 223; Nakayasu and, 294; Rosselli and, 192, 200; 223; Villa and, 151

untranslatability, 24, 34–35

utopia, 165, 267; avant-garde, 55; geopolitical, 254; progressivist, 332n106; Rosselli and, 161, 214

utopianism, 96, 126, 133, 154, 195, 239; the semiutopian, 136, 187

Urdu language, 264, 270, 273

Venice, 155, 171, 323n63, 338n58; St. Mark's Basilica, 15f

Venturini, Caterina, 173

vernaculars, 21–22, 29, 48, 70, 117, 122, 133, 205, 264, 272, 311n52; African, 351n128; Black, 262; Caribbean, 274–75; Chinese, 313n93; Dante's, 22, 174; Florentine, 137; international, 28; Italian, 152, 186; local, 112; minority, 30; national, 21, 23; nationalized, 85, 96; polyvernacular, 122, 130; Tuscan, 31

vibration, 45, 203–5, 211, 213, 226, 274, 312n70; Danielou and, 159; polyvernacular, 122, 130; radio, 234; Saussure and, 262; telegraph, 63

Victor, Divya, 24, 307n1

Villa, Emilio, 8, 30, 32–33, 38–40, 98–154, 217, 225, 328n33, 328n40; L'Adolescenza, 110, 114; autonomy of art and, 329n49; avant-garde and, 328n41; "Dichiarazioni del soldato morto," 231, 330n77; Disco Muto, 144–45, 148f, 150–51;

dis-sense and, 23; Duchamp and, 146; ideal nationality and, 20; Idrologie, 107, 150–52; mainstream publishers and, 160; Marinetti and, 330n71; Noigandres and, 331n100; Oramai, 119, 124; origins and, 114, 332n106; philology and, 107, 314n95; poetry of, 116, 130, 167; secularity of, 327n11; Semitic languages and, 104, 228; Trombetti and, 328n38, 329n44; Ytalyan, 39, 117, 122. See also English; Genesis; Italian; Latin; poetics; Tagliaferri, Aldo; Twombly, Cy

violence, 221, 246, 249; anti-Black, 288; of appropriation, 220; day-to-day, 282; domestic, 94, 282; of education, 258; of fait accompli, 188; governing, 168; hegemonic, 236; imperial, 68; kinship and, 280; police, 41; profane, 80; of Second Gulf War, 246; of self-referentiality, 34; slavery and, 289; transnational, 202

visual arts, 78, 111, 191, 276, 331n89, 348n69

Vittorini, Elio, 169, 205

vocabulary, 2, 4, 8, 188, 274; caged, 129; new, 91; Sumerian-Akkadian, 139; visual, 44

voice, 27, 54, 192, 194, 205, 252, 258, 261, 313n81, 342n149; active, 3; Albion, 208, 260; broadcasting, 92; collective, 346n31; human, 49, 271; maternal, 312n64; prelinguistic, 99; Rosselli's, 49, 163, 175, 205, 207–8, 210, 212; standardized English, 352n8; subjunctive, 298; as trope, 26; universal, 135; wireless transmission of, 52, 54, 58

wake, 283, 288; of disaster, 246–47; of Fascism, 38, 144; poetic, 36; work, 279, 288

war, 15, 58, 88, 96, 168, 185, 283, 301; Arab world and, 234; atrocities, 231; against barbarisms, 112; civil, 166, 220–21, 245, 250–51; crimes, 165; dead, 122; devastation of, 196; Fascist imperial, 69; horror of, 157; of information, 163; on language, 161; language reform and, 186; love of, 55; machinery of, 81, 123; Marinetti and, 59, 62, 83, 321n43; martyrs, 121; mechanical, 80; mother tongue and, 15; shortages, 78; veterans, 281; Villa and, 111, 120

Webern, Anton, 195. See also post-Webernism

"with a cat in the throat," 26, 207

Wolf, Uljana, 33, 35, 316n121

words-in-freedom/parole-in-libertà, 37, 57, 60, 62, 67, 78, 84, 90; fusedwords-in-freedom, 338n68

writing, 1, 33, 110, 135, 240–41, 293, 295; Adnan's, 221, 226–27, 229–31, 234, 238, 251, 254, 256, 282;

Arabic, 40, 223–24, 239, 242; archaic forms of, 183; barbarous, 129; carnality and, 176; Cixous's, 179; confessional, 340n94; critical, 235–36; Danielou's, 204; Diggs's, 279, 283; discomfortable, 267; drawing and, 40, 226, 247; Eliot's, 348n71; of migration, 314n100; modernist, 102; Munari's, 325n87; non-Latin, 224; nonnative, 34; oral, 338n67, 343n64; painting and, 40, 227, 229; plume of, 86; poetic, 329n49; of polyglots, 31; power of, 163; Rosselli's, 158, 171, 173, 178, 182, 207, 335n17; speech and, 3; translingual, 40; Twombly's, 133, 142–44; unmastery in, 4, 20, 24, 36, 138, 174, 188, 219, 260; visual aspect of, 244; women of color and, 20; xenoglossic, 2, 7, 38, 40, 219–20, 287, 290

xenoglossia, 2, 13, 19–20, 89, 102, 104, 186, 219–20, 226, 309n38, 346n31, 351n127; Adnan and, 40, 229, 251–52; Crawley's critique of, 130, 320n23; Diggs and, 264, 268, 290; as literary resource, 1; narratives of, 29; queer, 40, 229; Rosselli and, 7, 161, 179, 195, 210; translucency of, 131, 261; true, 46; Villa's, 122, 144

xenolalia, 13, 19, 102, 310n47, 320n23

Yiddish language, 18, 261, 273, 300

Yildiz, Yasemin, 23, 70

Zanzotto, Andrea, 103–4, 109, 113, 125

Zaum, 30, 314n95

Zevi, Bruno, 126, 338n58

Zukofsky, Louis, 13, 27, 205, 264